LIBERTY'S EXILES

Also by Maya Jasanoff

Edge of Empire

MAYA JASANOFF

Liberty's Exiles

The Loss of America and the Remaking
of the British Empire

Harper
Press

Harper*Press*
An imprint of HarperCollins*Publishers*
77–85 Fulham Palace Road
Hammersmith, London W6 8JB
www.harpercollins.co.uk

Visit our authors' blog: www.fifthestate.co.uk

Published in Great Britain by Harper*Press* in 2011

Maps on pages 2–4 created by Robert Bull

A catalogue record for this book
is available from the British Library

ISBN 978-0-00-718008-0

Printed and bound in Great Britain by
Clays Ltd, St Ives plc

In memory of Kamala Sen (1914–2005) and
Edith Jasanoff (1913–2007),
emigrants and storytellers

CONTENTS

MAPS

CAST OF CHARACTERS

(in order of appearance)

BEVERLEY ROBINSON AND FAMILY

A native Virginian, Beverley Robinson (1722–1792) moved to New York and married the wealthy heiress Susanna Philipse in 1748. He raised the Loyal American Regiment in 1777. After the evacuation of New York, Robinson settled in England, where he died in 1792. His widow and two daughters, Susan and Joanna, remained in England until their deaths. His five sons enjoyed profitable careers in different parts of the British Empire. The eldest, BEVERLEY ROBINSON JR. (1754–1816), lieutenant colonel of the Loyal American Regiment, settled outside Fredericton in 1787 and became a member of the New Brunswick provincial elite. FREDERICK PHILIPSE "PHIL" ROBINSON (1763–1852) was a career soldier who attained considerable prominence as a general in the Peninsular War and War of 1812, for which services he earned a knighthood. At the time of his death, General Robinson was the "grandfather" of the British army, the longest-serving officer on its books. The youngest son, WILLIAM HENRY ROBINSON (1765–1836), distinguished himself in the British army's commissariat department, for which he also received a knighthood. He married Catherine Skinner, daughter of loyalist general Cortlandt Skinner, and sister of Maria Skinner Nugent.

JOSEPH BRANT (THAYENDANEGEA) (1743–1807)

As a teenager in colonial New York, the Mohawk Indian Joseph Brant—or Thayendanegea in Mohawk—fell under the patronage of British superintendent of Indian affairs Sir William Johnson, who had married Brant's elder sister MOLLY (ca. 1736–1796). Brant was educated at Wheelock's Indian school in Connecticut, and fought for the British in both the Seven Years' War and Pontiac's War. During the American Revolution, Joseph and Molly Brant helped recruit Iroquois to the British cause. In 1783 Brant initiated the resettlement of dislocated Mohawks in Canada. From his new home on the Grand River (today's Brantford, Ontario), Brant tried to reunite Iroquois nations divided by the Canadian-U.S. border, and to establish a new Indian confederacy reaching to the west. He visited Britain twice, in 1775 and 1785, to advance Mohawk land claims; but as the 1790s wore on he found himself increasingly at odds with British colonial officials and saw his hopes for a western confederacy dashed. He died in 1807 and is buried next to the Mohawk Chapel in Brantford.

ELIZABETH LICHTENSTEIN JOHNSTON (1764–1848)

Elizabeth Johnston spent almost half her life on the move. An only child, she lost her mother at the age of ten and spent the early years of the revolution in seclusion while her father, John Lichtenstein, fought in a loyalist regiment. In 1779, she married WILLIAM MARTIN JOHNSTON (1754–1807), a loyalist army captain, medical student, and son of prominent Georgia loyalist Dr. Lewis Johnston. Johnston evacuated with the British from Savannah, Charleston, and East Florida, settling in 1784 in Edinburgh. In 1786 the Johnstons moved to Jamaica, where William worked as a doctor. The years in Jamaica were trying ones for Johnston; she went back to Edinburgh from 1796 to 1802, and in 1806 relocated to Nova Scotia (returning to Jamaica from 1807 to 1810 to wrap up business following William's death in 1807). She spent her last four decades far more rooted than her first, surrounded by her adult children and her father, who died in Annapolis Royal in 1813. Six of Johnston's ten children predeceased her, including her eldest son Andrew, of yellow fever in Jamaica in 1805, and her eldest daughter Catherine, in a Boston madhouse in 1819.

DAVID GEORGE (ca. 1743–1810)

David George was born a slave in Virginia. He ran away from his master in 1762, eventually ending up in the custody of Indian trader George Galphin at Silver Bluff, South Carolina. There, partly under the influence of George Liele, George converted to the Baptist faith and became an elder of the Silver Bluff Baptist Church. In 1778, George followed British forces to Savannah, where he worked as a butcher and continued to preach with Liele. With the British evacuations, George and his family traveled to Nova Scotia as free black loyalists. There George became an active evangelist, establishing a church at Shelburne and preaching to white and black audiences around the Maritimes. In 1791 George emerged as a leading supporter of the Sierra Leone Company's project to relocate black loyalists to Africa, and helped John Clarkson recruit colonists for the scheme. He was among the founding settlers of Freetown in 1792. George visited England in 1792–93, but otherwise spent the rest of his life in Sierra Leone, where he set up another Baptist church (the first in Africa) and died in 1810.

JOHN MURRAY, FOURTH EARL OF DUNMORE (1732–1809)

Dunmore was a Scottish peer whose father supported the Young Pretender in 1745. Despite their Jacobite sympathies, the family retained their title, and Dunmore served for nearly thirty years as a representative peer for Scotland in the House of Lords. He went to North America in 1770 as governor of New York, and became governor of Virginia in 1771. He achieved considerable notoriety for his proclamation of 1775, which granted freedom to patriot-owned slaves who joined British military service. Dunmore became a notable advocate of loyalist interests, promoting numerous schemes to continue the war (including those of John Cruden), and championing loyalist efforts to win financial compensation. He was appointed governor of the Bahamas in 1786, in which capacity he supported William Augustus Bowles's bids to establish the state of Muskogee. Dunmore was recalled from the governorship in 1796 and remained in Britain until his death.

GUY CARLETON, FIRST BARON DORCHESTER (1724–1808)

A career soldier, the Anglo-Irish Carleton joined the army in 1742 and assisted in the 1759 capture of Quebec, a place he would remain involved with for almost forty years. Carleton served as governor of Quebec from 1766 to 1778, and is best known for his role in authoring the 1774 Quebec Act. Loyalists knew Carleton best, however, in his position as commander in chief of British forces from 1782 to 1783, in which capacity he superintended the evacuations of British-held cities and helped organize the loyalist exodus. Carleton returned to Quebec as governor in chief of British North America in 1786 (and newly ennobled as Lord Dorchester). Though beloved by loyalists, Dorchester found himself at odds with developments in British imperial policy enshrined in the 1791 Canada Act. As at other points in his career, Dorchester clashed repeatedly with his colleagues, and resigned his position in chagrin in 1794. He retired to England in 1796 and lived in comfort as a country squire. His younger brother THOMAS CARLETON (ca. 1735–1817) was governor of New Brunswick from 1784 to 1817, though from 1803 until his death he governed in absentia from England.

GEORGE LIELE (ca. 1750–1820)

Liele grew up in Georgia as a slave. He was baptized in 1772 and became an itinerant Baptist preacher, serving as a spiritual mentor to David George. Liele was granted freedom by his loyalist master and spent much of the war in British-occupied Savannah. He there baptized Andrew Bryan, who went on to found the First African Baptist Church in Savannah. On the evacuation of Savannah in 1782, Liele traveled to Jamaica as an indentured servant to loyalist planter Moses Kirkland. He established the island's first Baptist church in Kingston, but during the 1790s became the subject of increasing persecution for his religious activities. After a charge of sedition failed to stick, Liele was imprisoned for three years for debt. Though he continued to be active in a range of commercial ventures, he never returned to public preaching after 1800, and his last years remain obscure.

JOHN CRUDEN (1754–1787)

Cruden emigrated from Scotland to Wilmington, North Carolina, sometime before 1770, where he joined his uncle (and namesake) in the trading firm of John Cruden and Company. During the war, Cruden served in a loyalist regiment and was appointed commissioner of sequestered estates in Charleston in 1780, which required him to manage numerous patriot-owned plantations and a labor force of several thousand slaves to produce supplies for the British military and for commercial sale. After Charleston was evacuated Cruden moved to East Florida, where he attempted to block the province's cession to Spain. In 1785, like many East Florida refugees, Cruden immigrated to the Bahamas, where he lived with his uncle on the island of Exuma. He continued to promote plans for the renewal of the British American empire. Cruden died, insane, in the Bahamas in 1787.

WILLIAM AUGUSTUS BOWLES (1763–1805)

Bowles was the most flamboyant loyalist adventurer of his period. He joined a loyalist regiment in 1777 but deserted in 1779 to settle with the Creek Indians. He married the daughter of a Creek chief and spent several years living in her village. After the revolution, Bowles began plotting to unseat political and commercial rivals in Creek country (which had become part of Spanish Florida). He was supported in these aims by Lord Dunmore and various other imperial officials. A first foray into Florida in 1788 ended in fiasco. A second, more ambitious expedition in 1791 brought Bowles closer to his dream of founding a pro-British Creek state, called Muskogee—but he was captured by the Spanish in 1792 and imprisoned in Havana, Cádiz, and the Philippines in turn. In 1798 Bowles escaped, via Sierra Leone, and returned to Florida for a final effort to establish Muskogee. Though this was the most successful bid of all—he built a capital in 1800 near present-day Tallahassee and presided over his domain for several years—he was betrayed in 1803 by Creeks under U.S. influence. He died in Havana, a Spanish prisoner, in 1805.

SUPPORTING FIGURES

Thirteen Colonies

Thomas Brown, loyalist commander, superintendent of Indian affairs.
Joseph Galloway, advocate of imperial union and loyalist lobbyist.
Charles Inglis, clergyman, loyalist pamphleteer, later bishop of Nova Scotia.
William Franklin, son of Benjamin Franklin, former governor of Pennsylvania, loyalist organizer.
William Smith, chief justice of New York and later Quebec, confidant of Sir Guy Carleton.
Patrick Tonyn, governor of East Florida, 1774–85.

Britain

Samuel Shoemaker, Pennsylvania refugee and friend of painter Benjamin West.
John Eardley Wilmot, MP and loyalist claims commissioner.
Isaac Low, former New York congressman and merchant.
Granville Sharp, abolitionist and sponsor of Sierra Leone settlement.

Nova Scotia

Jacob Bailey, clergyman and author.
John Parr, governor of Nova Scotia, 1782–91.
Benjamin Marston, surveyor of Shelburne.
Boston King, black loyalist carpenter.
"Daddy" Moses Wilkinson, black Methodist preacher.

New Brunswick and Quebec

Edward Winslow, lobbyist for creation of New Brunswick.
Frederick Haldimand, governor of Quebec, 1777–85.
John Graves Simcoe, governor of Upper Canada, 1791–98.

The Bahamas

John Maxwell, governor of the Bahamas, 1780–85 (active).
John Wells, printer and critic of government.
William Wylly, solicitor-general and opponent of Lord Dunmore.

Jamaica

Louisa Wells Aikman, member of loyalist printer family.
Maria Skinner Nugent, diarist, governor's wife.

Sierra Leone

Thomas Peters, Black Pioneer veteran, leader of resettlement project.
John Clarkson, organizer of loyalist migration, superintendent of
    Freetown, 1791–92.
Zacharay Macaulay, governor of Sierra Leone, 1794–99.

India

David Ochterlony, East India Company general, conqueror of Nepal.
William Linnaeus Gardner, military adventurer.

LIBERTY'S
EXILES

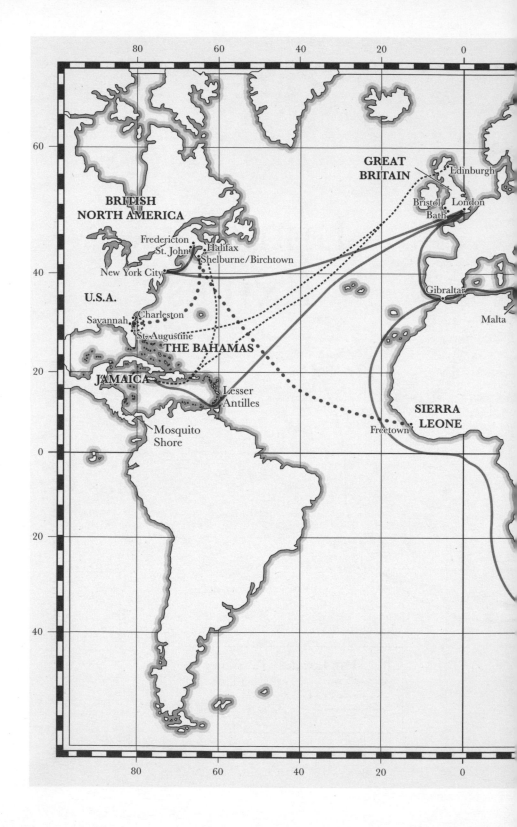

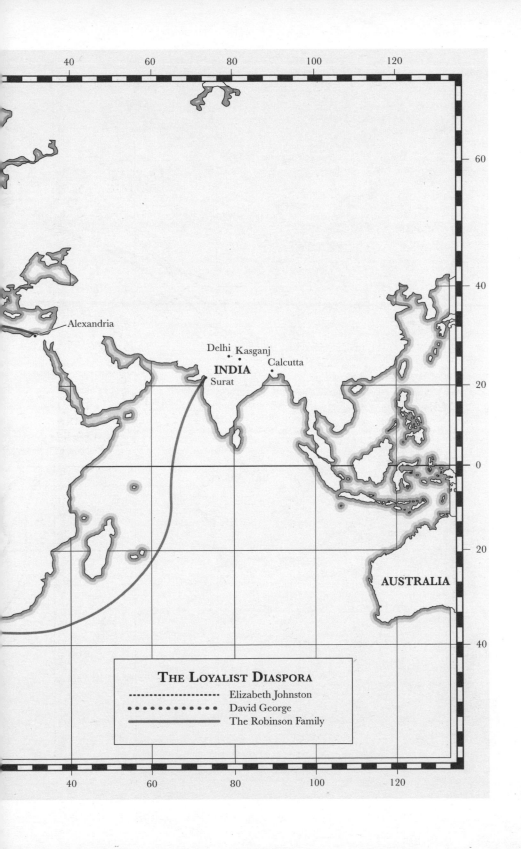

Alexandria

Delhi Kasganj

INDIA   Calcutta
Surat

AUSTRALIA

THE LOYALIST DIASPORA
.... Elizabeth Johnston
● ● ● ● ● ● ● ● ● ● ● ● David George
—————————— The Robinson Family

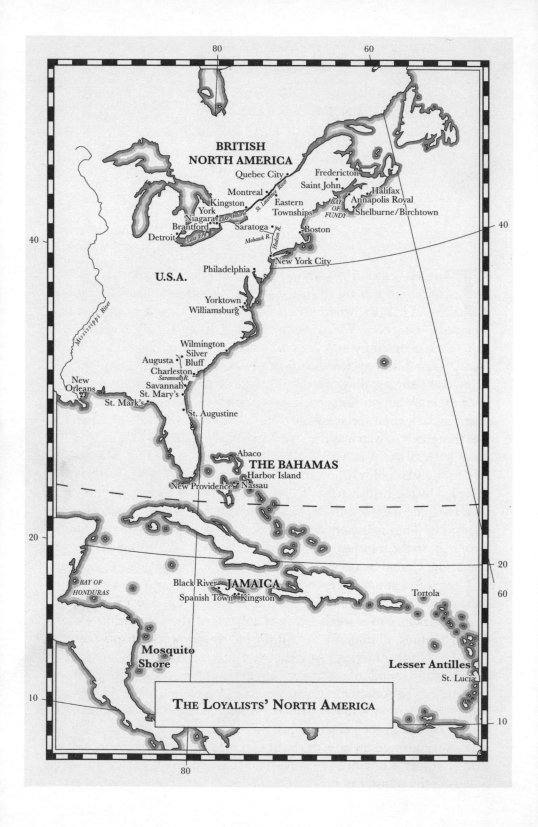

THE LOYALISTS' NORTH AMERICA

The Spirit of 1783

THERE WERE TWO SIDES in the American Revolution—but only one was on display early in the afternoon of November 25, 1783, when General George Washington rode on a grey horse into New York City. By his side trotted the governor of New York, flanked by an escort of mounted guards. Portly general Henry Knox followed close behind, leading officers of the Continental Army eight abreast down the Bowery. Long lines of civilians trailed after them, some on horseback, others on foot, wearing black-and-white cockades and sprigs of laurel in their hats.[1] Hundreds crammed into the streets to watch as the choreographed procession made its way down to the Battery, at Manhattan's southern tip. Since 1776, through seven long years of war and peace negotiations, New York had been occupied by the British army. Today, the British were going. A cannon shot at 1 p.m. sounded the departure of the last British troops from their posts. They marched to the docks, clambered into longboats, and rowed out to the transports waiting in the harbor. The British occupation of the United States was officially over.[2]

George Washington's triumphal entrance into New York City was the closest thing the winners of the American Revolution ever had to a victory parade. For a week, patriots celebrated the evacuation with feasts, bonfires, illuminations, and the biggest fireworks display ever staged in North America.[3] At Fraunces's Tavern, Washington and his friends drank rounds of toasts late into the night. To the United States of America! To America's European allies, France and Spain! To the American "Heroes, who have fallen for our Freedom"! "May America be an Assylum to the persecuted of the Earth!"[4] A few days later one newspaper printed an anecdote about a brief shore visit made by a British officer. Convinced that New York would be racked by unrest following the transfer of power, the officer was surprised to find "that every thing in the city was civil and tranquil, no mobs—no riots—no disorders." "These Americans," he marveled, "are a curious original people, *they know how to govern themselves, but nobody else can govern them.*"[5] Generations of New Yorkers commemorated November 25 as "Evacuation Day"—an anniversary that was later folded into the more enduring November celebration of American national togetherness, Thanksgiving Day.[6]

But what if you hadn't wanted the British to leave? Mixed in among the happy New York crowd that day were other, less cheerful faces.[7] For loyalists—colonists who had sided with Britain during the war—the departure of the British troops spelled worry, not jubilation. During the war, tens of thousands of loyalists had moved for safety into New York and other British-held cities. The British withdrawal raised urgent questions about their future. What kind of treatment could they expect in the new United States? Would they be jailed? Would they be attacked? Would they retain their property, or hold on to their jobs? Confronting real doubts about their lives, liberty, and potential happiness in the United States, sixty thousand loyalists decided to follow the British and take their chances elsewhere in the British Empire. They took fifteen thousand black slaves with them, bringing the total exodus to seventy-five thousand people—or about one in forty members of the American population.[8]

They traveled to Canada, they sailed for Britain, they journeyed to the Bahamas and the West Indies; some would venture still farther afield, to Africa and India. But wherever they went, this voyage into exile was a trip into the unknown. In America the refugees left behind friends and relatives, careers and land, houses and native streets—the entire milieu in which they had built their lives. For them, America seemed less "an Assylum to the persecuted" than a potential persecutor. It was the British Empire that would be their asylum, offering land, emergency relief, and financial incentives to help them start over. Evacuation Day did not mark an end for the loyalist refugees. It was a fresh beginning—and it carried them into a dynamic if uncertain new world.

JACOB BAILEY, for one, could give a vivid account of what led him to flee revolutionary America. Massachusetts born and bred, Bailey had since 1760 been an Anglican missionary in the frontier district of Pownalborough, Maine. While he ministered in what was then remote wilderness, in Boston his Harvard classmate John Adams voiced the colonies' grievances against Britain, and became a forceful advocate for independence. But Bailey had sworn what he regarded as a sacred oath to the king, the head of his church, and to renounce that allegiance appeared to him to be an act of both treason and sacrilege. Bailey struggled to maintain his loyalty in the face of mounting pressure to join the rebellion. When he refused to honor a special day of thanksgiving declared by the provincial congress, Pownalborough patriots threatened to put up a liberty pole in front of the church and to whip him there if he failed to bless it.[9] Another frightening omen came when he found seven of his sheep slaughtered, and a "fine heifer" shot dead in his pasture.[10] By 1778, the clergyman had been "twice assaulted by a furious Mob—four times haulled before an unfeeling committee. . . . Three times have I been driven from my family. . . . Two attempts have been made to shoot me." He roved the countryside to elude arrest, while his young wife and their children tried to get by with "nothing to eat for several days together." To Bailey the patriots were persecutors, plain and simple, a "set of surly & savage beings who have power in their hands and murder in their hearts, who thirst, and pant, and roar for the blood of those who have any connection with, or affection for Great Britain."[11]

Bailey certainly had a flair for sensational language. His melodramatic prose, however, spoke to genuine fear for his family's safety. Still unwilling to renounce the king—yet equally unwilling to risk imprisonment for refusing to do so—he saw only one more option before him, unappealing though it was. Before dawn one June day in 1779, the Baileys grimly "began to prepare for our expulsion." They dressed in a motley assortment of salvaged clothes, gathered up their bedding and "the shattered remains of our fortune," and made their way to a boat that would carry them to Nova Scotia, the nearest British sanctuary. In spite of all they had suffered, Jacob and Sally Bailey could not hold back their "bitter emotions of grief" on leaving their native country. Neither could they contain their relief, two weeks later, when they sailed into Halifax harbor and saw "the Britanic colours flying."[12] Bailey gave thanks to God "for safely conducting me and my family to this retreat of freedom and security from the rage of tyranny and the cruelty of opposition." Now they were in the British Empire; now they were secure. But the Baileys had landed "in a strange country, destitute of money, clothing, dwelling or furniture," and their future was in the hands of chance.[13]

This book follows refugees like Jacob Bailey out of revolutionary America to provide the first global history of the loyalist diaspora. Though historians have probed the experiences of loyalists within the colonies (and especially the ideology of articulate figures like Bailey), the international displacement of loyalists during and after the war has never been described in full.[14] Who were these refugees and why did they leave? The answers came in as many forms as the people themselves. Loyalists are often stereotyped as members of a small conservative elite: rich, educated, Anglican, and with strong ties to Britain—qualities captured by the pejorative label "tory," the nickname for the British Conservative Party.[15] In fact, historians estimate that between a fifth and a third of American colonists remained loyal to the king.[16] Loyalism cut right across the social, geographical, racial, and ethnic spectrum of early America—making loyalists every bit as "American" as their patriot fellow subjects. Loyalists included recent immigrants and *Mayflower* descendants alike. They could be royal officials as well as bakers, carpenters, tailors, and printers. There were Anglican ministers as well as Methodists and Quakers; cosmopolitan Bostonians and backcountry farmers in the Carolinas.

Crucially, not all loyalists were white. For the half million black slaves in the thirteen colonies, the revolution presented a striking opportunity when British officers offered freedom to slaves who agreed to fight. Twenty thousand slaves seized this promise, making the revolution the occasion for the largest emancipation of North American slaves until the U.S. Civil War. For native American Indians, too, the revolution posed a pressing choice. Encroached on by generations of land-hungry colonists, several Indian nations—notably the Mohawks in the north and the Creeks in the south—opted to ally themselves with the British Empire. The experiences of loyal whites, blacks, and Indians have generally been segregated into distinct historical narratives, and of course there were important differences among them.[17] But loyalists of all backgrounds confronted a common dilemma with Britain's defeat—to stay or go—and all numbered among the revolution's refugees. Their stories were analogous and entangled in significant ways, which is why they will be presented together here.

Perhaps the most surprising truth about loyalist refugees was how varied a role ideology might play in their decision-making. Though they shared an allegiance to the king and a commitment to empire, their precise beliefs otherwise ranged widely. Some, like Bailey, expressed sophisticated intellectual reasons for their position. For others, loyalism stemmed from a personal commitment to the existing order of things, a sense that it was better to stick with the devil you knew. Also widespread was a pragmatic opinion that the colonies were economically and strategically better off as part of the British Empire.[18] The extent and depth of loyalism points to a fundamental feature of this conflict that the term "revolution" belies. This was quite simply a civil war—and routinely described as such by contemporaries on both sides of the Atlantic.[19] Polarizing communities, destroying friendships, dividing families—most famously Benjamin Franklin, the founding father, from his only son William, a loyalist—this was the longest war Americans fought before Vietnam, and the bloodiest until the Civil War of 1861–65. Recovering the contingency, coercion, and sheer violence of the American Revolution explains why so many loyalists chose to depart—driven, like Jacob Bailey, by fear of harassment as much as by commitment to principle. By the same token, self-interest could be as powerful a motivator as core beliefs, as the cases of runaway slaves and Britain's Indian allies perhaps make most clear.

A range of reasons, ideological and otherwise, led all the people in these pages to the same defining choice: to leave revolutionary America.[20] This book sets out to explore what happened to them next. Of the sixty thousand loyalists who fled, about eight thousand whites and five thousand free blacks traveled to Britain, often to find themselves strangers in a strange land. The majority of refugees headed straight for Britain's other colonies, taking up incentives of free land, provisions, and supplies. More than half relocated to the northern British provinces of Nova Scotia, New Brunswick, and Quebec, helping to transform regions once heavily French to the English-dominated Canada of today.* A further six thousand or so migrants, especially from the American south, traveled to Jamaica and the Bahamas—carrying the vast majority of the fifteen thousand exported slaves with them. Some ranged still farther afield. The East India Company army would soon be sprinkled with American-born officers, including two sons of the notorious turncoat Benedict Arnold. An unlucky few ended up among the first convicts sent to Botany Bay, in Australia. And in

---

*From the American Revolution up to Canadian Confederation in 1867, these provinces were collectively known as British North America. "Canada" was synonymous with the province of Quebec until 1791, when it was divided into the provinces of Upper Canada (present-day Ontario) and Lower Canada (present-day Quebec).

perhaps the most surprising migration, nearly twelve hundred black loyalists moved to Africa, under the sponsorship of British abolitionists, to found the utopian settlement of Freetown, in Sierra Leone. In short, loyalists landed in every corner of the British Empire. Within a decade of the peace, the map of the loyalist diaspora looked much like the map of the empire as a whole.

A handful of studies have looked at specific figures and sites within this migration. But the loyalists' worldwide dispersal has never been completely reconstructed.[21] A key reason for this lies in the fact that history is so often framed within national boundaries. In the United States, the history of the American Revolution was written by the victors, who were chiefly interested in exploring the revolution's many innovations and achievements. Loyalist refugees simply fell outside the bounds of American national narratives. They received scant attention from British historians in turn, as embarrassing reminders of defeat— especially given the great triumphs in the Seven Years' War and the Revolutionary-Napoleonic wars that Britons could focus on instead. Loyalists loom largest, instead, in Canadian history, where they were hailed by some nineteenth-century conservatives as the "founding fathers" of a proudly imperial Anglo-Canadian tradition, and honored as "United Empire Loyalists," a title conferred by the imperial government on refugees and their descendants. But such treatments reaffirmed the "tory" stereotype and may well have contributed to later scholarly neglect.

There is also a practical reason that nobody has written this global history before. In the 1840s, Lorenzo Sabine, the first American historian who delved into this subject, lamented that "Men who . . . separate themselves from their homes . . . who become outlaws, wanderers, and exiles,—such men leave few memorials behind them. Their papers are scattered and lost, and their very names pass from recollection."[22] In fact, it is remarkable how much *does* survive: personal letters, diaries, memoirs, petitions, muster rolls, diplomatic dispatches, legislative proceedings. The challenge is putting it all together. Fortunately for twenty-first-century scholars (privileged with funding and access), technology has made it possible to pursue international histories in new ways. One can search library catalogues and databases around the world at the touch of a button, and read digitized rare books and documents on a laptop in one's living room. One can also travel with increasing ease, to piece together paper trails scattered across continents, and to see what remains of the refugees' worlds: the houses loyalists built on out-islands of the Bahamas, the precipitous slopes they cultivated above Freetown, or their gravestones, weathered in the Canadian maritime wind.

To look at the American Revolution and the British Empire from these vantage points is to see the international consequences of the revolution in a completely new way. The worldwide resonance of the American Revolution has traditionally been understood in connection with the "spirit of 1776" that inspired other peoples, notably the French, to assert their own rights to equality and liberty.[23] Tracing loyalist journeys reveals a different stamp of the revolution on the world: not on burgeoning republics, but on the enduring British Empire. Loyalist refugees personally conveyed American things and ideas into the empire. The fortunate brought treasured material objects: a finely wrought sugar box, a recipe book, or, more weightily, the printing press used by one Charleston family to produce the first newspapers in St. Augustine and the Bahamas.[24] But they carried cultural and political influences too—not least the racial attitudes that accompanied the loyalists' mass transport of slaves. One transformative export was the Baptist faith taken by black loyalist preachers from a single congregation in the Carolina backcountry, who went on to establish the first Baptist churches in Nova Scotia and New Brunswick, Jamaica, and Sierra Leone. In the most striking "American" transmission of all, loyalist refugees brought with them a discourse of grievance against imperial authority. In British North America, the Bahamas, and Sierra Leone, loyalist refugees beset hapless British governors with demands for political representation that sounded uncannily like those of their patriot peers. "Loyalist" these days often connotes a die-hard supporter of a cause, but American loyalists were certainly not unblinking followers of British rule.

Considering these kinds of revolutionary legacies brings into focus a remarkable period of transition for the British Empire, and helps make sense of a seeming paradox. The American Revolution marked the empire's single greatest defeat until the era of World War II. Yet in the space of a mere ten years, it bounced back to an astonishing extent. Building on earlier precedents, British power regrouped, expanded, and reshaped itself across the world—in Ireland and India, Canada and the Caribbean, Africa and Australia.[25] All told, the 1780s stand out as the most eventful single decade in British imperial history up to the 1940s. What was more, the events of these years cemented an enduring framework for the principles and practice of British rule. This "spirit of 1783," so to speak, animated the British Empire well into the twentieth century—and provided a model of liberal constitutional empire that stood out as a vital alternative to the democratic republics taking shape in the United States, France, and Latin America.

What did this postwar restructuring involve, and what role did refugee loyalists play in the process? The "spirit of 1783" had three major elements.[26] First and most visibly, the British Empire significantly expanded around the world—and loyalists were both agents and advocates of imperial growth. Historians used to portray the American Revolution as a dividing line between a "first" British Empire, largely commercial, colonial, and Atlantic, and a "second" empire centered in Asia and involving direct rule over millions of manifestly foreign subjects. But loyalist refugees bridged the two. As pioneer settlers in British North America, the Bahamas, and Sierra Leone, they demonstrated the continued vitality of the Atlantic empire alongside what has been described as the empire's "swing to the east." They also promoted ambitious expansionist projects elsewhere in the world, championing schemes to extend British sovereignty into Spanish America, or around the western borders of the United States. Far-fetched though some of these ideas can seem in retrospect, they hardly seemed so at a time when the future shape of the United States was very unclear, and Britain (among other European empires) was successfully establishing footholds in some of the most remote quarters of the globe. The first serious proposal to colonize Australia was put forward by none other than an American loyalist.[27]

Loyalist refugees also illuminate a second feature of the "spirit of 1783": a clarified commitment to liberty and humanitarian ideals. Although the American Revolution demonstrated that British subjects abroad would not be treated exactly as British subjects were at home, at least when it came to political representation, the revolution also had the effect of deepening an imperial guarantee to include all subjects, no matter what their ethnicity or faith, in a fold of British rights. Loyalist refugees became conspicuous objects of paternalistic attention. Black loyalists got their freedom from authorities increasingly inclined toward abolition, in self-conscious contrast to the slaveowning United States. Needy loyalists of all kinds received land and supplies in an empire-wide program for refugee relief that anticipated the work of modern international aid organizations. Loyalists even received financial compensation for their losses through a commission established by the British government—a landmark of state welfare schemes.

Yet liberal values had their limits, as loyalists discovered at close range. British officials after the revolution by and large concluded that the thirteen colonies had been given too much liberty, not too little, and tightened the reins of administration accordingly. This enhanced taste for centralized, hierarchical government marked the third component of the "spirit of 1783"—and one that loyalist refugees consistently found themselves resisting. Confronted with top-down rule, they repeatedly demanded more representation than imperial authorities proved willing to give them, a discrepancy that had of course undergirded the American Revolution in the first place. And for all that loyalists profited from humanitarian initiatives, they also ran up against numerous seeming contradictions in British policy. This was an empire that gave freedom to black loyalists, but facilitated the export of loyalist-owned slaves. It gave land to Mohawk Indian allies in the north, but largely abandoned the Creeks and other allies in the south. It promised to compensate loyalists for their losses but in practice often fell short; it joined liberal principles with hierarchical rule. Across the diaspora, the refugee loyalist experience would be marked by a mismatch between promises and expectations, between what subjects wanted and what rulers provided. Such discontents proved a lasting feature of the post-revolutionary British Empire—and another line of continuity from the "first" into the "second" empire, from the first major war of colonial independence to later anti-colonial movements.

Few could have predicted just how quickly the "spirit of 1783"—committed to authority, liberty, and global reach—cemented in the aftermath of one revolution would be tested by another. In early 1793, less than a decade after Evacuation Day, Britain plunged into war with revolutionary France in an epic conflict that lasted virtually uninterrupted till 1815. Fortunately for Britain, already tested by republican dissent in America, the "spirit of 1783" provided a ready set of practices and policies to pose against French models. In contrast to French liberty, equality, and fraternity, Britain offered up its own more limited version of liberty under the crown and hierarchical stability. This wasn't so much a counter-revolutionary vision as it was a post-revolutionary one, forged in part from the lessons of the war in America. In the end, it prevailed. Britain's comprehensive victory over France in 1815, on the battlefield and at the negotiating table, served to validate the "spirit of 1783" over French republican and Napoleonic alternatives, and to make liberalism and constitutional monarchy a defining mode of government in and beyond Europe.[28]

To this day, legacies of the British Empire's liberal constitutionalism endure alongside American democratic republicanism—making the "spirit of 1783" arguably just as important an influence in twenty-first-century political culture as the spirit of 1776. And yet, from some angles, maybe the spirit of 1776 and the spirit of 1783 didn't look so different. The post-revolutionary United States tussled with ambitions and problems remarkably like those faced by the British Empire from which it broke away: a drive for geographic expansion, competition with European empires, management of indigenous peoples, contests over the limits of democracy and the morality of slavery.[29] While the United States drafted its constitution, British imperial authorities developed constitutions for their colonial domains, from Quebec to Bengal.[30] While the British Empire made up for the loss in America by expanding into new colonies, the United States quickly embarked on empire-building itself, pushing west in a thrust that more than doubled the nation's size in just a generation. Though their political systems revolved around a fundamental divergence—one a monarchy, the other a republic—the United Kingdom and the United States shared ideas about the central importance of "liberty" and the rule of law.[31]

In 1815, Britain and its allies won at Waterloo; the British Empire was on top of the world. Loyalist refugees by then had carved out new homes and societies in their sites of exodus. After all the deprivation, the upheaval, the disappointment, and the stress, many surviving refugees, and even more of their children, eventually discovered a kind of contentment. Their trajectories from loss to assimilation mirrored the ascent of the British Empire as a whole, from defeat to global success. Loyalists who had left the United States for the British Empire were subjects of the world power that enjoyed international preeminence for the next century or more. They were, in this sense, victors after all.

THIS BOOK RECOVERS the stories of ordinary people whose lives were overturned by extraordinary events. To chronicle their journeys is also to chart them. The first three chapters describe the American Revolution as loyalists experienced it; the factors that caused them to leave; and the process by which most of them departed, in mass evacuations from British-held cities—an important yet little-known piece of revolutionary history. Chapters 4–6 follow the refugees to Britain and British North America (the eastern provinces of present-day Canada), to look at three features of loyalist settlement: how the refugees were fed, clothed, and compensated; how they formed new communities; and how they influenced the restructuring of imperial government after the war. Chapters 7–9 turn farther south, to explore the fortunes of refugees in the Bahamas, Jamaica, and Sierra Leone. Loyalists in these settings struggled against adverse environmental and economic conditions at the best of times, and the onset of the French Revolutionary wars only made things worse, by heightening conflicts over political rights and tensions around issues of slavery and race. The final chapter moves through the Napoleonic Wars and the War of 1812 to consider where loyalists stood a generation after their migrations began, from the place where they started—the United States—to the place that had overtaken America in imperial significance, India.

Since no one volume can contain sixty thousand stories, I have chosen to focus on a cluster of figures who capture different varieties of the refugee experience. Together they provide an intimate sense of what this exodus actually meant and felt like to its participants. The refugees belonged at once to a very big world—an expanding global empire—and to a surprisingly small one, in which scattered individuals retained personal connections over enormous distances of space and time. Remarkably many of these figures also moved more than once. Moving was part of the job for the imperial officials who recur in these pages, notably Sir Guy Carleton, commander in chief in New York and governor in Canada; and Lord Dunmore, governor of pre-revolutionary Virginia and the post-revolutionary Bahamas. For displaced civilians, however, repeated migrations underscored the dislocating effects of war, as well as the capacity of empires to channel human populations along certain routes.[32]

Elizabeth Lichtenstein Johnston, a middle-class loyalist from Georgia, was acutely aware of living in a world in motion. In her late teens when the war ended, Johnston led her growing family through the emptying British outposts of the south: Savannah, Charleston, and St. Augustine in turn. These journeys prefigured a longer postwar odyssey, when the Johnstons established homes in Scotland, Jamaica, and at last Nova Scotia, fully twenty years after their peregrinations began. The family of New York landed magnate Beverley Robinson provides an instructive parallel to the Johnstons, from a position of greater privilege. War reduced Robinson from sprawling acres in America to a modest dwelling in Gloucestershire. But he invested his remaining resources in placing his children in the military, one of the best mechanisms for upward mobility the British Empire had to offer.

Robinsons went on to thrive in imperial service everywhere from New Brunswick to Jamaica, Gibraltar, Egypt, and India. Some of Robinson's grandchildren even found fortune where their forebears had lost it, back in New York. Between them, the Johnston and Robinson families bring to life preoccupations shared by the majority of white loyalist refugees: to maintain social rank and respectability; to rebuild family fortunes; and to position their children for success. Their papers also give poignant insight into the emotional consequences of war on refugees coping with loss, dislocation, and separation.

Many refugees saw their journeys as devastating personal setbacks. But some realized that these turbulent times might offer great opportunities as well. Perhaps the most visionary of these dreamers was North Carolina merchant John Cruden, who watched both his fortune and British supremacy collapse around him, yet tirelessly promoted schemes to restore both. Cruden's projects to rebuild a British-American empire showed just how dynamic British ambitions remained after the war. In similar vein, Maryland loyalist William Augustus Bowles "went native" among the Creek Indians, and used his position between cultures to promote the creation of a loyal Indian state on the southwestern U.S. border. A more substantial effort to assert Indian sovereignty was led by Mohawk sachem Joseph Brant, the most prominent North American Indian to portray himself as a loyalist. From his postwar refuge near Lake Ontario, Brant aimed to build a western Indian confederacy that could protect native autonomy in the face of relentless white settler advance.

For black loyalists, of course, the losses inflicted by revolution were offset by an important gain: their freedom. This was the first step toward futures few could have imagined. David George, born into slavery in Virginia, found both freedom and faith as a Baptist convert in revolutionary South Carolina. After the war he emigrated to Nova Scotia, where he began to preach, quickly forming whole Baptist congregations around him. When he decided a few years later to seek a new Jerusalem in Sierra Leone, many of his followers made the journey with him. Networks of faith connected black loyalists around the Atlantic. George's spiritual mentor George Liele traced another line from the backcountry into the British Empire when he evacuated with the British to Jamaica, where he founded the island's first Baptist church.

To reconstruct these individual journeys, I have visited archives in every major loyalist destination to find refugees' own accounts of what happened to them. The interpretations people give of their behavior are usually refined in retrospect, and many of the writings loyalists produced about themselves had some agenda. This was manifestly the case for the single biggest trove of documents, the records of the Loyalist Claims Commission, set up to compensate loyalists for their losses. Every claimant had a vested interest in proving the strength of his or her loyalty, the intensity of suffering, and the magnitude of material loss. The best sources relating to black loyalists display another bias, having been shaped by British missionaries keen to advance an evangelical purpose. The most accessible sources concerning Indian nations were produced for and by white officials, placing an imperial filter over their contents. And then there were the usual distortions wrought by memory. Personal narratives written many decades after the war, like Elizabeth Johnston's, often emphasized tragedies, injustices, and resentments that lingered in the mind long after more benign recollections had faded. Early-nineteenth-century accounts produced in British North America, especially, could be skewed as heavily toward portraying loyalists as victims as competing accounts in the United States were toward presenting them as villains.

No sources of this kind are ever purely objective. But the way people tell their stories—what they emphasize, what they leave out—can tell the historian as much about their times as the concrete details they provide. The refugees' tragic discourse deserves to be listened to not least because it is so rarely heard. It captures aspects of human experience that are often left out of traditional political, economic, or diplomatic histories of this era, yet that are vital for understanding how revolutions affect their participants, how empires interact with their subjects, and how refugees cope with displacement. It inverts more familiar accounts to give a contrasting picture of alternatives, contingencies, and surprises. Nobody could predict at the outset how the American Revolution would turn out, whether the United States would survive, or what would become of the British Empire. For American colonists standing on the threshold of civil war in 1775, there would be a tumultuous, harrowing, and unpredictable journey ahead.

PART I

Refugees

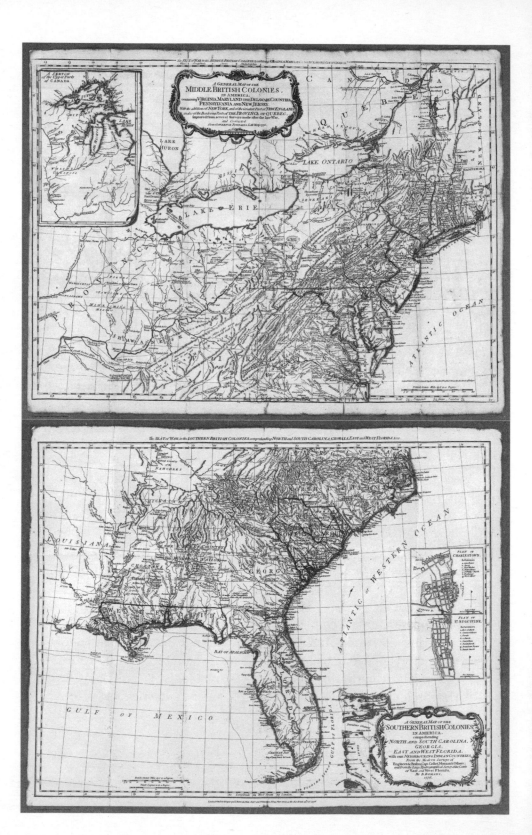

CHAPTER ONE

Civil War

THOMAS BROWN would always remember the day the American Revolution changed his life. It was the summer of 1775, the twenty-five-year-old's first on his own American land. He had arrived in the colonies a year earlier from the blustery English port of Whitby, with seventy-four indentured servants in tow, to start a plantation in the Georgia backcountry, near Augusta. The newcomers must have marveled on reaching this strange, subtropical landscape, where giant black oaks stood like sixty-foot columns holding up the sky.[1] Within nine months, Brown and his laborers had cut much of the forest into farms. He supervised his burgeoning 5,600-acre estate from a fine new great house, his tenants surrounding him in thirty-six farmhouses of their own. Horses filled Brown's stables; cattle and hogs got fat off his grass and feed. He applied to the governor for more land, sent away to Britain for another shipload of workers, and enjoyed "the pleasing prospect to observe that his affairs in that country were likely to succeed beyond his most sanguine expectations."[2] But another force was set to transform Thomas Brown's new world. He saw it coming one August day in the form of 130 armed men marching straight toward his house.

Brown knew, before coming to America, of the "troubles" that had been tearing up Anglo-American relations for a decade. A series of taxes imposed by Britain had triggered a heated conflict over the limits of parliamentary authority and the rights of colonial British subjects. Brown confidently reckoned that Georgia, a thousand miles away from New England, the center of unrest, had "no connection or concern" in

Opposite top: After Thomas Pownall, *A General Map of the Middle British Colonies in America*, 1776. Opposite bottom: Bernard Romans, *A General Map of the Southern British Colonies in America*, 1776.

such affairs. Even in 1774, investing his personal fortune and future in the American colonies looked like a good bet. But in April 1775, British and American troops exchanged the first shots of the revolution outside Boston—and no part of the colonies remained unconcerned for long. In Savannah and Charleston, the nearest major cities to Brown's estate, patriots formed associations to organize support for the rebellion, and approached Brown and his neighbors to join. Did he have anything to gain by doing so? Not really. The fact that he had recently arrived—and in 1775, 10 percent of the colonies' white population had immigrated within the last fifteen years—mattered less to his calculations than that he intended to spend the rest of his life in the colonies. He owed his land and status to the patronage of the Georgia governor; he also held a position as a local magistrate. Besides, he figured, surely this provincial uprising had little chance of success when met with the full military might of the British Empire. Whatever he may have thought of the principles at stake, self-interest alone pointed out Brown's choice. He refused patriot overtures, and signed on to a loyalist counterassociation instead. The next thing Brown knew, patriot invitations became demands, delivered by gangs like the one at his door.

Standing on the porch, the sticky heat clinging to him like a second shirt, Brown tried to put the men off calmly. He had no wish to fight his own neighbors, he said, but he "could never enter into an Engagement to take up arms against the Country which gave him being." The conversation quickly turned to confrontation. Some of the patriots "threatened that unless he would subscribe the association they would drag him by force to Augusta." Brown backed into the house to seize his weapons, "determined to defend himself as long as he was able against any violence." "It would be at the peril of that man who should attempt it!" he declared, brandishing his pistols. Six men lunged at him. Blades flashed, a gun fired, a rifle butt swung up over his head— and smashed squarely down onto his skull. Then blackness.[3]

What came next he would reconstruct later, from flashes of recollection in a semiconscious haze. Shattered head throbbing, body bleeding, he rattles over a track. They reach Augusta. He is tossed to the ground, his arms lashed around the trunk of a tree. He sees his bare legs splayed out in front of him, funny-looking foreign things, and he sees hot brown pitch poured over them, scalding, clinging to his skin. Under his feet the men pile up kindling and set it alight. The flame catches the tar, sears his flesh. His feet are on fire, two of his toes charred into stubs. The attackers seize his broken head by the hair and pull it out in clumps. Knives take care of the rest, cutting off strips of scalp, making the blood run down over his ears, face, and neck. Half scalped, skull fractured, lamed, slashed, and battered, Brown—remarkably—survives. Later, a doctor comes to the place where he is confined and bandages him up, setting his broken bones on course to heal. A sympathetic guard, moved by the spectacle of this badly damaged man, agrees to let Brown get away. He slips out of custody and rides over the border into South Carolina to take shelter with a loyalist friend.[4]

In years to come Brown frequently recalled how the patriots "tortured him in the most inhuman manner." He did not choose to describe how he was then carted through the streets of Augusta for public mockery—and how he, like many victims of such assaults, ultimately broke down and agreed to sign the association (an action he promptly renounced after his escape).[5] But the personal humiliation of giving in to his attackers could only have contributed to the passion of Brown's response. The incident turned him from a noncombatant into a militant enemy of the revolution. Within a matter of weeks, his feet so badly injured he could not walk, his head still wrapped in bandages, Brown rallied hundreds of backcountry residents to form a loyalist militia, the King's Rangers, and fight back. Physically and mentally brutalized by the patriots, Brown in turn earned notoriety as a particularly ruthless, vindictive loyalist commander.[6]

A rich historical tradition has portrayed the American Revolution first and foremost as a war of ideals—not a war of ordeals.[7] Yet for Brown and thousands more civilians caught in the conflict, this was what the revolution looked like: mobs on the march, neighbors turned enemies, critical decisions forced under stress. As the revolution gathered momentum across the colonies, one American after another faced a choice. Would they join the rebellion or stay loyal to the king and empire? Their answers had to do with a host of factors, including core values and beliefs, self-interest, local circumstance, and personal relationships. But no matter how contingent, their responses could have unexpectedly far-ranging results.

WHAT WAS a loyalist, and what kind of America and British Empire did loyalists want?[8] It is important to note at the outset that, as fellow American colonists, loyalists and patriots had more in common with one another than they did with metropolitan Britons. Both loyalists and patriots shared preoccupations with access to land, the maintenance of slavery, and regulation of colonial trade. Nor did their places of origin necessarily serve as a leading indicator of political difference. While Thomas Brown remained loyal, for instance, one of the indentured servants he brought from the Orkney Islands promptly ran off and joined a patriot militia.[9] Ultimately choices about loyalty depended more on employers, occupations, profits, land, faith, family, and friendships than on any implicit identification as an American or a Briton. At the start of the war, colonists often saw themselves both as American, in the sense that they were colonial residents, and as British, in the sense of being British subjects.

What truly divided colonial Americans into loyalists and patriots was the mounting pressure of revolutionary events: threats, violence, the imposition of oaths, and ultimately war. By 1776, the patriots renounced the king's authority, and developed fresh political and philosophical justifications for doing so—whereas loyalists wanted to remain British subjects, and wanted the thirteen colonies to remain part of the British Empire. On these fundamental points, loyalists could largely agree. Nevertheless, it would be a mistake to think loyalists were ideologically uniform—or that they simply wanted to preserve the status quo. In fact, many leading loyalists sought to reform the imperial relationship. They resisted the prospect of authoritarian rule, and were quick to defend their rights to representation. Indeed, during the colonial protests of the 1760s and 1770s, future loyalists and patriots alike spoke out in unison against perceived British tyranny. They tended to share provincial perspectives on rights and liberties, and a common language of grievance against the abuse of imperial authority. This would have important repercussions in the postwar years, when loyalist refugees found their expectations as British subjects to be at odds with those of their metropolitan British rulers.

The troubles in the colonies all started, strangely enough, with Britain's greatest imperial victory. Triumph in the Seven Years' War in 1763 brought the empire French Canada, Spanish Florida, valuable Caribbean islands, and an important foothold in India. But Britain had also racked up an enormous debt. To offset the costs, Parliament passed a series of measures in the colonies designed to promote imperial security and prosperity. Instead, it unintentionally provoked colonial resistance. Most notoriously, the Stamp Act of 1765, a seemingly innocuous tax on paper products, spectacularly backfired when Americans (and many Britons) denounced it as an abuse of imperial power, imposed by a parliament that did not adequately represent colonists. Many future loyalists were vocal opponents of the Stamp Act, though these protests also saw the first systematic attacks against American "tories," suspected of wanting to enhance royal and aristocratic power. Street gangs like the self-described Sons of Liberty smashed property and assaulted individuals—most vividly by tarring and feathering, a new hallmark of patriot justice.[10]

Violence was a familiar colonial phenomenon by the time a 1773 tax on tea touched off the worst trouble yet. One December night, Boston's Sons of Liberty, their faces streaked to resemble Indian warriors, stormed onto British tea ships anchored in Boston harbor and tipped the valuable cargo overboard. Parliament responded by passing the so-called Coercive Acts, closing the port of Boston and demanding repayment for the tea. Americans swiftly branded these the "Intolerable Acts." Delegates from around the thirteen colonies decided to convene a continental congress in Philadelphia and develop a coordinated response.

A few congressmen arrived in Philadelphia in September 1774 already primed for war. They must have cheered enthusiastically at a congressional dinner when the radical pamphleteer Thomas Paine— who had recently arrived from England to throw his support behind the patriot cause—raised a toast, declaring, "May the collision of British Flint and American Steel produce that spark of liberty which shall illumine . . . posterity"! But the majority of delegates would have cheered more comfortably when the company drank to the "Union of Britain and the Colonies on a constitutional foundation."[11] The prospect of war seemed to most congressmen an unnecessary, not to say suicidal, extreme. Far preferable was finding a way to assert colonial rights and liberties while remaining within the imperial fold.

The speaker of the Pennsylvania assembly, Joseph Galloway, offered Congress a compelling plan to achieve this.[12] Galloway agreed with most of his colleagues that the colonies—while they held "in abhorrence the idea of being considered independent"—could not adequately "be represented in the Parliament of Great Britain." Instead, Galloway suggested that America have a parliament of its own: a "Grand Council," to be headed by a president general. Made up of representatives from each colony, this American parliament would "hold and exercise all the legislative rights, powers, and authorities" required for running colonial affairs. It would also have the power to veto any legislation bearing on America produced by the British parliament. The colonies would thereby enjoy domestic self-government while retaining the benefits of imperial trade and protection. Such a "Plan of Union," Galloway argued, was the only way forward if the colonies wanted to stave off "all the horrors of a civil war" and the inevitable "ruin of America."[13]

Galloway's plan was the most significant colonial reform project on the eve of the revolution, though it did not come out of a vacuum. Galloway's mentor Benjamin Franklin had proposed a very similar idea himself twenty years earlier (developed with the governor of Massachusetts Thomas Hutchinson, later reviled as a "tory"), the Albany Plan of Union of 1754.[14] "Join, or Die," Franklin had inscribed under a memorable political cartoon showing the colonies as segments of a cut-up serpent—indicating the importance of continental union to American prosperity.[15] Galloway sent his own plan of union to Franklin, then living in London, who circulated the scheme among high-ranking British officials; Franklin's only objection was that it might embroil America in too many British imperial wars. Franklin's son William, the governor of New Jersey, wholeheartedly endorsed it. After all, it had much to commend it to American sensibilities. By granting the colonies control over virtually everything but the ability to go to war, Galloway's plan proposed a greater degree of autonomy for the American colonies than any other British domain enjoyed, including Scotland. His proposed American legislature would have fewer constraints than the Irish parliament, too. Most important, Galloway argued, his plan would aid the development of America itself. If the colonies were going to continue to grow and flourish, there had to be some overarching authority binding them together, in the spirit of Franklin's "Join, or Die"; perhaps, he suggested, an "American constitution."[16]

For one long late-September day in 1774, Congress debated Galloway's plan of union. The New York delegation was particularly well disposed toward it, with the respected lawyer John Jay speaking out clearly in its favor. It was "almost a perfect plan," declared an upstanding young South Carolina planter. Galloway congratulated himself that "all the men of property, and many of the ablest speakers, supported the motion." But not all his colleagues were convinced. "We are not to consent by the representatives of representatives," insisted Patrick Henry of Virginia.[17] Samuel Adams, the founder of the Sons of

Liberty, believed the colonies would do better by withdrawing from the British Empire altogether. When Galloway's plan came to a vote, five colonies voted in its favor versus six against—and the plan was tabled.[18] Instead of moving toward closer union with Britain, Congress issued a set of resolutions asserting Americans' entitlement to "all the rights, liberties, and immunities" of British subjects, in terms anticipating those of the Declaration of Independence.[19]

The closeness of the vote on Galloway's plan poses an intriguing "what if" for historians. What if one vote had gone the other way? What would have happened to the thirteen colonies if Galloway's scheme *had* been adopted? Ireland might provide one answer: following a series of reforms in 1782, the Irish parliament received something of the legislative freedom Galloway sought for America. In 1800, Ireland would be united with Great Britain outright and its parliament absorbed by Westminster. But a better answer would take shape in North America itself, in 1867, when the provinces of Canada, New Brunswick, and Nova Scotia united to become a federal, self-governing dominion within the British Empire. Canada—as this confederation was called—was the first example of "home rule" (autonomy over domestic policy) in the empire, and provided a template for self-government movements in later-nineteenth-century Ireland and India. In 1774 Philadelphia, Galloway advanced a model of imperial reform that anticipated home rule by generations. It was a prime example of how loyalists possessed dynamic political visions of their own.

Galloway could not have taken much comfort in seeing one part of his prophecy come true. By rejecting his plan—the last concerted American attempt to preserve ties with the British Empire—Congress moved inexorably closer to civil war. With tensions already near breaking point, it was mostly a matter of time before something touched off outright conflict.

The alarm came before dawn on the morning of April 19, 1775, when militia members in Lexington, Massachusetts, were rustled out of bed with news that British soldiers were coming from Boston to seize a patriot weapons store in nearby Concord. The militia mustered on Lexington Green as fast as they could and hastily readied their muskets as seven hundred well-disciplined British regulars marched, wheeled, and advanced toward them. Then a gun went off. Nobody knew who fired the "shot heard 'round the world" (as the poet Ralph Waldo Emerson would famously dub it), British redcoat or American militiaman.[20] But that didn't really matter. For despite their differences in power and purpose, the two groups of men were more alike than any other enemies they had faced. To them and thousands more now engulfed by war, the American Revolution did not look like a world-historical drama about the forging of a new nation. This was a bitter civil war about the division of an old empire. It accelerated a painful process in which British subjects were increasingly divided into opposing camps, as Americans and Britons.[21] The problem for loyalists was that they had affiliations to both, being at once rooted American colonists and committed British subjects.

FOR THE CONGRESSMEN meeting in Philadelphia, ideas and beliefs were an explicit subject of debate. But for the two and a half million Americans caught up in a civil war, ideas were hardened—if not superseded—by violence. The beginning of conflict was enough to push even some former congressmen to the other side, including prominent New York merchant Isaac Low. Though Low had resisted the abuse of imperial authority since the 1760s, he felt progressively alienated by the steps toward war. When the Second Continental Congress convened in May 1775, Low resigned his seat and stayed home; and when asked to purchase gunpowder for patriot troops a short time later, he withdrew entirely from government and soon lent his support to the British.[22] Within weeks of the skirmishes at Lexington and Concord, colonies established committees of safety that administered loyalty oaths to newly formed patriot legislatures. These oaths became a crucial marker of difference between patriots and loyalists. People who refused to swear them could be jailed, punished with property confiscation, or banished outright. Popular justice also followed those who failed to comply. Jacob Bailey, the Pownalborough minister, was comparatively fortunate that only his sheep and cows were attacked. At least two dozen others in 1775 shared the fate of Thomas Brown, by being tortured and publicly humiliated with tarring and feathering.[23]

Then there was the spreading violence of the war itself. Revolution reached five-year-old Catherine Skinner one night when soldiers broke into her house, yanked her from her bed, and plunged their bayonets into her mattress to see if her father was hiding underneath. Catherine's father, Cortlandt Skinner, New Jersey's last royal attorney general, had rebuffed patriot overtures (like Brown) and escaped to

British lines, leaving his family in the New Jersey countryside. Rebel raids trapped the Skinner family as prisoners in their own house; they hid in the cellar from gunshots, famished to the point of pain and tears. At last Catherine's mother managed to lead her ten youngest children to safety on her eldest daughter's farm. The days grew sharp and short, winter coming on. Every time they went into the fields they found another outbuilding burned, another of their pigs or cows poisoned by the rebels. The Skinners scraped through the winter of 1776–77 on stores of buckwheat buried beneath the hard-frozen ground. One frigid day the youngest of the family, a smiling boy of fourteen months, died. For days they kept the tiny body inside the house, unable to let him go with no priest to perform a funeral and no church accessible. In the end, Catherine's eldest siblings "carried the poor little thing out in the night and buried him in the corner of a field."[24] Traumatic scenes like this imprinted Catherine—and probably her younger sister Maria too—powerfully enough for her to recall them vividly more than sixty years later.

Loyalists closely monitored the progress of the war, sometimes hiding out to avoid confrontations, sometimes moving to seek shelter within British lines. Of course, at the outset it was reasonable to think that Britain would win the conflict handily. But a worrying indication to the contrary came when the British decided to evacuate Boston in March 1776 in the face of a patriot attack. In the orders to abandon the city, British general William Howe offered free passage to any loyalist civilians who wished to follow—unwittingly setting a precedent for many more evacuations to come. At least eleven hundred loyalists sailed with the departing troops for Halifax in Nova Scotia.[25] "By all accounts, there never existed a more miserable set of beings, than these wretched creatures now are," said George Washington, the commander in chief of the Continental Army. "Conscious of their black ingratitude, they chose to commit themselves . . . to the mercy of the waves in a tempestuous season, rather than meet their offended countrymen."[26] Washington's contempt aside, the refugees would have agreed with his portrayal of their woeful condition. Leaving behind almost all their property and personal connections, the Boston refugees were the first loyalists to experience mass evacuation—and the first group to discover the hardships of imperial exile.

In New York City, where British military efforts now concentrated, the assistant rector of Trinity Church, Charles Inglis, anxiously watched the situation deteriorate around him. As an ordained priest in the Church of England, Inglis (like Jacob Bailey) could not brook the prospect of forswearing his allegiance to the king who stood at the head of his church. But he felt sick at the sight of his country at war. In January 1776, Thomas Paine published the pamphlet *Common Sense*, a strident and hugely compelling argument in favor of American independence and republicanism. Inglis quickly scribbled out a deeply felt, intellectually grounded rebuttal called *The True Interest of America, Impartially Stated.* "I find no Common Sense in this pamphlet but much uncommon phrenzy," Inglis wrote. "Even Hobbes would blush to own its author for a disciple." Inglis vividly described the devastating consequences that he thought Paine's vision would have for America: "Ruthless war . . . will ravage our once happy land. . . . Torrents of blood will be spilt, and thousands reduced to beggary and wretchedness." What America needed instead, Inglis argued, was a reformed imperial relationship to secure American "Liberties, Property, and Trade." "No person breathing has a deeper sense of the present distresses of America, than I," he insisted, "or would rejoice more to see these removed, and our liberties settled on a permanent, constitutional foundation." But republicanism truly did seem to him a formula for anarchy, and independence a recipe for decline. He owed it "to God, to my King and Country" to resist. Where Paine had presented his text as the anonymous work of "an Englishman," Inglis—who was born in Ireland—published his pamphlet under the proud label of "an American."[27]

Inglis hoped that Paine's pamphlet, "like others, will sink in oblivion."[28] Instead it was a runaway sensation. Said to have sold half a million copies in 1776 alone—enough for one in every five Americans to own one—the pamphlet helped convert Americans en masse to the idea of independence.[29] Copies of Inglis's pamphlet, by contrast, were seized from the printer and burned in what Inglis condemned as "a violent attack on the Liberty of the Press." More outrages followed. The New York committee of safety ordered the loyalist-leaning governors of King's College—today's Columbia University—to empty out the college library so the facility could be turned into a barracks for Continental Army troops. In May 1776, suspected New York loyalists were rounded up and forced to hand over any weapons in their possession; the next month, more were seized by a mob, "rode on Rails, their Cloth's torn off, & much beaten & abused. Many were obliged to fly out of the City, & durst not return." By summer, Inglis and his friends were living in "the utmost Consternation and Terror" in the wake of a rumored plot to assassinate George Washington.[30]

And then, on July 4, 1776, Congress voted to adopt the Declaration of Independence. All patriot talk of union, reform, and British liberties was swept away, replaced by Thomas Jefferson's crystalline presentation of universal, "self-evident," and "unalienable rights." On paper, the declaration transformed thirteen British colonies into independent and "united States of America." It would take a lot more to make the United States real in practice, but the declaration had a critical effect on consolidating patriot and loyalist positions. From now on, independence was the dividing line: either you were for it or you were against it. Independence made anybody who aided or abetted the British into a traitor against the United States. It also came with a symbol attached. The language of the declaration turned King George III into the embodiment of everything patriots hated about British rule. For loyalists, by contrast, the king provided a focal point of unity; supporting him was the one thing they all believed in.

No more king, no more Parliament, no more British Empire: as news of the declaration whipped across America, people instantly understood its significance. Emblems of the king's authority came crashing down in an iconoclastic frenzy. Patriots marched through the streets of Boston tearing down inn signs, placards, and anything else bearing royal insignia. In Baltimore, they wheeled a statue of the king through the streets like a condemned man headed for execution and set it ablaze before a crowd of thousands. On Bowling Green in New York City, a crowd of soldiers and eager civilians looped ropes around a monumental equestrian statue of King George III, toppled it from its marble pedestal, chopped off the statue's head, and planted it on a spike of iron fence. Inglis recorded how the decapitated remains were paraded through the city to the Continental Army camp, where "the Declaration of Independency was read at the Head of several Regiments." Its valuable lead would be melted down into more than forty thousand bullets.[31]

Inglis remained frightened by "the critical situation of affairs" and "the most violent threats flung out against any who would presume to pray for the King." Fortunately for him, a deliverance of sorts was at hand. Preparing for an invasion of New York City, Royal Navy ships crowded into the harbor "as thick as trees in a forest."[32] In the last week of August 1776, thirty thousand British troops landed in Brooklyn in great red waves. They routed Washington's Continental Army on Brooklyn Heights and crossed the East River to seize Manhattan. Britain's comprehensive victory in New York almost ended the war on the spot—though through bad British decisions and good American luck, Washington escaped to fight another day. Instead, New York City became the central British base of operations for the rest of the war. It also became the largest loyalist stronghold in the colonies. Loyalists surged into this safe haven from surrounding war-torn areas.[33] In September 1776, when the British occupation began, the city contained a mere five thousand residents, many patriots having fled in the face of the British advance. Less than six months later, loyalist refugees had doubled the population, and soon New York played home to twenty-five to thirty thousand loyalists, making it the second largest city in the colonies.[34]

Refugees came to New York City in search of protection and stability, but these, they found, had a price. A few nights after the British arrival, a fire broke out on one of the slips at Manhattan's southeastern tip. Sheets of flame blazed up Broadway, consuming as many as a quarter of the city's buildings in its wake. British commanders concluded that the fire had been started by patriot arsonists, and promptly placed New York City under martial law; it remained under military rule until the end of the war.[35] Loyalists deeply resented living under military occupation, subordinated to the whims of raucous British troops.[36] (Not for nothing had the quartering of British soldiers in American homes been a long-standing colonial grievance.) In the fall of 1776, the disgruntled New York refugees presented a petition to the British commanders in chief complaining about martial law. "Notwithstanding the tumult of the times, and the extreme difficulties and losses to which many of us have been exposed, we have always expressed, and do now give this Testimony of our Zeal to preserve and support the constitutional supremacy of Great Britain over the Colonies," the petitioners stressed. "[S]o far from having given the least countenance of encouragement, to the most unnatural, unprovoked Rebellion, that ever disgraced the annals of Time; we have on the contrary, steadily and uniformly opposed it, in every stage of its rise and progress, at the risque of our Lives and Fortunes." In return for their loyalty, they argued, they deserved to be treated with "some line of distinction"—not the imperial iron fist that clenched them more tightly than ever.[37]

A frank declaration of *dependence*, this document conspicuously lacks the rhetorical grace and inspiration of the Declaration of Independence. But it gives clear insight into what a large cross section of American loyalists wanted from the British Empire. They had no wish to "dissolve the political bands" with Britain, as the Declaration of Independence had proclaimed. On the contrary, they sought "a speedy restoration of that union" between Britain and the colonies that had produced so much "mutual happiness and prosperity." At the same time, these New Yorkers were not backward-looking reactionaries. Their quest for a civil reunion with Britain would have inclined them toward plans like Joseph Galloway's, in which the colonies would gain greater autonomy. Nor were they unthinkingly "loyal" to what was effectively an army of occupation.

The "declaration of dependence" also nicely illustrates who these loyalists actually were. For three days in late November 1776, the petition sat on a table at Scott's Tavern in Wall Street, to be signed by anybody who wished. In all, more than seven hundred people came to put their names to the parchment—twelve times the number who signed the Declaration of Independence. The list of signatories ranged from grandees fat with land and capital to small-time local farmers and artisans. The very first signer, Hugh Wallace, counted among the wealthiest traders in the city; he and his brother Alexander, émigrés from Ireland, had cemented their self-made success by marrying two sisters of Isaac Low, the former congressman. Charles Inglis and New York's other principal clergymen followed immediately below. Representatives of New York's great landed families, the DeLanceys, the Livingstons, and the Philipses, also inscribed their names to the petition. The majority of signatures, though, belonged to the ordinary people who made New York run: tavern-keepers and carpenters, farmers from the Hudson Valley and New Jersey, Germans, Dutch, Scots, and Welsh. Here was the baker Joseph Orchard, who supplied the British army with bread, and the hairdresser and perfumer James Deas. Many signatories later joined up to fight: men like Amos Lucas, who left his farm on Long Island to join a loyalist regiment, and the Greenwich blacksmith James Stewart, a veteran of the Seven Years' War, who enlisted in the British army in 1777. While the petition recorded the social hierarchy of the times—with "leading citizens" at the top and their clients and subordinates below—it also demonstrated the social diversity of loyalism.[38]

As patriots united around the idea of an independent nation, loyalty to the king helped a parallel America coalesce around an ideal of enduring empire. Yet these New York loyalists confronted an ominous portent of what would become a recurring loyalist predicament. They found a place of safety, yes, but it was not necessarily a comfortable one. What they wanted from Britain was not always what British authorities would give them. And though they were not prepared to abandon the imperial connection altogether, they had no desire to be treated as supplicant minions either. It was one thing to experience such treatment in a time of war. But many would find, to their chagrin, that such disjunctures between loyalist expectation and British practice stretched on well into the peace.

It was no wonder, then, that colonists inclined toward the king could feel pressed between a rock and a hard place, reluctant to commit themselves openly to a loyalist cause that might bring nothing but punishment, property confiscation, dislocation, and discomfort in its wake. This was the dilemma that New York landowner Beverley Robinson wrestled with in the winter of 1777. The war had been going on for nearly two years, yet Robinson still could not figure out what to do. Born in Virginia, Robinson had come to New York in the 1740s as an officer in a colonial regiment—along with his childhood friend and brother officer, George Washington. There he met and married a member of one of New York's great landed families, Susanna Philipse. (Washington unsuccessfully courted Susanna's sister, who passed him over for a future loyalist.) The marriage made Robinson one of the largest landed magnates in the region. The Robinsons lived in style in the Hudson Highlands, sixty miles north of New York City. Collecting ample rents from contented tenants, surrounded by good friends and neighbors, and raising a spirited brood of two daughters and five sons, Beverley Robinson had every reason to believe that the 1770s would be some of the best years of his life. "Since the time of the golden age there never was more perfect domestic happiness and rural life than that which he and his family enjoyed," Robinson's fourth son, Frederick Philipse "Phil" Robinson, glowingly recalled.[39] Instead, Beverley Robinson found himself confronting the biggest decision he would ever have to make.

Would he openly declare his loyalty to the king, to whom he had sworn repeated oaths of allegiance as a militia officer and county judge? Could he continue to stay quiet? Or would he join many of his acquaintances in rejecting an imperial relationship gone sour? The stakes of his choice could not have been higher. In his heart of hearts, Robinson did not want his world to change—and why should he? As a patrician landowner he enjoyed a life as close to that of an English aristocrat as America could offer. Yet coming out as a loyalist would carry substantial risks for himself, his family, and his property. Besides, he cared deeply for his country and its future. If the colonies won the war and the United States became independent, he was not necessarily prepared to abandon New York in consequence.

Robinson was lucky that the rebels did not show up on his doorstep, as they had at Thomas Brown's. But in February 1777, matters came to a head when Robinson was summoned before a "Committee to Detect Conspiracies" and interrogated about his neutrality. One of the examiners was Robinson's old friend John Jay, the New York lawyer and congressman. "Sir," Jay told him soberly, "we have crossed the Rubicon and it is now necessary for every man [to] Take his part, Cast off all allegiance to the King of Great Britain and take an oath of allegiance to the States of America or go over to the Enemy for we have Declared our Selves Independent."[40] The dilemma cut Robinson to the core. "I cannot yet think of forfeiting my allegiance to the King," he wrote to Jay in distress after their meeting, and yet "I am as unwilling to remove myself or family from this place." He would take counsel one last time with his friends, he said, "on the unhappy & distracted state of my poor Bleeding Country." "If I am convinced that a Reconciliation cannot be had upon just & reasonable terms," Robinson concluded, "I will . . . content myself to share the same state as my Country. Nothing shall ever tempt or force me to do any thing, that I think . . . will be prejudicial to my Country."[41]

Robinson's struggle was agonizing for Jay too. Jay had long hoped for peaceful reconciliation with Britain himself—hence his support of Galloway's plan of union. Facing the Rubicon of independence, he crossed; but several close friends stayed back.[42] Hoping to prevent another ruptured friendship, Jay addressed a heartfelt appeal to Susanna Robinson, entreating her to persuade her husband to back down from declaring his loyalism. "Mr. Robinson has put his own & the Happiness of his Family & Posterity at Hazard—and for what? For the Sake of a fanciful Regard to an Ideal Obligation to a Prince . . . who with his Parliament . . . claim a Right to bind you & your Children in all Cases whatsoever." He invited her to consider what would become of the Robinsons if they remained loyal. "Remember that should you carry your numerous Family to New York Famine may meet you & incessant anxiety banish your Peace," he warned:

> Picture to your Imagination a City besieged, yourself & Children mixt with contending Armies—Should it be evacuated, where, with whom & in what Manner are you next to fly? Can you think of living under the restless wings of an Army? Should Heaven determine that America shall be free, In what Country are you prepared to spend the Remainder of your Days & how provide for your Children? These Things it is true may not happen, but dont forget that they <u>may</u>.[43]

Jay's warnings proved astonishingly prescient. But such visions could not change his friends' ultimate refusal, even in the face of civil war, to renounce the king. In March 1777, Beverley Robinson took his stand and joined the British outright. Though the Robinsons had long sat on the sidelines of the conflict, the family now threw themselves into war. Robinson raised a new provincial regiment (one of the brigades of loyalist soldiers attached to the British army), called the Loyal American Regiment, and served as its colonel. His eldest son, Beverley Robinson Jr., acted as the regiment's lieutenant colonel, and his second son as a captain.[44] When his fourth son Phil Robinson reached fighting age—thirteen—the youth took up a commission in a British infantry unit. Susanna Robinson and the other children retreated into occupied New York City for safety. There, at a small ceremony performed by Charles Inglis, the younger Beverley married Anna Barclay, the sister of another Loyal American officer. While the Robinson family fought to preserve their vision of imperial America, the state of New York confiscated Robinson's estates in the name of independence. In later years, Washington and his officers used the Robinson house as a headquarters, directing offensives against the British from the very same rooms in which he had dined and drunk as his loyal friend's guest.[45]

As BEVERLEY ROBINSON wavered over whether to take a stand in the war, a neighboring population of New Yorkers was already actively engaged in the British cause. They were Mohawk Indians, one of the many indigenous nations drawn into the American Revolution. For all that their experiences manifestly differed from those of colonists and slaves, they belong in the same frame as white and black loyalists for several reasons. Not least, Indian participation in the war loomed large in colonists' perceptions, and had some influence on their own choice of sides.[46] But this was not just a civil war among whites. It aligned and divided North America's native peoples too. For the Mohawks among others, fighting with the British led to outcomes that resembled and intersected with those of white and black loyalists—and ultimately pulled them, too, into the ranks of loyalist refugees.

On the frontiers of white settlement, the American Revolution did not look like a war about taxation and representation. This was a war about access to land, and it was triggered less by revenue-raising measures such as the Stamp Act than by the Proclamation of 1763, by which

Britain banned colonial settlement west of the Appalachians.[47] British officials passed the measure in part to stave off the inevitable violence between whites and Indians that accompanied expansion. To land-hungry settlers nothing could be more noxious. Decades of warfare between colonists and Indian "savages" had produced excruciatingly savage forms of warfare in turn—epitomized, for whites, by the practice of scalping.[48] (When Thomas Brown described "my head scalped in 3 or 4 places" on that August day in 1775, he deployed the worst slur available to colonial Americans: he likened his attackers to Indians.)[49] The violent history of Indian-white relations had important repercussions for frontier colonists' decisions about loyalty. One of the reasons Brown and his neighbors stayed loyal was because they counted on the British government to protect them from Indians. Yet one of the grounds patriots cited for rebellion was that the British had *failed* to protect them.

The coming of revolution presented Indians, too, with a choice. European powers had long relied on Indians to fight alongside them in colonial wars, and this was no exception. Both British and patriot agents worked to recruit Indians into their service, leaving Indians to weigh up their own questions of belief, conscience, and collective interest. Which side would enable them to protect their autonomy best? For no native population would such calculations be better documented, and perhaps more shrewdly measured, than the Mohawks. Because Indian nations in this period remained autonomous powers, historians have often resisted labeling those who fought for the British as "loyalists" instead of "allies." But the Mohawks' connection with Britain ran especially long and deep. In their own telling and that of their white peers, they could be considered loyalists too.

Part of a confederacy of Iroquois nations known as the Six Nations, the Mohawks had an alliance with Britain dating back to well before the revolution. The "Covenant Chain," as the Anglo-Iroquois alliance was called, was anchored both in treaties and in transformative personal relationships. For nearly twenty years it had been nurtured by Sir William Johnson, the enormously influential superintendent of Indian affairs for the northern department. The archetype of a successful Irish immigrant, Johnson had arrived in New York in 1738 with little more than a good connection (his uncle was a prominent admiral) and a dozen families he had recruited to settle on his uncle's lands. He ended up building a sprawling personal empire of 400,000 acres stretching across the Mohawk Valley. At his manor house, Johnson Hall, Sir

William lived in neo-feudal splendor surrounded by hundreds of tenant farmers. At the same time, in partnership with his third wife, Mary "Molly" Brant, a prominent Mohawk, he presided over a multicultural domain. The couple raised their eight half-white, half-Mohawk children in a house built in the best Georgian style, where they were served by black slaves and surrounded by white and Indian visitors. At regular Indian councils the Johnsons hosted sumptuous feasts for hundreds, to negotiate and seal deals around the council fire. Johnson's commanding influence among colonists and Indians alike allowed him to broker the Treaty of Fort Stanwix in 1768, which established a firm boundary between British and Indian lands in New York and Pennsylvania.

Johnson died in 1774, on the eve of his world's disintegration. But "Johnson" remained a name to conjure with in upstate New York. The office of superintendent would be assumed by his son-in-law Guy Johnson and his son Sir John Johnson in turn; another son-in-law acted as deputy superintendent. And while the Johnsons privileged the Mohawks in British policy, the Mohawks privileged the British in turn. When war erupted just months after Sir William's death, Molly Brant, the powerful doyenne of Johnson Hall, actively worked to rally the Iroquois to the British cause. Loyalism, to her, was the obvious stance: personal connections and anti-settler animosity, as well as considered self-interest, all pointed toward the British. The other Six Nations members followed the Mohawks' choice—with one notable exception. Acting on a calculation that the patriots might win the war, the Oneida Indians opted to join the other side. The American Revolution thus divided the Iroquois confederacy against itself, breaking the Six Nations into five versus one; it also split nations from within, with some villages remaining neutral while others went to war.[50]

Molly Brant's actions convinced the British that "one word from her is more taken Notice of by the five Nations than a thousand from any white Man without exception."[51] As such, the British repeatedly offered her special favors, such as houses and allowances to the tune of three to four thousand pounds per year.[52] New York patriots, meanwhile, provided different testament to Brant's influence. "Mary Brant (alias Johnson)" was one of only five women recorded on a list of loyalists formally stripped of their property under the New York State confiscation act. (The other four women were all Johnsons.)[53] However she may have characterized her own position, these British and American actions clearly portrayed Molly Brant as a loyalist.

But the relationship between the British and the Mohawks would be embodied most visibly in Molly's forty-year-old brother Thayendanegea—or as his non-Indian friends preferred to call him, Joseph Brant.[54] In Mohawk Thayendanegea means "two sticks," or "he who places two bets," and it was an apt name for a man who had come of age between cultures, welcomed into the mixed community of Johnson Hall by his sister Molly and treated almost as an adoptive son by Sir William. At the age of eighteen, Joseph, already a decorated veteran of the Seven Years' War, set out under Johnson's patronage for the well-known "Indian school" in Connecticut run by missionary Eleazer Wheelock. He later self-deprecatingly described his command of English, which he perfected at the school, as "half English half Indian," but there was some truth to the label, for Wheelock's school also helped Brant cement a double status.[55] Thanks to his ancestry and marriages, Brant enjoyed a high position in Mohawk society and politics, and lived in comfort on his parents' farm in the Mohawk Valley. At the same time, he associated easily with whites, became a devout Christian, and acted as interpreter to the Anglican missionary to the Mohawks, John Stuart.[56]

The revolution set Brant's cross-cultural role on an international stage. Soon he became chief sachem of the Mohawks, as Thayendanegea, and held a military commission as Captain Joseph Brant, the highest-ranking Indian in British service. He also learned to play the part of Anglo-Mohawk to dazzling perfection. In late 1775, Brant accompanied the superintendent of Indian affairs, Guy Johnson, to London, hoping to earn support for Mohawk land claims through a direct appeal to the king. "When he wore the ordinary European habit," a contemporary newspaper noted, "there did not seem to be anything about him that marked preeminence." But he knew how to make himself stand out. He sat for the popular society portraitist George Romney, crowned with a plume of scarlet feathers, cloak balanced over his left hand and tomahawk in his right, crucifix and gorget glinting around his neck. He charmed James Boswell, was presented at court, and was inducted into a celebrated Masonic lodge. As for his own impressions of London, it was the ladies that impressed him most, he said—and the sleek, swift horses.[57]

Spearheaded by the Brants, and building on the Johnson legacy, Mohawk participation in the Revolutionary War represented a genuine merging of multinational interests under the banner of the British Empire. As loyalists, the Mohawks would be able to call on a larger degree of support and patronage from the British than any other Indian nation. The British in turn relied on them to help secure the Canadian borderlands, the longest Anglo-American frontier. But loyalism did not ultimately shield the Mohawks when the war started to go against them.

The summer of 1777 was a savage one in the Mohawk Valley, as ferocious battles ripped the Iroquois confederacy apart. Patriot and Oneida forces sacked Molly Brant's home village of Canajoharie and looted her house; one officer made repeated visits to haul off wagonloads of her silk gowns and gold and silver ornaments. Patriots moved into the Mohawks' handsome houses and feasted on their stores of corn, cabbage, and potatoes.[58] But that year would be remembered more for another British offensive in New York. This campaign, led by General John Burgoyne, was designed to divide the colonies and win the war for Britain. In the event, things turned out quite differently. An unfortunate incident during the course of the British advance portended worse to come, when a young American woman was killed and scalped by British Indian allies. The episode fueled patriot hysteria against the British, linking the redcoats ever more closely with the redskinned "savages" they deployed.[59] Volunteers massed to the patriots, while Burgoyne's position steadily deteriorated. By October, the British army had dwindled from about eight thousand men to five thousand, and was confronted by an American force twice the size. Chased and bothered by American attacks, they reached the New York village of Saratoga, near Albany, so exhausted that they dropped to the sodden ground and slept through a heavy rain. On October 17, 1777, completely surrounded and under constant fire, General Burgoyne surrendered his army to the patriots.[60]

The British surrender at Saratoga was a turning point in the American Revolution. The top British commanders resigned in humiliation; the British government in Westminster became irreversibly divided. Most significantly, Saratoga brought America a crucial European ally, when France entered the war on America's side. Spain followed suit a year later. Suddenly, Britain was no longer simply fighting the patriots in North America. It was fighting its two biggest imperial rivals in a war around the world. The entry of foreign powers also had critical effects in deepening the sense of division between patriots and loyalists, Americans and Britons. It was no coincidence that persecution of loyalists measurably increased after Saratoga, manifested in a series of anti-loyalist laws. Within six months of the battle, six states had stiffened and expanded their test laws, enforcing loyalty oaths. In 1778 New Hampshire, Massachusetts, New York, and South Carolina all passed punitive laws allowing loyalists to be arrested or banished. Pennsylvania passed an act of attainder against "divers traitors." New Jersey established a committee of safety. Delaware prohibited trade with the enemy. Georgia implemented a vague but sinister law against "the dangerous consequences that may arise from the practices of disaffected . . . persons within this state."[61] And when the British strategically abandoned Philadelphia in June 1778, just nine months after they had captured it, thousands more loyalists became refugees—including Joseph Galloway and his daughter Betsy, bound for Britain.

It was not only whites who took flight. Saratoga very nearly sounded the death knell for Iroquois support of the British. "Upon the News of General Burgoynes Disaster," Molly Brant "found the five Nations very wavering & unstable." Still, she rallied her allies, reminding a Seneca chief "of the former great Friendship & Attachment which subsisted between him and the late Sr Wm Johnson, whose Memory she never mentions but with Tears in her Eyes" and of his promise "to live and die a firm Friend & Ally to the King of England and his Friends." So persuasive were her arguments on the chief "and the rest of the 5 Nations present, that they promised her faithfully to stick up strictly to the Engagements to her late worthy Friend, and for his & her sake espouse the Kings Cause vigorously and steadily avenge her wrongs & Injuries."[62] Mohawk loyalism prevailed. But Molly Brant and most of the Mohawks had by now become refugees themselves by fleeing west to the Canadian frontier for safety, sharing in a common loyalist fate.

EVER SINCE 1775, British officials had hoped for—if not expected and counted on—a large popular turnout among loyalists to bring the war swiftly to an end. About nineteen thousand loyalists joined provincial regiments, which compared reasonably well with the Continental Army's maximum force of twenty-five thousand, but fell considerably short of the combined American strength including patriot militias, to say nothing of the hordes of men required by the consistently troop-starved British.[63] After Saratoga, mustering loyalist manpower became more urgent than ever. Joseph Galloway and other prominent refugees in England persuaded British ministers, notably the colonial secretary Lord George Germain, that loyalists would still flock to the British flag if given the right support. The best prospects for this lay in the southern colonies of South Carolina and Georgia. Demographically, economically, and culturally, these colonies resembled the neighboring colonies of East and West Florida and the British West Indies—all of which remained loyal—about as much as they did those of New England, the hotbed of revolution. They had the highest ratio of slaves to whites in the colonies (hovering at about one to one), which tended to encourage a commitment to social stability among whites fearful of slave uprisings. Georgia, in particular, established in 1733, had a white population of only about thirty-five thousand, many of whom had close ties to Britain and the British Caribbean.[64] So it made good sense for Britain to turn its strategic attention south after the disaster of Saratoga.

John Lichtenstein (or Lightenstone, as he often Anglicized it) was exactly the kind of southern loyalist the British hoped would help. In 1762 Lichtenstein had immigrated to Georgia from the eastern fringe of Europe: he had been born in St. Petersburg, Russia, to a German Protestant minister. In Georgia he married Catherine Delegal, the daughter of one of the colony's first settlers, a Huguenot. Lichtenstein acquired a modest indigo plantation on Skidaway Island, south of Savannah, and a dozen slaves; he also earned a commission as captain of a government scout boat, patrolling coastal waterways. The Lichtensteins' only child, Elizabeth, born in 1764, remembered her Skidaway home as a veritable eden of "figs, peaches, pomegranates, quinces, plums, mulberries, nectarines, and oranges." But the idyll did not last. When Elizabeth was ten her mother died; and two years later, the outbreak of war upset her world again. Lichtenstein continued to command the scout boat until patriots demanded that he turn it over to them. He refused, staying loyal to the government to which he owed his livelihood. But the patriots confiscated the boat anyway, and Lichtenstein retreated to Skidaway.[65]

One morning in 1776, while he was shaving, Lichtenstein looked out the window to see a group of armed men approaching. Fortunately for him, one of his slaves valiantly distracted the party, giving him time to dress hurriedly and slip away in a small boat along with three slaves. The fugitives made their way to a British man-of-war anchored off Savannah. Lichtenstein sailed with the ship (which was also carrying Georgia's now deposed colonial governor, Sir James Wright) to the safe haven of Halifax, Nova Scotia. From Halifax, he joined the 1776 expedition against New York City, and there was formally commissioned in the quartermaster's office of the British army.

It was in this capacity that Lichtenstein became one of three thousand British and loyalist soldiers who, in the last days of 1778, landed in the swamps outside Savannah to commence Britain's southern offensive. For him and many of the men squelching through the rice fields, this was a homecoming. Lichtenstein knew the area so well that he helped the commanding officer, Highlander colonel Archibald Campbell, choose the spot to disembark. The British swiftly captured Savannah and established it as a bridgehead for further operations. Campbell marched toward Augusta to secure the backcountry, with the help of Thomas Brown's Rangers and other loyalist reinforcements. Sir James Wright returned to his post as governor, making Georgia the only revolting colony formally restored to crown control.

Through all this time, Elizabeth Lichtenstein had been tucked away from conflict on an aunt's plantation in the country. Now back in Savannah, Lichtenstein immediately sent a passport for his long-lost daughter to join him. She entered a city still marked by battle: the streets were strewn with papers torn from books and ledgers; feathers ripped from bedding skimmed across the dirt. So much seemed new to her—her father, for a start, whom she had not seen in three years, and whom she regarded with reverence and awe. City life, too, presented unfamiliar scenes to an "unsophisticated girl, quite new to the world, its customs and usages," who had spent the last few years effectively in hiding. Still, Elizabeth was no longer a child of twelve. At fifteen, she mixed with her father's new loyalist friends as a young adult. Indeed, much to her father's alarm, she promptly fell in love.[66]

Elizabeth stayed in Savannah with the family of Dr. Lewis Johnston, a Scot who had immigrated to Georgia in the early 1750s via a short sojourn on St. Kitts, where he had married the niece of a planter. Johnston managed an impressively varied career as a medical doctor, a wealthy planter, and a public servant, as a member of the governor's council and speaker of the assembly. When war broke out, the doctor and his family refused to break their allegiance and emerged among Savannah's most prominent loyalists. One of Johnston's younger brothers was Savannah's leading printer and refused to print patriot declarations in his newspaper. To protect himself and his precious typefaces, he shut down the press and took his materials into the backcountry for safety.[67] Dr. Johnston's sons carried the family politics onto the battlefield. One son, Andrew, joined Brown's Rangers and saw tough service on the Florida frontier. Another son, William Martin Johnston, escaped from Savannah on the same ship as John Lichtenstein—with whom he became good friends—and joined a loyalist regiment in New York. Before the war, "Billy" had been a popular if feckless medical student (studying under Philadelphia's celebrated doctor and patriot Benjamin Rush), more given to gaming than books. Stationed in occupied New York, the captain quickly became one of the city's "dashing fashionables," a charmer, flirt, and gambler. So it was no wonder that when Lichtenstein's twenty-five-year-old friend began paying court to young Elizabeth, ten years his junior—and when Elizabeth appeared responsive—the protective father promptly packed her back off to her aunt's secluded estate. William Johnston left Savannah on a military expedition into South Carolina; Elizabeth pined for him in silence.[68]

But a war that had divided so many others brought this couple together again. In early September 1779, a French fleet appeared off Savannah, and a Franco-American force laid siege to the city, outnumbering the defenders by five to one. William's regiment rushed to Savannah's defense. Elizabeth by then had returned to the city and was again staying with Dr. Johnston's family. When the shelling began, she and the elder Johnstons retreated to an island just offshore and huddled in a barn with fifty-eight women and children "who had each one or more near relatives in the lines." Fortunately for the besieged civilians, the bombs sailed straight over the defenders' heads and fizzled out in Savannah's sandy unpaved streets. After six days of bombardment, the French and Americans tried to take the city by storm, but were resoundingly repulsed. Loyalist civilians returned after the battle to find the roads "cut into deep holes by the shells," and their houses "riddled with the rain of cannonballs." But the Lichtensteins and Johnstons had made it through the ordeal untouched. Perhaps having survived the siege encouraged John Lichtenstein to relax his concerns about his daughter's personal future. The next month, Elizabeth Lichtenstein and William Johnston got married.[69] The union marked an enormous step up socially for the new Mrs. Johnston, from the middling plantocracy into a highly educated, politically influential, and well-off segment of the Georgia loyalist elite. In the years ahead William's family connections determined the course of the couple's life in significant ways.

Southern loyalists saw the reconquest of Georgia as a happy omen of wider victory to come. Indeed, for a time it seemed as if the setbacks of the previous years had been put into reverse. In 1780, the British captured Charleston, South Carolina, turning that city, too, into a safe haven for loyalists.[70] Where patriots had attainted prominent South

Carolina loyalists, forcing them into exile as enemies of the state, some now returned to retrieve their confiscated property.[71] Where patriots had imposed oaths of allegiance to the new state legislature, the British now made sure that hundreds of Charleston residents (including much of the city's Jewish community) signed certificates pledging to be "true and faithful Subject[s] to His Majesty, the King of Great Britain."[72] Where the patriots had earlier confiscated loyalist property, now patriot plantations and slaves were "sequestered," or requisitioned, for British use. A North Carolina merchant called John Cruden was appointed commissioner of these sequestered estates, and energetically set about managing them for maximum economic benefit to the British.[73]

The newly wed Johnstons especially enjoyed a period of upturn. William had been suffering from a "nervous complaint" triggered by a dangerous ride to Augusta to deliver military intelligence. He traveled to New York, in hopes that a more temperate climate would help him recover, and in a fit of "romantic folly" he insisted on bringing his bride across the war-torn country with him. The couple spent the summer of 1780 relaxing in the calm, British-held countryside of Long Island.[74]

But as the Johnstons' belated honeymoon reached its end, so did Britain's relative good fortune in the south. The strategy had called for the capture of Charleston in part to secure Savannah. Now, to maintain control over South Carolina, the general commanding the southern army, Charles, Lord Cornwallis, felt he had to conquer North Carolina, and to do that, Cornwallis believed he had to move north again into Virginia. Behind him, the Georgia and Carolina backcountry broke down into bitter conflict between patriot and loyalist militias. Thomas Brown felt the brunt of it. He had made Augusta into a loyalist base and cultivated Creek and Cherokee support in a new office as superintendent of Indian affairs for the south. In the autumn of 1780, patriots attacked Augusta, besieging Brown's forces in horrid conditions. By the time reinforcements came to the rescue, Brown had been lamed again by a bullet through both thighs, while Andrew Johnston, one of his most trusted lieutenants, lay among the dead. Patriots responded to the loyalists' pyrrhic victory by accusing Brown and his men of scalping the sick and wounded, summarily hanging prisoners of war, and kicking the decapitated corpses of their victims through the streets.[75]

Such appalling reports contributed to an increase in patriot insurgency across the interior of Georgia and the Carolinas and left the British struggling to contain what amounted to a guerrilla war. A few weeks after Augusta, a partisan battle at King's Mountain in North Carolina left the British hopelessly weakened in the rear. Meanwhile, Cornwallis's army staggered onward, low on supplies, manpower dwindling, harassed by patriot attacks.[76] And Virginia still lay ahead.

THE OLDEST and by far the largest of the thirteen colonies, in both area and population, Virginia sat at the geographic center of revolutionary America. Together with Massachusetts, Virginia formed one of the revolution's two ideological poles. It was the home of George Washington and Thomas Jefferson, among other founding fathers, and the heartland of America's slaveowning plantocracy. Just a day after the first shots of the war were fired in Massachusetts, conflict erupted independently in Virginia's capital, Williamsburg. Yet despite Virginia's prominence, few military actions took place there until Cornwallis invaded in 1781. Rather, the colony stood out as the epicenter of another revolution, whose shock waves were felt hundreds of miles away. David George was one of that revolution's twenty thousand black participants.[77]

Born a slave on a plantation in the Tidewater region of eastern Virginia around 1740, David went into the fields almost as early as he could remember, carrying water, carding cotton, picking tobacco with his callused fingers. His was a brutal boyhood: he watched his sister flogged until her bare back looked "as though it would rot." He saw his runaway brother hunted down with dogs, hung by the hands from a cherry tree, and whipped so violently that he might not have felt the stinging salt water poured into the open wounds. He heard his own mother struck by the lash, "begging for mercy." In his twentieth year, David decided to get away from all this. He walked through the night and all the next day and just kept on going, out of Essex County, out of Virginia, over the Roanoke River, over the Pee Dee, and on toward the Georgia border. There he worked peacefully for two years, until his master tracked him down again and David fled once more, as far as Augusta. Even there, five hundred miles away from his Virginia owner, David was not safe. After six months his master's son turned up to seize him, and David ran yet again. This time, he landed in the custody of a powerful Indian trader called George Galphin, at Silver Bluff, on the opposite bank of the Savannah River from Augusta.

The Irish-born Galphin, with his Creek Indian wife and mixed-race children, stood out as a sort of southern counterpart to Sir William Johnson. Silver Bluff was a veritable multiethnic kingdom in the backcountry, where the runaway David joined a diverse community with more than a hundred slaves who mixed relatively freely with both whites and Indians. He worked comfortably for a master who "was very kind to me," and met and married a part-black, part-Creek woman named Phillis. But David's years at Silver Bluff imprinted him most forcefully for another reason. In the early 1770s, a black preacher arrived in the woods to spread Baptist teachings to the slaves. David found himself alternately captivated and disturbed by the preacher's message. "I saw myself a mass of sin," he confessed, and realized that he "must be saved by prayer." After an exuberant meeting in a mill on Galphin's plantation, David and Phillis were baptized together in the millstream. David could hardly contain his ecstatic faith. Listening to another charismatic black Baptist, George Liele, preach in a cornfield, David felt an overwhelming urge to lead prayers himself. Liele encouraged the new convert to follow his passion. With Galphin's permission (notable in an era when many planters were wary of their slaves being exposed to Christian teachings), David began to preach to the slaves at Silver Bluff—adopting his mentor Liele's first name George as his own surname. Soon he presided there over America's first black Baptist congregation.[78]

By the time war broke out in 1775, Virginia seemed comfortably distant to David George. But the repercussions of conflict disrupted his enclave in time, for reasons originating in the very place from which he had fled. British military fortunes did not get off to a good start in Virginia. The governor, John Murray, fourth Earl of Dunmore, bore part of the blame. Despite being born into considerable privilege as a member of the Scottish aristocracy, Lord Dunmore came of age acutely aware of the precariousness of fortune. In 1745, his father had supported the bid of Charles Edward Stuart ("Bonnie Prince Charlie"), the Jacobite pretender, to reclaim the British throne from the Hanoverian king George II. The choice to stay loyal to the Stuarts cost many prominent Jacobites their titles and more. Though Dunmore's family managed to avoid serious sanctions, the near miss must have informed his subsequent hard-nosed pursuit of power and personal gain. Appointed governor of New York in 1770 and governor of Virginia a year later, he was perhaps best known for his aggressive approach to land acquisition—achieved through war against the

Indians—and he quickly acquired a reputation for autocracy, arrogance, and self-interest. These qualities were displayed the day after Lexington and Concord, when Dunmore ordered his men to remove the gunpowder from the Williamsburg magazine, to protect it from possible rebels. His unilateral move alienated moderates and patriots alike.[79] Armed volunteers demanded the return of the gunpowder; Dunmore responded by booby-trapping the magazine with a spring-loaded gun, wounding three men who tried to break in. The Virginia capital bayed for the governor's blood. Under cover of night, Dunmore and his family fled to the safety of a British frigate in the James River.

Dunmore did not mean this as an admission of defeat. He promptly turned HMS *Fowey* into the headquarters of an extraordinary government in exile, using the fleet to launch operations against patriots in Hampton, Norfolk, and other coastal towns. Hundreds of loyalists rowed out to join this waterborne outpost of British Virginia—as did runaway slaves, who were also given sanctuary. Soon Dunmore governed a "floating town" inhabited by three thousand people on board nearly two hundred ships.[80] Patriots denounced Dunmore for "throwing the affairs of this colony in extreme confusion, by withdrawing himself unnecessarily from the administration of government." But that was not the worst of it. For Dunmore also appeared to be "exciting an insurrection of our slaves" by putting guns in the runaways' hands.[81]

If the prospect of Indian attacks struck terror into frontier colonists, slave rebellions formed the stuff of nightmares for whites in every British colonial slave society. Since 1774 anxious patriots had rumored that the British might arm the slaves, inciting revolt from within the very bosom of American homes.[82] Now Dunmore did just that. On November 7, 1775, he issued a proclamation that declared "all indented Servants, Negroes, or Others (appertaining to Rebels) free, that are able and willing to bear Arms, they joining His Majesty's Troops, as soon as may be."[83] Within two weeks of the proclamation, Dunmore reported that two to three hundred slaves had joined him on his ships. He formed the runaways "into a Corps as fast as they come." Called the "Ethiopian Regiment," these black soldiers went into battle wearing uniform badges that boasted "Liberty to Slaves," a slogan chilling to the white patriot champions of liberty.

Dunmore's proclamation may have stemmed more from pragmatism than principle. The offer of freedom, limited as it was to patriot-owned slaves, brought valuable recruits into British service and dealt a huge blow to rebel morale, without openly undercutting the support of loyalist slaveowners. Motives aside, however, the proclamation's social impact is hard to underestimate. From one mouth to the next, talk of freedom spread across the plantations of the south—and the slaves began to run. Single mothers led their children to the British; old and young traveled side by side; entire communities sometimes ran away together, dozens of slaves escaping from single plantations. Dunmore's Ethiopian Regiment quickly numbered more than eight hundred men, and might have attained twice that strength were it not for a smallpox epidemic that killed hundreds on board Dunmore's fleet. In pointed irony, some of the most prominent patriots lost their own slaves to the British. Several of George Washington's slaves ran from Mount Vernon to the floating town. So did several belonging to Virginia burgess Patrick Henry—known for his patriotic rallying cry "Give me liberty, or give me death!"—who cited Dunmore's proclamation as a reason that Americans should declare independence.[84]

By July 4, 1776, though, Dunmore's floating town was decimated by disease, and there was no improvement in sight. Dunmore was forced to retreat to New York with his Ethiopians. Despite the governor's die-hard instincts, his effort to preserve royal authority in Virginia had become a farce, another lost cause for the onetime Jacobite. But Dunmore's proclamation took on a life of its own. By inviting African Americans to join, it dramatically changed the character—and the material strength—of loyalist support for the British. British military commanders promptly repeated the promise of freedom to slaves who would fight. When the British bombarded Wilmington, North Carolina, in the spring of 1776, so many slaves ran to join them that General Sir Henry Clinton formed them into another black regiment, the Black Pioneers. (One of those Wilmington runaways, Thomas Peters, would later emerge as a significant leader of black loyalists in exile.) All told, approximately twenty thousand black slaves joined the British during the revolution—roughly the same number as the whites who joined loyalist regiments. Though hopes of a great white loyalist surge would prove elusive to British commanders, Dunmore and others harbored enduring fantasies of blacks helping to save the colonies for Britain.

News of black liberation wound into the southern backcountry, as far as Silver Bluff and the ears of David George and his friends. George's master Galphin had come out as a patriot—or in George's more muted phrase, an "antiloyalist." Galphin was appointed Indian commissioner by the patriots, a position in which he vied with his loyalist counterpart Thomas Brown for Creek support. Because of Galphin's efforts, Creek backing for the British remained uncertain as the redcoats advanced into the backcountry. But when the British army encamped opposite Silver Bluff, the choice for Galphin's black slaves was clear. On January 30, 1779, David George and his family—among ninety of Galphin's slaves—crossed the Savannah River to the British camp, to earn their freedom as black loyalists.[85] The Georges made their way to British-occupied Savannah, where David found work as a provisioner and butcher and Phillis did laundry for the British soldiers. Better yet, from George's point of view, he was reunited in Savannah with his spiritual mentor George Liele. Together they continued to preach, knitting together a community of faith among other runaway blacks. Such ties among black loyalists, as among white loyalists, would provide an important sense of togetherness in years to come and destinations unknown.[86]

By 1781, with northern offensives abandoned and the southern advance under General Cornwallis running into trouble, the British army's mass liberation of slaves had come, in some minds, to look more strategically necessary than ever. In August 1781, a sergeant in the Black Pioneers named Murphy Stiele had a brush with the supernatural. He was sitting in the regimental barracks on Water Street in New York City when he heard a piercing yet disembodied voice. It instructed Stiele to tell General Clinton (now commander in chief) to "send word to Genl. Washington That he must Surrender himself and his Troops to the King's Army, and that if he did not the wrath of God would fall upon them." If Washington refused, Clinton "was then to tell him, that he would raise all the Blacks in America to fight against him."[87] For two weeks the voice pestered Stiele, until he relayed his message to the commander in chief. Stiele's vision of blacks thronging to the British standard—a very particular version of those recurring hopes of loyalist support—must have given Clinton pause, since he had always promoted British recruitment of slaves. Such an influx might be just the thing to rescue Cornwallis's campaign.

During Cornwallis's march, black slaves had continued to join the British—including almost two dozen belonging to the author of the Declaration of Independence himself, Thomas Jefferson. Yet despite these arrivals, Cornwallis did not have enough manpower to bring the "wrath of God" down on anyone. He commanded about six thousand

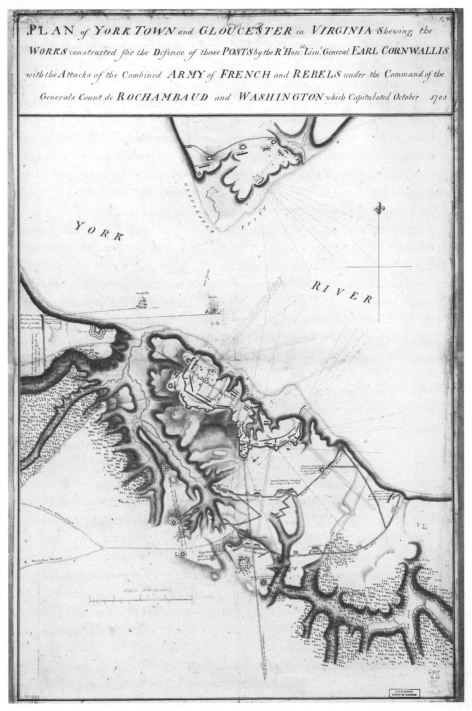

Plan of York Town and Gloucester in Virginia, Showing the Works
Constructed . . . by the Rt. Honble: Lieut. General Earl Cornwallis,
with the Attacks of the Combined Army of French and Rebels, 1781.

soldiers, and his resources were fast running out. Cornwallis decided to set up camp on an exposed peninsula near Williamsburg and wait for reinforcements.[88] The men labored through the heat to dig fortifications around the new post, called Yorktown. Smallpox and typhus ravaged the camps, afflicting the blacks—most of whom had not been inoculated for smallpox—in especially large numbers. Provisions were so short that almost everyone, including hundreds of loyalist civilians in the British lines, suffered from anemia.[89] By late summer, little more than half Cornwallis's men were fit for duty. Then, on the last day of August 1781, scouts caught sight of a fleet approaching—only to discover that it was not the hoped-for British reinforcements, but the French. The enemy navy closed in on the British by sea. Meanwhile, Washington was racing overland from Pennsylvania to pin the British in by land. Two weeks later, a combined force of sixteen thousand French and American soldiers camped outside Yorktown. The outnumbered British army, and the loyalists in their care, were trapped. "This Place is in no state of defence," reported a desperate Cornwallis to General Clinton. "If you cannot relieve me very soon you must be prepared to hear the worst."[90]

The bombing started in the night of October 9, blowing up the carefully constructed earthworks in cascades of dirt, as the French and Americans advanced methodically toward the British positions. Inside the lines, Yorktown became a lurid scene of fire and blood. Deserters straggled out from the besieged camp reporting that the soldiers within were worn out "with excessive hard duty & that they are very sickly." Loyalists, black and white, suffered through an ordeal of hunger and sickness as the dead and wounded mounted around them. To spare resources, Cornwallis ordered the slaughter of the horses, expelled smallpox patients from the hospital, and drove away many of the blacks who had run to the British.[91] But the food was gone. The ammunition was gone. The reinforcements had not come. It was time to seek terms. On the anniversary of Saratoga—a coincidence not lost on the Continental Army—Cornwallis sent a messenger with a flag of truce to negotiate his surrender.[92]

At two o'clock in the afternoon on October 19, 1781, Cornwallis and his army marched out of Yorktown to surrender to George Washington and his French allies. They emerged from their blasted hell in neat ranks, with "arms shouldered, colors cased and drums beating a British or German march."[93] Legend holds that the band played a tune called "The World Turned Upside Down." In retrospect, it seems almost too good to be true, since from some perspectives, the world order really had been inverted. The underdog had triumphed, the mighty empire had faltered. The song would have held special resonance for contemporaries. The ballad had originally appeared in the English Civil War, more than a century earlier, when conflict had divided Britons on the question of royal and parliamentary power.[94] The tune could have reminded its listeners of what so many of those who lived through the American Revolution had already experienced. Civil wars often overturn their participants' worlds—and sometimes those can never be uprighted again.

Despite the brutality that had unfolded at Yorktown, Cornwallis and Washington agreed quickly on mutually acceptable terms for the surrender and the fate of British prisoners of war—often a sticking point in such negotiations. But one group of Yorktown survivors found themselves entirely unprotected. In the draft terms of capitulation he sent to Washington, Cornwallis specified that "Natives or inhabitants of different parts of this country, at present at York[town] and Gloucester, are not to be punished on account of having joined the British army." In his view, the surviving loyalists who stumbled out of the ravaged encampment had already been punished enough. But Washington bluntly replied that "this article cannot be assented to."[95] It was the only one of Cornwallis's requests that he rejected outright. Loyalists had chosen the British. Now they would have to cope with the consequences of their choice.

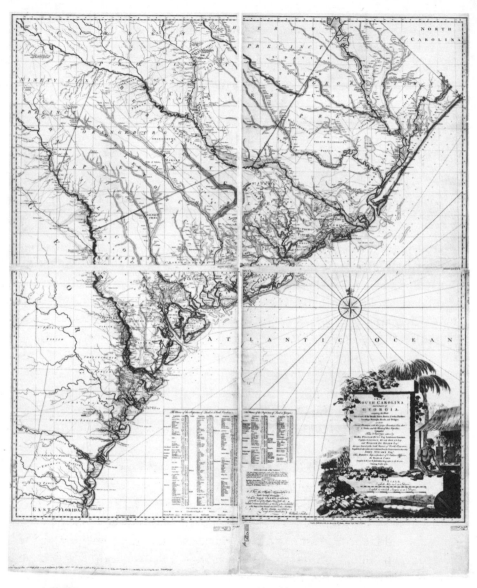

William Faden, *A Map of South Carolina and a Part of Georgia*, 1780.

CHAPTER TWO

An Unsettling Peace

A CROSS THE ATLANTIC, when news of Cornwallis's surrender reached the embattled British prime minister Lord North,
he took it "as he would have taken a ball in his breast." "Oh
god! It is all over," he exclaimed, throwing his arms into the air and
pacing frantically about the room.[1] He was—at one level—right. Yorktown is conventionally understood as the endpoint of the war. It was
the last pitched battle between the British and Continental armies, and
led directly to the peace negotiations that resulted in British recognition of American independence.

But as even North must have known, it would take more than surrender to end this war. Beyond America, Britain's global conflict
against France and Spain raged on. Yorktown did not pull back the
British forces sweating it out in southern India against French-allied
Tipu Sultan. It did not relieve the British soldiers defending Gibraltar
and Minorca against the Spanish. Crucially, it did not stop the French
fleet that had trapped Cornwallis in Virginia from cruising into the
Caribbean and threatening Britain's valuable sugar islands. Within
America, too, hostilities continued to an extent not often appreciated
in standard histories of the revolution. The war between Lord Corn-
wallis and George Washington may have ended in the trenches outside
Yorktown, but Thomas Brown's war was not over, nor was Joseph
Brant's. From the outskirts of New York City to the Florida borderlands, partisan fighting nagged and gnawed at American communities.
After Britain ceased offensive operations in January 1782, this was
more than ever a civil war, waged by loyalists, patriots, and Indians.

Loyalists responded to news of Yorktown very differently from
North. At first, some didn't even believe it. "A Hand Bill from Jersey of
the Surrender of Lord Cornwallis . . . shocks the Town," wrote New
York's loyalist chief justice William Smith in his diary six days after

Yorktown. "I give no Credit to it," he comfortably concluded, "but suspect an Artifice to prevent the Insurrection of the Loyalists or some Operations on our part."[2] The fifty-three-year-old jurist was a skeptic by nature, which was one reason that he, like Beverley Robinson, had delayed taking a public stand until he was summoned before a patriot committee and forced to choose between swearing allegiance to the republic or moving to British-occupied New York City. When push came to shove, Smith moved to New York. Of course, he quickly recognized the awful truth about Yorktown when veterans arrived in New York bearing eyewitness accounts of the battle and the miserable "Fate of the [loyalist] Refugees left there to the Mercy of the Usurpers." But as Smith and other influential loyalists saw it, there was still no reason to consider the war over or lost. Smith and his friends concocted various strategies to "balance the Southern Disaster" with further British attacks. "There are 40 Thousand Men . . . here, including Canada and [St.] Augustine," insisted one, and "if we had made a right Use of them all would have been well, and . . . there is still no Cause to despair."[3] A somewhat different plan for a troop surge was suggested by John Cruden, the commissioner for sequestered estates in Charleston. Raise an army of ten thousand freed slaves, he said, and America could yet "be conquered with its own force." Cruden sent the proposal to his patron Lord Dunmore, who enthusiastically forwarded it to General Henry Clinton.[4]

Even if Britain stopped fighting, loyalists believed that British rule in the colonies could still be saved. Britain could refuse to grant the colonies independence and instead offer them some kind of self-rule, rather like Joseph Galloway's plan of union, or an analogous proposal by William Smith to create an American parliament.[5] This had been the thrust of British peace initiatives during the war, which had granted virtually everything the colonists had requested up to 1775, and even floated the possibility of admitting American representatives into the House of Commons. Though Congress had dismissed the most significant British overture, the Carlisle peace commission of 1778, insisting on independence as a prerequisite for further talks, Smith, Galloway, and others still held out for an imperial federal union.[6] Loyalists could perhaps take some comfort in knowing that King George III himself was so strongly opposed to independence that he threatened to abdicate if it were granted. "A separation from America would anihilate the rank in which the British empire stands among European States," he declared, "and would render my situation in this country below continuing an object to me."[7]

Partly because of the range of possibilities still in play after York-town, it took a year for British and American negotiators to work out a preliminary peace treaty, and another year until a definitive peace was signed and British troops evacuated. Historians tend to fast-forward through these two years as if their outcome were inevitable. But for loyalists in America, especially those who had already fled to British-occupied cities, these years of peacemaking proved just as stressful as the years of war. Loyalists saw their hopes for a continued British rela-tionship with the colonies dashed, one after another. They wanted renewed military offensives; but Britain declared a cessation of hostili-ties. They wanted the colonies to remain part of a confederated empire; Britain acknowledged U.S. independence. They wanted pro-tection from reprisals and security of property; the Anglo-American treaty left many feeling just as "abandoned" by the British as the York-town loyalists had been. They wanted to preserve the British Empire, and instead they watched the British start to leave. By the middle of 1782, loyalists in British-occupied New York, Charleston, and Savan-nah confronted urgent choices about where to vest their own futures: in the United States or in other quarters of the British Empire. In a cli-mate of persistent violence and uncertainty, the majority chose to evac-uate with the British. Yet the wrenching results of the peace also left them feeling deeply frustrated with the British authorities who bro-kered it. Loyalists thus often went into exile harboring grievances against the very same government they relied on for support. Their disheartening final months in America laid the groundwork for a recurring pattern of discontent elsewhere in the British Empire, with repercussions as far afield as Nova Scotia, Jamaica, and Sierra Leone.

It was to be as much in European political and diplomatic councils as on a Virginia battlefield that loyalist dreams came crashing down. Back in Westminster, support crumbled for the war effort and the wavering government of Lord North. After all, many Britons had never wanted to go to war in the colonies in the first place. The "friends of America" included some of the greatest politicians of the age, such as the eminent political philosopher Edmund Burke. They also included future leaders William Pitt the Younger, elected to Par-liament in 1781 at the tender age of twenty-one, and Charles James Fox, a radical aristocrat, who ostentatiously dressed in buff and blue, the colors of Washington's army. Though North's political adversaries had long been stymied by their own internal rifts, the opposition regrouped after Yorktown and emerged determined to bring the war in America to an end.[8]

Late one February night in 1782, a venerable general rose from the narrow wooden benches of the House of Commons to speak out against a war "marked in the best blood of the empire," "traced . . . by the ravaging of towns and the murder of families; by outrages in every corner of America, and by ruin at home."[9] He went on to propose a motion to end "the farther prosecution of the offensive war on the continent of North America, for the purpose of reducing the revolted colonies to obedience by force." At half past one in the morning, Parliament voted in favor of the motion by a slim margin of nineteen votes.[10] Two weeks later, North failed a vote of "no further confidence" (the first use of such a measure in British history) and submitted his resignation.[11] In North's leavetaking meeting with King George III the next day, the king, resistant to the bitter end to the idea of American independence, dismissed his prime minister coldly, saying, "Remember, my Lord, that it is you who desert me, not I you."[12]

In June 1782, the new prime minister, William Petty, Earl of Shelburne—another friend of America—took the critical decision to acknowledge American independence. This concession made sense from a metropolitan British perspective, because the future of the thirteen colonies was only part of a larger strategic picture involving France and Spain. It mattered less to Britain whether the United States was independent than whether it remained in a British, as opposed to French, sphere of influence. For loyalists, though, this was the worst news yet, ending any prospect of continued imperial ties. It also raised the next major challenge for administrators. How would the colonial relationship actually be dismantled? This question had two distinct parts. One was addressed in Paris, where British and American peace negotiators began to hash out the details of U.S. independence. There were borders to be drawn. There were economic relationships to be untangled, from trade privileges to the resolution of transatlantic debts. Then there was the issue that most gripped the loyalists' attention. What provisions would be made to protect them from legal and social reprisals, and compensate them for their confiscated property?

Meanwhile in North America, British officials had to figure out how to phase out Britain's physical presence on the ground. There were about thirty-five thousand British and Hessian troops to be withdrawn, and substantial British garrisons in three cities—New York, Charleston, and Savannah—to be dismantled. These cities also held at least sixty thousand loyalists and slaves living under British protection, whose welfare had to be taken into account. A further difficulty was that Sir Henry Clinton had resigned his position as commander in chief immediately after Yorktown, leaving nobody actually in charge of superintending this huge task. The job description for his successor was as awe-inspiring as it was unenviable: it required nothing short of deconstructing the apparatus of an empire from the bottom up. Who could be entrusted with it? Fortunately the king and his ministers, despite their many differences, readily agreed on whom to appoint. Sir Guy Carleton, veteran military officer and colonial administrator, was their man.

OF ALL the British officials who influenced the fate of refugee loyalists, Sir Guy Carleton was far and away the most significant, and also the most trusted and well liked. (Lord Dunmore, for instance, who continued to be involved in loyalist affairs, rarely commanded either trust or affection.) As the primary manager of Britain's evacuation from the United States, Carleton bore the brunt of responsibility for the refugees and slaves under British protection. His actions determined their futures to an extent unrivalled by any other policymaker, and his ideas defined the shape of the loyalist migration in crucial ways. So what sort of a person was the new commander in chief? Horace Walpole, one of Georgian Britain's sharpest commentators, estimated Carleton to be "a grave man, and good officer, and reckoned sensible"—a sight better than any of the ineffectual commanders who had preceded him.[13] Many of those who met the general agreed with Walpole's assessment. Stiff and closed in demeanor, Carleton may well have chilled less commanding souls when he looked down his long, severe nose at them from an imposing height (for the era) of six feet. But if anybody could have glimpsed behind the general's ungiving façade as he traveled down to Portsmouth on April 1, 1782, and waited for the *Ceres* to sail to New York, they would surely have detected confidence and at least a whiff of self-congratulation. For Carleton had been to North America before, three memorable times—and this appointment, coming on the heels of a long period in the political wilderness, represented a personal vindication.

Carleton was himself a creation of the British Atlantic world, and his pre-revolutionary experiences in North America shaped the attitudes he brought to his later career. Born outside Londonderry in 1724 into the ranks of the Anglo-Irish landed gentry, Carleton, like so many other boys from ambitious families on the margins of the British Isles, joined the army as a teenager—a path chosen by his brothers as well. He soon became close friends with another officer two years his junior, James Wolfe. While Carleton doggedly served out his lieutenantcy, Wolfe shot up through the ranks, impressing his seniors and fighting in some of the period's key battles. Soon Carleton's friend had become his most important patron. In 1758, Wolfe got Carleton appointed quartermaster-general on a campaign the younger man was to command against the French in Canada. They sailed out in 1759— Carleton's first voyage to North America—and together spent a frustrating summer laying siege to the city of Quebec. In September 1759, Wolfe plotted a daring assault on the fortified capital, hoping to take it by storm. As the morning mist rose on the day of the attack, Carleton stood in the front line of redcoats on the Plains of Abraham, outside the city walls, commanding an elite detachment of grenadiers. By afternoon, he had fallen wounded in the head. His friend Wolfe lay dead. But the battle had been won, and it proved a significant victory indeed. Thanks to the capture of Quebec, the whole of French Canada was ceded to the British Empire in the 1763 Treaty of Paris. In his will, Wolfe left "all books and papers" to Carleton, and a handsome legacy of £1,000.[14]

Carleton would not figure in the phenomenally popular 1771 painting *The Death of General Wolfe* produced by the American-born artist Benjamin West, which catapulted Wolfe (and West) to stardom—and Carleton must have felt the loss of his friend's patronage power at least as much as the loss of his companionship. By then, Carleton had returned to Quebec as imperial governor and brigadier general. He took up his post within the stone-walled capital almost seven years to the day after he had fought on the battlefield outside it. As he surveyed the city from the windows of the crumbling old Château Saint-Louis, Carleton might have felt he had returned full circle in one further respect. As a colony overwhelmingly composed of white but Catholic, non-Anglophone subjects, Quebec resembled no part of the British Empire so much as his native Ireland. Carleton applied himself to learning French, and to managing the competing interests of the majority French Catholic population (the *habitants*) and the small but vocal community of Anglophone Protestant merchants. British forms of government "never will produce the same Fruits as at Home," Carleton decided, "chiefly because it is impossible for the Dignity of the Throne, or Peerage, to be represented in the American Forests." As such, he systematically supported preserving

French systems in place of introducing British laws and institutions "ill adapted to the Genius of the Canadians," and equally strongly upheld the power of authoritarian direct rule.[15] In 1770, he traveled to England to consult with the government on how to reform Canadian administration. These discussions culminated in the Quebec Act of 1774, widely understood as a milestone in British imperial legislative efforts to accommodate culturally and ethnically alien subjects.

Carleton returned to his post later that year, bringing with him a charming new wife—aristocratic, French-educated, and thirty years his junior—their two small sons, and clarified powers under the Quebec Act. While maintaining French civil law and ensuring freedom of worship for Catholics, the Quebec Act also ostensibly protected French Canadian interests by entrusting sole legislative authority to the governor and council. There was to be no elected assembly, no trial by jury, no habeas corpus—measures, according to Carleton, that French Canadians had no wish for. Edmund Burke, among others, condemned the measure as despotic, but as one minister quipped back, "if despotic government is to be trusted in any hands . . . I am persuaded it will be as safe in [Carleton's] as in anybody's."[16] Carleton himself, highly satisfied with an act drawn up in large part to his own design, was pleased to find that most Québécois welcomed its terms.[17]

The trouble was that Anglo-Canadians—to say nothing of British subjects in the thirteen colonies—did not. They saw it as both overly authoritarian and an affront to their own rights and interests. The discontents tearing apart the American colonies to the south soon made their way into the coffee houses of Canada. Reports told of travelers from Boston being intercepted and searched on the roads by Canadian dissidents who were trying to sever communication between British officials. Agents from Massachusetts infiltrated the province to organize antigovernment resistance. A few days after the battles at Lexington and Concord, Anglo-Canadian patriots in Montreal poured black paint over a bust of George III, topped it with a mitre, and hung a rude sign around it reading, "Behold the Pope of Canada or the English Fool."[18] Though the *habitants* did not rally en masse to the patriots, much to Carleton's relief, they also appeared unresponsive to his efforts to form a militia for provincial defense.[19]

Neutrality is all well and good until you get invaded. Ill-equipped, and reluctant to recruit large numbers of Indians (as some British officials encouraged him to do), Carleton had just about managed to fend off guerrilla raids with his limited troops. But in September 1775 the

Continental Army invaded Canada, under the command of Generals Benedict Arnold and Richard Montgomery, and sped against the onset of winter toward Quebec. Would it have encouraged or chastened the governor to know that he himself had successfully besieged the city he now endeavored to defend? Before dawn on the last day of 1775, the hungry, half-frozen Americans assaulted the city with a stinging blizzard blowing at their backs. By the time the late sun curved into the sky, it was all over. As in 1759, the leading attackers had fallen outside the walls: Arnold with his left leg shattered, Montgomery dead in the snow. But the American painter John Trumbull's attempt to immortalize the episode with *The Death of General Montgomery* enjoyed less success than his teacher Benjamin West's depiction of Wolfe. Because this time it was Quebec's defenders who won, securing the province in the British Empire. Years later, Carleton would find himself lending the lamed Arnold a supportive arm, as the American limped into his first audience with the king.[20]

With the American invasion repelled, and the *habitants* having rejected a diplomatic overture from Congress to join the revolution, Carleton launched a counteroffensive into New York. In October 1776 he smashed the patriots at Lake Champlain and joined forces with Burgoyne. But, seeing "the severe season approaching very fast," he withdrew into Canada for the winter.[21] Burgoyne and others chastised him for not proceeding farther south to Fort Ticonderoga, a fatal blunder (they said) that allowed the Americans to get away. Whether or not they were right, the decision proved fatal for Carleton's career. He had already made an enemy out of the influential colonial secretary Lord George Germain. Fortified by Burgoyne's hostile reports, Germain fired Carleton from his military command and tried to recall him from the governorship. Carleton preemptively resigned his positions in 1777 and returned to England in disgust.

His sixth Atlantic crossing carried him toward an uncertain future, his reputation tarnished and position reduced. Yet leaving North America ultimately put Carleton in the most advantageous situation he could have hoped for. One by one British generals fell in America, while Sir Guy and Lady Maria, comfortably distant from a badly managed war, made the rounds of London society, cementing their connections among the British elite. Carleton, without knowing it, had also landed in a fortunate political position. His abilities had made him an enduring favorite of the king, and now his feud with Germain endeared him to the parliamentary opposition as well. The appointment as commander in chief of British forces in North America offered an especially sweet satisfaction after his earlier dismissal from military command. And it must have been even better to know that his rehabilitation had helped force his hated rival Germain out of office.[22]

So as he faced America again in the spring of 1782, Sir Guy had much to reminisce about. But it was time to confront the challenges ahead. He cracked open the seal on his instructions from the prime minister and read about his mission. The most "*immediate* object to which all other considerations must give way" sounded deceptively simple: Carleton was to withdraw "the garrison, artillery, provisions, stores of all kinds, every species of public property" from New York, Charleston, and Savannah, as well as St. Augustine in East Florida if he saw fit. Meanwhile, in his role as a peace commissioner, he was to placate the Americans as much as possible in order "to revive old affections and extinguish late jealousies"—part of a hearts-and-minds offensive designed to separate the Americans from the French. There was one group of people who were to command his closest attention. Carleton must extend his "tenderest and most honourable care" to the loyalists, by helping them move to "whatever other parts of America in His Majesty's possession they choose to settle."[23]

The mission was defined clearly in outline, but executing it would be daunting indeed. He had up to 100,000 soldiers and civilians in British-held cities to evacuate. Yet he possessed scant resources with which to provision them, no clear instructions on where actually to send them, and fewer than fifty ships at his disposal. And for all that hostilities had officially ceased, Carleton discovered a different reality on the ground. From New York to the swamps and forests of the lower south, the civil war continued, clouding over the impending evacuations with violence.

To RECOVER the conflicts that continued in America during the months after Yorktown is to understand the passion with which some loyalists clung to, and fought for, their version of British America. Equally important, it helps explain why so many loyalists chose to follow the departing British. Wartime violence had pushed thousands of loyalists into British lines, for what they hoped would be a temporary stay. But as internecine conflict continued into peacetime, present danger and the threat of future reprisals made loyalists fear for their long-term welfare in the United States. It transformed their displacement into an international diaspora.

Carleton landed in New York on May 5, 1782, to find himself

immediately swept up in a controversy that revealed the depth of factional animosity still raging in the colonies. It centered in part around one of New York's leading loyalists, William Franklin, the last royal governor of New Jersey, and the only son of patriot statesman Benjamin Franklin. How long ago it seemed that father and son had flown a kite together, the wet string twirling and pulling in William's hands as the square of stretched silk bobbed, fluttered, and caught the currents up toward the storm clouds. For thirty years the Franklins had been close partners in life and work, moving together to London and back and sharing in the early upbringing of William's son, Temple. But the coming of war opened an unbridgeable rift between them. Benjamin Franklin broke with British authority, signed the Declaration of Independence, and moved to Paris, where he now served as a peace commissioner and one of the United States' most revered public figures. William Franklin, though no friend to arbitrary power, and a champion of imperial reform, could not bring himself to renounce his loyalty to the king—and endured two years as a patriot prisoner for his refusal. During his time in jail, his beloved wife Elizabeth fell dangerously ill, but Washington denied Franklin permission to visit her. She "died of a broken heart" before her husband could see her. Equally painful for William, Benjamin had essentially adopted Temple Franklin as his own and taken the lad to Paris, where Temple acted as secretary to the American peace commission. The relationship between Benjamin and William Franklin would never be restored, and stands out as the highest-profile example of how this civil war tore families apart.[24]

William Franklin arrived in New York City after his release from jail, battered, disappointed, and ready to fight back. His efforts to organize loyalists were formalized in 1780 with the creation of a so-called Board of Associated Loyalists, which sponsored paramilitary "companies of safety"—a counterpart to patriot committees of safety—to protect loyalists in the hinterland.[25] Under the board's patronage, partisan fighting ravaged the greater New York area well after Yorktown. On an early spring day in 1782, a patriot captain named Joshua Huddy, notorious for his rampages through central New Jersey, was found swinging from a tree at Sandy Hook. A paper pinned to his chest declared, "We, the Refugees, have with grief long beheld the cruel murders of our brethren, and . . . determine to hang man for man, as long as a refugee is left existing. . . . UP GOES HUDDY FOR PHILIP WHITE." A loyalist captain had ordered the execution—apparently on William Franklin's instructions—in retaliation for the summary killing of another loyalist, Philip White, some days earlier. Outraged by the incident, George Washington demanded that the perpetrator be handed over for punishment or else he would order a British prisoner of war executed in his stead. To make matters worse, the officer selected for American retribution—a Yorktown prisoner—turned out to be the poignantly young and impressively well-connected Charles Asgill, heir to a baronetcy. Before long the New York spat had become an international incident, with Prime Minister Shelburne asking Benjamin Franklin to intercede personally on Asgill's behalf.[26]

When the new commander in chief arrived in New York City, patriots were screaming for justice, loyalists were up in arms to protect their own, and British regulars were incensed at the idea of an innocent officer falling victim to Washington's *lex talionis*. On his very first day on shore, Carleton spent two hours closeted with William Franklin and William Smith discussing the case. Asgill was ultimately relieved thanks to a direct appeal from his mother to a different American ally, Queen Marie Antoinette. Washington did not come out well from the affair: his unforgiving stance verged on downright cruelty. But William Franklin came out looking worse. As the sordid details of the case emerged before boards of inquiry and a court-martial, Franklin appeared vengeful and injudicious, denting his reputation as a sage leader. It was a thoroughly souring experience for the former governor. The news, which reached America in midsummer 1782, that Britain had agreed to recognize American independence—that Franklin's father had won—only compounded his despair. In August 1782, William Franklin sailed to England for a life in exile, carrying with him—"for a Pretext," thought William Smith—"a Petition to the King from the Loyalists, deprecating the Separation of the Empire and imploring Protection," a list of grievances against the government whose asylum he sought.[27]

The Asgill affair was just the first instance of the violence still haunting America that Carleton had to contend with. On the western edges of New York and Pennsylvania, Britain's Indian allies had been caught up in another ongoing partisan struggle. After Saratoga, Molly Brant had moved to Niagara with the other Mohawks from her village. Like many a refugee, she found herself "not at all reconciled to this place & Country," for it "at first seemed very hard for her to leave her old Mother . . . & friends behind and live in a Country she was an entire Stranger in."[28] Still, she continued to muster support for the British, and was rewarded in turn with a house built for her on Carleton Island, at the far eastern tip of Lake Ontario. Joseph Brant fought in an intensifying series of offensives and counteroffensives: patriots led a scorched-earth campaign across the Finger Lakes region; Indian war parties and loyalist militias swooped down on patriot outposts ranging all the way from the Mohawk to the Ohio rivers.[29] Brant's raids in one month alone resulted in ninety people captured and killed, more than a hundred houses destroyed, and five hundred cattle and horses seized.[30] Such vicious frontier war attested to an animosity between white colonists and Indians too entrenched for a formal Anglo-American cease-fire to eliminate. These hatreds boiled over in what was probably the largest massacre of civilians during the entire American Revolution, five months after Yorktown. In far western Pennsylvania, patriots captured a village of pacifist Moravian Delaware Indians and methodically murdered every one, striking each male victim first with a blow to the head, as livestock were stunned before slaughter, then tearing off their scalps.[31] Carleton's ability to neutralize frontier violence would have special bearing on the future of the refugee Mohawks.

Of all the theaters of continuing conflict, however, the fiercest was also the one of most immediate importance to Carleton. In the deep south, loyalists fought desperately to preserve British power. William Johnston and his father-in-law John Lichtenstein remained at the forefront of these efforts, by commanding cavalry brigades that patrolled the swampy outskirts of Savannah. Two weeks after Yorktown, Johnston and his men were relaxing at their base when they saw three hundred patriots advance from the woods. Rapidly surrounded—and doubtless not eager to follow the fate of his brother Andrew, slain at Augusta—Johnston was on the verge of surrendering his sword to the opposing commander when a patriot soldier struck out at one of Johnston's men. Fired up by the insult, Johnston promptly began a vigorous defense of their position. Fortunately the outnumbered loyalists were soon rescued by a detachment of Thomas Brown's Rangers, commanded by a Johnston family friend named William Wylly.[32]

Johnston's brush with death was just one of many such episodes in the southern civil war. "The rage between Whig and Tory ran so high, that what was called a Georgia parole, and to be shot, were synonyms," recalled one American officer.[33] Patriots and loyalists struck truces that held only as long as tempers. Brown may never have embraced his reputation for savagery, but another loyalist officer described with positive pride how he ranged through the Carolina borderlands burning his enemy's houses, stringing up deserters from trees, taking hostages, and stealing slaves and horses.[34] All this fighting left the Carolina and Georgia backcountry "so completely chequered by the different parties" that no livestock, not even any squirrels or songbirds, animated the land; just the bald, red-headed turkey vultures, tearing at the corpses.[35] In the spring of 1782, American forces encamped a few miles outside Savannah, busily fomenting desertion from the British ranks. Thomas Brown sortied from the city, intending to link up with three hundred Indian allies and drive the Americans back. But Brown failed to make the connection and his skirmish ended in stalemate. A few weeks later, the Indians were also rebuffed and the surviving warriors streamed into the safety of British lines. The struggle to save British rule in Georgia was over.[36]

This was the backdrop against which Carleton set in motion a momentous train of events: the evacuations of British-held Savannah and Charleston. Carleton saw this step as "not a matter of choice, but a deplorable necessity in consequence of an unsuccessful war."[37] There simply were not enough British troops to hold these cities, let alone send badly needed reinforcements to the Caribbean. In early June, 1782, a letter from Carleton marked "<u>Secret</u>" reached British headquarters in Charleston. "A day or two after the receipt of this letter," it warned the commanding officer Alexander Leslie, "you may expect off the bar of Charles-Town a fleet of Transports: these I send for the evacuation of Savannah, and of St. Augustine; to bring off not only the Troops, with the Military and public Stores of all sorts; but the Loyalists who choose to depart with their effects."[38] General Leslie immediately forwarded the news to Savannah, asking Georgia governor Sir James Wright to notify "the King['s] Loyal subjects . . . to provide for whose ease and accommodation on this distressing occasion . . . has been an object of prime consideration with the Commander-in-Chief."[39] Two months later Leslie faced exactly the same task when he was ordered to evacuate Charleston.

What looked like a strategic necessity to Carleton looked like a disaster to the thousands of loyalists in both cities. News of evacuation prompted outcry and anguish. A mere five hundred more troops, Governor Wright believed, could "have drove the Rebels entirely out of the Province."[40] Yet instead the British were abandoning it. "The distress and misery brought on His Majesty's Loyal Subjects here, you cannot conceive," Wright reported, "and the very great property given up . . . I apprehend your Excellency has no idea of."[41] In Charleston, a handbill authored by a self-styled "Citizen" (not, notably, a "subject" of the British crown) wryly proposed various ways loyalists might try to curry favor with the incoming patriots:

> [O]ne man intreats his wife or some friend to write letters inter-cessory for him;—then, there is another person has a cousin of his wife's aunt now in the American camp; . . . and last of all, one pleases himself with the charming thought, that he was always a friend to the American cause in his heart—though perhaps he now and then does duty at the City Guard in a Red Coat.[42]

But British withdrawal was no jesting matter for most loyalists. They heard terrifying reports of what was happening outside the city limits, of loyalists hunted down and murdered by vindictive patriots.[43] Confiscation acts passed by the Georgia and South Carolina patriot legislatures in 1782 expelled some five hundred prominent loyalists as traitors on pain of death, taking their property, and subjecting "divers other persons" who "did . . . traiterously assist abet and Participate in . . . treasonable Practices" to similar penalties.[44] And when delegations of loyalist merchants went to meet with patriot authorities to find out what treatment they might expect if they stayed on, the answers were far from encouraging. Savannah loyalists were told they could take "reasonable time . . . to dispose of their property and settle their pecuniary concerns," but that the Continental Army could not prom-ise total protection, and of course "traitors" (vaguely defined) could always be prosecuted under the Confiscation and Banishment Act.[45] Similar terms in South Carolina convinced Charleston merchants that the patriots were "retaliating upon & punishing the innocent."[46] Prospects hardly seemed any brighter for the hundreds of humbler refugees, such as those dwelling in Charleston's makeshift camp of "miserable huts." Eight hundred "distressed refugees" were dependent on cash handouts from the British army, and had scant hopes of finding much better if they returned to their war-ravaged homes.[47]

What were they to do? Here was a country coming out of civil war, with the possibility of anti-loyalist reprisals, and the good chance that their property had been seized or destroyed in their absence. There were the British ships, offering free passage to fresh domains. Amid so much confusion, one thing at least was clear. Loyalists who left would enjoy the security of remaining in the British Empire. Within a matter of weeks of the evacuation orders, the majority of civilians in Savannah and Charleston made up their minds to go.

In the twenty-first century, such scenes of mass human displacement, of cities emptying out, have come to seem depressingly common consequences of war. But in the 1780s there were simply no British precedents for civilian evacuations on this scale. Nor have any histories of the American Revolution described the British withdrawals in detail. Yet what unfolded on the ground during the last months of British power in America held up a startling mirror to the familiar images of United States nation-making. For while American patriots considered how to fashion the thirteen colonies into a United States of America, following Thomas Paine's injunction to "begin the world over again," thousands of refugees set off into the British Empire, as one loyalist put it, "to begin the world anew."[48]

So where would they go? For many white loyalists in Savannah and Charleston, the choice of destination hinged on one overriding consideration to do with a very special kind of property, at once portable, valuable, and alive: slaves. The question of how best loyalists might sell or employ their slaves crucially influenced decisions about whether and where to go into exile. During the war, most refugees who had left the colonies had traveled to Britain or Nova Scotia. But in Britain, slaveowning had been effectively illegal since the early 1770s, while Nova Scotia, a preferred locale for New England and New York refugees, was seen as climatically unsuitable for southern plantation slaves. Jamaica and other British West Indian islands seemed a better option, but these well-settled islands had little uncultivated land available, and were known for their high cost of living and high chance of dying of tropical disease.

That left only one British territory as an attractive possibility for southern slaveowners: the neighboring loyal province of East Florida. More or less similar to Georgia in climate and ecology, and unfolding in mile upon mile of uncultivated land, East Florida appeared to loyalist planters like the last best hope for reproducing their existing lifestyles. The ambitious governor of East Florida, Patrick Tonyn, enthusiastically encouraged loyalist immigration. "Upon the unfortunate defeat of Earl Cornwallis" he issued a proclamation inviting "the distressed and persecuted Loyalists in the neighbouring Colonies" to "become settlers in this Province."[49] Hundreds had already arrived. The only trouble was that in Carleton's initial orders, St. Augustine had also been slated for evacuation. Dismayed loyalists and sympathetic officials chorused in protest against the measure, as did Governors Wright and Tonyn.[50] Under loyalist pressure, Carleton canceled the evacuation on the grounds that Florida would give loyalists "a convenient refuge, whither the most valuable of their property may without much difficulty be transported, and in a Country where their Negroes may continue to be useful to them."[51] East Florida henceforth became the destination of choice for southern loyalists—underscoring the importance of property concerns, and slavery in particular, in determining the course of the loyalist exodus.

Loyalists in Savannah were the first to confront a situation that would be replayed on successively larger stages in the months ahead. Seven thousand white civilians and slaves prepared to depart in less than four weeks' time. How or if loyalists readied themselves psychologically for leaving can never be really known, but there were concrete chores aplenty. The city's neat grid of angles and squares turned into a moving mosaic. Days became busy with selling and packing, transactions and farewells. Soldiers piled up military stores and ordnance below the fort walls to be rowed out to the coast. Slaves hauled furniture and baggage and gathered by the hundreds to ship out with their masters. Ultimately almost all of the five thousand enslaved blacks in Savannah would leave, transported from the city as loyalist property. On July 11, 1782, the garrison trooped into flatboats and rowed around the grassy curves of the river mouth to the sea. "Nothing can surpass the sorrow which many of the inhabitants expressed at our departure," a New York soldier noted in his diary, "especially those ladies whose sweethearts were under necessity of quiting the town at our evacuation; some of those ladies were converted and brought over to the faith, so as to quit as well and follow us."[52]

If it is hard to know just what went through the minds of departing loyalists, it is especially difficult to gain insight into the attitudes of the majority of people who left, those five thousand or so enslaved blacks, who outnumbered the white migrants by more than two to one. George Liele, though, part of the tiny minority of free blacks to evacuate, did provide some account of what made him go. Liele may have found a higher solace in his journey, for he followed two masters to the seafront—if you counted the one in heaven as well as the one on earth. For about three years, Liele had been living in Savannah as a free man, ever since his former owner, a loyalist who had manumitted him before the war, had been killed, his hand blown off by a patriot bullet. Liele may well have worked in Savannah as a carter, like many other free blacks, helping to provision the British as his friend David George was doing from his butcher's stall. But the labor that really consumed Liele (and George) was the Lord's: preaching among the blacks in town, as he had done in the cornfields, clearings, and barns around Silver Bluff. Though David George moved his family to Charleston in anticipation of disruptions in Savannah, Liele stayed on and preached till the very end of the British occupation.

Freedom, Liele had learned, could be a precarious condition. Once, he had been jailed by whites who did not believe his old master had really freed him. Only by presenting his manumission papers did he get released, with the support of a white benefactor, a backcountry planter and loyalist officer called Moses Kirkland. (It was Kirkland who had taken in Thomas Brown after the latter's torture in 1775.) Liele owed Kirkland something more. Liele's wife and four small children had all been born slaves, and Kirkland apparently helped him purchase their freedom. In return, Liele agreed to renounce a portion of his own liberty by indenturing himself to Kirkland for a period of a few years. Now the British were leaving Savannah, Kirkland was banished, and George Liele was "partly obliged" to follow, no longer a slave, and yet neither entirely free. Like everyone else, he had important preparations to make before his departure. Standing in the shallows of the Savannah River in the shadow of the city walls, Liele baptized Andrew, Hannah, and little Hagar Bryan, three slaves belonging to a loyal Baptist, bringing three new members into the church. As the Lord willed that Brother George would carry the word beyond American shores, now it was for Brother Andrew to continue his work among Georgia blacks.[53]

On July 20, 1782, Liele and his family sailed on the first convoy out of Savannah, bound for Port Royal, Jamaica.[54] His reason for evacuating with the British might seem clear—to protect some limited freedom for himself and his family. But the moment Liele stepped on board he would have seen overwhelming evidence of why so many whites left: to protect their enslaved property. The sloop *Zebra* (a suggestive name given the racial breakdown of its passengers) and its twelve flanking ships carried a mere fifty white loyalists on board. The vast majority of its passengers were nineteen hundred blacks, almost all of them slaves.[55] Whole slave communities sailed out together:

more than two hundred belonged to governor Sir James Wright alone, the remnant of an enslaved labor force numbering more than five hundred souls that Wright had once put to work across eleven plantations. They had survived the war only to be transported to Jamaica in the custody of one of Wright's associates, Nathaniel Hall, there to be hired or sold into the notoriously punishing conditions of Caribbean slavery.[56]

The next day, a second evacuation fleet left for St. Augustine. This convoy would also be numerically dominated by slaves; Georgia's lieutenant governor John Graham took charge of no fewer than 465 black men, women, and children belonging to himself and others.[57] Thomas Brown, meanwhile, escorted another, more unusual nonwhite contingent. About two hundred of the Creek and Choctaw warriors who had fought with him against the patriots were returning to their villages, after spending a year at war.[58] Their presence on board represented a rare British concession to southern Indian allies, and a unique counterflow within the exodus: for them, and them alone, this voyage out was a voyage home. The St. Augustine convoy also carried most of William Johnston's extended family: his father Lewis Johnston Sr., his brother Lewis Jr., and his sisters with their husbands and children. The Johnstons had a strong reason to favor Florida. With seventy-one enslaved men, women, and children in his household, Lewis Johnston Sr. figured as one of the largest slaveowners among the Georgia refugees.

Elizabeth and William Johnston, though, joined the fleet bound for Charleston with William's regiment. It was an unusual choice for Elizabeth to go to Charleston with William, rather than to St. Augustine with her in-laws—not least because she was then seven months pregnant, and passed up the offer from a patriot friend of William's to stay in Savannah under his protection until she was "fitter for moving." But the Johnstons had already been apart for much of their short married life, and Elizabeth wanted no more of it. She had suffered the loneliness of raising their firstborn son, Andrew—a "handsome sweet fellow" with a "large proportion" of his father's "passionate temper"—while William was away at war. And she had acquired another reason to wish William close at hand. For beyond her watch, William had fallen into his old habit of gambling, "a vice so destructive and ruinous in its nature" that it threatened to wreck their growing family.[59] He did not reveal the alarming extent of his losses to his wife, but wrote to her father with hangdog contrition, imploring Lichtenstein to support the family in their need.[60] What was worse, William's behavior opened a rift with his own father and sisters. "You know not how wretched you have made me," Elizabeth opined, "and tis cruel to distress a Father whose sole wish & care, is to see his children happy."[61] Dr. Lewis Johnston, with his wealth and influential connections, was not a man to be alienated lightly. A rift with him would cut off the young couple from their best source of support and patronage.

So when British power collapsed around her in Savannah, Elizabeth Johnston followed her impulse and her spouse: "My husband would not like the separation, and I positively refused to remain." Not once did she mention the issues of principle involved in leaving her home. Nor, more strikingly, did she note the obvious impetus for her extended family's departure. Every single one of Johnston's close male relations had been proscribed under the Georgia Confiscation and Banishment Act, including William Johnston, his father Lewis, and her father John Lichtenstein. In her own telling, Johnston did not leave for reasons of political sentiment but for emotional ones, the bond of conjugal love.

The Johnstons arrived in Charleston to find that city, too, in the throes of pre-evacuation mayhem. Day in, day out, British officials coped with shortages of food, rum, ships, and cash; rising disorder and falling morale; and more than ten thousand civilians clamoring for relief and reassurance. "The perplexity of civil matters here is so much beyond my abilities to arrange, that I declare myself unequal to the task, nor have I the constitution to stand it, from morning till night I have memorials and petitions full of distress, &c. &c. before me," moaned Charleston commander General Leslie.[62] Patriot advances had cut off the city's food supply, forcing Leslie to send forage parties out to raid the countryside for grain.[63] Soldiers grew restless and undisciplined, falling "into all kinds of dissipation," and, increasingly, running away.[64] An attempted deserter was hanged before a crowd of two thousand; two other men were flogged with "500 lashes each at the most public parts of the town and then drummed out of the garrison, for harboring two deserters."[65] Conditions among the impoverished refugees were not much kinder. From November 1781 to November 1782, a neighborhood coffin maker crafted 213 wooden boxes for the loyal dead: a poignant list of spouses, grandparents, and, especially, children; for a teenager named "America," and for individuals of whom no more was recorded than their heights.[66]

Within a week of the publication of evacuation orders in August, 1782, 4,230 white loyalists announced their intention to depart with the British, along with 7,163 blacks, chiefly slaves.[67] Following the Savannah precedent, East Florida was the destination of choice. But in Charleston, a far larger and more economically developed city than Savannah, the evacuation of so many slaves posed special complications.

During the British occupation, about a hundred patriot-owned estates with five thousand slaves had been "sequestered" and run for the benefit of the British military by the loyalist commissioner of sequestered estates, John Cruden. Now, with evacuation imminent, many loyalists whose own slaves had been seized by the patriots wanted to take sequestered slaves as compensation. Logical though the swap might appear, it was also illegal, since loyalists had no title to these patriot-owned slaves. To make matters more difficult, hundreds of black loyalists lived and worked in Charleston—David George and his family now among them—who had legitimate claims to leave with the British as free people. Patriots balked at the prospect of any of their valuable slaves, sequestered or freed, sailing off into the empire. How could Britain evacuate blacks so as to prevent wrongful seizure of patriot-owned slaves, on the one hand, while upholding promises of freedom to black loyalists on the other? Leslie wrote to Carleton for instructions. "In whatever manner we may dispose of such of them who were taken on the sequestered estates," he felt, "those who have voluntarily come in, under the faith of our protection, cannot in justice be abandoned to the merciless resentment of their former masters."[68] Carleton emphatically agreed: "Such as have been promised their freedom, must have it."[69]

With loyalists and patriots clamoring for fair allocation of property, and blacks both free and enslaved facing him with their plight, Commissioner John Cruden had his hands full and his capacities stretched. Not least, Cruden was terribly in debt: numerous people had failed to pay him for hired labor and produce from the sequestered estates, and his public accounts were £10,000 in arrears.[70] (He and his younger brother had meanwhile racked up such personal expenses that their poor father, a Presbyterian minister in London, had asked his brokers to stop extending the boys credit.)[71] But John Cruden had always been one to see the bright side of things—witness the proposal he had sent to his patron Lord Dunmore, after Yorktown, to raise an army of free blacks and continue the war. When provisions were running low in Charleston in the summer of 1782, Cruden equipped a flotilla of galleys and dispatched them into Low Country waterways to seize patriot grain supplies.[72] In the months ahead Cruden would do whatever he could to ease loyalists' distress—even when his ideas and methods became unconventional indeed.

Cruden prided himself on his management of the sequestered estates, many of which he averred were "in higher Cultivation than when I took them into my Charge, [and] would have been torn to pieces by needy Creditors" without his care. Surely, he thought, it would be simple enough to resolve disputes over slaves. Putting forward his own version of the golden rule, he endeavored to return all sequestered slaves to their patriot owners "in the hope & firm belief that it will produce a similar effect on them by Exerting them to restore the property of the British Subjects."[73] Cruden thus vigilantly policed loyalists from taking away patriot-owned slaves that did not belong to them. He trusted patriots to be equally respectful, in turn, of loyalist property and the freedom of black loyalists. To him there was no contradiction between upholding the rights of slaveowners in one domain and supporting the liberty of free blacks in another: that was what honor was all about.

As the first ships prepared to sail from Charleston in October 1782, Leslie and the patriot governor of South Carolina agreed on terms respecting the exchange of prisoners and the transfer of sequestered property. "All the Slaves, the Property of *American* Subjects in *South Carolina*, now in my Power, shall be left here, and restored to their former Owners," ordered Leslie, "except such Slaves as may have rendered themselves particularly obnoxious by their Attachment and Services to the *British* Troops, and such as have had specifick Promises of Freedom." To placate the patriots and "in order to prevent the great Loss of Property, and probably the Ruin of many Families," he volunteered to pay a fair price for black loyalists whose former owners contested their cases.[74] But the enormous numbers of blacks claiming freedom as loyalists made Leslie blanch at the "monstrous expense" that would be involved.[75] Instead, Leslie appointed a board of inspectors to interrogate blacks who had "come in under the faith of various Proclamations and promises, in hope of obtaining their freedom," and judge their veracity.[76] American inspectors were given the right to search outbound ships for illicitly removed slaves. Leslie's handling of this issue provided an important model for the still larger evacuation of blacks that Sir Guy Carleton would soon superintend in New York.

David George and his family were among those whose freedom was confirmed by the board, and numbered among an estimated fifteen hundred free blacks evacuated from Charleston.[77] George was impressed to discover that his family, just like the white refugees, was entitled to free passage to other British domains. They sailed on one of the first convoys out of Charleston, at about the beginning of November 1782.[78] Though the majority of ships were bound for New York or St. Augustine, the Georges had a more unusual destination. They and their five hundred or so fellow passengers were headed for Nova Scotia, where they would be among the first of thousands of loyalist refugees who flooded into the British North American province in the year ahead.[79]

Coincidentally, William Johnston may have been one of the officers who cleared George for departure. As one of eleven men appointed to Leslie's board of inspectors, William spent some of his last days in Charleston hearing out the stories of black women and men who had fled from slavery. Elizabeth Johnston gave birth to the couple's first daughter, Catherine, in the comfort of a stately sequestered house. Around her in the emptying city, "everything is in motion, and turned topsy-turvy." "It is impossible to describe what confusion, people of all denominations, seem to be in," one soldier noted. "The one is buying everything he can to complete his stock of goods, the second is searching for a passage to some other garrison of His Majesty's troops; the third is going from house to house to collect his debts."[80] Though the Johnstons had no property to handle in Charleston, they also faced fresh choices. William's regiment was due to ship out to New York City, along with most of the Charleston garrison. Far away and likely facing imminent evacuation itself, New York made little sense as a destination for Elizabeth and the children. This time they decided that she would head for St. Augustine separately and stay with William's relatives until he could join them there, to establish their first real family home.[81]

In early December 1782, Elizabeth Johnston stepped into a small boat with her toddler son, infant daughter, and a black nurse, and rowed out into the harbor to board a Florida-bound schooner. It was like cruising into a jigsaw puzzle. Above her loomed the curved wooden walls of a city afloat, dark with slime and tar, the outlines of figures scurrying along decks and rigging, canvas sails stretched on a lattice of masts. Skiffs and rowboats traced ripples across the water, ferrying loyalists and slaves, barrels of food and supplies, furniture and livestock—even the valuable bells of St. Michael's Church—to the waiting ships.[82] More than twelve hundred white loyalists and twenty-six hundred blacks plashed out to join a convoy bound for Jamaica. Another group of two hundred black loyalist soldiers gathered to sail for Saint Lucia. A few hundred individuals, including various government officials, joined a convoy for Britain. Finally, on the afternoon of December 12, the soldiers began assembling on the city wharfs to board the transports for New York. Two days later, the Americans formally reoccupied Charleston, while the Johnstons swayed out to sea in opposite directions: he with the garrison to New York City, she to join the rapidly growing loyalist community in East Florida.[83]

Together, the evacuations of Savannah and Charleston set more than twenty thousand loyalists, slaves, and soldiers on the move: so many people separated, so much left behind, so many lives bent on unpredictable routes. What unfolded during these evacuations exposed contradictions that would follow the refugees into exile. Loyalists left for reasons of pique as much as principle, primed to find fault with the administrators they nonetheless relied on. Free blacks and slaves traveled on the same ships, leaving their status open to confusion and abuse. The Johnstons and the Georges, who had been evacuated twice, pointed to another recurring phenomenon: many of these refugees would end up moving again and again. Yet for all that their emigration, with its many uncertainties, could make loyalists worry about the worst, it could also promise change for the better—a chance to rebuild fresh lives as British imperial subjects. Though less frequently voiced than anxieties and laments, some refugees offered more optimistic assessments of evacuation. Out of so much loss, one might find something new. That was how John Cruden saw things when he sailed for St. Augustine, his dreaming not yet done. "This moment," he felt, was "perhaps the most important the World Ever beheld."[84] And what was the value of being on earth at such a time as this, if not to capitalize on its opportunities?

As the ships sailed out of Charleston, one year after Yorktown, loyalists had come to terms with the reality of defeat and begun, literally, to move on. The war was over, U.S. independence assured. At least eight thousand white and black refugees had already settled in other British colonies, notably East Florida. But there were still some loyalist hopes hanging in the balance. What would the United States provide for loyalists by way of protection against retaliation and compensation for their losses? It was up to the peace commissioners in Paris to hash out the answers, which would have great bearing on the decisions of loyalists still uncertain about whether to stay or go.

The terms of Anglo-American peace rested in the hands of a mere five men, each of whose personal attitudes would carry significant weight. The seniormost member of the American peace commission was Benjamin Franklin, who was joined in Paris by the New York lawyer John Jay and John Adams of Massachusetts. A fourth American commissioner, South Carolina planter Henry Laurens, would come to meet them later. The British side in the negotiations was superintended by just one man, Richard Oswald, appointed to the post by the prime minister, Lord Shelburne. Oswald had striking, not to say surprising, credentials for the job. Nearly eighty years old, the Glasgow-based merchant had built a fortune in the Atlantic trade, primarily shipping tobacco to Britain from the Chesapeake and slaves to America from a trading fort he and his associates owned on Bunce Island, in Sierra Leone. Oswald had invested significantly in East Florida land. Above all, he had many close American friends, including Franklin and Laurens. Indeed he was so much a "friend of America," in this sense, that many did not think he could be trusted to speak loudly enough for British interests. Other government ministers sent a deputy to keep tabs on him, Henry Strachey, a deft civil servant who had cut his teeth as secretary to East India Company commander Robert Clive, and who, like Oswald, owned a sprawling estate in East Florida and had close ties with Laurens.[85]

In hotel suites, over dinner tables, and in letters crisscrossing the quarters of Paris, the negotiators wrangled over how to disentangle the thirteen colonies from the British Empire. By the late fall of 1782, only a few sticking points remained. Americans wanted access to the cod-rich shores of Newfoundland, and to clarify the western and northern boundaries of the United States. Many Americans owed money to British creditors, and there was some debate over how these debts should be resolved. But the most nagging outstanding question concerned the loyalists: what, if anything, would the United States do to compensate them? Bit by bit solutions were brokered. Oswald conceded the fishing rights. The two sides agreed to mark the western border of the United States at the Mississippi River. John Adams then helpfully observed that the question of debts should be treated separately from the question of loyalist property—a decision that "struck Mr. Strachey with peculiar pleasure; I saw it instantly smiling in every line of his face"—and insisted, as a point of Yankee honor, that all American prewar debts be paid.[86]

That left the loyalists. Moral responsibility aside, Lord Shelburne and his ministers knew that failing to secure concessions for the loyalists would open them up to attack from their political opponents, and he instructed Oswald and Strachey to take the issue seriously.[87] But as they sat down to negotiate this last point—the only diplomatic obstacle left between war and peace—they may not have realized what firm resistance they would face in one of their American counterparts. Benjamin Franklin adamantly opposed granting anything to the loyalists. Even Jay and Adams were surprised by Franklin's passion on the subject: "Dr. Franklin is very staunch against the Tories, more decided on this point than Mr. Jay or myself," Adams noted.[88] And as the weeks wore on, Franklin's resolve seemed only to harden. If Britain demanded compensation for loyalist property, Franklin threatened, then he would demand that Britain pay reparations to the United States for all the damages of war. Loyalists had spent years "wantonly burning and destroying farm houses, villages, towns," he said, and he flatly refused to give them anything back. "It is best for you to drop all mention of the refugees," he declared to Oswald.[89] Either accept his terms, or keep fighting the war. It was easier, apparently, for two nations to agree on every major issue defining their relationship than it was for one father to forgive betrayal by his son. Franklin's resistance to compensating loyalists would be reflected in his own last act toward William. In his will, Franklin pointedly left William only the land he owned in Nova Scotia (the premier loyalist haven) and a clutch of books and papers. "The part he acted against me in the late war will account for my leaving him no more of an estate he endeavoured to deprive me of," explained the embittered father.[90]

Franklin's challenge worked. The preliminary articles of peace included only a limp nod in the loyalists' direction. Article V stated that "Congress shall earnestly recommend it to the legislatures of the respective states to provide for the restitution of all estates, rights, and properties, which have been belonging to real British subjects." That is, Congress would ask the states nicely to give loyalists their property back—but it was entirely up to the states to act as they saw fit. At Franklin's insistence, the article was phrased only to extend to those loyalists "who had not borne arms against the said United States," in a stroke excluding thousands of loyalist military veterans from consideration.[91] The phrase "real British subjects" would also later cause friction among loyalists who saw it as setting up an invidious hierarchy among British subjects, instead of presuming them all to be equally "real."

In late November 1782, as the final draft of the treaty was being drawn up, the fourth American peace commissioner arrived in Paris just in time to introduce one last self-interested clause. Henry Laurens had sailed for Europe two years earlier to negotiate a loan with Holland when his ship was intercepted by the Royal Navy and he was imprisoned in the Tower of London on a charge of treason. He endured fifteen months of confinement in a tiny stone cell, intermittently sick, closely monitored, taunted by guards who played "The Tune of Yankee Doodle . . . I suppose in derision of me."[92] He ultimately secured his release thanks to the lobbying—and bail money—of none other than Richard Oswald, his old friend and associate. Joining his colleagues on the eve of the treaty's signing, Laurens proposed a further detail to be inserted into the text. Britain, he said, must agree to evacuate "without causing any Destruction or carrying away any Negroes, or other Property of the American Inhabitants." Oswald, who had traded slaves with Laurens for decades, had no objections, and the phrase went in—with considerable consequences to come for black loyalists.

On November 30, 1782, the five commissioners gathered in Oswald's suite at the Grand Hotel Muscovite to sign the preliminary articles of peace. Many contemporaries were surprised by Britain's generosity toward the former colonies—but prognosticators saw things differently. At a gathering at Franklin's house afterward, a Frenchman taunted the British delegation with the prospect that "the Thirteen United States would form the greatest empire in the world." "Yes," Oswald's secretary proudly replied, "and they will *all* speak English, every one of 'em."[93] Whatever greatness the future might hold for the United States, language itself ensured that it would share with Britain a connection that no other major foreign power could match. In British eyes, the peace achieved an all-important goal, namely to secure the United States in a British sphere of influence, against its rival France. And there was something more. For if, as many then expected, the United States failed to cohere as a single nation, the treaty put Britain in a good position to pick up the pieces. The months of fighting after Yorktown had shown how surrender alone did not end a war. To those in the know, the generous terms of the treaty hinted that it would take more than this peace to end British ambitions in and around the United States.

With the American agreement in hand, British negotiators promptly concluded peace with France and Spain, swapping territories in a familiar eighteenth-century game of diplomatic poker. France and Britain agreed to return more or less to the status quo ante bellum. Of greater consequence to loyalists, Britain arranged to cede East and West Florida to Spain in exchange for continued possession of Gibraltar. In September 1783, Britain signed the definitive peace treaties with the United States, France, and Spain collectively known as the Peace of Paris. On parchment, the American Revolutionary War was over. But on the ground in North America, the evacuations were far from finished.

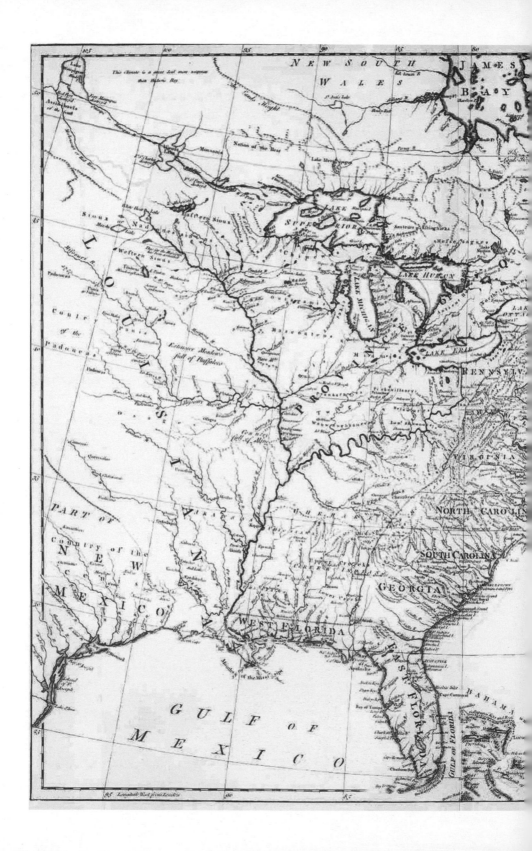

William Faden,
*The United States
of North America
with the British
and Spanish
Territories
According to the
Treaty of 1783,*
1785.

CHAPTER THREE

A New World Disorder

O N MARCH 2 5, 1783, American newspapers published the preliminary articles of peace among the belligerent powers. Patriots tolled bells, raised toasts, and set off fireworks to celebrate the formal end of an eight-year war. To the forty to fifty thousand loyalists remaining under British protection in New York City and East Florida, however, the news might as well have been printed on black-edged paper, as death announcements usually were. The thirteen British colonies were no more. And on what terms! Even the British home secretary must have realized how much he was asking when he urged Sir Guy Carleton to "use every conciliatory Effort in your power to obtain the full Effect of the 5th Article"—Benjamin Franklin's noncommittal nod toward property compensation—"whereby so much was necessarily trusted to the good Faith of the Congress."[1] Entrusted to faith indeed. The war was over, U.S. independence granted, and now no compensation guaranteed for loyalists at all—Article V of the peace would go down in infamy among loyalists as the greatest betrayal of their interests yet. And loyalists in East Florida would face still worse news when they learned that Britain had agreed to hand their haven over to Spain. Yet to whom else but the British government could these loyalists turn for help? Such was the climate of frustration in which the last and largest British evacuations took place, from New York City and East Florida.

Carleton himself had always resented that the peace negotiations took place in Paris, not in New York—and, by extension, that he had been prevented from playing a major role in them. In New York he had become fast friends with leading loyalists who embraced him as a guardian of their interests. Carleton formed an especially close connection with William Smith, and had long shared Smith's hopes for some kind of imperial federation with America. Right up to the eve of peace, he told Smith he was "convinced that the Reunion is at our Command, and that if there is a Rent of the Empire it will be our own Folly."[2] He felt the treaty to be almost a personal blow, and was "much affected by the dishonorable Terms" respecting loyalists. Adding insult to injury, the feeble provisions now placed on *his* shoulders the burden of trying, as Whitehall instructed him, to refresh "Harmony and Union between the Two Countries." He had resisted American independence in the first place; now he had to use his "judgment" and "humanity . . . to effect the conciliation of Individuals, and a cordial oblivion of all personal Injuries committed, or supposed to have been committed on either Side."[3] But all those years in Quebec had taught Carleton much about colonial governance, and out of the wreckage of this civil war he envisioned creative ways forward. He would do all he could for American loyalists, because his own sense of loyalty—and his own vision of empire—depended on it.

Up till now, Carleton had managed evacuations of American cities from a distance. Now by far the largest and most complex surrounded him, on a scale totally overshadowing those of the south. Withdrawing from New York City posed an awesome set of logistical challenges. Winding down a military garrison twenty thousand men strong, entrenched for seven years, was daunting enough. There were cannon and ordnance for a whole fortified city to be packed and loaded, stablefuls of horses to be shipped, forage and provisions for thousands to be located and sent. And this was only half Carleton's job. Also in New York there were some thirty-five thousand loyalist civilians, almost all of whom, if Savannah and Charleston offered any example, would probably seek to leave. Where would he find the ships to carry them, or rations to feed them? Where would they go and what equipment did they need to get settled? In his New York headquarters Carleton found himself pulled in as many directions as the refugees would travel. He managed a constant stream of entreaties from the disabled and dispossessed. He monitored Indian diplomacy and persisting hinterland violence. He processed requests for aid from Florida, from Jamaica, from Quebec and Nova Scotia. He corresponded with British officials, urging them to adopt generous policies toward the migrants. Yet under these extraordinarily pressured conditions, Carleton and his staff improvised a series of measures that laid the foundations for an Atlantic-wide program of refugee relief.

When the southern evacuations commenced, Carleton had proposed that the British government grant tracts of land to loyalist refugees, free of charges and quitrents, in Nova Scotia, Florida, and other relatively sparsely settled provinces. Some precedent for this could be found in mid-eighteenth-century Nova Scotia, when land confiscated from French Acadians had been redistributed to Anglophone settlers; similar offers of land had also been extended to veterans after the Seven Years' War, as a good way simultaneously to encourage colonization and provide gainful employment for demobilized soldiers, who were seen as a potential source of social instability. But Carleton's land-for-loyalists scheme fitted into a larger plan for imperial reconstruction. The loss in America, he felt, had made it "indispensably necessary to establish the most close & cordial connection with the provinces which have preserved their allegiance." Giving land to loyalists in British North America and elsewhere would ensure that "every man will readily take arms for its defence, & by these means only they can be preserved. Not only quit rents and fees of office of every sort shou'd be dispensed with, but no taxes shou'd be imposed in future by Great Britain."[4] The policy thus had a twofold purpose: it rewarded a population whose loyalty had already been confirmed, while reinforcing loyalty and security elsewhere in the British Empire.

In January 1783, an association of New York loyalists dispatched agents to Nova Scotia to scout out a settlement at a place called Port Roseway, an undeveloped harbor about a hundred miles south of Halifax. Although Nova Scotia governor John Parr had not yet received instructions from London about land grants, he offered to provide the refugees with 400,000 wooden boards to build new houses. The planks would be the beginnings of a veritable loyalist metropolis. Initially about six hundred loyalists had joined the Port Roseway Association intending to emigrate. When their fleet prepared to sail at the end of April 1783, "upwards of seven thousand" people had signed on to go.[5] Carleton's commissary-general, the able London merchant Brook Watson, processed an imposing list of goods for the pioneers: adzes and saws, water buckets and grease buckets, calipers and pincers, cartridges, powder, shot and shell, lanterns, locks, and ladles.[6] Ships from Britain set out to meet the settlers, heavy with hatchets and hoes, and all the shingles, "gimblets," and "wimble bits" they might need.[7] As the first New York evacuation fleet sat well-stocked and ready to sail in the harbor before him, Carleton wrote to Governor Parr expressing his pleasure that "we are able to give these deserving people, some refuge, which I trust they will amply repay by that increase of wealth, and commerce and power, which they may give in future to a greatly diminished Empire."[8] A few months later, Carleton learned that British ministers had approved his recommendations about land grants. The key elements of loyalist resettlement—free passage, provisions and supplies, and access to land—were all in place.

Carleton did not mention another, equally significant dimension of the loyalist exodus to Nova Scotia that he worked hard to facilitate: the emigration of black loyalists. While white loyalists had been devastated by Article V of the preliminary peace treaty, it was Article VII—Henry Laurens's stipulation forbidding Britain from "carrying away any Negroes, or other Property"—that terrified the blacks. News of the peace, remembered Boston King, a former slave from South Carolina, "diffused universal joy among all parties, except us, who had escaped from slavery and taken refuge in the English army; for a report prevailed at New-York, that all the slaves . . . were to be delivered up to their masters." King had already endured much to "feel the happiness of liberty, of which I knew nothing before." He had run away to Charleston from a cruel master, and survived the physical ravages of smallpox and the discomforts of military service. Toward the end of 1781 King had made his way to New York, where, unable to find the tools to resume his trade as a carpenter, he moved from master to master in domestic service, struggling just to keep clothes on his back. At least he had his freedom. But King and his peers spent the spring of 1783 haunted by the spectacle of "our old masters coming from Virginia, North-Carolina, and other parts, and seizing upon their slaves in the streets of New-York, or even dragging them out of their beds." Consumed by "inexpressible anguish and terror," some black loyalists in New York were too frightened to eat, and "sleep departed from our eyes."[9]

It could not have encouraged them to see the handbill posted around New York City on April 15, 1783, reproducing the text of Article VII together with Carleton's orders that "no Person is permitted to embark as a Refugee, who has not resided Twelve Months within the British Lines, without a special Passport from the Commandant."[10] Three officers were to examine every departing ship for property—that is, people—illicitly removed. Some of the black loyalists had certificates attesting to their military service; but many of them did not. Was this how their runaway journeys would end: with abduction on the streets, or reenslavement at the docks?

But Carleton had insisted during the evacuation of Charleston that slaves promised freedom should have it—and his word held just as firmly now in New York City. He implemented his own version of the commission General Leslie had established in Charleston, to assess the cases of blacks claiming freedom. Every Wednesday from ten till two, members of this committee (made up of four British and three American representatives) sat in Fraunces's Tavern on Pearl Street to hear out disputes over former slaves. Those cleared by the board received a printed certificate of freedom signed by the commandant of New York, General Samuel Birch. Then at the docks, inspectors entered the names of all departing blacks into a sprawling register, together with their ages, former owners' names, brief physical descriptions, and notes—ironically enough, much the same information recorded for slave sales. The register, known as the "Book of Negroes," forms a genuinely exceptional document of exodus; nothing like it exists for the thousands of white loyalist refugees. The reason for such careful bookkeeping was that these migrants were also exceptional compared to whites. They could be considered property as well as people. The volume that recorded the black loyalists' freedom thus reinscribed their former status as slaves.[11]

British assurances of freedom held good. But Americans were none too pleased. On a Tuesday morning in early May 1783, Carleton sailed up the Hudson on the aptly named *Perseverance* toward the broad waters of the Tappan Zee, to hold a conference with George Washington. The commanders had exchanged chilly letters for a full year, but this was their first meeting in the flesh. Sizing each other up on the shore, each man may have been disconcerted to detect a hint of himself in the other: standing roughly eye to eye at about six feet tall, big-nosed and thin-lipped, exuding authority as much by their braided uniform coats and tall boots as by their innate gravitas. The commanders had pressing items of business to discuss, including the ongoing depredations of partisan raiders in the countryside, the exchange of prisoners of war, and the timetable for evacuation. But Washington started off the conference by lecturing Carleton on what, to him, was the most urgent matter of all: the removal of human property from New York. Carleton calmly explained that a fleet had already embarked for Nova Scotia with registered black loyalists on board. "Already imbarked!" exclaimed a startled Washington. (He might have been yet more surprised to know that one of the blacks embarked, Harry Washington, had once belonged to him.) Carleton replied that he could not abide by anything in the treaty "inconsistent with prior Engagements binding the National Honor, which must be kept with all Colours."[12]

That evening, from his quarters in Orange, Washington wrote Carleton a letter bristling with rebuke:

> I was surprized to hear you mention that an Embarkation had already taken place in which a large Number of Negroes had been carried away. Whether this conduct is consonant or not to, or how far it may be deemed an Infraction of the Treaty, is not for me to decide. I cannot however conceal from your Excellency, that my private opinion is that the measure is totally different from the Letter & Spirit of the Treaty.

He demanded to hear from Carleton exactly what procedures had been put in place to prevent such miscarriages in future. But Carleton could match his counterpart's accusations point for point, meeting outrage with moral superiority. It was odd that Washington should be "surprized" by the news, Carleton dryly observed, when everything had been conducted in the most open manner. All the ships for Nova Scotia had been inspected, and the only disputes "arose over negroes who had been declared free previous to my arrival. As I had no right to deprive them of that liberty . . . , an accurate register was taken of every circumstance respecting them." Besides, he concluded, "Had these negroes been denied permission to embark, they wou'd, in spite of every means to prevent it, have found various methods of quitting this place, so that the former owner wou'd no longer have been able to trace them, and of course wou'd have lost, in every way, all chance of compensation." In short, he had acted entirely in keeping with the spirit and letter of British law. "The negroes in question . . . I found free when I arrived in New York, I had therefore no right . . . to prevent their going to any part of the world they thought proper."[13]

Back on Pearl Street, the commission continued its weekly work under the hospitable roof of Samuel Fraunces—reputedly part black himself. They handed out certificates of freedom by the hundreds, and at the waterfront the register of names grew apace, with the particulars of "stout" and sometimes "sickly wenches," "likely girls," "fellows" both "feeble" and "fine." By the time the commissioners finished, more than two thousand names had been entered into the Book of Negroes. Boston King sailed for Port Roseway with his certificate in hand and his new wife, Violet, twelve years his senior, by his side, among the 132 free blacks (Harry Washington included) looking for a new life beginning on *L'Abondance*. Members of the Black Pioneers, including Murphy Stiele, who had been haunted by voices about a great black army winning the war, and Thomas Peters, a future leader of black loyalist refugees, took their tickets to freedom on the *Joseph* bound for Annapolis Royal.

Carleton's principled defense of the black loyalists stands out for its clarity of conviction, and highlights an emerging contrast between certain American and British attitudes toward slavery. Carleton's handpicked personal secretary, Maurice Morgann, was an articulate abolitionist, who in 1772 published Britain's first proposal for a gradual emancipation of slaves in the West Indies.[14] Carleton himself was not an abolitionist as such; he had not explicitly set out to free the slaves. His actions spoke in part to a sense of personal honor. Promises had been made, promises must be kept. But they also reflected his commitment to a concept of national honor—and the paternalistic government's responsibility to uphold it—that would rapidly gain momentum among the rulers of the postwar British Empire. His time as governor of Quebec had honed his belief, in common with a number of his fellow administrators, that an empire of diverse subjects was best ruled by a strong executive. After all, he might well have thought, what was imperial power for, if not to be exercised by the rulers who had it on behalf of those subjects who did not?

FEW OF THE thirty-five thousand or so loyalist civilians in New York City could have expected their lives would ever come down to a choice between emigration and endangerment. Through the spring and summer of 1783, they sifted through a competing series of promises and threats, deciding if, when, and where to go. In the words of "The Tory's Soliloquy," a satirical patriot verse published in various American newspapers: "To go or not to go—is that the question? / Whether 'tis best to trust the inclement sky / That scowls indignant o'er the dreary Bay / of Fundy . . . or stay among the Rebels! / And, by our stay rouse up their keenest rage, / That, bursting o'er our now defenceless heads, / Will crush us."[15]

News of the peace brought patriots back into New York City to reclaim their property, but loyalists making the reverse journey found conciliatory feelings in notably short supply. "Almost all those who have attempted to return to their homes have been exceedingly ill treated, many beaten, robbed of their money and clothing, and sent back," Carleton told the British ministry.[16] In Westchester County, an elderly member of the prominent loyalist DeLancey family had been beaten "in a most violent manner" and told to "run to Halifax, or to his damned King, for that neither he nor one of his breed should be suffered to remain in the Country."[17] Another town announced that loyalists "shall not be permitted to continue longer than seven days, after being duly warned to retire, on pain of experiencing the just punishment due to such infamous parricides." Citizens of Poughkeepsie declared that loyalists deserved nothing "from this country but detestation and chastizement. The spirit of 75 still beats high, and *must* beat high, or American freedom is no more."[18] An author calling himself "Brutus" issued a sinister warning, widely reproduced in regional newspapers, "TO All Adherents to the British Government and Followers of the British Army Commonly called TORIES." "Flee then while it is in your power," he ordered, "for the day is at hand, when, to your confusion and dismay; such of you as reject this seasonable admonition, will have nothing to deliver them from the just vengeance of the collected citizens."[19]

Offsetting such worrying reports, positive propaganda appeared in the New York press under the signature of loyal emigrants, boasting about their new climes. A settler at Port Roseway described quantities of fish veritably leaping from the water: trout, salmon, cod, "hollaboat (a most delicate fish indeed)," and herring so numerous that "I am told that a single person with a scoop net, may take twenty barrels in one day."[20] "Often I thank God I came to this place," said another, "and I sincerely think Port Roseway, in a little time, will be one of the most flourishing capital places in North America."[21] From Saint John, on the Bay of Fundy, an emigrant boasted of the bracing climate, fertile soil, and a toothsome menagerie of "Moose, (which I think excels any beef) Hares, Rabbits, Partridges, Pidgeons."[22] Loyalists on St. John's Island (today called Prince Edward Island) declared, "We were told, as perhaps you may be, the worst Things possible of the Country; such as, that the People were Starving; We should get nothing to eat, and should ourselves be eaten up by Insects. . . . We have found the Reverse too true. . . . Come and see, and depend on the Evidence of your own senses."[23] And if none of these northern locales appealed, there were also the turquoise-bordered islands of the Bahamas, an archipelago that "wants only inhabitants, and a small degree of cultivation, to render it as flourishing as any of the West-India Islands."[24]

By late summer 1783, New York City witnessed a continuous parade of loyalist departures, and some patriot returns. It must have been an eerie thing to watch one of the largest cities in America turning inside out. "No News here but that of Evacuation," one bemused (undoubtedly patriot) commentator wrote, "This . . . occasions a Variety of physiognomic, laughable Appearances.—Some look smiling, others melancholy, a third Class mad. To hear their Conversation would make you feel merry: Some . . . represent the cold Regions of Nova-Scotia as a new-created Paradise, others as a Country unfit for any human Being to inhabit. Tories are vexed with Tories; they curse the Powers to whom they owe Allegiance, and thus render themselves *rebellious.*"[25] Advertisements crowded the columns of the *Royal Gazette* announcing sales and business closures, and informing loyalists when and at which wharf to board their ships. British regulars and Hessians packed their gear and began to leave by the regiment-load. Cannon came down from the ramparts, munitions were crated up. The commissary's office sold off its surplus stock: 63,596 pairs of shoes and 68,093 pairs of worsted stockings, 10,100 shoe buckles, 21,000 needles.[26] On summer Wednesdays and Saturdays, the Wagon Office auctioned its draught and saddle horses, carts, and equipage.[27]

Colonel Beverley Robinson had an especially close look at the loyalist plight during these last hectic months of British occupation. As one of three inspectors of refugees, he and his colleagues visited and assessed the needs of hundreds of "distressed Loyalists" who had poured into the city from as far away as Florida. The inspectors distributed nearly £9,000 (New York currency) to 529 refugees for the first quarter of 1783 alone.[28] He surely knew personally some of the 212 New Yorkers on that list, reduced to destitution from positions of perfect comfort. Now he, like them, had to decide where to locate his family in future.

The Robinsons had fought a good war. Colonel Robinson himself played a role in one of the revolution's most notorious incidents, the 1780 defection of Continental Army general Benedict Arnold to the British. As patriot commander of West Point, Arnold had taken up residence in Robinson's confiscated house, just across the Hudson River from the fort, and there plotted to surrender West Point to the British. Robinson was the perfect British decoy to establish contact with Arnold. Sailing up to West Point on the British warship *Vulture*, he solicited a meeting with Arnold on the pretext of personal business related to the house, and Arnold made his infamous escape to the British on the *Vulture* a short time later. Soon enough, Robinson's eldest son Beverley Jr. was campaigning behind the turncoat general in Virginia. Meanwhile his sons Morris and Phil Robinson had become patriot prisoners of war. The colonel spent eighteen months trying to get the boys released and succeeded at last "in consequence of the embers of friendship that still remained unextinguished" between himself and George Washington.[29]

American independence, Robinson could see, would force "the Loyalists of America to depend on the mercy of their enemies for the restoration of their possessions, which we are well assured they will never grant." The terms of the peace treaty only confirmed his view that a future in the United States would be untenable. Robinson's Loyal American Regiment had been promised land grants in Nova Scotia. His men, like the majority of loyalist veterans, traveled north together to settle tracts assigned by regiment, trading in their comradeship in arms for neighboring farms. The colonel himself preferred to go to Britain, "with the hopes that the government . . . will not suffer us to starve but allow us a small pittance."[30] (His New Jersey counterpart Cortlandt Skinner made the same choice, moving his large family to England while his former regiment settled in the Saint John River valley.)[31] But as Robinson confessed in an embarrassed memorial to Carleton, "my circumstances are so very distressing that I cannot leave this place, without some assistance from Government." He required a six-month advance on his pay to actually make the move.[32] In the late summer of 1783, Robinson set off for England with his wife, daughters, and some of his sons. Beverley Jr. went to Nova Scotia with the Loyal Americans, while Phil remained garrisoned in New York City with his British infantry unit. This parting of the ways scored a painful line in the Robinson family, one among many clans dispersed by emigration. In years to come, the scattered relatives remained connected through affectionate, newsy letters—but several would never meet again.

Of course, in New York as in other British-held cities, not all loyalists left. Some families chose to split the challenges of staying and going, with female family members remaining in situ to pursue property claims (in some states, dower property had been excluded from confiscation) and men going on ahead to scout out new places of residence. Yet considering how much stronger the pull of stasis can be over change, the striking thing is just how many people did choose to go. Ultimately the total recorded exodus of New York loyalists to Nova Scotia alone amounted to nearly thirty thousand. A further twenty-five hundred or so traveled to Quebec and to Abaco, in the Bahamas.[33] All told, the evacuation of New York City may represent the largest (proportionate to population) civilian transfer in American history.

Not many loyalist civilians were left in New York by November

1783, when Carleton fixed the date for his own departure. The fleet waiting off Staten Island on Evacuation Day was Britain-bound, carrying government personnel, along with the remaining troops and refugees. Nineteen-year-old Phil Robinson was among the last British troops to march out of the city on Evacuation Day, "the only one of the family that witnessed that most humiliating scene."[34] Carleton's confidant William Smith also lingered till the bitter end. He wrote up a power of attorney for his wife, Janet, who was staying on to manage family affairs, drafted his last will and testament, packed his trunks, and rowed out with Carleton to the *Ceres*—the same ship that had carried the commander in chief to America eighteen months before. Crammed into a cabin "where five pens are scribbling around one Table," Smith wrote fondly back to Janet on shore. "Give yourself not a moment's uneasiness," he reassured her. "Every Comfort is to be found here." Still, Smith could not hide his impatience to set off, especially when they remained inexplicably at anchor a week later and he watched the celebratory fireworks exploding over Bowling Green. Writing yet "another Farewell" to his wife, he hoped that "no Accident happens by the Fireworks which I see. . . . Adieu to you all. Imbrace Harriet, and tell her I shall never forget to love her, if she loves you and obeys all your commands. Yours ever ever WS." Two days later the *Ceres* rounded Sandy Hook and headed into the open sea.[35]

With it, the British occupation of the United States officially ended. Henceforth the story of loyalist refugees would continue in other parts of the British world, from Halifax to Nassau, to London and to cities yet to be founded. But even with New York City formally surrendered, the loyalist exodus was not finished. For at the southern tip of British North America, on the beaches of East Florida, loyalists were about to perform the last, least expected, and most vigorously contested evacuation of all, as they learned in horror that their asylum was to be ceded to Spain. From hopeful place of refuge to last point of departure, East Florida bridged two phases of the refugee experience, linking the displacements initiated by war to the ongoing quest for a haven in peace.

IT HAD TAKEN Elizabeth Johnston three tedious weeks to travel down the Georgia coast to St. Augustine, boxed up on shipboard, always in motion, even in her sleep. When at last they turned into the St. Augustine inlet, they felt a stomach-dropping thud as their boat struck a sandbar. Fortunately, they managed to clear the obstruction, which was more than could be said for another Charleston convoy, wrecked against the shoals and ruining many refugees' carefully exported property. Half a dozen ships keeled askew on the sand, sentinels of loss. Johnston's first impressions of this flat, foreign place were not good. She found all her in-laws "much dissatisfied with their situation," grumbling over their future prospects. Little Andrew had been sick; the weather seemed "constantly wet or cloudy," and as she wrote her husband, she "repent[ed] sincerely of not going with you to New York . . . for what is life when separated from my kind William."[36]

But a touch of sun and time to settle in soon awakened Johnston to the charms and curiosities of this "very salubrious" spot. She would have recognized dozens of familiar faces from Savannah there, though Georgia this was not: she could see that much in the compressed shells of the coquina stone houses, the balustrades of the former Convento de San Francisco, now the army barracks, and the colorful presence of Minorcans and other Mediterranean islanders who had been recruited a decade earlier as laborers for the settlement of New Smyrna, farther south. Now and then she glimpsed the exotic wife of Andrew Turnbull, the entrepreneur behind that scheme, a "lady of Smyrna, who always retained the costume of her country, a majestic, noble-looking woman." Johnston enjoyed promenades along the broad, pointed ramparts ringing the city, the breeze slapping against her skirts. And what a pleasure it was, after the supply shortages of wartime Savannah and Charleston, to feast on fish caught fresh from the sea! "I never was in better health and indeed never was so fleshy as during my . . . residence there," she later remembered. Best of all, William got leave for a brief visit from New York, and they could plan their future face-to-face.[37]

By the start of 1783, twelve thousand loyalists and slaves had settled in East Florida.[38] Although the governor, Patrick Tonyn, struggled to support so many refugees "without provisions, money, cloathing, or implements of agriculture, and in the most deplorable circumstances," he welcomed their arrival as the commencement of "a happy Era to this province."[39] Tonyn glowingly forecasted the expansion of his realm to the south and north, augmenting the growing communities on the St. John's and St. Mary's rivers. Britain had acquired the territory from Spain at the end of the Seven Years' War, and it had been rapidly carved up in a speculative frenzy with a few hundred British landlords, many of them aristocrats and grandees, claiming more than 2.8 million acres among them. The peace commissioner, Richard Oswald, secured a grant for twenty thousand acres. Governor Tonyn's "dear friend" Henry Strachey, the deputy British peace commissioner, owned ten thousand acres, while Tonyn himself bagged another twenty thousand.[40] But few landlords had actually settled their lands (Strachey and Tonyn were exceptions), leaving the province's potential largely untapped.

The vast claims already staked on East Florida's most attractive land was surely one reason wealthy new colonists like Dr. Lewis Johnston, Elizabeth Johnston's father-in-law, were "much dissatisfied" on first arriving in the province; other fertile prospects lay still less accessibly in Indian country.[41] Another cause for dissatisfaction may have been the knowledge that so few British plantations had met with any success. New Smyrna presented a frightful spectacle of how things could go wrong. This palmetto-fringed eden became a latter-day heart of darkness. Malaria and malnutrition killed off colonists by the hundreds, while its founder, Andrew Turnbull, turned slave driver, enforcing a deadly labor regime by whips and chains.

Yet even as New Smyrna failed—its survivors had all withdrawn to St. Augustine by 1777—the rewards of colonization in East Florida seemed closer than ever.[42] Governor Tonyn knew that the influx of loyalist and slave workers might be just what the province needed to tip over into prosperity. To cater to loyalists' demands for land he devised a scheme to escheat smaller plots from within large grants. Thomas Brown, a member (with Dr. Johnston) of Tonyn's governing council, settled many of his old soldiers around the St. John's River—and earned ten tracts in the region for himself amounting to 100,000 acres, dwarfing the fifty-six hundred acres he had lost in Augusta.[43] While rich loyalists hired out their slaves for money, poorer settlers built themselves thatched huts and log cabins and got to work girdling trees and clearing ground for corn and rice.[44] St. Augustine took on cosmopolitan trappings such as Tonyn had not enjoyed in a decade of living there, thanks to refugees like the entrepreneurial South Carolina printer William Charles Wells. Wells had dismantled his family's printing press in Charleston (used to print Charleston's leading prewar newspaper) and brought it with him to St. Augustine. There he successfully reassembled it—thanks to invaluable diagrams in a book called *The Printer's Grammar* and "the assistance of a common negro carpenter"—to publish Florida's first newspaper in early 1783. In his spare time, Wells managed and acted in a troupe of theatrically minded army officers, who staged amateur productions "for the benefit of the distressed Refugees."[45]

Could it be that loyalists would achieve in East Florida what two decades of imaginative British colonization efforts had not: making profitable plantations out of subtropical swamps, flourishing towns from struggling outposts? Tonyn certainly hoped so, as one of many officials who embraced this refugee crisis as an opportunity for colonial expansion. John Cruden, the onetime commissioner for sequestered estates in Charleston, was another. Now a displaced refugee in Florida, Cruden enthusiastically shared Tonyn's visions for East Florida's future. The difference was that Cruden's enthusiasm had begun to border on mania. Still committed to his mandate as commissioner, he made a point of tracking down slaves whom loyalists had illegally removed from South Carolina. March 1783 found him on the Caribbean island of Tortola, well known as a clearinghouse for slaves, where he discovered that "many Negroes the property of the inhabitants of the Southern Provinces, have been offered for sale, and by people who have no right to dispose of them."[46] From Tortola he returned to St. Augustine but found his efforts to retrieve sequestered slaves thwarted by obstructions from the governor and council.[47] Governor Tonyn did not understand Cruden's passion to restore property to patriots who, in Tonyn's view, had done loyalists such wrong. Equally important, the land speculator in Tonyn, "whose chief study is to inrich himself at the Expence of many," had no desire to compromise his province's invaluable labor force.[48] By May, Cruden was in New York seeking Carleton's support instead. In June he proceeded on to London to solicit the endorsement of government ministers.[49]

This cause might seem an odd preoccupation for an ardent loyalist—and, judging from his writings, a quasi-abolitionist too—but it was in keeping with both Cruden's sense of justice and his personal ambitions. His transatlantic peregrinations undoubtedly involved genuine outrage at the capture of so many slaves by loyalists who had never legally owned them. They also reflected an aggressive desire for self-advancement and official recognition. Cruden stands out as an example of how adverse circumstances encouraged some refugees to think up creative alternatives, even when those involved unusual alliances and causes.[50] However peace turned out, Cruden could see some way for himself and his fellow loyalists to profit from it. His ideas would only grow more grandiose with time.

In the event, in April 1783 the news of the peace treaty hit East Florida loyalists like a hurricane. Article V of the peace with the United States, which neutered the possibility of receiving compensation from the states, paled for them next to Article V of Britain's peace treaty with Spain and France, by which Britain agreed to cede East and West Florida to Spain, with no strings attached. It had seemed like a reasonable arrangement to British diplomats, who were more committed to keeping the strategically valuable Gibraltar than the economically disappointing Floridas. But the treaty yanked the ground from beneath the refugees' feet. They had already undergone the ordeal of leaving their homes under duress, often more than once, and accepted the challenge of starting over in an underdeveloped land. Now even this hard-won asylum was denied them—and by their own government at that. Unless loyalists were prepared to swear allegiance to the king of Spain and practice Catholicism, they had eighteen months to gather up their possessions and go.

"The war never occasioned half the distress, which this peace has done to the unfortunate Loyalists," Elizabeth Johnston wrote, "no other provision made than just recommending them to the clemency of Congress, which is in fact casting them off altogether." Her father-in-law Lewis became "unwell both in body and mind as he lets this news of a peace prey too much on his spirits but how can it be avoided, with such a Family, and such prospects enough to distract him."[51] At a dinner a few nights after the terrible news arrived, John Cruden recalled the emotional reaction when the assembled refugees drank to the king's health: "How he [the king] must have felt had he seen the Company; two of the Gentlemen were so much agitated that they covert their faces with their handkerchiefs, but they could not conceal the Tears that trickled down their Loyal Cheeks."[52] For another young Georgia loyalist, news of the peace was

> the severest shock our Feelings have ever had to struggle with. Deserted as we are by our King, banished by our Country, what Recourse is left us in this Combination of Calamities. . . . Heavens! What distress! That men who not only possessed the Necessaries, but all the Luxuries of Life . . . should become Vagrant, & be plunged in the Torrent of Misery & Despair by the Parliament of Britain, who having no further Occasion for their Services, treat them with Contempt and mock their sorrows.

"We are all cast off," he opined. "I shall ever tho' remember with satisfaction that it was not I deserted my King, but my King that deserted me."[53]

This plaint captured the essence of loyalist anguish. The doors of "our Country," America, were bolted to them. And now, far worse, their own king had shunned them. After so "many scenes and passages through and during the late war," one loyalist "could not put any faith" in the news until he "saw the King's speech" in print: it was only on reading his sovereign's words, endorsing the peace, that he accepted the reality of this outrageous betrayal.[54] The deeply emotional, almost histrionic character of East Florida loyalist outpourings suggests what a profound attachment imperial subjects felt to the figure of the king. They also gave voice to the psychological power of a blow by which thousands of individuals already traumatized by many years of war and migration were forced to move once more. This further displacement carved mental wounds that flared up in years and destinations to come.

White loyalists were not the only Floridians who felt traduced by their sovereign. Talk of East Florida's cession swirled into Indian country, where Creeks long allied with the British could not believe what they were hearing. Aghast at the news, they held a conference with Governor Tonyn and Thomas Brown, the superintendent of Indian affairs. "We took up the Hatchett for the English at a time we could scarce distinguish our friends from our Foes," remembered one Creek chief:

> The King and his Warriors have told us they would never forsake us. Is the Great King conquered? Or does he mean to abandon Us? Or does he intend to sell his friends as Slaves, or only to give our Lands to his and our Enemies? Do you think we can turn our faces to our Enemies, and ask a favour from them? No. If he has any Land to receive us (We will not turn to our Enemies) but go [to] it with our friends in such ships as he may send for us.

Another chief recalled how he had learned at his father's knee about his people's bonds with the British, a connection so deep the two groups intermarried "and became one flesh." For him, too, a life in exile seemed better than one overshadowed by the United States or Spain: "If the English mean to abandon the Land, we will accompany them. We cannot take a Virginian or Spaniard by the hand. We cannot look them in the face."[55] These protests were reinforced by the new leader of the Creeks, Alexander McGillivray. As his unlikely name suggested, McGillivray was part Scottish: his father was a prominent loyalist

Indian trader in Augusta; his mother was half French, half Creek. McGillivray held a position among the Creeks analogous to Joseph Brant among the Mohawks, an Indian leader with strong links to white society, committed to guarding his nation's interests in the face of white empires.[56] "I conceive we have a right to protection & support from the Nation whose cause has drawn the vengeance of an enraged multitude upon us," he wrote to Brown. The Creeks had fought "from principles of Gratitude & Friendship to the British Nation," and it was both "cruel & unjust" after eight years of loyal service "to find ourselves & country betrayed to our Enemies & divided between the Spaniards & Americans."[57]

Brown, for his part, found it difficult to look his Indian friends in the face: "The situation of our poor unfortunate allies most sensibly affects me. They were ever faithful to me. I never deceived them." They had fought side by side since the very beginning of the war, and he felt his own personal honor undercut by the decision to abandon them to Spanish rule.[58] Brown understood that some chiefs had sworn to resist, and worried that "through rage and disappointment they will wreak their vengeance on the unfortunate unhappy residents in their land." "However chimerical" it might seem that the Creek "very seriously proposed to abandon their country and accompany us," there were in fact some precedents for such movements. When the Spanish left Florida in 1763, the Yamassee Indians followed them to Cuba; and now in Canada a Mohawk loyalist settlement was taking shape under British sponsorship. Brown suggested to Carleton that the Creeks "might be conveyed to the Bahamas," where they could start afresh under British protection.[59]

But the Creeks were not black loyalists: Carleton did not feel that British promises had been breached with "those deceived Indians as you are all so fond to stile them." If they wanted to go to the Bahamas, then he would provide the ships to take them, but it would be much better to "dissuade them from a measure destructive of their happiness."[60] Instead, Brown and his colleagues tried to soften relations between the Indians and the Spanish, and preserve Indian goodwill toward Britain as a bulwark against the Americans. On Brown's urging, Alexander McGillivray accepted a commission in Spanish service, and became a silent partner with the Scottish merchant firm that retained the valuable monopoly on the Florida Indian trade.[61] Governor Tonyn prided himself on the thought that "in the Breasts of these unenlightened Savages, there remains deeply rooted, an unextinguishable spark of ardent Love, and faithfull attachment, to the British name; which may rise into a Flame, and be improved to advantage, on some future occasion."[62] How valuable such enduring loyalty might prove remained for later British officials to discover.

For all that East Florida loyalists hoped against hope that something in the treaty might yet be reversed, the eighteen months allotted for their departure were fast vanishing, along with any semblance of civic order. The northern frontier between Florida and Georgia had become a bandit-ridden no-man's-land, raided by Americans coming south and ravaged by lawless quasi-loyalist gangs. Loyalists lived in fear of attack by disgruntled Indians. "The whole of the People in the Province are in the utmost Confusion, nothing going on but robbing and plundering," reported one refugee.[63] And where on earth were they to go? Tonyn remained "perfectly in the dark" until the spring of 1784 about what the arrangements for evacuation would actually be.[64] Tonyn described the loyalists as

> quite at a loss how to dispose themselves. The West India Islands are stocked, and it requires a greater capital than in general they are possessed of to form settlements in them. . . . [T]he Bahama Islands are mere rocks, fit only for fishermen, and the Inhabitants live chiefly by wrecking. Nova Scotia is too cold a climate for those who have lived in the southern Colonies, and intirely unfit for an outlet, and comfortable habitation for owners of slaves.[65]

Dr. Lewis Johnston set off on an exploratory mission to the Bahamas to size up the possibilities for settlement there. Johnston had lived briefly in St. Kitts before his immigration to Georgia, so he had some experience of the West Indies. But the Atlantic archipelago of the Bahamas was quite different. What "they reckon here their best lands," he reported, were merely "poor sandy soil," holding little promise for long-term rewards. "My Expectations tho' by no means sanguine being so cruelly disappointed," Dr. Johnston returned to St. Augustine "as much at a loss as ever where to direct my steps with my unfortunate Family."[66]

On his father's instructions, William Johnston traveled to Britain (probably with an evacuation fleet from New York) to resume his medical studies in Edinburgh. His departure left Elizabeth emotionally overwrought, brooding alone in her room, spinning anxious fantasies of what might become of him, of them. She scrawled plaintive screeds begging, "May this bitter separation be our last." William's half-pay as a loyalist captain would not be enough to support them all in Britain, so Elizabeth and the children continued to depend on his father's protection. Yet month after month Lewis Johnston remained "still in suspence where his next route will be," while he tried to sell his slaves in a suddenly glutted market. "Probably if your Father disposes of his Negroes," Elizabeth wrote to William in early 1784, "he may go to Scotland tho' I have my fears on that head, as he seems to have an Idea of Jamaica, from the Flattering accounts the Loyalists there give of their large crops of Indigo." To add to her worries, she was pregnant again—"I have grown lusty in every sense of the word"—and "the uncertain state we are in at present makes me unhappy in the dread of my near Lying in when your Father leaves . . . and I will remain here, rather than go to sea so near my time, in short, we are all distracted not knowing how to resolve."[67]

A full ten months after learning about the cession of East Florida, Lewis Johnston at last managed to sell his slaves and made up his mind to move to Scotland. Elizabeth and her children would travel with him. He also sold William's slaves to Thomas Brown, for £450, with the exception of one, Hagar, whom Elizabeth "kept as a nurse, for the expected stranger who I hope will shortly make its appearance."[68] Her departure for Britain came not a moment too soon. William's most recent letter had upset her on numerous fronts, beginning with his accusation that she did not write to him often enough. ("Believe me," she insisted, "I have had you constantly in my mind, and suffered so much anxiety on account of our distressing separation, that tis impossible I could omit a single opp[ortunit]y of writing.") Nor was his letter sensitive on other points: "I am hurt at your not mentioning the then little invisible, nor your wishing for my safe delivery, as you must have known my situation before you left me." Worse, far away from his family's supervision, William had not yet moved on to Edinburgh, but remained unaccountably in "that seducing City" of London, "full of temptations"—specifically the gaming table—"which Americans of your disposition <u>cannot always resist.</u>"[69]

Boarding the worm-eaten boat at St. Mary's a few days before her twenty-first birthday, the Elizabeth Johnston who sailed from Florida in May 1784 had matured from the woman who had arrived there fifteen months earlier. This had been a cruel introduction to her career as a refugee: learning to appreciate her new surroundings just in time to

discover she must leave them, and then experiencing months of haunting worry and doubt. She carried a different newborn in her arms
now—Lewis, born in March—and she had coped as a single parent
when her "volatile" eldest son Andrew broke his leg and when Catherine, "the greatest vixen in Florida," fell dangerously ill. Her own father
was as distant as her husband, also in Britain; she had to make do on little money and her in-laws' support. And she had come to feel separation from her husband as an intolerable strain. Increasingly she worked
to "fortify my mind with that strengthener religion (which is the only
resource in cases of real distress)"—just as she increasingly dreaded the
prospect of moving and being away from William. As she embarked at
Florida for her first Atlantic crossing, she little knew how many more
voyages and separations there would be to come.[70]

THE JOHNSTONS were relatively privileged, as refugees went:
notably, they were among only a handful of Floridians (about 2 percent) who opted to travel to expensive, far-off Britain, supported by the
proceeds of their slave sales.[71] The majority of Florida loyalists, including Thomas Brown with his newly purchased slaves, chose to immi-
grate to the Bahamas despite the negative reports, since at least it was
nearby and had available land. "British promises" had "been violated in
every instance," declared one loyalist officer. "Stripped of our property, drove from our homes . . . robbed of the blessing of a free and
mild government, betrayed and deserted by our friends," now they
were "thrown on the wide world friendless and unsupported." One
thing he knew: "whenever Great Britain sees it her interest to withdraw her force and protection from us," then it would. No more promises for him. A few days later the disaffected officer and seven other
loyalist families pushed off into the coastal waterways in flatboats, to
find new fortunes at Natchez on the Mississippi, altogether beyond
British reach.

The deep sense of injustice felt by so many East Florida loyalists is
worth listening to not just as an expression of personal distress. It triggered political aftershocks as well. These would later become especially evident in the Bahamas, where doubly displaced refugees arrived
harboring a deep sense of betrayal. In East Florida itself, it was enough
to push some loyal British subjects to the brink of radical action.
"Should England be engaged in another War (as she shortly must be),"
warned a Georgia loyalist, "let her not expect that, out of thousands of

us Refugees, there will be one who will draw a sword in her Cause. . . . The People are so exasperated they cannot now endure the Name of an Englishman." Anger moved him to contemplate nothing short of a coup against the Spanish. "Perhaps the Dons may find themselves deceived in their Expectations of taking Possession of this Country. We have a fine Body of Provincial troops here, equal to any in the World," he said, and together they could resist. Rumors told of a plot among the loyalist troops to mutiny, arm the slaves, and "put every white Man to Death that opposed them keeping the Country to themselves as they will rather die than be Carried to Hallifax."[72]

These particular schemes did not materialize. But in the hands of loyalist visionary John Cruden, similar ideas took on an extraordinary life of their own. As loyalists were leaving Florida in the spring of 1784, Cruden crossed the ocean in reverse, returning from a sojourn in Britain to the land that he loved. The cession of East Florida foiled all of Cruden's business plans for trade in St. Augustine. He had always been dedicated to the idea of fairness, hence his actions concerning black loyalists and slaves. But what wrongs had now been committed against the white refugees, and "the poor Indians, whom we have cherished . . . and who have been shamelessly deserted." (Some of whom, "singular as it may appear," he believed to be "descended from the ancient Britons" and "speak the Welsh language.")[73] He acknowledged that it would no longer be possible to overturn the treaty and keep the Floridas entirely. Yet redress, rewards even, might still be seized. Arriving at the mouth of the St. Mary's River, Cruden dreamed of a community reborn. A scrap of paper survives to tell of his ambitions. "At a meeting of the Delegates of the Loyalists on the St. Mary's River," the fragment reads, "It was unanimously Resolved that in the present State of the Loyalists Mr. Cruden should be Vested with Dictatorial powers, and untill such time as another Mutiny could be held with propriety, that the Loyalists should consider Every act of His as their President binding upon them." It was signed, "John Cruden, President, United Loyalists." If Britain wouldn't give East Florida to loyalists, well then, loyalists could take some of it for themselves. By establishing an independent state for loyalist refugees, Cruden, the newly appointed dictator of St. Mary's, would strike a blow for justice for his own kind, just as he had always strived to achieve for others.[74]

East Florida governor Tonyn knew something of what was afoot. Cruden and his friends, Tonyn informed his superiors in Whitehall, had been concocting "plans suggested by their inflamed imaginations, and finally they foolishly hit upon the diabolical design of seizing this government by force and setting themselves in opposition to the Spanish." To break up the conspiracy, Tonyn hoped to exploit potential rifts between Cruden and the other denizens of the region, the infamous bandits who had been resisting authority for years. By granting Cruden permission to raise a "posse" against the banditti, Tonyn prided himself on "having been able to avert the catastrophe . . . without resorting to the calamitous and dangerous necessity of using force, which might have bathed us in blood."[75] He assured his Spanish counterpart, Vicente Manuel de Zéspedes, that "the Government of Spain, have nothing to fear from Mr. Cruden"; all his talk was just the British habit of free speech at work. But it must have given Tonyn some secret pleasure to know that the Spanish would inherit a domain shot through by the continuing consequences of loyalist discontent, turmoil on the borders, and an Indian population inclined toward the British. And even he had not adequately gauged the extent of Cruden's schemes.

On July 12, 1784, the Spanish flag rose over the Castillo de San Marcos to volleys of musket fire and cannon salutes; the Minorcan community's priest held a mass and a full *Te Deum* was sung, "all of which was experienced with complete happiness by ourselves," reported Zéspedes, "and with applause by the new Catholic subjects." (Approximately five hundred of East Florida's pre-revolutionary population of Mediterranean-born colonists decided to remain under Spanish rule.) The transfer of power was formally complete. But "in the swamps and thickets" around the rivers in the north, Cruden and his "desperadoes" worked to build an independent loyalist state.[76] "There are twelve hundred men embodied between the St. Mary & St. John's Rivers in Florida," Cruden's younger brother James reported to the British ambassador in Vienna, and another twelve hundred in Nassau and Natchez, "all of whom are in perfect readiness to cooperate in the prosecution of his purpose." "Agents are dispatched into the Indian Country," he explained. "Commissioners are appointed to associate the Loyalists, who have resorted to Nova Scotia . . . proper persons are sent to Charles Town, and Philadelphia, to sound the disposition of the Continental Officers; from these arrangements, added to the anarchy that prevails universally throughout the Continent, the most sanguine hopes of success are entertained.[77] "America shall yet be ours," swore John Cruden, "but the House of Brunswick do not deserve the sovereignty of it."[78] It was time to turn to Spain.

In all the thousands of petitions produced by loyalist refugees, perhaps none conveys more clearly the sheer desperation loyalists felt after defeat and perceived betrayal by Britain as the appeal that John Cruden addressed to King Carlos III of Spain in October 1784:

> Abandoned by that Sovereign for whose cause we have sacri-ficed Every thing that is dear in life and deserted by that Coun-try for which We fought and many of us freely bled . . . We . . . are Reduced to the dreadful alternative of returning to our Homes, to receive insult worse than Death to Men of Spirit, or to run the hazzard of being Murdered in Cold blood, to Go to the inhospitable Regions of Nova Scotia or take refuge on the Barren Rocks of the Bahamas where poverty and wretchedness stares us in the face Or do what our Spirit can not brook (pardon Sire the freedom) renounce our Country, Drug [*sic*] the Religion of our Fathers and become your Subjects.

Cruden went on to entreat the Spanish king to grant loyalists "the Jurisdiction and the sole discretion of the internal Government" for the area between the St. John's and the St. Mary's rivers, in exchange "for which we will gladly pay a reasonable Tribute to Your Majesty and Acknowledge You as Lord of the Soil," defending the province "against Every power but our Mother Country."[79]

For Cruden's greatest quarrel was not with Spain, or even with Britain, but with the United States and the republican patriots who had wrecked his world. He barraged Spanish authorities with letters assuring them of his benign intentions; he had styled himself dictator merely "to prevent Your Government from having any apprehension at frequent Meetings, Customary as you know to us, but not so in the Dominions of Spain."[80] At the helm of his proposed loyalist state, Cruden promised to resist an enemy common to Britain, Spain, and American loyalists alike: republicanism. The reason his brother James was in Vienna was to woo the Hapsburg emperor Joseph II to this imperial coalition. ("He hates Republicans," Cruden noted.) "How-ever much you might be disposed to consider my plan Visionary and too Extensive," Cruden told the Spanish, "it is not impossible that such a grand wish may be laid as may pave the way for a happy, cordial, and lasting Union between Britain and Spain." Together, American loyal-ists and the empires of Europe could vanquish the upstart republican United States and restore the power of crowns.[81]

Zéspedes had no fewer illusions than Tonyn about Cruden's "abounding fanaticism": "I regard him as a mere visionary," he said, and his only worry was that Cruden's ideas "will perhaps have a great influence on the large number of impoverished and desperate exiles from the United States, who find no means of subsistence in the Bahama Islands." When Cruden wanted to go to Nova Scotia in 1785 to muster further support, Zéspedes was only too happy to give him a passport just "to be forever rid of him."[82] The Spaniard must have been irked when he continued to receive letters from "this restless soul" not from far-off Canada but from the Bahamas, just a few dozen miles offshore. From his new perch Cruden continued to transmit his schemes to correspondents west and east, informing Lord North, for instance, that "with but a very little help, I will D. V. not only bring Hence the lost sheep, but open the Gates of Mexico to my Country."[83]

John Cruden would never return to Florida, and fewer and fewer people credited his talk. Yet for two reasons it would be unfair to write off his plans as meaningless ravings. First, Cruden's far-out ideas emerged from a set of destabilizing experiences shared by thousands of other loyalists, and suggested how the revolution had the ability, however paradoxically, to radicalize loyalist politics. The British evacuations really had inverted loyalists' worlds: cast out from their homes, then cast out again from their haven, it was little wonder that some grasped for extreme alternatives. Personal trauma intensified a sense of political grievance. The second reason to take Cruden's plans seriously was that his contemporaries did too. High-ranking British officials read his letters, while Zéspedes came to believe that Governor Tonyn personally had some hand in the plot.[84] This attested to a deep skepticism among European powers about the territorial integrity of the United States. If the United States fell apart, as many people expected it would, Britain, France, and Spain all wanted to scoop up the fragments. What Cruden essayed in Florida was just the first in a series of British projects to assert control in this region. Soon Cruden's shoes would be filled by a Maryland loyalist called William Augustus Bowles, who solicited British support for another loyal independent state, to be peopled primarily by the Creeks. And within less than a decade, Cruden's suggestion of an imperial coalition against republicanism would become real when the French Revolutionary wars brought Britain and Spain together as allies against the French republic.

Throughout 1784 loyalists and slaves migrated out of East Florida on flatboats, in ships, and through back ways in the wilderness. An official estimate counted 3,398 whites and 6,540 blacks leaving East Florida for other British domains. A further five thousand were "imagined to have gone over the Mountains to the States &c.," where most of them disappear from historical view.[85] Governor Tonyn's own drawn-out departure played out in miniature the strains and reluctance with which the evacuations had taken place. The eighteen months allotted for withdrawal by the treaty expired in March 1785, at which time Tonyn expected that "this arduous and vexatious business, will be fully and completely accomplished in the course of a few weeks." But he required (and received) a four-month extension actually to finish the work, and it was only in August 1785 that he could report, from on board the *Cyrus* at the port of St. Mary's, that "I have discharged my mind of a heavy burden, by the dismission of the last division of Evacuists." Tonyn continued impatiently to wait to "emerge, out of this most disagreeable situation" and sail for England. And then, it was as if Florida itself held him back. On September 11, 1785, the wind picked up enough to carry the *Cyrus* over the first sandbar, then shifted direction suddenly, dashing the ship against the bar. Taking in water at a rate of six inches per hour, the frigate crawled back to shore for repairs. Tonyn spent an uncomfortable two months at St. Mary's until new vessels arrived from the Bahamas to fetch him.[86]

On November 13, 1785—two years after Evacuation Day in New York, four years after Yorktown—Tonyn and the last of the Florida refugees finally put out to sea. "It is shocking and lamentable," Tonyn had written on leaving St. Augustine, "to behold a Country once in a flourishing state now in desolation—a once beautiful City lying in ruins; these . . . may be compared to my own misfortunes, and those of a deserving, considerable Loyal People, who from a condition of happiness and affluence . . . are by a cruel reverse in human affairs reduced to indigence and affliction."[87] If he and his fellow passengers looked back to shore, they might have seen heaps of cast-off planks scattered over the sand. Unable to sell their houses to incoming Spaniards, loyalists had dismantled the frames, hoping to take them away for reassembly in the Bahamas or elsewhere—but there was not enough room for them on the ships.[88] Rebuilding a house would be hard enough. Rebuilding lives and communities posed an altogether more daunting task. But when the last Florida refugees faced the Atlantic before them, at least they were heading in a promising direction. They were bound for Britain, where the blueprints for reconstructing loyalist fortunes—and imperial ones—were being drawn up.

PART II

Settlers

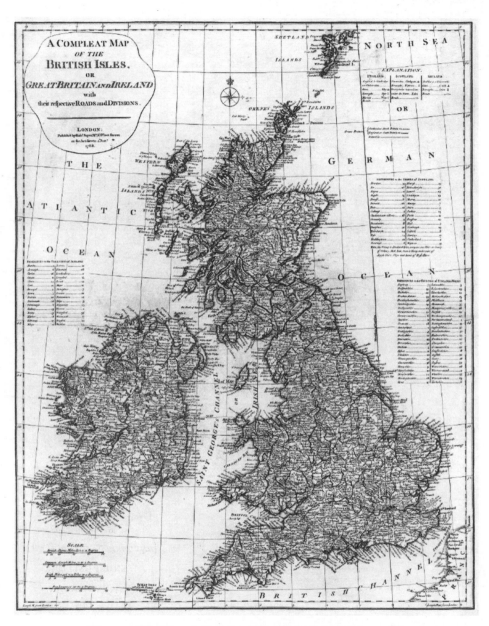

Thomas Kitchin, *A Compleat Map of the British Isles*, 1788.

CHAPTER FOUR

The Heart of Empire

"How shall I describe what I felt, when I first set my foot on British ground?" soliloquized Louisa Wells, a young loyalist refugee from Charleston, when she disembarked on the shores of Kent in 1778. "I could have kissed the gravel on the salt Beach! It was my home: the Country which I had so long and so earnestly wished to see. The Isle of Liberty and Peace." After what she had endured, Wells had good reason to feel relieved. The daughter of Charleston's leading printer, a loyalist, she had stayed in the war-torn city to protect the family property against confiscation "as long as one stone stood upon another," while her relatives fanned out in a loyalist diaspora in miniature.[1] Her parents went to England; her brothers William and James to East Florida, bringing the family press with them; and her fiancé, a former apprentice of her father's, to Jamaica. Wells painstakingly liquidated family assets in Charleston and invested the proceeds in easily transportable indigo, only to have her cargo seized by patriots as she prepared to sail for England. Then her ship itself was captured as a suspected privateer. She finally made it across the Atlantic, five months after leaving Charleston, plagued by bad weather and fear of French attack.

Britain may not have been the closest place, geographically, for American loyalists to seek asylum, but as the center of the imperial world, it was in some ways the most obvious. During the war, Britain served as a primary destination for loyalist refugees. It commanded a strength of attachment that no other locale could match, based in language, religion, culture, and for many white loyalists, blood. Yet few if any expressed sentiments resembling Wells's when they got there. Far more often, they echoed the paradox embedded in her statement.[2] Her "home," as she put it, lay in a locale she had "long and so earnestly wished"—but never yet actually managed—to see. For all that many

Americans had been raised to consider Britain as "home," this was emphatically a foreign country.[3] The tension between familiarity and difference would be the first of several paradoxes loyalists encountered in Britain, as their dearest, most trusted refuge proved an oddly alienating place.

What a new world this was! Nothing in America could prepare the provincial newcomers for the sensory experience of Georgian London, one of the largest, most diverse cities on earth. "[I]t is absolutely impossible for any American, who has never lived in London, to have any idea of it," pronounced one colonial visitor.[4] "[N]otwithstanding the grand Ideas I had formed of it," a Massachusetts exile explained, London "far exceeded my expectation"—for better and for worse. The best of the city showed itself in elegant squares and town houses and in the graceful greenswards of St. James's Park, often "throng'd by loyalists."[5] The capital offered an inexhaustible series of things to see and do. You could squeeze into a crowd of theatergoers to watch David Garrick play Hamlet.[6] You could visit the British Museum and handle ancient manuscripts, peer at fossils, and wonder at the curiosities recently brought from the South Seas by Captain James Cook. You could pay your respects at the tomb of General Wolfe in Westminster Abbey, and admire grand historical canvases by Benjamin West and other prominent painters at the Royal Academy. You could make the rounds of London churches to hear celebrated divines preach, or visit the law courts and listen to eminent jurists try cases. You could fill your ears with the swelling choruses of Handel's *Messiah*, "the most sublime piece of music in the whole world."[7]

But as loyalists reveled in all these activities, they found London to be overwhelming too. Refugees felt buffeted by the crush of humanity in the streets as they navigated among "coaches, carts and waggons etc. continually passing repassing, meeting and jostling," and swerved around beggars and hawkers, constantly alert for pickpockets.[8] In London's East End—where the majority of black loyalists ended up— "Whores Rogues & Sailors" clogged the filthy lanes, while cargoes from India, America, and Africa were unloaded onto docks as busy as whole villages.[9] Unrelenting grey skies and saturating damp left the Americans depressed and prone to illness. One complained that very few Britons upheld "ancient Hospitality" and "pittied the fate of the Refugees."[10] "The shyness reserve and unconversibility of native Englishmen is notorious," grumbled another.[11] London seemed an altogether pushy place, where everyone looked out for themselves and foreigners were incidental distractions. Partly for this reason, many loyalists chose to reside in Bristol, Bath, and smaller towns, where prices were lower and the pace of life slower. Loyalists also tended to keep their own company, living near one another and frequenting common haunts. A refugee from Maine found quarters in South Kensington with three Massachusetts exiles, and dined regularly with an "American club" of fellow New England loyalists. Coffee houses—the New England, New York, Carolina, and others—served as their lifelines to America, sources of news, debate, gossip, and convenient places to receive precious letters from home.[12]

During the war loyalist refugees sadly recorded the anniversaries of their departures from America, and looked forward to a peace that would let them go home.[13] But the war's end and the unsatisfying treaty seemed to slam the door to return shut. Instead thousands more refugees arrived on British shores. Because of the high cost of living in Britain, its distance from America, and the incentives offered for settlement in British North America and the Bahamas, only about 15 percent of white loyalist refugees, or around eight thousand, chose to migrate to Britain—less than twice the number of black loyalists who ended up there, often as a result of their military service. The majority of white loyalists crossing the Atlantic were of middle-class status or higher. Their central objective was to win compensation for their lost and confiscated American assets. Joseph Galloway and William Franklin, formerly advocates for imperial union, became leading lobbyists for government relief. Loyalists also leaned on patrons to try to secure new jobs, and endeavored to place their children in good schools and on promising career paths. Unsure about how much financial support they might win, or where they might profitably settle, even privileged loyalists found life in Britain uncomfortable. Still, they were fortunate compared to the smaller number of refugees who arrived in Britain in more desperate straits. For hundreds of indigent newcomers—the disabled, the illiterate, single mothers, and former slaves—relief could make the difference between starvation and survival.

And yet as loyalists across the kingdom clamored for assistance, Britain was in a poor position to grant it to them. "Nothing can be worse than this rich, devoted, ill govern'd Island," growled one fed-up refugee as he approached the tenth anniversary of his exile in 1784.[14] Parliament seemed in perennial tumult, with a series of ministries undercut by rivalry and infighting. The costs of war had brought the national debt to its highest level ever, at £232 million (or £25 billion in current terms). Britain's territorial concessions in the Peace of Paris appeared to its critics to reveal weakness in the face of European rivals. American independence also raised troubling metaphysical questions about what the relationship between nation and empire would look like in the future.[15] With the loss of the thirteen colonies, fewer and fewer imperial subjects resembled the British, in ethnicity, religion, culture, or language: Bengal, in eastern India, with perhaps twenty million inhabitants, was easily the largest domain in the British Empire. Nor, as the war had demonstrated, could Parliament claim to represent virtually its white settler colonists in the same manner it represented those in the British Isles. Imperial government had been shaken, but it remained to be seen how it would adapt.

Loyalist refugees brought the social and material consequences of defeat straight to the empire's heart. Having lost their personal property, livelihoods, and homes, they put a human face on Britain's own loss of the thirteen colonies. How would the refugees, and the empire to which they adhered, manage to regroup? Postwar Britain became the center of a parallel process of reconstruction. Individual loyalists sought to reestablish themselves with financial aid and new positions, while British authorities set about reforming imperial government and expanding into new domains—laying the foundations of the "spirit of 1783." But for all that these projects harmonized in many ways, loyalists in Britain ran up against one contradiction after another. Though they strongly identified as British subjects, they felt estranged in this foreign land. Convinced that they deserved compensation, they grew frustrated in their quest for support. And while a newly expanding empire presented them with a panoply of career opportunities overseas, they struggled to make a go of it in Britain itself. The refugees in Britain benefited from imperial recovery, while experiencing firsthand the challenges that went with it.

AMERICANS IN LONDON frequently commented on the spectacular trappings of state power. From the palace of Westminster to St. James's Palace, from the offices lining Whitehall to the grim brown bulk of the Tower, it was hard not to be awed by the government's sheer architectural heft. Then there were its personalities. A number of loyalists attended debates in the House of Commons to watch gifted politicians in action, men like the eloquent Edmund Burke, the passionate

Charles James Fox, and the precocious William Pitt the Younger, who in December 1783 became Britain's youngest prime minister at the age of twenty-four. Some caught sight of Queen Charlotte at the theater, with her "lustures of Diamonds" glittering by candlelight. Others spotted King George III riding through the streets in a state coach, pulled by eight white horses bedecked in royal blue ribbons.[16] A select few loyalists even had the chance to be presented to the royal family at court levees. No other refugees, however, encountered the monarch in quite the way that Samuel Shoemaker did, one day at Windsor Castle.

Shoemaker was a Pennsylvania Quaker, former mayor of Philadelphia, and a pillar of the New York City loyalist community during the war. (He had served with Beverley Robinson as an inspector of refugees in the occupied city.) Shoemaker left New York in the last evacuation fleet, with Carleton, William Smith, and a number of other associates, and arrived in Britain to find many of his refugee friends already getting settled. He had not seen his fellow Pennsylvanian Benjamin West, however, in at least twenty years, not since the painter had moved to Britain in 1763 to further his career. In the intervening decades, as Shoemaker lived through the breakdown of imperial relations in Pennsylvania, his old friend West surged to prominence as the greatest image-maker of British imperial might. A founder of the Royal Academy, of which he would be president for nearly thirty years, West was now history painter to the king, with whom he was a personal favorite.

Shoemaker enjoyed a fond reunion with his long-lost friend and visited the Wests at their residence in Windsor Castle. One afternoon, he was loitering outside in hopes of catching a glimpse of the royal family on their way to chapel when West popped out from the castle with surprising news: the king had just asked to meet Shoemaker personally. Flustered, Shoemaker had no time to overcome his shock before West whisked him into the royal presence. And suddenly there he was: the leader of the empire, the personification of loyalist hopes and patriot hatred, goggle-eyed King George III himself, with Queen Charlotte and four of their daughters in tow. "Mr. S. you are well known here, every body knows you," said the king, instantly calming Shoemaker's nerves. Why, the king wanted to know, was "the Province of Pennsylvania . . . so much further advanced in improvement than the neighbouring ones" that had been settled earlier? Shoemaker, "thinking it wd. be a kind of compliment to the Queens countrymen &c," generously suggested that it was due to hardworking German colonists. The king returned the favor, saying that Pennsylvania's prosperity must be "principally owing to the Quakers." For another forty-five minutes Shoemaker happily chatted with the king and queen—partly in German—about America, his family, and more. The Hanovers swished away, leaving their loyal subject smitten. "I cannot say but I wished some of my violent countrymen could have such an opportunity as I have had," Shoemaker reflected in his diary. "I think they would be convinced that George the third has not one grain of Tyrany in his Composition, and that he is not, he cannot be that bloody minded man they have so repeatedly and so illiberally called him, it is impossible, a man of his fine feelings, so good a husband, so kind a Father, cannot be a Tyrant."[17]

Shoemaker's unusually long, informal encounter with the king brought him as close as any loyalist to a man so many Americans had only fantasized about, for good and ill. His positive impression of his sovereign gestured toward an important if perhaps surprising outcome of the American Revolution for the monarchy. Although King George III had fervently opposed recognizing American independence, the secession of the thirteen colonies—along with those former subjects who condemned him as a "tyrant"—actually strengthened his symbolic power in the rest of the empire. The king's popularity surged in Britain in the years immediately following the war.[18] Imperial officials overseas, in turn, increasingly used ceremonies, symbols, and celebrations to cultivate emotional connections to the monarchy.[19] In many domains royal authority would be fortified at the expense of elected legislatures, a palpable manifestation of the "spirit of 1783."

But loyalists' connection to the king overlaid a more ambivalent relationship to Parliament and other branches of government. Their quest for compensation brought these tensions to the fore. In Britain as in America, loyalist concerns centered on the noxious Article V of the peace treaty. The prime minister during the treaty negotiations, Lord Shelburne, had feared that failing to provide adequately for loyalists might give ammunition to his political opponents. He was right. When the treaties with the United States, France, and Spain came up for debate in the House of Commons, the opposition fiercely denounced their terms. Britain's generous territorial concessions were bad enough. Even worse, Lord North (now in opposition) opined, the poor treatment of loyalists "awakens human sensibility in a very irresistible and lamentable degree": "Never was the honor of the nation so grossly abused as in the desertion of those men, who are now exposed to every punishment that desertion and poverty can inflict." His allies promptly chimed in. This "gross libel on the national character," proclaimed Edmund Burke, "in one flagitious article plunged the dagger into the hearts of the loyalists." One MP's "heart bled. . . . It was scandalous, it was disgraceful!" It was, another asserted, "a lasting monument of national disgrace." The MP and playwright Richard Sheridan read aloud woeful petitions from loyalists in Florida, theatrically "breathing in the most animated style," to underscore their outrage. In short, as an opposition member passionately summed up:

> Europe, Asia, Africa, and America, beheld the dismemberment and diminution of the British empire. But this, alarming and calamitous as it was, was nothing when compared with another of the crimes of the present peace—the cession of men into the hands of their enemies, and delivering over to confiscation, tyranny, resentment, and oppression, the unhappy men who trusted to our fair promises and deceitful words.[20]

Few could have doubted where all this invective would lead. In the winter of 1783, the House voted to censure the peace treaties, delivering a crippling declaration of no confidence in the ministry. Shelburne promptly announced his resignation, leaving another government broken on the wheel of civil war. (He would be replaced in April 1783 by a coalition anchored by the unlikely duo of Lord North and the radical Charles James Fox.[21] This government also proved short-lived and fell at the end of 1783, leading to the premiership of William Pitt.)

Although the issue of loyalist compensation helped bring down the Shelburne government, it must be said that the loyalists' own sturm-und-drang rhetoric did not always win them friends. In the later years of the war, many politicians had grown weary of loyalists' chimerical visions of faithful Americans rallying to the British flag; British opponents of the war increasingly blamed the loyalist lobby (and especially Joseph Galloway) for unnecessarily prolonging an unsuccessful conflict. "They talked and acted like foolish gamesters," said one MP, "whose passions bound them more strongly to persevere the more their losses galled them."[22] In a notably measured speech closing the treaty debate, the Derbyshire lawyer John Eardley Wilmot vowed that he would "share with them my last shilling and my last loaf" but cautioned against paying too much attention to loyalists who continued to inveigh against the peace. "I do not think it was to be expected," he said, "that at the end of a successful rebellion, in which this country had been beaten, that those who were victorious should on any terms give up their estates and possessions again to those with whom they had been contending." Since the majority of loyalists remained within the United States, the stipulation (in Article VI) that no punitive action be taken against them seemed to Wilmot to "provide effectually and completely for much the greatest part of the American loyalists." As for loyalist refugees who failed to get adequate compensation in the United States, he presumed that "the honour and justice of the [British] nation" would see to it that they were provided for by other means.[23]

Wilmot had closer insight into the predicament of loyalist refugees in Britain than just about anyone. During the war, the Treasury had been making ad hoc pension payments to hundreds of refugees, rising in some years to nearly £70,000. These allowances had been intended for "temporary" relief. But the end of the war opened up a seemingly endless vista of further spending. Shortly after taking office, Lord Shelburne had appointed Wilmot and another MP, Daniel Parker Coke (both of whom opposed the war but were otherwise independent of party affiliations), to assess the merit of the individual claims. Working late into winter nights, they filtered through hundreds of cases, interviewing loyalists and vetting their testimonials—a task made the more "difficult as well as invidious" by having to weigh up "the relative Claims, losses, and situations of so many persons" whose property lay "in a *remote* part of the world." They finished their job at the end of January 1783 as debates on the peace treaty were about to commence, having pared down pension payments by a third.[24]

Short-term subsistence payments, though, were a quite different matter from compensation for property confiscated, damaged, or abandoned. What should or would any ministry do about this? Loyalist refugees were quick to supply an answer: the government should provide restitution from Treasury funds. In a well-coordinated lobbying initiative, refugees appointed a board of agents, headed by former Georgia governor Sir James Wright and composed of Galloway and other well-known figures to represent each colony. The agents set about arguing for "their Right to receive compensation from this Government."[25] An anonymous pamphlet entitled *The Case and Claim of the American Loyalists, Impartially Stated and Considered*, published by the loyalist agents—and probably authored at least in part by Galloway—laid out their rationale. The social contract, the pamphlet observed, mandated that *"protection and allegiance are reciprocal duties between the State and the subject."* "As perfectly subjects of the British State, as any man in London or Middlesex," loyal Americans were "as much bound by all the obligations and duties of the society, and consequently as much entitled to the protection and justice of the State" as any other Briton. The king's failure to protect loyalists, they contended, entitled them to financial compensation in return. And since the British government had decided to acknowledge American independence "without securing *any restitution whatever* to the Loyalists," then "natural justice" dictated that British taxpayers should assume the costs. The pamphlet went on to argue that loyalist losses also fell under the principle of eminent domain, citing influential eighteenth-century political theorists as support. In closing, they produced (rather strained) precedents of analogous British government compensation: to planters on St. Kitts and Nevis after a French invasion in 1706; and to Hanoverian loyalists for property destroyed in the Jacobite rising of 1715.[26]

The lobbying worked. In July 1783, Parliament passed an act formally appointing a commission "to enquire into the Losses and Services of all such persons who have suffered in their Rights, Properties, and Professions, during the late unhappy Dissensions in America, in consequence of their Loyalty to His Majesty, and Attachment to the British Government." MPs John Eardley Wilmot and Daniel Parker Coke were obvious choices to serve as commissioners, given their prior experience with claims; they were joined on the committee by two veterans of the war, who had served at Saratoga and Yorktown respectively, and by an ambitious civil servant called John Marsh.[27] Together the five men were to verify each claimant's loyalty, ascertain the value of his or her property, and recommend an amount for compensation. (The final decisions for payment rested with Parliament.) The act gave loyalists nine months in which to submit claims, and allowed the commission two years to process them. In mid-September 1783, the Loyalist Claims Commission opened the doors of its office in Lincoln's Inn Fields and welcomed in its first deponents.[28]

For all that loyalist agents volunteered precedents, the Loyalist Claims Commission was actually just as *un*precedented in scale as all the other provisions—land grants, free passages, rations, and supplies—already made for refugees. This relief program was born in a period when public welfare scarcely resembled its modern forms. Military pension schemes were just taking shape; the central plank of state charity, the Poor Law, dated to the days of Queen Elizabeth I; and many other kinds of aid, such as orphanages, depended primarily on private initiative. Private support had proved just as important as government assistance in coping with the only two previous refugee crises Britain had faced on anything like the same scale: the influx of fifty thousand or so French Huguenots in the late seventeenth century (who introduced the word "refugee" into the English language), and that of thirteen thousand destitute Palatine Germans who fled to England in 1709.[29] Never before 1783 had the British government itself accepted financial responsibility to this extent for refugees. Now it assumed a burden of potentially millions of pounds when the British national debt had never been higher—underscoring the extraordinary nature of this commission.

Of course, American loyalists differed from Huguenot and Palatine refugees in a crucial respect: they were British subjects. Those earlier refugee crises had triggered debates about immigration and the rights of aliens. The reception of the loyalists, though, touched on a different question—one that had partly underpinned the American Revolution itself. Was there any distinction between the rights of British subjects at home and those of subjects abroad? American loyalists said no. They grounded their case for compensation in the presumption that British subjects were all the same no matter where they resided. But British authorities offered a more equivocal answer. Though British law traditionally distinguished only between subjects and aliens, Article V of the peace treaty referred to "real British subjects"—implying some sort of differentiation among kinds of subjects. Loyalists bridled at this logic: "To affirm of a person, that he is more a subject or less a subject is to speak neither good English, nor good law," observed one.[30] British officials, however, did not see loyalists as being "as perfectly British subjects as any in London or Middlesex." As Parliament framed it, loyalists got compensated not because they had a *right* to such aid, but because Britain had a moral responsibility to provide it. Parliament sought to uphold "the honor of the nation," protect the "national character," and fend off "national disgrace." This overarching moral concern helps explain why so many politicians who had earlier condemned the loyalist lobby for obstructionist behavior during the war now turned around in support of loyalist compensation.

If the claims commission thus made an unusual intervention in support of British subjects, it made an equally important statement about how the state conceived of its responsibilities. This was not a broad-based declaration about subjects' rights; it was an assertion of the state's paternalistic duties. As such, it represented another variation on what was fast becoming a familiar theme, in which colonial demands sat uneasily with metropolitan provisions. And it paved the way for a claims process that ended up frustrating many of those loyalists whom it had been designed to help.

MORTLAKE, once a quiet village on the south bank of the Thames and now enveloped by the suburban terraces of greater London, was far in all senses from Beverley Robinson's Dutchess County estate, but the colonel and his family put the best face on their new situation.[31] Arriving in England in the late summer of 1783, they decided to settle outside London to keep their costs down. Even in Mortlake, the once wealthy Robinsons could only afford to rent "a small old fashion house or rather part of a Bake house ready furnished for 12/pr week." In one half of the humble dwelling lived the baker who "supplys the whole village [with] bread." In the other half lived the colonel, his wife Susanna, and their daughters Joanna and Susan. Inelegant though their new surroundings were, Robinson wrote to his daughter-in-law Ann that "we have been very comfortable in it. . . . We are in a very good neighbourhood, & have got acquainted with several very Polite & agreeable families who treat us with a great deal of respect & Hospitality."[32] It helped to know the boys were reasonably well provided for. The eldest, Beverley Jr., had settled in Nova Scotia with Ann and their children. The youngest son, William, bunked on the spare bed in Mortlake until he went to Geneva to train for a career as a military commissary. Twenty-year-old Phil Robinson was now camped with his regiment in Staffordshire, enjoying a riotous life with his rakish brother officers. The young lieutenant was "quite as wild as ever," Joanna Robinson noted. "He is yet a most intolerable gallant he has made great devastation in the hearts of the Stafford fair. It is impossible for the Leopard to change its spots."[33]

Nor were the Robinsons short of company. They quickly discovered one chief consolation of exile: being able to share it with friends. American friends, relatives, and connections lived all around them. Fellow New York loyalist Isaac Low (who had been a delegate to the First Continental Congress), took a house in Mortlake with his wife; and nearby in East Sheen lived some of the Robinsons' only British friends, Helen and Brook Watson, who had been commissary-general in New York. Susanna Robinson's brother Frederick Philipse was in London, while her sister's family lived "very comfortably" in London and later Bath.[34] Though the Robinsons rarely traveled up to London themselves, they received frequent visitors, including Samuel Shoemaker, William Smith, and Peggy Arnold, Benedict Arnold's wife, who rode out to Mortlake on horseback. "She is grown amazingly lusty but it becomes her better than I thought it did when I first saw her in London," Joanna decided.[35]

Yet there was no compensating for the loss of the nearest connections of all. The permeating February chill seemed to have seeped into Joanna Robinson's spirits the day she wrote to her brother Beverley Jr. in Nova Scotia, aching with images of what she had left behind: "Our parting scene at New York will never be effaced from my memory, it is needless to tell you the pain it gave me, if you will judge of me by your own feelings."[36] She and her parents desperately tried to preserve their emotional bonds with the younger Beverley and his family. "Mama never sees a fine child but it costs her a sigh and sometimes a tear on the recollection of her seperation from her sweet grandchildren," Joanna told her brother, while the colonel pleaded with his daughter-in-law: "Pray take all methods in your power to prevent Hinky Pinky [Henry] from forgeting me, tell the dear little fellow I think of him day & night, and often all night for he is constantly before me in my dreams." The English Robinsons were delighted to learn of the birth of Beverley and Ann's third son in Nova Scotia. "God bless him I love him dearly already, but not so as to endanger my Hinkys nose," glowed the colonel. Their pleas for every detail of "who he is like, what signs & tokens happened at his birth, what assistance you had, how long you was Ill, what friends with you, & who nursed you" had to serve as surrogates for the grim fact that they might never see the newest Robinson in their lifetimes.[37]

"What a charming country this would be if we had but the means of living well in it, as it is it requires a great deal more philosophy than I am Mistress of to be content," concluded Joanna.[38] Her words captured a sentiment shared right across the loyalist exile community. Cut off from their old jobs and sources of income, unable easily to find substitutes in Britain, and unsure whether they would win enough compensation to make staying there viable, "the American Loyalists," Joanna reported, "are dispersing themselves about the kingdom some are gone to Chester some to . . . Yorkshire and some wandering about uncertain of their fate."[39]

Fate, for many hundreds of refugees, now rested in the Loyalist Claims Commission's office in Lincoln's Inn Fields. Rumors that the government might compensate loyalists had reached New York City before the evacuation, which allowed some refugees to hit the ground running with their claims.[40] Just a month after Samuel Shoemaker arrived in London, he found himself waiting in the foyer of the home secretary Lord Sydney's office with Sir Guy Carleton and "a number of those calld Refugees attending to be introduced." Beverley Robinson was there. So were the Wallace brothers, Hugh and Alexander, wealthy Irish-born merchants who had settled in New York in the 1750s and married sisters of fellow businessman Isaac Low. Reverend Charles Inglis, erstwhile rector of Trinity Church in New York, was another face familiar to all. All these men were seeking preferment of some kind; Shoemaker, for instance, wanted Sydney's recommendation in securing "a genteel allowance for my support until the matter respecting compensation for my losses is determined."[41] Over the months to come he interspersed his frequent visits to the Treasury and Loyalist Claims office by socializing with his American friends and touring the London sights.

The drawn-out process of filing claims, giving evidence, and waiting for a response held many loyalists in an anxious state of suspended animation. The former congressman Isaac Low articulated the strains of this nerve-racking predicament more fully than anyone. Attainted by the state of New York, Low and his wife Margaret sailed for Britain on the last evacuation fleet. The "violent rough passage" they endured served as gloomy omen for what followed.[42] Margaret was nearly constantly ill in London, while Isaac found "Nothing but Disorder and Confusion here which is very discouraging to us poor wanderers."[43] Their only joy was being reunited with their son, Isaac Jr., whom they had sent on to England ahead of them. A "robust," lively adolescent, the younger Isaac was "of great Use as a Guide in returning the Visits of our Friends and I really believe he knows more of London the few months he has been here than I should in as many Years." Low's own thoughts, though, were "so much engrossed with our present embarassed Situation, that I can't attend to the Course, or remember the names of the Streets two Days together." He struggled to support his family on a sum so small it would "soon take wings and fly away."[44] "To have nothing to do and to live altogether upon the little stock I can rake together are most disagreeable Circumstances."[45] While he waited for a response from the claims commissioners, he relied on loans from his younger brother Nicholas, a successful businessman still in New York, and on Nicholas's help in selling off what little American property he had managed to preserve.

In April 1784, Low received a glimmer of good news from the commissioners. He had been awarded "the <u>handsome</u> allowance of £140 St[erling] Pr annum untill my Claims are considered"—but he underscored "<u>handsome</u>" sarcastically, for this was not enough to help him decide "how to dispose of myself. At present I am all Suspense."[46] Now and then, that summer in Mortlake, Low had bright moments when he could persuade himself that "a moderate Share of the one Thing needful"—money—"and we should regret nothing but the absence of the dear Friends we left behind us."[47] But "how, where, or when" he might reestablish his position "are Questions which I cannot for a moment banish from my thoughts"; and at times he could not hold back the crashing waves of despair "least all should be lost."[48] It is hard not to hear Low's personal experience speaking between the lines of some advice he delivered to two married slaves he had left behind in New York. Though the Lows had taken care not to separate the couple, placing them with friends who would treat them "more like Children than Servants," the pair had "express[ed] a Desire of being free unless they could live with us again." "I certainly think they would be great Fools at their Time of Life to be set adrift in the world to seek a precarious Subsistence," Low cautioned. "If they could but see . . . how much better they live than the poor white Labourers in this Country, they would bless their lucky Stars, and not have a wish to alter their Condition."[49]

Of course, Low's disappointments stood in proportion to his expectations. Plenty of people would have regarded an income of £140 as a princely sum. For all his apparent poverty, Low did manage to maintain his residence at Mortlake, and kept at least one servant, Anne, a slave brought from New York. Low also made it a priority, as many loyalists in Britain did, to further his child's career no matter what the cost, and placed Isaac Jr. in a first-rate school in Kensington "at the extravagant price of £100 pr annum."[50] What so tormented refugees like Low was not just the palpable fact of having slipped from affluence, it was the paralyzing fear of falling still further, into bankruptcy and the social wilderness of disrepute.

While the Robinsons and Lows adjusted to modest suburban living, other refugees must have found it hard to imagine how things could get any worse. Across the congested slums of Mile End, Wapping,

Stepney, and Southwark hundreds of desperately poor refugees struggled simply to get by. In plaintive letters and memorials, refugees who
had any access to influential figures—or just to pen and paper—
detailed their troubles to the Loyalist Claims Commission. The worries that plagued Isaac Low, for instance, had already come true for one
New Yorker whose husband, a merchant, had lost his fortune to the
vicissitudes of war, and fled from both his creditors and his family. His
wife found him in London two years later, in "very distressed circumstances," and soon, with the threat of prison hanging over him, he vanished once more, leaving his wife and three small children down to
their last shift of clothes and "in daily pursuit of bread."[51] Even worse
off was a Boston woman, also abandoned by her husband, who tried to
scrape by with her children "on two pennyworth of bread a day and
1 lbs. of beef a week," but got hauled off into the miasmatic wards of
Newgate Prison for debt.[52]

A number of the poorest white refugees in Britain had actually been
born in the British Isles, but typically on its geographical margins, and
turned up in London as dispossessed and disconnected as many a
native-born North American. One Irishman spent the first months of
his exile struck down with "ague" in County Londonderry, and when
he traveled to London to pursue his quest for compensation, he too
got locked up in Newgate for debt. An illiterate Highlander filed a
claim for three houses and land he had lost in North Carolina; but,
aged over seventy, sweating on a mattress in a London slum with a
fever he could not shake, he must have doubted he would live to see
government aid come his way.[53] Another Highland Scot arrived in
London lamed, without his wife—who died a refugee in Nova Scotia—
and without the estate he had built for himself outside Savannah. This
native Gaelic speaker could not even file his own claim: he barely
understood English and needed an interpreter to help him.[54]

But of all the poor loyalists eking out a living in postwar Britain, the
largest group was in many ways the most conspicuous: black loyalists,
as many as five thousand of whom, overwhelmingly male, arrived in
England as demobilized sailors, soldiers, servants, and more. After
what some had been through in the war, it was a miracle they made it
there at all. Shadrack Furman, a free black Virginian, had worked as a
provisioner for British troops and then as a guide and informant, in
which role he was captured by patriot troops. Refusing to disclose
intelligence, Furman was sentenced to five hundred lashes. For many
victims this spelled certain death, but the unlucky Furman survived,

flayed down to the muscle, deranged by an ax blow to the head, blind in both eyes and lame in one leg. This scarred and knotted wreck of a man staggered to Nova Scotia and then to England, where he fiddled on the streets for spare change.[55] Benjamin Whitecuffe of New York had an equally dramatic tale of wartime survival. He too had been born free, the offspring of an American dream: Whitecuffe's mulatto father traded in his own sloop around Long Island Sound and managed a good-sized pasture and orchard besides. During the war his father and brother joined the patriots; but Benjamin volunteered as a British spy. Captured by the rebels, it was straight to the gallows for him. For fully three minutes, with the blood pounding in his head and blotting out his sight, Whitecuffe swung heavily above the ground while his neck, amazingly, withstood the tug of the rope. Cut down by passing British troops, the hardy young Whitecuffe went on to elude another brush with execution, to capture by a privateer, and naval service off Gibraltar, before finding himself in London, with a white English wife and no work.[56]

While middle-class loyalists successfully impressed their problems on the power brokers of Westminster and Whitehall, the striking spectacle of black loyalists like a Yorktown veteran called Peter Anderson— in his own words, "realy starving about the Streets Havin Nobody to give me a morsel of bread & dare not go home to my Own Country again"—gave many Britons pause.[57] To some, these blacks "begging about the streets of London, and suffering all those evils, and inconveniences, consequent on idleness and poverty," fueled only racist hostility.[58] But for a number of do-gooders, the "Black Poor," as this community became known, invited a different response. The most sustained efforts to help the Black Poor would be spearheaded by the well-known philanthropist Jonas Hanway, who had earned a fortune in the Russia trade and used it to imprint thousands of neglected lives. His earlier projects had included the Marine Society, which he established to train up poor lads for naval service; the Foundling Hospital, where he served as governor; and a crusade on behalf of abused and stunted little chimney sweeps. Hanway could not stomach the prospect of the Black Poor shivering through another London winter—any more than he could stand to drink tea, a "pernicious custom" that he devoted his least successful campaign to trying to eradicate.[59]

In the first weeks of 1786, Hanway summoned a group of his wealthy businessman friends to form a "Committee for the Relief of the Black Poor." Taking up their headquarters in a coffee house opposite the Royal Exchange, the committee launched a fund-raising effort to help the black loyalists and their hungry peers. "The greater part of them, have served Britain, have fought under her colours," one newspaper appeal ran, "and . . . depending on the promise of protection held out to them by British Governors and Commanders, are now left to perish by famine and cold, in the sight of that people for whom they have hazarded their lives, and even (many of them) spilt their blood." How could Christian, patriotic sensibilities stand unmoved? Contributions quickly flowed in to the committee, from benevolent grandees like the Duchess of Devonshire and Prime Minister William Pitt, right through to humbler well-wishers who could afford only a sixpence or a donation of wooden bowls and spoons. By the end of January 1786, more than two hundred poor blacks had queued up outside the committee's three soup kitchens to receive simple meals. Two hundred and fifty of them sloshed back home in newly issued shoes and stockings.[60]

Like many humanitarian initiatives of the era, this one owed its success in part to human empathy and the tug of Christian kindness. But it explicitly tapped into another, widespread feeling as well: the sense of collective responsibility for loyal subjects, the sense of national honor, that was enshrined in the Loyalist Claims Commission. It simply wasn't fair, the reasoning went, for black loyalists who had served Britain to end up penniless on British streets—any more than it was fair for loyalists to go uncompensated for their losses; any more than it was fair for black loyalists to be deprived of their promised freedom; or any more than it was fair, growing numbers of Britons thought, to ship black captives around the Atlantic as slaves to begin with. It was no coincidence that the committee received its largest single donation from a group of Quaker abolitionists, or that Granville Sharp, Britain's leading antislavery campaigner, kept in close touch with the committee's activities. The participation of abolitionists in this relief effort would have vital long-term consequences for black loyalist refugees.

For as needy blacks formed ever longer lines at the White Raven and Yorkshire Stingo taverns, waiting for broth, bread, and a sixpence to take home, committee members recognized that soup kitchens and clinics could only be a stopgap measure. The navy might employ some, but with postwar depression producing high levels of white unemployment, the prospects for jobless throngs of blacks seemed especially bleak. Some of the Black Poor volunteered their own solution. Perhaps their best chances for success did not lie in Britain at all, but in other British domains. Maybe they could go to Nova Scotia, where thousands of other black loyalists like David George and Boston King were settling? Or somewhere warmer, where all shivering would cease— such as the very place from which their forebears had been stolen, the west coast of Africa? This intriguing possibility found an enthusiastic champion in the person of Henry Smeathman, an entomologist who had spent four years in Sierra Leone. Smeathman had for some time advocated British colonization at the mouth of the Sierra Leone River, one of the largest natural harbors in the world—and the site of Bunce Island, one of Britain's largest slaving stations. In an impressive piece of salesmanship, Smeathman rapidly persuaded the committee to send the Black Poor to Sierra Leone as pioneer colonists. By spring 1786, the committee secured support from the British Treasury and Navy Board to transport the Black Poor overseas, equipped with supplies for a new settlement.[61]

From a committee meeting in a London coffee house to a fleet of ships ready to sail from Greenwich, all in a matter of months: this big, expensive, and frankly nebulous scheme advanced astonishingly quickly. It provides stunning evidence of the capacity and willingness of both the British state and private investors to launch colonial under-takings on the basis of little more than an interesting idea. Still, it is hard to imagine the scheme moving ahead with quite the same speed if the British government were not already so well practiced in transport-ing and supporting thousands of loyalists around the world—or if the British public were not already primed to sympathize with loyalist suf-ferings. Hanway himself would not live to see the results of the plan: he died in September 1786 with the destination and contours of the expe-dition yet to be finalized. (A month before his death, Hanway recanted on the merits of Sierra Leone, anticipating conflict with the Bunce Island slave traders, and tried to persuade the committee to settle the Black Poor in Nova Scotia instead.)[62] But henceforth taken over by Granville Sharp and the abolitionists, the project he set in motion evolved into one of the strangest and most enduring utopian experi-ments of its era.

MEANWHILE, thousands of loyalists, black and white, female and male, still waited to hear the result of their official claims. The submis-sion deadline for the Loyalist Claims Commission had originally been set for March 25, 1784. By then, the commissioners had already received 2,063 claims, which when tallied up sought compensation for lost property valued at £7,046,278, and for unrecoverable debts total-ing £2,354,135. "This was an alarming sum," gasped John Eardley Wilmot—approaching one billion pounds in current terms—and thousands more loyalists still hoped to file.[63] To accommodate further claims, Parliament extended the deadline to 1786, and renewed the commission's mandate annually until its work was finished. A total of 5,072 individuals submitted memorials of some kind and the commis-sion examined 3,225 claims in full.[64]

The records of the Loyalist Claims Commission form the largest single archive of evidence about the loyalist side of the American Rev-olution.[65] Within these thousands of bundles lurk extraordinary stories of wartime devastation, adventure, and personal trauma. It was here, for instance, that Thomas Brown told of his torture; that John Lich-tenstein explained how he had been chased off his plantation; and that Molly Brant described the seizure of her property and flight to Niag-ara. The claims yield up arresting images of the American Revolution as civil war. They also give unusual insight into colonists' material worlds, forming a sort of unsystematic colonial Domesday Book. From these pages tumble forth the vanished goods of American households: rum puncheons, damask bedspreads, carpenter's tools, old brass coffee pots, slick new saddles, favorite garnet earrings. These inventories of objects may seem at first blush to have little in common with the per-sonal narratives of hardship that accompany them, but together they make a powerful statement about the nature of the American Revolu-tion. Though some historians have portrayed the revolution as a rather staid affair, lacking the violence and mass property transfers of later revolutions in France and Russia, the record provided by displaced loyalists shows that, for at least one substantial group of Americans, this was an unequivocally turbulent event.

All these records must of course be read in light of the specific cir-cumstances for which they were produced—that is, read with caution. Nor does this mass of documents, subjective and unrepresentative as it is, form a reliable basis for drawing statistical conclusions about the composition or distribution of the loyalist population during the war.[66] What it does show, however, is not only that loyalism extended right across the American social spectrum, but that loyalists of all profiles, on both sides of the Atlantic, successfully made their plight known to the commission.[67] Four hundred and sixty-eight of the 3,225 claims preferred were filed by women, and forty-seven by black men.[68] Some three hundred claims were lodged by people who could not even sign their own names.[69] The numbers are especially noteworthy when one considers the logistical challenges involved in filing a claim. Though the commissioners put announcements in major British and Irish newspapers and informed government officials in North America, many loyalists only found out about the commission by word of mouth, sometimes too late.[70] Pursuing a claim required a considerable investment of time and money. It did not help that claimants were initially required to testify in person, which could entail costly trips to London. Hundreds relied on attorneys, agents, or family members to advance their cases for them. William Johnston submitted memorials on behalf of his brother Lewis Johnston Jr., who had moved to the Bahamas, while Dr. Lewis Johnston Sr. traveled down personally from his new residence in Edinburgh to present evidence.[71]

The wording of the commission's brief, to investigate losses suffered "in consequence of . . . loyalty"—and not merely through the depredations of war—meant that claimants had to establish a direct link between their allegiance and losses. Though claims varied significantly in length and detail, they tended to follow a formula. A 1783 pamphlet called *Directions to the American Loyalists in Order to Enable Them to State Their Cases by Way of Memorial to the Honourable the Commissioners* provided loyalists with a helpful fill-in-the-blank template:

> To the Honourable Commissioners . . . The MEMORIAL of A— B—, late of the Province of C— in America . . . *Humbly Sheweth* . . . That on the breaking out of the Civil War in the said province of C—, the Memorialist exerted himself in opposing the people who usurped the powers of Government, and was imprisoned by them, and in great danger of losing his life, until he made his escape from prison, and got on board his Majesty's ship of war D—, commanded by E— F—, Esq., lying at G— in the said Province of C—.[72]

And so on. After a précis of the claimant's experiences and sufferings as a loyalist, a claim typically continued with a description of lost property, income, and debts. (The pamphlet even provided specific forms for loyalists to claim compensation for runaway slaves who had been granted freedom by British troops.) The crucial final component to every case consisted of testimonials from character witnesses, who could vouch for the strength of the claimant's loyalty, and from neighbors, business partners, or family friends who could attest to the value of lost property.

In their Lincoln's Inn Fields headquarters, the five claims commissioners confronted mountains of paper and a monumental task. Vetting thousands of personal stories, usually heavier on hearsay than hard evidence, challenged even their experienced administrative minds. Before they started their hearings, the commissioners met with the loyalist agents in London to learn about values and prices in America. How much was an acre of cultivated land worth in Tryon County, New York, or Bucks County, Pennsylvania, or Ninety-Six District, South Carolina? How much did a bushel of Indian corn fetch in New Jersey in 1778, or a hefty Virginia hog ready for slaughter, or the mahogany furniture in a Boston house? As their inquiries proceeded, the commissioners realized that some of the information they needed could never be reliably obtained at thousands of miles' remove, so they dispatched an agent, a lawyer named John Anstey, to the United States to make inquiries on the spot. Anstey spent nearly two years in the United States gathering records in situ and interrogating loyalists' neighbors, relatives, and deputies. In 1785, two of the commissioners personally traveled to British North America to take evidence from claimants and witnesses settled there.[73]

The commission quickly developed a bureaucratic apparatus to handle the cases—and a bureaucratic attitude to match, as William Smith discovered to his annoyance when he went to submit his papers. He handed over his "bundle" to the secretary, who promptly found flaws in Smith's presentation and "said it ought to conform to the printed Instructions." Smith, who was of course a distinguished lawyer, insisted that it did, on which the secretary "pettishly observed that the Instructions must be complied with and asked me what I thought they were given for. I answered doubtless to instruct the Ignorant." After some further bickering, the secretary officiously accepted the papers, told Smith that probably "it would not be taken into Consideration for 2 years," and sent him away.[74]

The claims office became a hub of activity as loyalists cycled in and out, presenting their own cases or giving evidence in support of others. Here was Dr. Lewis Johnston, testifying about his and his son's lost income and property; there was Benjamin Whitecuffe, to describe his near death in the noose.[75] Reading the notebooks of Commissioner Daniel Parker Coke is like reading a loyalist who's who, as prominent loyalist advocates all took their place before the commission's desk: officials like Lord Dunmore and Lord Cornwallis; loyalist leaders like William Franklin and Joseph Galloway; loyalist military officers like Beverley Robinson and New Jersey general Cortlandt Skinner. Going into the office to testify for a fellow New Yorker, William Smith bumped into Sir Henry Clinton coming out, and they chatted about the peace settlement. (Clinton thought that "America would belong to England yet.")[76] Samuel Shoemaker spent several long sessions giving the commissioners "some information respecting several of my Countrymen which I did very candidly."[77] The day he presented his own case, with Joseph Galloway as his primary witness, Shoemaker saw another friend in the foyer and summoned him in to offer extra information.[78] These personal hearings were the claimants' best chance to impress their case on the commissioners, and they presented whatever testimony they could muster. One loyalist explained "to the Commissioners in the fullest manner, the sufferings of the whole Fam[il]y for our Loyalty, Shewd them my Scars, & they were pleased to reply that, such merit certainly ought not to go unrewarded by Government."[79]

Though Shoemaker was distressed to discover that some of his acquaintances had dishonestly inflated their losses ("since the commencement of the late troubles, it seems as if honesty and virtue had almost left us," he complained), only a handful of claims would be dismissed as outright frauds.[80] At the same time, the high standards of evidence required to prove a claim, with its emphasis on good connections and detailed documentation, made it incredibly difficult actually to win compensation. Proving a case was no mean feat even for well-positioned claimants. Isaac Low was told that he had to produce "the Certificates of the actual Sales of our confiscated Estates"—documents that could only be procured by his brother in New York.[81] Shoemaker had to return "with a list of debts owing to me in Pennsylva[nia] that I apprehended would be lost, or any other addition to my acct. of losses that I could support."[82] Testifying for Beverley Robinson and Robinson's brother-in-law Roger Morris, William Smith was quizzed minutely on matters such as the provisions of the Morrises' marriage settlement.[83] The structure of the commission especially marginalized the illiterate, the poor, and the poorly connected even while it opened up for them the tantalizing prospect of aid.

Given these standards, it was hardly to be wondered at that most of the black claimants received paltry payments of five, ten, or twenty pounds—if they received anything at all. The commissioner's response to one William Cooper, who said he had lost a house and land worth £500, was not atypical. They dismissed his claim out of hand, deciding that "in all probability not a single fact as stated is true; all these blacks say that they were free born and that they had property, two things that are not very probable; we did not believe one syllable of his case."[84] Implicit in the commission's judgment, in several of these cases, was the notion that black loyalists had already received freedom and thus did not really merit any further reward. A little more than half the black claimants received relief payments, usually thanks to testimonials they could provide from respected commanding officers. Only one black claimant successfully won compensation for his property losses. Charleston fishmonger Scipio Handley told how he had escaped hanging as a spy (a common experience for these black men, who had often been deployed as messengers and informants) and nearly lost his leg to a war wound; he provided a written schedule of losses, and produced a reliable witness. For all his sufferings and for his carefully produced claim, Handley received a grand total of £20.[85]

Female claimants also tended to be disadvantaged by the system. Few of them possessed the legal documents sought by the commissioners, or could rehearse the particulars of livestock, merchandise, or land values in as great detail as their male peers—although they were generally much more specific than men at itemizing their household goods.[86] One Jane Gibbes of South Carolina, who had been married to no fewer than three loyalists in succession, appeared before the commissioners to claim compensation for her second husband's estate. Though witnesses confirmed that Gibbes's late husband "was a grand Loyalist"—slaughtered on his own land by a mob of 163 men—the value of his holdings and proof of its confiscation could not be demonstrated to the commissioners' satisfaction, and much of the claim was disallowed.[87] Still harder to prove was the claim of a woman like Jane Stanhouse, a modest Scottish-born spinster who supplemented her income as a schoolmistress by taking in needlework. Known to have sheltered loyalist soldiers in North Carolina, Stanhouse had to flee to New York, losing what small property she had. In England, "an entire stranger," Stanhouse could produce no witnesses, and her claim was rejected "as there is no reference from the Treasury."[88]

And so the paperwork, the inquiries, and the judgments ground forward. By the time the commissioners prepared to announce their first set of recommendations for payment, in the spring of 1785, "the poor Exiles here are in status quo, waiting their Day of Judgment, more in anxious, then sure & certain, hope. Many of them, so streighten'd, 'tis a wonder how they rub through."[89] Parliament accepted the commission's report and voted £150,000 to settle the claims already examined. Loyalists eagerly pored over the results. The big winner from the first round of payments was Susanna Robinson's brother, Frederick Philipse, awarded nearly £17,000. Joseph Galloway and Cortlandt Skinner received several thousand pounds each. Isaac Low, like many others, briefly took heart from the news of these handsome payments, thinking it boded well for his own pending case. But a darker clue lay in the sums awarded to his brothers-in-law: Hugh and Alexander Wallace received little more than £1,500 between them, despite having been among the most prosperous merchants in prewar New York City.[90] "Fine doings," Alexander raged to Nicholas Low in New York. "It cost me double the sum to bring myself & family to England & to support them in London to prove my losses. . . . Damn them all & your good people who passed the law to deprive us of our property."[91]

From one slow season to the next the claims commission deliberated over its recommendations, and the dividends awarded seemed, to once prosperous loyalists, less and less satisfactory. Loyalist agents wheeled out familiar arguments in protest: "under the fundamental laws of the British Constitution," they asserted they had "not only an equitable but a lawful right to a just compensation for their estates and property." But instead of gaining a fair settlement, "it is impossible to describe the poignant distress under which many of the American Loyalists now labour. . . . [T]en years have elapsed since many of them have been deprived of their fortunes, and with their helpless families reduced from independent affluence to poverty and want; some of them are now languishing in British Gaols . . . others have already sunk under the pressure and severity of their misfortunes."[92] In the meantime, a New York refugee complained, "the Americans here help to keep up one anothers spirits, they have little else to do."[93] Little else but wait for more of the commission's reports to come through—and more disappointments. "If you have one that is satisfied with his dividend on your side of the Water, it is more than I can say on this," wrote another London-based loyalist to his brother in New Brunswick; "the pittance is so small to many that they refuse, & despise it with contempt, while others die with broken hearts, and the smallness of their dividends. Some have run mad with dispair & disappointment. Many that were men of repute, good livers, & had a right to expect from £500 to £1000 were reported for £7 10., £8, £9, £10, £11, £12 & so on up to £40 or £50."[94]

Melodramatic though these laments might sound, they accurately described the reality experienced by Isaac Low and his brothers-in-law the Wallaces. By 1785, Alexander Wallace had settled with his family in Waterford, Ireland: "I cannot say I like it so well as I once liked N. York: but this place answers with me & I am perfectly content & happy."[95] His brother Hugh stayed with them, ardently hoping to win compensation soon so that he could rejoin his beloved wife in New York. But Hugh was "far from the person he was when you last see him," Alexander informed Nicholas Low, "his mind is much troubled, with his Misfortunes."[96] "If ever man was to be pitied, he is, his losses hang heavy on him & his being from his wife hurts him much."[97] By the summer of 1786, with only £300 compensation in hand and the prospect of being able to travel back to America fast receding, Hugh Wallace found his health collapsing. "Another attack of his disorder"— perhaps a small stroke?—left him unable to walk or ride; soon he could barely sit up for more than half an hour at a stretch.[98] His family watched this once vigorous man simply dissolve away. By autumn 1787, Hugh was so frail that "his man servant carries him from Room to Room in his arms as a Child. Indeed he is in every respect as helpless as a Child & his memory very bad." The next winter he was dead, his losses unrewarded, his widow left to grieve on the other side of an ocean.[99]

Back in Mortlake, Isaac Low waited for news of his own dividend. It would be £1,700, he learned, a handsome sum by anybody's reckoning (worth about one hundred times that in today's purchasing power)— but as with his earlier pension, far less than he had counted on. He responded first with despair, ready to "set myself down for a ruined Man," then with anger at the "palpable Injustice" done him.[100] Low thought he had presented unimpeachable witnesses and testimony (so much, indeed, that the commissioners found his papers "to be too voluminous and not sufficiently clear"), and could only explain the disappointing result by conjuring spectral visions of "insidious" enemies whispering "Malice" in the commissioners' ears.[101] Yet there was one blot Low could never erase: "I found on my own previous Examinations, that my having been in Committee and Congress, was a great stumbling Block." Condemned as a loyalist in New York, now that Low was in Britain the former congressman found himself discriminated against as a seeming onetime patriot.[102]

Low strenuously protested the commission's judgment for as long as he could: he asked his brother in New York to "muster all my Friends, and to cram Mr. Anstie with Evidence (as they do Turkeys in this Country with Paste) to prove . . . that all my Efforts, in all Situations, was to conciliate and preserve Peace . . . and above all, to pre-

vent a Separation of the two Countries."[103] Grudgingly he took his
money, resigned himself to the thought that he would never return "to
breath my native air," and started a new career in London as an insur-
ance underwriter.[104] After four years in Britain, at least "the Gloom
which oppressed me begins to dispel as the prospect opens of earning a
subsistence, and passing away the Remainder of my Days in this Land
of true Liberty."[105] But the black beast of "Despondency" trailed him
as surely as his own shadow; and Low could never really quiet a mind
agitated by need, smarting from injustice, and troubled afresh by the
high risks of his new profession. Low literally worried himself sick. On
a visit to the Isle of Wight to recover his health, he died, crushed by
loss. "To see all the fruits of his Industry, set at to nought through the
cruell treatment he experiencd on both sides [of] the Atlantic brought
on an anxious mind, which hurried him to the Grave," Isaac Jr. wrote
to his uncle in New York. He lifted his father's concerns onto his own
capable, Kensington-educated shoulders instead.[106]

All told, the British government awarded loyalists £3,033,091—
worth about £300 million today—on a total volume of losses claimed
amounting to £10,358,413. Receiving compensation for lost property
were 2,291 loyalists; a further 588 earned pensions to make up for lost
income.[107] Hundreds of loyalists began and ended the claims process
with far fewer resources, and far fewer chances of winning help, than
Isaac Low. Yet for all that those disadvantaged claimants received min-
imal payments, it was Low and his peers who came away from the
experience with the greatest sense of disappointment. Their dissatisfaction hinged on that discrepancy between loyalist and metropolitan
attitudes that had underpinned the commission from the outset. Inad-
equate compensation just opened afresh the wounds of being a
refugee, and enhanced the sense most refugees had of being strangers
in Britain. They saw compensation as a right. What they got instead
was charitable relief from a self-consciously paternalistic (and penny-
pinching) state. How much happier must have been broken, blind, and
confused Shadrack Furman, awarded an annual pension of £18 for life:
enough, perhaps, to shelve his catgut fiddle for a while and stay off the
streets, with a fire and a fresh loaf of bread.

AS THE CLAIMS commission wound down its business in the late
1780s, many loyalist refugees had discovered Britain to be a disappointment. But though they may not have recognized it as clearly, they

also sat at the center of an empire reshaped by the "spirit of 1783." In June 1788, Prime Minister William Pitt rose in the House of Commons to open the debate on the liquidation of the last remaining loyalist claims. He addressed a legislature in the middle of a thrilling session, preoccupied by affairs that well reflected the changes under way in the post-revolutionary British world. The most significant issue was reforming the East India Company, the commercial body that had effectively morphed into an imperial state by administering Bengal. Since the American Revolution, Company activities had fallen under increasing scrutiny and parliamentary oversight. In March 1788, regulatory efforts culminated in a spectacular impeachment trial of Warren Hastings, governor-general of Bengal, on a charge of "high crimes and misdemeanors." Hundreds of spectators filed into Westminster Hall to watch Edmund Burke, who spearheaded the prosecution, launch a gripping piece of political theater. For four consecutive days, Burke held his audience transfixed with a speech detailing Hastings's alleged rapacity, corruption, blackmail, and worse. As he described alleged British torture of Indian women, using terms "more vivid—more harrowing—and more horrific—than human utterance on either fact or fancy, perhaps, ever formed before," the MP Richard Sheridan's wife fainted dead away in shock; Burke himself was seized with a stomach cramp and had to retire for the day.[108] A few days later, when Sheridan took to the boards, tickets to the trial were said to be selling for fifty guineas each.

As if the Hastings trial were not dramatic enough, in May 1788 Pitt introduced into Parliament a contentious subject that had been sweeping through the nation's churches, coffee houses, and drawing rooms. For generations, slave ships had cruised in and out of Liverpool, Bristol, and other British ports as part of a triangular trade with Africa and the Americas. The British public had seemed little bothered. But starting in the 1770s, abolitionists circulated tales of the ghastly conditions on board these ships, portraying the slave trade as a national disgrace. Suddenly, after the war, it was as if thousands of heads looked up together, recoiled, and spoke out at once. Petitions poured into Parliament from every corner of Britain, calling for an end to the transatlantic slave trade. In 1788, Pitt secured a unanimous resolution from Parliament to debate the matter in its next session, and in April 1789 the Yorkshire MP William Wilberforce introduced the first abolition bill in British history.[109]

Disparate though these proceedings might seem, the Hastings trial and the rise of abolitionism were both every bit as closely related to the loss of America as the issue of loyalist compensation. Though both reform efforts predated the American Revolution, the loss of the colonies injected them with fresh relevance and ethical force. The secession of more than two million white American subjects drove home the fact that the British Empire was a majority nonwhite enterprise. Bengal and other areas ruled by the East India Company were the empire's most populous domains, and the company itself was one of the empire's largest governing institutions. With the memory of American mismanagement still raw, it seemed more vital than ever, especially to "friends of America" like Burke, to reform Indian government to prevent corruption and abuse of power. At the same time, the American Revolution removed half a million slaves from the British Empire, and a major interest group in the form of American slaveowners. Abolitionists were able to draw a moral contrast between Britain, where slaveowning was unenforceable following the 1772 Somerset case, and a United States in which slavery would be constitutionally protected. Together these causes illustrated the paternalistic impulses of the "spirit of 1783," toward increasingly centralized authority and clarified ideals of liberty and moral purpose.[110]

By 1788 the transformative effects of the American Revolution for the British Empire were also discernable in a third arena, reflecting the final element of the "spirit of 1783." This one could be traced on the imperial map. For while Britain compensated loyalists for their losses, it began to compensate for its own loss of the thirteen colonies by expanding into new territories. And while thousands of loyalist refugees built new settlements around the Atlantic, one loyalist in Britain helped launch what was perhaps the period's most consequential colonial undertaking, on the other side of the earth.

New York–born James Mario Matra had arguably seen more of the world than any American alive. As an able-bodied seaman in the Royal Navy, Matra had circumnavigated the globe with Captain James Cook from 1768 to 1771 on the *Endeavour*, a pioneering voyage of "discovery" widely understood today to have initiated British imperialism in the Pacific. But no active steps had yet been taken to colonize the most promising territory Cook identified for settlement: Australia. "We almost universally have a strong affection for our Native Soil," Matra recognized, and "few of any Country, will ever think of settling in any foreign part of the World, from a restless mind, & from romantick views."[111] But when he saw his fellow loyal Americans become refugees, Matra spotted an opportunity to achieve two goals in one. With so many exiles questing for a new home, he suggested, why not settle them in New South Wales, on Australia's east coast? Temperate and sparsely inhabited, New South Wales was like an antipodean reflection of North America. And the American refugees would make ideal colonists. They were already uprooted, self-evidently loyal, and in many cases familiar with the kinds of labor needed to create a settlement. Matra assured British ministers that "the most intelligent, and candid Americans . . . all agree that under the Patronage, and Protection of Government, it offers the most favourable Prospects that have yet occurred, to better the Fortunes, and to promote the happiness, of their fellow Sufferers, & Countrymen."[112]

"Matra's Plan," as authorities termed it, became the template for Britain's colonization of Australia—though in the event, his scheme took another turn. Before the revolution, Britain had been transporting convicts to the American colonies as indentured laborers, but U.S. independence made it impossible to continue this practice. Officials desperately needed a fresh outlet for Britain's disgustingly over-crowded prisons. Recognizing an even better opening, Matra swiftly modified his plan for a loyalist "asylum" in Australia, and proposed that New South Wales be developed as a penal colony instead. So Australia was not to be a loyalist haven in the end—though the First Fleet that sailed for Botany Bay in 1787 carried seven unlucky black loyalists among the prisoners.[113] But as the convicts cut back the gum trees and fragrant eucalypts to pitch their tents at Sydney Cove in the spring of 1788, they enacted a version of the same process loyalist refugees performed from the banks of the Saint John River to the Sierra Leone estuary.

So by the time Parliament debated the outstanding loyalist claims in June 1788, the "spirit of 1783" had demonstrably marked the refugees' world. Just five years earlier in the peace treaty debates, MPs had wrung their hands at the division of the empire, Britain's loss of international standing, and the betrayal of national honor. Now relief efforts showcased British humanitarianism while administrative reforms sought to ward off colonial discontent from India to Ireland. Widened geographical expansion made the empire a Pacific entity as well as an Atlantic one. And while in 1783 the "abandonment" of the loyalists had seemed to encapsulate everything that went wrong with British America, by 1788 Britain's treatment of the loyalists seemed to exemplify the virtues of this rejuvenated empire. Summing up the work of the Loyalist

Claims Commission, Edmund Burke reminded his colleagues that "the loyalists had no claim upon the House founded in strict right"; rather "the House was bound in honor and justice to take their claims into consideration." Compensating loyalists did "the country the highest credit. . . . It was a new and noble instance of national bounty and generosity."[114]

Burke's use of the adjective "new" deserves notice. The American Revolution made clear that overseas subjects—even white ones—would not necessarily be considered as extensions of those in the metropolis, in the way that American colonists had once hoped to be treated (though that did not stop overseas subjects from seeking enhanced rights and representation). What they got instead was embedded in Burke's idea of "national bounty," a phrase that touched on the fundamental ethos of this post-revolutionary empire. British officials self-consciously advertised their moral responsibility toward overseas subjects. It did not matter if you had white skin or black, the logic went, wore saris or moccasins, kneeled in a mosque or took Catholic communion: you would still win imperial protection and responsible government. As loyalists discovered, you could even win freedom and financial support. The refugees got paid for their losses for the same reasons some politicians hoped to protect Bengali subjects from rapacious governors, and abolitionists hoped to protect African slaves from death on British ships. "Whatever may be said of this unfortunate war, either to account for, to justify, or to apologize for the conduct of either Country," the claims commissioner John Eardley Wilmot wrote with satisfaction decades later, "all the world has been unanimous in applauding the justice and the humanity of Great Britain . . . in compensating, with a Liberal hand, the Losses of those who suffered so much for their firm and faithful adherence."[115] Thanks to the Loyalist Claims Commission, loyalists had gone from reminders of defeat to points of pride, testaments to British munificence. And though there were no real precedents for the Loyalist Claims Commission, it provided a meaningful example in turn when the French Revolution brought thousands more refugees to British shores for asylum. Wilmot helped form a committee for émigré relief, many of whose members had previously been involved in aiding American loyalists.[116]

Debates concluded, payment schemes drawn up, the Loyalist Claims Commission presented its twelfth and final report to Parliament in 1789, and the Treasury duly paid out the final dividends. No matter how much loyalist refugees received, simply finishing the claims process marked the end of a long road. To a few of the most fortunate, substantial payments meant that they could continue living in Britain in relative comfort. Yet even Beverley Robinson, who received a magnificent £25,000, one of the largest sums awarded, felt disappointed by his settlement.[117] The resolution "seems to have affected him very much in his spirits, pray God it may not injure his Health," his youngest son William observed. Too old now for military service or government positions, if any were even available, Robinson could only hope that "possibly from constant application & dancing attendance he may get some addition to his allowance."[118] The best compensation for privileged loyalists like Robinson and his friends came from seeing their children succeed. His eldest son Beverley Jr. was becoming a pillar of the British North American elite. Three other sons were well placed in trade and military administration. Phil Robinson, though prevented by lack of money from fulfilling an ambition to study in Germany, continued his romping career through the ranks of the British army.[119] Beverley Robinson's successes with his children notably contrasted, though, with the fate of another disappointed refugee, William Franklin. Now permanently settled in London, Franklin took little pleasure from his reunion with his only son Temple in 1792. Raised for many years by Benjamin Franklin, the young man had become a stranger to William, shiftless and dissolute. Father and son became about as estranged as William and Benjamin had been. William found pleasure instead in raising Temple's illegitimate daughter as his own.[120]

For many other loyalists in Britain (though the historical record is not detailed enough to allow for precise estimates), compensation helped propel new journeys. Some looked back across the Atlantic for fresh opportunities. In 1786, Sir Guy Carleton was named governor in chief of Canada, and William Smith followed his patron to Quebec, to serve as chief justice. Reverend Charles Inglis had years of lobbying rewarded with an appointment as the first bishop of Nova Scotia in 1787. Hundreds of humbler refugees left to become farmers, tradesmen, and lawyers in British North America among their friends and former neighbors from the thirteen colonies. Benedict Arnold joined this reverse migration, exchanging his costly life in Britain for what he hoped would be a profitable commercial career in Saint John, New Brunswick.[121] And for a few loyalists, including Samuel Shoemaker, the stay at "home" in Britain ended in a return to the "home" they had fled. Despite off-putting reports of chaotic conditions in the early

American republic, and lingering fears about punitive action, they braved the dangers and headed for the United States.

The experiences of the Johnston family provide especially good insight into the choices made by middle-class refugees in Britain. Since their departure from East Florida in 1784, they had been living in Edinburgh, where William completed his medical education and Elizabeth enjoyed setting up, at last, something resembling a family home. In the spring of 1785 she bore another "fine boy," while William went to London "to form some plan as to where he should finally practice." He may never have seen his new son, for just three months later the baby was dead of thrush—lifted by God, Elizabeth consoled herself, "from a world of sin and sorrow." She had given birth to four children in four different cities in about as many years. Now she planted her first gravestone in Scotland's alien soil. With William's training finished and the claims payments made out (their fathers were rewarded with about £1,000 each), the Johnstons contemplated a fresh set of options for their future.[122] Lack of money and access to positions compromised their prospects for a comfortable life in Britain. William Johnston turned to his patrons for help. One "handsome offer" came from Archibald Campbell, William's commanding officer at the capture of Savannah.[123] Campbell had just been appointed governor of Madras: would William like to join him in India? It was a tantalizing prospect. India tended to mean one thing to the hard-up, ambitious British men who sailed there: the chance to live richly overseas and retire with a tidy fortune. That made getting into East India Company service highly competitive, and an appealing option for loyalists who could manage it. But then, the chances of not coming back at all were considerably higher, for India also had a well-earned reputation as a white man's grave.

A different lead was dangled by another of Johnston's wartime patrons, former Savannah commandant Alured Clarke. Clarke was due to travel out to Jamaica as its new governor. How would William like to set up a practice there?[124] Jamaica, too, had sickness aplenty, and fewer legends about incredible wealth to offset its risks. It was also, though, a much more familiar possibility for the Johnstons than Asia. Its slave-based plantation society resembled the one they had left in Georgia and shared cultural and social ties with the American south. William Johnston's own parents had met and married on St. Kitts.

So which was it to be, the Indies east or west? The Johnstons could pick between two distinct spheres of opportunity within a single global empire. In October 1786, Elizabeth traveled to the Scottish port of Greenock, where she had landed just over two years before, to take passage for another unknown. She was sad to leave Edinburgh, where she had "met with much kindness and affection"; and she must have felt a tighter tug on leaving her firstborn son Andrew, who stayed behind to get a good Scottish education in his grandfather Dr. Johnston's care. But this departure signaled an important step toward self-sufficiency. No longer forced to move by war, and no longer dependent on William's father, the Johnstons could stay together and—at last—stay put. Boarding the ship with her children Catherine and Lewis, Elizabeth especially welcomed her impending reunion with William, who had gone on ahead, leaving her racked by familiar fears that they were "never to meet again."[125] But on the other side of the indigo Atlantic he was waiting for them, in the white-shuttered governor's house of Spanish Town, Jamaica.[126]

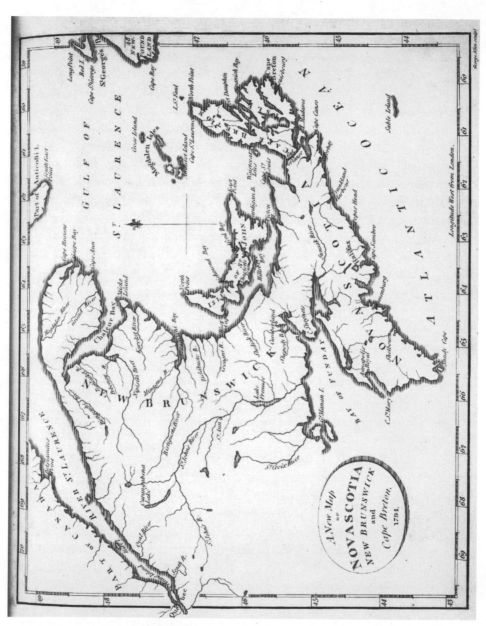

Jedidiah Morse, *A New Map of Nova Scotia, New Brunswick, and Cape Breton*, 1794.

CHAPTER FIVE

A World in the Wilderness

HE *LYON* keeled and swayed from Gravesend across the roiling Atlantic, no sooner cleared of one storm than thrown into the churning belly of the next. Charles Inglis, the former rector of New York's Trinity Church, monitored the "violent Tempests" through deep-sunk eyes, his hollow cheeks tight with strain, as he held close his children Peggy and Jack and clenched his hands together in prayers for safe passage. Six weeks and three thousand miles later, a purple strip of land lined the horizon, and the coves and cusps of the Nova Scotia shoreline came into view: a forbidding contrast to the gentle downs and crumbling chalk cliffs they had left behind. Inglis sailed into Halifax in October 1787, offering up "Praise to the Almighty for thus bringing me in safety to my destined place of residence"—much the same language used by another loyalist clergyman, Jacob Bailey, eight years before.[1]

Inglis's journey from England to Nova Scotia had been as rough as it was roundabout. He had never even expected to be in Britain in the first place. Though he and his wife had both been attainted by the state of New York, when news of the peace treaty reached the city in the spring of 1783, Inglis sought to have the judgments against his family reversed so they could safely remain there. But the New York assembly denied his request: after all, Inglis had been one of the city's most outspoken loyalists throughout the war. Effectively banished from New York, Inglis made plans to travel to Nova Scotia, where he hoped to serve as a missionary for the Society for the Propagation of the Gospel. Along with fifty-four other prominent loyalist civilians "desirous of continuing to enjoy the benefits of the British Constitution," he signed a petition asking Sir Guy Carleton for land grants in Nova Scotia on the same generous terms (five thousand acres each) granted to veteran officers. (This document, known as the "petition of fifty-five," attracted outrage from humbler loyalists, who saw it as an arrogant assumption of privilege by the elite.)[2] He packed up his library and household furniture and dispatched them to Annapolis Royal with his servants, preparing to follow shortly himself. But then, as New York seethed around him during the last weeks of British occupation, Inglis's plans took a terrible set of turns. His wife Margaret had been bedridden for several months with a mysterious but lingering illness. As she languished in discomfort during those squalid August days, every one of the three Inglis children suddenly contracted measles, which was often fatal. Inglis faced the horrifying prospect of his entire family being wiped out. What was worse, precisely this had happened to him twenty years earlier, when his first wife died in childbirth, followed by their twins. This time fortunately the children recovered; but on the last day of summer, the long-suffering Margaret was dead.[3]

By now the only ships Inglis could find out of New York were heading not for Nova Scotia but for England. Hurriedly rearranging his plans through the haze of mourning, Inglis dispatched one daughter to England ahead of him and arranged to leave another daughter, too weakened by sickness to travel, with her grandmother in New York. On October 21, 1783, he stepped into the pulpit of St. George's Church to preach his last sermon in New York City. "Finally Brethren Farewell," read his chosen text. "Be perfect; be of good comfort; be of one Mind; live in peace; and the God of Love and Peace be with you." A few days later, he boarded a Britain-bound ship with his six-year-old son.[4]

With so many New York friends also in Britain, including the Robinsons, the Lows, and William Franklin, Inglis's exile was by no means solitary. Like them, he took advantage of the move to Britain to place his children in good schools, investing in their future while his own remained uncertain. Armed with testimonials from Carleton and William Smith, Inglis secured a pension of £175 from the Treasury until his loyalist claim could be reviewed. But even with the pension in hand, London life was far from easy. His children got sick again, and he himself endured nearly a year of debilitating illness. Still, he tirelessly pursued a new objective: to establish a bishopric for the growing province of Nova Scotia—and to be appointed to that position himself. In Britain he held numerous meetings with the archbishop of Canterbury and others, patiently working to build support for the plan. After more than two years of urging, Inglis insisted that "the State of Things in the Colonies called for the immediate Presence of the Bishop," and pleaded, "If I was not appointed, I wished to know it soon, because I had a Family (two Children) to remove, & adjust my Affairs for leaving London, which became absolutely necessary for sake of my Health, & on other accounts."[5] He waited fully four years before the Privy Council approved the episcopate. At last, one summer Sunday in 1787, all that hardship was crowned with success when Inglis was consecrated at Lambeth Palace as bishop of Nova Scotia, the first colonial bishop ever created in the British Empire. Two weeks later, the Inglises sailed back to North America.[6]

Going to Halifax was not quite going home for the Inglis family, but under the circumstances of exile, it was the next best thing. They were quickly welcomed by friends old and new. The bishop and his children stepped off the ship and straight into the governor's own carriage, which drove them through the unfamiliar streets to a friend's house. Inglis dined with Governor Parr, received calls from loyalist connections, and promptly wrote to his friend in Annapolis Royal to reclaim "my servants & furniture," which he had sent on from New York four years earlier.[7] He was especially excited to renew his acquaintance with a distinguished visitor to Halifax, Prince William Henry, the king's third son (and future King William IV). In 1783, New York loyalists had gone weak at the knees when the teenage prince, a midshipman in the Royal Navy, arrived with his ship in Manhattan. Now in Halifax, a seasoned lieutenant fresh from Caribbean service with Horatio Nelson, the prince inspired equal devotion among the local loyalist elite. Bishop Inglis fawned anew over the "slender, genteel, affable, and sprightly" prince, and in a long private conversation "assured him of my inviolable attachment to his Majesty & personal affection. That I loved the man, whilst I reverenced the sovran [*sic*]—that no circumstance in my appointment gave me more pleasure, than thereby having it in my power to diffuse more extensively principles of loyalty."[8]

The new bishop wasted little time widening the reach of the Church of England in the province. In the summer of 1788, he set off on a tour of his new dominion. Traveling first to Windsor, about forty miles northeast of Halifax, he scouted out appropriate plots for a new church and a school. He then crossed the peninsula to Cornwallis, near Annapolis Royal, where he found the church on a rudimentary footing, within a largely dissenting community. Even at Annapolis itself, the oldest European town in Nova Scotia, and one of the largest sites of loyalist settlement, Inglis found "things not duly prepared for administering Confirmation. . . . The Church here is of a moderate size, built by the Inhabitants, & is just a finishing—the Chancel, pews

& pulpit not yet built." He conversed at some length with Jacob Bailey, who had been minister at Annapolis since 1782. Though Bailey had supported a rival candidate for the bishopric, Inglis observed he "appears to be a meek, inoffensive man," and decided not to chastise him for this error in judgment. At least in Annapolis Inglis was reassured to find that the "inhabitants appear to be the most decent & regular I have yet seen in the province. Their behaviour in time of Divine service very proper. They sing well."[9]

The scattered hamlets above the marshes might well have reminded Inglis more of his birthplace in Ireland than of his adult home in New York City. But though the surroundings were new to him, many of the faces were familiar. A few miles outside Annapolis, Inglis stopped to visit Cornelia DeLancey, the sister of Beverley Robinson Jr.'s wife Ann. Mrs. DeLancey's pious mother, one of Inglis's dearest New York friends, had just died. Grieving her mother (and perhaps unleashing the pent-up stresses of her notoriously unhappy marriage), DeLancey was so overcome by the visit of her former pastor that "on seeing me, [she] bursted into tears." Together the pair mused on where the years had taken them since New York, and where they might lead yet; DeLancey's husband had just been appointed chief justice of the Bahamas.[10] The next day, Inglis sailed down the Annapolis Basin to Digby, nestled on the southern curve of a shimmering bay. There he "was most affectionately received by the Inhabitants, who were all Loyalists. Many of them were formerly members of my congregation, & seemed to vie with each other in manifesting their affection & esteem," although he was disappointed to note "they are very poor, & I fear will continue so, unless they disperse, & settle on farms."[11]

The spectacle on the opposite shore of the Bay of Fundy, recently constituted as the province of New Brunswick, presented an impressive contrast. Inglis cruised into the city of Saint John, a craggy town with busy wharves at the harbor mouth and fine houses lining the ridge above. And to think it was all brand-new! "Scarcely five years have elapsed since the spot on which it stands was a forest," Inglis marveled; yet with "upwards of 1000 houses . . . it affords a striking instance of what industry is capable of doing." With a population composed almost entirely of loyalists, and revolving around the Atlantic trade, Saint John seemed like a miniature New York, a city transplanted. Inglis again paid many calls on "my old acquaintance. . . . Here as at Digby the Congregation is made of Loyalists—many of them were my former parishioners."[12]

The bishop rounded off his tour by proceeding up the meandering

Saint John River to the capital of New Brunswick, Fredericton. Late summer, when rich sunlight haloed the overripe trees, was the perfect season to visit this place, as tranquil as the river that flowed gently past the barracks square. As the guest of Governor Thomas Carleton—Sir Guy's younger brother—Inglis enjoyed the best of what the small capital could offer, from casual walks on the riverbank to genial dinners with the local elite. One day Inglis crossed over to Nashwaaksis, opposite Fredericton, to visit "my old acquaintance & friend" Ann Robinson. She and Beverley Jr.—whose wedding ceremony Inglis had performed in New York—had arrived in Fredericton a year earlier from Nova Scotia and carved out an impressive estate. Ann had just delivered the couple's seventh child, and because of her recent confinement, Beverley had shielded her from the bad news of her mother's death. Perhaps it mitigated the shock to hear of it now, from the trusted minister's lips. Inglis left the British Empire's newest capital thoroughly impressed with its potential: "All seemed to be busily employed. Each thought his own employment, & his farm the best."

What Bishop Inglis saw on his summer tour in 1788 was a colonial society created almost overnight. Thirty thousand loyalist refugees— with about twelve hundred slaves—had flooded into these provinces in the space of eighteen months. As he noted, their work was far from done: churches unfinished, schools not built, farmlands in the first seasons of cultivation. But many of the settlements Inglis visited had been virgin woods just five years earlier; the rest had been demographically changed by the great loyalist immigration. Business partners from New England and New York reestablished their concerns in Halifax, Shelburne, and Saint John. Veterans of disbanded regiments traded swords for spades and settled as neighbors on adjacent land grants. Inglis's parishioners from New York prayed together in Nova Scotia and New Brunswick—retaining communities of faith, though Inglis may not have known it, in the same way that black loyalists did in their villages on the edges of white settlements.

Nowhere did loyalist refugees transform their surroundings on the same scale or with the same enduring significance as in the provinces of British North America. Later historians would come to see them quite simply as the "founding fathers" of British Canada. This characterization has to do in large measure with their influence on politics and government. Their impact in these spheres became apparent as early as 1784, when British authorities responded to the mass immigration by dividing Nova Scotia in two, to create the province of New Brunswick. With a white population overwhelmingly composed of refugees, New Brunswick was the closest thing loyalists had to their own state; and elite loyalists hailed it as an opportunity to fashion their own imperial answer to the United States. Meanwhile, refugee Mohawks essayed a new settlement around Lakes Erie and Ontario, where Joseph Brant tried to establish an autonomous Indian domain between the American republic and British Empire. In these arenas west of the Bay of Fundy, refugees helped shape a loyal America, as it were, in contrast to the republican America they had fled.

But if you toured the Canadian provinces in the 1780s, as Inglis did, you would also see change impressed on the land itself. This transformation would be most evident in Nova Scotia, which received the largest infusion of refugees by far. The loyalist community at Port Roseway, in particular, consisting of the largely white town of Shelburne and the adjacent black village of Birchtown, became the shock city of the exodus, springing up virtually overnight. How did loyalist refugees make the wilderness a new world? In its effects on Nova Scotia's human and environmental landscape, the loyalist influx resembled white expansion elsewhere in North America, as well as the contemporary colonization of Australia.[13] Yet this wasn't just any colonial undertaking. It was also a major refugee crisis that posed particular challenges for government, and heightened tensions between settlers and authorities. And the refugees' imprint was all the more notable when set in the context of earlier British efforts to colonize Nova Scotia. For this province had already been altered by a British imperial project one generation before—an episode not of settlement, but of displacement.

ON THE OLD European maps they called the place Arcadia, for the first explorers who charted the shores had seen its tall pine forests and verdant marshes as pastoral fantasy made real. In pure if apt coincidence, the native Micmac Indians used the suffix -*akadie* to indicate a "place of abundance"—making it so much the easier for "Arcadia" to slip, on the tongues of the French who settled there, into the simpler *l'Acadie*. They planned to make this corner of North America into a New World idyll.[14]

In the first years of the seventeenth century, French colonists established a settlement called Port Royal on the gentle shore of the Annapolis Basin, notched into the coast behind the Bay of Fundy. They dyked and sluiced the marshes into farms and orchards, protecting their crops from the eighteen-foot tides of the bay. They protected their settlement also, with a stone fort surrounded by star-shaped earthworks, to resist any attack from the sea. Their hamlets were humble, but the smallness of their numbers and simplicity of their circumstances belied the wealth that surrounded them. Under the glinting surface of the North Atlantic waters swam silvery cod, millions of them. Pulled in seemingly endless abundance from the ocean, the fish were slit, dried, packed into barrels with salt, and shipped to Europe and the West Indies, where they nourished rapidly growing slave populations. The land hosted fortunes, too, in the scampering creatures of the woods. Indians brought bundles of sleek beaver furs and other pelts to trade with the Europeans for kettles and hatchets, needles and knives.

Resource-rich and with long, accessible coasts, French-settled Acadia quickly attracted the attention of the ambitious and more numerous colonists in Massachusetts, just a few days' sail to the south. Opportunistically acting against the backdrop of European war between Britain and France, New England adventurers conquered Port Royal twice in the space of fifteen years and renamed it Annapolis Royal (after Queen Anne). By the Treaty of Utrecht in 1713, Britain formally won possession of most of Acadia from the French. In British eyes, this rough, bluff terrain had less the look of an Arcadia than of Scotland: on English maps it was named Nova Scotia, appropriately enough for the northern neighbor of New England. And just as residents of Hanoverian Britain worried about forging a union with Jacobite-leaning Scotland, Nova Scotia's eighteenth-century colonizers also had to come to terms with a white population of suspect loyalties.[15]

Considering how large the rivalry between Protestant Britain and Catholic France loomed in European and imperial politics, it was only to be expected that the relationship between Nova Scotia's new Anglophone rulers and their French Acadian subjects should prove tense. Acadians insisted on their neutrality in the face of British and French pressures, recognizing the authority of the British government while refusing to swear undying loyalty to the crown. But neutrality did not always count for much in the calculations of competing European empires. Acadia remained a focal point of French colonial desire. To the British and New Englanders, meanwhile, Nova Scotia looked like the natural extension of the colonies along the eastern Atlantic seaboard. They hoped to turn it into a beacon for Protestant emigrants from the British Isles and beyond. Such settlement would of course come at the expense of indigenous peoples—as North American colonization invariably did.[16] But its sponsors also championed a program of settlement as a self-conscious effort to assert Protestant Anglophone dominance over the Acadians.

On a July day in 1749, the newly appointed governor of Nova Scotia, Colonel Edward Cornwallis (uncle of Charles, Lord Cornwallis), sailed in a sloop of war around the Chebucto promontory on Nova Scotia's eastern shore, followed by thirteen transports loaded with more than twenty-five hundred colonists. The site had been promoted by Massachusetts lobbyists because of its deep-water harbor. ("Chebucto" means "big harbor" in Micmac.) The emigrants got to work cutting down trees, putting up tents and huts, and laying lines for the streets of a new town. They called it Halifax, for the president of the board of trade who authorized the scheme.[17]

A few days after the British disembarked, Acadians from nearby villages came to investigate the activity in the harbor. Cornwallis had been given a declaration to deliver to them. "In His Majesty's Name," Cornwallis told the Acadians that "in hopes . . . to induce them to become for the future True and Loyall Subjects, [the king] is graciously pleased to allow that the said Inhabitants shall continue in the free exercise of their Religion." But imperial tolerance rarely came without strings attached. Freedom of worship would be granted to the Acadians "provided" that they "take the oaths of Allegiance appointed . . . by the Laws of Great Britain," submit to the new government's "Rules and Orders," and "give all possible countenance and assistance" to British-sponsored colonists.[18]

Cornwallis's speech to the Acadians contained the seeds of a fast-growing conflict. With Anglo-French war a more common state of affairs than peace, the Acadians refused to agree to British demands that they take up arms in defense of the province—in defense, that is, against their own Francophone Catholic neighbors in Quebec. Resisting the British oath of allegiance, some Acadians began to flee the province. Others began to fight back. Faced with organized Acadian protest, British officials decided to adopt a policy similar to one recently prosecuted in Scotland, where after the Jacobite rising of 1745, British forces had swept through the Highlands confiscating land, destroying villages, and deporting suspected insurgents. The same would now be inflicted on Nova Scotia's "rebel" Catholics. In the late spring of 1755, British troops seized the French fort of Beauséjour, strategically poised on the isthmus that links peninsular Nova Scotia to the mainland. Renamed Fort Cumberland—after the royal duke in charge of slashing and burning the Highlands—the fort became the headquarters of anti-Acadian operations. Their land, houses, and live-stock would be confiscated, and, a British colonel informed the shocked residents of the Acadian community at Grand Pré, "you your-selves are to be removed from this province."[19] In groups of no more than one thousand people each, the Acadians were to be scattered across the American colonies from Massachusetts to Georgia.

The roundups started in the summer of 1755, a season when even a warm day in Nova Scotia may be clipped by a crisp maritime wind, and rain often mists over the waterlogged land. Hundreds of Acadians were held prisoner in the cellars of Fort Cumberland, awaiting forced ship-ment. From nearby Fort Lawrence, a lucky few dozen prisoners suc-cessfully escaped through a tunnel dug out with smuggled-in knives and spoons. In the vicinity of Annapolis Royal, British officers had to sift through a mixed Anglo-French community picking out Acadians to deport. When the transports appeared off Grand Pré, men were sent on board first, "praying, singing, and crying," followed some weeks later by the women and children, who were packed onto the ships in "a scene of woe & Distress."[20] In the wake of the evacuations, British and New England troops plundered Acadian hamlets, wrecked property, and burned whatever was left, thereby denying shelter to any escapees. By the end of 1755 alone, seven thousand people—about half the Acadian population—had been shipped off from Nova Scotia for the thirteen colonies. Despite an official dictum that whole families should travel together, the twenty-year-old commissary at Fort Cum-berland, Brook Watson, lamented that "I fear some families were divided and sent to different parts of the globe, notwithstanding all possible care was taken to prevent it."[21] Nearly three decades later, as commissary-general in British-occupied New York, Watson worked hard to provision the loyalist refugees and help stave off, for them at least, the worst of the sufferings he had witnessed among the Acadians.

The expulsion and dispersal of the Acadians held a mirror up to the experience of the refugee loyalists, to reveal a pattern of transconti-nental migration recognizable in outline, but terribly distorted and reversed. The whole scheme stood in stunning contrast to the image of a tolerant, multiethnic British Empire increasingly promoted in the wake of the Seven Years' War. Like American loyalists, Acadians refused to swear loyalty oaths; but their refusal was met with organized state-sponsored violence. The majority of Acadians relied on the char-ity and goodwill of hosts in the thirteen colonies who were very like their original antagonists, though more than a thousand Acadian refugees ultimately found asylum in their soi-disant mother country,

France. Like the Black Poor in London a generation later, these refugees—packed into the slums of French Atlantic port cities—were tapped as colonial pioneers and shipped off to populate outposts as far afield as the Falkland Islands. A more successful venture took shape on the Gulf coast of Louisiana, where Acadians became "Cajuns," rebuilding their community in a subtropical wetland thousands of miles from the northern arcadia they had left. From Louisiana's *nouvelle Acadie* to old *Acadie* in the north, later generations remembered the expulsion as *le grand dérangement*, embedded in an oral tradition of stories and songs.

The Acadian removals left an ominous shadow over the land reached by loyalist refugees thirty years later, as well as tangible legacies. In 1758, the Nova Scotia assembly legalized the government's confiscation of Acadian lands and restricted the role Catholics could play in provincial civil society. Instead, Acadian land was used to attract Protestant colonists, chiefly from New England. Each head of family who settled there was offered a thousand acres, free of quitrent for ten years. This land redistribution formed a clear precedent for the grants later extended to loyalist refugees. Nova Scotia, like East Florida, became the site of a land rush, as colonial and British officials issued 3.5 million acres to speculators. (Several individuals invested in both colonies.) The Proclamation of 1763, by which Britain prohibited North American settlement west of the Appalachians, further encouraged colonial migration to the north: Nova Scotia's population more than doubled in a dozen years.[22] These settlers, known as the planters, put a British colonial stamp on Nova Scotia that would be extended and deepened by the loyalists.[23]

On the eve of the American Revolution, two Yorkshire farmers visited this "Land of Liberty and Freedom" to investigate its potential for British emigration.[24] They judged the terrain promising for growing corn and rearing cattle. Halifax, recently a frontier outpost struggling through snowbound winters, had become a respectable capital, with a crown of stone fortifications, state buildings, and fine homes with large, leafy gardens. In place of the Acadians, now a largely Protestant white population approaching twenty thousand lived scattered across the province in small villages—among several thousand Micmac, Abenaki, and other Indians.[25] A small number of Acadians had actually returned, invited back to work on the dikes that only they knew how to maintain. Yet with such a small population on so much land, Nova Scotia remained far from flourishing, its promise as the next big thing of British North America still largely unfulfilled. Such was the landscape—depopulated in one imperial tragedy—that would provide a home for the subjects of another imperial upheaval in 1783. Could loyalist refugees turn this underdeveloped province into a thriving, profitable colony?

NOVA SCOTIA often made a poor first impression on Anglo-American arrivals, and the refugee Reverend Jacob Bailey and his family were no exceptions. As they sailed toward Halifax in June 1779, in flight from Maine, they winced at the altogether "unpleasing aspect" of this windy, barren region, with its "starving and misshapen" trees. But the Baileys were quite a sight themselves. They had escaped from New England with little more than the rags on their backs. Bailey vividly described his costume of battered shoes "which sustained the marks of rebellion and independence," rusty black trousers, an over-sized coat so stained "that it might truly be stilled [styled] a coat of many colours," and a "jaundise coloured wig" topped with a limp beaver cap. When their boat tied up at the Halifax quayside, so many people stopped to gape at the strange new arrivals that Bailey delivered an impromptu speech from the quarterdeck: "Gentlemen we are a company of fugitives from . . . New England, driven by famine and persecution to take refuge among you, and therefore I must intreat your candor and compassion to excuse the meaness and singularity of our dress."[26]

They were not to remain outsiders for long. No sooner had Bailey delivered his off-the-cuff introduction to the curious onlookers than he spotted a familiar face: one of the Baileys' neighbors from Maine pushed through the crowd, hailing his long-lost friends. Escorted by their countryman, the Baileys looped through Halifax's impressively "wide and regular" streets, taking in the "singular appearance" of the buildings about them, to the home of another former neighbor. Within hours of their arrival, they sat cheerfully around a hospitable table, fortifying themselves with hot tea and fresh white bread, and receiving visits from a series of old acquaintances and local dignitaries. Bailey's hostess promptly ordered him a new pair of shoes and stockings—"the sight and possession" of which "British manufactures gave pleasure to my inward man"—and the next day, the family found lodgings of their own on Pleasant Street, "the most elegant street in the town," in a tidy house with a wallpapered parlor.[27] Flanked by hawthorn trees and giving onto verdant groves "extremely pleasant to the sight and grateful to the smell," the Baileys' new residence made them feel as if they were more "in the midst of a woody country, than in the heart of a populous town."[28] The Nova Scotia assembly promptly voted fifty pounds for the family's relief, nicely completing their first week's welcome in this northern "land of freedom."[29]

Jacob Bailey found much to praise in his new home. "Notwithstanding the inhabitants are a mixture of several nations," he remarked, "besides english, scotch, Irish, Hessian and American soldiers with a large number of Indians, yet I was never in a town so regular and well governed. You may walk the streets all night without perceiving the least disturbance or noise, and what will astonish the New England puritans, you will scarce hear an oath as you are passing the street."[30] But his enthusiastic portrayals concealed the difficulties faced by this city in wartime. Despite the hopes imperialists vested in the harbor city, Halifax's moment of greatness (like Nova Scotia's more generally) had always seemed to be somewhere around the next corner. By the 1770s its population was actually shrinking. And the civic order Bailey so admired reigned in part because since 1775 Halifax, like the British garrison towns in the thirteen colonies, had been under martial law. Prices, always high because of the city's relative remoteness, shot up under the pressures of wartime dearth; the arrival of troops and loyalists following the 1776 evacuation of Boston had doubled rents.[31] Residents complained that "their Fields and Gardens had been plunder'd, the enclosures pulled down by the Soldiers."[32] Few refugees shared Bailey's positive assessment of the place, and many left as soon as possible for the apparently more congenial climes of Britain. Halifax was "a place I heartily wish none of my Friends may be driven to against their Wills," wrote one Bostonian, "As for those who chuse to come here I have Nothing to say to them."[33]

While Halifax residents found plenty to complain of, war made conditions even more difficult for those in the isolated settlements along the coast, regularly raided by New England privateers. They cruised into harbors, stole small boats, and sometimes landed to loot the towns—actions that some patriots deplored as likely to "occation more Torys than 100 such Expeditions Woud make good." In Liverpool, on the south shore, repeated attacks succeeded in frightening a relatively neutral population into action. It wasn't just that the Americans seized boats and guns—it was the shamelessness with which they did it, coasting into the harbor "with Drum and fife going, and whuzzaing." Liverpool's magistrate organized his fellow townsmen into posting night guards and coming up with a response plan for attack. By

1780, Liverpool had been fortified with a small detachment of regulars and fitted out a privateer of its own.[34]

With so many of its inhabitants having come from New England in recent decades, Nova Scotia might have seemed, on the face of things, to be a likely candidate for becoming a fourteenth American state. In 1775, the residents of Yarmouth petitioned the Nova Scotia government for formal neutrality, pointing out, "We were almost all of us born in New England, we have Fathers, Brothers & Sisters in that country, divided betwixt natural affection to our nearest relations, and good Faith and Friendship to our King and Country." (The government rejected their request as "utterly Absurd and inconsistent with the duty of Subjects.")[35] Bailey, who was appointed to a parish near Annapolis soon after his arrival, complained about the suspect loyalties of the "true sons of New England" he encountered there.[36] But Nova Scotia, geographically detached from the lower North American colonies, did not catch the revolutionary fire. Trade relationships bound the province far more tightly to Britain than to the thirteen colonies, making the prospect of joining the Americans economically unattractive. Then too, Nova Scotia's political culture, forged in a later, less politically conflictual era than New England's, made provincial governors more willing to negotiate and reach compromise with British authorities. (Similar factors help account for why the British West Indies also did not join the revolution.) So Nova Scotia remained loyal—but more by default than by declaration. This meant that though it offered a plausible asylum for loyalist refugees, the assertive loyalism of newcomers like Bailey stood in contrast to the more neutral sentiments of many prewar inhabitants.[37]

In the fall of 1782, a new governor arrived in Halifax to assume the reins of command. John Parr, like so many other colonial officials of the period, was an Irish-born army officer, blooded on the battlefields of Culloden and Minden.[38] Nearing sixty, Parr expected the job to be just the sinecure he desired at the end of a long military career. He reached his post in October in a moment of unusual calm, suspended between the cessation of hostilities with American patriots and the great influx of refugees to come. Settling comfortably into one of three governor's residences, he beamed with pleasure at his handsome income, his accomplished French chef, and well-stocked cellar, "determind to be happy and to make everyone so who comes within my line."[39] Within a matter of months, his vow would be tested to an extraordinary degree.

No sooner did Parr take office than he received a letter from Sir Guy Carleton informing him of the imminent arrival of more than six hundred loyalist refugees. Following Carleton's advice, Parr planned to give three hundred acres to every individual man, five or six hundred acres to each family, and to provide the newcomers with food, wooden boards, and other supplies. New townships were to be laid out with two thousand acres set aside for the church, and another thousand acres for a school.[40] Parr looked forward to welcoming these additions to the population, "especially to the Working people of whom there is great want."[41] It was a good thing he did, since the early trickle quickly swelled. In January 1783, the agents for the Port Roseway Association in New York came to scout out their settlement, for which they then had some fifteen hundred subscribers.[42] Refugee fleets began arriving from New York in April. By June 1783, Parr reported that "there have arriv'd in different places upwards of seven thousand persons including men women and children"; ten weeks later, the figure had become "upwards of 12,000 Souls." By the end of September, he said, "by Conjecture the whole already arriv'd may amount to upwards of 18,000 persons."[43] In late November he had revised his estimate upward to "venture to say, they considerably exceed 25000 souls," crowding into Halifax, Annapolis, and the new settlements at Port Roseway and Saint John.[44] When surveys of the Nova Scotia population were completed in the late summer of 1784, they counted more than twenty-eight thousand new inhabitants—twice the number of prewar settlers established in the province.[45] By the end of the migration, at least thirty thousand refugees had come into Nova Scotia, including approximately three thousand free blacks and twelve hundred slaves.[46]

Only a minority of the newcomers, mostly merchants and professionals, lived in Halifax. Few of them warmed quickly to the provincial capital. A Boston lawyer grumbled to another exile, "The weather is . . . abominably dull and the Town looks as Solitary compared with New York as Newport used to do when we were there. Every thing is intollerably dear and the old Inhabitants are accumulating wealth at a great rate by the exorbitant prices which they extort from the Strangers."[47] He did not wish on anybody "this stupid insipid, extravagantly dear and horrid rainy stormy hole."[48] As in Britain, many relied on friendship to lighten the hardships of exile. *Mayflower* descendant Edward Winslow, formerly the muster-master general of loyalist regiments in America and one of the most prominent leaders of the Nova Scotia refugee community, wrote cheerfully to his best friend in London that "we are now making regular arrangements for the Winter's amusement—Whist Club, Saturday's Club, &c &c &c." to tide them through the long December nights.[49] "This is a Young Climate," Winslow reported, "it has all the marks of Virginity about it. It breaks wind furiously. Spits a little. We however contrive to manage it."[50]

Much as some loyalists complained about Halifax, however (and it must be noted that Winslow and his friends were both remarkably privileged and rather curmudgeonly by temper), life for the refugees in other parts of the province presented far more serious challenges. Arcadia this was not, decided Colonel Robert Morse, chief British military engineer in North America, sent by Sir Guy Carleton in 1783 to scout out Nova Scotia's potential for loyalist settlement. The coast alone, with its "high, bold, rocky" cliffs, looked so "stony and barren" it was "commonly called an Ironbound Shore." As for "the interior of this country," Morse opined, it was "so much unknown that very little description can be given of it." Only a handful of real roads traversed the forests; the rest of the byways were "simply cuts through the Wood, with Trees marked to discover them." "From bad Weather, and other Obstructions common through a Country entirely in Wood," it took Morse fully two weeks to struggle across the one hundred miles separating Port Roseway on the south shore from Annapolis Royal on the opposite coast—and that was in congenial summer weather. There was promise in the land, to be sure, and some of Morse's findings echoed the optimistic reports circulating in New York newspapers in the summer of 1783. He envisioned sprawling orchards of apples, plums, and pears, pointed to bounteous wild fruits and nourishing populations of moose and black bear, and admired acre upon wooded acre of strong, straight timber. Yet so much of the terrain remained unbroken wilderness that it was hard to see how it could be turned quickly into farmland, while those areas already settled seemed to be in a sorry, "neglected state," a problem he attributed to "want of Industry, Money, and perhaps . . . protection."[51]

Despite Commissary-General Brook Watson's best efforts in New York to provide loyalists with food and supplies, most refugees arrived with few possessions to prepare them for the conditions in which they now found themselves. Jacob Bailey in Annapolis—population approximately twelve hundred—watched nine shiploads of New Yorkers disembark into a town barely able to contain them: "Every habitation is crowded, and many are unable to procure any lodgings." Remembering his own flight, he felt particular sympathy for the higher-class individuals who had "left large possessions in the colonies" only to find themselves in a "destitute condition, render[ing] them very affecting objects of compassion."[52] It did not help that so many of the New York refugees arrived in the late autumn, leaving Parr scrambling to get them "under Cover, before the severity of Winter setts in."[53] The Nova Scotian weather delivered a particularly nasty shock to arrivals from St. Augustine, "the poorest and most distress'd of all Beings, without a Shilling, almost Naked, and destitute of every necessary of life." "Charity has made me venture to give them warm Cloathing, with other things to prevent them from perrishing by the severity of this Climate," said Parr.[54]

During the war, the most "Sickly & Naked" refugees had been placed in the Halifax poor house and provided with clothes at municipal expense.[55] The sheer number of needy loyalists now swarming over the province called for response on a much larger scale. Carleton had promised Nova Scotian migrants twelve months' food rations, at the end of which time, it was hoped, they would be able to support themselves from their own crops. But the magazines at New York held only six months' worth of food for the émigrés, while Nova Scotia's farms could not alone make up the shortfall.[56] By the beginning of the winter of 1783–84, a provisioning crisis loomed. Though ministers in distant Whitehall seemed oblivious to the problems of supply, provincial officials confronted dearth up close in the refugees' drawn, hungry faces. Thousands of loyalists "must suffer extreme distress if deprived," wrote Major General John Campbell, one of the officials most closely involved in refugee relief, and "it becomes a very unpleasant task to refuse them, especially as the refusal has the appearance of a violation of public faith." As an emergency measure, at the height of winter he made the executive decision to buy an extra month's worth of provisions to distribute. He also dispatched a team of muster agents to travel through the settlements "to examine the Claims of every individual and to discriminate between such as are able to obtain a subsistence and the real objects of distress."[57] Through the spring and summer of 1784, the muster agents journeyed from one village to the next, counting residents and vigilantly separating out the small number of apparent fraudsters from among the thousands of loyalists who had a legitimate claim on government provisions.[58] In this as in other enumerative exercises (the assessment of loyalist claims and the registration of black loyalists, to name two), government relief was closely allied with government caution.

By April 1784, Nova Scotians had still not heard anything from Britain on how to resolve the food shortage, while the situation on the ground grew "serious and alarming." "Multitudes . . . will inevitably perish, unless the Royal Bounty of Provisions should be continued for some time longer," Campbell exclaimed, and forwarded an impassioned petition from New York loyalists complaining that "the condition of the poorer people who compose the bulk of the Loyalists is more pityable than when they quitted New York." "The sudden stoppage of the rations of so many thousand indigent people, most of whom are destitute of any trade or employment by which they can gain a livelyhood," he warned, "will raise commotions of the most dangerous tendency, especially as they considered the national faith pledged to them by the Commander in Chief at New York, for at least one years provisions from their landing."[59] Only in the late summer of 1784 did Campbell receive instructions from Whitehall approving of his purchase and extending the offer of government-supplied provisions by one further year.[60]

So famine would be averted. But a larger structural obstacle to loyalist settlement remained: the allocation of land grants. The promise of land had been the most powerful incentive luring refugees to Nova Scotia to start with. Yet as administrators and refugees alike discovered, it was one thing to offer every loyalist a certain number of acres—and quite another thing actually to dole the acreage out. Not least, preexisting territorial claims had to be resolved before any new allotments could be made. Fortunately for loyalists, few of the huge land grants made in Nova Scotia in the 1760s had been developed according to the stipulated terms, but surveyors still had to determine which ones could now be forfeited or escheated for noncompliance and reassigned.[61] A further claim on the land had been staked in the name of the king himself. The region's rolling forests of balsam fir allow one Nova Scotia county today to dub itself the "Christmas tree capital of the world." In the eighteenth century, dense evergreen woods made this region a valuable source for naval timber. By act of Parliament, "all White Pine Trees in Nova Scotia" and other valuable trees were "reserved to the Crown."[62] No forested areas could be cleared without a license from the surveyor-general of the king's woods, Sir John Wentworth.

As loyalist refugees spilled off their transports, two types of surveyors worked their way across the province, assessing land on both sides of the Bay of Fundy. Wentworth and his deputies tracked through the forests deciding which areas would be reserved, which opened for settlement. This was arduous work even in what turned out to be a relatively mild winter of 1783–84, as they dragged their boots through slush and clinging mud and sailed from point to point around the shore through incessant squalls. In later winters they would push through snow as high as their waists, stinging their faces when the sharp winds blew. After one such foray Wentworth's team staggered back into Halifax "having consumed all our provisions, and worn out the Men, to such a Degree, that they fell sick."[63]

The job of identifying lands to escheat and drawing up new townships fell to the surveyor-general of Nova Scotia, Charles Morris. Morris's father had held the position before him, but even the elder Morris—who had laid out the city of Halifax and helped mastermind the Acadian expulsions—had not faced the kinds of challenges confronted by his son in 1783.[64] Severely short of staff, supplies, and support, Morris advanced more than £1,000 of his own money and all his personal stamina to fulfill his mandate. By the end of 1784, he and his subordinates had defined nearly 1.2 million acres for escheating, approximately one-fifth of the land that had been granted during the midcentury boom. It was little wonder he found the job "next to Egyptian Slavery," and his gargantuan task would only be compounded by complaining loyalists and deputies clamoring for pay.[65]

Yet as rapidly as the surveyors worked, and as fully as government authorities tried to provide food and shelter, conditions for many refugees that first winter in the north remained rudimentary. In Annapolis Royal, Jacob Bailey fitted out his church "for the reception of hundreds, and multitudes are still without shelter in this rigorous and stormy season. Nearly four hundred of these miserable exiles have perished in a violent storm, and I am persuaded that disease, disappointment, poverty, and chagrin, will finish the course of many more before the return of another spring."[66] On Christmas Day 1783, one loyalist veteran, who had arrived at the mouth of the Saint John River with his regiment earlier in the summer, noted sadly that it was "the seventh Christmas since I left my beloved parents," the seventh since he had been "driven from my native home." He himself had much to be thankful for: already settled on a good lot, a few miles from the river's mouth, he counted his blessings "that I am now comfortable, where I daily see those who have neither house nor home, and scarcely nourishment or clothing to guard them against the attacks of this rigorous season of the year."[67] Farther upriver a girl from New York huddled under a government-issued tent and remembered how "the melting snow and the rain would soak up into our beds as we lay."[68] "Amazing discontents" swept across the camps on the Saint John River mouth for the simple reason that the blankets distributed to the refugees—rejected army surplus—were burned and full of holes, none "whole to cover the space of twelve inches."[69] Even in Halifax, comparatively well equipped with housing stock and food, loyalist veterans were "Daily & Nightly picked Up in the Streets in a perishing State & sent to the poor House afflicted with various Disorders."[70]

As Colonel Morse, the engineer, traveled from one refugee encampment to the next, he saw much that made him nervous: "If these poor People, who from want of Land to Cultivate and raise a subsistence to themselves, are not fed by Government for a considerable time longer, they must perish. They have no other country to go to. No other asylum."[71] Edward Winslow, the former muster-master from Massachusetts, formed an equally dismal view when, acting as land agent for loyalist regiments, he toured the communities of ex-soldiers on the banks of the Saint John River. He described to an old friend how

> I saw all those Provincial Regiments, (which we have so frequently mustered) landing in this inhospitable climate, in the month of October, without shelter and without knowing where to find a place to reside. The chagrine of the officers was not to me so truly affecting as the poignant <u>grief</u> of the men. Those respectable serjeants of Robinson's, Ludlow's, Cruger's Fannings &c, (once hospitable yeomen of the country) were addressing me in a language which almost murdered me as I heard it.
>
> "Sir, We have served all the War. Your honor is witness how faithfully! We were promised land, we expected you had obtained it for us, we like the country—only let us have a spot of our own, and give us such kind of regulations as will hinder bad men from reigning us."[72]

On receiving another of Winslow's angst-ridden reports about "the distressing State of the unfortunate Loyalists," Brook Watson in London forwarded it to an able Home Office secretary with the simple plea: "For Godsake see these matters effectually done away and guarded against for the future."[73]

For those who witnessed it—to say nothing of those who composed it—the flood of loyalists transformed Nova Scotia by doubling its settler population, filling forests with tent camps. It juxtaposed hopeful visions of colonial prosperity against spectacles of appalling hardship; it set the generosity of official promises against the cold reality of the possible. "This year is the crisis and in it Nova Scotia will take its cast,"

declared Sir John Wentworth in April 1784, "either to be a Noble Substitute to Britain for those lost [colonies] or it will become an Addition
to her burthens, and the Source of future troubles." Wentworth could
not yet predict any better than anyone else which outcome it was to be.

OF ALL the loyalist communities hastily developed in British North
America, the most impressive was the one at Port Roseway, south of
Halifax. This project was unusual among refugee settlements insofar as
the prospective migrants had taken great pains, before leaving New
York, to prepare for their exodus by sending scouts to investigate the
site, and assembling boatloads of supplies. But no amount of advance
preparation could stave off the sheer physical difficulties of creating a
new town from scratch. To this extent what unfolded at Port Roseway
served as a representative example of the material challenges confronted by so many refugees to British North America and beyond. It
proved typical in a further respect too. For the refugees brought more
than tools, horses, and grain with them from America. They brought a
set of attitudes, chiefly about land and about relations between black
and white, that sparked conflict both between loyalists and British
authorities and among loyalists themselves. The settlement of Port
Roseway provides a remarkable case study in problems and tensions
that would be reprised across the loyalist diaspora.[74]

In the spring of 1783, while Carleton and Watson attended to the
refugees' final pre-departure demands in New York, officials in Nova
Scotia prepared for their arrival. On April 21, Charles Morris
appointed a doughty fifty-three-year-old Massachusetts loyalist called
Benjamin Marston to survey the new town at Port Roseway. The job
made Marston a pivotal figure in the site's development, and gave him
keen insight into the travails of settlement—all of which he recorded in
a sharply observant diary, the best single source documenting these
events. A Harvard-educated merchant and cousin of fellow loyalist
refugee Edward Winslow, Marston actually had no prior experience as
a surveyor. If experience as a loyalist refugee were any qualification,
though, he had earned the position many times over. Chased by a
patriot mob from his home at Marblehead in 1775, Marston had fled
to Boston and in the space of just one year "lived in a town beseiged, on
board ships, both of war & others, have been at sea, in ye West Indies,
have lain in ye woods, have travelled by land & carried my baggage on
my back," was captured by a privateer, and endured a stint in jail.[75] In

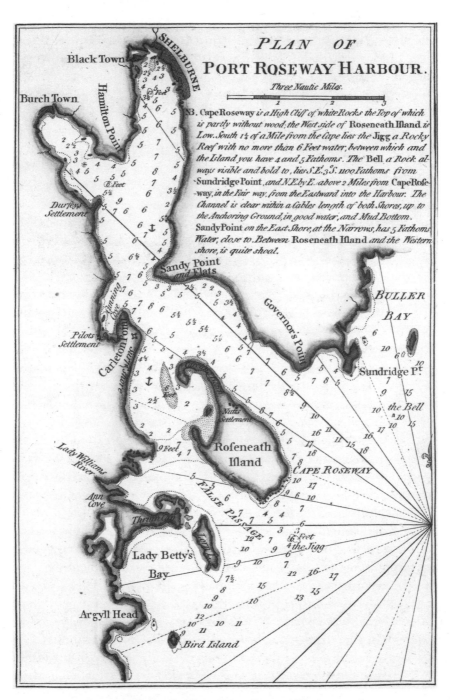

PLAN OF

PORT ROSEWAY HARBOUR.

Three Nautic Miles.

SHELBURNE

Black Town

Burch Town

Hamilton Point

Durfey Settlement

NB. Cape Roseway is a High Cliff of white Rocks the Top of which is partly without wood; the West side of Roseneath Island is Low. South 1¼ of a Mile from the Cape lies the Jigg a Rocky Reef with no more than 6 Feet water, between which and the Island you have 4 and 5 Fathoms. The Bell a Rock always visible and bold to, lies S.E.⅜.S. 1100 Fathoms from Sundridge Point, and N.E.by E. above 2 Miles from Cape Roseway, in the Fair way, from the Eastward into the Harbour. The Channel is clear within a Cables length of both Shores, up to the Anchoring Ground, in good water, and Mud Bottom. Sandy Point on the East Shore, at the Narrows, has 5 Fathoms Water, close to. Between Roseneath Island and the Western shore, is quite shoal.

Sandy Point and Flats

Governor's Point

BULLER BAY

Sundridge Pt.

the Bell

Finning Cove

Pilots Settlement

Carleton Point

Nutts Settlement

Roseneath Island

CAPE ROSEWAY

Lady Williams River

9 Feet

Ann Cove

Thrum Cap

FALSE PASSAGE

Lady Betty's Bay

the Jigg

Argyll Head

Bird Island

Captain Holland, *Plan of Port Roseway Harbor*, 1798.

the coming years he undertook numerous risky trading voyages from Halifax to the West Indies, in the course of which he was captured and jailed twice more. But a simple expedition around Nova Scotia in 1781 triggered his greatest ordeal of all.

On the return voyage from Annapolis to Halifax, Marston's leaky ship *Britannia* foundered in the ice near Cape Sable, a short distance south of Port Roseway. Gathering up their small stock of provisions, Marston and his crew set off on foot for Halifax, 130 miles away. It was mid-December, a bitter season of freezing nights and deep snows. The first night they "lodg'd comfortably" in the woods and feasted on a quarter of a duck and half a boiled flour dumpling each. The next days they walked. By the fourth day—despite the happy discovery of a few ounces of cocoa in their baggage—they trudged onward with "very heavy hearts our provision growing lower & lower." They saw nobody, heard no human sound, just the roar of the wind in the trees. By the tenth day, Marston could trek no farther. He gave his comrades his share of meat—freshly cut from their faithful dog Tiger, slaughtered the night before—and urged them to go on without him. They left him "very unwillingly"—for as everyone knew, to be alone in such circumstances was tantamount to a death sentence. All night and all the next day, then another night and day again, Marston lay helpless in the woods, gnawing on dried moosemeat, his thoughts spiraling into delirium. And then, footfalls, voices: two Indians standing above him. Rescue. Marston staggered into the Indian village "very Lame & very much exhausted wth fatigue & long fasting." He returned to Halifax in March 1782, clutching the weather-beaten diary in which he had recorded his experiences.[76]

Back in Halifax, Marston found his business dwindling to a standstill, his options and his cash spent.[77] The job offer of surveyor could not have come at a better time. Marston immediately set off down the coast, stopping on the way to collect surveyors' instruments. On May 2, 1783, he cruised into the forked harbor of Port Roseway. Rippled sheets of water ran into the horizon between dark wedges of land. Spindly herons strutted among the reeds. Wading onto the pebbly beach and into the tangled grass, he observed with relief that the soil looked more fertile than reports of the area had suggested. But Marston knew a thing or two about the Nova Scotian wilderness, and there would be labor aplenty in making this place a town. Tracking through the undergrowth on their first day ashore, Marston and his colleagues "fell in with a monstrous she-Bear," who fortunately turned and ran off into the woods.[78]

The next afternoon, the sails of the refugee fleet came into sight. By nightfall, thirty transports stood at anchor, carrying, Marston was told, three thousand people in their hulls. Marston set up a marquee on shore, and together with his assistants and settlers' representatives he spent a day combing over the area to determine on which side of the harbor they would lay down the town. But the following day, "the Multitude" of refugees rejected the surveyors' choice, "because— say they—'tis a rough uneven peice of Land—so they propose to mend the matter by choosing 3 men from every Company to do the matter over again." They ended up resolving on exactly the same site, on the northeastern finger of the harbor.

This would be just the first of many mounting frustrations Marston endured as he dealt with the refugees. (Even Sir Guy Carleton, back in New York, had lost his temper over their incessant complaints and demands. "It could not be supposed that Government would set a number of people down there, 'and say <u>we will do nothing more for you</u>, you may starve,' " he snapped. " '[I]f any were dissatisfied they had better <u>not go</u> if they could do better for themselves.' ")[79] On the first day of work Marston noted with pleasure that "the People began very chearfully to cut down the Trees—a new employment to many of them"—but in less than a week he grumbled about the "people turning very indolent." It wasn't that he had no sympathy for the settlers' predicament: none of them, after all, had been trained for this kind of work. "They are upon the whole a collection of characters very unfit for the business they have undertaken," he noted. "Barbers Taylors Shoemakers & all Mechanics bred . . . to live in great Towns—are inured to habits very unfit for undertakings w[hi]ch require hardiness, resolution, industry & Patience." Felling trees, uprooting stumps, moving boulders, draining marshland—it was arduous, Marston recognized, for those "who have come from easy Situations to encounter all the hardships of a new plantation."[80]

But Marston's sympathy had its limits. The disorganized mass of humanity pouring off the transports appeared an altogether "miserable sett" of characters. "These Poor People are like sheep without a Shepherd," he complained. "They have no [men] of abilities among them." Even their so-called leaders, the captains of each company of loyalists, had been plucked from "the same Class" as the settlers themselves and seemed little more than "a Sett of low lived dirty fellows whom meer accident has placed in their present Situation."[81] The title of captain "made many men here <u>Gentlemen</u> & of course yr wives & daughters <u>Ladies</u> whom neither Nature nor Education intended for that Rank."

"Real authority," Marston sniffed, "can never be supported without some degree of real superiority."[82] Meanwhile the makeshift tent village where they lived became a brewing, stewing, smelly place, littered with ashes and waste, and rudimentary taverns every few hundred paces. They drank and they drank, they drank and they sang ("such a damn'd noise"), and when they finished singing they had fistfights and boxing matches in the streets. On the king's birthday, the rambunctious settlers managed practically to burn the whole place down with a "nonsensical feu du joie." Two of the captains nearly fought a duel; others boasted that "they were going to effect a settlement without ye assistance of ye <u>Clergy</u> intending to have none of that order among them for the present." Truly, Marston sighed, "the D[evi]l is among these People."[83]

You could almost see the snobbery dripping from Marston's pen: the Harvard-educated New Englander sneering at New York riffraff. But there was something more about these loyalists that sharpened the edge of Marston's critique. For from the very first day when the loyalist "mob" had challenged his decision about where to site the town, Marston believed that this was not only a disorderly crowd—it was a radical one. "This curs'd Republican Town Meeting spirit," he growled, "has been the ruin of us already & unless checked by some stricter form of Governm[en]t will overset the prospect wch now presents of retreiving our affairs." "Too much Liberty," Marston knew, was a dangerous thing. He had seen its face in the mob that attacked him in Massachusetts; he had suffered its repercussions in patriot prison cells and in the wilderness, not many miles away, where he lay starving just eighteen months before. He could recognize the risks of freedom among these working-class refugees. In order for the loyalist colony to have any chance at success, he thought, "this curs'd levelling Spirit must be crush'd by every man whatever, or we shall be for reb[ellio]n soon."[84] So, on the rough ground of Port Roseway, Benjamin Marston clearly articulated what would become a recurring official commentary on loyalist refugees: American loyalists could shockingly resemble American patriots.

Granted, the equalizing aims of their "curs'd Republican principles" quickly broke down when Marston held the first lottery for town lots. "The idea of owning land is some how or other exceedingly agreable to the human mind," he noted; but there is nothing like competition over space to ignite animosities. "The Association from N York are a curious sett," Marston decided. They chose a committee that promptly excluded hundreds of refugees from entering the lottery at all.[85] The original settlers wanted to claim all the best lots for themselves, in order to sell them off at a profit to newer arrivals. Speculation in land grants became rampant, "so little do the Loyal Refugees have to do with <u>common honesty.</u>" Soon Marston was handling "a hundred applications in a day about bad house Lots & bad water Lots. Were I to enter into them all I should be constantly moving the people from one end of the Land to the other."[86] "My head is so full of Triangles, Squares, Parallelograms, Trapezias, & Rhomboidses that the corners do sometimes almost put my eyes out."[87]

All this hassle, though, attested to the stunning advances being made in turning the woods of Port Roseway into a full-fledged town. In late July 1783, Governor Parr sailed into the harbor, swore in five justices of the peace, a notary public, and a coroner, and gave the town a name: Shelburne.[88] (It was an insensitive choice, considering how many loyalists blamed Lord Shelburne for betraying them in the peace treaty.) Even before Parr cruised away again, new transports were arriving with hundreds more settlers from New York and beyond. By the end of the year, Shelburne's population had reached at least eight thousand, rivaling that of Halifax.[89] Governor Parr boasted that Shelburne was

> the most considerable, most flourishing and the most expeditious [town] . . . that ever was built in so short a space of time. . . . 800 Houses are already finished, 600 more in great forwardness, and several Hundred lately begun upon, with Wharfs and other Erections, upwards of 12,000 Inhabitants, about 100 sail of vessels, a most beautiful situation, the Land good, and the finest and best Harbour in the World. I have not a doubt of it's being, one day or other, the first Port in this part of America.[90]

Marston himself took a moment to acknowledge the fruits of the settlers' efforts when McGragh's Tavern hosted a ball in honor of the queen's birthday in January. "About 50 Gentlemen & Ladies . . . danced—drank tea—& play'd at cards in a house wch stood where 6 months ago was an almost impenetrable swamp," he mused, "so great has been the exertions of the settlers in this New World. The room was commodious & warm, tho in the rough the whole was conducted with good humour & satisfaction."[91]

While Marston justly congratulated himself on the progress made at Shelburne, he could have been equally satisfied by developments unfolding on the opposite side of the harbor. The stream of refugees arriving in Shelburne included hundreds of the black loyalists evacuated from New York, including the South Carolina runaway Boston King and his wife Violet. When the Baptist preacher David George came to Shelburne in the summer of 1783, having made his way to Nova Scotia from Charleston, he was pleased to find "numbers of my own color" already in residence.[92] Governor Parr had ordered that, instead of receiving allotments within Shelburne, the blacks should have a nearby settlement of their own. At the end of August 1783, Marston went over to the northwestern fork of the harbor with the commander of the demobilized Black Pioneers "to shew him the ground alloted for his People." "They are well satisfyed with it," Marston noted with pleasure, and he promptly began to lay out a sister township to Shelburne, to be named Birchtown after the commandant who had signed off on the black loyalists' certificates of freedom in New York.[93]

At Birchtown, a parallel loyalist community quickly took shape. Muster rolls from January 1784 show 1,485 free blacks living in and around Shelburne—making this one of the largest free black settlements in North America.[94] Where the Port Roseway associators had by and large been city dwellers unprepared for hard labor, these former slaves—like Boston King, a trained carpenter—possessed valuable skills for the work of settlement. "Every family had a lot of land," remembered King, "and we exerted all our strength in order to build comfortable huts before the cold weather set in."[95] Their initial allotments may have been smaller than those of the whites—a half or quarter acre each—and their resources fewer. Some could not complete their houses before winter began, and lived through the harsh months in shelters dug down into the earth and covered with crude slanted canopies of logs. Yet while in Shelburne the loyalists remained "much at variance with one another—a bad disposition in a new settlement," the black loyalists of Birchtown sustained an apparently close-knit community.[96] And if the devil was among the white loyalists of Shelburne, God glowed over the blacks and Birchtown.

They called the Methodist preacher Moses Wilkinson "Daddy Moses," less for his age (just thirty-six) than for the charisma he exuded—spinning ecstatic visions of salvation despite his own blinded eyes, a legacy of the smallpox he had survived in Lord Dunmore's floating town. During the war this former slave from Virginia had attracted a strong following among black loyalists, many of whom, such as George Washington's runaway slave Harry Washington, had traveled to Nova Scotia with him on the very same evacuation ship from New York. Once at Birchtown, Violet King would be the first of Daddy Moses's new converts, "so overwhelmed with anguish of spirit" by her experience that she became physically sick. Boston King struggled with salvation too, especially when he saw his coworkers assembling twice daily for prayer meetings. One January day King heard his friends relate the parable of the sower ("A sower went out to sow his seed: and as he sowed some fell by the way side . . . some fell upon a rock . . . some fell among thorns . . . and other fell on good ground, and sprang up, and bare fruit an hundredfold") and found himself overcome by a rush of enlightenment.[97] In the dead of a winter night, he trudged out into the snow and fell to his knees, "lifting up my hands, eyes, and heart to Heaven" to make a covenant with God. Before long, the Kings had joined the Methodist exhorters of Birchtown, and "the work of the Lord prospered greatly among us."[98]

The Methodists were not the only Christian community to flourish among the black refugees in Nova Scotia. David George quickly established a Baptist congregation too. It was God, as usual, who had guided him toward Shelburne. His family's journey aboard the evacuation fleet from Charleston had been arduous, twenty-two days during which the blacks were "used very ill on board." Halifax, their first point of arrival, appealed to George little more than it did to many white loyalist refugees. "Coming almost naked from the burning sands of South Carolina, to the frozen Coast of Nova Scotia, destitute of almost every necessary of life" (as Parr described the Charleston refugees), the Georges would have been woefully unprepared for the climatic shock of Nova Scotia in December.[99] What was worse, George saw no chance in this heavily white city "to preach to my own color." Hoping for more fertile ground in the new settlement at Port Roseway, he traveled south to join that burgeoning community in June 1783. "There were no houses then built," just a clearing in the woods—but that was enough for George. On the first night he arrived he walked out into the encampments and began to sing. Every night for a week he continued to sing hymns, attracting more and more curious onlookers, both white and black. His first Sunday in Shelburne, so many people attended George's morning service that "after I had given out the hymn, I could not speak for tears" of joy.[100]

Though many in this hardscrabble frontier town remained skeptical of the earnest black preacher, an acquaintance who knew George from Savannah—a white man—generously gave the Georges permission to build on his land. By the end of the summer, David, Phillis, and their children lived in a "smart hut" of stripped poles, collected their daily food rations like everyone else, and received a quarter-acre land grant of their own. Best of all, a stream ran through the lot, just as George had hoped, "convenient for baptizing at any time." His congregation prayed and grew and built. As snow melted off into spring, "the worldly Blacks, as well as the members of the church," cut down wood, sawed boards, chipped shingles, invested their few spare coppers in buying nails, and gradually the frame and fittings of a meeting house took shape. This would be the first Baptist church in Nova Scotia: a lineal descendant of the congregation formed a decade earlier in the backcountry at Silver Bluff. Among George's congregants, there flourished another American import at least as powerful as the "town meeting spirit" that Marston had identified among the whites.[101]

But a third American inheritance was also at work on the forked harbor: racial animosities. When George arrived in Shelburne he discovered that "the White people were against me." Part of the problem was that the fifteen hundred free black loyalists of the area lived alongside several hundred black slaves—a portion of the approximately twelve hundred slaves brought by white loyalists to Nova Scotia.[102] Deeply rooted ideas connecting servitude and skin color remained alive and well among the white loyalists of Shelburne. Such attitudes peered out, for instance, from the engineer Robert Morse's comparatively well-intentioned proposal for the Nova Scotia government to hire black loyalists on public works projects, "for it is known by experience that these Persons brought up in Servitude and Slavery want the assistance and Protection of a Master to make them happy; indeed to preserve them from penury and distress."[103] In reality, as former slaves relatively unused to wage labor, black loyalists frequently ended up pressed into work at exceptionally low wages. Many Birchtown blacks became indentured to whites in Shelburne, working under conditions that replicated their former positions of slavery. David George encountered another face of prejudice when he tried to baptize a white couple. Their relatives "raised a mob, and endeavoured to hinder their being baptized," and the woman's own sister "laid hold of her hair to keep her from going down into the water."[104]

The fraught business of land allocation continued to catalyze tensions among the refugees, and would have particularly negative consequences for the blacks. Severely short-staffed, Marston could not keep up with the need and demand for lots; yet in Shelburne as elsewhere, "many of the Refugees refus'd to carry the [surveying] Chain to lay out their own Land without exorbitant payment."[105] Every time he held a land lottery the complaints piled up. Some loyalists kept selling their lands at speculative prices, violating the terms of the royal bounty; others fraudulently entered children into the drawings. Still others resented restrictions placed by Wentworth on cutting clearings in nearby forests. Given the hostilities swirling about this place of hardship, it was dismally predictable that many whites especially resented the sight of former slaves receiving the same kinds of concessions they themselves were struggling to realize. Shortly after Marston began to survey Birchtown, "the <u>People</u>" of Shelburne appointed a surveyor of their own, who tramped about the area "with a pocket compass & codline" laying out fifty-acre lots. Blithely absorbing Birchtown into his assessment, the rival surveyor sold off lots to white loyalists "on ye Black men's ground" without "even a shadow of a license."[106]

Marston might have taken some grim satisfaction at knowing he'd seen trouble coming all along—if not, perhaps, anticipating exactly what form it would take. On July 26, 1784, "a Great Riot" burst out in Shelburne: "the disbanded soldiers have risen against the free Negroes to drive [them] out of Town because they labour Cheapr [than] they (ye soldiers) will." In scenes reminiscent of the revolution they all had fled, more than forty former soldiers stormed onto David George's land, swinging hooks and chains seized from ships. In the space of a few hours, they demolished George's house and twenty or so others belonging to free blacks, and threatened to burn the Baptist meeting house to the ground. Benjamin Marston rushed to the barracks for information and discovered that he too—the focal point of so much loyalist discontent—was imminently "threatned by the Rioteers." Before the day was out he clambered onto a boat among the newly constructed wharves and pushed off for Halifax and safety. For days afterward, he learned, the rioters would comb the countryside in search of the hated surveyor, ready to hang him on sight.[107]

While the town erupted around him, David George stood his ground. From his freshly built pulpit he continued to preach, undaunted when the mob came in "and swore how they would treat me if I preached again." He went on preaching until they returned with sticks and clubs; they struck and beat the pastor until they "drove me into a swamp." Under cover of night, George returned to Shelburne to collect his family and together they slipped across the river on the town's western edge—as he had slipped away so many times in his runaway years—and over to Birchtown, where he hoped they might be safe.

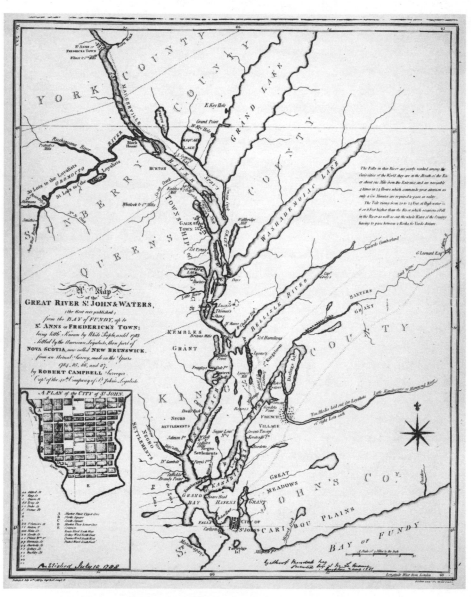

Robert Campbell, *Map of the Great River St. John & Waters*, 1788.

CHAPTER SIX

Loyal Americas

S HELTERING UNDER TENTS, subsisting on government-issued rations, and waiting impatiently for land of their own, Nova Scotia refugees discovered with exceptional immediacy what loyalists had been finding ever since the outbreak of war: their expectations from the British did not always square with the reality. What happened in Shelburne would be replayed in various versions around the sites of loyalist exodus. Land grants, at the heart of the Shelburne troubles, proved to be the single most potent source of discontent among loyalist refugees already severely tested by deprivation. Tensions over race formed another recurring theme, and would later inspire a dramatic sequel for the black loyalists of Birchtown, when the opportunity arose to emigrate to Sierra Leone. Most of all, the problems in Shelburne demonstrated how the formation of a new settlement wasn't just a physical challenge. It was a political one as well. Refugees had fled north united by their loyalty to the king and searching for continued security under British rule. Yet as the case of Shelburne showed, they could also sharply diverge between loyalists who favored centralized authority (like Benjamin Marston) and those who resented it (like the rioters who threw him out); and American loyalists could easily fall into conflict with imperial agents (of whom Marston was one). When opinion ranged so widely among loyalists—when even loyalists could become rebels, as Marston saw it—how could the British Empire actually manage to govern them? Nowhere would this question become more pressing, or be more systematically addressed, than in the provinces of British North America west of the Bay of Fundy.

From the comfortable distance of Whitehall, British ministers surveyed the development of British North America with pleasure. "His Majesty feels great satisfaction that the disputes and disagreements which had subsisted amongst the New Settlers have entirely subsided," Lord Sydney, the home secretary, wrote approvingly to Governor Parr of Nova Scotia in early 1785. He was pleased to see that the region fulfilled its primary goal of providing "a comfortable Asylum" for loyalists. Even better, Sydney harbored great ambitions "that they will, under the Protection of His Majesty's Government, become the Envy of the Subjects of the Neighbouring States."[1]

Some of Sydney's loyalist subjects shared his optimistic vision for British North America. "Lord Sidney's declaration quoted in your letter, 'That he will make Nova Scotia the envy of the American States,' has excited a kind of general gratitude," reported Massachusetts loyalist Edward Winslow from Nova Scotia. Winslow had recently returned from his depressing visit among the disbanded soldiers in the Saint John River valley, where he had witnessed firsthand the refugees' winter deprivation and hardship. But Winslow was also the sort of person who saw crisis as an opportunity for change:

> Such an event as the present, never happen'd before—perhaps never will happen again. There are assembled here an immense multitude (not of dissolute vagrants such as commonly made the first efforts to settle new countries,) but gentlemen of education—farmers, formerly independent & reputable mechanics, who by the fortune of war have been deprived of their property. They are as firmly attached to the British constitution as if they never had made a sacrifice. Here they stand with their wives and their children looking up for protection, and requesting such regulations as are necessary to the weal of Society.

With proper government, he averred, "Yes—By God! We will be the envy of the American States."[2] In his view it wasn't the United States that would inspire the world with visions of liberty and prosperity. It was the loyal, imperial provinces of British North America that could stand as a model, and Winslow laid out one of various projects for how.

His primary concern rested with the refugees he knew best, the struggling veterans along the Saint John River. Winslow placed the blame for their trying conditions squarely on the shoulders of Governor Parr in Halifax, whom he thought a remote and unsympathetic figure, who wasn't working fast enough to provide assistance. "The only possible means of effectual relief," Winslow believed, was to divide Nova Scotia in two and give the refugees on the western side of the

Bay of Fundy a government of their own. The creation of a new province, he argued, would let loyalists in the Saint John River valley enjoy a government both physically closer to hand (getting to Halifax entailed an arduous voyage by land and sea) and more responsive to their needs than Governor Parr appeared to be. And it wouldn't hurt that a new provincial administration would also conveniently produce a fresh slate of salaried offices that Winslow and his officer-class friends were busily positioning themselves to fill.[3]

In a lobbying effort that resembled earlier loyalist initiatives for financial compensation, Winslow successfully mobilized transatlantic support for his plan. Sir Guy Carleton, in particular, was won over by the scheme, which he hoped would form part of a larger restructuring of British North American government. Key ministers in London also gradually came around, despite the resistance mounted by Parr and his associates and the fall of the Fox-North administration, which was relatively sympathetic to loyalist interests. After seeing the parliamentary opposition effectively use the abandonment of the loyalists to bring down the Shelburne ministry, the new government under William Pitt could not afford to ignore the ever louder loyalist protests from across the Atlantic.[4] In June 1784, the Privy Council passed an order splitting Nova Scotia, just as Winslow wanted. Henceforth, Nova Scotia ended at the Bay of Fundy and the isthmus of Chignecto, which connected the peninsula to the mainland. The territory west of the bay, up to the borders of Quebec, became the province New Brunswick. (The same order also constituted Cape Breton Island as a separate province, but few loyalists migrated there and it would be united with Nova Scotia in 1820.) The partition of Nova Scotia—a strategy that in other, later contexts became a preferred British solution to colonial tensions— provided striking evidence of the loyalists' transformative impact in the north. They had succeeded in redrawing the map.

Spem Reduxit read the motto for the new province: Hope Restored. At Shelburne and Birchtown, and along the Fundy shores and Saint John River banks, loyalists had constructed new towns in the woods. New Brunswick gave them—or to be more precise, an elite among them—the chance to construct a whole colonial state along their preferred lines. American loyalists had never simply been reactionaries; many had advocated imperial reform in the thirteen colonies. The newly populous British North America now provided an arena for loyalist refugees and British authorities alike to advance fresh schemes for imperial government. So what would this loyal America look like?

Three different answers could be found in the settlements west of the Bay of Fundy. The creation of New Brunswick presented one clear expression of loyalist ambitions, with the establishment of a loyalist-majority state. An instructive point of comparison developed among the Mohawk refugees in Quebec. Receiving grants of land around the Great Lakes, the Mohawks sought not just to rebuild their villages, but to reestablish a confederation of Indian nations under the protection of the British Empire. Meanwhile, the emigration of approximately six thousand white loyalists into Quebec, though less numerically significant than the thirty thousand refugees who flooded into the Maritimes, inspired British authorities to reform government in that province, too, in an attempt to ward off the problems that had undone imperial rule in the thirteen colonies. The result was a piece of constitution-making with far-reaching consequences for the structure of British North American government.

Each of these projects made manifest a consequence of the American Revolution long recognized in Canada but less often noted in the United States: the revolution inspired the consolidation not of one country but of two.[5] While a republican America took shape to the south, loyalists and British authorities refashioned an imperial America in the north. These schemes for British North America shared the features of the "spirit of 1783" articulated across the British Empire, committed to territorial expansion and paternalistic government. In particular, they elucidated forms of imperial liberty in contrast to the republican liberty of the United States. As such, the loyalist migration helped lay the foundations of the distinctive liberal order discernible in Canada to this day.[6] Yet just as the process of nation-making in the United States provoked intense internal conflict, so the postwar development of British North America proved a highly contentious process. For all that loyalists coalesced around a generic commitment to monarchy and empire, they held widely varying views about what the empire should actually do. These three visions for the North American provinces, at once experiments in imperial possibility, opened up three contests over the nature and limits of imperial power, centering around popular representation, Indian sovereignty, and Anglo-Protestant hegemony in turn.

IF YOU STAND above the bend in the river, on the north side of the city of Saint John, you can watch a peculiar phenomenon overcome the water below. The whitecapped rapids rushing down toward the Bay of Fundy gradually calm and flatten, then begin to swirl up again—only this time flowing upstream instead. These so-called reversing falls are produced by the massive Fundy tides, which surge so high here (more than twenty-five feet) that they actually have the power to change the river's course. The Saint John's churning currents provided a fitting backdrop for the unsettled fortunes of the loyalist refugees living along its banks.

Loyalists had first thrown up their tents, wigwams, and rudimentary cabins at the river mouth in the summer of 1783. When New Brunswick's first governor sailed into the harbor less than eighteen months later, he saw an impressive town of nearly fifteen hundred frame houses. It was called Parrtown, at Governor John Parr's desire.[7] The new governor might have been equally pleased by the smaller settlement on the other side of the harbor, which was named Carleton, in honor of loyalists' hero Sir Guy. For the governor not only shared widespread loyalist skepticism of Parr; he was a Carleton man through and through. He was Sir Guy's younger brother, Thomas.

Just shy of forty years old, Thomas Carleton had enjoyed a more cosmopolitan if less glittering career than his brother. After serving in the European campaigns of the Seven Years' War, Thomas was sent to Gibraltar, a dreadful posting where he felt "shut up with a set of Gourmands" in a "horrid Prison."[8] Instead he secured leave to travel and embarked on an unusual circuit around the Mediterranean, visiting Minorca and Algiers, Italy and France—a tour that must also have honed his notable linguistic fluency: Carleton spoke Spanish, French, Italian, and German. In 1773, Carleton followed the lead of other adventurous Western military officers by volunteering in the Russian army, which was then fighting a major war against the Ottoman Empire. On the banks of the Danube, he had the chance to watch imperial history in the making, when the Russians repelled the Ottomans and forced them into the humiliating Treaty of Kuchuk Kainarji—widely recognized as the first serious blow to Ottoman stability. Entering the Turkish camp after the defeat, and then journeying on to Constantinople, Carleton saw firsthand how even the mightiest empires could be shaken.[9]

He passed the winter of 1774–75 in St. Petersburg, far from the rumblings of revolution that Sir Guy was handling in Quebec. But the American Revolution called Thomas across the Atlantic soon enough. Thanks to his brother's sponsorship, he served as quartermaster-general of the northern army and lived in New York City during the last months of the British occupation. After the war, Thomas joined his brother and influential loyalists in lobbying for a reconfiguration of North American government. While Sir Guy trained his sights on the top, aiming to be the first governor-general of a restructured British North America, Thomas worked the same circle of patrons to nab a junior office for himself. Thanks to his connections and the peerless Carleton name, he earned the appointment of lieutenant governor of New Brunswick, a position he would hold until his death in 1817.[10]

Carleton disembarked at Parrtown to a seventeen-gun salute and huzzahs from an eager crowd. "Long live the king and the governor!" they roared, and presented him with an address congratulating him on his "safe arrival to this new world." The city residents welcomed him as the very man to "check the arrogancy of tyranny, crush the growth of injustice, and establish such wholesome laws as are and ever have been the basis of our glorious constitution." What they did not necessarily expect was that the governor's vision of the best way to achieve all this was to rule from the top down, in concert with a small circle of appointed advisers.[11] Carleton's council was composed entirely of officer-class and landowning loyalists, men like and including Edward Winslow. Together they set about fashioning the neo-feudal oligarchy of their dreams, crafting a government that would be, in Winslow's revealing phrase, "the most Gentlemanlike one on Earth."[12]

Authorized by Whitehall to rule without an elected assembly for as long as necessary, Carleton and his council laid down the foundations of provincial order, issuing proclamations, answering petitions, clamping down on cross-border smuggling. Finding that "many families are yet unsettled," Governor Carleton extended the royal bounty of provisions to loyalist refugees for a further two years.[13] He continued to make land grants, taking care "to prevent any Persons disaffected to us and our Government from becoming settlers" by issuing lots only to those who took a loyalty oath.[14] Edward Winslow's cousin Benjamin Marston was one of several refugees attracted to the new province from Nova Scotia. In January 1784, Marston had celebrated the queen's birthday in Shelburne by noting his satisfaction at the great progress of settlement. Exactly one year later, he celebrated the same holiday in newly built Parrtown by attending the governor's "Ball & Supper at the Assembly Room" with "Between 30 & 40 Ladies near 100 Gentlemen. . . . The business was as well conducted as such an Entertainment could be—where so large a Company were to be entertained in so small a Room."[15]

The oligarchy's approach to government was underlined by Carleton's choice of a capital. In the winter of 1785, he went to investigate the settlements about seventy-five miles upriver at a place called St. Anne's Point. Loyalists there had endured a brutal winter. One eleven-year-old refugee vividly remembered the "oh, so cold" morning when her father guided them from their tent through the snow-choked woods, to the shelter he had raised in the forest. "There was no floor laid, no windows, no chimney, no door, but we had a roof at least," and with "a good fire" they survived into spring.[16] Many of her peers did not; a handful of their weathered grave markers still jut from the ground like broken teeth. But Carleton saw great potential at this bend in the river, and determined to fix the capital on the spot. In a stroke, St. Anne's Point became the city of Fredericton, "the Metropolis of New Brunswick."[17] There were two strategic reasons for Carleton's decision. By setting up an inland capital, the governor ensured the development of the provincial hinterland and a steady traffic up and down the Saint John River. He also created a capital suited to the "gentlemanlike government" he and his friends craved, dominated not by the merchants at the river mouth but by a landed elite. Beverley Robinson Jr. became an archetypal member of this group when he and his family moved to Fredericton in 1787 and, on their new estate opposite the city, resumed the genteel lifestyle the Robinsons had enjoyed in colonial New York.[18] Robinson was duly appointed to the governing council himself.

Fredericton was intentionally distant, in more ways than one, from the hoi polloi of the port. The rank-and-file refugees in Saint John had been growing restive at the government's autocratic style. They took early umbrage at the "petition of fifty-five" elite New Yorkers, including Charles Inglis, who requested giant 5,000-acre land grants, which they said they needed to maintain their positions of social prominence.[19] The ordinary men and women who composed the majority of refugees said this arrogant demand would force everyone else "either to content themselves with barren or remote Lands Or submit to be Tenants to those, most of whom they consider as their superiors in nothing but deeper Art and keener Policy."[20] As a satirical verse in an early Saint John newspaper decried, "A seven years war, a shameful peace / Brings us no nearer a release . . . / No recompense for service past, / The future too, an airy blast; / A piece of barren ground that's burnt, / Where one may labour, toil, and grunt."[21] Many refugees saw the establishment of New Brunswick itself as just another concession to the interests of the loyalist elite. And Carleton's failure to call an election for a provincial assembly did little to reassure them that their needs would be well met.

Early in his tenure, Carleton sought to assuage popular discontent by incorporating Parrtown and Carleton into the "City of St. John (which name has . . . been adopted in compliance with the desire of the Inhabitants)," under a charter modeled on that of pre-revolutionary New York City. The move (which Winslow reported "has prevented a serious representation from the people") gave Saint John its own municipal government with authority to legislate over trade, as well as establishing a court of common pleas and a local police force.[22] Many city residents, however, might have been worried on learning the attitude with which their governor had adopted the measure. "I think on all accounts it will be best that the American Spirit of innovation should not be nursed among the Loyal Refugees," Carleton observed to his London superiors. Why open the door to popular debate in matters where "the Crown alone is acknowledged to be competent"? He contemned the situation of neighboring Nova Scotia, in thrall, as he saw it, to an assembly composed of fractious New Englanders. In New Brunswick, "where a great proportion of the people have emigrated from N York and the Provinces to the Southward," Carleton hoped instead to "take an early advantage of their better Habits, and, by strengthening the executive powers of Government discountenance its leaning so much on the popular part of the Constitution." "A firm and orderly Government," he felt, would soon work its magic "in the manners of the people, & the introduction of the habits of decorum & Industry over the remains of dissipation so long maintained among them by the late war."[23]

Yet even Governor Carleton had been in North America long enough to know that executive authority had its limits. He "cautiously avoided" taking steps that "could lead to the belief of an intention to govern without an Assembly." Sooner or later, he would actually have to summon one. In October 1785, almost a year after he took up his post, Carleton issued the writs for New Brunswick's first election. In eighteenth-century Britain and America, the right to vote was usually granted only to men who met a minimum property qualification. Because all New Brunswick's settlers had arrived so recently and so many land claims were still pending, however, Carleton took the unusual step of extending the franchise to "all Males of full age who have been Inhabitants of the Province for not less than three months." (All *white* males, that is: New Brunswick's free blacks were bluntly excluded.)[24]

The governor may have hoped this unusually democratic measure would ease the "violent party spirit" that had long plagued Saint John.[25] But for ten years now, most of the refugees had lived through war and often martial law, without any semblance of political participation. The 1785 election seemed to release a collective sigh of relief. Benjamin Marston superintended the voting at Miramichi, on the far northern edge of the province, where he now acted as sheriff and surveyor. No friend of democracy, Marston saw shades of Shelburne in a community where "most of the People are illiterate & ignorant & much given to drunkeness. . . . They want two Things—Law to keep them in order & Gospell, to give them some better information than they seem to have." He was chagrined, if not surprised, when the residents returned "an ignorant cunning fellow" and a notoriously radical lawyer as their chosen representatives.[26]

In Saint John, especially, the election unleashed resentments that had been mounting since the earliest weeks of settlement. The geography of the city itself reinforced social and political divisions. In the streets around the waterfront, the so-called Lower Cove, lived shopkeepers, carpenters, laborers, and seamen who had tended to resent the authoritarian style of the governor and council. They produced a slate of candidates headed by a New York military veteran who had been one of the leading opponents of the "petition of fifty-five." On the higher ground sloping up toward Fort Howe, the Upper Cove, dwelt the provincial officeholders, lawyers, and educated professionals, who sponsored a government ticket anchored by the New Brunswick attorney general.

Voting began one November afternoon at McPherson's Tavern in the Lower Cove, with men filing into the room six at a time to register their votes. Two days later, in the interests of balancing out the tally, the sheriff shifted the polling place to the Mallard House Tavern in the Upper Cove, a stronghold of government support. Meanwhile at McPherson's, the Lower Cove voters continued to swig ale and talk politics. Talk became debate, debate turned into taunts and threats, threats provoked a brawl between rival supporters. Angry words flew around the tavern: "Let's go up—they are at Mallard's. Damn 'em—we'll Mob them." Seizing canes and pickets, somewhere between forty and one hundred Lower Covers left the tavern and marched up the streets to Mallard's. "Huzza for the Lower Cove!" they shouted, and tried to force their way past the government supporters guarding the door. "Come on, my boys, we'll soon dislodge 'em!" yelled one, hitting the man who held him back. Within moments, the protest became a riot: stones hurled through windows, clubs and fists smashed into faces, shattered glass, crockery, bones. The melee ended only when troops rushed down from Fort Howe, pulled the sides apart, and carted the protestors off to jail.[27]

Governor Carleton blamed the election riot on radicals bent on "intoxicating the lowest Class," and congratulated himself on the "decisive measures" he had taken to "check this licentious spirit." After a temper-cooling pause of one week, the polls reopened "and the Election is now conducted in the most peaceable manner."[28] Authority could suppress a riot easily enough. But when the sheriff counted up the votes, the result was less easily contained: the Lower Cove candidates had won by a margin of more than 10 percent. This was hardly the outcome Carleton and his circle had expected—and they had no intention of letting it stand. Instead of admitting the six Lower Cove candidates into the assembly as an opposition party, the government decided on a different tactic. They held a recount. Across a cheerless Christmas week of 1785, the sheriff pared through the returns, disallowed almost two hundred votes in favor of the Lower Covers, and installed the government ticket.

To supporters of the opposition, the news came like a knife in the back. "The House of Assembly . . . *ought to be tore limb from limb*," raged one distressed voter—who was promptly arrested for inflammatory speech, and made to apologize to the house on his knees.[29] Writing in the *Saint John Gazette*, a self-styled "Americanus" offered an emotional plea to his countrymen. "I . . . have been all my life a Loyalist," he insisted, yet how bleak this asylum had become: "We scarcely dare view tomorrow. Our Provisions almost gone. Our lands not brought into Cultivation. Our Loyalty suspected." "My distressed Countrymen," he urged, "Be firm in the protection of the Birth Right handed down to you, and supported by our happy Constitution . . . upon no Account . . . lose sight of what you are. In Fine, let the world know, as you know, the Rights you are jealous of" as "Descendants of Britons." The identity of "Americanus" would never be revealed, but the printers were charged with seditious libel and the newspaper shut down.[30]

Petitions against the election results promptly circulated around the province. The largest, signed by 327 men—nearly one-third of the electors of Saint John—sounded a clarion of discontent. "We have proven ourselves to be the most faithful and Loyal Subjects to the best of Governments," the petitioners insisted, and yet

we have publicly seen British Subjects confined in Irons. . . .
The Military introduced & unnecessarily & unlawfully patrolling the streets, during an Election. . . . Taxes levied by the
Incorporation Contrary to Law. . . . The freedom of Election
violated . . . in the most public manner. . . .

We most positively affirm these Proceedings to be unjust,
Injurious to the Freedom of Election, manifest Violations of the
Rights of the People & Subversive of the first Privileges of the
British Constitution.

Armies in the streets, unlawful arrest, unfair taxation, unjust elections:
the scene might as well have come straight out of the thirteen colonies
on the eve of the revolution. So might the loyalists' rhetoric. In much
the way that American patriots invoked the British constitution in
pleading for just representation, Saint John loyalists protested recent
events as a violation of their rights as British subjects. Their outrage
was directed at the king's colonial representatives, not against the king
himself: to this extent they remained loyal (as had the majority of
Americans before 1776). Indeed, their best hope for redress rested precisely with King George III. They called on the monarch to dissolve
the assembly and call a new election, thus ensuring that their "most
essential Rights can be preserved."[31]

In substance and in language, it was as if the proto-revolutionary
rumblings of the 1760s had migrated with the loyalists from the thirteen colonies to New Brunswick. But Governor Carleton had no
intention of backing down. Swiftly branding the opponents of government as disloyal, he pitted loyalist against loyalist. To stop antigovernment petitions from gaining momentum, the assembly passed "An Act
against Tumults and Disorders, upon pretence of preparing or presenting Public Petitions . . . to the Governor"—effectively making
such petitions illegal. When four men came to present the protest document to the assembly, they were duly arrested. They went to trial
together with the detained Mallard House rioters and the seditious
newspaper printers, and were "severally convicted and punished" for
their insolence.[32] "I can venture to assure your Lordship that faction is
at an end here," Carleton declared in the spring of 1786. The important difference between loyalist Saint John and revolutionary America
was not so much in the content of the protest. It was that this time,
imperial government won. Authority, it seemed, trumped a popular
call for liberty. The falls had been reversed.

The 1785 election in Saint John would be one in a series of vivid political clashes around the empire between American loyalist refugees and British authorities. What lessons did its participants take away? To Lord Sydney in Whitehall, the whole thing could have been avoided if Carleton had not been so democratic in the first place, and "had confined the Electors to such Persons only as were in Possession of lands . . . as by that means many of the more refractory and disorderly of those (who I suppose were of the lowest orders of the People) would have been excluded."[33] The upheaval appeared to offer further proof—as if the American Revolution had not been proof enough—that a little democracy could be a dangerous thing. Carleton, in retrospect, would doubtless have agreed. To him, the unrest thoroughly vindicated an authoritarian response to protest. "Considering the motly description of persons collected here from the various departments of the Army, and the disorderly conduct many of them have been habituated to during a long Civil war," he observed, "it seems of the last consequence to hold the Reins of Government with a strait hand, and to punish the Refractory with firmness."[34]

Yet the tumults in New Brunswick also plainly revealed that political schisms among British subjects did not simply end with the war. They highlighted an important continuity, forged by loyalist refugees, from the pre-revolutionary into the post-revolutionary British Empire. A commitment to "British rights" could be held with equal sincerity by people with otherwise divergent views of what those rights actually were.[35] Such differences continued to split British subjects on both sides of the Atlantic. Decades later, one of the British sergeants at Fort Howe—who may have helped break up the Mallard House riot—remembered the 1785 election as a milestone in his own political genesis. He described how, in an effort to tip the election further in favor of the government ticket, Upper Covers had considered extending the vote to the soldiers in the garrison (a measure of dubious legality). "Our *Officers* were, of course, of the Upper Cove party," the sergeant recalled, but when the enlisted men were asked which side they supported, "my six grenadiers thundered out from under their great hairy caps, 'for the Lower Coves, Sir, to be sure!' " "It was odd enough," he reflected, "that we should have had this unanimous feeling in favour of the popular party in the Province; but we had it, and all the cats o'nine tails at the command of the Holy Alliance would not have rooted it out of our hearts."[36] The sergeant's name was William Cobbett, and when he recorded this memory in the years after Waterloo, he had emerged (after many years as a staunch conservative) as one of the leading English radicals of his age. However much he may have distorted his rec-ollections to suit, Cobbett mobilized these memories of the 1785 elec-tion in the service of the ideals for which he would become famous, as a champion of parliamentary reform in Britain itself.[37]

And what about the loyalists? What the election demonstrated most strikingly of all was that "loyalists" could come in many political shapes and sizes. They agreed on one thing: they upheld the authority of the king—at least as long as the king did his part by them in turn. In this key respect, loyalists *were* loyal; and this was one vital reason why the government did prevail. But monarchism would be about the only principle binding together a disparate population of American refugees. Edward Winslow and his friends were delighted to see dissent suppressed and "gentlemanlike government" confirmed. They wanted loyalist New Brunswick to be a stable, hierarchical alternative to the seeming anarchy of the republican United States. But the "envy of the American States" did not look so appealing to the denizens of the Lower Cove, or to the veterans in their makeshift dwellings upriver—or to black loyalists like the former sergeant Thomas Peters, squeezed onto poor lots on the fringes of Saint John and Fredericton and excluded from voting altogether. Faced with government repression reminiscent of the pre-revolutionary thirteen colonies, one of the printers convicted of seditious libel decided to return to the United States—which was, at least, his home. Such political differences make it entirely impossible to portray all refugee loyalists as convinced "tories." Rather, in testing the limits of government power, they waged contests over liberty and authority that would continue to inflect the region's political culture and find echoes elsewhere in the loyalist diaspora.

THE MEMBERS of the New Brunswick elite were not the only loyalists to cultivate bright expectations of what the post-revolutionary British Empire could provide. On and around Lake Ontario, another group of refugees—the Mohawks—pioneered their own alternative to the United States, and in the process articulated another variation on the theme of liberty and sovereignty within the empire. As Joseph Brant and his followers saw it, the attraction of resettling in Quebec wasn't just about land. It also had the potential to provide the foundation of a new Indian confederacy in and around the Great Lakes, linking the Iroquois with nations ranging far to the west. Here, Brant and others hoped Indians might establish an autonomous domain between the empire and the republic. Might, that is, if they played their hand right, as the British Empire's independent allies and as its loyal subjects.

To the Iroquois nations allied with Britain, the peace treaty of 1783 had appeared as devastating as it had to so many white loyalists. Not only did it make no special provisions for Indians against the menacing, land-hungry Americans; it simply did not mention them at all. Furthermore, the treaty required Britain to abandon its forts among the Great Lakes, an act that would remove an important bulwark of protection for Indians against U.S. expansion. Worst of all, the borders fixed between Quebec and the United States ceded extensive Indian territory to New York State, in flat contravention of the 1768 Treaty of Fort Stanwix. Recognizing how appalling these terms would be to the Iroquois, British officials tried to keep the news secret from their allies for as long as possible—and when at last they revealed the awful truth, they attempted to dull the blow by issuing the Indians with eighteen hundred gallons of rum.[38] As one Mohawk spokesman declaimed, the king "had no right Whatever to grant away to the States of America, [the Mohawks'] Rights of properties without a manifest breach of all justice and Equity, and they would not submit to it."[39] "England had Sold the Indians to Congress," said Joseph Brant.[40] So much for being loyal.

The Iroquois saw the peace as an even greater betrayal of their interests than southern Indians had regarded the cession of Florida. For as alarmed as the Creeks, and others felt at being surrendered into Spanish hands, that was still better than falling directly under the rule of the United States. Decades of conflict over land had been capped by eight years of a war that, in Indian country, seemed little better than a catalogue of what later generations might dub war crimes. Unremitting violence had sent hundreds of Iroquois over the border into Quebec in exactly the way black and white loyalists fled to British-held cities for security. At the war's end at least two hundred Mohawks from New York's Fort Hunter lived at La Chine, below Montreal, while another large community clustered on the western frontier, near Niagara, at a place dubbed "Loyal Village" by British authorities.[41] Now these Iroquois migrants performed the same depressing calculations as other loyalist refugees about where to settle permanently.

Yet for all their distress, the Iroquois enjoyed an important advantage over the southern Indian nations. Situated in the borderlands between British Canada and the United States, they straddled a vital imperial frontier. In the south, British agents had primarily wished to retain Indian allegiance to protect trade and to support nebulous future initiatives against the United States or maybe Spain. In the north, where the British Empire bordered the United States, the British had an active investment in retaining Indian loyalty. The Mohawks' location thus placed them at the crossroads of British and American interests. The Americans wanted to lure them back to the Mohawk Valley, neutering their potential for making trouble on the frontiers; the British hoped to keep the Mohawks on the Canadian side of the border, thereby preserving the alliance. Chased by two suitors, the Mohawks could compensate for their relative vulnerability by playing the powers off each other.

The Mohawks had a further asset, one that Joseph Brant was especially well positioned to exploit. Because of their long connection with British imperial officials, they could mobilize personal relationships to broker a better future. Not only did Brant enjoy kinship with two successive superintendents of Indian affairs, Guy Johnson and Sir John Johnson, and a position in the Indian department himself; he also found a relatively sympathetic interlocutor in General Frederick Haldimand, governor of Quebec since 1778. Haldimand, unlike his predecessor Sir Guy Carleton, actively cultivated Iroquois support—and he shared the Indians' sense of betrayal at the terms of peace. "My soul is completely bowed down with grief at seeing that we (with no absolute necessity) have . . . accept[ed] such humiliating boundaries. I am heartily ashamed," Haldimand confessed—unwittingly echoing the sentiments of Thomas Brown, Indian superintendent for the south, on learning of the abandonment of the Creeks.[42] In much the way that Sir Guy Carleton insisted on abiding by British promises of freedom to the black loyalists, Haldimand felt personally committed to maintaining British support for the Indians. His own personal dignity, as well as Britain's national honor, stood on the line.

During the trying months of 1783, Haldimand, like his counterparts in East Florida and Nova Scotia, coped with a steady influx of loyalist refugees from the American states. While some of those heading to Nova Scotia brought rudimentary supplies with them, the overwhelming majority of migrants into Quebec were virtually destitute: by the end of 1783, one tally suggested that more than three thousand refugees stood in need of basic clothing.[43] Sadly, Haldimand had painfully few resources at his disposal. His office laid out a series of brutally simple cost-cutting strategies:

> Sick & infirm women with young children & those whom from
> their situation, cannot go out to service. Instead of alowing

them lodging money seperately to be placed togather [*sic*] in one or two houses. Wou[l]d be a considerable saveing in regard to Fireing & Lodging Money. . . . Some of Those, might also be usefully employed in making blankett coats Leggins &c. at a Fixt & Cheaper rate than the Canadians. Royalists getting into service (as so great wages is given in this province) to be struck off fireing & provisions if they big [beg] sickness are obliged to leave their places to be taken care off till again provided for. The same rule might be observed in regard to trades people or artificers.[44]

Inspectors of refugees were instructed to distribute full rations only to "those objects whose necessities <u>absolutely</u> require it."[45] Refugee complaints soon followed. Without government relief, they pleaded, "we shall not be able to over come the Seveir and approaching hard Winter," suffering as they were in "a Strange and Disolate Place where they can get nothing to Work to Earne a Penney for the Support of Each Other, . . . much more the Bigger part of us Without one Shilling in our Pockets and not a Shew [shoe] on our feet."[46] One inspector told of another "very sickly" group of refugees, of whom "several died owing as they think for the want of provision & Cloathing"—only to be reprimanded "for representing the distresses of the Loyalists."[47]

Such desperate economizing toward white loyalists made Haldimand's concessions to the Indians even more striking. For against the backdrop of dearth and want, he assumed a major extra expense on the Indians' behalf: he arranged to give Mohawk loyalists a land of their own. In the autumn of 1783, the Indian agent Daniel Claus (a son-in-law of Sir William Johnson, and another close connection of Joseph Brant's) traveled to La Chine to encourage the Mohawk refugees there to remain in British Canada, rather than return to their ravaged ancestral lands in New York. It was, he recognized, "a disagreable proposal . . . to a people who lived at their ease, upon a rich Tract of Country, left them . . . by their ancestors from Time immemorial." He also knew how hard it would be for them to abandon "the Graves of their deceased Friends and Relations to be demolished and abused by their Enemies." But Claus successfully persuaded the community to "pitch up on a good spot" in British domains "where they and posterity might spend their days undisturbed."[48] At the invitation of British officers, Joseph Brant and some Mohawk associates selected a site on the Bay of Quinte, near present-day Kingston. "With great Chearfulness" Haldimand arranged the purchase of this land from the Mississauga Indians for the Mohawks, and granted provisions to carry them through the first hard seasons: "I have always Considered the Mohawks as the first Nation deserving the attention of Government and I have been particularly interested for their Wellfare & reestablishment."[49]

Though personal conviction may have informed Haldimand's actions at least in part, he justified his expense to Whitehall on strategic grounds. This settlement, he argued, might ensure the Mohawks' loyalty for generations to come. By the end of 1784, more than fifty-six hundred white refugees had clustered at Kingston (then called Cataraqui) and along the Saint Lawrence River as far as Sorel, on sixteen settlements so hastily formed they were known by number.[50] Haldimand hoped that the Mohawks could be folded into this band of new villages, becoming a sort of loyal anchor to the chain of British-allied nations that he wanted to set as a buffer between Quebec and New York. As an extra means of ensuring Mohawk support, Haldimand ordered adjacent houses built in Kingston for Joseph and Molly Brant.[51] All these measures stood out as relatively unusual in the context of Anglo-Indian relations, evidence of how desperately the British needed the Mohawk alliance to ensure imperial security. Placed in the context of provisions for loyalists, however, Haldimand's treatment of the Mohawks appeared less exceptional. By granting the Indians land, Haldimand extended to them the same central concession the British government gave to other loyalist refugees. Such actions demonstrated afresh that British officials saw the Mohawks not only as sovereign allies: they were also loyalists, and won privileges accordingly.[52]

So where did that leave the Mohawks themselves? Joseph Brant intended to make the most of the Mohawks' double role. The question that most concerned him was how much autonomy he would be able to carve out on the strength of it. He had always believed the British offered more for the Mohawks than the Americans. That judgment would only be confirmed by unsatisfying negotiations with the United States to reclaim Iroquois lands. A fresh treaty of Fort Stanwix, signed in 1784, further hemmed in the Iroquois, and confirmed Brant's desire—in line with Haldimand's—to keep the Mohawks on the British side of the border.[53]

For Brant, however, the attraction of the British Empire wasn't about cozy assimiliation into Canada, as British authorities may have hoped. Rather, he saw the empire as the best arena in which to rebuild Mohawk sovereignty. Empire could provide land, land could provide a foundation for unity—and unity, he knew, meant power. One of the first things Brant did after learning about the peace treaty was to reach out to the nations to the west, hoping to form an Indian confederacy even greater than the Six Nations had once been. At a giant conference at Sandusky, in the Ohio Country, representatives from dozens of nations, including the Creeks, met to discuss their position, pressed between the British Empire and the United States. Brant delivered a compelling speech in support of unification under Britain's aegis. At the end of the meeting, thirty-five nations pledged their support to an Iroquois-led confederacy.[54]

With this vision of western cooperation in mind, Brant set his sights on a different tract of land for Mohawk settlement. It lay on the Grand River, between Lakes Erie and Ontario, a good strategic spot from which Brant could communicate easily both with Indian nations to the west and with neighbors in New York State. Haldimand paled at the prospect of a further expensive land acquisition. But still feeling guilty over the peace treaty, and eager to retain Brant's support, he agreed to buy the territory. In October 1784, "in consideration of the early attachment to [the King's] cause manifested by the Mohawk Indians, and of the loss of their settlement which they thereby sustained," Haldimand authorized the purchase of the Grand River tract and granted it to the Mohawks for "them and their Posterity . . . to enjoy for ever."[55] This expenditure for the Indians would be among his last: three weeks later, Haldimand returned to Britain, recalled from his governorship for overspending.

In the middle of 1785, the Indians of Loyal Village traveled to their new imperial home. (The two hundred or so Mohawks who had originally come from Fort Hunter opted to remain at the Bay of Quinte with their own leader.) The grant marked a significant achievement for the Indians: this was to be the ground on which they could rebuild their personal livelihoods and reestablish their collective power. But Joseph Brant's business with the British Empire was not yet done. For like other loyalists, the Indians not only wanted a new place to live, they wanted compensation for what they had lost in the United States. The Mohawks had repeatedly approached the British government with their claims, but to no avail. Fed up with delays, Brant decided to cut straight to the heart of the empire. While his people settled down on the Grand River, Brant sailed for Britain, determined to pursue the issue of compensation in person.

Shortly before Christmas 1785, the British press heralded the arrival in London of "Colonel Joseph Brant, the celebrated King of the Mohawks." As ever, Brant maneuvered in two guises: as Thayenda-negea, "King of the Mohawks," he undertook "an embassy to the British Court," while as Joseph Brant he deployed his Anglicized charm and social connections to win favor. Taking up lodgings with his friend Daniel Claus, Brant promptly sought an audience with Lord Sydney. There he laid out the case for Mohawk compensation—speaking in Mohawk, with an old military colleague acting as inter-preter. On behalf of "the whole Indian Confederacy," he said, "We were struck with astonishment at hearing we were forgot in the treaty."[56] In the same terms used by other loyalist refugees, he asked Sydney to respect "the claims of the Mohawks for their losses . . . in consequence of their faithful attachment to the King, and the zeal they manifested in supporting the cause of His country against the rebel-lious subjects in America." British officials had promised him "that their losses should be made good," he concluded, and it was past time for them to follow through.[57] As he waited for an official answer to the Mohawks' collective claim, Brant pursued his and Molly Brant's per-sonal claims for compensation, in the amount of about £1,200 each. He also sought the half-pay (pension) that his position in the Indian department entitled him to but that he had never actually received.

Meanwhile, as on his visit to London in 1775, Brant found himself lionized by high society. People clamored to meet this brown-skinned warrior prince from the North American woods, one of the many indigenous imperial subjects whom late-eighteenth-century Britons embraced as real-life "noble savages." If the response to him hadn't much changed, though, how much had Brant himself? Ten years after he had been painted by George Romney, Brant sat again for a portrait, this time by the American-born artist Gilbert Stuart. Plumed again in red feathers, he sports a medallion with the king's image beneath his shining gorget. But where the younger Brant, in Romney's canvas, looked his viewer in the eye with a kind of sultry swagger, this Brant's gaze drifts downward. He has been visibly aged by a decade of conflict: his left eye droops, creases outline his chin, sagging flesh bunches above his collar. At a glamorous costume ball, guests admired Brant's appearance in Mohawk dress, with half his face streaked in scarlet paint. An Ottoman diplomat at the party, thinking that Brant was wearing a mask, reached out and grabbed the Mohawk's nose to yank away his presumed facial covering. Suddenly an "appalling war-whoop" sliced through the room. The buzz of conversation stuttered into silence, as Brant whipped his tomahawk from his belt and swung it about the Turk's head, the steel blade flashing in the lamplight. For one breath-catching moment, the company stood suspended—until Brant replaced his weapon, and they broke into a din of relief. Nobody could ever quite figure out whether Brant meant it all in fun or not; maybe the danger was part of his appeal.[58]

Four months after his audience with Lord Sydney, Brant received his long-awaited response about Mohawk claims for compensation. The king, explained Sydney, denied the "right of individuals to compensation for losses sustained by the depredations of an enemy." But "as a proof of his most friendly disposition toward them," and with "due regard to the national faith, and the honor and dignity of his crown," the king agreed as a special favor to compensate the Mohawks regardless.[59] The king's response demonstrated exactly the same logic that Parliament had shown toward other loyalists. Mohawks had no more "right" to compensation than any other loyalists—but the "national faith" would see right done by them in the end.

Brant returned to Canada later in 1786 flush with winnings great and small: a silver snuffbox given to him by Charles James Fox, a gold watch, a locket with his portrait in miniature, a pair of caged canaries. He had secured his half-pay as a retired captain. Better yet, he had received £2,100 in goods and bills, handsome reimbursement for his and Molly's losses.[60] As for the British promises of compensation to the Mohawk nation, those would also gain material reality. He reached the Grand River to find the new Mohawk village, "Brant's Town," nicely taking shape. A tidy settlement of log houses with glass windows, surrounded by well-farmed fields and mills, Brant's Town resembled the Mohawk Valley villages they had left behind. A schoolhouse had been built at British government expense. At the center of the village stood the largest monument to the Anglo-Mohawk relationship: a trim white clapboard church, with a sharply angled façade and square steeple, set off by pointed finials. When the missionary John Stuart (with whom Brant had lived in the 1770s) visited the "mohawk village on the grand River" a couple of years later, he found "about 700 souls," most of them "my old Parishioners," lodged among "a great Number of good Houses."[61] He was especially pleased to find the church equipped with rich crimson fittings, a pipe organ, and a resonant bell imported from England. The royal arms hung over the pews, while the silver communion vessels, Stuart might have noted, were the same ones he had once used in his chapel at Fort Hunter, in New York.

To Stuart and other white visitors, Brant's Town appeared a model of Anglicized civilization among the savages. "Indeed, I was so pleased by that Country," Stuart declared, "that I was strongly tempted to remove my Family to it."[62] Brant, for his part, played the lordly role to perfection on his Grand River manor. His elegantly furnished house was ringed by a neat picket fence, and a British flag flew out front. When he entertained white company, he raised toasts to the king and queen with glasses of madeira served by his black slaves, who were kitted out with frilly neckerchiefs and silver buckles on their shoes. After dinner, he led his guests through expertly danced Scotch reels and entertained them with tales of his military exploits. The man who had cut a swath through London society never failed to impress white callers at Brant's Town with his "civilized" deportment and hospitality.[63]

But Brant's Town was also, in a sense, Thayendanegea's town. (The Mohawks called it Ohsweken.) For all that Brant took satisfaction at the sight of the flourishing church, school, and farms, it must have been equally gratifying to watch his vision of a broad Indian confederation begin to come alive. Within a year of the move to Grand River, nearly two thousand Indians lived on the reserve—not just Iroquois, but Algonquian groups and even a handful of Creeks and Cherokees, settled in their own small villages by nation.[64] Shortly after his return from Britain, Brant attended another major Indian council at which the participating nations reaffirmed their solidarity and issued a pacific overture to the United States. It seemed, at least for now, that his new Indian confederacy was successfully taking hold on the borders of the British Empire and the American republic.

One can never really know how much Brant struggled with his joint role, the need to be at once Mohawk leader and loyal British subject. Nor, frustratingly, do many sources survive to attest to the attitudes of the majority of Indians who lived under his authority. Did they see the Grand River settlement—as New Brunswick's advocates were inclined to understand their own province—as a victory snatched from the jaws of defeat? Peace, they had surely learned, could prove as challenging a thing as war. In an ideal world, Brant thought, he could "unite the Indians together and make such a peace between them and the United States, as would remove all prejudices and enable us to set quietly down on our seats, free from apprehensions and jealousy."[65] But this was no ideal world. The Mohawks had lost their native lands, villages, and property. They had lost, to varying degrees, real political independence in a reshaped landscape, pressed between British and American states. In later years, Brant would have much to complain of in the actions both of the British, who increasingly hemmed in Indian land rights, and of his fellow Iroquois, who steadily trickled east into New York State, abandoning his model society.

Still, it seemed clear to Brant that living in the midst of the British Empire as allies or subjects was a better option than dwelling in the reach of the republic, ravenous for Indian land. In the mid-1780s, he had only to compare the Mohawks' situation with that of the Oneidas who had chosen to stay on the American side of the border. They returned to their scorched homelands but proved unable to fend off New York speculators. The British Empire had one major thing to recommend it to the Mohawks: it provided a nominally protective umbrella for Indian interests. And for all the limits placed on Indian expansion in the empire, Brant's vision of a British-allied Indian confederacy became an influential forerunner for subsequent attempts to assert Indian sovereignty—from the well-known ambitions advanced by the Shawnee leader Tecumseh in the Great Lakes, down to plans for a loyal Indian state in the Mississippi Valley promoted by the loyalist and adoptive Creek William Augustus Bowles. The step away from the United States remained, for the Mohawks, a step forward. What they did not yet know was how limited the prospects for real power would be in the British Empire too.

WITH NOVA SCOTIA's boundaries redrawn to accommodate loyalists, and the Mohawks resettled on new land, a third cluster of settlements—in the province of Quebec—invited a further question about the governance of British North America after the loyalist influx. How would the increase in English-speaking Protestant residents affect a province with a French Catholic majority population? In some ways this would have the most far-ranging consequences of all. For British administrators it slotted into a broader concern about how best to organize and govern what now remained of Britain's empire in North America. Primary responsibility for addressing it fell to the one man who had already done so much to accommodate *habitants* and aid loyalist refugees alike. Guy Carleton's challenge now was to see if he could achieve both goals at once.

Each time Carleton returned to North America he arrived in a grander station than before. He had first set foot on the continent as a young colonel; next he came as a general and colonial governor; and then he arrived as Sir Guy, knight of the Bath and commander in chief. After the war, Carleton hoped to advance another step. Joining the circle of loyalist refugees lobbying for reform of British North America, he promoted the partition plan for Nova Scotia and the creation of an all-powerful governor-general to superintend all the provinces. While Thomas Carleton was dispatched to New Brunswick, Sir Guy intended to claim the premier position for himself.[66]

The job as such was Carleton's for the taking, but there were two snags. First, the Pitt ministry resisted the idea of creating a governor-generalship with the extensive authority Carleton had in mind, which would have given him virtual autonomy from London. (At exactly the same time, the powers of the governor-general in India were being hotly debated in connection with East India Company reform.) Second, more intractably, Carleton set a stiff asking price for accepting the post: he wanted an aristocratic title to go with it. It was more than mere vanity that motivated Carleton's demand. He knew that a title was the best way to assert power in the British world: "An English peer had a more eligible Standing than any crowned Head."[67] If he was going to be responsible for rebuilding the postwar empire in America, he needed all the authority he could muster. This task, he felt, demanded more than a general; it required an aristocrat. Through two drawn-out years of negotiations, he insisted on a peerage while the king and government equally persistently refused. At last, Carleton's stubborn patience prevailed. Though he did not get all the powers he had hoped for as a governor-general, he did get the aristocratic title he craved, to become the first Baron Dorchester. He chose his style to evoke a semi-imagined ancestral connection to a small Oxfordshire village (not the better-known Dorchester in Dorset); selected a motto to underscore his military accomplishments; and devised a coat of arms with a pair of beavers rampant, acknowledging his ties to North America. Fortified with the accoutrements of aristocracy, the newly minted Lord Dorchester sailed west once again, as governor in chief of Britain's continental North American empire.[68]

Dorchester (as he would henceforth be known) understood the contours of his position about as well as anyone. In a light moment in London, he and his former secretary Maurice Morgann "had been amusing themselves with the Probability of the Restoration of the Empire" in America. "It was their Idea that no Government was the Offspring of Theoretic Premeditation but of Accident, Contingency

& Distress."[69] Like many Europeans at the time—to say nothing of his loyalist friends—Dorchester thought it likely that the United States would break up, and that parts of it might fall back into European hands. Even if the nation did survive, nobody could yet predict which power—the United States, Britain, Spain, or France—would gain control of the strategically vital regions of the Great Lakes and the Mississippi Valley. At the same time, Dorchester recognized the intrinsic challenges that the independent United States posed to British North America. In population and economic development, British North America compared very unfavorably with the United States. New York State alone had about two and a half times more people in it than all of neighboring Quebec.[70] Dorchester also knew, as the architect of the Quebec Act, how difficult it could be to reconcile the competing interests of British North America's ethnically diverse population. The arrival of more than thirty-five thousand refugees made British North America into even more of a mosaic of white, black, and Indian residents, speaking several tongues and worshipping in many churches. All that the newcomers seemed to share were varying degrees of deprivation and discontent. Now Dorchester had to assimilate these embodiments of "accident, contingency & distress" along with British North America's prewar residents to form a stable, viable imperial state.

Returning to the Château Saint-Louis for his third tenure as governor, Dorchester looked out over a familiar view of rooftops and weathered stones and the vertiginous drop down to the river below. Yet he encountered in 1780s Quebec a reconfigured political and social scene. Although the *habitants* still outnumbered Anglophone settlers by a ratio of five to one—and more like forty to one in the St. Lawrence River valley—the six thousand or so loyalist refugees in the province formed an influential interest group.[71] As in New Brunswick, the loyalist elite was especially well represented in the governor's own entourage. Notably, Dorchester's longtime collaborator William Smith accompanied him to Quebec to serve as chief justice, and provided an influential source of policy advice. Dorchester's official instructions reflected the changed priorities of post-revolutionary British North America. Whereas in the 1770s he had been told to ease Anglo-French relations, and attended closely to the interests of the French Catholic majority, now he held an almost diametrically opposed assignment: to propose reforms to government that would cater to the increased Anglophone population.

This commission reflected a central lesson that British officials drew from the American Revolution. The empire needed reform, constitutional reform. Government had already been restructured in Ireland and India; similar reformist impulses influenced the rising opposition to the Atlantic slave trade. Dorchester and his advisers now brought the reforming mandate to British North America. William Smith had a clear diagnosis of Quebec's problems: "This Country by a Mistaken Policy had been locked up from the State Physicians: King Lords & Commons."[72] British North America, he thought, should become the seat of a strengthened and revamped British constitution, designed to prevent the problems that had brought down the empire to the south. That meant, at base, strengthening the authority of the crown (and the king's executive representatives) over and above the power of colonial assemblies—a desideratum already manifested in New Brunswick, among other sites of loyalist exodus. In the case of Quebec, in particular, it also meant privileging the British community over the French. In the courts, Smith promptly set about asserting the primacy of English civil law over French Canadian law in cases involving loyalists. Charles Inglis's confirmation as bishop of Nova Scotia cemented the institutional significance of the Church of England in the provinces, despite the fact that the white population was largely composed of Catholics and dissenting Protestants. Dorchester and Smith also put forward a new system of free primary school education in Quebec designed to raise the *habitants* out of their "State of *base Barbarism*."[73] In one arena after another, the powers of the establishment were reinforced, and British interests trumped French.[74]

Both these priorities would be enshrined in the reform that Parliament ultimately passed into law, the Constitutional Act of 1791—also known as the Canada Act—a foundation stone in modern British imperial government. Largely authored by the secretary of state in London, Canada's new constitution transparently represented the authoritarian attitudes of the Pitt administration. The act reads in part like a retort to the American Revolution—and to the fresh troubles brewing in revolutionary France—by explicitly bolstering the powers of church, aristocracy, and king. In particular, it directed that a full one-seventh of land in all new townships would be reserved for the Church of England, a source of future concern not just to French Catholics but to Methodists and other Protestant nonconformists. Although it provided for elected assemblies, it also established influential legislative bodies, modeled on the House of Lords, to be composed of appointed members. It even allowed the king to create a hereditary

aristocracy in Canada. For all these reasons, the act has been interpreted as a counter-revolutionary measure, of a piece with turns to
authoritarianism around the empire.[75] (In British political history, the
debate over the bill would best be remembered as the moment when
the longtime friendship between the radical Charles James Fox and the
increasingly conservative Edmund Burke—already strained by con-
flicting views on the French Revolution—definitively ruptured in a
dramatic showdown on the floor of the House of Commons.)[76]

In the event, Dorchester himself played a relatively small role in
fashioning the terms of this legislation as compared with the Quebec
Act, which he had effectively drafted. This was telling, since the
Canada Act countered the spirit of the Quebec Act in one vital way.
(Officially, indeed, it repealed parts of the Quebec Act, deemed "in
many Respects inapplicable to the Present Condition and Circumstances of the said Province.") Whereas the Quebec Act had provoked
Anglo-Americans by extending civil liberties to French Catholics, the
Canada Act made a clear statement in favor of Anglophone—and
specifically loyalist—interests. Following the model of partition in
Nova Scotia, it divided Quebec in two. Henceforth the eastern part of
the region became Lower Canada (present-day Quebec), retaining its
overwhelmingly French Catholic population. In the west, the new
province of Upper Canada (present-day Ontario) was dominated by
Anglophone, Protestant settlers, most of them loyalist refugees. Under
the old provincial boundaries these colonists had languished on the
thinly settled fringe of a province dominated by Catholic *habitants*.
With the creation of Upper Canada, loyalist refugees earned an
administration of their own—making Upper Canada the western
equivalent of New Brunswick. In a further concession to loyalist interests, land tenure rules in Upper Canada were defined so as to facilitate
settlement with very low fees attached. The division of the provinces
took a major step toward transforming this frontier, within a generation, into the heartland of Anglophone Canada.

But perhaps the most revealing way to understand the Canada Act
is in relation to the emerging United States. It was not so much a
counter-revolutionary gesture, in the conventional meaning of "reactionary," but a post-revolutionary response to a changed political landscape.[77] Famously, the "British constitution" remains an unwritten
one, resting not in a single foundational text but in an evolving series of
documents and precedents. The Canada Act stands out as one of several instances where post-revolutionary British administrators sought

to make explicit the constitutional terms for imperial rule, over white as well as nonwhite subjects. Nor was it coincidental that Britons wrote this constitution for Canada at exactly the same time that Americans fashioned a republican constitution for the United States. Civil war made Britons and Americans alike rethink the basis of North American government, and record those thoughts in foundational documents.

How well did the new imperial constitution sit with its North American subjects? In pre-revolutionary British America, the idea had been that colonial subjects were virtually represented in the British parliament at Westminster. This act, instead, effectively cloned Westminster and transplanted it in Canada. But not all loyalists embraced what, in legislative terms, was a distinctly metropolitan British creation. As one Kingston loyalist grumbled, "A Government should be formed for a Country, not a country strained and distorted for the Accommodation of a preconceived and speculative scheme of Government."[78] Dorchester himself had mixed feelings about the act. Although he "agreed the Colony could not rise but upon British Principles," he balked at the pace and nature of change. "*Doucement, doucement*," he urged an eagerly reformist Smith.[79] Dorchester especially resisted dividing the province, partly on the grounds that this would estrange French Canadians. Throughout his twenty years of governing in North America, he had promoted a kind of rule that sheltered varied ethnic groups under a canopy of imperial authority. These were the values he saw enshrined in the Quebec Act, and the principles he upheld when he superintended the evacuation of the black loyalists. The Canada Act seemed, though, to marginalize this priority. Dorchester—who shared his brother Thomas's taste for oligarchy—also objected to the formation of another provincial assembly, as partition would entail. Instead, he continued to advocate creating a single overarching governor-general, and coauthored a proposal to this effect with Smith, which partly resembled Smith's earlier idea for an American parliament.[80]

Their rival plan for reform to some extent anticipated the recommendations of the Durham Report of 1839 for "responsible government" and the union of Upper and Lower Canada—a key moment in the ascent of liberalism in British North America.[81] But it was a telling reflection of Dorchester's lack of influence over the 1791 Canada Act that he was not even in North America when it came formally into effect. Nor did he approve of the man appointed to serve as Upper Canada's first lieutenant governor. Dorchester had favored his old friend Sir John Johnson for the post—a natural choice given Johnson's ties to the Mohawks and his prominence among the white settlers of Upper Canada, many of them veterans from his own disbanded loyalist corps. The British government chose instead John Graves Simcoe, a thirty-seven-year-old Revolutionary War veteran and member of Parliament. Simcoe had seen extensive service in North America as colonel of the Queen's Rangers, but had few ties to the loyalist elite. This was an advantage, as far as British administrators were concerned—it made him more likely to promote the metropolitan version of government than to indulge in provincial variations—but the appointment came as another slap in the face to Dorchester. Chagrined by these events, Dorchester sailed home on leave before Simcoe reached Canada. The two men would clash repeatedly in years ahead over issues of policy and chain of command, culminating in Dorchester's resignation in 1794.[82]

Unlike Dorchester, with his vision of an authoritarian, multiethnic empire, Simcoe came to Canada committed to building a new Britain in the west.[83] He proudly declared that "this province is singularly blessed, not with a mutilated Constitution, but with a Constitution . . . [that] is the very image and transcript of that of Great Britain."[84] The land might be undeveloped, the people poor, but with British constitutional principles guiding his hand he could shape, he hoped, an imperial utopia.[85] Distancing himself yet further from the American refugees, Simcoe decided to locate the capital of Upper Canada not at Kingston, the largest town in the province, but to found a new town altogether, and camp at Niagara in the meantime. Before leaving Britain, he had prepared for this wilderness government by buying (from the estate of Captain James Cook) a "canvass house similar to that sent with the Governor of Botany Bay."[86] Elizabeth Simcoe, his wife, animatedly documented their western progress in a journal she kept for four of their young daughters, whom they had left behind in Devon. She described how the "canvas house" became almost comfortable with partitions raised and a stove to warm it. Between its stretched fabric walls, the Simcoes held quasi-viceregal court. They hosted visitors from Joseph Brant—charismatic as ever, sporting an English coat smartly draped with a crimson blanket—to Prince Edward, the king's fourth son, then stationed in Canada with his regiment. They played endless rubbers of whist, and drank tea from a china service shipped from England. While John Simcoe toured the western reaches of the province, Elizabeth spent her days at Niagara much as she might in England, drawing, riding, reading the latest works on chemistry and art, and collecting plants and butterflies to send to her daughters.[87]

In the summer of 1793, the Simcoes crossed Lake Ontario to the site the governor had chosen for his capital. Elizabeth admired the landscape of vine-covered poplars and firs, giving way to sparkling sandbanks along the lakeshore. As she explored the creeks and inlets around the Toronto peninsula, only the quiet plash of canoe paddles interrupted the bustle of the living wilderness, with loons howling and wild ducks flapping out from the rushes.[88] To loyalists in Kingston, Governor Simcoe's dream of building "a second London" on this remote spot looked like a "piece of political Quixotism . . . perfectly Utopian."[89] But the governor would not be dissuaded: soldiers of the Queen's Rangers (Simcoe's old regiment) set to work clearing the forests and laying down roads, preparing a military base that could double as an administrative capital. Simcoe named the frontier settlement York.[90] By the time the city was incorporated as Toronto in 1834, it had become the cultural and commercial center of Upper Canada.

Later generations of Ontario conservatives hailed Simcoe for the very things that many of his loyalist contemporaries condemned: they saw him as the founding father of a particularly British, and anti-American, version of Canadian government.[91] Yet for all that he came bearing a set of metropolitan British attitudes, Simcoe made one fundamental concession to his North American context. He helped make Upper Canada more "American" still. Simcoe recognized that the secret to economic success and security lay in increasing the province's population—especially with flourishing New York State to compete with just over the border. In the way that Nova Scotia's governors had once looked to New England for colonists, Simcoe sought to attract new residents for Upper Canada from the United States. With so many Americans migrating west in those years, he thought, surely some could be drawn to settle in Upper Canada if the land prices were right. He could hardly hope for better pioneers. In their ethnic range, their religious beliefs, their familiarity with the climate and the land, they differed not at all from the loyalist refugees. All they had to do was accept the British monarchy in place of the American republic. And that, Simcoe congratulated himself, ought to be easy to do. "There are thousands of the inhabitants of the United States whose affections are centered in the British Government & the British Name," he believed.[92] Besides, what was the Canada Act if not a perfected version of a British constitution tried, tested, and found true? The United States was so young it had barely stumbled through its first steps; its constitution had only just been ratified, and its future shape remained unclear.

Just weeks after landing in North America, Simcoe issued a proclamation inviting Americans across the border. In exchange for a simple oath of allegiance to "the King in his Parliament," settlers could receive grants of two hundred acres for a third the cost associated with land in the American west.[93] "A great many settlers come daily from the United States, some even from the Carolinas," noted Elizabeth Simcoe.[94] Ultimately some twenty thousand "late loyalists" streamed into the region, part of the huge surge of white settlement into the North American west, and helping to shift British North America's own Anglophone population center away from the Maritimes. Upper Canada might be a British province, but as this influx from the United States demonstrated, its people remained emphatically continental American in origin. (Only after 1815, with the border closed to Americans, would immigrants from the British Isles outnumber U.S. arrivals in British North America.)[95] To be sure, some American loyalists returned permanently to the United States; but no evidence suggests that this occurred in anything like the great numbers for the immigration to Canada.[96] More often, loyalists paid temporary visits to the United States and kept up relationships with family, friends, and business associates—further reinforcing the ties among North American kin and neighbors. War had divided Americans into patriots and loyalists, and a new border divided empire from republic. But peace drew divided communities together as well, around a common quest for land, profit, stability, and security. As pioneers on a North American frontier, Upper Canadian loyalists shared more with their counterparts south of the border than they did with the British officials who ruled them—a position that would be complicated and sharpened by the War of 1812.[97]

At the same time, Canadian residents prided themselves on having achieved under British rule a comfort their U.S. counterparts had not. "When any stubborn Difficulty occurs here, we have one general Remedy which we use on every Occasion," reflected the missionary John Stuart in Kingston; "that is, 'How happy are we, compared with the Subjects of the distressed, & divided States?' And the great Influx of Inhabitants from the american Frontiers (with melancholy Complaints of Taxes, Poverty & Tyranny) confirms us in an opinion which 'tis our Interest to cherish."[98] Stuart had a point. American patriots had waged a war against taxation without representation. Yet here in British North America, it seemed that American loyalists had won that very struggle. With the creation of New Brunswick and Upper Canada, loyalists had nominally gained greater representation through the formation of two new administrations and assemblies. That there were decided limits on popular participation, in turn, seemed only an advantage to loyalists when they compared their situation with conditions south of the border, replete with rampant electioneering, libelous newspapers, and sporadic political violence. (All of which phenomena encouraged some U.S. leaders to become more authoritarian themselves.)

The issue of taxation presented a still more favorable contrast with the United States, in their view. In Upper Canada, with an administration and defense forces heavily subsidized by Britain, loyalists and immigrants received ample grants of cheap land and paid virtually no taxes. In the United States, saddled with war debt, state governments charged far more for land, and demanded substantially higher taxes in turn: New Yorkers in the 1790s paid five times more tax on their land than their peers in Upper Canada. In short, to be an American gave you purchase on active citizenship—but you literally paid for it. To be a British subject in Canada meant acquiescing to imperial authority, but cost you little in terms of tax burden.[99] (And when those tax burdens did change in the 1820s, it helped foment rebellion in Upper and Lower Canada just as it had in the thirteen colonies in the 1770s.) A century later, loyalist descendants in Canada would still take pride in being "the lightest-taxed and the freest people on the American continent."[100] The equation of freedom from taxes with freedom more generally remains a resonant definition of liberty in Anglo-American political culture.

Of course, Stuart knew there was no such thing as an easy life on the frontier. He had seen crop failures plunge the community into need; he had lost one of his own children in frigid Montreal, in the harsh conditions of exile.[101] As a refugee himself and minister to so many more, he also knew how displacement and loss could haunt the mind even after the body moved on. British rule was no panacea. In Kingston and York, as in Saint John and Shelburne—as in pre-revolutionary Philadelphia and Boston—loyalists bridled against perceived infringements of their rights and alien policies imposed from outside. Simcoe soon clashed with loyalists in the Upper Canada assembly who wanted to hold New England–style town meetings. His plan to phase out slavery in Upper Canada met resistance from loyalists in turn, many of whom had brought slaves from America, and had little sympathy for the abolitionist ideology so rapidly winning converts among metropolitan Britons, Simcoe among them.[102] The Canada Act in some ways sowed as many problems as it solved, enshrining commitments to Anglicanism and a tendency toward oligarchical rule that provoked intensifying opposition in the years to come.[103] Imperial rule could always make enemies out of its own loyal subjects.

So what, then, did loyalism mean in post-revolutionary British North America? The answer came down to the core tenet around which loyalists had always coalesced. However "American" loyalist refugees remained in political temperament, they were not ultimately anti-imperial: they did not want to break their ties with the king or British Empire. By the time Simcoe founded York, a decade after the British evacuation of New York, white, black, and Indian refugees had fashioned viable, enduring alternatives in British North America. They had, for a start, survived. From conditions of serious deprivation—hunger, homelessness, exposure in harsh climes—they had built houses, docks and mills, churches and schools. They enjoyed a clarified and expanded provincial government. They were united under a monarchy that offered protection; they had access to ample land at low cost. Indeed, for the most marginal of British subjects, imperial authority could be a welcome thing, by offering protection against white colonial neighbors. Black loyalists like David George, persecuted by racist fellow refugees, could turn for defense to British laws upholding his freedom. The Mohawks could appeal to the crown in pursuit of land and a degree of sovereignty much harder to achieve in the majoritarian republic to the south.

In some sense post-revolutionary British North America presented an answer to the great "what if" question of the American Revolution: how might the thirteen colonies have looked without independence? British North America witnessed neither reactionary reversal nor mere status quo. An influential interpretation of the genesis of Canadian political culture portrayed loyalists as importing American liberalism into Canada, only with a "tory touch" that delayed the emergence of popular democracy.[104] But the refugees' quests for political place in 1780s British North America suggest a less teleological way of understanding their impact. What really distinguished British North Amer-

Beverley Robinson's house in the Hudson Highlands. After the Robinsons left in 1777, the house was used as a Continental Army headquarters. It burned down in 1892, not long after this drawing was published.

George Romney, *Joseph Brant (Thayendanegea)*, 1776. Brant sat for this portrait on his visit to London in 1775–76.

Elizabeth Lichtenstein Johnston around the time of her marriage, ca. 1780.

Dunmore Proclamation, 1775. This document, promising freedom to patriot-owned slaves who joined British forces, launched the emancipation of black loyalists.

By his Excellency the Right Honourable JOHN Earl of DUNMORE, his Majesty's Lieutenant and Governour-General of the Colony and Dominion of Virginia, and Vice-Admiral of the same:

A PROCLAMATION.

AS I have ever entertained Hopes that an Accommodation might have taken Place between *Great Britain* and this Colony, without being compelled, by my Duty, to this most disagreeable, but now absolutely necessary Step, rendered so by a Body of armed Men, unlawfully assembled, firing on his Majesty's Tenders, and the Formation of an Army, and that Army now on their March to attack his Majesty's Troops, and destroy the well-disposed Subjects of this Colony: To defeat such treasonable Purposes, and that all such Traitors, and their Abetters, may be brought to Justice, and that the Peace and good Order of this Colony may be again restored, which the ordinary Course of the civil Law is unable to effect, I have thought fit to issue this my Proclamation, hereby declaring, that until the aforesaid good Purposes can be obtained, I do, in Virtue of the Power and Authority to me given, by his Majesty, determine to execute martial Law, and cause the same to be executed throughout this Colony; and to the End that Peace and good Order may the sooner be restored, I do require every Person capable of bearing Arms to resort to his Majesty's S T A N-DARD, or be looked upon as Traitors to his Majesty's Crown and Government, and thereby become liable to the Penalty the Law inflicts upon such Offences, such as Forfeiture of Life, Confiscation of Lands, &c. &c. And I do hereby farther declare all indented Servants, Negroes, or others (appertaining to Rebels) free, that are able and willing to bear Arms, they joining his Majesty's Troops, as soon as may be, for the more speedily reducing this Colony to a proper Sense of their Duty, to his Majesty's Crown and Dignity. I do farther order, and require, all his Majesty's liege Subjects to retain their Quitrents, or any other Taxes due, or that may become due, in their own Custody, till such Time as Peace may be again restored to this at present most unhappy Country, or demanded of them for their former salutary Purposes, by Officers properly authorised to receive the same.

GIVEN under my Hand, on Board the Ship William, off Norfolk, the 7th Day of November, in the 16th Year of his Majesty's Reign.

D U N M O R E.

G O D   SAVE   THE   K I N G.

Sir Guy Carleton, ca. 1780.

Black loyalist certificate, 1783. These certificates were issued to black loyalists at the evacuation of New York City, guaranteeing their protection by British officials and licensing their emigration.

NEW-YORK, 21ˢᵗ April 1783.

THIS is to certify to whomſoever it may concern, that the Bearer hereof _Cato Ramsay_ a Negro, reſorted to the Britiſh Lines, in conſequence of the Proclamations of Sir William Howe, and Sir Henry Clinton, late Commanders in Chief in America ; and that the ſaid Negro has hereby his Excellency Sir Guy Carleton's Permiſſion to go to Nova-Scotia, or wherever elſe _He_ may think proper. —

By Order of Brigadier General Birch,

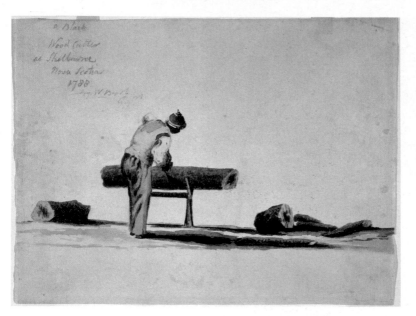

William Booth, *A Black Wood Cutter at Shelburne*, 1788.
This may be the only surviving contemporary image of a black
refugee. The black loyalist Boston King worked as a carpenter
around Shelburne, not unlike the figure shown here.

William Booth, *Part of the Town of Shelburne*, 1789. This watercolor depicts
the Nova Scotia loyalist metropolis at its height.

James Peachey, *Encampment of the Loyalists at Johnstown, a New Settlement, on the Banks of the River St. Laurence in Canada*, 1785. An unusual glimpse of a loyalist refugee camp.

Elizabeth Simcoe, *Mohawk Village on the Grand River*, ca. 1793. Brant's Town as seen by the Upper Canada governor's wife. The Mohawk Chapel is at the right of the image, and the large house at the left, with the British flag in front, is likely to have been Joseph Brant's.

Mohawk Chapel, Brantford. This was
the first Anglican church established in
the province of Quebec. Joseph Brant is buried
next to it.

William Augustus Bowles, 1791.

Rodney Memorial, Spanish Town,
Jamaica. This structure, commemorating
Britain's triumph in the 1782 Battle of
the Saintes, can justly be considered the
largest British victory monument of
the Revolutionary War.

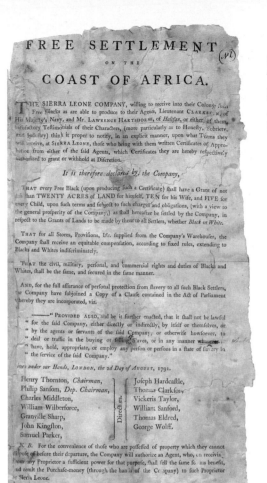

FREE SETTLEMENT

ON THE

COAST OF AFRICA.

THE SIERRA LEONE COMPANY, willing to receive into their Colony such Free Blacks as are able to produce to their Agents, Lieutenant CLARKSON, of His Majesty's Navy, and Mr. LAWRENCE HARTSHORNE, of Halifax, or either of them, satisfactory Testimonials of their Characters, (more particularly as to Honesty, Sobriety, and Industry) think it proper to notify, in an explicit manner, upon what Terms they will receive, at SIERRA LEONE, those who bring with them written Certificates of Approbation from either of the said Agents, which Certificates they are hereby respectively authorized to grant or withhold at Discretion.

It is therefore declared by the Company,

THAT every Free Black (upon producing such a Certificate) shall have a Grant of not less than TWENTY ACRES of LAND for himself, TEN for his Wife, and FIVE for every Child, upon such terms and subject to such charges and obligations, (with a view to the general prosperity of the Company,) as shall hereafter be settled by the Company, in respect to the Grants of Lands to be made by them to all Settlers, whether *Black* or *White.*

THAT for all Stores, Provisions, &c. supplied from the Company's Warehouses, the Company shall receive an equitable compensation, according to fixed rules, extending to Blacks and Whites indiscriminately.

THAT the civil, military, personal, and commercial rights and duties of Blacks and Whites, shall be the same, and secured in the same manner.

AND, for the full assurance of personal protection from slavery to all such Black Settlers, the Company have subjoined a Copy of a Clause contained in the Act of Parliament whereby they are incorporated, viz.

———" PROVIDED ALSO, and be it further enacted, that it shall not be lawful
" for the said Company, either directly or indirectly, by itself or themselves, or
" by the agents or servants of the said Company, or otherwise howsoever, to
" deal or traffic in the buying or selling Slaves, or in any manner whatsoever,
" have, hold, appropriate, or employ any person or persons in a state of slavery in
" the service of the said Company."

Given under our Hands, LONDON, the 2d Day of AUGUST, 1791.

Henry Thornton, *Chairman,*		Joseph Hardcastle,
Philip Sansom, *Dep. Chairman,*		Thomas Clarkson,
Charles Middleton,	*Directors.*	Vickeris Taylor,
William Wilberforce,		William Sanford,
Granville Sharp,		Thomas Eldred,
John Kingston,		George Wolff.
Samuel Parker,		

N. B. For the convenience of those who are possessed of property which they cannot dispose of before their departure, the Company will authorize an Agent, who, on receiving from any Proprietor a sufficient power for that purpose, shall sell the same for his benefit, and remit the Purchase-money (through the hands of the Company) to such Proprietor at Sierra Leone.

Sierra Leone Company handbill, 1791. To help recruit volunteers, this document, laying out the terms of the proposed West Africa settlement, was circulated among black loyalists in Nova Scotia.

Sketch of Freetown, ca. 1798. Virtually no pictures show Freetown in its very first years, so it is all the more remarkable that this one was produced by William Augustus Bowles during his brief sojourn in the African capital.

Left: Gardner family tomb, Kasganj. This mausoleum, in late Mughal style, was erected by New York–born William Linnaeus Gardner for his eldest son. Gardner and his wife are buried in the foreground.

Below: Benjamin West, *The Reception of the American Loyalists by Great Britain,* ca. 1812. This engraving, published as the frontispiece to a book about the Loyalist Claims Commission, beautifully illustrates the "spirit of 1783" as rendered by the most famous British history painter of his day, Pennsylvania native Benjamin West.

ica from the United States was not the pursuit of liberty, but the persistence of loyalty. Both polities shared a commitment to life, liberty, and property; both polities had vigorous internal disputes about how best to achieve such goals.[105] In British North America, loyalty to the monarch and the empire provided an important foundation for unity on the eve of another revolutionary war, with France. At the same time, in British North America as in the United States, a diverse, multiethnic population struggled to find common ground. (The War of 1812 would soon test togetherness on both sides of the border.) And in British North America as elsewhere in the British world, popular expressions of liberty were contained by rule from above. Loyalists in British North America discovered what their peers in Britain were also learning—that what refugees wanted from the British Empire was not always what they got. It remained to be seen whether their counterparts to the south, in the Bahamas and Jamaica, would fare any better.

PART III

Subjects

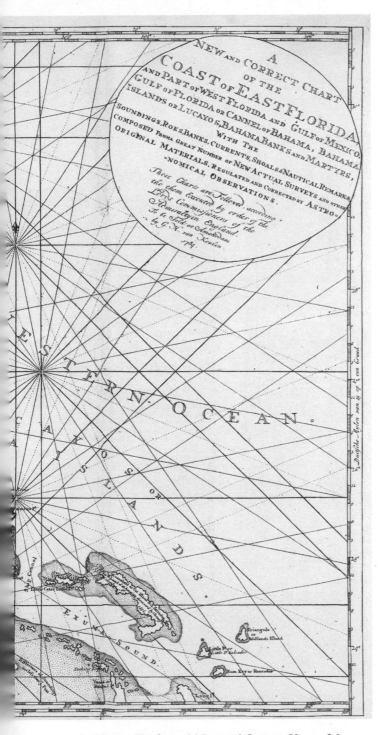

G. H. van Keulen, *A New and Correct Chart of the Coast of East Florida* (detail), 1784.

CHAPTER SEVEN

Islands in a Storm

FROM HIS NEW vantage point on the Bahamian island of Exuma, John Cruden, the former commissioner of sequestered estates in South Carolina, could see great things brewing on the horizon. Despite his best efforts to carve out an independent state for loyalists in East Florida, his fellow refugees had dispersed around the Atlantic. Cruden traced many of their routes himself. He had visited Britain to seek payment for expenses incurred on the sequestered estates. He had been to the West Indian island of Tortola—not a site of white loyalist refuge, but a well-known center of slave traffic—as part of his righteous crusade to chase down patriot-owned slaves stolen by departing loyalists. He had gone to Nova Scotia to file a claim with the loyalist claims commissioners sitting in Halifax, and to pursue business ventures with American friends resettled in Shelburne. And together with a thousand of the refugees from East Florida, he had found himself a new home at last, in the Bahama Islands. As a multiply displaced person, Cruden understood intimately, and from many vantage points, the trials and strains that dislocation wrought on loyalist refugees. But "the keen blasts of Adversity that I have Experienced for years," he felt, had "given vast scope to my mind . . . my reason is aided by Revelation Misfortune has matured my judgment."[1] "It requires no Spirit of Prophecy, nor gift of Divination, to foretell Events," Cruden declared. "We are on the eve of a grand Convulsion," and it was critical for Britain, and the loyalist refugees, to "make the most of the times & of Circumstances."[2]

As he sat on arid little Exuma in 1785, Cruden penned schemes for imperial renewal of ever more ambitious proportions. He had already tried his hardest to hang on in America, with his attempt to cling to a corner of East Florida. In an "Address to the Monarchial and Thinking Part of the British Empire," dedicated to Lord North, Cruden suggested several new ways Britain might turn the loyalist exodus to its imperial advantage. Refugees in the Bahamas could develop the islands' valuable salt ponds, and utilize their strategic location for Atlantic trade. Free blacks could travel to Central America and revive British possessions there, while the abolitionist project to settle black loyalists in West Africa, he glowingly declared, could let Britain prove "to the whole World, that we are worthy of the most dignified title on Earth . . . Friend & protector to ye Liberties of mankind."[3] It might seem contradictory that a man who so avidly worked to return stolen slaves to their former masters should also safeguard black freedom. But both these causes—protecting private property on the one hand, and personal liberty on the other—conformed entirely with the "spirit of 1783" and stood as pillars of the emerging political philosophy of liberalism.

Cruden's most passionate crusade, though, reflected another element of the "spirit of 1783": a drive toward geographical expansion. He urged British ministers to compensate for the loss of the thirteen colonies by pouncing on territory elsewhere in North America. Indeed, tapping into the widely held opinion that the United States might quickly disintegrate, Cruden believed that if Britain played its cards right, it could yet "bring the Americans back again."[4] The plausibility of such proposals surely helped explain why high-placed figures such as Lord North and Lord Cornwallis kept Cruden's screeds among their papers rather than promptly discarding them. Similar ideas would only gain momentum when Cruden's prediction of a "great Convulsion of Empire" actually came to pass, with the beginning of the French Revolution and the outbreak of Anglo-French war in 1793.[5]

Each of the plans John Cruden set forth in the Bahamas indicated the islands' particular place in the geography of loyalist exodus. In the Bahamas as in Nova Scotia and New Brunswick, loyalist refugees formed the majority of the population, with pronounced effects on the islands' landscape, economy, and demography. Also as in British North America, refugees regarded imperial authorities with mistrust. But there were several points of divergence between the loyalist societies north and south. Unlike British North America, in the Bahamas the twenty-five hundred or so white refugees were significantly outnumbered by the movable property many had struggled so hard to secure: some six thousand slaves. This demographic imbalance added a racial dimension to political conflicts in the islands, when white slaveowners found that their views on how to manage slaves stood in contradiction with the more paternalistic opinions of their rulers. Furthermore, where loyalists in British North America fashioned a sort of imperial reflection to the United States, some loyalists in the Bahamas—Cruden among them—envisioned a quite different relationship with their prominent neighbor. They wanted to use the Bahamas, a mere sixty miles or so off the coast of Florida at their closest point, as a staging post for seizing parts of North America back. Competing positions on slavery and expansion etched a fault line among loyalist refugees in the Bahamas, between those who aimed to establish a plantation society much like what they had left behind in the American south, and those who advocated the entrenchment and extension of a more paternalistic style of rule. These latter attitudes would gain a powerful advocate in the governor of the Bahamas from 1786, Cruden's old patron and former Virginia governor Lord Dunmore.

The visionary quality of John Cruden's thinking pointed suggestively toward a final defining characteristic of refugee life in the Bahamas. By 1785, Cruden, long manic, had become a maniac. His acquaintances commented on the signs. "John Cruden is here, for what purpose God knows," one of his friends in Halifax told another. "I think him mad. . . . He seems to be the same good hearted sensible Man we once knew him, but too wild in his politicks, which have turned his Head."[6] A male business partner must have been at least mildly surprised to receive letters from Cruden expressing the hope that "Providence will enable me soon to prove how much, and how ardently I Love you" ("as <u>David loved Jonathan</u>," he explained elsewhere) "and that the day will yet come, when we shall meet to part no more."[7] His strangest fantasies, though, or at least his most widely repeated, flew off into the realms of millenarianism. For Cruden's ambitions for the British Empire did not stop with reconquering the United States. "If the Jews could be brought to unite in Earnest," he continued, "& assist the Emperor & the Empress of Russia against the Turks, it is impossible to say what we might do."[8] Reestablishing British power in America, as Cruden began to see it, would pave the way for the restoration of the Jews—not in the Holy Land, but along the Mississippi. From imperial renewal to the Second Coming: now that would be a "grand Convulsion" indeed.[9]

All this, to be sure, was the product of a single, rattled mind. Still, social outliers can help cast light on social norms. As Cruden grasped ever more frantically at ways to piece together a world that had been shattered, his mad meditations presented a striking case study in the psychological effects of displacement. He noted himself how his ordeals had "matured" his thinking. Almost half of the Bahamas' refugees had, like him, been multiply unsettled by the cession of East Florida. They arrived in the islands mentally marked by the strains of repeated migration, aching with a sense of betrayal, and primed for discontent. The legacy of trauma among these refugees set the stage for an especially dramatic clash between loyalists and rulers in the Bahamas, a clash of opinions about what the British Empire should stand for. What had appeared in British North America to be a spectrum of loyalist political views became in the Bahamas a polarized opposition between those who contested imperial authority and those who sought to assert it. How did these factions take shape, and which one would prevail?

IT DID NOT look like much from the sea, this new world—a strip of limestone and coral peeping up from water so clear you could trace the ripples of sand in the ocean floor. But after five punishing weeks riding the uncharted swell, land was land to the approaching sailors, land was life. They stumbled off the ship and fell to their knees on the beach, praying and planting banners emblazoned with green crosses and crowns. The admiral called it San Salvador, for it must have seemed to them like salvation indeed.[10]

Christopher Columbus and his crew thought they had landed in India on October 12, 1492, when in fact they had navigated into the reefs of the Bahamas. Largely flat, unprepossessing, and without any sources of fresh water, the Bahama Islands have nothing of the spectacular tropical lushness of the West Indies. (They lie in the Atlantic Gulf Stream, not the Caribbean, and are mostly above the Tropic of Cancer.) But Columbus would not be the only outsider to see something providential in these stony protrusions from the sea. In the 1640s, the Bahamas' first Anglophone settlers, a group of self-styled adventurers from Bermuda, colonized an island they named Eleuthera—from the Greek word for "free"—aiming to establish a model republic with freedom of worship. A later wave of Bermudans renamed one of the larger islands of the archipelago New Providence, on which they founded the Bahamas' capital, Nassau.[11]

The American loyalists who approached the islands three centuries after Columbus belonged to a long line of colonists who hoped the

Bahamas might bring heaven-sent rewards. They also reinforced a history of close ties between the Bahamas and continental North America. It was no coincidence that the settlement on Harbor Island, off Eleuthera, strikingly resembled the fishing villages of Massachusetts in architectural style.[12] Culturally as well as ecologically, the islands shared more with places like Nantucket or the Outer Banks—or, of course, Bermuda—than with the British West Indian islands of Jamaica or Barbados, with their sugar plantations and giant slave labor forces. By the time of the American Revolution only about seventeen hundred whites and twenty-three hundred blacks (about half of these free) lived on New Providence, Eleuthera, and Harbor Island.[13] Some scraped by on scavenging from the wrecks of ships dashed against the treacherous reefs. Others managed to eke out a living from fishing, whaling, catching turtles, and cutting timber. In the islands' most lucrative business, seasonal workers raked salt from the glistening ponds that slicked and crusted the southernmost islands. These prewar residents would come to be called "conchs," after the marine snails they ate, tough twists of flesh nestled in rose-lipped shells.[14]

While the West Indies represented an economic powerhouse of the eighteenth-century British Empire, the Bahamas remained decidedly marginal to imperial calculations. The poorly defended islands were frequently attacked by Spain, and depended heavily on trade with nearby American ports for subsistence. So it was hardly surprising that Bahamians (like many Nova Scotians) saw the American Revolution primarily in pragmatic terms, as a threat to security and commerce, rather than in ideological ones. The revolution arrived in the Bahamas early one March morning in 1776, in the form of seven American warships off New Providence. When the governor called out the militia to defend Nassau, many of the men had no weapons, while others simply failed to show up. Two cannon fired as an alarm at Fort Nassau ended up falling off their mountings; in Fort Montagu, just east of town, "there was not a Barrel of Powder or length of Match Stuff" available for use.[15] On hearing that three to four hundred American soldiers had landed on the beach, the fort's outnumbered defenders promptly returned to their houses to protect their personal property. The patriots took Nassau without a single shot. Two weeks later they left again, many of them drunk to the point of senselessness on all the captured wine they had guzzled.[16]

Despite such farcical scenes, and an apathetically loyal population, the Bahamas would be the site of a signal loyalist victory, in what turned out to be the very last action of the war. In 1782, Spain formally conquered the Bahamas. Loyalist refugees in nearby East Florida grew restive at the proximity of this Spanish occupying force. One impatient South Carolina loyalist called Andrew Deveaux decided to take matters into his own hands. Believing that "we have everything to fear, and nothing to expect from the British Empire, but what springs from our own . . . generous exertions," Deveaux began "beating up for volunteers to go to take New Providence."[17] Approaching Nassau, Deveaux skillfully masked the paltry size of his "handful of ragged Militia"— perhaps seventy men in all—by sailing back and forth to his ships and appearing to land fresh boatloads of troops each time.[18] The Spanish defenders felt sufficiently threatened that they abandoned Fort Montagu without a fight (as the Bahamians had done in 1776). On April 18, 1783, Deveaux raised the British flag over Nassau.[19]

Deveaux's capture of the Bahamas was a proud testament to loyalist entrepreneurship, and underscored the contrapuntal relationship between the islands and the mainland. The only problem was that he was too late.[20] Not only had hostilities in North America formally ended four weeks earlier, but under the terms of the preliminary peace treaty signed in January 1783, Spain had already agreed to return the Bahamas to Britain. The loyalists were fighting for something that had already been won. The main effect of the adventure was to provide some positive distraction for refugees in East Florida reeling from the shocking news of the province's cession.[21]

The exploit also helped direct attention to the Bahamas as a location for loyalist resettlement.[22] The Bahamas had not initially appealed to Florida-based refugees. The only loyalist settlement thus far had been pioneered by a group of about fifteen hundred New Yorkers who moved to Abaco, one of the northern islands, in the summer of 1783.[23] To most refugees, the Bahamas seemed little more than "barren Rock[s]."[24] Dr. Lewis Johnston confirmed this negative impression when he made his investigative mission from St. Augustine in the summer of 1783. He quickly saw why Bahamians had not bothered to develop agriculture on the out-islands, "and never visit them with any other View than wrecking Turtling and cutting Timber."[25] The soil quality was far too poor to establish sugar plantations as in the West Indies, or to cultivate rice and tobacco as in the American south. Yet many of the Florida refugees, Johnston included, had one overriding objective. They needed to find a place where they could put their slaves to work. For all that the Bahamas may have seemed unpromising for settlement, Nova Scotia made even less sense, with a "climate . . . not being calculated for Southern Constitutions, or for the employment of the Slaves." Jamaica and Barbados were already crowded, with very little land available. The Bahamas had the advantage of being "nearly in the same Latitude" as Georgia and South Carolina, "very thinly Inhabitated, and but little Cultivated."[26] Caught between a "barren rock" and the hard place of Nova Scotia, the majority of Florida refugees chose the rock.

In late 1783, the British government decided to buy out the islands' hereditary proprietors, and—as in British North America—offer loyalists "Tracts of Land . . . (gratis) proportioned to their former situation, and ability to cultivate them."[27] This was the first of several parallels between the experience of the Bahamas refugees and that of their peers in the Maritimes. Next came the arrivals. Bahamas governor John Maxwell, like Governor Parr in Nova Scotia, suddenly found himself coping with the makings of a refugee crisis.[28] By the middle of 1784, transports from Florida were disgorging refugees and slaves onto New Providence by the hundreds. "They are sitting themselves down, where they can; and without order," reported Maxwell, "as I unfortunately do not know, whether the Purchase of the Soil has been made by Government."[29] Many stayed in more or less rudimentary conditions around Nassau; others migrated to the dry, empty out-islands, to tear back the scrub and try their luck at planting. All told, more than six thousand loyalists and their slaves arrived in the Bahamas, doubling the prewar population and raising the ratio of black to white inhabitants from a little more than one to one to two to one.[30]

For all that the Bahamian climate was more forgiving than that of Nova Scotia, the undeveloped islands had little to offer destitute arrivals. By the spring of 1785 there was such a shortage of food that officials urged East Florida governor Patrick Tonyn to stop sending any more refugees.[31] (When John Cruden, plotting his coup against the Spanish takeover of Florida, had asked the Bahamas governor for provisions, he was put off with a sharp reminder that "the Provisions remaining are for those Loyalists, who are expected here.")[32] The islands remained so dependent on imports that the wreck of a single British supply ship off Nassau was enough to push the hungry refugees to the brink of famine.[33] Nor was there sufficient housing available to accommodate them. Despite being the largest town in the islands, Nassau had "but one tolerably regular street," lined with simple wood houses. A visiting German naturalist discovered all the buildings "filled with refugees excaped from North America." He could only locate lodgings for himself in a "quite barn-like" dwelling outside of town; many refugees still lived in tents.[34]

On Abaco, where the New York loyalists settled, the situation was not much better. They laid out a town—named Carleton after their benefactor Sir Guy—and entertained high hopes for a place praised in the New York press for its potential to be the next big plantation economy. But they soon discovered the country to be "not . . . so fertile as had been expected," and that it would be "impossible for them to clear the Land, Plant it, and Reap the Fruits of their Labour Sooner than Twelve or Fourteen months."[35] As in the other Carleton, on the Saint John River, dearth fueled dispute. They "had been but few days on shore," reported one official, "when dissention got among them, which by degrees rose to such a height, they were on the point of taking arms against each other." Hopelessly divided by a fight over food distribution, some of the Carleton settlers split off to found a rival town at Marsh's Harbour.[36]

"It will be a difficult Task, I imagine, to please so dissatisfied a People," Governor Maxwell anticipated.[37] That was an understatement. The troubles on Abaco foreshadowed what turned out to be the most significant resemblance between loyalist societies in the Bahamas and British North America: conflict between disgruntled refugees and the officials responsible for helping them. Echoing their peers in the north, the newly arrived Florida refugees promptly began complaining about provisions, land allocation, and political representation. And like Governors Parr and Thomas Carleton before him, Maxwell became a focal point of loyalist rage.

It all started with the food. The distribution of rations, like the distribution of land, was a perennial source of tension between refugees and government across the diaspora. But in the Bahamas, the issue took on a special twist, due to the islands' proximity to the United States. Responding to a petition from refugees complaining about food supply problems, Maxwell suspended an order in council against trade with the United States, thus allowing American ships to bring desperately needed provisions into Nassau.[38] Little did he anticipate the loyalist response. "This, in their Opinion, is a monstrous offence," Maxwell discovered. Some refugees were so angered by the sight of U.S. ships in the harbor that they tried to tear the stars and stripes down from the masts.[39] Maxwell condemned such behavior as "contrary to the peace of our Lord the King and in open violation of all public Order and decorum," and issued a proclamation "strictly commanding and enjoyning all His Majesty's Leige Subjects, to refrain from such dishonourable and illegal practices."[40] "I have often been called upon, when I commanded a Regiment, to prevent Riots when Bread was scarce, but that was before I had to do with Loyalists," he mused. "Who would have thought, that giving them Bread cheap would, at the same Time, give them offence?"[41]

Within a day or two of these incidents, somebody strolling down Nassau's Bay Street would have spotted curious handbills pasted up. They had almost certainly been printed on the press belonging to the Wells family from Charleston, which John Wells had recently brought with him from St. Augustine and now used to publish the Bahamas' first newspaper, the *Royal Bahama Gazette*.[42] The handbill made a "proclamation" of its own, satirizing Maxwell's, and pretending to be in his voice:

> Whereas I have in Violation and direct Opposition to the Order of His Majesty in Council permitted sundry Vessels the property of Rebels to enter and dispose of their Cargoes in this Island. And Whereas some of those people called Refugees or a name equally hatefull to me Loyalists have . . . showen [*sic*] their dislike to this part of my Conduct . . . I do hereby declare, that . . . I shall . . . mark such loyal and dutifull Conduct to His Majesty (while it is so opposite to my Interest) with my highest displeasure.[43]

Maxwell's loyalist enemies were convinced that the governor favored the prewar "conch" inhabitants over the needy newcomers. They accused him of opening the port to American ships not so as to help them, but to benefit himself and his conch friends financially. For how could it possibly help them to admit the very Americans who, in their eyes, had chased them into exile?

Maxwell lost no time branding his enemies in turn. His ideal society, not unlike that espoused by his fellow Anglo-Irishmen the Carletons, rested on authority, hierarchy, and an agrarian economy. "When I mention the Word, Loyalists, in General Terms," he took care to note, "I always mean to except out of their general bad Behaviour many among them, who are quiet & orderly."[44] He especially admired the refugee planters "who have set themselves down on the out-Islands with large Families and ten, twenty or one Hundred Slaves." It was the urban professionals—merchants, printers, lawyers—who caused all the trouble, and the East Florida refugees especially. (He thought they received tacit backing from Governor Tonyn, who coveted the Bahamas governorship for himself.)[45] "They are the most tormenting, dissatisfied People on Earth," Maxwell despaired.[46] "If I am to judge from what I have at present (a very few excepted) they are the Scum & Refuse of our unfortunate Army," and "if the Remainder, that intend coming here, are of the same Sort, Civil Government is in Danger."[47] The only way to deal with such people, Maxwell concluded, was to suppress them with a show of military force. The trouble was, he had no force to show: British troops assigned to garrison the islands were still in Florida and would not arrive for several months yet.

On a late July day in 1784, another handbill appeared in Nassau. "The peculiar Situation of the LOYAL REFUGEES, now in the Bahama Islands," it read, required "their steady and united Exertions to preserve and maintain those Rights and Liberties, for which they left their Homes and their Possessions." The document announced a "General Meeting of the Loyalists from the Continent of North-America" to discuss loyalist concerns. The list of fifteen signatures at the bottom instantly confirmed Maxwell's prejudices. They included three lawyers, a doctor, several merchants, and a few wealthy planters, and they had all come via St. Augustine. The president of the group, James Hepburn, had been attorney general of East Florida and an anti-Maxwell agitator from the moment he arrived. The printer John Wells was another signatory, here appearing to act out his newspaper's motto, "not bound by any masters."[48] The meeting was to be hosted by none other than Lewis Johnston Jr., Dr. Lewis Johnston's son and William Johnston's brother, who may have been primed for dissatisfaction with the Bahamas by his father's negative reports.[49]

Through the summer of 1785, loyalist grievances snapped like water drops on a hot skillet. Hepburn and two other lawyers, believing that they were unjustly excluded from practicing law, stormed into the courthouse and assailed the chief justice with such "a Torrent of Billingsgate Language" that proceedings had to be adjourned. The court remained suspended for several months while tempers cooled.[50] On another occasion, Hepburn showed up at Governor Maxwell's house and accused the governor of so betraying his duty that his authority had become meaningless. Maxwell, equally quick with extremist language, retorted that "if this Conduct is not a very high Misdemeanor, not to say, Treason, I don't know what is."[51] Meanwhile, Maxwell juggled complaints about land allocation, on the one hand trying to honor the prior claims of prewar settlers, on the other placating loyalists who, "Where they see a vacant Spot, say, they <u>must</u> have it, and <u>will</u> have it: it is 'promised to them' that is their Language."[52]

And then there were the riots. One Sunday morning, loyalist agitators stood outside the church with "Drums beating the Rogue's March, so as to drive the people out of the Church." Occupying the premises, they "amused themselves" in the dead of night "with Ringing the Bell, as if the Town had been on Fire."[53] Such disruptions continued for weeks, invariably originating "from the Houses and Tents of the Loyalists."[54] In a scene that could have unfolded in revolutionary America, a mob of "both White and Black Men armed" appeared one night at the gates of the chief justice's house, shouting "Fire" and threatening to shoot the inhabitants.[55] Yet with the courts suspended and no troops at his disposal, Maxwell was effectively powerless to retaliate—an authoritarian lacking the necessary instruments of authority.[56]

The protestors won a victory of sorts: Maxwell was recalled from his position and sailed home with evident relief in the spring of 1785. His successor as acting governor was James Edward Powell, a genial man "far advanced in his dotage," and himself a loyalist refugee from Georgia.[57] Powell hoped that now "tranquility and mutual confidence would take place of Rancour and resentment."[58] But Maxwell had already, before leaving, set in motion the greatest controversy yet between loyalists and government. In late 1784 he dissolved the house of assembly and called an election for a reconstituted house, with eleven new representatives for the recently settled out-islands. Among the freshly elected members taking their seats in February 1785 were the notorious James Hepburn and a number of his discontented loyalist friends.

In his first speech to the assembly, Governor Powell promised to "have no retrospect to whats past, But hope that Harmony and mutual confidence may be restored in future." No sooner had he finished his remarks than Hepburn leapt up to present a clutch of petitions from his associates. Each petitioner claimed he had been elected to the assembly by a handsome majority, only for the provost marshall "falsely, wickedly, and illegally" to install a rival candidate (representing the conchs) in his stead. Hepburn and six other members stomped out of the chamber in protest, "without leave of the Speaker, in a very abrupt manner."[59] Summoned to appear before the house and give their reasons for withdrawing, Hepburn and his friends refused, saying they "did not <u>chuse</u> to attend the House while there were persons in it <u>illegally</u> chosen." In retaliation, the sitting members ordered that the loyalist protests be "burned by the hands of the Common hangman as a most wicked false and scandalous reflection upon the authority and dignity of this House." The next day, in a graphic performance of the power of the state, the public executioner ignited the offending documents in front of the courthouse.[60]

Provocative handbills and news reports in Wells's *Gazette* once more circulated around the islands. Agitated loyalists convened an emergency meeting in Nassau to give vent to "the intolerable grievances under which they and their constituents groan." The departed Governor Maxwell, they contended, had used "the utmost Art & influence . . . to prevent His Majesty's loyal subjects lately settled in these Islands from obtaining any share in the Representation." The elections had been conducted in "a direct flagrant & intolerable breach of the Constitution and Laws." The assembly did not represent them, and they in turn were "not bound by any Laws the Assembly might pass." They called on Powell to dissolve "the present Assembly as illegal and unconstitutional" and appoint a committee (from a group of loyalist protestors) "to transact business" in its stead.[61]

Refusing to abide by the law, calling for the suspension of regular government: these were revolutionary challenges. And they called themselves loyalists? The escalating conflict left ministers in Whitehall scratching their heads. "It is not a little extraordinary," marveled Lord Sydney, "that Men who profess to have suffered for their Loyalty to the Crown, and adherence to the British Constitution, should so far forget themselves, and the Duty they owe to His Majesty, as to be guilty of the most daring attempts against His Royal authority, and that Constitution."[62] Governor Maxwell, with appropriate resources, might have suppressed the protests with a crackdown like Carleton's in New Brunswick. But Powell, himself a loyalist and more diplomatic than his predecessor, refused to lose his cool. He thanked the loyalist petitioners for their "Attachment and firm Adherence to the British Constitution" and prorogued the assembly for the summer, enjoining the members to "use your utmost endeavours to heal the divisions that hath and continue in some degree still to subsist."[63] His moderation yielded only moderate rewards. After a four-month break, the assembly successfully ejected seven of its most obstreperous members. But disputes over selection of representatives outlasted the aging Powell himself, who died in the winter of 1786, passing on the tense legacy to yet another governor.

None of this protest was unique to the Bahamas in substance. Bahamas refugees appealed to the British constitution in defense of their rights, spoke out against its abuse, and deployed the printing press, the petition, and the law in their cause. All of these were characteristic forms of protest in pre-revolutionary America and around the British world. Yet there was something distinctive in the style of this Bahamian protest, with its explosive public outbursts, riots and assaults, and proto-revolutionary councils. Why was it all so hysterical? Reflecting on the dispatches from Nassau, Lord Sydney volunteered an explanation. Given "the disagreeable state in which many of the Loyalists upon the Bahama Islands are represented to be," he suggested, it was hardly surprising that the once affluent refugees should keenly "feel the difference between their former and present situation and that their Temper and Disposition should be sowered from the unpleasant change."[64] Of course, all loyalist refugees dealt with deprivation, dislocation, and dispossession. But it was no coincidence that the most refractory Bahamian loyalists had come from East Florida in particular. Not only did they carry the physical and psychological legacies of war. (Thomas Brown, for instance, arrived in the Bahamas so plagued by migraines as a result of the 1775 attack that in an extreme attempt at relief he underwent trepanning, a procedure in which a hole was cut into his skull.)[65] These doubly displaced refugees came bearing enormous resentment against their own government for abandoning Florida. And perniciously reminding them of the gulf between where they came from and where they now were, loyalists in the Bahamas lived under the shadow of the United States, so close and yet so far. Proximity to the United States was a source of such consternation to some refugees that they attacked American flags, yet it was a source of ambition to others, like Cruden, who imagined using the Bahamas as a base for imperial expansion.

All these circumstances help explain how it was that these American loyalists came as close as any refugees yet to emulating American patriots in a final, vital respect: they seemed prepared to take up clubs and pistols if necessary, to make a decisive break from their governor. Indeed for a time it even seemed that the loyalist agitators might prevail over imperial authority. Until, that is, authority arrived in the form of a ruler few would forget. Lord Dunmore, the former governor of Virginia, was coming back across the Atlantic.

PERHAPS THE Earl of Dunmore had been in an especially good mood in 1761 when he commissioned a new folly for his estate at Airth. He had recently been married, and chosen to represent Scotland in the

House of Lords—a particular honor given that his father had been disgraced for supporting the Young Pretender in 1745. Certainly this was a folly if ever there was one. Up close, it looks like a stone carver's masterpiece, an elaborate confection of exquisitely crafted tongues and curls of stone. From a distance, it looks like a joke. The intricately sculpted structure represents a gigantic pineapple, four stories high, a favorite eighteenth-century decorative motif blown out of proportion, and a strange evocation of the tropics against the glowering lowlands sky. What Dunmore could not possibly have known was that twenty-five years later he would be governing a land of pineapples—one of the few tropical species successfully cultivated in the Bahamas.[66]

Lord Dunmore loved to do things big. As governor briefly of New York, and from 1771 of Virginia, he embraced his chance to make a mark, prosecuting expansionist campaigns against the Shawnees in the Ohio Country and—by no means incidentally—acquiring a phenomenal four million acres of American land for himself. His efforts to quash revolution in Virginia had been equally assiduous, from his extraordinary floating government on the Chesapeake to that controversial 1775 proclamation offering freedom to slaves. Though Dunmore had been forced to abandon the floating town in 1776, he was unceasing in his efforts to win the war. On both sides of the Atlantic, he became a leading advocate for loyalist causes and for continued British offensives. Among the projects he supported was one, advanced after Yorktown, to seize the lower Mississippi Valley and turn it into a loyalist asylum.[67] Another was Cruden's 1782 plan to raise a large black army. Dunmore was Cruden's most prominent patron for a reason, for he, like Cruden, refused to see 1783 as an end to British prospects in the United States or its southern borderlands. Their world was simply too dynamic to acknowledge any defeat as final.

When Powell's death created a vacancy in Nassau's Government House, Dunmore seemed to many an ideal candidate to replace him. (Maxwell, who was officially on leave in Dublin, was politely informed that the ministry had decided to replace him with "some Person entirely unconnected with the present Inhabitants of those Islands.")[68] The earl was experienced in North American administration, he enjoyed considerable loyalist support, and he had been actively questing for another governorship. Dunmore greedily accepted the appointment and crossed the Atlantic in 1787. A priori, Bahamian loyalists welcomed him: here was a man whom they felt they could rely on to promote loyalist over conch interests, a primary source of tension under Maxwell. But they soon discovered that the new governor had competing interests of his own. To begin with, there were his authoritarian tendencies, stronger even than Maxwell's, and his relentless search for personal gain. More provocatively, there was the issue for which Dunmore had become notorious in Virginia—freeing black slaves—a somewhat dubious credential in the eyes of white Bahamian slaveowners. Finally, there were Dunmore's ongoing dreams of restoring imperial control on the North American continent, an ambition that as governor of the Bahamas he was especially well placed to pursue. For all that Dunmore had made a name as a friend to loyalists, none of these objectives squared neatly with the desires of his agitated new subjects.

By the time Dunmore reached Nassau, the influx of refugees had caused the city to burst its seams. A 1788 map commissioned by the assembly gives a nice overview of Nassau at this time.[69] The city center, anchored by Fort Nassau, contained public buildings including the church and assembly; Vendue House, built in 1787 for slave sales; and an open-sided structure gloriously labeled the Bourse, which served as a public marketplace and meeting place.[70] Eight or ten busy wharves lined the waterfront, and new streets ran inland as far as Government House, poised on a hill just south of the city center. The enlarged city was divided neatly into 214 lots, many of them owned by loyalist refugees. Nearly a quarter of Nassau real estate belonged to forty-eight different women, both white and black. Twenty-seven lots belonged to "free negroes" and people "of colour"—an important reminder that up to half of the Bahamas' prewar black and mixed-race population was free. A small number of black loyalists now joined them, including an associate of David George and George Liele's called Brother Amos, who established the first Baptist church in the islands.[71] Although overwhelmingly black shantytowns skirted the city limits, Nassau itself, on paper at least, looked strikingly racially integrated. From his corner lot on Princes Street, a white loyalist called Isaac DuBois could see the façade of Government House from his front windows. If he looked out the back of his house, he could see that of his black neighbor Thomas Maloney; if he looked to the right, he saw the property of Henry Evans, another black; and diagonally opposite he glimpsed the land of Rebecca Darling, a woman "of colour." (A few years later, DuBois would be almost entirely surrounded by black neighbors when he moved to Freetown, Sierra Leone.)

The out-islands at the time of Dunmore's arrival had changed even more dramatically. By terms announced in 1785, loyalist men and women could claim rent-free grants of forty acres each, plus a further twenty for every additional person in a household—slaves included. Because land came in proportion to slave ownership, the biggest planters from America had some chance of reproducing their positions in the Bahamas. Thomas Brown was among these fortunate few. In 1775 he had been master of almost six thousand acres in the Georgia backcountry, with 150 indentured servants in his employ. In 1785 Brown claimed sixty-four hundred acres in the Bahamas, mostly on the salt-rich Grand Caicos, and had 170 slaves to work them (including those he had bought from William Johnston in Florida).[72] Brown's ability to match his prewar circumstances was of course relatively unusual; his land grants were among the largest made to any loyalist. The majority of refugees made do with more modest tracts, usually of less than two hundred acres each.[73] In contrast to Brown's workforce of 170, the mean number of slaves on Bahamaian plantations was fewer than thirteen. Cumulatively, however, the refugee immigration completely altered the landscape of the islands. Loyalists—or more precisely, their slaves—brought thirteen thousand acres of land under cultivation in just a few years, nearly quadruple the prewar total.[74]

They did not grow sugar as in the West Indies, or rice as in the Low Country, or tobacco as in the Chesapeake. Instead they turned to a crop new to many of them: sea island cotton. Cotton would be the great white hope of Bahamian planters. First sown on the islands in 1785, the cotton crops of 1786 and 1787 yielded 150 and 250 tons respectively. William Wylly, a Georgia loyalist and author of the best general description of the islands for this period, supplemented his position as the Bahamas' solicitor-general by turning cotton planter on Abaco. He boasted of an annual output that "has infinitely exceeded their [the planters'] most sanguine expectations." He enthused about the fortunes of one planter, who with "no more than thirty-two slaves" had managed to produce fully nineteen tons of the crop, "worth on the spot 2660l., which is nearly double the whole value of the negroes by whose labour it was made."[75] But chances were good that when Wylly walked among his waist-high cotton plants that season or the next, he would have noticed a worrying thing nestled among the triangular leaves: striped, squiggling chenille bugs. These ravenous little caterpillars first blighted Bahamian cotton crops in 1788, and proved a relentless scourge in years to come.

Some loyalists may have seen a cruel irony in the coincidence of the chenille bug infestation with Lord Dunmore's arrival, for within weeks the governor had started to look like something of a plague himself. In charge of land grants, Dunmore promptly established himself within the ranks of the Bahamian landed elite by issuing himself a handsome 5,355 acres and granting another seventeen hundred acres to one of his sons. But the governor shared less with loyalist planters when it came to his attitudes about slave labor. As the man who first promised freedom to slaves during the American Revolution, Dunmore was not pleased to discover that in the Bahamas "the Negroes, who came here from America, with the British General's Free Passes, [are] treated with unheard of cruelty, by <u>men</u> who call themselves <u>Loyalists</u>. Those unhappy People after being drawn from their Masters by Promises of Freedom, and the Kings Protection, are every day stolen away from these Islands, shipped, and disposed of, to the French at Hispaniola."[76] John Cruden had already resumed the "disagreeable and distressing" task of hunting down blacks seized by loyalists "in Violation of the most positive Orders of Government."[77] To help stamp out such practices altogether, Dunmore issued a proclamation—his very first act on shore—promising to establish a tribunal to investigate black claims to freedom.

It was not quite the incendiary blast of his 1775 proclamation in Virginia, but Dunmore's order immediately had loyalists up in arms. The importation of slaves by loyalists had more or less doubled the ratio of slaves to whites in the islands.[78] As early as 1784, the assembly had responded to the sharp increase in the black population by passing a harsh new legal code against slaves and free blacks, resembling that of the American southern states. Suddenly here was a new governor spontaneously granting concessions to blacks instead. "The New Inhabitants considered Lord Dunmore as a Friend to the Negroes," one contemporary observed.[79] Dunmore noted dryly that "this enquiry has given umbrage to some persons here who had detained several of those poor unhappy people under various pretences in a state of slavery."[80] "Umbrage" was putting it mildly. In Nassau, a group of white loyalists burst into the house of a free mulatto and savagely attacked her. A loyalist arrested for his part in the incident swore "he would burn every house belonging to the free negroes in that quarter of town."[81] On Abaco, Thomas Brown was arrested as one of the ringleaders of a race "Riot" and was henceforth seen as "an open Opposer of Lord Dunmores Administration."[82] The racial violence prompted Dunmore to sail to Abaco himself with his "Negro Court" in tow, to assess the merits of black loyalist claims. (Though as it turned out, the governor's promises achieved little: of the thirty claimants who came to court, only one was judged to be free.)[83]

The controversy over the management of slaves—with Dunmore upholding, in principle, the right of black loyalist over white—proved just the opening salvo in an escalating war between the governor and white loyalists, between the forces of authority and the appeal to rights. Dunmore's knack for alienating his subjects flared up next over the perennially vexed issue of political representation. In early 1788, loyalists across the islands petitioned Dunmore to dissolve the assembly—a natural move, they argued, following the appointment of a new governor. New Providence loyalists made the case that they "consider themselves *unrepresented* in the present Assembly; and that the Planting and Commercial interests of the Colony are in the same Predicament." Loyalists from Exuma pleaded that they were "deprived of the Right of legislative representation." The cotton planters on Long Island stated "that many of the present members of the House of Assembly were illegally chosen"; on Cat Island, loyalists felt "excluded from a representation in the Legislative Councils" and thus shut out from the "blessings of Liberty" promised by the British constitution. In the most detailed petition, Abaco loyalists called attention to the fact that they had come to the islands "convinced that in the most obscure and remote part of His Majesty's Dominions, they would enjoy those inestimable Rights and Privileges of the British constitution." Yet, they lamented, "there is scarce a Planter, a Merchant, or an American loyalist in the Lower House of Assembly." To all these wordy requests, Dunmore delivered more or less the same terse reply: "Gentlemen, I do not think it expedient for His Majesty's service to dissolve the House of Assembly at this period."[84]

Dunmore's petitioners did not accept his rejection lightly. Solicitor-General William Wylly, for one, would stand for none of it. Wylly had only arrived in the Bahamas a little before Dunmore, but the Georgia native and erstwhile Florida refugee was closely connected to many of his new neighbors. (Both William and his brother Alexander had fought in Thomas Brown's Rangers, in which capacity Wylly had rescued William Johnston from patriot attack outside Savannah in 1781.) Wylly was quickly schooled in local politics when the chief justice (a Dunmore partisan) approached him with the dark warning that he should "take a party." Standing his ground as an independent, or at any rate refusing to align himself with Dunmore, Wylly found himself swept into jail on an accusation that he had called the justice "a damned liar." Thomas Brown, part of the anti-Dunmore faction, offered an affidavit in Wylly's defense; and Wylly's lawyer, another leading anti-government loyalist, managed to get Wylly off in a trial that exposed the farce of his arrest in the first place.[85] Lord Dunmore responded by effectively closing down the courts.

Standoff turned into stalemate. To Dunmore, the loyalist "party" that so plagued him, like Maxwell before him, appeared a selfish bunch of hucksters, horse thieves, smugglers, and troublemakers primarily concerned with keeping stolen slaves.[86] The only way to ensure such people's obedience, he determined, was to nip their demands in the bud. In a grand demonstration of authority, Dunmore launched the construction of batteries and fortifications across the out-islands, as well as a massive new fort to the west of Nassau, called Fort Charlotte. The fort's mighty, cannon-studded bastions may have been intended to inspire as much awe among New Providence's residents as among its putative assailants. For "had we a war with America tomorrow," Dunmore worried, "the Loyalists . . . would be those I should have the greatest reason to fear."[87]

To agitated loyalists, Wylly foremost, Dunmore represented the worst of a bad aristocracy, (Scottish) tyranny personified: "obstinate and violent by nature; of a capacity below mediocrity . . . ignorant of the Constitution of England, and of the Rights of British subjects; his principles of Government are such as might naturally be expected from the lordly despot of a petty Clan." Wylly's charges against the governor resembled those made by American patriots against reviled governors in the thirteen colonies. Dunmore's suspension of the courts and refusal to call an election betrayed the most fundamental rights— such as habeas corpus—that British subjects held dear. To make matters worse, "his private life" was no "less reprehensible than his publick character."[88] The governor's nepotism knew no bounds: he got one son elected to the assembly in a by-election, and would later unilaterally appoint another son to be lieutenant governor. Dunmore's pineapple in Airth was nothing compared to the folly of his island fortifications, whose costs spiraled to a staggering £32,000, eight times the original estimate, draining public funds.[89]

What could a loyal Bahamian do? Wylly directed his appeals to British ministers, hoping "that Justice might be obtained" in London "for injuries offered to British Subjects, *in the most distant parts of the Empire.*"[90] But in Nassau, Dunmore continued his near-absolutist regime—and Wylly feared that worse was to come. He rounded off his catalogue of complaints against Dunmore "with a charge that may perhaps appear *incredible*." For, Wylly declared, registering his shock in italics, "His Lordship has endeavoured to alarm the minds of the people by circulating strange reports of *conspiracies* entered into by the *Loyalists* (those Loyalists who have bled so freely in the cause of their King and Country) *to throw off their allegiance to Great Britain, . . . in order to put themselves under the protection of a Rebel Congress.*"[91] How could Dunmore accuse the loyalists—the *loyalists*—of being in secret collusion with the United States? And who knew what outrages he might commit next?

The awful truth for Wylly was that not only did Dunmore claim to possess evidence of a loyalist plot against the state—and by extension a justification for imposing martial law, which Dunmore longed to do.[92] The governor himself was also becoming rapidly embroiled in an intrigue that transposed Bahamian rivalries into North America. Dunmore had long supported some of the most radical ideas for reasserting British sovereignty on the continent. In the Bahamas he was especially well positioned to facilitate such projects. And now, in place of mad John Cruden, Dunmore had found a perfect new collaborator to advance them, in the form of a dynamic young loyalist called William Augustus Bowles.

HE MUST HAVE demonstrated himself to be a reliable provider by bringing meat and deerskins for his prospective bride, perhaps also a blanket and some clothes. He might have built a house for them to live in, too, a neat foursquare dwelling with white- or red-plastered walls and a roof of cypress bark.[93] With his broad shoulders and strong features, he certainly looked like a good enough warrior, yet at about sixteen years old, the groom was only just a man, not even fully grown. And for all that his skin had darkened under the Florida sun, no amount of weathering could obscure a revealing mark of his ancestry: his deep-set eyes twinkled blue.[94]

Many teenage boys in colonial America might have fantasized about such a life, inverting all those bloodcurdling tales they had been reared on: running away to live with the Indians, dressing in buckskins, wielding tomahawk and scalping knife, savoring imagined woodland freedoms of sex, violence, and drink. The precocious Maryland-born William Augustus Bowles had done all this in his teens and more.

(Even this marriage to the daughter of a Creek chief was his second; he had fathered at least one child already by a Cherokee first wife.)[95] Bowles had begun his adventures at the age of fourteen, in 1777, when he earned a commission as ensign in a regiment of Maryland loyalists. But he adapted poorly to a military career that combined immense boredom with exceptional discomfort. In late 1778, his regiment traveled to Pensacola to reinforce the city against an anticipated Spanish attack. He hated this steaming, stinking, sickness-filled port, judged by a fellow officer to be a hell on earth: "Satan and all his angels should be banished to this place."[96] Stir-crazy and insubordinate, Bowles quarreled with his commanding officer and got struck from the rolls. When a delegation of Creek Indians who had come to Pensacola to collect presents from the British returned to their villages, Bowles "threw my red Coat with indignation into the Sea" and traveled with them.[97]

Bowles became one of hundreds of white men to dwell among the Creeks in the later eighteenth century.[98] (The Creek leader Alexander McGillivray was the son of one of the most prominent, Scottish trader Lachlan McGillivray.) Bowles "went native" to the extent of forming a Creek family, and when he led a Creek war party to the defense of Mobile, a contemporary described him "grown out of recollection, and in every respect like a savage warrior."[99] But he never renounced his allegiance as a British subject. In 1780, Bowles even ended up rejoining his loyalist regiment, which meant that at the end of the war he was entitled to a land grant for his service. He chose to move to the Bahamas, close to his adoptive southeast. Circulating restlessly in the postwar years between the Bahamas and the North American mainland, Bowles became another of those loyalist refugees—like John Cruden—whose wartime wanderings anticipated a peripatetic postwar life.

In April 1788, Bowles appeared in Nassau with an alarming tale. On a recent visit to Georgia, he had met a fellow veteran who owned land in the Bahamas. The officer "urged him [Bowles] very strongly to call upon Messrs. Johnston, Hepburn, Cruden and some others" once he returned to the islands. "These and some others were principal leaders of a strong Party in the Bahamas," his acquaintance told him, and they were about to put into motion a daring plan. The officer pulled out a sheaf of letters to explain. These described a soaring scheme "of rendering the said Islands independent of Great Britain." Seceding from the British Empire, the new loyalist rulers of the Bahamas would "open their Ports to all the world; have an extensive

Commerce, and moreover derive great profit and advantage from the Salt Ponds with which the said Islands abound." Everything was in place for the project; all the plotters had to do was set a date "to rise and possess themselves of the Government." At the bottom of the documents, Bowles read the confident signature of the man who had penned them: John Cruden.[100]

The encounter left Bowles convinced that "there has been, and is now, a design to wrest this Colony from the Dominion of Great Britain." Indeed he was quite certain that the ongoing conflict over seats in the house of assembly "was not with any real design of obtaining a representation of the People, but to discover by this means the strength and number of their Party." Not democracy, but a coup d'état: here was Dunmore's evidence of a loyalist conspiracy against his regime. And it was especially convenient that Bowles swore to all this in a deposition just days after William Wylly's trial. A charge of treason (even if it hinged on the words of crazy Cruden) would surely shut down the loyalist antigovernment agitators once and for all. In the event, Bowles's sensational accusations advanced no further. Not least, by the time he testified, John Cruden was gone for good; in September 1787, Cruden died in the islands for which he harbored such great hopes, just thirty-three years old.[101] But the symbiotic relationship Dunmore and Bowles forged over the case soon evolved in ways that would have made Cruden proud.

Though Bowles and Cruden probably never met, they shared more than a moment of virtual connection through the pages of Cruden's treasonous letters. For like Cruden, Bowles believed that Spanish authority could be overturned in Florida, and saw the Bahamas primarily as a jumping-off point from which to do so. The difference was that Bowles wanted to achieve this conquest in the name of, and with the support of, the Creek Indians. The American Revolution had thrown Creek society into flux, transitioning from traditional ways of life toward an economy more oriented around plantation agriculture and slave ownership.[102] Creek chief Alexander McGillivray personified this shift. Like Joseph Brant, McGillivray invariably impressed whites with his fine Charleston-educated manners, fair complexion, and European dress. He forewent the winter hunting pursued by most Creek men in favor of managing an estate on the Gulf of Mexico, and spent summers on his sprawling plantation at Little Tallassie, complete with apple orchards, large herds of livestock, and a labor force of sixty slaves. Meeting McGillivray in 1790, Abigail Adams (whose husband

John was then vice president) was impressed that he "speaks English like a Native"; but he spoke to his fellow Creeks through an interpreter. Bowles presented a self-conscious contrast to this, portraying himself—to white audiences at least—as every inch the Indian hunter and warrior. The only surviving portrait of him depicts a decidedly Byronic figure in a ruffled shirt, silver armbands cinching its billowing sleeves, thick coils of beads looped around his neck, and an elaborate ostrich-plumed turban. Though some fellow whites found his Indian dress "ridiculous" and "slovenly," the showy guise also helped him attract white support. He hoped his British ties, in turn, would help him garner a following among the Creeks.[103]

Bowles's ambitions in Florida dovetailed beautifully with Lord Dunmore's. Since the peace of 1783, the Indian trade in Spanish Florida had been controlled by a firm called Panton, Leslie and Company. Headquartered in Nassau, the company was strongly affiliated with Dunmore's Bahamas enemies—including Thomas Brown, who had helped secure its monopoly when he was superintendent of Indian affairs. Dunmore wished to unseat the company for reasons largely to do with Bahamian politics and personal profit. Bowles, meanwhile, had his own reasons to topple Panton, Leslie. The firm's silent partner in Indian country was none other than McGillivray, Bowles's greatest rival in his bid to gain ascendancy among the Creeks. With Dunmore's backing, Bowles led an expedition into Florida a few months after the Wylly affair, designed to oust Panton, Leslie from the region.[104] Unfortunately for him the foray quickly became a fiasco. On warnings from Thomas Brown, Spanish authorities turned McGillivray against "that villain Bowles," who was "no more than the foolish instrument of veritable scoundrels."[105] McGillivray gave Bowles some "wholesome advice" designed to "dismiss him from this Country forever," and threatened to "cut off his ears" if he did not oblige.[106]

But neither Bowles nor his patron Dunmore were daunted by failure. Rather, they found further common ground in Bowles's bigger plans for the future of Florida. Offering a compelling variation on projects that Dunmore had long endorsed, Bowles envisioned a whole new state rising from the swamps under his personal leadership. He called it Muskogee. Muskogee, as he sketched it out to the governor, was to be an independent Indian state, free of Spanish rule, secure against American incursions, and a haven for anyone loyal to British ideals. It would achieve this comfortable position thanks to an alliance with the British Empire, making it a sort of southern counterpart to

Joseph Brant's confederacy. And Britain would benefit from the relationship in turn by gaining access to the Mississippi. Dunmore liked what he heard. With the governor's blessing, Bowles returned to Creek country in 1789 to start bringing Muskogee to life. So it was that what started as a local conflict among Bahamian politicians spilled over into commercial rivalries, Indian affairs, and a test of the meanings of loyalty itself.

At Coweta, on the Chattahoochee River (now the border between Alabama and Georgia), Bowles convened a council of Creek, Seminole, and Cherokee representatives. He began to style himself "Estajoca," or "Director General of the Creek Nation." "The unanimous voice of twenty thousand warriors" (or so he flattered himself) acclaimed him as their leader and commissioned him to go on an embassy to London.[107] Bowles set off on an Atlantic circuit to win British aid, retracing the journeys of many loyalist refugees before him. From the Bahamas, he headed to Nova Scotia to attract imperial administrators to the idea of a loyal western alliance between Muskogee and the Iroquois. He successfully recruited Governor Parr to his plan in Halifax, helped by the fact that he presented it at the height of an Anglo-Spanish war scare, and proceeded to Quebec to meet with Lord Dorchester.[108] Though Dorchester had always been wary of Indian alliances, and tried to dissuade Bowles from going to London, even he acknowledged that Creek aid would be invaluable in the event of war with Spain.[109] With Dorchester's reluctant blessing (and at his expense), Bowles and his small entourage crossed the Atlantic and arrived in London at the end of 1790.

There, despite adverse diplomatic developments, Bowles confidently proposed what was surely the grandest pro-British scheme for seizing North American territory since the American Revolution. In a petition to King George III, Bowles stressed his dual role as both "leader of an independent and populous Nation" and a British subject of proven loyalty. "I have always preserved my Allegiance to your Majesty and my affection to this Country," Bowles assured his sovereign, and now he was in a rare position to demonstrate it by bringing a vast region of North America into the imperial embrace.[110] Bowles volunteered more specific propositions to the foreign secretary. With appropriate British backing, he calculated it would take just two months to drive "the Spaniards from the whole country of the Floridas and that of New Orleans." From there, he "would proceed without delay to Mexico, and in conjunction with the Natives declare it independent of the Spaniards" (a promise that uncannily echoed John Cruden's onetime boast that he would "open the Gates of Mexico to my Country").[111] As to the loyalty of Muskogee to the British crown, officials could rest easy. Just look at the rest of the empire, Bowles observed: look at India. He pointed to the example of Robert Clive, the East India Company general who had brought Bengal under British hegemony. Clive had sworn that the only way to secure the Indian subcontinent was to use local troops, and Bowles thought "the Maxim . . . as good in America as in Indostan." In the same way Britain maintained control in India with an army of native sepoys, it could sustain its enlarged American empire with Creek and other indigenous manpower. "The Americans are now waiting their opportunity to seise the remainder of the British Colonies," Bowles concluded. The time was right for a preemptive British strike.[112]

Whether it was the strength of his passion or (more likely) the smallness of his budget, Bowles managed to secure limited British permission to move forward with his plans.[113] (Whatever else, Muskogee must have seemed more plausible than the scheme for a British-sponsored rising across South America advanced by the Venezuelan revolutionary Francisco de Miranda a few months earlier.) Bowles returned to Nassau and from there set sail for Florida, with the red-and-blue Muskogee banner he had designed himself rippling from the mast. This time fortune was kinder to Bowles's expedition. He successfully rallied further Indian support, and boasted to Dunmore that he was vested "with full power to transact all business of the nation and direct their future councils."[114] His deputies scored a critical strategic victory by seizing a Panton, Leslie warehouse. While Dunmore delivered confident reports to London that "one of the finest Countrys in the world" was about to be opened to Britain, McGillivray and his associates scrambled to preserve their influence, urging the Indians to back away from Bowles: "He calls himself an Englishman, but be assured he is none; he tells you that he Came from the King of England, but when did you See an officer of that King Come to you in poverty & rags."[115] But soon McGillivray had to retreat to Pensacola in the face of what was fast becoming a dangerous challenge to his authority. Confronted with such upheaval in their domains, Florida's Spanish governors decided to negotiate with Bowles.[116]

In early 1792, Bowles cruised into New Orleans on a Spanish vessel to speak with his opponents. As he stepped out into this cosmopolitan city between the river and the gulf, he must have felt his life's ambition about to come true: Muskogee to be recognized, the Mississippi gained for the British Empire. Bowles insisted to the Spanish governor of New Orleans that he, rather than McGillivray, should be recognized as the leader in Creek country. He would make Muskogee a bulwark against the United States, he promised, and a committed friend to the empires of both Spain and Britain—invoking, like Cruden before him, the common interests of European empires in the face of a republican rival. The governor appeared receptive and told Bowles to meet with superior authorities in Cuba to finalize an agreement.

But when Bowles disembarked in Havana, under the imposing fortress of Morro Castle, he realized with a thud that he had been tricked. The Spanish had no incentive to support Bowles's grand pro-British plans when they already enjoyed good relations with the Creeks through McGillivray. Luring him to Cuba was a way of pulling him into captivity. Just weeks before, Bowles had looked set to lead the Floridas to loyal independence in a greater British world. Now he was a Spanish prisoner, soon to be transferred from Cuba to Cádiz, and then to the Philippines, as far from Muskogee as the Spanish Empire could take him. Instead of becoming lord of Muskogee, Bowles became surely the only American loyalist to be exiled in southeastern Asia. Stranded in that Pacific archipelago, on the other side of the world from the Bahamas, Bowles must have gained a visceral appreciation for the power of global empires. Only a near miracle could bring him back to Muskogee.[117]

HE WOULD OFTEN be described as the "adventurer" Bowles, and at one level the dismissive epithet was appropriate. Bowles's failed attempts to establish the state of Muskogee rendered him something of a shooting star across the Bahamas scene, blazing brightly and fast flaming out. For all its exceptional qualities, however, Bowles's career brilliantly illuminated the persistence with which refugee loyalists— like the British Empire to which they adhered—sought to translate losses into gains.

It also highlighted the divisions embedded within Bahamian loyalist society, around competing ideas about what the British Empire ought to do for its subjects. Hepburn, Brown, Wylly, and others articulated an oppositional rhetoric of rights and representation very similar to that of American patriots. At the same time, they imported their slaves in large enough numbers to transform the Bahamas' racial composition, just as they imported American racial attitudes which they aimed to put into law. Dunmore and Bowles, though (and Cruden at his sanest), espoused a competing image of what the British Empire stood for. In line with the "spirit of 1783," they envisioned a multiethnic community united in loyalty under a tolerant, protective crown—a conception of empire historically more congenial to metropolitan authorities than to provincial white settlers. Dunmore, the man who freed slaves in Virginia, acted as a lightning rod for conflicts over race in the Bahamas thanks to his comparative tolerance of black claims to freedom. The collision of opinions during his governorship set a precedent for conflicts over race and slavery between white Bahamians and British authorities that would long outlast him.

It also formed a backdrop of controversy against which William Augustus Bowles posed a vivid contrast. Here was a white American loyalist hoping to lead his adoptive Indian brethren to territorial independence, with British aid. This head-spinning combination attested to the cosmopolitan possibilities of the British Empire as a place in which a man like Bowles—or like Joseph Brant or Alexander McGillivray—could successfully portray himself as at once a loyal imperial subject and as the leader of a sovereign Indian nation. All these men hoped that the same empire that offered paternalistic protection to blacks would provide support for North America's indigenous peoples, in the face of U.S. encroachment. But in the intensely divided political environment of the Bahamas, Bowles's plans proved especially provocative, by deepening battle lines already dug around slavery and representation. Such interlocking tensions make the Bahamas a striking case in point of why the stories of loyal whites, blacks, and Indians have to be explored together to be understood in full.

Territorial ambitions like Bowles's can sometimes seem hard to take seriously, especially considering the small forces involved and the very large areas they hoped to control, often at great distances from metropolitan centers. Yet the American Revolution fueled precisely such expansionist thinking among British subjects. After all, the British Empire had always built itself up by capitalizing on the weaknesses of its imperial rivals, of which the United States, with its shaky frontiers, was now one. Besides, when loyalists had built cities in the Canadian wilderness, when the Iroquois established a new domain in the Great Lakes, when free blacks pioneered a settlement in Sierra Leone, and when British subjects colonized Australia and governed Bengal, then why wasn't Muskogee also a plausible prospect? However outraged Bahamian loyalists might have been by Bowles as a character, they could not write off his enterprise as such. That was just the problem. Bowles emerged from the same turbulent late-eighteenth-century climate that fostered numerous other imperial visionaries, from John Cruden to Francisco de Miranda, and acted as a forerunner in turn to nineteenth-century U.S. filibusters who sought to carve their own chunks out of Spanish America. (Just a decade after Bowles's capture, U.S. vice president Aaron Burr plotted the conquest of the lower Mississippi Valley and Mexico along rather similar lines.) All these projects revealed visible points of convergence between apparent opposites, Anglo-American loyalists and rebels, between the British Empire and the expansionist American republic.

When some loyalists demonstrated against imperial authority to the point of breaking with it altogether, and others championed schemes designed to expand and entrench it, it was clear that loyalism itself could connote a wide range of things. By the time of Bowles's arrest, war with republican France would make loyalty and the containment of dissent more urgent than ever to British imperial authorities. With the threat of a French attack on the Bahamas, and anxious that popular agitation might take a dangerously republican turn, Dunmore could no longer resist a fresh election. In 1794, for the first time in a decade, Bahamian voters chose a new house of assembly. The results at last confirmed the refugee planter ascendancy in the islands, by eliminating Dunmore's old supporters and electing a number of his long-standing rivals; William Wylly was appointed chief justice. Renewed fears of slave uprisings, triggered by the 1791 revolution on Saint Domingue, inspired a series of tougher racial laws, designed to keep blacks and whites safely apart, and trumping Dunmore's paternalistic policies. Provoked at last by the continuing protests against Dunmore, his massive expenditures, and his unavoidably irregular (not to say corrupt) behavior, Whitehall recalled the hated governor in 1796. Dunmore returned to Britain under a cloud, his own loyalty ironically tainted by a personal scandal, when one of his daughters had married—without royal permission—one of King George III's sons.[118]

And so Dunmore's vision of empire may have been defeated in the local context of the Bahamas. But the white loyalist settlers' dreams of a cotton-rich plantation society proved equally elusive. The sandy Bahamian soil Dr. Lewis Johnston had disdained never became more fertile. The chenille bug continued to burrow into the cotton bolls.

Hurricanes regularly wrecked houses and crops, while sustaining rainfall too rarely came. By 1800 most planters had abandoned their struggles with cotton and turned to a more diverse, if less lucrative, assortment of corn, peas, and other grains.[119] (In a remarkable illustration of the Bahamas' contrapuntal relationship with the mainland, sea island cotton would be reintroduced from the Bahamas into the American south, where its fortunes became the stuff of legend.) Some of them cashed in and moved on. In 1805, Thomas Brown developed a third 6,000-acre estate, a counterpart to those he had owned in Georgia and the Bahamas, on the island of St. Vincent, on land recently seized from the indigenous Caribs.[120] In stark contrast to British North America, the Bahamas never took off as an agricultural economy. The islands flourished best in their position as maritime center, way station, and offshore hub—a role they continue to play more than two centuries later.

For all that Dunmore had prepared for war with his extensive bulwarks and barricades, Fort Charlotte—the jewel in his crown of fortresses—would never fire its guns in battle.[121] Manning the bastions facing the blank ocean, bored soldiers carved their initials into the sun-baked walls, waiting for attacks that never came. Like the folly in Airth, it still stands there, a relic of dated ambitions. In the end, despite loyalist efforts to make it otherwise, the Bahamas remained marginal to imperial interests. For the important challenges for the British Empire, like the real profits and possibilities, lay in a different quarter of that aquamarine sea. It was on the Caribbean island of Jamaica, Britain's richest colony, that loyalist refugees would experience most acutely the disjuncture between hopes and realities, and the pressures of living in an empire once more consumed by revolutionary war.

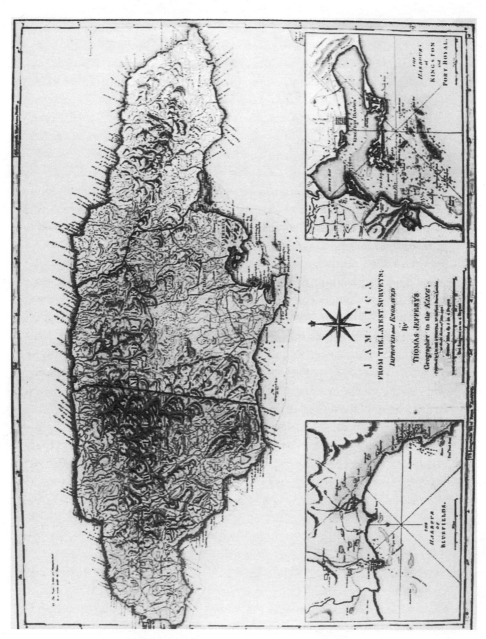

Thomas Jefferys, *Jamaica, from the Latest Surveys*, 1775.

CHAPTER EIGHT

False Refuge

ITS BEAUTY could take your breath away. From the sparkling surface of the water your gaze swept sharply up to the craggy Blue Mountains, climbing into the clouds. Over the rippled slopes fell a living green blanket, textured in the weird vegetable forms of the tropics: giant ferns and tufted bromeliads, flap-eared plantains, muscular trees draped in epiphytes, careening stands of bamboo, and sinewy palms. When you turned past the outer lip of the harbor you floated over the broken stones of the old capital of Port Royal, mostly destroyed in a 1692 earthquake. The gleaming sand swept around the shoreline to Kingston, Port Royal's replacement, the greatest British metropolis in the Caribbean. Gulls sliced circles around the masts, the sun cut the water into liquid diamonds. No wonder loyalists were captivated by it. "Such hills, such mountains, and such verdure; everything so bright and gay, it is delightful!" gushed one new arrival on cruising toward this spectacular landscape.[1] An eighteenth-century aesthete effusively compared the bay of Kingston to the bay of Naples, with the Blue Mountains standing in for Vesuvius and the submerged ruins of Port Royal like a phantom Pompeii under the transparent sea.[2] Others let the "grandeur and sublimity" simply overcome them, knocking language from their lips.[3] Whatever else loyalist refugees knew of this lush island, they could see it wasn't the thirteen colonies anymore.

Of all the British colonies to which loyalists migrated during and after the revolution, Jamaica presented the most immediately attractive destination. The very fact that refugees did not regularly complain about going there, as they did about Nova Scotia and the Bahamas, said much about its appeal. It was the most populous, developed, and richest British island in the Caribbean, and its slave-based plantation system made it an obvious choice for slaveowning southern loyalists in particular. South Carolina refugee Louisa Wells, for one, who had

escaped from Charleston to join her parents in Britain, openly fantasized about traveling "to the scorching Torrid Zone." That was partly
because she found her British "Isle of Liberty and Peace" cold and
dank, and promptly fell ill. It was also because Britain lay on the wrong
side of the Atlantic: Wells's fiancé, Alexander Aikman, had moved to
Jamaica, and she longed to join him there. In 1781, Wells braved the
dangers of another wartime Atlantic crossing to do so—only to get
captured by the French and imprisoned for three months. Undaunted,
she took passage for Jamaica again, this time as a passenger on board a
slave ship.[4]

She arrived with nostrils clogged by the stench of packed bodies, of
vomit, waste, and sweat, barely concealed by pungent vinegar-swabbed
decks, and with an all too vivid sense of the desperate conditions under
which the vast majority of immigrants to Jamaica—captive Africans—
journeyed to an isle of slavery and violence. The patterns of black
migration in the British Atlantic have been well mapped by historians,
to reveal the contours of a community transformed by dislocation.[5]
Wells's voyage pointed up the irony in the fact that this colony, based
on forced migration, now served as a haven for American refugees.
Displaced by war, she belonged to a group whose movement—though
not coerced in anything like the manner of slaves—also fell short of
fully voluntary. It was a telling portent of the many unsettling contradictions loyalists would soon encounter in Jamaica.

To Wells, fortunately, Jamaica offered a happy asylum: she found
Aikman thriving, and they married in early 1782. Aikman had started a
newspaper when he reached Kingston—the *Jamaica Mercury*, soon
renamed the *Royal Gazette* and emblazoned with the royal arms—and
from 1780 gloried in the position of official printer to the crown. His
paper joined the diaspora of publications that fanned out from the loyalist Wells family's single Charleston printshop, to East Florida, the
Bahamas, and now Jamaica. While his brother-in-law John Wells
printed assaults on imperial rule in Nassau, Aikman became a pillar of
the Jamaican establishment, acquiring plantations and fine houses, and
serving as a member of the house of assembly from 1805 to 1825.[6]

Yet the Aikmans' successful transition from South Carolina to
Jamaica was fairly exceptional among the three thousand loyalist
refugees who came to the island. For all Jamaica's evident advantages
as a site of loyalist settlement, it posed adverse contrasts with British
North America and the Bahamas. Refugees in the former, after all,
remained in North America, and comprised the majority of the popu-

lation in Nova Scotia and New Brunswick; loyalists also formed a majority in the Bahamas, which remained environmentally and culturally more similar to (and connected with) the former southern colonies than Jamaica. In terms of ecology and population structure alone, going to Jamaica was like going to a tropical moon. The refugees were doubly a minority, enveloped within Jamaica's creole white society, which was itself numerically overwhelmed by slaves, in a ratio of black to white dwarfing that of pre-revolutionary South Carolina and Georgia. American refugees had trouble finding land, employing their slaves, and preserving their health in a notoriously disease-ridden environment (which may help account for the relative absence of records documenting loyalist lives in Jamaica). In place of an ideal haven, loyalists quickly ran up against the harsh realities of Jamaican life: the elusiveness of its legendary wealth, the violence of its slave-based society, the decimating forces of disease, and a permeating sense of vulnerability from within and without. Contradictions between expectations and realities formed a defining theme of the refugee experience across sites of loyalist exodus, but nowhere would these contrasts appear more starkly than in Jamaica. They were practically built into the society itself.

Jamaica signaled many things to an eighteenth-century Anglo-American. First and foremost was opulence. A thousand miles away from Britain's other West Indian colonies of Barbados and the Lesser Antilles, Jamaica formed the third corner of a compact triangle of imperial wealth based on sugar. Cuba and Saint Domingue, each about a hundred miles from Jamaica, yielded profits just as dramatic for Spain and France as Jamaica did for Britain. It was the wealth of these rivals, in fact, that first lured Britons to the western Caribbean. They came not as planters, but as pirates. In 1655, Britain seized Jamaica as part of a smash-and-grab expedition against the Spanish, and for decades to come the island functioned primarily as a buccaneering base. "The Dunghill of the Universe, the Refuse of the whole Creation . . . the Place where Pandora fill'd her Box," snarled one satirist of this rowdy, lawless society. It was no wonder that people interpreted the 1692 earthquake that destroyed Port Royal as divine retribution against the "very *Sodom* of the Universe"—especially given how much they preferred what replaced the buccaneer-dominated society, namely the plantation economy of imperial dreams.[7] But Jamaica's proximity to French and Spanish colonies kept it at the center of one of the eighteenth-century's biggest imperial war zones. Vulnerability to outside attack was one reason that Jamaica, like other British West Indian colonies, remained emphatically loyal in the face of the American Revolution.

Soon, the planters' source of wealth outstripped even the greatest of pirates' hoards. It came packed in an unassuming green stalk, about as thick as a child's wrist. Sugarcane fed an increasingly insatiable British sweet tooth. (Average Britons in the 1780s consumed twelve pounds of sugar per person per year, three times as much as their grandparents.)[8] "A field of canes, when . . . it is in arrows (or full blossom), is one of the most beautiful productions that the pen or pencil can possibly describe," enthused the planter and writer William Beckford.[9] He might as well have said the most lucrative, for to its owner a field of ripe sugarcane was tantamount to a field of profits. Sugar was gold in the eighteenth century. Jamaica's trade in sugar and rum helped make the island the wealthiest colony in the late-eighteenth-century British Empire. On the eve of the American Revolution, when per capita wealth for a white person in England averaged about £42, and about £60 for whites in the thirteen colonies, white Jamaicans enjoyed a per capita net worth of £2,201.[10] The only other British imperial domain that could rival Jamaica in terms of profitability was India, and even there, opportunities for adventurous Britons to come back loaded with diamonds and gold (like the great nabob Robert Clive) were tapering off by the end of the century. At only forty-four hundred square miles—about the size of Connecticut, and significantly smaller than Cuba or Hispaniola—Jamaica could lay claim to being, after French Saint Domingue, the second richest colony on earth.

And yet Jamaica's opulence rested on the inherently abusive system that enabled such fortunes in the first place. All that wealth depended on a slave labor regime of remarkable proportions. If you lop off a section of sugar cane and gnaw at it, you can just about suck out some of its sweet juice. But processing these fibrous stalks into bulk sugar requires an enormously labor-intensive process of harvesting, grinding, boiling, molding, and crystallizing—every stage of which was performed by slaves.[11] As consumption of sugar increased, so did the labor force required to produce it. By the end of the American Revolution, about 210,000 slaves outnumbered the island's eighteen thousand whites by a ratio of nearly twelve to one. This ratio of black to white was fairly typical of British Caribbean colonies, but stood in startling contrast to the former thirteen colonies, where no state had even a black majority in 1790.[12]

Greatly outnumbered by its own slaves, the white minority went to appalling extremes to secure its authority. White Jamaica survived on a reign of terror. To be sure, slave discipline in the American colonies— to say nothing of the penalties regularly dispensed by the British criminal justice system—seems horrifying enough in retrospect. But even by contemporary standards, Caribbean violence was of another order. A dispassionate record of Jamaica's everyday sadism survives in the diaries of plantation overseer Thomas Thistlewood, whose thirty-seven-year-long career on the island ended with his death in 1786. By then, Thistlewood had scored tens of thousands of lashes across slaves' bare skin, practically flaying some of his victims alive. He had had sex with 138 women (by his own tally), almost all of them slaves. He had stuck the heads of executed runaways on poles; he had seen cheeks slit and ears cut off. He routinely meted out punishments such as the following, for a slave caught for eating sugarcane: "had him well flogged and pickled, then made Hector shit in his mouth."[13] Such incredible barbarity symptomized the panic that pervaded Jamaican white society: the fear that the black majority might rise up and slaughter them in their beds. Thistlewood would not have blinked at the sentences imposed on slaves convicted of participating in Tacky's Rebellion of 1760, the largest slave uprising in the eighteenth-century British Empire: some gibbeted in iron cages, others slowly roasted over open flames.[14]

The sheer demographic shock of Jamaica's slave society must have struck black loyalist George Liele even before he disembarked. The very same ships that carried his family away from Savannah to a fresh start in freedom carried almost two thousand other blacks onward into continued slavery. The racial composition of the loyalist exodus to Jamaica shows what a central place slavery held in white loyalists' calculations: the approximately three thousand white refugees who moved to Jamaica managed to export with them fully eight thousand slaves. Liele and his family belonged to a tiny number of free blacks amid the Jamaican immigrants. Even then, Liele's own autonomy was hemmed in by his indenture to Moses Kirkland, the officer who had helped him purchase his family's freedom—a reminder of how the boundaries between slavery and freedom could be blurred. Stepping off the *Zebra* convoy in August 1782, the Lieles joined about ten thousand mixed-race "free people of color" and free blacks living on Jamaica.[15] As Liele made his way through Kingston's streets, mud-clogged by the summer rains, he must have marveled to find himself, for the first time in his life, in a city where black faces outnumbered white. He was now in a society where he counted in the racial majority (divided though it was by ethnic cleavages), yet where that majority was brutally subordinated by law and violence. Liele knew, from his months in a Georgia jail, that being a free black in America was hard enough. What would freedom bring him here?

Landing on this alien island would have been equally striking for Liele's fellow Savannah evacuee Elizabeth Johnston. In 1786, a year after William Johnston had left Scotland for Spanish Town, she steeled herself for another Atlantic passage and set off with their youngest children to join him in Jamaica. Though this had been the couple's longest period apart, Johnston said little this time about her eagerness to see her husband; the farewells she had made in Scotland may have tainted her happiness. She had left behind her own father in Edinburgh, her close circle of in-laws, and her first real family home. Most wrenchingly, she left her firstborn son Andrew, who stayed with his grandfather Dr. Lewis Johnston to be educated in Edinburgh's celebrated schools. Whether she felt transported by the gorgeous strangeness of the setting, Elizabeth Johnston never later told. All she recorded about her arrival on Jamaica was its date: December 15, 1786. It was the fifth place she had inhabited in as many years. Still just twenty-two years old, she had spent her entire adult life in transit, unsettled by the resonating aftereffects of the American Revolution. In something of the way Liele's indenture made his emigration less than voluntary, Johnston's movements fell into a shaded zone between free choice and force of circumstance. Her time on Jamaica would only enhance her tendency to understand all her migrations as trials.

Elizabeth Johnston remained mute about the island's beauty, never mentioned sugar once, and rarely referred to the slaves who surrounded her. (As a white woman on Jamaica, Johnston belonged to an especially small minority in a society with twice as many white men than women.)[16] But she was quickly schooled in another inescapable feature of Jamaican life: death. This island was a morgue. Tropical diseases such as yellow fever and malaria led to mortality rates among whites as high as one in eight, supporting one visitor's casual observation that "once in seven Years there is a Revolution of Lives in this Island. . . . As many die in that Space of Time as perfectly inhabit it."[17] Of course that was why William Johnston had come to Jamaica in the first place. As a doctor, he filled the one profession guaranteed to thrive under any adverse circumstances. But the same mortal forces that supported the Johnston family financially also came to haunt them personally throughout their residence in Jamaica.

It was easy enough to understand why up to two-thirds of wealthy planters lived comfortably far away in Britain, leaving a small core of white overseers, bookkeepers, lawyers, and doctors to staff their estates. Arriving white loyalists notably resembled their Jamaican peers in a crucial respect: they were people pushed by circumstance to run high risks in hopes of high rewards. White Jamaicans saw themselves, too, as exiles of a sort, sojourners rather than settlers. "Europeans who come to this island have seldom an idea of settling here for life," remarked the Jamaica planter and historian Bryan Edwards. "Their aim is generally to acquire a fortune to enable them to sit down comfortably in their native country."[18] Yet the island's very advantages served as disadvantages for loyalist refugees, who in any case saw "their native country" as closed to them—underlining the degree to which their own choice to settle in this place was made under duress. Land was not just there for the taking, as in British North America or the Bahamas. In a well-supplied labor market, there were surprisingly few places for striving refugees to put their slaves to work. And though they represented a significant enough increase in the island's white population—perhaps as much as a sixth—to earn special treatment from Jamaican authorities, they also invited competitive resentment from fellow whites.

Loyalist refugees in Jamaica thus arrived in an island of opposites and extremes. Jamaica had survived the dangers of war, its sugar output kept increasing, and its economy diversifying; it seemed on the surface a perfect place for the refugees to rebuild. But restrictions on trade with the United States left Jamaicans reeling and resentful. Provision shortages, combined with severe drought, led to a famine that reputedly killed at least fifteen thousand slaves.[19] You might be forgiven for thinking that nature itself was out to get Jamaica. Almost every year in the 1780s screaming hurricanes swept away crops and houses like chesspieces off a game board, and left the lushest landscapes "visibly stricken blank with desolation," brutally exposing how fragile even the largest fortunes might be.[20] However hard you tried to focus on the opulence, you could not get away from the violence. It charged relations between white and black. It infected bodies from within. It burst out of the very heavens. And less than a decade after the British evacuations from the United States, it threw Jamaica—and the loyalist refugees—into the cockpit of another revolutionary war. Struggling to carve out a niche on Jamaica, loyalists hit up against the disjunction between aspirations and realities in such intractable form that some of them would end up moving on again. If by the 1790s the American Revolution looked like the first chapter in what historians have called an age of democratic revolutions—continuing in France and Saint Domingue—loyalist refugees in Jamaica gained hard-won insight into how the revolution had also set off an age of imperial migrations.[21]

DOMINATING THE main square of Spanish Town stands a remark-able monument to imperial confidence. It consists of a heroic statue, sheltered under an elaborate cupola and flanked by sweeping colon-nades. The figure's giant toes alone, splayed wide apart in sandals, con-vey an aura of command. Every part of his Roman costume, from skirt to tunic to luxuriously billowing cape, emphasizes his powerful physique. His left hand rests on a sword and shield, and his right fist points determinedly ahead, clenching a baton. Not many passersby could understand the somewhat inelegant Latin inscribed on its pedestal—to Admiral Lord George Rodney, who restored well-being to Jamaica and peace to Britain—but the gist of the thing was clear enough.[22] The Rodney Memorial, as this glorious ensemble is called, represents an anomaly in the historical vestiges of the American Revo-lution. It is the greatest British *victory* monument of the war. Nothing better demonstrates how differently the American Revolution looked from the British West Indies than it did from the thirteen colonies—and by extension, how different the outlook of loyalist refugees would be from that of their Jamaican hosts.

While thirteen British colonies in North America rebelled in 1775, the other thirteen colonies that Britain possessed in the Americas, north and south of the future United States, did not. None remained more staunchly loyal than the West Indian islands, of which Jamaica was the largest.[23] Although Jamaica traded with the thirteen colonies for food and timber, these commercial ties were overshadowed by the island's dependence on the protectionist British sugar market. (Jamaicans particularly resented American smugglers who circum-vented British tariffs by importing cheaper molasses from the French West Indies.) Economically, it had nothing to gain from joining the American Revolution. Strategically, it had much to lose. Unlike Amer-ican colonists, who resented the stationing of British troops on their soil, Jamaicans positively welcomed British garrisons to protect them from their own slaves. The memory of Tacky's Rebellion was still fresh when a slave conspiracy in the fateful month of July 1776 underscored how much Jamaicans depended on British forces. Though rumored to have been encouraged by American patriots, this plot in western Jamaica owed much to the fact that half the islands' soldiers were in the process of shipping out for North America.[24] Martial law and the usual savage executions successfully suppressed the would-be rebellion; but the incident still haunted Jamaicans when a massive slave revolt broke out on nearby Saint Domingue in 1791. To a small white population heavily reliant on Britain, anti-imperial revolution—especially when it was a revolution by slaves—felt like a nightmare come to life.

Jamaica also needed Britain to guard it from the external dangers posed by war. These came perilously close to the island in the winter of 1781–82, when the French fleet, fresh from its triumph at Yorktown, cruised out of the Chesapeake and into the Caribbean. The seemingly unstoppable force seized the British colonies of St. Kitts, Nevis, and Montserrat in quick succession, and had Jamaica next in its sights. Jamaica's resourceful governor, Archibald Campbell (who assumed that position after his successful command in Savannah), busily worked up a strategy for island defense, calling on all whites, free blacks, and selected "confidential slaves" to support British troops.[25] Jamaican creoles shuddered at the prospect of an imminent invasion; it was rumored that the French carried "50,000 pairs of handcuffs, and fetters" to capture their slaves. Fortunately for them, the Royal Navy under Admiral Rodney was in pursuit. Early on an April morning, a superior British force caught up with the French in a channel between Dominica and Guadeloupe called "the Saintes." Boldly breaking through the line of French ships, Rodney scored a decisive victory, capturing the French admiral de Grasse himself. In a stroke, Rodney saved the richest colony in the empire and handed Britain a valuable bargaining chip in the peace negotiations.[26]

Recognizing the historical significance of the Battle of the Saintes (as it became known), the Jamaica house of assembly voted to spend £1,000 commissioning a statue from one of London's finest sculptors.[27] But like all such monuments, the Rodney Memorial is a splendid half-truth. For one thing, the beginning of the war had found the admiral rather ingloriously hiding out from his creditors in France, ruined by gambling losses. When he conquered the Dutch island of St. Eustatius in 1781, he plundered it so rapaciously that he provoked transatlantic outcry as well as costly lawsuits. More seriously, Rodney was so busy ransacking St. Eustatius that he failed to intercept the French fleet on its way to Yorktown.[28] The Battle of the Saintes allowed him to salvage a reputation badly shaken by his earlier errors. Instead of being the rogue who helped lose America, Rodney became the hero who saved Jamaica. And since Jamaica was Britain's most profitable colony, and the Caribbean its most valuable imperial region, this battle mattered more from the perspective of the British Empire as a whole.

So when the evacuation fleet from Savannah landed in Port Royal, four months after the Battle of the Saintes, it brought the haggard faces of defeat to an island basking in victory. (At least one Jamaican newspaper concealed from its readers the fact that this actually was an evacuation fleet, and the beginning of the end of British rule in the thirteen colonies.) Over the next six months, ships from Savannah and Charleston unloaded thousands of disoriented refugees and slaves into the streets of Kingston and the nearby capital, Spanish Town, in varying states of need. With approximately twenty thousand residents, Kingston was the largest city in the British Caribbean, and the third largest city in English-speaking America, after New York and Philadelphia.[29] It outclassed Savannah and Charleston, to say nothing of Nassau or Halifax, with its extensive city plan and the proud buildings of a colonial cosmopolis: well-appointed barracks and spacious parade, an imposing church complete with pipe organ and clocktower, a free school, and—like Spanish Town—a handsome synagogue. The city's broad streets were lined with two- and three-story brick houses, designed for the climate with covered galleries and patios. "The most luxurious epicure" would find everything available in Kingston's overflowing markets. At a concert or ball in the city's two finest taverns, Ranelagh and Vauxhall, you could almost imagine yourself in the London pleasure gardens for which they were named. Even the county jail merited distinction: it formerly belonged to a mathematician who installed an observatory there, "little suspecting . . . that it would be converted into a receptacle for unfortunate persons, who are here precluded from almost every other amusement than that of star-gazing."[30]

The refugees made a startling impression against this prospering scene. "Affecting and unusual spectacles of Misfortune and Misery were exhibited in all parts of the town," locals opined. It is impossible to tell from the scant surviving record what percentage of newcomers arrived in poverty, but given the migration patterns from Savannah and Charleston, whereby wealthier loyalists opted to move to East Florida, it seems fair to speculate that disproportionately many of the

whites arriving in Jamaica were relatively poor. With the vast majority
of the three thousand white refugees remaining in Kingston, parish
authorities formed the front line of relief. Dozens of loyalists were
admitted into the poor house, and many others received ad hoc pensions. Kingston residents, moved by the sight of such sufferings, took
up a subscription that raised just over £1,000 on behalf of the
refugees.[31] Another observer, Prince William Henry, passing through
Jamaica on naval duty, was so shocked by the sight of the destitute
masses spilling off the evacuation fleets that he offered "a handsome
sum" from his own funds "for the relief of those refugees from South
Carolina."[32] His royal example inspired a legislative sequel. In February 1783 (the same week that it commissioned the Rodney Memorial),
the house of assembly passed a bill "to exempt from Taxes for a limited
time such of his Majesty's subjects of North America as from motives
of Loyalty have been or shall be obliged to relinquish or abandon their
possessions in that country, and take refuge in this Island with Intent to
settle."[33] That last qualification—"with Intent to settle"—stands out.
British officials had long fretted over how to maintain Jamaica's white
population, ravaged as it was by disease and absenteeism. Deficiency
laws, mandating that planters maintain a minimum number of whites
on their property, had proved hapless at best. Loyalist refugees thus
appeared as attractive candidates for long-term residence. The question was how actually to integrate them.

Alexander Aikman printed 460 copies of the act, which quickly
made its way around the refugee community.[34] In a sort of miniature
version of the Loyalist Claims Commission, refugees filed cases to
prove their loyalty, losses, and intention to settle. Successful claimants
received certificates confirming their tax-exempt status. These documents open a rare window onto the composition of the Jamaica loyalist refugees. (At least 169 certificates survive, though fifty-one of these
belong to a different group of claimants included in the act: settlers
displaced from British outposts in the Bay of Honduras and the Mosquito Shore.)[35] At one level, they expose the refugees' geographical
and social diversity. There were migrants who had initially evacuated
from Boston in 1776, like William Parker, "an inhabitant of that place
from his infancy as a loyal subject to his Britannick Majesty." There
were New Yorkers like Robert Stuart, a loyalist veteran who found he
"cou'd not remain in New York after the evacuation of that place"; and
Israel Mendes, with his family of eight, who joined a Jewish community in Kingston at least as thriving as the one he had left in colonial

New York. Benjamin Davis of Philadelphia, "one of the people called Quakers," had escaped prosecution in Pennsylvania, fled to Charleston, and sailed to Jamaica from there. Two claimants from West Florida had been imprisoned in Havana after the capture of Pensacola.[36]

Two-thirds of the certificates, however, belonged to loyalist refugees from Georgia and South Carolina, and together form an important record of the larger if still more obscure component of the influx into Jamaica: loyalist-owned slaves. George Liele's patron Moses Kirkland landed in Jamaica with forty-one slaves, whom he hoped to employ in indigo planting, as he had back in America. The widow of an attainted Georgia loyalist, Helen McKinnon, also managed to extract forty-one slaves from her husband's confiscated property, while Susannah Wylly (William's mother) arrived with thirty-seven, "a part of her slaves and that of her children (being all British subjects), . . . which have been employed in Kingston and in the county in jobbing." Several claimants brought not only their own slaves but those consigned to them by associates. In addition to the eighty-nine slaves of his own that Samuel Douglas of Augusta brought from Georgia, he carried 113 belonging to a pair of London merchants, "all of which slaves to the number of 202 have for some time past been employed on the Public Works." William Telfair, also from Augusta, brought sixty-six of his and his wife's slaves, as well as 112 owned by South Carolinian William Bull, whose family already owned land in Jamaica. Then there was Nathaniel Hall, the largest slave trafficker in the list. He came with fifty-six of his own slaves, 102 belonging to the imperial official William Knox, 217 of Georgia governor Sir James Wright's, and thirty-seven more besides—"all of which said negroes amount[in]g in the whole to 412 have since their arrival been employed in St. Thos. in the East."[37] Altogether, the eighty-one claimants from South Carolina and Georgia brought 1,359 slaves to Jamaica—a ratio of one to sixteen whites to blacks, higher even than the Jamaican average.

Skewed so strongly toward wealthy southern slaveowners, the certificates make for a curious record of distress. On the one hand, all of these testimonials document real losses and the real problems and deprivations of being a refugee, whether one had left behind thousands of acres or the humblest of houses. On the other hand, those who had lost the largest amount of property had also often preserved the most, in the movable form of their slaves. Owning dozens of slaves made them well-off by any eighteenth-century standards. Their successful bids for tax exemption (like many of the cases rewarded most fully by the Loyalist Claims Commission) seemed to prove the maxim that to those who have, more shall be given. Were these really the starving refugees so in need of government relief?

Jamaican creoles did not let this anomaly pass without comment. The tax relief measure had dragged Kingston parish revenues down, even as the loyalist influx brought its population noticeably up. Soon the parish was struggling to make ends meet. In the fall of 1784, the exasperated members of the vestry encouraged the church warden to ship, at parish expense, "such persons off the island, who are desirous of going and are like to become burdensome"; it was cheaper to pay for them to leave than to pay for them to stay.[38] The vestry followed up with an impassioned petition to the house of assembly. They commended the tax relief law for its "honourable motives." But seventy "apparently wealthy" refugees, they noted, living in "elegant" houses "in some of the best situations in town," had been exempted from taxes—while the indebted parish had spent more than £2,000 on relief, and its poor house was filled to bursting.[39] A year later, the vestry repeated its plea in still stronger terms. The law had been intended "for the consolation of the Poor, or such as were bereft of all property," they noted; but the successful petitioners for tax relief "have been employed in very lucrative departments." "Vague Itinerants and volatile fugitives, ought not to be discharged from [taxes] by virtue of national munificence, or the specious appreciation of Loyal and Distressed refugees."[40]

The house of assembly did not ultimately meet the Kingston vestry's demands—quite possibly because it had a host of other petitions to deal with, all grappling with postwar economic vicissitudes.[41] With the thirteen colonies lost, Jamaica mattered more than ever to the British imperial economy. At the same time, American independence had unfortunate consequences for Jamaica when the British government sharply restricted trade with the United States. Supply of basic provisions fell, prices rose. The opposite phenomenon overtook the sugar market: exports increased while prices trended downward, and high wartime duties remained frustratingly in place. In retrospect, many people would point to the American Revolution as the beginning of the end for the West Indies as the epicenter of the British Empire.[42] Soon enough the Jamaica house of assembly addressed petitions of its own directly to the king, seeking tax reductions and freer trade. It was hard enough to cope with commercial regulations, war debts, supply shortages, and hurricanes. The American refugees added yet another financial burden. Was it really "advisable at this time," they asked, "to give Berth to a New Spirit of Emigration and Adventure" by encouraging loyalists to settle in Jamaica?[43] Though not numerous enough in Jamaica to permeate political life as they did in British North America and the Bahamas, loyalist refugees nevertheless made a mark on Jamaican politics too. As focal points of Jamaica's postwar distress, they came to embody the predicament of a society coming to terms with its own altered position in a changing imperial world.

All the while, the refugees quested for opportunities for themselves and their slaves. Some Americans had trouble adjusting to tropical conditions. One South Carolinian had brought fourteen slaves and intended to start a plantation, but at sixty-two years old, "being very corpulent (upwards of 280 weight) is very unwieldy and inactive" and "unable to work."[44] In keeping with provisions made for refugees elsewhere, Whitehall had instructed Governor Campbell to make ungranted lands available for the loyalists.[45] The trouble was, there was virtually no land to be had. When the three months of food rations supplied for the Charleston refugees ran out in April 1783, even the slave-rich loyalists were not yet in a position to provide for themselves. The weather that season had been "excessive and uncommon dry," they complained, their slaves had fallen sick, and anyway they had "no land of their own here to employ them on." Though they tried to hire out their slaves for money, either on private plantations or public works projects, they found this difficult since "the return of peace has greatly lessened the demand for Negro labour."[46]

Nathaniel Hall, with more than four hundred slaves to place, was initially fortunate in this respect. He had connections to the influential planter Simon Taylor, who was fast becoming the richest man in Jamaica, if not indeed the whole British Empire.[47] On the "very strong" recommendations of Hall by mutual friends, Taylor reported that "I have distributed his negroes among my Friends where they can be maintained."[48] But Taylor was disappointed at the results. The American slaves, he decided, were simply not up to the kind of labor expected on a Jamaican plantation. "In respect to the American Negroes," he counseled a friend,

> I advise you to have nothing to do with them on any acct. I have never seen a single Gang of all that have been brought out to this Island that has turned out well. They are a set of soft Angola and Mundigo Negroes who are too lazy ever to provide provi-

sions for themselves and who have always been used to be handfed & if not give themselves up & take to dirt-eating which is inevitable Death.[49]

Sugarcane required tougher, hardier men, he thought; slaves "seasoned" to the particular physical challenges of the Jamaican work environment, slaves not from Angola or Sierra Leone but (here acknowledging the ethnic differences within the black Jamaican population) from the Gold Coast and the Bight of Biafra, primary depots for Jamaica-bound slaves.[50] Hall, in turn, soon complained to one of the slaves' owners, William Knox, that he could no longer locate sufficient employment for them in Jamaica. Finding his carefully exported human property an increasingly "burthensome possession," Knox arranged through Hall to send the majority back to the United States to be sold.[51] It is hard enough to follow the fortunes of loyalist refugees in Jamaica, and reconstructing the trajectories of loyalist-owned slaves proves even more difficult. But this example reveals that some endured a fate at least as bad as staying on Jamaica: they were shipped out again, with all the physical and psychological brutalization that the process entailed, on another stage in an ongoing cycle of migrations. Even for loyalist-imported slaves, Jamaica proved a deceptive place of residence.

What, meanwhile, were the landless white refugees to do? Here they were in the most profitable colony in the British Empire. Yet the richest failed to break into an already congested planter society, and the poorest still relied on charity handouts from the parish. It was then that they began to hear of a tempting possibility. In the western parish of St. Elizabeth, along the Black River, rumor told of unclaimed crown lands stretching across twenty thousand acres or more. The soil would be perfect for sugarcane, it was said, or maybe the indigo that many loyalists had grown in South Carolina before the war. The only problem was, it was currently a waterlogged morass. "Could it be drained," the planter Edward Long had optimistically suggested in 1774, the St. Elizabeth morass "might form many capital plantations. No attempt of this sort has yet been made . . . but it promises to yield a very great return for any of the proprietors, who shall have spirit, ability, and patience, sufficient for prosecuting such an experiment."[52] For Jamaica's dispossessed refugees, the experiment seemed well worth running. With Governor Campbell's support, a project came together to drain the St. Elizabeth morass and divide it into land grants for Jamaica-based loyalists.

Mangrove thickets choke the Black River and its tributaries into an impenetrable maze of roots, a network of water and wood. If you pause for just a moment, the insects swarm into a tornado above your head, whine past your ears, and prick your fingers and wrists. Crocodiles lurk among these opaque channels. Lazy, brown, bump-backed things, they seem as benign as floating branches, until in an instant they can thrash up from the water with enough force to snap a small child in two. This was the weird wetland world that engineer Patrick Grant cruised into late in 1783, with a team of slaves and his surveyors' tools, and a mandate from the governor to chart the morass into lots for loyalist refugees. For nine months, the surveyor pursued his task, trudging and sloshing through the swamps, laying out his lines and ignoring as best possible the complaints of nearby landowners, who used the dry patches now and then to graze their cattle. In the autumn of 1784, Grant staggered back to Spanish Town exhausted but satisfied. He lay before the assembly his hard-won map of 28,040 acres divided into 183 lots, and a bill of £3,660 for his pains.[53]

Loyalist refugees signed up to claim the St. Elizabeth lots and eagerly waited for the house of assembly to issue their patents to the land—a pro forma process, they assumed. But the assembly hit a snag: Grant, they thought, was charging too much for his work. They decided to launch an inquiry into his actions—and by extension into the legitimacy of this settlement scheme, initiated by the now departed governor Campbell. Interrogating the assemblyman for St. Elizabeth, a house committee asked whether he thought there was enough "dry land interspersed among the waters . . . to make 183 comfortable settlements?" He did not. "Are you of the opinion," they continued, "that any living creatures besides fish, frogs, Dutchmen, and amphibious animals, can exist in the district?" He was not. "Are you of the opinion that this spot . . . can be drained, so as to make it useful for the habitation of man?" He was not. Even if he were given the land for free, he said, he would not take it.[54]

For a whole year the investigation remained suspended while the assembly was out of session. By the time it resumed the inquiry in late 1785, loyalists had grown tense with impatience. Not surprisingly, some of the largest refugee slaveowners in Jamaica had subscribed to the scheme—people like Moses Kirkland, Nathaniel Hall, and his wife—imagining in the dark morass the ideal solution to their labor problems. Every month without land, to them, was another month at a loss. A humbler South Carolina tailor called Robert Frogg was one of several loyalists who preemptively moved to St. Elizabeth with his slaves anyway. Poor Frogg's efforts to start draining the swamps prompted one local resident to jest that "the land thereabouts were so unhealthy, that even a frog could not live there." Such reports only confirmed the assembly's dismal view of the scheme. At the end of 1785, two years after Grant began his survey, the house judged that "the morass land . . . laid out for the refugees from America, cannot be drained for cultivation, but at such a considerable expense as to make it highly improbable that they will ever be drained." It refused to grant patents to the land, and closed the book on Jamaica's one and only officially sponsored land scheme for loyalists.[55]

"Frog" puns notwithstanding, nobody seems to have joked about the double meaning of "morass." The metaphoric resonance may have been just too painful for the loyalists involved. No episode more succinctly captures the contrast between the refugees' reception in Jamaica and that in other parts of British America. Land grants sat at the center of British provisions for loyalists in the Bahamas and British North America. In Jamaica, the one effort to provide land began in farce and ended in tragedy. Combined with the complaints from the Kingston parish vestry, the house of assembly's refusal to follow through with the land grants confirmed Jamaicans' cool response toward the plight of the American refugees.

It was especially ironic that this land of opulence, rooted in slavery, should prove so unsatisfying for the largest slaveowners among the refugees—people who must have been attracted to this island precisely because of its storied wealth. Unable to procure land, unable to hire out their slaves profitably, American planters found it far more difficult to adjust to Jamaica than professional men like Alexander Aikman and William Johnston, who could at least get jobs for themselves. (Again, though a breakdown of refugees by occupation and status remains elusive, the absence of other conspicuous successes like these suggests they remained a rarity.) News of the disappointing conditions on Jamaica circled quickly back to the mainland, as returns of the East Florida evacuation make clear. In contrast to the thousands who poured in from Savannah and Charleston, a mere 196 whites set off for Jamaica from St. Augustine—many of them intending only to use the island as a way station, en route to the "Spanish Main." For them, the largely unknown possibilities of Central America appeared preferable to the known lack of opportunities on Jamaica.[56] Ultimately, more Florida refugees decided to migrate to the tiny island of Dominica than to Britain's Caribbean gem, attracted by promises of land grants from the governor. Though the lands were "very bad, being in general Tops of Mountains, and so situated as not to allow of cultivation," at least they were on offer—and a mountaintop was surely better than a morass.[57]

AT DUSK, the tropics grew deafening as nature transitioned from day to night: cawing birds, scuttling animals, the rhythmic crescendo of rattling insects. Bats dipped and ducked in the twilight; sticky-toed geckos scuttled over walls; vultures swooped into the trees and hunched up their ruffled shoulders to sleep. In the humid air mosquitoes condensed like a rising mist. They homed in on warm bodies as if some deep intelligence guided their needle-noses to blood. If you weren't careful, you'd step back indoors to find every patch of bare skin inflamed with bites.

Mosquitoes were pests, but nobody yet knew they were killers too: carriers of deadly yellow fever and malaria. The sinister little *Aedes aegypti* mosquito alone, dispensing the yellow fever virus into the human bloodstream, helped kill more white people in the eighteenth-century Caribbean than any single other cause. Smallpox, dengue fever, yaws, hookworm, dysentery, tetanus: all the plagues that made Jamaica such a death trap also made it a beacon of opportunity for the newly trained Dr. William Johnston. He came to Jamaica with justifiably high hopes for his career. He enjoyed the influential patronage of the governor; he held credentials from Edinburgh, the best medical school in the British world; and while his compatriots discovered that Jamaica had little room for more planters, Lord knew it always needed doctors. The governor generously "attached him nominally to some regiment"—a sinecure from which Johnston reaped a salary of 20 shillings per week plus handsome supplements for his family. Soon he accepted an invitation from James Wildman, a member of Jamaica's governing council, to serve as physician on Wildman's estate at Liguana. (Wildman was a powerful if slightly dubious patron: as attorney to one of Jamaica's richest absentee owners, William Beckford, he and his brother had rapidly amassed—or rapaciously swindled, it was alleged—a fortune off commissions, and persuaded Beckford to give them a substantial plantation outright.)[58] Johnston's quick ascent may have helped inform a veteran Jamaican doctor's gripe that "this country owing to the vast number of Medical people who were either *refugees*, or deprived of employment by the place, is so perfectly overrun with them that almost every small plantation has got its Doctor."[59]

Diseases affected blacks and whites differentially (notably, blacks had greater immunity to yellow fever and malaria than whites), but black or white, free or slave, nobody could escape the pervasiveness of death in Jamaica, least of all the doctors who tried to cheat it. By the 1780s, terrible mortality rates among West Indian slaves had become an incriminating piece of evidence for British abolitionists, who latched onto the fact that slave deaths consistently outpaced births to argue that slavery needed to be ameliorated, if not eliminated outright. Planters, in response, became increasingly concerned to reduce slave mortality.[60] Existing records suggest that at any given time, half the slaves on a sugar plantation might be afflicted with some injury or illness. Johnston's tasks likely involved regular visits to an estate hospital, staffed by black attendants, where he would treat and diagnose slaves on the sick list. He may also have administered smallpox inoculations, an increasingly widespread practice on Jamaican plantations. Another of his duties would have been to fill out an annual report on the causes of death of slaves, required by Jamaica's consolidated slave law of 1788—a grim record of how man and nature conspired to keep slaves dying young.[61]

Johnston continued to treat white patients as well. A pan-American yellow fever epidemic in 1793 proved a bonanza to his practice, when his merchant clients in Kingston called on him to attend the sick sailors on their incoming ships. Yellow fever produces internal bleeding and jaundice; it starts with a headache, then fever, nausea, and vomiting. When the vomit turns black and gritty with blood, it is almost over: the victim is usually dead within days. Dr. Johnston eschewed the technique of bloodletting that other doctors prescribed for the disease; though as he dosed one heaving patient after another with calomel, a mercury solution given as a purgative, his treatment may have harmed as much as it helped.[62] "Sometimes there were seventeen or more funerals a day," Elizabeth Johnston remembered with distress. At their family house in Halfwaytree, just outside Kingston, she had a large Jamaica-born brood of young children to worry about: Eliza, born in 1787, a year to the day after Elizabeth Johnston's arrival on Jamaica; Laleah Peyton in 1789; then John (1790), Jane Farley (1791), and James Wildman (1792). Johnston congratulated herself that none of her family contracted yellow fever. But their resistance to the island's diseases would not last much longer. By the end of 1793 the Johnstons' youngest daughter, Jane, was dead of scarlet fever, aged two.

You could not avoid death, but you could try to come to terms with it. As if to replace the lost child, the Johnstons named their newest infant, born in 1794, Jane Farley as well. With her, the Johnstons weren't taking any chances: because of William's constant exposure to smallpox, he arranged to have the baby girl inoculated. Although the procedure had become widespread in Jamaica by then (as in Britain), there was always some risk that, rather than developing antibodies to fight off the controlled infection, the patient might contract a fatal case of smallpox instead.[63] Parents anxiously monitored the incisions where the virus had been applied to make sure infection did not spread. The second Jane Farley Johnston, just three months old, was not so lucky. "After lying on my lap for some time on a pillow, a very sad spectacle, one sore being quite black, she died in my arms," her "angelic blue eyes" never to open again. William carried the small body from Elizabeth's lap and she collapsed on the floor, convulsed in grief and prayers.[64]

She had lost two children already—one in Edinburgh, another in Jamaica—but this bereavement touched Elizabeth Johnston more deeply than any other. Perhaps it had something to do with the sense that she could have stopped it, that she had actually approved (and probably watched) when the fatal germs were applied to her child's soft, satin limbs. But to be there in that strange, suffocating place, with nothing familiar around her, "having no female relation to be with me, only black servants, and having to think about and direct everything for so many little ones"—it seemed too much to bear. "Much exhausted in mind and body," she fell into a serious depression. Not long after the baby's death, the Wildmans offered to adopt the Johnstons' daughter Eliza and take her with them to Britain as their own. "We could not for some weeks make up our minds to part with her," Johnston confessed, as they wrestled with a dilemma that faced generations of parents in inhospitable imperial outposts. Was it better to keep the children close at home, exposed to tropical dangers—or to send them thousands of miles "home" to distant Britain? Deciding it "best for the child," the Johnstons dispatched Eliza to England with the Wildmans. For much the same reasons, they sent their eldest daughter Catherine back to Edinburgh at her grandfather Dr. Johnston's request.[65]

As the inexorable pressures of mortality closed in around them, the Johnstons discovered Jamaica to be a false refuge for them too. Though William Johnston succeeded where many southern refugee planters did not, by quickly carving out a professional career, the hostility of the alien environment broke down his family both physically and psychologically. In 1796, a "debilitated" Elizabeth Johnston admitted defeat. She decided to return to Edinburgh with the children, as "a duty both to their health and their morals," while William, who "could not possibly leave his practice," stayed on in Jamaica alone. Fully forty years later, the grief still welled up inside her when she remembered "the morning of that sad day when I heard that the boat was come to take us on board," for another separation, another Atlantic crossing. "I hardly think I was in my senses. I uttered screams that distressed my poor husband to such a degree that he would then . . . have been glad if I had given up going. He begged me . . . to let him go on board and bring our things back, but all I could say was, 'It is too late!' "[66]

But as the figures on the docks dwindled into blurs and dots, and the ruins of Port Royal shimmered away beneath the ship, and the green Blue Mountains receded into gray outlines, she drew strength from a fresh source. In her darkest hours of mourning and isolation, Johnston had been saved. She saw the arms of an unfamiliar God stretched out to embrace her: a loving, accessible presence, the God of the Baptists. The old Anglican pieties she had been trying to console herself with since Florida seemed merely "cold morality" to her now. She found solace in "the preaching of the Dissenters, which has been the means of awakening many a poor soul."[67] Like millions of others in the later-eighteenth-century Atlantic world, Johnston had been caught up in the evangelical tide known as the Second Great Awakening. Her own path to conversion, through personal upheaval and distress, seemed to crystallize the larger process of recovery across an Anglo-American world torn by war. She had lost so much in Jamaica; but this discovery she could carry with her always.

FOR THIS island of death was also increasingly an island of Christian faith. The spiritual comfort Elizabeth Johnston discovered in her personal trials would be repeated thousands of times over in 1780s Jamaica as evangelical Protestant missionaries began to convert the brutalized slave population in large numbers. What was more, those missionaries were black themselves—and black loyalists from America at that. While white refugees had imported thousands of slaves but themselves blended anonymously into Jamaican society, died, or left, a handful of free black loyalists, importing their religious sensibilities, made an indelible mark on the island. Their activities tied Jamaica into a growing Atlantic-wide network of black evangelicalism, a vibrant and enduring consequence of the loyalist dispersal. At the forefront of these missionary activities was George Liele, who brought to Jamaica a version of the same Baptist teaching that his protégé David George was spreading in Nova Scotia and New Brunswick.[68]

Like William Johnston, Liele had the good fortune to arrive in Jamaica with a personal recommendation to the governor—but in his case, it was to be an indentured servant. Indebted to loyalist Moses Kirkland for the purchase price of his family members, Liele had effectively been obliged to follow Kirkland to Jamaica in 1782. "Promising to be my friend in this country," Kirkland arranged for Liele to work in the comparatively congenial employ of Governor Archibald Campbell. After two years, Liele managed to pay off his indenture, and Campbell provided him with "a written certificate from under his own hand of my good behaviour." Knowing the power of paper in British colonial society, Liele also made sure to procure "a certificate of my freedom from the vestry and the governor . . . both for myself and my family." Fully seven years after his manumission in wartime Georgia, he could declare himself beholden to no man, and prove it legally to anyone who asked.[69]

Truly free at last, Liele set himself up as a "farmer," bought a team of horses and wagons, and worked as a carter with the help of his three growing boys. But the real measure of success, as far as George Liele was concerned, lay in another domain. Around September 1784, Liele began to preach once more. He preached on the Kingston racetrack and in the open air in Spanish Town, while black loyalist colleagues such as the New York barber Moses Baker carried the good word deeper into the interior. Just as the charismatic Liele had done a decade earlier in the moss-draped glades of the Carolina backcountry, he quickly drew followers around him in Jamaica. His "words took very good effect with the poorer sort, especially the slaves," who had rarely if ever been exposed to such preaching—though many retained a culture of African spirituality. The ghastly conditions of slaves' lives, steeped in violence and permeated by death, surely enhanced their receptiveness to Liele's message. He baptized converts in the river at Spanish Town, in the salt waters of Kingston harbor, in the streams and creeks that braided through the countryside. In Kingston he started a nascent church in a small private house, with just "four brethren from America besides myself." Soon he counted 350 supporters in his congregation, a few of them white, and his followers around the country numbered at least fifteen hundred, "some living on sugar estates, some on mountains, pens, and other settlements," mostly enslaved, largely illiterate.[70]

"There is no Baptist church in this country but ours," Liele announced proudly in 1791, and he could now point to the rising walls of an actual chapel to prove it. The project was a testament to Liele's capacities not just as a preacher but as an institution-builder. His tight community of faith in the American south had been scattered when many of its members followed evacuating British forces. Yet from an evangelizing point of view, dispersal was the best thing that could have happened to them. Through letters from around the Atlantic, Liele proudly kept track of David George's activities in British North America; of the successes that another black loyalist, Brother Amos, enjoyed in the Bahamas; and of how Andrew Bryan, whom he had baptized himself, continued to win black converts in Savannah. His own church in Kingston provided a vital base in this expanding international black organization.

To build the chapel proper, Liele knew that asking for contributions from the destitute slaves "would soon bring a scandal upon religion," and his free black congregants hardly had money to spare. Though his parishioners devotedly pulled together their pennies and bits, Liele reached beyond the black community—as he had done before in America—to solicit contributions from Jamaican whites. "Several gentlemen, members of the house of assembly, and other gentlemen," contributed a quarter of the funds that Liele used to purchase three acres in eastern Kingston and start building. His church walls were eight feet high when he reached out again, this time to Baptists in Britain. His congregation was growing fast and strong, he told them. All he needed was a little more money to put on a roof, and "this building," he assured his sponsors, "will be the greatest undertaking ever was in this country for the bringing of souls from darkness into the light of the Gospel."[71] Completed in 1793, a good two decades before white Baptists established a permanent mission, Liele's chapel was the first Baptist church in Jamaica.

Liele pitched his appeals to British dissenters perfectly, since many were coming to see missionary activity as the best way to cleanse the British Empire of the stain of slavery. His activities did not go over so well, however, in a colony run by white supporters of slavery. As one of Liele's white patrons explained, "the idea that too much prevails here amongst the masters of slaves is, that if their minds are considerably enlightened by religion or otherwise, that it would be attended with the most dangerous consequences." All that talk of equality in the eyes of the Lord, all that talk of freedom in salvation—it sounded suspiciously like revolutionary language to slaveowners, who worried that missionaries might incite their slaves to revolt. And how much more they must have worried when those missionaries were black, and former slaves to boot. Liele understood the opposition he faced. He knew how David George had been hounded out of Shelburne, how Andrew Bryan in Savannah had been arrested and savagely whipped; he remembered how Jamaicans "at first persecuted us both at baptisms and meetings."[72] Ever the diplomat, Liele took pains to assure white audiences that he posed no challenge to slavery as such. He admitted no slaves "into the church without a few lines from their owners of their good behaviour toward them and religion."[73] Converting slaves, he stressed, was about enlightenment, not revolution. He was a loyalist, after all: he had no stated desire to overturn the order of empire itself.

Such pledges could hardly have come at a more critical time. The same year Liele began constructing his church, Jamaica was rocked by news of a giant slave rebellion on Saint Domingue. Citing the right to equality promised by the French revolutionaries' Declaration of the Rights of Man and of the Citizen, slaves swept across the north of the French colony, burning canefields and killing two thousand whites in their wake. The rebellion became the opening act of the Haitian Revolution, which ultimately led to the establishment of the second republic in the Americas. (Some of the leaders of the Haitian Revolution had fought alongside the French and Americans in Savannah in 1779, perhaps gaining an early taste of republican principles there.) These events seared themselves into the consciousness of blacks and whites throughout Atlantic slaveowning societies. On Jamaica, a mere hundred miles away from Saint Domingue, the neighboring revolution had an especially pronounced effect. Blacks in Jamaica followed these events with keen interest, while white Jamaicans tried to suppress the news—which frightened them as much for being a slave revolt, tapping into a deep well of white Caribbean terror, as for being a republican one.[74] Proximity to Saint Domingue made Jamaica an asylum again, this time to black runaways and white refugees fleeing Saint Domingue with *their* slaves.[75] Following the outbreak of Anglo-French war in 1793, Jamaica also came to serve as the staging post for a series of British interventions on Saint Domingue. Through all the bloodshed, tangled alliances, and regime changes that followed in Saint Domingue, one lesson at least was clear to white Jamaicans. This was dangerous, it was close at hand, and nothing like it could be allowed to happen here.

Liele made sure to stress his congregation's loyal participation in island defense efforts. "The whole island under arms," he observed in late 1791, "several of our members and a deacon were obliged to be on duty; and I being trumpeter to the troop of horse in Kingston, am frequently called upon." But the rapidly changing circumstances of war seriously compromised his position for two reasons. First, simply being a free black in Jamaica became much harder under the tightened discipline of a government more than ever concerned to police runaways, itinerants, and deserters—figures often presumed to be vectors of revolution.[76] "It is scarcely safe for a man of colour to appear in public," a Kingston newspaper warned, as early as 1791.[77] One particular segment of Jamaica's free black population, the Maroons, became a special source of anxiety for British officials.

In the western interior of Jamaica stretches Cockpit Country, an eerie landscape of scooped valleys and egg-shaped mountains. On the hilltops of this hidden world lived communities descended from runaway slaves, called the Maroons, who had successfully won quasi-independence from British rule in the 1730s. They were allowed to remain unmolested in five reserved towns, as long as they agreed not to harbor fugitive slaves but rather helped to catch them. The revolt on Saint Domingue made the imperial state especially concerned to manage interactions between the Maroons and other blacks. Much to the Maroons' anger, authorities imposed fresh restrictions on them to try to keep them apart from slaves. In 1795 (a year in which British authorities also confronted slave uprisings on St. Vincent and Grenada), Maroon resentment exploded when the Maroons of Trelawny Town struck back at the British. Hiding out among the dips and rises of the cockpits, they waged a successful guerrilla war against a British force five times their size. Only when the British shifted to unconventional tactics, by importing a hundred snarling bloodhounds from Cuba, did they manage to hunt down their elusive enemy. In defeat, the Maroons were promised the right to remain on the island if they agreed to beg on their knees for forgiveness, and to move to wherever else on Jamaica the government decided to send them. But citing a breach of the treaty, the governor reneged on his word: he decided to send the troublesome Maroons away from Jamaica once and for all. In a bleak counterpoint to the expulsion of the Acadians, British authorities rounded up 568 Trelawny Maroons and shipped them off under military escort to the opposite end of British America: Nova Scotia.[78] The defeat and deportation of the Maroons vividly demonstrated the lengths to which the imperial government would go in enforcing racial hierarchy, underlining the difficulties facing any free black on Jamaica during these years of war and revolution.

And George Liele was suspicious not only because he was free and black. His activities as a preacher set a second mark against him. The close connection between abolitionists and evangelicalism had made certain forms of Christian teaching seem, in the eyes of many Jamaican planters, almost as subversive as republicanism. One Kingston mob even burned the radical Thomas Paine in effigy next to a figure of the evangelical abolitionist William Wilberforce.[79] Persecution against Liele (as against other preachers) intensified in the revolutionary climate. Though Liele got permission from Spanish Town authorities "to make mention of their names in any congregation where we are interrupted," this did not prevent a range of outrages. Once during a service, a man rode his horse straight into Liele's chapel and up to the altar, issuing the mocking challenge, "Come, old Liele, give my horse the sacrament?" while the animal whinnied and snorted before the cross. Another time, three men strode over to the communion table, seized the sacramental bread, and distributed it while cursing and swearing. In 1794, a new sedition law put an end to Liele's preaching altogether. After a sermon on some text at best peripherally suggestive of abolitionist sentiments, Liele was charged with "uttering dangerous and seditious words" from his pulpit. He was hauled off to prison, loaded down with heavy iron chains, and his feet locked in stocks.[80] His colleague Moses Baker was arrested for quoting the words of a Baptist hymn: "We will be slaves no more, / Since Christ has made us free, / Has nailed our tyrants to the cross, / And bought our liberty."[81]

So after all that loyal volunteering to defend the British Empire both in America and in Jamaica, after all those certificates and testimonials to his freedom, here was George Liele back in jail again—a slave no more, but a prisoner nonetheless. (Perhaps he and Baker indulged in stargazing from the Kingston jail.) At his trial, despite concerted efforts to prove that he was trying to incite a slave rebellion, Liele was acquitted of the charge of sedition. But his opponents found another way to take him out of action: he was imprisoned for debts incurred while building the church, and confined for more than three years.[82]

In the space of just a decade, George Liele thus confronted as directly as any one individual could the twinned objectives of the post-revolutionary British Empire, toward moral righteousness and top-down rule—the two faces of paternalism.[83] Liele had come to Jamaica as an embodiment of a particular humanitarian promise: by affiliating himself to the British during the war he had secured his freedom and been transported in (nominal) liberty with his family to another British territory, at British expense. His work as a Baptist preacher tied him into a larger community committed to a program of individual and collective moral uplift. Liele seemed a perfect illustration of the self-image, championed by abolitionists among others, of a British Empire that would give all its free subjects, regardless of ethnicity, British liberties, the rule of law, and the chance to partake in cultural enlightenment. And in his repeated assertions of loyalty during the heat of the Haitian Revolution, Liele appeared to be living proof (with how much sincerity it is hard to say) of how such policies could tighten diverse subjects' bonds to king and empire, not strain them.

But when the Caribbean blew up in a new revolution, Liele found himself staring into the authoritarian face of the British Empire. An empire of law and of liberty some might claim it to be, but this was still an empire that practiced mass enslavement, and Britain was the world's preeminent slave-trading nation. As the activities of governors like Lord Dunmore or even Lord Dorchester had suggested, humanitarian sentiment and restrictive rule were by no means mutually exclusive. Loyalist refugees in New Brunswick and the Bahamas had felt the fist of authority close around issues of political representation in the 1780s. In Jamaica in the 1790s, with republicanism and slave revolt rattling the gates, the suppression of dissent became an imperial imperative. Through sedition laws, the deportation of the Maroons, and other repressive measures, the Jamaican government clamped down (as the Pitt ministry was doing in Britain) on the circulation of potentially subversive individuals, information, and rhetoric. Liele's prosecution in 1794 was just part of a larger campaign against suspected dissidents. In 1802 the house of assembly passed a law banning "the preaching of ill-disposed, illiterate, or ignorant enthusiasts, to meetings of negroes and persons of colour, chiefly slaves"—another effort to limit the spread of evangelical language.[84] Partly because of such legislation, Liele himself never returned to regular public preaching after the 1790s.

While the laws tightened, however, the Lord's work went on. As Liele languished in jail, the Baptist movement took on a life beyond him. Another black preacher broke away to form a rival chapel that quickly developed a strong following of its own.[85] By the time white British Baptist missionaries began arriving on the island in the 1810s, they found a thriving black evangelical community that had folded African traditions into its ecstatic Christian worship. Hostilities between planters and preachers continued well into the nineteenth century, outlasting the institution of slavery.[86] But in a climate of such violence and terror, the preachers had an inbuilt advantage. The language of salvation, brought from America, offered an effective antidote to the imperial realities of slavery and death.

MORE THAN a decade after it was commissioned, and after an extravagant £30,000 had been spent, the Rodney Memorial basked in the Spanish Town sunshine, complete. It spanned the main square between the governor's residence on one side and the house of assembly on the other. But for all that Rodney's marble hand pointed straight at the windows of her house, the governor's wife Maria Nugent did not mention the structure at all when she described her surroundings in her diary. Perhaps that was because by the time she and her husband, newly appointed governor George Nugent, arrived in Spanish Town in July 1801, the Battle of the Saintes already seemed remarkably remote. The French Revolutionary wars had been raging for the last eight years (the length of the American Revolution), unprecedented in the annals of British warfare for their international extent and scale. The Nugents' four years of married life had been totally overshadowed by conflict. The couple had previously been stationed in Ireland, where as a general in the British army, George Nugent helped suppress the French-backed nationalist rebellion of 1798. Their time in Ireland left them "heartily sick, tired, and disgusted," said Maria, "having witnessed . . . all the horrors of a civil war." Conflict-ridden Jamaica was the last place they wanted to be posted next. But duty called, and, "like good soldiers, we made up our minds to obey." Not for nothing did she don "a full Lieutenant-General's uniform" for formal dinners at sea, complete with gold epaulettes adorning her scarlet coat.[87]

During a residence of four years in Jamaica, Nugent kept a diary that splendidly captures what it was like to live in such a magically beautiful yet dangerous place, a place where dances and sumptuous dinners continued against a backdrop of massive military mobilization, and where the "only three subjects of conversation" were "debt, disease, and death."[88] Her diary remains one of the most detailed and accessible sources on white Jamaica for this period. Nugent's preoccupations strongly resembled those of her rough contemporary Elizabeth Johnston, despite their considerable differences in social rank. (The two women overlapped on Jamaica for three and a half years, though it is not clear they ever met.)[89] They shared the same anxieties about raising children in such a dangerous climate. They shared a feeling of isolation as white women on an island dominated by "the blackies" (Nugent's preferred term) and by creole planters whose dissolute habits both women deplored. In this alienating context, "religion" became for Nugent, like Johnston, "my greatest source of happiness."[90] And they shared another important if less obvious trait: Nugent, like Johnston, was an American loyalist refugee.

Maria Nugent, née Skinner, had been raised to soldier on. She may not have remembered the night back in New Jersey in 1776 as clearly as her sister Catherine did, when the rebels came looking for her loyalist father General Cortlandt Skinner. She had been only four years old to Catherine's five then, and the Skinner family had experienced many upheavals since. They spent the last years of the American Revolution in British-occupied New York, and evacuated to London in 1783. There, like their friend Colonel Beverley Robinson and his family, the Skinners lived in straitened but genteel circumstances, on property salvaged from America and compensation from the Loyalist Claims Commission. Though a civilian before the war, General Skinner—also like Robinson—positioned his children in the military, a good vehicle for social advancement. His sons got commissions in the army and navy, and his four youngest daughters married military men in turn. Maria's sister Catherine formalized a family tie to the Robinsons when she married the colonel's youngest son, William Henry Robinson, in 1794. The new war brought several family members back to the New World. Catherine joined her husband on his postings as a military commissary in the West Indies, while Catherine and Maria's youngest brother worked briefly as a customs collector in Jamaica, before dying there of fever.

Maria Nugent's diary has made her a touchstone for historians of Jamaica, but positioning her within the context of American loyalist refugees illuminates a pattern evident across the diaspora, and repeated by generations of British imperial servants. Migrations, once set in motion, can be hard to stop. The conditions that brought Nugent and her relatives to the Caribbean echoed and reflected the circumstances that had carried the family to Britain in her girlhood. Dispossessed and displaced by one war, the family now strove to recuperate its fortunes as servants in another, children making up for what parents had lost. Set against the example of Elizabeth Johnston, Nugent's passage through Jamaica also helps make sense of the island's position on the loyalist refugees' map. The colony might serve as a relatively attractive, lucrative—and temporary—posting in a longer imperial career, which was how Nugent and her relatives approached it. But loyalist refugees like Johnston, who intended to settle on Jamaica long-term, needed to do more than rebuild lost fortunes. They sought to rebuild some semblance of a home. In this respect, Jamaica proved an unreliable substitute at best.

Less than six months after Nugent sailed into Kingston for the first time, Elizabeth Johnston landed in Jamaica again, drawn back from Edinburgh by news that her husband was ill. Her years in Scotland had been dominated by concerns about her two eldest children, Andrew and Catherine, whom she had left as innocent pre-adolescents but returned to find wayward teenagers, eighteenth-century style. Handsome, popular Andrew, at fifteen years old, had been cajoled into studying medicine, but—like his gambler father before him—easily found other diversions (such as a talent for ice skating) and became a perennial source of worry to his parents. Fourteen-year-old Catherine had developed a "wild and giddy" streak—encouraged, according to her mother, by unfettered access to a lending library and a taste for unsuitable novels. "When she heard I was coming to Edinburgh, she imagined me like a heroine in a romance," said Johnston. But reality proved less rosy, and the mother and daughter, separated at a formative moment, never forged a successful adult bond.[91]

Returning to the family house at Halfwaytree in 1802, the Johnstons' Jamaican travails began anew, as illness and further partings haunted the family.[92] For once, the Johnstons were together in December 1805, when the prodigal Andrew—now, like his father, a doctor in Jamaica—traveled from his practice to join them. The visit signaled a reconciliation between the parents and their feckless son, who seemed at last to be shaping up into a responsible adult. But on his way to Halfwaytree Andrew developed a terrible headache and stopped over in Kingston to recover. Instead he grew rapidly sicker, and soon he began vomiting up black: the fatal sign of advanced yellow fever. Though he lay dying just a short distance away from his parents, Andrew "could not, bear to see our grief, and begged that we would not come." He died within a week. "To describe my anguish is impossible," said Johnston. He had been a disappointment in life, yet his death carved a wound that could never heal.[93] To make matters worse, Andrew's death pushed Catherine into a serious "nervous illness." Treated with heavy doses of laudanum, she began hallucinating—in keeping with Jamaica's strange dangers—"that there was an insurrection of the slaves, that they had set fire to the house, and that the bed she lay on was in flames."[94]

The place killed Johnston's infant daughters and her firstborn son; it drove her eldest daughter to the edge of insanity. She herself understood her Jamaican ordeals as divine trials, and prayed her way forward. (Did anything other than health considerations ever inform her and William's frequent decisions to separate? Johnston's one-sided account makes it impossible to know.) From a modern psychological standpoint, it is more tempting to see the family's continuing struggles as an illustration of how trauma gets played out across generations. Johnston, a child when the American Revolution began, had been a loyalist essentially because her father was. Now the consequences of the Johnstons' loyalism, in the form of repeated separations and migrations, cast long shadows over their childrens' lives in turn. Andrew and Catherine had done nothing more in the American Revolution than be born, in British-occupied Savannah and Charleston respectively. Yet the effects of displacement—raised by people other than their parents, struggling to form connections with their nuclear family, shunted around the Atlantic—seemed to mark them at least as deeply, and tragically, as their parents.

The Johnstons immigrated to Jamaica because of professional opportunities—the same factor that moved the Nugents and the Robinsons around the British Empire. Yet the years in Jamaica infused Elizabeth Johnston with an almost emotional compulsion to leave, fueling a cycle of separations that seemed to take on a life of its own. So it was that one spring day in 1806 saw William Johnston pacing the Kingston docks, looking for a ship to carry his family, once more, away from this ill-starred island. With the trade restrictions of the 1780s largely lifted, the harbor was full of vessels bound for New York.[95] Northern, healthy, and easy to reach (to say nothing of personally familiar to him), New York City seemed a suitable enough destination to William. He began scoping out available cabins, when he ran into a friend. "Why Doctor," his friend exclaimed on hearing the plan, "I wonder you who are a loyal subject do not prefer sending your family to a British province." Evidently this invocation of loyalism touched some chord in William, for he promptly booked a passage for the family to Halifax instead. "Send us to Nova Scotia!" Elizabeth cried when he came home with the news. "What, to be frozen to death? Why, better send us to Nova Zembla [in Baffin Bay], or Greenland."[96] Maybe she remembered the dismal accounts of the place that had circulated through St. Augustine back in 1784. But what she didn't count on was that by now Nova Scotia had become home to so many fellow loyalists that it would be her last and most congenial destination of all.

When the Johnstons set off on their next journey, most loyalist refugees in Jamaica had either moved on or faded from the record. A clutch of the old morass-subscribers (including one Lachlan McGillivray, cousin to Creek chief Alexander) had struck out into the forests of Central America to shape settlements in present-day Belize.[97] Others shifted elsewhere in British America, and presumably some to the United States; and many, of course, died. The loyalists' failure to find a berth in Jamaica had to do in part with intrinsic obstacles such as the lack of available land, and in part with their marginal position within a larger creole society that remained guarded toward them at best. The loyalists' tale also mirrored a crucial shift in Jamaica's position more generally. After the dual disruptions of the American Revolution and the Haitian Revolution, the planters' profits and political clout would never be the same. The ascendancy of metropolitan over creole interests became manifest in 1807 when, after thirty years of passionate campaigning by Wilberforce and others, Britain abolished the slave trade. The West India lobby wasn't only trumped by metropolitan morality. It was also increasingly overshadowed by rival imperial locales. Before the American Revolution, Jamaica had been the economic powerhouse of the British Empire. By the end of the French wars a generation later, that position had been ceded to India.

George Liele, though, stayed put in Jamaica, despite the persecution he faced as a free black and a Baptist. If indeed he ever wished to leave, he may have found the cost of a passage to Britain or North America prohibitive. In Jamaica, the work of evangelizing was hard but it was ample and necessary; besides, his brethren had already established missions elsewhere in the western Atlantic. And maybe, reading between the lines of their optimistic reports about congregation-building, Liele knew that the furrow of a black loyalist would be just as hard to plow wherever else he might go. Liele's namesake in Nova Scotia, David George, could have told him tales of hardship aplenty. Indeed, for David George and his followers—unlike for Liele—the pressure of living as free blacks in British North America had become intolerable by the 1790s. So when the promise of another land appeared before them, they were ready for a fresh exodus.

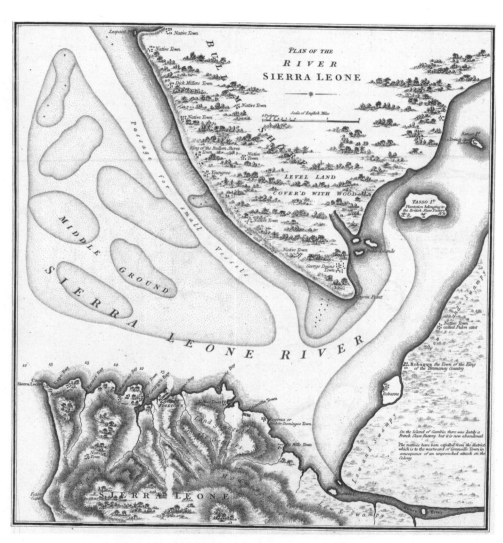

William Dawes, *Plan of the River Sierra Leone*, 1803.

CHAPTER NINE

Promised Land

D AVID GEORGE returned to Shelburne in 1790 on a wooden sled, built for him and pulled across the slush by his "brethren," since his legs were so badly frostbitten he could hardly feel them anymore. It had been six years now since George had been driven out of town in the great riot of 1784. After five months lying low in Birchtown, he had ventured back into Shelburne, cutting his way with a whipsaw across the ice-blocked river between the settlements. He discovered his residence destroyed and the Shelburne meeting house "occupied by a sort of tavern-keeper, who said, 'The old Negro wanted to make a heaven of this place, but I'll make a hell of it.' " But with dedication and divine goodwill, George managed to reclaim his church from its sinful tenant and preside over "a considerable revival of religion" in Shelburne.[1]

As word of this inspiring black preacher spread, George decided to transmit the Lord's word farther in turn. He traveled to Saint John, New Brunswick, where he baptized black loyalists before a fascinated throng of white and black onlookers. But some city residents, uncomfortable at the spectacle, insisted that he get a license to preach from Governor Thomas Carleton. George proceeded to Fredericton to do so. With help from a white loyalist he had known in Charleston, he secured a certificate granting "permission from his Excellency the Lieutenant-Governor to instruct the Black people in the knowledge, and exhort them to the practice of, the Christian religion." The governor himself sent regrets for being too busy to come and watch George baptize in Fredericton. The next time George preached in Saint John, "our going down to the water seemed to be a pleasing sight to the whole town." Some of his new converts "were so full of joy" at his return that "they ran out from waiting at table on their masters, with the knives and forks in their hands, to meet me at the water side." Up and down New Brunswick, and on the coasts of Nova Scotia, George preached and baptized, planting the seeds of new congregations.[2]

George's message must have shone a rare flash of hope for his converts during difficult years of dearth and readjustment. His success at congregation-building among the refugees, who were still coping with the unsettling consequences of war, resembled George Liele's experiences in Jamaica. So, though, did various attempts to restrict and harass him—a sign of the anxiety white loyalists felt even here, far from the West Indies, about vocal blacks and their potentially disruptive teachings. To be sure, the climate for blacks in British North America was substantially better than it was for the enslaved black masses in Jamaica. The majority of George's parishioners were black loyalists, officially free, and they lived in a province where slaveowning was legal but nowhere near as widespread as in the West Indies. That said, the conditions of life for black loyalists in Nova Scotia and New Brunswick stood in bleak contrast to those of their white refugee neighbors. Their promised land delayed and their independence hemmed in, many blacks grew dissatisfied enough to contemplate a new move altogether, in which David George would play an important role.

Among the thousands of loyalists grumbling about the drawn-out process of getting land grants in the Maritimes, the three thousand or so black loyalists had greatest cause for complaint. Although they had been told they would receive land on the same terms as white refugees, their grants were invariably smaller, worse located, and slower in coming. Blacks did not hesitate to use that favorite British device, the petition, to call attention to their situation. Shortly after arriving in Nova Scotia, two former sergeants in the Black Pioneers addressed a petition to Governor Parr asking him to honor General Clinton's promise that the blacks should earn "land & provitions the same as the rest of the Disbanded Soldiers." One of those sergeants was named Thomas Peters, and this was the first in a remarkable series of measures he would undertake to better the situation of his peers. By the time Parr instructed the surveyors to improve the location of the Black Pioneers' grants, another winter's snows were piling up, making it impossible to lay out the twenty-acre farm lots Parr decreed they should have. The surveyors hastily drew up one-acre town lots for the blacks and left it at that. This was a relatively typical allotment; in the best cases, blacks received parcels of fifty acres in regions where whites drew between a hundred and four hundred each. Compared to their former conditions of slavery, black loyalists could see their position as a glass half full. Compared even to the struggling white refugees around them, though, they may have seen their glass half empty. Peters, for his part, abandoned his quest for a good grant in Nova Scotia and crossed the Bay of Fundy hoping to do better for himself in New Brunswick.[3]

Largely landless and propertyless, black loyalists had to find other ways to support themselves in British North America. The blacks who rushed from their masters' tables to be baptized by David George were among the many refugees who were employed as domestic servants. In Shelburne, the surveyor Benjamin Marston hired a number of blacks to construct the barracks and other public buildings. Others deployed their skills as coopers, smiths, and sawyers; they swept chimneys, cut hair, and made sails, ropes, and shoes. Boston King, one of the early Birchtown settlers, just about managed to eke out a living as a carpenter, crafting wooden chests and salmon-fishing boats on commission before securing steadier work as a house-builder, for £2 and a couple of barrels of preserved fish per month. King's life was far from easy, but he felt good about his relative fortune "upon vieweing the wretched circumstances of many of my black brethren at that time, who were obliged to sell themselves to the merchants, some for two or three years; and others for five or six years."[4] For the sad truth of the free blacks' plight was that many of these former slaves—who had rarely if ever before been paid for their work, or knew the luxury of commanding their own time—promptly ended up back in temporary bondage to white masters.

Although there are crucial differences between indentured servitude and slavery—not least, indentures have a time limit—indentured black loyalists in Nova Scotia and New Brunswick worked alongside black slaves in a culture that easily conflated the two categories. It did not help that the polite language of British officialdom labeled the estimated twelve hundred slaves brought into the Maritimes by white loyalists as "servants." (This term was also intended to ward off controversies with the United States over stolen slave property.)[5] Abuses against free black laborers racked up fast. Employers routinely did not pay them as promised; in a few cases blacks were tricked into signing away their labor for much longer periods than they thought. Whites took black children into their households, "and when the Parents ask for the child they are told—'have not I maintained your Child for this last year or years you must pay me a Dollar pr. Month for its bound or I shall keep him till he can pay me himself.' "[6] Blacks also endured a perennial threat of reenslavement. In the worst violations of liberty, some black loyalists were simply seized and sold back into slavery in the United States or the Caribbean.[7]

"The place is beyond description wretched," said an aghast white visitor to Birchtown in 1788, "their huts miserable against the inclemency of a Nova Scotia winter. . . . I think I never saw such wretchedness and poverty so strongly perceptible in the garb and countenance of the human species as in these miserable outcasts."[8] And by now, five or six years into their postwar freedom, the black loyalists themselves must have felt beaten down by the sheer battle to get by. Even the energetic David George had almost been destroyed by the inhospitality of Nova Scotia. While he was returning from another preaching circuit around the province, his boat was blown off course in the same region where Benjamin Marston had been shipwrecked some years before. Adrift in the bitter sea, he felt the cold bite into his uncovered legs until they grew white, then purple, sharply painful, then numb. He wondered if he would ever have the use of them again. As he hobbled off the wooden sled and back into his Shelburne church in 1790, supported by his parishioners, he could only hope that things might somehow get better by spring.

For all that British promises to the black loyalists had been made in good faith, by 1790 it was clear that the reality of their situation fell grievously short of their hopes—the starkest version yet of a cruel contrast that loyalist refugees had been encountering across the British Empire. Some found spiritual relief in David George's emotional preaching, others in the words of blind "Daddy Moses" Wilkinson and itinerant Methodist exhorters including Boston King. But could black refugees in British North America win earthly consolations as well? Thomas Peters, the former sergeant, would try to find out.

Peters, about fifty years old in 1790, was a Yoruba from present-day Nigeria, who had been brought to America as a slave in 1762. He had attempted to run away several times in his early years of enslavement, so when the British appeared off Wilmington, North Carolina, in 1776 with promises of freedom to patriot-owned slaves, he and his family were quick to respond to them. He served throughout the war in the Black Pioneers. After the war, he emerged as the most persistent spokesman of black loyalist complaint in British North America. Despite barely being able to sign his own name, Peters regularly delivered petitions in Nova Scotia and New Brunswick asking for black loyalists' rights to be respected. By 1790, he too was growing desperate as colonial officials ignored his appeals. He began to consider going over their heads and lodging his complaints directly with higher authorities in Britain (as Joseph Brant, among others, had done to advantage). Then somebody passed on to him a snatch of overheard conversation.

It drifted up from a Nova Scotia dinner table, perhaps belonging to one of those slick, prosperous loyalists who had managed to snap up the best lots of land and build a fancy house fast, one of the white refugees who could afford to hire black refugees to wait on him. Around the edges of this particular table hovered a black attendant, quietly serving and clearing, when somebody mentioned a familiar name: that of the abolitionist Granville Sharp. His ears perked up. Sharp was known across the Afro-British world thanks to his role in the 1772 legal case that had effectively ended slavery in England. What the waiter heard next enticed him even more. Sharp, the dinner guests said, was sponsoring a scheme to settle free blacks in Africa, on the coast of Sierra Leone. The blacks were to have land and liberty under a free government, and prove to the world that an African colony without slaves could be as valuable a commercial partner for Britain as the African slave-trading posts that Sharp so abhorred. Some black settlers had already set off for Sierra Leone, funded by the British government.[9]

Strange as it might have sounded, it was of course true. Granville Sharp was now in charge of the scheme launched in London by the Committee for the Relief of the Black Poor to establish a free black settlement in Sierra Leone. Hearing about the project now, in North America, only enhanced Peters's determination to deliver his next petition personally to top British administrators. A hundred black families in New Brunswick and another hundred people in Nova Scotia deputed him (he said) to travel to London and "represent their unhappy situation . . . in the hope that he should be able to procure for himself & his fellow sufferers, some establishment, where they may attain a competent settlement." Some of them wanted their land grants honored in North America; the rest were "ready and willing to go wherever the wisdom of Government may think proper to provide for them as free subjects of the British Empire."[10] They might not have received their promised land in Nova Scotia, but this promised land of freedom in Africa sounded like too good a chance to miss. In the autumn of 1790, Thomas Peters sailed from Nova Scotia to London with his petitions, to find out whether black loyalists in British North America might join the Sierra Leone settlement.[11]

Peters's activities would culminate in the final and farthest-ranging major branch of the loyalist exodus: a second collective migration by black loyalists in British North America to West Africa. From start to finish, the Sierra Leone project replayed scenarios that had been acted out across previous loyalist settlements—showing that even this apparently extraordinary enterprise in colonization had important antecedents and parallels. Nevertheless, there were key contextual differences which made what unfolded in Sierra Leone an especially vivid case study in the possibilities available to—and the limits placed on—loyalist refugees in the British Empire. Not only did the Sierra Leone colonists seek to assert free black sovereignty in the shadow of a major British slave-trading station; they also represented an advance guard of British colonization in a region dominated by indigenous powers. Most significantly, the black loyalists set off for Africa not in the 1780s, in the immediate aftermath of the American Revolution, but in the 1790s, in the era of the French Revolution. Their settlement took shape against the backdrop of a fiercely ideological war between Britain and France. The wars pitted Britain's "spirit of 1783" against the more radical, egalitarian—and, in British eyes, destabilizing—promises of republican France. This had important repercussions for the black loyalists in Sierra Leone. It meant that when they feuded with *their* governors over issues of rights and taxation—just as refugees in British North America and the Bahamas had done before them—their protest held explosive potential. It turned the Sierra Leone loyalists into the most potentially revolutionary challengers to imperial authority of all.

OF COURSE, Thomas Peters had no way of anticipating any of that in 1790. Nor did he yet know, when he traveled to London that fall, what had happened to the black refugees who had already gone to Sierra Leone: the three hundred or so destitute blacks in Britain who signed up in 1786 to travel to Africa under the aegis of the Committee for the Relief of the Black Poor.

This hapless band of emigrants got an unpleasant foretaste of trouble before they even left England. Though the expedition had been organized impressively quickly, its departure was held up for four months by one delay after another: administrative delays, embarkation delays, bad weather, and bad luck. Cooped up inside the cramped ships, the emigrants endured conditions little better than those of a prison hulk. They subsisted on awful rations of salted food, and lacked warm clothes to cover themselves with as winter fell. About fifty people died of fever before they got under way. A public feud broke out between the expedition's commissary, the enterprising former slave Olaudah Equiano—the first black to receive any such appointment from the king—and another agent whom Equiano accused of skimming off Treasury funds. Ominous columns against the project appeared in London newspapers, alleging that the blacks were being transported against their will—whether to a penal colony, or back into slavery, nobody quite could say, but "they had better swim to shore, if they can, to preserve their lives and liberties in Britain, than to hazard themselves at sea with such enemies to their welfare."[12] It did not make Granville Sharp's charitable mission any easier when the first fleet of prisoners bound for Botany Bay simultaneously began preparing to sail. In some minds, there was little difference between the convicts on board one fleet and the charity cases on board the other.[13]

So when at last, after the four months of waiting and two months at sea, they made out the tall, dark silhouette of the West African coast in the spring of 1787, it was a particularly gratifying spectacle. They turned into the mouth of a giant bay, shaped like a flexed arm, and cruised into one of the largest natural harbors in the world. On their left, white beaches skirted the low-lying forests of the Bulom Shore. On their right, where they intended to establish their "Province of Freedom," high mountains rippled into thick folds. When Portuguese explorers had first seen these peaks in the fifteenth century, they thought the humpbacked crests resembled the shape of a reclining lion. They named it Serra Lyoa (Lion Mountains), and continued on their course, charting out the future routes of the Atlantic slave trade. The free black settlers who approached Sierra Leone in 1787 became the first people of African origin systematically to reverse that human traffic, in the first "back to Africa" project in modern history.

The colonists disembarked at a cove called Frenchman's Bay—promptly renamed the more patriotic St. George's Bay—cut a track into the bush, and planted a British flag. The next day a local Temne subchief, known to the Europeans as King Tom, came down to have a "palaver" (a term for meeting used in Africa) and soon agreed to a treaty granting the new settlers a huge tract of land. Quite aside from the fact that the treaty revolved around woefully mismatched European and African understandings about land ownership, Tom was only a subordinate ruler, and lacked authority to make this agreement in the first place. A year later, the settlers finalized the grant of the land with King Tom's superior, King Naimbana. In this 1788 treaty, Naimbana agreed to cede land to "the free community of Settlers . . . lately arrived from England," promised to protect them "against the Insurrections and Attacks of all Nations or people whatever," and made over to them a portion of the valuable customs duties paid by ships anchoring in the harbor. In return, he received several suits of embroidered clothes, a telescope and a "mock Diamond ring," two hefty wheels of cheese, and the usual tributes of tobacco, guns, and rum.[14]

By the time Naimbana fixed his mark to this paper, though, more than a quarter of the settlers were dead. The much-delayed fleet had arrived squarely in time for the annual rains that batter crops, slick the mountainsides into sheets of clay, and produce stagnant pools breeding bacteria and bugs. The unlucky arrivals camped under torrential rains in a tent settlement they called Granville Town. Sharp had provided them with a *Short Sketch of Temporary Regulations* ("short" being nearly two hundred pages long) detailing how the colony should be managed, right down to the prayers to be said on each day and the specific wording of indenture certificates. Based around an idealized form of Anglo-Saxon communal government he called "frankpledge," Sharp envisioned a state divided into "tithings" made up of ten families each, and "hundreds," composed of ten tithings; elected representatives from these blocks (called tithingmen and hundredors) would meet in a common council, not unlike a New England town meeting, to organize labor and defense. A black loyalist from Philadelphia, the city of brotherly love, was duly elected the first leader of this "*land of freedom, like England, where no man can be a slave.*"[15]

But it wasn't so easy to create a "Province of Freedom" when, just a few miles up the Sierra Leone River, sat one of the largest British slaving stations in West Africa, on Bunce Island. As many as fifty thousand slaves passed through Bunce Island's holding pens before sailing across the Atlantic in chains—many of them, in the 1780s, bound for Jamaica. (Richard Oswald, the British negotiator behind the Peace of Paris, was one of the Bunce factory's principal proprietors, and his American counterpart Henry Laurens acted for many years as Charleston agent for Bunce Island slaves.) The slave traders lived in a grand multistory stone house and amused themselves with rum, mistresses, and playing rounds on the island's two-hole golf course.[16] It was a rather stylish existence until you looked out the factory windows and saw hundreds of captives in the yard below, chained in circles, feeding themselves from troughs of rice.[17] As the free blacks of Granville Town got hungrier, sicker, and wetter, it was not so surprising that many of them ran off to join the European slavers and enjoy such luxuries as regular meals. The slavers, in turn, were busily influencing King Tom's successor, King Jimmy—who profited from the slave trade—to turn against the abolitionist-sponsored settlement. In late 1789, provoked by a conflict with the crew of a British ship, King Jimmy ordered the remaining residents of Granville Town to evacuate and burned their huts to ashes.

From Province of Freedom to proverbial fiasco: "God grant I never may again, witness so much misery as I was forced to be spectator of here," lamented an English visitor named Anna Maria Falconbridge on seeing the Granville Town survivors a short time later.[18] Granville Sharp despaired when he heard about the colony's destruction. But he was not one to brood for long. He had already started to form a joint-stock company that would take over the Granville Town land and manage the settlement henceforth as an explicit experiment in moral mercantilism. By giving land to free black colonists and conducting an "honorable trade" in their produce, Sharp's company would demonstrate that free African labor was a profitable enterprise, undercutting the social and economic basis for the slave trade. What was more, they would spread "civilization" on the back of commerce, using their model society (and evangelical faith) to introduce "light and knowledge in a Continent which has been kept in misery by the slave trade."[19] Though the strong pro–slave trade lobby in Britain prevented it from winning a royal charter, the Sierra Leone Company was officially incorporated in July 1791. Its directors included all the abolitionist luminaries of the time—among them Sharp, William Wilberforce, and the indefatigable publicist of the antislavery movement Thomas Clarkson—while scores of merchant investors underlined its profit motive. The company dispatched Alexander Falconbridge (Anna Maria's husband), a former slave-ship surgeon turned abolitionist, to renegotiate the land deals and revive the settlement. All they needed now were new colonists to populate it.

Enter Thomas Peters, who arrived in England toward the end of 1790. London was by far the biggest city he had ever seen, a chaos of faces and noises, bustle and jostle. Yet even this cosmopolis was not so big that a new black man in town talking about rights would not soon become known to Granville Sharp. Peters quickly tracked down both his old company commander and General Sir Henry Clinton, who referred him in turn to Wilberforce and Sharp. On Boxing Day 1790, Peters submitted two petitions to the secretary of state William Grenville, with an endorsement from Clinton urging Lord Grenville to "suffer the poor Black to tell his own melancholy Tale."[20] One petition denounced government failures to provide decent land grants. The other, framed with Sharp's help, delivered a broad denunciation of Nova Scotia's "public and avowed Toleration of Slavery . . . as if the happy Influence of his Majesty's free Government was incapable of being extended so far as America to 'maintain Justice and Right' in affording the Protection of the Laws & Constitution of England." Black loyalists had been "refused the common Rights and Privileges of the other Inhabitants," Peters protested, invoking the language of British rights so often used by dissatisfied loyalists. They had "no more Protection by the Laws of the Colony . . . than the mere Cattel or brute Beasts," he concluded, and "the oppressive cruelty and Brutality of their Bondage is . . . particularly shocking irritating and obnocious to . . . free People of Colour who cannot conceive that it is really the Intention of the British Government . . . to tolerate Slavery in Nova Scotia."[21]

To ministers in London, Peters's petitions actually looked fair enough: it seemed to them that the metropolitan initiative to award freedom and land to black loyalists had been distorted by provincial practice—a familiar discrepancy by now in loyalist settlements. Lord Grenville forwarded Peters's petition to Governors Parr and Thomas Carleton, instructing them to investigate his complaints and make the blacks "some atonement" for the "unaccountable delay" in getting their lands.[22] Lobbied by Sharp and the Sierra Leone Company, Grenville went one step further. If the blacks were fed up with Nova Scotia, they would find a ready welcome in the Province of Freedom: the Sierra Leone Company would give them land, and the British government would pay for their passage to West Africa—a notable reiteration of their promises to loyalists in the United States nearly a decade before. None of this, to be sure, demonstrated a government commitment to abolitionism as such. William Wilberforce was on the verge of suffering a serious parliamentary defeat in the spring of 1791 when he tried to introduce a bill to abolish the slave trade. But when Peters secured these concessions from the ministry, the French Revolution had already set into motion dynamic new concepts of liberty, equality, and fraternity—while the slave rebellion on Saint Domingue would soon provide a frightening demonstration (to a British Empire dependent on slavery) of just how violent the French version of liberty could be. Peters's complaints gave ministers a good chance to showcase Britain's more contained version of liberty instead, by underwriting a specific grant of freedom to a specific group of former slaves.

Now that the government had authorized a new expedition to Africa, who would actually organize it? Thomas Peters could help recruit settlers from among the disgruntled black loyalists, but some

Sierra Leone Company official would have to manage the logistics of transporting them across the Atlantic. Abolitionist Thomas Clarkson proposed the perfect candidate: his own younger brother John. Twenty-seven years old, John Clarkson had spent half his life in the navy, serving through the American war; he had been in the West Indies under Admiral Rodney and seen plantation society up close. Recruited to the abolitionist cause in the 1780s, he spent six months in France in the heady days before the revolution gathering testimony against the slave trade. An officer and an abolitionist, John Clarkson was also a consummate gentleman: Wilberforce praised him as "a young man of very great merit & a thousand good qualities both professional & personal."[23] Clarkson's integrity mattered a great deal. Loyalist refugees of all stripes shared a tendency to malign the authority figures above them. Sir Guy Carleton was a rare exception, garnering widespread respect for his efforts to do right by the refugees. John Clarkson would be another. No matter what grievances they harbored toward other white officials, most black loyalists—with the significant exception of Thomas Peters—came to see gentle John, full of conviction and competence, as their Moses. Given what an improbable exodus he was to lead them on, such confidence in his leadership would be a vital ingredient for success.

In August 1791, Clarkson sailed for Nova Scotia in the aptly named *Ark*. His brother and Wilberforce sent long lists of instructions to guide him into the unknown. "Don't talk about the abolition of the Slave Trade, except where you are <u>sure of your Company.</u>" Don't call the loyalists "Blacks or Negroes," but "<u>Africans</u> as a more respectable way of speaking of them." Watch out for Falconbridge, the commercial agent, "hot, rash, & impetuous." Watch out for Thomas Peters, so "you will not be implicated in any Errors he may fall into." "In the Rivers in Africa take Care of the Alligators and in the Land of the Snakes." Write notes on local customs and practices. Write regular letters home—if necessary in code. Keep an eye on public morals. Keep a diary.[24] The last piece of advice proved particularly well taken: Clarkson's journal provides a wonderfully intimate record of how this final British government–sponsored migration of American loyalists unfolded.

Clarkson arrived in Halifax in the first week of October 1791, pleased with the city's "pretty appearance from the sea," and dined with Governor Parr. Though Parr had been instructed to give his support to Clarkson's mission, he seemed more interested in "pushing about the Bottle, a favourite employ of his" than in encouraging the earnest young man. Neither Parr nor Thomas Carleton, in New Brunswick, had taken kindly to Thomas Peters's complaints—especially once he carried them to London. Replying testily to Whitehall's instructions that he remedy the black loyalists' situation, Carleton insisted that they had "been allowed every privilege of free British subjects," that they had been given their land but failed to cultivate it, and that "none of the Blacks in this province" had deputed Peters to speak on their behalf.[25] Parr also vigorously defended his administration's actions. Clarkson "could plainly see that the governor would rather I should not succeed in my business than otherwise, probably from an Idea that if the People were averse to leaving the Province it would be a good argument to prove that they were content, and that their complaints were groundless."[26]

But such obstructions if anything fortified Clarkson's resolve. He distributed a handbill declaring the terms of the Sierra Leone Company's "FREE SETTLEMENT on the COAST OF AFRICA." Every free black man, it promised, would get twenty acres of land, ten for his wife, and five for every child; as well as food rations to tide them over until they could support themselves. It was understood that the land would be free of charges and quitrents for at least some period of time (as it had also been offered in Nova Scotia).[27] Clarkson traveled around the black townships of Nova Scotia to sell the plan. When Boston King, now living in the black village of Preston, near Halifax, heard about the emigration scheme his own first thought—unusually among his peers—was that he had no reason to go. He had finally found himself a well-paying job (as a domestic servant) and he was making great inroads as a Methodist preacher. But King had bigger ambitions in life. "Recollecting the concern I had felt in years past, for the conversion of the Africans, I resolved to embrace the opportunity." He volunteered himself to the recruiters and explained his desire to preach in Africa—which of course the devout Clarkson was only too delighted to hear.[28]

With more than two hundred names already on his rolls, Clarkson sailed to Birchtown, still the largest black town in British North America. Here he again encountered official resistance to the scheme, in the form of the very man appointed by Parr to help him, Stephen Skinner, a New Jersey loyalist. A younger brother of Cortlandt Skinner, Stephen had emerged as one of the leading merchants in Shelburne: a signal recuperation of his fortunes after years as a patriot prisoner, and after a notorious prewar career as treasurer of New Jersey, during which he was accused of embezzling thousands of pounds.[29] Skinner objected to the Sierra Leone scheme, he said, on the grounds that the settlers "will suffer as the first did who embarked for the same place in 1786." But his deeper worry was that the emigration plan "has had such an Effect on the minds of the Blacks that I am fearfull the whole to the amount of 12 or 15 hundred will leave the province a loss that I think will be severely felt."[30] The departure of so many cheap laborers would have a serious impact on the Shelburne economy. Skinner apparently declared that "he would give the Blacks two [years'] provisions himself if they would stay in this Country and shd [do] everything in his Power to prevent their going."[31] At the same time he helped circulate rumors about the horrors awaiting emigrants in Africa: murder by savages, death by disease, or that perennial threat, as David George heard it, "that if we went away we should be made slaves again."[32]

No sooner had Clarkson disembarked at Birchtown than a black man, about fifty years old, came enthusiastically over to greet him. Spring had worked its miracles and now David George's legs had healed, and a new form of deliverance seemed to be at hand. He launched into a passionate description of the "abject state of servitude" free blacks were living in and the malign tales whites were spreading about Sierra Leone; "if it was known in the town that he [George] had conversed with us in private," George portentously told Clarkson, "his Life would not be safe, he cautioned us from appearing in the Town or Country after it was dark."[33] But such threats did not dissuade George from the emigration plan any more than they did Clarkson. He handed Clarkson a long list of names of people who had already expressed interest in going, and recommended that Clarkson hold a public meeting in Birchtown the next day. By addressing the nasty reports head-on, George said, he could assuage black concerns and win countless volunteers.

Clarkson walked into Daddy Moses's Methodist meeting house that October morning and climbed into the pulpit to find between three and four hundred people packed onto the humble benches before him. Here they were, the living, breathing results of a British imperial promise, skeptical, angry, jaded, desperate, and yet just possibly hopeful. And despite his convictions and his faith, he felt his resolve for a moment falter. Who was he to influence "the future Happiness, welfare, and perhaps Life of these poor Creatures"? Who was he to tell them to abandon their hard-won homes and follow him to a place none of them had ever seen? But as they looked expectantly at him, so many focused eyes in so many worn, tired faces, his confidence that he *could* offer them something better returned. He laid it all out from the beginning, as clearly as possible. Thomas Peters had delivered their grievances to London, and the government had listened. The black loyalists had three options. They could get their local land claims resolved, as the king had commanded, and stay in Nova Scotia. They could join another black regiment and serve in the West Indies, with all the usual benefits attending military service. (Not surprisingly, this option did not hold much appeal.) Or they could choose what Peters had opted for himself, the course that Clarkson undertook to lead, the project that so many aspirations had already been invested in: they could establish a settlement in Sierra Leone and, under the clearly out-lined terms, live there in freedom and farm on free land without any attached fees or rents. Weigh it well, he told them; do not sign up unless you are absolutely sure. This journey will be no easy thing. But I give you my word I will see to it you get your land, and I will stay until every one of you is satisfied.[34]

At the end of Clarkson's speech in Birchtown, even Stephen Skinner had to admit the fairness of the proposals, and "wholly acquitted" Clarkson of the aspersions he had cast on him before. For the next few days the two men received family after family in Clarkson's Shelburne lodgings, and inscribed their names into the ledger of recruits.[35] Are you quite sure, Clarkson asked each one, you are ready to leave every-thing behind? Do you understand the terms being offered you? He was startled when one black man, born in Africa and speaking only broken English, candidly admitted, "No, Massa me no hear, nor no mind, me work like slave, cannot do worse Massa in any part of the world; there-fore am determined to go with you Massa if you please." "You must consider that this is a new settlement & should you keep your health, must expect to meet with many difficulties if You engage in it," Clark-son reminded him. "Me well know that Massa, me can work much, and care not for Climate, if me die me die, had rather die in my own coun-try than this cold Place."[36] In the most poignant case of all, a slave came to register his wife and children, who were free. "With Tears streaming down his Cheecks he said tho' this seperation would be as death to himself, yet he had come to a resolution of resigning them up for ever." Clarkson was so moved by the man's story that he tried to purchase the slave's freedom so he could come to Africa too.[37]

Within three days, five hundred men, women, and children had signed up to go. From Birchtown and the other Nova Scotia settlements to New Brunswick, where Thomas Peters was rounding up emigrants, about twelve hundred people gave in their names. Together they represented fully a third of the entire free black community in these provinces. And every one, it seemed, came with a story of woe— summarized by Clarkson in a list of "reasons given by the free Blacks for wishing to leave Nova Scotia." While the Book of Negroes, listing black departures from New York, represents the most complete register of loyalist emigration from the thirteen colonies, the documents surrounding the black loyalist migration to Sierra Leone yield the most systematic record of *why* loyalist refugees chose to journey on. There was also a larger structural explanation for the black loyalists' readiness to emigrate once more. Displacement from America marked a new phase in the longer series of movements many had already undergone as slaves. Their second collective exodus speaks to the recurring logic of dislocation within a community of people used to being on the move.[38]

It may seem strange that these most marginal of British subjects generated the longest paper trails. In part it reflected their unusual status. As a group of people who also at various points might have been considered property, they did double duty in the archives of an empire obsessed with recordkeeping. In part, too, it reflected their absolute clarity of purpose. Black loyalists in British North America had explicit grievances with their provincial governments, and even more serious complaints with the behavior of white loyalists, their fellow American refugees. Yet as their participation in this scheme signaled, they preserved their faith in the word of the king and the promises of the British Empire. Or at least in such promises as they were embodied in the likable, trustworthy form of John Clarkson.

IT WAS HARD to play Moses, Clarkson felt, as the dimensions of his task kept expanding. In Halifax, he almost single-handedly managed a rerun in miniature of the British evacuations from Savannah, Charleston, and New York. The total number of emigrants was much higher than he had originally anticipated, which made it hard to assemble enough ships and provisions. Back in Britain, Clarkson's brother Thomas had been busily circulating a diagram of a slave ship, every inch of white space dense with little human figures to show the appalling crowding on board. The image was one of the most effective weapons in the abolitionist arsenal, and John Clarkson was especially sensitive about ensuring that conditions for the black passengers on his ships bore no resemblance to it. He rejected vessels that didn't have enough space between the decks, and insisted that ventilation shafts be cut into others; he mandated a strict hygienic regimen of fumigation and multiple cleanings per day. He took equal care over the passengers' diet, plotting a nutritious weekly rotation of salt fish, beef, pork, and vegetables—not just the horrid weevily hardtack that sustained the Royal Navy.[39]

In December 1791, the emigrants assembled in Halifax, organized by village into temporary barracks. With Christmas just a few days away, Thomas Peters sent in another petition requesting that "as it is the larst Christmas day that we ever shall see in the amaraca" they be granted "one days alowance of frish Beef for a Christmas diner."[40] At least this was an easy enough request to fulfill; but when the embarkations began that same week Clarkson struggled to keep up with all the rest. Could they bring pets? Could they bring pigs? (Yes, and no.) Could they travel on the same ship as this family or that? Clarkson was so "greatly teazed in arranging them" it left him "dread[ing] what anxiety and trouble I shall have in fixing these people on our arrival in Africa."[41] To the mental pressure of accommodating all these demands came the physical strains of rushing about the icy streets, checking in on the stuffy barracks, and rowing among the ships in an open boat, as snow fell from above and the sea chilled him from below. Clarkson got headaches, a violent cold, and then a raging fever he could not shake for months.

While the white Moses wrestled with logistics, black leaders kept up morale among the emigrants. After Clarkson's Birchtown speech, David George had led his parishioners en masse to sign up for the expedition. All but a handful joined the project. Testament to George's own eagerness to be gone, he sold his meeting house and lot, site of so much hard work, for a mere £7. He never missed a chance to keep preaching, though, and while they waited in Halifax to depart he spoke in chapels and houses across the city, and led his congregation in hymns that filled the barracks with some of the finest harmonies that Clarkson could ever recall hearing.[42] Birchtown's Methodist preacher Daddy Moses, living up to his name, had gathered his spiritual children behind Clarkson as well. He preached to them so passionately that when Clarkson wandered into the barracks one day and heard him, Daddy Moses "worked himself up to such a pitch that I was fearful, something would happen to him."[43] For these devout black loyalists the journey at hand really did appear to be an exodus of biblical proportions, from their Egypt of North American bondage to an Israel in Africa.

It was good they had their faith to reassure them once their voyage got under way, on January 15, 1792. For the next seven weeks they retched, ached, and shivered, tossed by tempests the likes of which even the veteran sailors among them had never seen. Boston King watched the swell smack up over the decks and wash a man overboard. Seasickness and fever ravaged the passengers below, King's wife Violet among them. She recovered, an answer to her husband's fervent prayers, though sixty others did not, including three of David George's church elders and Clarkson's personal manservant.[44] Other nightmares may have haunted them too. More than fifty had been born in Africa—Thomas Peters included—which meant that they had almost certainly made a previous Atlantic crossing in chains, shoved belowdecks on slave ships.

"There was great joy to see the land," said David George, when at last it appeared before them.[45] They disembarked at the overgrown site of the original Granville Town and promptly busied themselves "clearing away the wood to build the town which is to be called Free Town." On the first Sunday ashore, the Sierra Leone Company's Anglican minister delivered a sermon on the text of Psalm 127, "Except the Lord build the house, they labour in vain that build it," while not far away, David George's followers gathered around to hear him preach "the first Lord's day, it was a blessed time," under a canvas sail stretched for cover. In due course they built a proper meeting house with wooden poles and thatch.[46] This was the first Baptist church in Sierra Leone, and the last node in what was now a transatlantic network of spiritual communities created by black migrants who once had worshipped together in the glades at Silver Bluff.

Traveling on the same boat as George, Clarkson had heard his shipmates' cheers and volleys on the sight of land. But it was "not in my power to describe my sensations at this moment, for I knew not what the next hours"—or weeks, months, years—"might produce."[47] Fortunately, the Temne did not attack them when they landed, as Clarkson had feared. Instead he discovered a different unwelcome piece of news: orders from the Sierra Leone Company appointing him superintendent of the new colony. The position was the last thing he wanted. "I had positively declared before I left England, that nothing should induce me to continue in Africa," he moaned to the deaf pages of his diary, "or to undertake anything more than collecting the people in America and afterwards seeing them properly conducted to Sierra

Leone."[48] He had been sick and stressed for months, and he longed to sail home to England to recover and rejoin his patiently waiting fiancée. "But what can I do?" When he considered the real "affection & regard" he felt for the loyalists, "and my ardent zeal for the civilization of the surrounding nations, and Africa . . . I have made up my mind to take the consequences . . . and to remain with the poor Nova Scotians till the Colony is established or lost."[49]

What unfolded on the African peninsula pitted great ambitions against ample difficulties. The work of making Freetown reprised the central features of loyalist settlement in British North America and the Bahamas. The colonists contended with an alien environment, with preexisting residents, and with one another. Their troubles revolved in part around the consistently contentious matter of land allocation, a source of strife in every loyalist settlement. But most of all, the newcomers wrangled with the government appointed to manage them. For Clarkson quickly learned, as so many governors had before him, that loyalist refugees were not unreflectingly "loyal" to dictates from above. These settlers, like their white peers in Nassau and Saint John, had ideas about rights and representation at odds with their rulers' more authoritarian style.

Through a near-constant tremble of fever, Clarkson labored to apportion land, organize working parties, and placate various constituencies. Freetown's first lots took shape: David George and Thomas Peters received nine acres each, Daddy Moses seven; most of the other men gained six acres apiece, while women and children received two to four.[50] As in other sites of exodus, shortages of food and supplies compounded the challenges of adapting to a strange physical environment. Here there were especially exotic dangers. One day a baboon seized a twelve-year-old girl from her tent. Leopards prowled out from the bush. Giant snakes slithered among the huts.[51] Even before the rainy season, disease worked its deadly way through Freetown. "It is quite customary of a morning to ask, 'how many died last night?' " noted Anna Maria Falconbridge.[52] They had been on shore just three weeks when Violet King fell ill, "helpless as an infant," and went out of her mind with delirium. Her husband and friends sat around her in prayer, when she "suddenly rose up" and said "I am well: I only wait for the coming of the Lord." As their voices chorused up in the confident cadence of an old Wesleyan hymn she quivered and cried out with them, and "expired in a rapture of love"—embraced by the faith that had seized her soul at Daddy Moses's meeting house in Birchtown.[53]

Every evening as the noise of crickets and bullfrogs made "the town and woods ring," Clarkson mustered his dwindling energies to record the trials of his day.[54] "There are so many Circumstances which happen in the Course of the Day to plague and vex me that I am almost tired of my life," he confessed.[55] First he had to manage relations between the settlers and the Temne. Soon after landing he held a palaver with Naimbana to smooth the way for Freetown's expansion, making the earnest promise that "I would never have come to Africa to take their land without paying for it."[56] He also tried to accommodate the remaining survivors from Granville Town, who felt marginalized and resentful of the new administration. Then there were the other Europeans. It was bad enough that the slave traders held court just a short distance away, to Clarkson's continued horror. The Sierra Leone Company had dispatched a small governing council from London, a motley bunch of men divided by infighting, in some cases suspiciously racist, and in two instances hopeless alcoholics.[57] In June 1792, Clarkson eagerly welcomed some new white arrivals, notably the loyalist Isaac DuBois. Hailing from Wilmington, North Carolina—the same town as Thomas Peters—DuBois, like the black loyalists, traveled to Sierra Leone as a multiple migrant, having initially settled in the Bahamas. He had abandoned his cotton-planting efforts there and now hoped for better luck in Freetown, a rare white settler in this free black colony. Clarkson appointed DuBois manager of the storehouse and town militia, and came to rely heavily on his competence.[58]

Of all the challenges facing the new settlement, though, the greatest came from the settlers themselves. Wilberforce had warned Clarkson to beware of Thomas Peters, recognizing that the impulses that had led Peters to London made it unlikely he would remain a passive subject in Freetown. Sure enough, within a fortnight of landing, Peters came to Clarkson "and made many complaints; he was extremely violent and indiscreet in his conversation and seemed as if he were desirous of alarming and disheartening the people."[59] Peters started attending Methodist meetings, and "invariably after the Meeting is over addresses the People and complains that the promises made to him in London have not been complied with."[60] The delays in getting their land allocated made the black loyalists all the more receptive to Peters's rhetoric, for, "ill treated through life," they "began to think they should be served the same as in Nova Scotia."[61] "You know Governor, the state you found us in in Nova Scotia & New Brunswick," they reminded Clarkson. "King George was good to us, God bless him and gave us many Articles to comfort us and gave us promises of land . . . but yet after being there for many years we never received them."[62]

Clarkson soon found that the settlers, "having imbibed strange notions from Thomas Peters as to their civil rights," became fractious and reluctant to work.[63] "The trouble the Blacks give me in coming for orders, in bringing complaints &c. daily increases," Clarkson said. "I am often so harrassed that in my weak state I am ready to faint. . . . I have scarcely put a stop to one evil when others arise."[64] On Easter Sunday 1792, Clarkson learned of a plot by Peters to take over the government. He immediately called a meeting "under a Great Tree"—perhaps a spreading cotton tree, like the one that defines central Freetown today. With the settlers assembled before him on the red ground—as six months earlier they had gathered in the Birchtown pews—he turned to Peters and "said, it was probably either one or other of us would be hanged upon that Tree, before the Palaver was settled." In sharp terms, Clarkson persuaded the settlers that "the Demon of Discord" would bring "misery and guilt," and "blast . . . every prospect of bettering the condition of the Black population throughout the world."[65] A few days later the settlers agreed to a declaration "purporting that whilst they reside in this Colony, they will live obedient to its Laws which will be made conformable to those of England as far as local circumstances will permit."[66]

And then suddenly, in June, Thomas Peters died: a quick victim of the pernicious fevers of the place. His death removed the most strident political presence among the loyalists, and Clarkson's single greatest source of trouble. But the legacy of this community leader did not so rapidly vanish. A month later, reports circulated of Peters's ghost strolling the streets of Freetown.[67] His political vision lingered, too, of a colony in which blacks would hold the reins of their own government rather than remain the misled subordinates of a white imperial administration.

Clarkson continued to exert all his diplomatic skills in managing concerns about rights and about land. He had unwittingly paved the way for the most serious conflict between settlers and the Sierra Leone Company by promising, in Birchtown, that the black loyalists would not be charged quitrents on their land grants. It later turned out that the company had quite different ideas. Meanwhile, Clarkson agreed to a request that blacks be allowed to serve on juries alongside whites. He responded positively to a complaint from David George and other leading citizens about the decision to site public buildings on the waterfront, remembering how in Nova Scotia "they were all excluded from ye Water by the white gentlemen occupying all the Water Lots."[68] The biggest problem stemmed from delays in clearing and granting the promised twenty-acre farm lots. The settlers never ceased to tell Clarkson how they had never received their grants in North America. But Clarkson knew that even if they put all their muscle-power to work (which they did not), a thousand machetes could not possibly cut back enough jungle by summer's end. Instead, Clarkson hammered out a compromise by which the settlers took smaller lots as a temporary measure, until more ground could be cleared.

Shattered by illness and strain, Clarkson received permission to sail to England on leave at the end of 1792. As he looked over his time in Africa, he could take pride in the fact that Freetown had survived its first year: a vital achievement, especially in the wake of Granville Town's failure. The colony would remain. But he was also leaving unresolved problems in the hands of a cadre of white officers who proved unsympathetic, inept, or both. Clarkson's immediate successor, William Dawes, was an austere evangelical who had just completed a stint as an officer in the penal colony of Botany Bay. It wasn't the most promising qualification for governing a group of people trying to escape the memory of enslavement and injustice. Equally unpropitious was the background of Dawes's replacement, Zachary Macaulay, who had spent five formative years working on a Jamaican sugar plantation. Though still in his twenties, the fiercely religious Macaulay struck even his supporters as "inflexible" and "illiberal," sometimes "chilling."[69] The rest of the colony's councilors descended into strife and dissipation. Alexander Falconbridge, the only one of them with long experience in the region, steadily drowned himself in alcohol. After a drinking binge one day in December 1792, he died. "I will not be so guilty as to tell a falsehood on this occasion, by saying I regret his death, no! I really do not," wrote his widow Anna Maria, soured by years of his abuse.[70]

Through all the disputes that divided them, the black loyalists—Peters excepted—had looked on Clarkson as an honest broker, and more: their Moses. His departure attracted outpourings of sorrow and goodwill. Naimbana sent an ox and an Arabic prayer for a safe passage. Black settlers came by the dozens to present their beloved superintendent with humble offerings for his journey: yams, eggs, onions. Phillis George brought a handsome donation of three chickens and four eggs, while her husband David was the leading signatory of another petition.[71] Addressed to the Sierra Leone Company directors, the text described (in the broken writing its authors had learned as adults) how Clarkson "ever did behave to us as a gentilmon in everey rescpt [respect]. . . . Our ardent desier is that the Same John Clarkeson Shold returen Back to bee our goverener." Until that time, "we pray that his Excelency John Clarkson might Be preserved safe over the sea to his frinds and return to us again."[72]

David George also made preparations to leave. From their first meeting when Clarkson stepped off the boat in Shelburne and through their voyage together to Sierra Leone, the two men had become good friends. Clarkson often came to hear George preach, and sometimes joined his prayer meetings; George named his youngest child after Clarkson. Maybe they had been discussing homecomings on board the *Lucretia* one day, en route to Africa, when it struck George to ask his friend "if I might not hereafter go to England?" George "wished to see the Baptist brethren who live in his country." Clarkson agreed to take him if the chance ever arose. Now George packed his trunks too, "preached a farewel sermon to the church" and appointed deputies to carry on in his absence.[73] A few days after the black loyalists' first Christmas in Africa, Clarkson and George cruised out of Freetown together, on another journey charted, as they would have been inclined to see it, by God and the British Empire.

ON A SEPTEMBER morning in 1794, seven ships entered Freetown harbor with British flags flying. They were a welcome sight in the settlement, where supplies were short and ships (if not part of the inevitable slave traffic heading upriver) might bring much-needed provisions. "Multitudes" gathered on the waterfront to watch the unexpected fleet draw near, while from his balcony the new governor Zachary Macaulay made out the details of the boats through his telescope. They were rigged and built in the British style, he saw, they bristled with guns, and the sailors on one frigate were training a cannon—straight up at him! He darted inside as shots zinged past. Within moments the ships had run down what turned out to be decoy British flags and put up their real colors instead: the French Revolutionary tricolor. They fired off a broadside straight into Freetown. David George, who had been to Britain and back unscathed, was in the crowd of people screaming, pushing, scrambling away from the hail of shells. Though Macaulay ordered a white cloth hung over his balcony as a flag of truce, the bombardment continued for an hour and a half.

Storehouses, offices, dwellings, and the Anglican church all exploded into ripping flames and eye-watering smoke. Then came the plundering. French sailors grabbed rum, money, food, anything valuable they could carry. They smashed the printing press and the apothecary's shop, trampled Bibles into the dirt, seized and slaughtered hogs and chickens by the hundreds. The *sans culottes* even snatched clothes off residents' backs—leaving George shirtless and his family "almost naked." At the end of the day a young child was dead; two settlers had their legs blown off. By the time the French forces left two weeks later, Freetown—barely two years old—lay in ruins.[74]

For all the similarities between the founding of Freetown and other loyalist settlements, the French attack on Freetown underscored a central difference. This was the 1790s, not the 1780s: the French Revolution had plunged Britain into a bitter global war, and reframed debates over liberty and authority. For black loyalists, the French attack was an awful addition to the challenges they faced in developing this colony. For their white rulers, the episode confirmed how important it was to maintain discipline, order, and loyalty among imperial subjects at a time when another revolution threatened to unseat British power altogether. The early years of Freetown showed how the coming of the French Revolution hardened the lessons British rulers had drawn from the American Revolution. It also polarized imperial subjects afresh around loyalty to the existing order versus resistance in the name of greater liberty.

Governor Macaulay had asked the French commander to spare Freetown from plunder on the grounds that it was a neutral colony, and that the black settlers were "not Englishmen." Black loyalists begged the French to restore some of their possessions, "telling them we was Americans from North America" and thus (they claimed) French allies. All's fair in war. But once the French left, such assertions appeared more suspicious than not. Macaulay not only demanded that the blacks assume some of the cost of the destroyed Sierra Leone Company property; he imposed a new loyalty oath before he would grant them medical assistance or employment. "We was British subjects eighteen & twenty years before we came here," the indignant settlers retorted, and since "after our arrival hear we all took the Oath of Allegiance to our King and Country, we therefore refused to comply."[75] As loyal British subjects, they should get British rights with no questions asked. To them, Macaulay's maneuvers worryingly resembled those familiar white efforts to deny them land and rights in Nova Scotia and New Brunswick. Daddy Moses and his congregants summed up their distress in a plaintive letter to John Clarkson: "In Your Being here we wance did call it Free Town but since your Absence We have a Reason to call it A Town of Slavery."[76]

If only Clarkson were still with them! During his year as governor he had been able to use his close relationship with the loyalists, one founded in genuine mutual respect, to defuse tensions about land allocation and rights. For years to come, Freetown's black residents sent him emotional letters describing their disappointments and begging for his return. "Times is not as it was when you left us," they said sadly.[77] "We Believe that it was the handy work of Almighty God—that you should be our leader as Mosis and Joshua was bringing the Children of Esaral [Israel] to the promise land," wrote another correspondent— "but Oh that God would Once more Give you A Desire to come & visit us here."[78] What they did not know was that Clarkson himself had fallen out of favor with the Sierra Leone Company directors, who objected to what they saw as his preference for settlers' interests over company profits. Not long after his return to Britain, the directors dismissed him as governor. "Thunderstruck" by the move, Clarkson nevertheless kept his grievances to himself lest he enhance public disapproval of the entire Sierra Leone Company project. He wrote back to his black friends in Freetown and told them that his recent marriage prevented him from returning.[79]

Clarkson had sworn that the settlers' coveted farmlands would be distributed within a few weeks of his departure. Unfortunately his successors did not comply. He had been gone less than two months when the black loyalists rose up again to protest the delays. "Mr. Clarkson promised in Nova Scotia that no distinction should be made here between us and white men"; they reminded Clarkson's replacement, Governor Dawes, "we now claim this promise, we are free British subjects, and expect to be treated as such."[80] In Clarkson's absence, Isaac DuBois became their strongest white ally. A fellow American refugee, he must have presented a sympathetic contrast with the stern British evangelical officers. Though DuBois had fared little better as a cotton planter in Sierra Leone than in the Bahamas, his managerial competence quickly earned him respect and stature in the colony. He also discovered surprising personal fulfillment. In early 1793, DuBois declared himself "happyly joined in the bonds of wedlock"—to the freshly widowed Anna Maria Falconbridge. They married less than three weeks after her first husband's death. She "made no apology for my hastiness . . . for deviating from the usual custom of twelve months *widowhood.*"[81] He, for his part, didn't mind that the minister failed to keep the news discreetly to himself (as he had been instructed to do), but "carried it piping hot to the ears of every one he met." "I am happy," DuBois said, experiencing an improbable flash of fortune compared with the ample disappointment he had known as a loyalist refugee.[82]

DuBois helped the settlers draft yet another petition of protest. "Mr. Dawes seems to wish to rule us just as bad as if we were all Slaves," it read, laying out familiar complaints about land and other abuses.[83] Doubtless hoping to repeat Thomas Peters's past political success, the black loyalists elected two representatives to carry the petition personally to Sierra Leone Company directors in London. They reached England in August 1793 and met with the chairman of the board. Though at first they found him "very kind" and "compassionate," he strictly told them their "complaints were frivolous and ill grounded."[84] The newlywed Isaac and Anna Maria DuBois arrived in England a short time later, and once again DuBois helped them make their case. But the directors rejected the settlers' demands, blocked them from meeting with Clarkson, and packed them off back to Sierra Leone as quickly as possible. For his pains, DuBois was dismissed too.[85] When Anna Maria wrote up an account of her journeys to Sierra Leone, she was so put off by the company's treatment of both her husbands that she actually came out *against* the abolition of the slave trade, the company's founding principle.

The black emissaries returned to Sierra Leone to find Freetown once again in ferment. This time tensions had been whipped up by a confrontation between black settlers and the white captain of a slave ship, a consequence of the uneasy proximity of Freetown to Bunce Island. Governor Macaulay managed to suppress a public riot by putting a cannon at his gate and offering free passage back to Halifax (on a former slave ship) for anybody who wanted to go.[86] Nobody did— though a cluster of disappointed Methodists decided to move off company land altogether and start afresh, where "we may be no longer in bondage to this tyranious Crew."[87] The episode helped confirm Macaulay's opinion that the Methodists were more troublesome than David George and his Baptists. For George by now stood out as one of Freetown's most contented denizens, his loyalism strengthened by his experiences in Africa and Britain. All those white plots he had complained of in Nova Scotia seemed as distant as Birchtown itself. Authority had done well by him now: he had been kindly received during his visit to England, and enjoyed the support of British Baptists as he continued to grow his church. He also prospered in more earthly pursuits, holding a license to operate a tavern out of his house.[88]

George did not protest, for instance, during the next major upset between settlers and government. It concerned quitrent, which Macaulay insisted that settlers pay on their freshly allocated grants. As early as 1783, Sir Guy Carleton had advised that no rents or fees be assessed on land grants for loyalists: he knew well that Americans viewed such charges as a form of taxation, and that "quit-rents will, in all cases, sooner or later become a source of popular disquiet."[89] Macaulay's measure turned out to be every bit as provocative among black loyalists in Sierra Leone as Carleton had predicted. Many of them clearly remembered John Clarkson's vow, made from Daddy Moses's pulpit back in Birchtown, that there would be no fees on land in Sierra Leone. Here was yet another violation of British promises. Boston King wrote to Clarkson telling him that many families were "thinking of going when the R[a]in is over & it appire [appears] that their chief reason is because the Company require quit rent for their Lands."[90] A 1796 election of hundredors and tithingmen saw substantial gains made by candidates opposed to Macaulay.[91]

As vocally as they resented this form of taxation, the Freetown settlers also continued to seek greater representation. When the hated Macaulay at last departed in 1799 (taking a number of Africans with him for a bracing dose of British civilization), black loyalists seized the chance to claim more autonomy. Resuming an old grievance, they demanded the right to appoint their own judges—a request that the company government, not surprisingly, rejected. But coming on the heels of years of dissatisfaction, this controversy pushed some Freetown residents to the brink. Unwilling to stand for continued infringements and restraints, some of the hundredors and tithingmen launched what amounted to a loyalist coup. In September 1800, they issued their own legal code, effectively setting themselves up as an independent government.[92] They elected their own governor in the person of Isaac Anderson, one of the emissaries who had gone to London in 1793. And they gathered up their guns. The black loyalist rebels took up a position on a bridge just outside Freetown, with the tacit support of King Tom, the Temne subchief, ready to fight for their alternate government.

For one steamy week, black settlers around Freetown had to choose once more between staying loyal or joining a rebellion. It was the largest armed challenge to imperial authority posed by any refugee loyalist community—and offered a rare insight into what purchase loyalty retained among these British subjects. David George balked at the spectacle before him. Even he had been moved to the brink of rebellion a few years earlier by a contentious marriage law, designed to clamp down on "loose" sexual morality among the blacks; but he had backed away at the prospect of violence.[93] Fear of violence, if nothing else, prevented George from joining this rebellion too. The episode confirmed his loyalty to authority, in much the way revolution had done for his old friend George Liele in Jamaica. About half the settlers around him, however, took an opposite position. They had struggled for freedom on both sides of the Atlantic, and were unwilling to see their attempts at self-assertion end in the same old repression that had quashed them so many times before.

But if the black loyalists were not prepared to submit, neither was the white government. Intervening before King Tom could become openly involved, the governor launched a forceful strike against the rebels. In a battle at the bridge, British troops swiftly routed the rebels, killing two and capturing thirty more. The rest were mostly hunted down from the bush. Isaac Anderson, the would-be first black ruler of a self-governed Freetown, met justice at the end of a rope. Among the two dozen rebel leaders banished from the colony for involvement in the uprising was Harry Washington, who had run away from George Washington's Mount Vernon some twenty years before. Also banished was the self-named former slave British Freedom.[94] The African-American revolution in Freetown was over—and the quest for expanded liberty, however American or British, cut short.

THE 1800 rebellion was the culmination of a series of conflicts around subjects' rights that had erupted in Freetown since its founding. It highlighted how Freetown itself, established a decade after the surrender at Yorktown, entrenched patterns made manifest across the loyalist diaspora. Like the troublesome East Florida refugees in the Bahamas, Freetown's black loyalist settlers had experienced a double displacement, and internalized a mistrust of British authorities in North America that proved extremely difficult to overcome. Their attempts to achieve greater political representation (and reduced taxes) resembled analogous efforts by white loyalists in British North America and the Bahamas. They used the same tools to demand their rights—petitions, delegations, elections—deployed by their white peers. Faced with intransigence from their white rulers, some of these

frustrated settlers even made the ultimate break with imperial authority that American patriots had done before them, and instigated armed
rebellion.

But this wasn't 1776, or even the mid-1780s; it was 1800. William
Wilberforce, who had been one of the guiding spirits behind the
colony, snidely commented that the black loyalists in Sierra Leone
were "as thorough Jacobins as if they had been trained and educated in
Paris."[95] (He might as well have said Port-au-Prince, since what the
rebels sought resembled what the Haitian revolutionaries were fighting for: a government by and for free blacks.) Likening American
loyalists to French revolutionaries, Wilberforce revealed the anti-
democratic attitudes that accompanied his paternalistic antislavery
crusade. His jibe also called attention to the French Revolution's role
in sharpening the edges of the "spirit of 1783." The wars enhanced the
exercise of top-down authority in the British world, hemmed in individual liberties, and provided a pretext for territorial expansion.
Around the empire, as loyalist refugees from William Wylly to George
Liele discovered, the French wars tested British subjects' loyalty
afresh.

So it was not surprising that the Freetown colonists, founding their
settlement in the turbulent 1790s, ran up against the "spirit of 1783"
with unusual force, for better and worse. This was especially evident in
their encounters with imperial authority. Not only were the lines
between rulers and ruled etched in white and black; as war continued,
metropolitan government tightened its grip. In 1799, the Sierra Leone
Company petitioned Parliament for a royal charter to solidify its rule.
Parliament had rejected the company's request for a charter in the
1780s, largely under the influence of the proslavery lobby. By 1799,
though, the influence of that lobby had declined, while the prospect of
French republicanism destabilizing regimes in and beyond Europe
made Parliament look more kindly on any request to enhance centralized authority. In 1800, the Sierra Leone Company received a charter
granting it direct rule over Freetown. States routinely underwrite the
power of arms with the power of law. As if on cue, the charter arrived
in Freetown just weeks after the September rebellion. It eliminated
hundredors and tithingmen outright, marking the end of even the illu-
sion of representative government for the black loyalists. Following
the abolition of the slave trade in 1807, the Sierra Leone Company
itself was dissolved and Freetown turned into a crown colony, administered directly by Whitehall.

The imposition of crown rule pointed in turn to a second aspect of the "spirit of 1783" carried to new lengths (literally) by the black loyal-ists: expansionist initiatives. Their transatlantic exodus extended British rule into a hitherto largely uncolonized part of the African con-tinent. As a colony of settlement, Freetown came into being in contrast with the utilitarian British slaving stations on the West African coast, and acted as a bridgehead for further imperial incursion. (Freetown also served as a model for the neighboring colony of Liberia, founded by American abolitionists in the 1820s.) The black loyalists' migration established a template for subsequent black arrivals. In 1800, a second group of free blacks joined the loyalists in Freetown: Jamaican Maroons. The Maroons had already followed in the footsteps of the black loyalists once, as exiles in Nova Scotia, where they settled in one of the villages largely vacated by the black loyalists in 1791. But Nova Scotia was a far, cold cry from Cockpit Country, and the unhappy Maroons petitioned every official they could, asking to move to a warmer climate. The Sierra Leone Company welcomed their request, seeing the Maroons as a good group with which to augment—and dilute—Freetown's population of obstreperous loyalists. The Maroons arrived in Freetown, with exquisite coincidence, just as the rebellion of 1800 was in full swing. On government orders, they disembarked in time to help suppress the rebels—part of a classic imperial strategy of divide and rule. After the abolition of the slave trade in 1807, a third group of blacks came to Freetown in the form of "recaptives" liberated by the Royal Navy from intercepted slave ships. Within twenty years of the black loyalists' arrival, they had become a minority in a city of their own making, and would be known as the "Nova Scotians" to dis-tinguish them within an increasingly diverse population.[96] The label obscures their connection to the United States and a history of revolu-tion, which may be one reason it stuck.

It can be easy—especially in light of the region's more recent history—to relate the story of Freetown as a chronicle of broken promises and thwarted hopes. Yet in spite of the limits placed on their autonomy, in spite of the diminution of their influence, "Freetown" actually meant something to its free black founders. These black migrants demonstrated more clearly than any other loyalist refugees the continued purchase of the third element in the "spirit of 1783": a commitment to liberty and humanitarian initiatives. Freetown marked the last stage of these refugees' transcontinental journey out of bondage. In the thirteen colonies, most of them had been chattel slaves. In Nova Scotia they were nominally free, but constrained in various ways: many had become indentured to whites, never received adequate land grants, and been excluded from civic participation. In Sierra Leone, they remained free and did one step better again: they got their land, as well as various civil rights such as the ability to choose representatives and sit on juries.

And for all the difficulties in founding this place, the colonists could point to one unmistakable achievement: Freetown actually survived and grew. For contrast they had only to look at the wreckage of Granville Town, or at another colony essayed at exactly the same time by a breakaway faction of the Sierra Leone Company, on the nearby coast of Guinea. That project, misbegotten from the outset, ended in disaster within a year, with all its colonists either dead or evacuated. One of the first victims was the colony's surveyor—none other than Benjamin Marston, the man who had laid out Birchtown nearly a decade before. He died on the West African coast, a world away from North America, yet just three hundred miles from many of the Birchtown blacks he had once helped to settle.[97] It was a poignant if accidental reminder of the fragility and the interconnectedness of refugee lives.

If Marston had had the chance to see Freetown, he might have recognized there a range of loyalist opinion similar to that he had once observed in Shelburne. British promises of liberty did not reach as far as Thomas Peters or the 1800 rebels wanted. But while conditions in Freetown pushed some to revolt, they strengthened the loyalty of others.[98] David George, for one, had been as outspoken as anyone about the abuse of his rights back in Birchtown. In Sierra Leone, however, he rarely protested. With freedom and property secured, systematic persecution at an end, and a promising arena for preaching before him, George had little reason to wish his government otherwise. Boston King appeared to share his positive outlook. King, like George, had also had the chance to visit England, and spent two memorable years there sponsored by British Methodists. In the meeting houses of London and Bristol, King "found a more cordial love to the White People than I had ever experienced before," for "in the former part of my life I had suffered greatly from the cruelty and injustice of the Whites." He decided that "many of the White People, instead of being enemies and oppressors of us poor Blacks, are our friends, and deliverers from slavery."[99] To be sure, this was exactly what King's white audience wanted to hear, and he must have known it. Still, living in a free black society gave King a security and confidence he had never enjoyed before. Never again would he be flogged and tortured as he had been in South Carolina, or regularly haunted by nightmares of his master coming back to snatch him, as he had been in New York. Never again would he be "pinched with hunger and cold" in snowbound Birchtown.[100] Political aspirations imported from North America may not have taken root in Africa, but that did not make the colony a failure, or even necessarily a disappointment to its inhabitants. Indeed, the evangelical Christianity imported by loyalists including George and King proved to be quite compatible with the Sierra Leone Company's civilizing mission.

At least one other loyalist who came to Freetown must have heard resonance in the city's hopeful name. One spring evening in 1798, Governor Zachary Macaulay had stepped onto his piazza to discover "a very singular & interesting personage" standing in the twilight. "He was meanly clothed, but his air & manner had somewhat very commanding and prepossessing in them. . . . [H]is eye was strongly expressive of firmness and intrepidity, and of a Spirit capable of daring enterprize." Macaulay "was at some loss even to conjecture from what part of the World he could have come," when the stranger introduced himself: " 'My name Sir,' " he said, " 'is William Augustus Bowles, I am a Chief of the nation of Creek Indians.' " Freetown meant something to Bowles because it marked his own release from captivity. Bowles had last flashed across British imperial authorities' consciousness in 1792, when he was taken prisoner by the Spanish and shipped to the Philippines. In 1798, his Spanish captors decided to transfer him to their French allies and put him on a ship bound for Europe. As the vessel cruised up the West African coast, Bowles watched and waited for any chance to escape. When a rival craft drew up alongside his own, he saw the near miracle he needed. Collecting his wits and a small bundle of clothes, he slipped away onto the adjacent boat—and when that ship in turn sailed to Freetown, Bowles stepped back into the British Empire, a free man.[101]

Bowles enjoyed Macaulay's hospitality and sketched a pleasing picture of Freetown, with tidy white houses nestled comfortably against the mountains.[102] The city brought the "spirit of 1783" to life, a pioneering colony in a new imperial domain. And as he looked out toward the Atlantic from the edge of another continent, Bowles felt his own expansive dreams revive. He and the black residents of the town around him had been among sixty thousand loyalists dispersed by the American Revolution. Together, they had challenged, benefited from, and helped shape a renewed British Empire. Now that another revolutionary war was redefining regimes around the world, what role would any of them continue to play in the British Empire going forward?

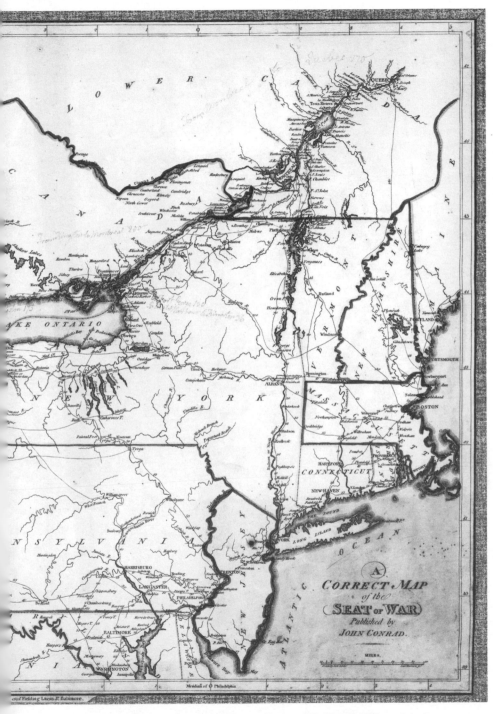

Samuel Lewis, *A Correct Map of the Seat of War*, 1815.

CHAPTER TEN

Empires of Liberty

A T THE TURN of the century loyalist refugees spanned the British Empire, from tens of thousands settled across the revivified provinces of British North America to a tiny handful in Australia, the empire's remotest edge. Wherever they had moved, by the early nineteenth century all had been touched in some way by the "spirit of 1783." They had also seen the empire tested anew by war with France. For the Sierra Leone colonists, among others, war led to a tightening of imperial rule. For the scattered members of a single refugee family—the Robinsons of New York—it occasioned a remarkably immediate appreciation of the empire's global reach.

Beverley Robinson, the family patriarch, had retired to England in 1783 to seek compensation for his confiscated estate, and position his children on promising career paths. He died in 1792, in the placid Gloucestershire village of Thornbury, near Bath. But had the New Yorker survived into the new century, he would have been thrilled to see how well his investment in his children paid off. Imperial service carried the Robinsons around the world in a diaspora of their own. Robinson's fourth son, Frederick Philipse "Phil" Robinson, now acted effectively as head of the family in England. A career soldier, Phil had participated in the last act of the American Revolution, by marching out of New York City on Evacuation Day, and was in from the beginning of the French Revolutionary wars, fighting in a 1793 offensive in the West Indies. Invalided home in 1794, Phil had since then enjoyed unusual stability for a soldier in wartime, stationed in England as an officer in charge of recruiting. While his mother and two unmarried sisters resided quietly at Thornbury, his brothers dispersed. Two circulated about the empire on military service. Two others lived in New Brunswick, including the eldest, Beverley Robinson Jr., on his large estate outside Fredericton, a confirmed member of the provincial elite.[1]

One evening in November 1799, Phil Robinson sat in the glow of a good fire at home in Bedford with his wife, mother, and sister, who were visiting from Thornbury. As the Robinsons gossiped in the parlor, a young man arrived at the door. He was a stranger to them—yet he looked somehow familiar too. The caller turned out to be Phil's own nephew Henry, Beverley Jr.'s second son. The last time any of them had seen "Hinky Pinky"—as his grandfather fondly used to call him—he had been learning to take his first steps in British-occupied New York City. Now, sixteen years later, here was Henry Clinton Robinson all grown up and fresh off the boat from New Brunswick. For a moment they froze in mutual shock, Henry tongue-tied, and old Mrs. Robinson "rather overcome at first" at the startling, wonderful sight of her grandson. "But a plentiful shower of tears relieved her," Phil wrote excitedly to Beverley, "and allowed her to join us in ten thousand enquiries." "Henry could not answer us fast enough," filling them in on all the news from North America, about his parents and many siblings. "We are all delighted with him," reported the proud uncle, "and will endeavor to supply the place of those he left behind."[2]

The domestic contentment around the hearth at Bedford contrasted with an external reality the Robinsons could never forget. The British Empire was at war. Phil encountered its demands almost every day as he strove to find healthy volunteers to fill the army's ranks in this ever-widening conflict. Even Henry's forty-five-year-old father, Beverley Jr., had been called up on militia duty in New Brunswick, an experience that brought him back with a jolt to his first days as a soldier, in the American Revolution. Now Henry carried a new generation of Robinsons into a new revolutionary war. With help from his well-connected relatives, he secured an ensigncy in a good regiment and was promptly swept up into a career that captured the global dimensions of combat.

His campaigning started in the Mediterranean. He sailed into the "most Grand" harbor of Valletta, Malta, marveling at the fortifications that jutted into the water like shark's teeth.[3] From there, his regiment traveled onward to a more stunning destination still: Egypt, which had been occupied by the French since 1798. Henry there participated in Britain's first major military offensive in the Middle East. He wrote to his uncle Phil, breathlessly describing his adventures. "His astonishment at every thing he saw seemed to have been excessive, and with reason," Phil reported to Beverley Jr., "for so many, rapid, and striking changes of situation perhaps never before happened to a lad of his age;

from the banks of peaceable <u>St Johns river</u>, through scenes of warfare to <u>Egypt!</u>"[4] The heat, robed and wrapped figures billowing down parched streets, the dryness, muezzins calling, camels chewing, the sun, more heat, and so much glaring sand: New Brunswick could not be farther away. But whenever Henry spent time with another loyalist's son in his regiment, "we would always Transport ourselves to America" in the imagination.[5]

Henry returned to Malta to hear of the impending Treaty of Amiens, signed by Britain and France in 1802. But it was an uneasy, short-lived peace, soon broken by Napoleon Bonaparte's ambitious plans for French expansion. Henry meanwhile went on to Gibraltar, as hateful a posting now as it had been forty years earlier when Thomas Carleton did his best to get away from it.[6] "This is a miserable Hole des[titute] of all kinds of society except [a] variegated Assemblage of those Red Coated Beings who pass for Votives of Mars but may more properly be nominated Disciples of Bacchus," Henry complained.[7] A new governor had just been appointed to clean things up, in the person of Prince Edward, Duke of Kent. The duke had spent much of the last decade in British North America, where he befriended many loyalists; Phil Robinson "once was a favorite with him."[8] Henry also earned the duke's positive notice. Unfortunately his regiment did not. The duke's crackdown on indiscipline ended up provoking a mutiny, led by members of Henry's regiment. While the duke was recalled to England for his actions, the regiment suffered a worse reprimand. They were sent to the deadliest posting in the British world: the West Indies.

Henry put the best face on it: "The pleasing Idea of being so much nearer my Beloved Parents & the fair Prospect of my soon seeing them bears down every objection I should have in going." With luck, he told his parents, "the Regiment may have the good fortune to be Quarterd in Jamaica," where "Uncle William writes me he can be of more service to me there than any other place" and "General Nugent is Governor who you know married Aunt Williams Sister."[9] Stationed in Tobago, Henry sent cheerful reports (and boxes of pineapples) back home: "I am well & in high spirits," he told his mother. "The Island is very healthy & so am I."[10] But by early 1805, Henry was dead, victim of the "Fatal West Indies." His death came on the heels of that of a younger brother, also in military service, who had drowned in New Brunswick.[11] His anguished mother wrote to her sister-in-law in England, "I have yet scarcely firmness enough to speak upon subjects which rend my heart asunder . . . how is our once happy Family dis-

jointed, two of the most flourishing Branches cut off forever. . . . I feel
at this moment as if every prospect I had of happiness was Buried with
my Children."[12]

Phil Robinson suffered too, for he considered both his nephews as
sons, and "this second loss so recently after the first, is a more severe
trial than the strictest & coldest philosophy can bear up against."[13] And
yet, while he grieved over the double tragedy, he could also report
good news to his brother Beverley. "A very great change has taken
place in the fortunes of the Robinsons in this country." Their brother
Morris earned a lucrative appointment as assistant barrack master at
Gibraltar, effectively chief of staff. The youngest brother, William
Henry Robinson, landed the position of commissary-general in
Jamaica, which was so well paid that Phil could "look upon William as
established for life."[14] Phil, for his part, had been promoted to lieutenant colonel and would later set off on a career-making tour of his
own as a leader of British forces in the Peninsular War. Jamaica, Portu-
gal, Gibraltar, Egypt—this was just the beginning for the Robinson
family. Between 1800 and 1815 they served in virtually every major
theater of the Napoleonic Wars—including the one that encompassed
their former home. In 1812, war broke out between Britain and the
United States, reprising the conflict that had scattered the Robinsons
three decades before. Phil Robinson sailed for North America to fight
for the British, even as some of his nephews had moved back to settle
in New York.

As the American Revolution receded into a previous century, how
did loyalists fit into a changing imperial world? The Robinson family's
transcontinental mobilization suggested an answer. By the early nineteenth century, many loyalist refugees had become assimilated into the
British Empire to the point that their own American origins were
largely obscured. Less and less distinguished them as American loyalists but the fact that they had been born in the colonies as British subjects and opted to move elsewhere in order to remain so. The refugees'
absorption into the enlarged empire would be most vividly personified
by the handful of loyalists who made their way to India. There, they
entered a domain so vast and varied as to constitute an empire in itself,
and became in some cases so bound up in what they found as to "go
native" altogether. Their routes out of America paralleled the empire's
own eastward turn, as India supplanted the American colonies as the
economic and strategic center of the British Empire.

Yet while a smattering of loyalists participated in the empire's Asian ascent, most refugees had remained in the Atlantic world, half of them in North America alone. Their experiences underscored how, despite the increasing importance of South Asia, the Atlantic remained a vital part of this global empire, especially for framing modes of governance. For loyalists in North America, the early nineteenth century brought its own version of closure. It wasn't so much that their ties to home loosened over time—indeed some (the Robinsons included) returned to the United States. It was that the political and social landscape of North America itself was being transformed, on both sides of the U.S. border. How much had changed since the revolution—and how much had not—was driven home in 1812 when Americans and British subjects were once again divided by war. The War of 1812, in part a legacy of the American Revolution, stemmed from enduring tensions between Britain and the United States. Like that earlier conflict, it called on British subjects to assert their allegiance to empire, and sharpened the distinctions between British subjects and American citizens. But where the revolution had triggered mass migration, the War of 1812 had a consolidating effect among whites, blacks, and Indians in British North America. It put a period on the journeys of the majority of refugees, while altering the resonance of loyalism in North America henceforth.

By definition, the loyalists' divergent paths trailed off in many directions. But if one wanted to take stock of where they stood a generation after their dispersal, one could gain excellent perspectives from the poles of the once and future empire: North America and India. Seen from these vantage points, at opposite ends of a global empire, it was clear how far both individual loyalists and the British Empire had come since 1783. But neither the empire, nor what it meant to be a loyalist, was quite the same.

IN HIS BRIEF LIFE, Henry Clinton Robinson had crossed continents in British service, from North America to North Africa, from the Mediterranean to the Caribbean. His eldest brother, though, crossed a significant if nearer imperial frontier. "After a quick tho very blustering passage, my dearest mother, I arrived here . . . in perfect health," Beverley "Bev" Robinson III wrote home to New Brunswick in 1796, "and found my native City and future home in a situation to receive its fugitives again."[15] His "native city" was of course New York, where he was born and baptized by Charles Inglis in 1779. He probably did not remember much of the place he had left at the age of four, and in any case he returned to a city transformed. The United States' population had roughly doubled since his birth, and New York City's had doubled in just the last decade. The city had served briefly as the new nation's political capital, and stood out as its commercial center. Ships for Europe, the West Indies, and points east packed the harbor; brokers trading stocks and bills filled the rooms of Tontine Coffee House on Wall Street, precursor to the New York Stock Exchange.

Bev had come to New York to study law, and within a few years he had qualified and considered himself "an Independent Citizen," able to support himself comfortably.[16] (His success encouraged another brother, Morris, to join him in New York in 1802.) In 1805, Bev married Fanny Duer, the sister of his law partner William Duer. Their union marked the bridging of an earlier generation's reluctant divide. Where Bev Robinson's father and grandfather had raised their own loyalist regiment during the revolution, the Duers' father was a New York congressman and their grandfather was a prominent patriot general.[17] As Bev and Fanny eagerly awaited the birth of their first child, Bev urged his father to come to New York for a visit. He longed "to ride with you over one of the finest countries in the world," and fantasized about family reunions in blooming bowers and orchards. And when days grew short and cold, "the winter evenings we should pass most delightfully round my little fire side, and in the day time you could indulge your curiosity in visiting the haunts of your youth, and observing the vast growth and improvement of your native City."[18]

That his father had fled New York at the end of a civil war, attainted by his "native" state, did not seem to faze Bev. He was too young to remember those tense last months of British occupation, when loyalists worried they would be ostracized, prosecuted, or worse. His bright outlook demonstrated just how much had changed since then. Violence against loyalists largely tapered off by 1784—thanks in part to the fact that so many in the British-occupied cities had actually left, but testament, too, to the ideological flexibility and allegiances that had made so many colonial Americans hesitant to take sides to begin with.[19] Instead, old oppositions between patriots and loyalists became subsumed by party political divisions, with former loyalists identifying overwhelmingly with the Federalists, who favored a strong central government. (Their Republican opponents, tellingly, accused them of wishing to reinstate a monarchy.)

The chief conflicts over loyalist reintegration took place not in the streets but in the courts. One thorny issue concerned how to define who was an American citizen and who was a British subject. Because British law held that all natural-born subjects (including Americans born in the colonies before 1776) were perpetually bound to their sovereign, it was difficult to disaggregate American citizens from the mix. Loyalists became a crucial test population for defining citizenship in American courts, as a series of cases established a principle of volitional allegiance, whereby individuals born before 1776 gained the right to choose between citizenship and subjecthood. (Controversies around these definitions would swirl up again in the years leading up to the War of 1812.)[20] Another, more immediate legal matter had to do with reprisals against loyalists. Article VI of the Treaty of Paris mandated that no state was allowed to prosecute loyalists for their wartime affiliations. The treaty also stopped short of including a measure, advocated by Congress, to prevent exiled loyalists from returning.[21] Many states, however, objected to these articles as unfair federal violations of state sovereignty and passed anti-loyalist laws anyway, in direct contravention of the treaty's terms.[22] New York, the largest British stronghold during the war, witnessed especially intense disputes over what rights and protections former loyalists might enjoy. Property confiscations from loyalists actually *increased* in New York after the Treaty of Paris was signed.[23] Alexander Hamilton, coauthor of the *Federalist Papers*, began his career as a lawyer in New York City in 1782 defending former loyalists against hostile laws.[24] "The world has its eye upon America," Hamilton declared in an influential essay, and insisted that the new republic "justify the revolution by its fruits" by accommodating its former dissenters.[25] This type of argument ultimately prevailed. By the time Bev Robinson returned to New York in the late 1790s, legal sanctions had largely been repealed or suspended. He, like many relatives of attainted loyalists, fought for years in state courts for the restitution of confiscated property and unpaid prewar debts, with some success.

The reintegration of loyalists into the United States mirrored a larger process of reconciliation taking place between Britain and the United States. Britain had always wanted to preserve good relations with the United States, partly so as to prevent the republic from falling into a French orbit. The United States, for its part, relied on Britain as its most important trading partner and literally could not afford to compromise the relationship. The outbreak of war between Britain and France in 1793 added new urgency to both sides' concerns. Though the United States declared neutrality, hoping to be spared the costs of war, the conflict pressed the young republic, as George Washington put it, "between the rocks of Scylla and Charybdis, for more pains were never taken . . . to embroil us in the disputes of Europe."[26] War brought to the fore a number of issues between Britain and the United States that had lingered unresolved since 1783. Americans were especially aggrieved that Britain maintained its forts in the Great Lakes, instead of having withdrawn from them as the Treaty of Paris mandated. (Britain justified this on the grounds that the United States had not provided adequate compensation for loyalists.) American slaveowners continued to clamor for compensation for slaves stolen during the evacuations, while British merchants and loyalists still wanted their prewar debts properly paid back.

In 1794, the former peace commissioner John Jay (now chief justice of the U.S. Supreme Court) traveled to London to negotiate a compromise. He worked out an agreement in which Britain gained sought-after trading privileges and agreed to withdraw from the western forts, and that established commissions to adjudicate border issues and war debts. (An abolitionist, Jay did not press the matter of compensation for stolen slaves.)[27] Because of its perceived generosity to Britain, the Jay Treaty was one of the most provocative documents in early American history. Thomas Jefferson denounced it as "nothing more than a treaty of alliance between England and the Anglomen of this country against the legislature and people of the United States."[28] And yet the fact was that the United States had more to gain economically and strategically from conciliation with Britain than it did from conflict. By the end of the 1790s, Americans were no longer calling for war with Britain—instead the United States hovered on the brink of war with France.

But this harmonizing of interests between white loyalists and patriots, and between Britain and the United States, conspicuously left out one group of Britain's revolutionary allies: Indian nations. For the Mohawks and the Creeks, among others, the end of the revolution had brought no end to violence; it bled into an ongoing series of frontier conflicts.[29] Some British officials, notably Upper Canada governor John Graves Simcoe, wanted to continue using Indian allies to defend British North American borders against the United States. But by agreeing in the Jay Treaty to pull out of the Great Lakes forts, British metropolitan policymakers essentially sold out the Indians to the larger objective of Anglo-American reconciliation. When American troops marched against Joseph Brant's western Indian confederacy, Simcoe was unable to send British soldiers to assist. Defeated at the

Battle of Fallen Timbers in 1794, the confederacy ceded most of present-day Ohio to the United States.

From his reserve at Grand River, Joseph Brant continued to maneuver between empires. Britain's withdrawal from Fort Niagara by the terms of the Jay Treaty left him staring unprotected at an American army on the border of Iroquois land. His fragile autonomy seemed to be splintering. A tragedy within the bosom of his own family only compounded the sense that things were falling apart. In 1795, Brant's troublesome son Isaac flew at him in a drunken rage, wielding a knife. Brant deflected the blow, only to end up striking his son in the head with the blade. Isaac died of the wound two days later. For years afterward, Brant kept the dagger on his bedroom mantelpiece, a haunting reminder of how hopes could go horribly wrong.[30] He began to drink. He tried to lease or sell Iroquois land to white loyalist settlers, to raise much-needed revenue for the Mohawks. But the British would not let him: after the cession of the forts, imperial authorities in North America sought to tighten their control around Indians, hoping thus to ensure their loyalty in the event of any future conflict with the United States. Brant repeatedly talked about going to London once more to make his case, as he had in 1775 and 1785. But he was losing his leveraging power as well as his health, and never made the trip.[31]

While Brant felt his influence ebb away in the north, another test for the potential of British-Indian alliances took place among the Creeks in the south, spearheaded once again by William Augustus Bowles. The self-appointed Director-General of the Creek Nation made his way from Freetown to London in 1798—courtesy of a £10 loan from Zachary Macaulay to pay his passage—to find British ministers once more receptive to plans to oust the Spanish from North America.[32] Bowles quickly revived his scheme for Muskogee, the would-be Creek loyalist state in the southwest. Renewing his London connections (Lord Dunmore, now living in Britain, insisted that Bowles come to dinner "dressed as Eastajoca ought to be"), Bowles made the rounds at Whitehall and garnered a new set of half-promises of support. In 1799, he set off across the Atlantic again, at British government expense.[33]

He returned to his Creek wife's village after an absence of seven years. Things had changed in Creek country: his old rival Alexander McGillivray was dead; now the U.S. superintendent for Indian affairs actively worked to "civilize" the Creeks and turn them into slaveowning planters and consumers.[34] Bowles's message, though, was the same that it had always been. Unite behind Muskogee, he urged his peers, unite behind Britain, and earn real autonomy in the face of U.S. settler incursion and Spanish rule. In the spring of 1800, Bowles and three hundred Indians struck a major blow for Muskogee by seizing the Spanish fort at St. Mark's on the Gulf of Mexico. At the swampy Seminole village of Miccosukee, near present-day Tallahassee, Bowles began to build his long-dreamed-of capital, with plans for a newspaper, a university, and more. He plotted the terms of Muskogee's constitution. Though the document was never finished, it offered a fine expression of Bowles's commitment to a broadly British version of constitutional rule, charting a middle course between republicanism and absolutism. He also hoped to attract a new kind of loyalist to Muskogee. The French Revolution had sent about 200,000 French émigrés into exile, while a further fifteen thousand refugees had arrived in the United States from Saint Domingue.[35] As Bowles envisioned it, Muskogee could be a haven for any and all such displaced persons who wanted good land under a liberal government.[36]

But the same shifting regimes that had facilitated Bowles's ascent would also bring about his downfall. Policy and administration changes on both sides of the Atlantic, compounded by the 1802 peace of Amiens, brought his lattice of international support tumbling down. Ultimately, the Creeks themselves lost faith in this flamboyant character. Sensing the weakening of local backing for Bowles, the U.S. Indian agent decided to eliminate this troublesome rival once and for all. He struck a deal with the Creeks granting them debt forgiveness in exchange for a cession of land—and for their agreeing to turn over William Augustus Bowles. At an Indian council in May 1803, a Creek contingent seized Bowles, clapped him into handcuffs (forged specially for the purpose by a local blacksmith), and transferred him to the Spanish. In a sinister piece of déjà vu, Bowles was shipped back to Havana's Morro Castle, where he had been jailed eleven years before. This time, though, there would be no miraculous escape. Whether through illness, poisoning, or self-inflicted starvation, Bowles wasted into a skeleton of his former self. He died in Havana in late 1805. His adopted people, the Creeks, would end up paying a terrible price for their relationship with the American republic, when they fractured into civil war.[37] U.S. forces, partly under the command of Tennessee colonel Andrew Jackson, swooped into the middle of the conflict, using it as an excuse to expand into Indian country. With Americans hysterically denouncing their enemies as "British savages," just like a generation before, Jackson commenced his ascent to the status of national icon on a pile of Creek bodies.[38]

Bowles's project proved the last great attempt to carve out a pro-British loyalist state in what would soon be U.S. territory, the end of a line that ran back to John Cruden and Lord Dunmore. Two years after Bowles's death, Joseph Brant also died, wrestling with the British imperial government.[39] Though Brant's vision of a western Indian confederacy would endure under the leadership of Shawnee chief Tecumseh, the Mohawks' subordination to the imperial government steadily increased. The deaths of Bowles and Brant closed an era in which it looked like the Creeks or Iroquois might effectively operate as autonomous powers between empires.

And as they fell victim to growing American ambitions and waning British support, the Indians gestured toward the greatest convergence between Britain and the United States of all: a resemblance in imperial ambitions. The same spring Bowles was captured, the United States bought the Louisiana Territory from France, practically doubling the country's size overnight. The purchase sealed the transformation of the world's largest republic into a striving continental empire—an "empire of liberty," as Thomas Jefferson described it, united in language, belief, and culture, an empire of free trade, self-government, and natural rights.[40] To Jefferson and his contemporaries there was no contradiction at all between the concepts of republic and empire. They lived in a world of empires, and their nation was every bit as much the product of an imperial age as it was the harbinger of a republican one.

Yet what was the British Empire if not a self-perceived "empire of liberty" too? Parallels are often drawn between American and French forms of republicanism. American imperialism, though, despite its distinctive features as a continental power, drew on no model more strongly than the British. American and British imperialists alike saw themselves as spreading a less coercive form of liberty than Napoleon, for instance, with his tyranny of the sword. The Indians' fate underscored the contradictions built into the very concept of an empire of liberty. But it also helped explain why America and Britain, and patriots and loyalists, could appear to reconcile so rapidly after their civil war. Differences of style aside, their aspirations toward dominion and liberty were, in substance, very much the same.

It had seemed natural enough to Bev Robinson in the first decade of the nineteenth century—flourishing in New York City while his brothers fought and died for the British Empire—that Britain and the United States should enjoy harmonious relations and common interests. He believed that "every American must find his security in the welfare & stability of the British Government."[41] How, then, could it be that just a few years later these apparently natural partners found themselves at war? Perhaps Bev could have turned to his younger brother Morris for insight. Morris had also moved to New York and done well for himself, and married a sister of Bev's (patriot-descended) wife. But while Bev proudly called himself "an American," the Nova Scotia–born Morris never forgot that in New York he was living "in a strange Country."[42] And while Bev confidently predicted great things ahead for the United States if it remained allied with Britain, Morris gloomily observed (in 1806), "I should not be at all surprised if in a few years the United States should be involved in a Civil War."[43] The war that did break out, in 1812, confirmed and qualified the effects of the American Revolution for white loyalist descendants such as himself, for North American blacks, and for Indians alike.

Morris's prophecy—echoed by others on both sides of the Atlantic—reflected rising tensions between Britain and the United States. By 1807 the Jay Treaty had expired and efforts to negotiate a replacement failed. Three chief problems beset Anglo-American relations. First, Britain provoked the United States by imposing the Orders in Council in 1807, which banned neutral powers (the United States of course among them) from trading with France. Second, there was ongoing disagreement about the definition of American citizens and British subjects. Britain claimed that twenty thousand British subjects were serving in the American merchant marine, many of them carrying dubious citizenship papers issued by American officials.[44] It felt fully justified in ordering the overstretched Royal Navy to intercept American ships and impress sailors on board on the grounds that they were British subjects—even though to the United States such actions seemed an outright violation of national sovereignty. A third concern centered around the status of Indian nations on U.S. frontiers, whose initiatives and autonomy the United States assumed Britain continued to support (with reason, in the case of Tecumseh).

By the early 1810s, resentment against Britain inspired a loud faction of republicans in Congress to call for war—making them America's original "war hawks." The majority of Britons wanted nothing less than war with the United States. They were more than otherwise engaged. Napoleon's empire by then reached from the Mediterranean to the Baltic, from Andalucia to the borders of Russia. Britain was dragged down by a bitter campaign in Spain, and was stretched thin trying to protect its possessions in the West Indies, Africa, and Asia. Things on the home front were not much better. In a blow to national confidence, the immensely popular (albeit half blind and rheumatic) King George III definitively lost his mind in 1810, leading to the appointment of his notoriously debauched eldest son as prince regent. Economic distress ran high; in 1811–12, disgruntled workers unleashed a wave of attacks on mills and factories, smashing mechanical looms in the name of a mysterious "Captain Ludd." Then, on a May day in 1812, Prime Minister Spencer Perceval walked into the lobby of the House of Commons and a man stepped out from a doorway and coolly fired a pistol into his chest. Perceval died almost instantly, the only British prime minister ever to be assassinated. His successors promptly repealed the controversial Orders in Council, hoping to ease relations with the United States. But they were too late. Five days earlier, President James Madison had signed a declaration of war against Britain.

The U.S. war hawks hailed the War of 1812 as a second war of independence. (Given that the American population had roughly tripled since 1775, a high percentage of Americans would not even have remembered the first one.) Many Britons, by contrast, regarded it as a stab in the back. But in some ways Morris Robinson came closer to the mark with his prediction that the United States would erupt into a "civil war." Indeed, New England Federalists were so opposed to the war that they threatened to secede. In British North America, meanwhile, the war would crucially test the loyalties of imperial subjects. And though this was a war between the United States and Britain, it was also, like the American Revolution, a war fought by and among North Americans, white, black, and Indian. It would have pronounced effects for all these groups, and on forging a sense of togetherness in the United States and British North America alike.

The United States and the British Empire shared a poorly fortified land border thousands of miles long: "all frontier and little else," groaned the Duke of Wellington.[45] In 1812, as in 1775, conquering Canada was a primary U.S. objective. With only a few thousand British regulars on hand, British North America had to rely heavily on Indian auxiliaries and local militia units for its defense.[46] The Maritime provinces, fortunately, were well protected by the Royal Navy and unlikely to be attacked; they provided much-needed supplies to the rest of British North America. Lower Canada's Francophone majority appeared to share British hostility to the United States, and as in 1775, they remained tacitly loyal.[47] Anglophone Upper Canada, however, was another story. Its strategic location, embracing the Great Lakes, meant that it would receive the brunt of an American invasion. Yet 80 percent of its 100,000 or so residents had been born south of the border. Could these so-called late loyalists be counted on to fight for the empire? For that matter, what about the original loyalists? In 1789 Lord Dorchester had conferred upon them the title of "United Empire Loyalists," intended to be a mark of distinction, and extended free land grants to their children, thereby hoping to secure another generation's attachment to the empire.[48] Nevertheless, the province had been rocked by vigorous if inchoate popular challenges to government. An example of the kind of trouble rulers feared came when the Upper Canada assembly voted down a request by British general Isaac Brock to suspend habeas corpus in the interests of wartime discipline—a measure that had already been authorized in both Britain and the United States.[49]

British anxieties about North American loyalty did not easily subside, and recruiting Upper Canadians into the militia remained a problem throughout the war. Inevitably some British subjects did defect to the Americans; others (a reversal of the more familiar twentieth-century phenomenon) moved to the United States to avoid military service. Many simply stayed quiet, uninterested in taking sides in this unwanted war.[50] But the threat of enemy invasion drew Canadians together too. British North Americans took heart from the knowledge that Federalists and New Englanders opposed the war (a fact heavily emphasized in the Canadian press), and championed the merits of their orderly government over America's republican mayhem.[51] A proclamation from the U.S. army promising that Upper Canadians would be "emancipated from Tyranny and oppression and restored to the dignified station of freemen" left Canadians scoffing at the hypocrisy. *Theirs* was the free government; republicanism imposed the tyranny of the majority, and a high tax bill to boot.[52]

Though Thomas Jefferson, among others, assumed that the U.S. conquest of British North America would be "a mere matter of marching," the campaigns quickly proved him wrong.[53] An American offensive against Montreal was abandoned when militiamen, who were not required to fight outside their states, refused to cross the border. At Detroit and Niagara, General Brock stopped American advances with help from Indian allies. In October 1812, at Queenston just below Lake Ontario, Brock faced a U.S. invading army three or four times larger than his own. The New York militia poured across the Niagara River in boatload after unstoppable boatload—until the sight of the returning dead and wounded reminded the soldiers that they were not obliged to cross, and they stayed back. The day ended in victory for the British, though it also ended the life of General Brock. Shot down as he rushed up Queenston Heights, Brock became a latter-day General Wolfe, earning apotheosis as one of British North America's first great heroes.[54]

Thesc early victories helped rally an initially diffident Upper Canadian population behind the war. So did a memorable defeat. In April 1813, the Americans launched a raid across Lake Ontario to York. John Graves Simcoe's dreamed-of "second London" had not developed much beyond a small town, but York was nevertheless the provincial capital, complete with public buildings, a substantial garrison, and weapons stores. Overwhelmed by the assault, the British decided to retreat, blowing up the fort's powder magazine as they left. Hundreds of Americans were killed and wounded in the explosion. Enraged American soldiers went on a looting spree, ransacking every unoccupied house they could find and vindictively burning the Upper Canada parliament to the ground. The sight of the flames engulfing the seat of government proved hard to forget—especially when it became the first of many demonstrations of the "burning system of the Americans."[55]

What happened in York served in turn as precedent for an iconic episode in American national mythology, when the British admiral Alexander Cochrane ordered his forces to "lay waste" coastal towns in the Chesapeake until the United States compensated Upper Canada for damages. In August 1814, the British decided to march directly on the U.S. capital, Washington, D.C. Washington's terrified residents could hear the guns pounding from a few miles away, and fled in anticipation of the British attack. In the White House, First Lady Dolley Madison insisted on taking a full-length portrait of George Washington with her for safekeeping. Finding it too cumbersome to unscrew from the wall, she ordered the frame broken and the canvas taken out and rolled up. The talismanic image offered her scant protection in turn, though: at a tavern outside the city, she was turned away by Washington refugees angry at her husband for dragging them into this mess.[56] The battle-worn British stumbled into the abandoned city in darkness and got to work visiting upon Washington the same treatment that the Americans had inflicted on York. Army pyrotechnic experts supervised the burning of the Capitol by firing Congreve rockets through the windows. British forces entered the White House, where they discovered—and happily consumed—a dinner for forty, before going from room to room, setting the trappings and furnishings alight. All night the city burned. Even to the troops who performed it, watching "the pride of the Americans" go up in flames was a disturbing spectacle. But war was a disturbing thing—and the British never forgot that the Americans had started this one.[57]

By then, the British position had significantly improved thanks to the fact that the conflict in Europe seemed at last to be coming to a close. Napoleon had disastrously retreated from Russia, and after four years of grueling combat in the Iberian Peninsula, British forces had swept the French out of Spain. Emboldened by these events, British commanders determined to end the war in America decisively. Thousands of Peninsular War veterans sailed to North America as reinforcements, Phil Robinson among them. He reached North America with new facings on his uniform and new medals on his chest, promoted to brigadier general for his valiant service in Spain. It was his first visit to the continent of his birth since the evacuation of New York City in 1783.

British strategists planned to finish the war where it started, on the Canadian frontier. If things had gone according to plan, Robinson would have played a big role in winning it. He commanded one brigade in a bid to dominate Lakes Champlain and Ontario, but the planning was botched and the offensive ended in disgrace.[58] And so it was that the last act of the War of 1812 unfolded, instead, in what William Augustus Bowles might have hailed as a dream come true, when a British fleet appeared in the Gulf of Mexico to take control of the Mississippi. In the last days of 1814, British soldiers disembarked in the bayous around New Orleans. They advanced into the city on January 8, 1815, against an American force commanded by Andrew Jackson. Relentless American fire mowed down the British attackers, line after redcoated line falling mangled to the ground. At the end of the battle more than two thousand British troops were dead, missing, or wounded, as compared with a mere seventy-one American casualties. The appalling carnage awed Jackson's backwoods fighters. "I never saw the like of that!" exclaimed a Kentucky militiaman. A Scottish soldier snapped back, "That's nowt, man; if you'd been wi' us in Spain, you would ha' seen summat far war!"[59]

The grizzled veteran's dismissive remark served as an effective epitaph for the Battle of New Orleans. The American victory had come too late to matter. Two weeks earlier, with Britain feeling confident in its victory over Napoleon, British and American negotiators had signed a peace treaty at Ghent, ending the War of 1812 and reaffirming the status quo ante bellum. The Anglo-American war was over. After at least fifteen thousand combatants had been killed or wounded, on paper it had barely changed a thing.

THE TERMS of the peace treaty confirmed the way the British generally interpreted the War of 1812, as an ultimately inconsequential (if bloody) affair, an unwanted sideshow to the primary struggle against France and its allies. But for its participants in North America this second Anglo-American conflict had more lasting significance. Fought in and among communities divided by civil war just thirty years earlier, the War of 1812 crystallized the legacies of the American Revolution for three groups of sometime loyalists: black slaves, British-allied Indian nations, and white British North American refugees.

The clearest way in which the War of 1812 replayed a revolutionary script took place in the spring of 1814, when Admiral Cochrane issued a proclamation inviting Americans to defect. Any takers, he promised, would be welcomed into the British armed forces or have the chance to go "as Free Settlers to the British possessions in North America or the West Indies where they will meet with due encouragement."[60] Though Cochrane did not say it in so many words, everyone who saw his fleet lurking in Chesapeake Bay knew what type of volunteers he meant to attract: this was an invitation to slaves. Neither blacks nor whites had forgotten Lord Dunmore's 1775 proclamation; indeed, American-owned slaves had been running to the British since at least 1813, in some cases as far as Nova Scotia. As Cochrane cruised along the same inlets where Dunmore had recruited Daddy Moses, Harry Washington, and hundreds of other blacks forty years earlier, more than three thousand slaves made their way to the British. What happened to them after the war also followed the revolutionary precedent. The British government resettled two thousand "Refugee Negroes" in the very same Nova Scotia villages that had been founded by the black loyalists. Other slaves who joined the British military took up land grants in the newly acquired British colony of Trinidad, becoming colonial pioneers much as their black loyalist counterparts had done in Nova Scotia and Sierra Leone.

The management of these runaway slaves vividly illustrates how, in

spite of all the ways that freedom had been compromised for black loy-
alists in the British Empire, British promises still held at least some
attraction for American slaves thirty years after the revolution.[61] There
was one instructive difference, however. In the American Revolution,
Sir Guy Carleton had resisted George Washington's demands that
Britain should either give back or pay for the black loyalists. In the
War of 1812, doubtless mindful of the revolutionary controversy, the
British government distanced itself from Cochrane's declaration.
When the United States lodged a compensation claim for evacuated
slaves, Britain did not return the runaways—that would be a violation
of promises too far—but after a process of international arbitration, it
agreed to pay American slaveholders approximately $1.2 million for
the 3,601 liberated slaves.[62] Paying for the slaves' freedom in this
instance underscored the novelty of Britain's refusal to do so during
the American Revolution. It adhered instead to the contemporary
norm of paying for manumission, an example that would be followed
on a giant scale in 1833 when slavery was abolished in the British
Empire and the government compensated slaveowners to the tune of
£20 million. Here was a powerful demonstration, as if slaves needed
one, of how the British "empire of liberty," like the United States—
where all the New England states, New York, and New Jersey had abolished slavery by 1804—might honor black freedom in some domains,
while underwriting enslavement in others.

For Britain's Indian allies, the War of 1812 marked a far bleaker
contrast for the worse with the aftermath of the American Revolution.
After the revolution, British officials had sought to use Iroquois as
allies against the United States in the north, and offered limited support to Indian initatives in the south. Brant and Bowles had felt personally the whittling down of British aid in the early 1800s. Though
some British officials championed an Indian buffer state under Tecumseh at the outset of the War of 1812, by the end of the war all such talk
had ceased. For the truth was that by 1815 the British no longer
needed Indians as buffers against the United States. Peace confirmed
national boundaries, and effectively laid to rest all those earlier expectations that the United States might fragment. Britain gave up its territorial aspirations to control the Great Lakes and the Mississippi.
Instead, as white settlement on both sides of the Canadian-American
border became more entrenched, earlier patterns of collaboration and
negotiation between whites and Indians got fixed on a map of lands
divided and claimed.[63] On the southern U.S. frontier, the War of 1812

had a similarly conclusive effect on British designs. The Creeks bore especially painful witness to what happened when Britain withdrew support. In 1814 Andrew Jackson forced them into the humiliating Treaty of Fort Jackson, by which they ceded more than half their territory to the United States and agreed to move west. Retreating British forces on the Gulf coast did try to leave one thing behind for their embattled allies: a well-built fort on the Apalachicola River, right in the heart of Bowles's Muskogee. For a short time after the peace, "Negro Fort," as this site came to be known, attracted a cosmopolitan community of Choctaws, Seminoles, and especially runaway slaves, a bastion of self-government against the forces of U.S.-sponsored "civilization." But this little haven was destroyed on Jackson's orders in 1816.[64]

For a third group of participants, white loyalists in British North America, the War of 1812 consolidated the revolutionary inheritance most explicitly of all. Americans have conventionally understood the War of 1812 as a crucible for national identity, a position cemented in 1931 when "The Star-Spangled Banner"—penned by Francis Scott Key during Britain's bombardment of Baltimore—was adopted as the U.S. national anthem.[65] But it was in British North America, as much as in the United States, that the war could really be said to have transformed a collective identity—in something of the way the American Revolution had achieved south of the border. For Upper Canadians, especially, the War of 1812 posed several analogies with the position of American colonists during the revolution. It made them choose between imperial and republican regimes; it asked them to fend off invasion by a substantially larger power; and it required many residents to balance their personal, local loyalties with their allegiance to the state. Only this time, the supporters of the empire won. The conquest of Canada, the major U.S. war aim, ended in defeat.[66] Canadian nationalist historians folded the "loyal" defenders of Upper Canada in 1812 together with the United Empire Loyalists of the revolutionary era, thus effectively rewriting the earlier story of defeat with a redemptive tale of resistance and unity.[67] As a rallying point for postwar identity, the War of 1812 helped make "loyalty" to empire—rather than, say, "freedom" or "liberty"—the central concept in British North American political discourse for at least a generation to come.[68]

But the privileging of loyalty also opened up a contest over its meanings. For some, loyalty formed the basis for an inclusive definition of who could belong in British North America. U.S.-born "late loyalists," French Canadians, and Indians could all be comfortably embraced into the fold of British subjecthood as long as they were loyal. For others, loyalty served as a litmus test for excluding precisely such groups from full British rights. Not long after the war, these opinions collided in an Upper Canadian controversy called the "alien question," over whether or not Americans who immigrated after 1783 could become naturalized British subjects.[69] One of the leading spokesmen against naturalizing Americans was John Beverley Robinson, the precocious attorney general of Upper Canada and a distant cousin of the New York Robinsons. Robinson's attitudes epitomized an emerging sense of Anglo-Canadian distinctiveness rooted in hostility toward the United States. A second-generation loyalist and a first-generation Canadian patriot, Robinson was born in Upper Canada in 1791 to refugee parents, fought with Brock at Queenston, and spent two years studying law in England. (Phil Robinson was "most exceedingly happy" to meet him there and hoped "to have the pleasure of introducing you to some more Robinsons e'er we both quit this country.")[70] The stay in the imperial heartland confirmed young Robinson's patriotic (not to say chauvinistic) sensibility, as he made clear when a British friend "chose to Twit me with the term Yankee, seeming to think it applied to all [North] Americans." "My being born in Canada made me just as much a Yankee as if I had come from the Orkneys," he snapped back, horrified that "the people of Canada" might be "so confounded with the people they so detest, & with whom they have so long been fighting."[71]

John Beverley Robinson's attitudes typified the Canadian "tory" vision of loyalism that took shape after 1812. He and his fellow conservatives celebrated loyalists—whether the United Empire Loyalists or the loyal fighters of the War of 1812—as founding fathers of a tub-thumpingly imperial Canada. Theirs wasn't just the British North America of light taxes and stable government many loyalists championed before 1812. Their British North America was a stalwart defender of empire, fiercely monarchical, and thoroughly anti-American.[72] Loyalism, to them, had some of the resonances associated with the term today (and its use in Northern Ireland in particular), connoting die-hard support for empire. So effectively did Upper Canadian conservatives rebrand the meaning of loyalism after the War of 1812 that they helped entrench an abiding perception of revolutionary era loyalists as conservatives. But this portrayal was misleading at best, and captured only a subset of the opinions that American refugees might have recognized as their own.

In cementing the legacies of the American Revolution for loyalists in North America, the War of 1812 also seemed to replace certain tensions with a kind of truce. Both British North America and the United States of America emerged from the conflict thinking it had won, with fortified self-images as realms of liberty. South of the border, the United States promised its citizens an empire of individual liberty and democratic government—while continuing of course to exclude slaves and in most cases Indians from full participation. North of the border, British North America presented an empire of ordered liberty, anchored in hierarchy and constitutional monarchy, and ostensibly inclusive of multiethnic difference. Whatever their future disputes, these rival empires, reflecting each other across a lengthening land border, would never formally go to war again.

For however firmly the War of 1812 divided the British Empire and the United States, reprising aspects of the American Revolution, it was neither a war of independence nor a revolution. At its end there were no mass migrations of refugees. Instead, there were individual homecomings. With his tour of duty in Upper Canada complete, Phil Robinson—recently knighted for his valiant service—decided to visit his childhood home. As he traveled down the Hudson Valley for the first time since adolescence, the primal familiarity of the landscape came rushing back over him, the smell of known earth, the rustling creeks, reddening autumn leaves. Staying with long-lost cousins, Phil continued his pilgrimage into the past by searching out the wet nurse who had cared for him in infancy. The old woman, now eighty, did not recognize him, "but when I made myself known to her she was quite overcome."[73] Then he went to find the house. How would it look after all these years, if indeed it even stood? His sister-in-law Catherine Skinner Robinson had gone to visit her own birthplace in Amboy, New Jersey, "but no trace remained of my father's house—not one stone was left upon another. It was a grass plain!"[74]

Then he saw it: the long white wooden house in three connected parts, with neat shutters and a tidy pair of dormers, nestled at the base of rugged Sugarloaf Mountain. The cherry tree was noticeably taller now, and the willows on the road (dubbed "Arnold's willows" for his father's infamous friend) looked blasted and weathered.[75] Otherwise, the scene stood "so little altered" from his memory that "it brought tears into my eyes and many a heavy sigh from my heart." Phil felt like he was thirteen again, "when I left that Vale of Peace and Comfort." He remembered those low-ceilinged rooms when they rang with the voices of his parents and their friends; he remembered how he and his siblings had enjoyed "the most perfect Domestic Happiness" of a kind he had never felt since.[76] How insouciant they had been then, and comfortable, as befitted the children of a confident colonial elite, tucked safely into a world little larger than this ring of hills.

But it was 1815 now, and those were glimpses from another century. The British Empire had changed as much as he had, now as palpably an Asian entity as an Atlantic one, more centralized in its structures, more purposefully liberal in its governing style. General Sir Frederick Philipse Robinson turned to his own son beside him, and together they walked away.

WHILE THE WAR of 1812 served as a conclusion of sorts to the story of loyalist refugees in North America, the routes of a handful of other loyalist migrants pointed toward a broader reorientation of the British Empire in this period. These figures, like the empire that employed them, turned to the east, to South Asia.

Phil Robinson's mother Susanna was at home in Thornbury one February evening in 1810 when she heard another unexpected knock on the door, and saw another half-familiar youth step into the room. A decade after Henry Clinton Robinson had turned up from North America, here was her grandson William Robinson, another of Beverley Robinson Jr.'s sons from New Brunswick. "O how happy Grandmama was to see me she cryed like a Child," William wrote home on his first evening in Thornbury. "You my Dear Father is her first thought, notwithstanding the length of time that you have been separated, her affections are as strong as when you first left her." Following in the footsteps of his deceased elder brother Henry, William, barely sixteen years old, had also come to Britain on his way to war. He too was swept up into his large family's capacious embrace. His grandmother and aunts regaled him with old family stories. "Uncle Phill is the most agreeable man I ever met with he keeps us constantly on the laugh," and his uncle William Henry Robinson so "very much like papa in every thing he is always cracking his jokes" that the lad felt instantly at home.[77] Then Phil did the same thing he had once arranged for Henry, by placing young William in a good regiment. William set off in his smart new blue uniform for war. But he would travel to where no Robinson had gone before. He sailed for India.

Since at least the 1750s, India had been the coming concern in the British Empire. The loss in America made it the primary investment. That wasn't to say that the British Atlantic empire was finished—as loyalist refugees knew better than most. British North America, in particular, continued to provide templates for colonial government that would be employed as far away as Australia. Yet by the end of the century it was plain that imperial interests in the Atlantic world were being offset by increasing commitments in and around India—a trend the Revolutionary-Napoleonic wars would only confirm. Within India, fear of French rivalry provided an excellent pretext for British military expansion. Beyond India, Britain won a strategic chain of way stations to the subcontinent: Malta, the Cape of Good Hope, Ceylon, and Singapore. By 1815 India was to the British Empire pretty much everything the North American and Caribbean colonies had been forty years earlier: the largest, most economically valuable, and strategically significant domain, and the one most influential in turn on metropolitan politics and culture.

With one big difference: this wasn't an empire of settlement, like British North America and now Australia. It was an empire in disguise. Even at the peak of British rule, around 1900, there were only about a hundred thousand Britons living in India—a tiny minority in a population of nearly 250 million. Until 1858, British interests were managed by the East India Company, a private trading company accountable to its directors and shareholders—albeit subject to increasing parliamentary oversight. The company also maintained a private army of 200,000 Indian sepoys, making it one of the largest standing armies in the world. And the biggest fiction of British rule in India was that it wasn't really there. The Mughal emperor in Delhi and his subordinates nominally governed most of north India; the rest of the subcontinent was divided into hundreds of independent principalities. Indian courts seduced Britons with their exotic opulence, especially once they were safely folded into British suzerainty. One by one, indigenous states fell under more or less direct British control, beginning with Bengal in the 1750s, and moving into the Mughal provinces of Awadh, Hyderabad, and Arcot. Tipu Sultan of Mysore, once Britain's most serious challenger in south India, was killed in a spectacular storming of his capital city in 1799. The largest threat to British power in western India, the Maratha confederacy, was subdued by 1818 in a series of bitter wars.

Parliamentary regulation in the 1780s had helped end the rampant fortuneering of the "nabobs" (Anglicized from the Persian term

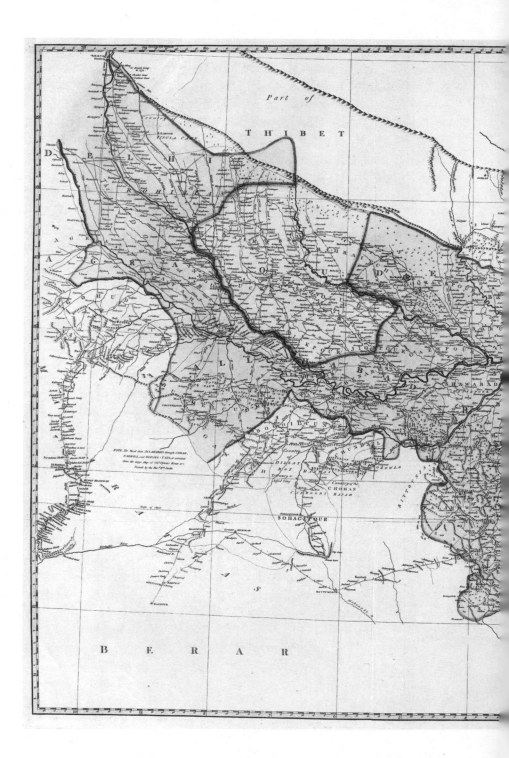

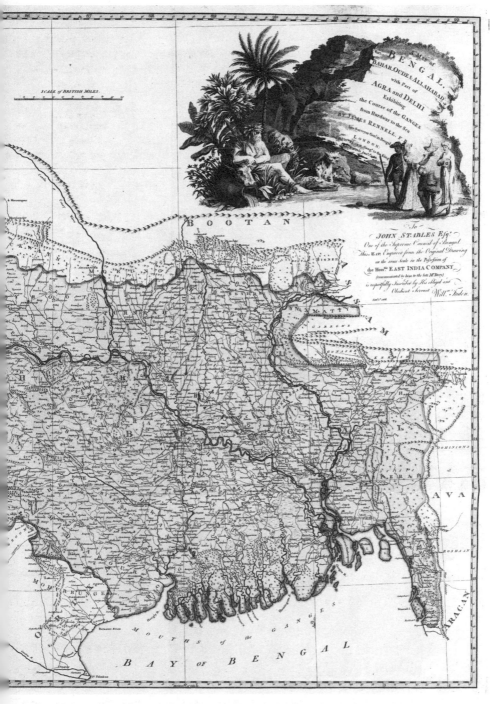

James Rennell, *A Map of Bengal, Bahar, Oude, & Allahabad,* 1786.

nawab), the Anglo-Indian counterpart to the sugar barons of the Caribbean. But India became the location of choice to make a reputation, holding pride of place on the imperial career ladder. Revolutionary war veterans Alured Clarke and Archibald Campbell both held high offices in India after serving as governors of Jamaica. John Graves Simcoe was promoted from his position in Upper Canada to commander in chief of India, though he died before he took up the post. Most famously, Lord Cornwallis redeemed his embarrassing loss in America with an influential term as governor-general of India from 1786 to 1793. (Just five years after Yorktown, when an East India Company captain founded Britain's first outpost in Malaysia, he named its fort Cornwallis after the new governor-general.) Cornwallis's tenure was rated such a success by the East India Company that he was reappointed and returned to India in 1805, where he died soon afterwards.

As an attractive if risky arena for upward mobility, India particularly appealed to ambitious but somewhat marginalized individuals, like down-at-heel gentry, Scots, Irish Protestants—and American loyalist refugees. The East India Company army was soon sprinkled with American-born officers—as Maria Nugent saw firsthand.[78] In 1811, six years after leaving Jamica, she accompanied her husband to India, where he had just been named commander in chief. She had at least two nephews in company service, and also enjoyed a reunion in Calcutta with her elder brother Philip Skinner, a general in the British army.[79] At Mathura, outside of Agra, she spent a pleasant evening with the Company paymaster Edward Arnold and his sister Sophia. What she didn't note in her journal was that the Arnolds were also children of loyalists: their parents were none other than Benedict Arnold and his second wife Margaret (Peggy) Shippen.[80] In 1799, Benedict had sent Edward to Bengal "under the Patronage of Lord Cornwallis." Peggy was "much distressed in parting with her eldest Son," but the parents thought it a "necessary" step—necessary to make money— "and we have no doubt of his doing well If he retains his health."[81] Three years later, Edward's younger brother George also joined the Bengal army.

Sophia Arnold may have come to India for a piece of social positioning of her own, as part of what was uncharitably called the "fishing fleet" of women who went to find a husband in India's male-dominated white society. The strategy tended to be successful: even eighteen-year-old William Robinson, garrisoned at Surat in western India, cruelly thought about marrying a white widow in the vicinity, "not, because I like her, but because she has a d—n' large Fortune."[82] Sophia married one of Edward's fellow officers in 1813.[83] But the shortage of marriageable European women was one reason that many white men developed long-term relationships with Indian companions.[84] Edward Arnold provided comfortably in his will for "Mahummedy Khaunum a native Woman living with me."[85] When George Arnold died in India in 1828, he left a substantial inheritance for his British widow and child, but he also bequeathed an annual income for "Settural Khanum a Native woman who lived in my House for ten years & a half," and a large legacy for their nearly fifteen-year-old daughter.[86] Benedict Arnold's half-Indian granddaughter, baptized Louisa Harriet Arnold, enjoyed about the best future a Eurasian girl in those years could. In the 1830s Louisa went to Ireland as the ward of her aunt Sophia's widower and married a British architect in 1845. Her name by then had been changed from Arnold to Adams, and her dubious ancestry was not spoken of.[87]

What if—an ambitious loyalist officer like Phil Robinson might have asked himself—what if he had turned farther east, and joined the East India Company army instead? What would his fortunes and his life course have looked like then? One of his most celebrated contemporaries in India, General Sir David Ochterlony, had been born in Boston in 1758. His maternal relatives became prominent loyalists, while David sailed to India as a cadet in 1777. Instead of marching to defeat on American battlefields, Ochterlony expanded the frontiers of British rule in Asia, most famously by leading the conquest of Nepal in 1814–16. He earned a baronetcy for his success, but he often preferred to go by the Persian title he had gotten from the Mughal emperor— Nasir ud-Daula, or "Defender of the State"—during his years as British resident in Delhi. There wasn't a trace of New England puritanism about Ochterlony, who giddily embraced the habits of a Mughal nobleman. Legend held that this hookah-smoking, turban-wearing, chutney-eating Bostonian had thirteen Indian wives, who processed around the city with him every evening on thirteen elephants.[88] Even if it had become less common for Europeans to return from India and live like "nabobs" in the West, Ochterlony was one of many westerners who stayed in India and chose to live like a Mughal nawab in the East.[89]

But Phil Robinson could have discerned an even closer parallel in the career of a loyalist refugee raised not eighty miles away from him, William Linnaeus Gardner, born in 1771. Gardner's mother, Alida

Livingston, hailed from the grandest of the old New York landed families; in fact, Robinson and Gardner were distantly connected through marriage.[90] At Livingston Manor, north of the Robinsons' Hudson Valley estate, Gardner's maternal grandfather presided over hundreds of square miles of land, approximating the European aristocracy so closely that he bore the informal title of "lord." Several of the Livingstons were active patriots; one even signed the Declaration of Independence. But others leaned toward loyalism, including Alida, who had married a British army officer, Major Valentine Gardner. By 1779, Valentine Gardner was campaigning with the British through South Carolina, and Alida left her father's house with young William to join him. The family tried to sail to Britain later that year, but was captured en route and remained in America until the evacuation of New York.[91] At the end of the war the Gardners joined the loyalist exodus out of America, and William earned his first commission in the British army, aged just thirteen years old. Before he reached twenty he decided to pursue his military ambitions where he had the best chance of advancement. With some obliging string-pulling by Lord Cornwallis, Gardner transferred regiments and reached India in 1790.[92]

Gardner spent his twenties in a peripatetic, fitful military career. Maybe it was the uprootedness of his wartime childhood that made him keep casting about for something different. With his mother's death in 1791 he inherited land in New York, and considered returning to the United States. He also contemplated settling in Britain, where his father now lived in some style. But around 1798, in Surat, Gardner's life took a decisive turn. The young officer had undertaken to help the family of the deceased nawab of Cambay (Khambat) reclaim their position from a usurper. As Gardner sat through tiresome diplomatic negotiations, he noticed a curtain at the end of the council room twitch aside. Behind it "I saw, as I thought, the most beautiful black eyes in the world." They belonged to the nawab's thirteen-year-old daughter, Mah Munzel ul-Nissa. Her eyes "haunted my dreams by night and my thoughts by day." Obsessed, Gardner "demanded the princess in marriage"; her relatives, recognizing his official status, grudgingly consented to this white Christian's proposal. Because of the restrictions of purdah, Gardner never saw his wife's face until their wedding day. When at last he raised her veil and "beheld the bright eyes that had so bewildered me," he was not disappointed. "I smiled: the young Begum [noblewoman] smiled too."[93]

There was no question of going west now. Instead, Gardner

became more and more deeply embedded in India, when he resigned his British commission and joined the Maratha warlord Jaswant Rao Holkar, becoming one of dozens of white officers recruited into indigenous armies. After the Maratha defeat, Gardner raised a cavalry regiment for the East India Company called Gardner's Horse.[94] He led the unit behind his fellow American Ochterlony into Nepal, commanded it on operations against the Pindaris in central India, and joined the British invasion of Burma in 1825. Between imperial campaigns, Gardner returned to his family at Kasganj, on the Ganges southeast of Delhi, where they lived on an estate given to his wife by the Mughal emperor. Here the Anglo-American officer became "half an Asiatic," hung up his uniform and put on pyjamas, banished European food from his table, and reveled in the happy disorder of a "house filled with Brats . . . from Blue Eyes and fair hair to Ebony and Wool."[95] His favorite granddaughter was named "the Morning Star" in Hindustani; but whenever they used her English name—Alida, after William's mother, and a popular Livingston family name—he heard a little echo from New York. He determined never to leave India, "a country far preferable to the cold climate, and still colder hearts of Europe."[96]

Maria Nugent would have been shocked to see her fellow American thus "gone native" in Mughal India. It had been startling enough to meet Gardner's cousin Edward in Delhi—whose perfectly English brother Lord Alan Gardner was renting the Nugents' house in Buckinghamshire—dressed in Indian clothes and "immense whiskers," and refusing to eat beef or pork, "being as much Hindo[o] as Christia[n], if not more."[97] But Fanny Parkes, the wife of an East India Company civil servant, spent time with Gardner in the 1830s and was utterly captivated by this "kind, mild, gentlemanly, polished, entertaining companion" . . . "such a high caste man!"[98] Parkes kept pressing Gardner to write an autobiography. "If I were to write it," he said, "you would scarcely believe it; it would appear fiction."[99] Though he did not often talk about "my Yankee country," the first chapter of his personal epic would, of course, have begun with the American Revolution.[100] Without it he might have been an heir on the Hudson. Yet here he was, a squire in Hindustan—New York lost and India found.

Gardner died in 1835, not long after Parkes met him, and his beloved begum passed away just one month later. They were buried side by side (her head toward Mecca) next to the tomb they had raised for their eldest son a few years before: an onion-domed Mughal mausoleum encased in white marble. The marble has been stripped away now, but the monument rises still above Gardner's old farmlands, an enduring memorial to the merging of cultures across continents. Gardner's journey from America to Asia followed the larger trajectory of British imperial expansion during his lifetime. It was, of course, a relatively rare one among American loyalist refugees. But for all that Gardner may have traveled farther than most, he was in another sense a representative member of the American exodus. Absorbed, like so many others, into an expanded global dominion, he was another colorful piece in the kaleidoscope of empire, refracting and revolving its subjects in an interconnected world.

Losers and Founders

O n June 18, 1815, Britain and its Prussian allies defeated the French at Waterloo, bringing the Napoleonic Wars to an end. Everything about that June day—from the magnitude of the triumph to the magnitude of the costs, with casualty figures (typically for these wars) in the tens of thousands—presented a different spectacle from the closing scene of Britain's last big war, the dolorous march out of New York City in 1783. Victory in 1815 helped usher in Britain's greatest age of global hegemony. Peace talks held at the Congress of Vienna restored constitutional monarchies and empires in and beyond Europe rather in line with British liberal ideals, charting a middle way between republicanism and absolutism.[1] Moreover, Britain and the United States forged a relationship that brought Britain many of the benefits of imperial rule in America without the costs. Around the empire, Britain seemed to have consolidated a form of imperialism able to withstand republican (and totalitarian) challenges. Around the world, Britain's international ascendancy looked unrivaled. All told, it was a remarkable vindication of the "spirit of 1783." Loyalist refugees, too, seemed to have reached an analogous peace. By 1815, major loyalist migrations had stopped. From North America to India, surviving refugees and their children were absorbed into the British Empire, and even in some cases reintegrated in the United States. The loyalist exodus was over.

So what did all those losses, displacements, and overturned lives amount to in the end? Was it fair to see the loyalists' trauma, like the empire's (with the loss of the thirteen colonies), ending a generation later in a kind of triumph? A vivid reply in the affirmative was provided by Benjamin West, the celebrated American-born painter of British imperial scenes, in an allegorical image called *The Reception of the American Loyalists by Great Britain*. Though it may never have existed in freestanding form, the image appeared as a painting within a painting in an 1812 portrait of the loyalist claims commissioner John Eardley Wilmot, and an engraving of it was published in 1815 as the frontispiece to a memoir by Wilmot about the commission's work.[2]

West presents a flattering picture of the loyalists' place in a resurgent empire. At the right of the frame, a larger-than-life Britannia extends her benevolent hand over a diverse throng of refugees. (An elderly West and his wife, though they had immigrated well before the revolution, stand at Britannia's knee.) Among the figures are prominent white loyalists, such as William Franklin. The group also includes an American Indian, every inch the "noble savage" with a statuesque physique and costume of skins, feathers, and beads. Under his right arm, he shelters (in the words of the accompanying text) a "Widow and Orphans, rendered so by the civil war," while behind him huddle a number of blacks, "looking up to Britannia in grateful remembrance of their emancipation from slavery." The key explains that the two figures holding up Britannia's mantle represent "Religion" and "Justice." Cherubs floating above the scene busily bind up the fasces of the Anglo-American relationship, tested anew by the War of 1812. But another emblem requires no clarification: the crown, focal point of imperial loyalty, caressed by a refugee's outstretched hand.

Here was the British Empire as its rulers in 1815 wanted it to be seen, a clear expression of the "spirit of 1783" triumphant. This was a hierarchical empire, with the king at the helm, the law and the church close behind. White men stand closest to the seat of power, and women and nonwhite subjects obediently follow. This was a benevolent and multiethnic empire: an empire ostensibly protective of black freedom and inclusive of indigenous peoples, an empire extending humanitarian relief to the poor and powerless. This was an empire suffused with national pride, and an empire that seemed able to heal the breaches of war with the United States (an issue of personal concern to West). Anyone who turned past the frontispiece to read Wilmot's book would discover in its pages an account of the Loyalist Claims Commission that suggested how compensating loyalists had been a way for Britain to compensate for defeat. But those who did not look beyond West's image might well be forgiven for failing to recognize that there had ever been a defeat in the first place. The loyalist refugees, in his depiction, were poster children for British imperial success.

Many refugees, especially in British North America, could probably identify with this happy picture. Elizabeth Johnston, at last, was

among the contented. By the time Johnston rehearsed the events of
her life for her memoirs in 1837, she was seventy-three years old. Her
sight was dimmed by cataracts, and her memory twisted around old
traumas like a tree growing around barbed wire: all those movements,
all those separations, and so many deaths (including William's, in
Jamaica in 1807). She had come of age during a civil war, and spent
decades of her adult life coping with dislocation and bereavement. Yet
there was no anger in Johnston's recollections, nor any nostalgic long-
ing for her lost home; if anything, she sounded rather self-satisfied.
For she had rooted herself in a new home now. "Little did I . . . think
that I and all my family would ultimately settle in Nova Scotia," she
recalled. While she achieved a stability and social comfort she had
never before known, her surviving children became prominent members of Nova Scotia's professional and political elite, in some cases
achieving positions of higher status than they could ever have plausibly
enjoyed had they remained in the United States.[3] After all their trials
and migrations, the Johnstons had arrived—and evolved from American loyalists into British North American patriots. To follow Johnston's narrative, in keeping with Canadian tory interpretations of the
loyalist influx, these losers were winners in the end.[4]

An assessment of such refugees' lives as charting a course from
defeat to success continues to be compelling, because it helps, among
other things, to explain a notable difference between the American
refugees and other conspicuous groups of "losers" and exiles. As the
revolution receded, so too did the refugees' rich language of lament.
They and their descendants did not spawn a transnational discourse of
having participated in a common upheaval. They did not maintain a
folklore of loss in songs or poems, in the manner of the Acadians. They
did not raise secret toasts, like Jacobites, to the restoration of the
monarchy in America. They did not collectively nurture an equivalent
of the "lost cause" ideology so prevalent among southerners after the
American Civil War. Nor did all refugees, even in British North America, share the anti-Americanism articulated by some. For unlike other
refugee communities, the loyalists began and ended their journeys as
subjects of the same crown. Their position as British subjects was the
one thing they had never lost. The absence of mournful voices in later
generations speaks, in its eloquent silence, to the loyalists' absorption
into an empire able to quiet them.

At the same time, it would be facile to suggest that the image of
empire presented by West (or the perspective of any single loyalist,

such as Elizabeth Johnston) was the only way to look at the results of the exodus. West might use loyalist refugees to portray the "spirit of 1783" as a positive compound of hierarchical rule, liberal ideals, and transcontinental reach. But many refugees had also gained visceral understanding of the flip side of the "spirit of 1783": authority could be oppressive, promises could go unfulfilled, and global expansion might facilitate recurring displacement. Indeed, every one of the things celebrated in this image has a darker aspect. The Loyalist Claims Commission, to name the most obvious, was indeed a notable manifestation of humanitarian impulses—but it left many loyalists frustrated, and left the majority out altogether. Black loyalists did get their freedom, as the picture proudly conveys, letting British authorities claim the high ground of principle over their American peers—but black freedom had been constrained in all kinds of ways in practice, and slavery, of course, endured. As for the Indians, by the time this was painted, the British Empire may still have looked more benign on the whole than the United States, but prospects for real Indian sovereignty under Britain's aegis were fast disappearing.

Finally, while West foregrounded loyalists' ethnic and social diversity—and by extension the centrality of such inclusiveness in British self-perceptions—his image completely obscurs a preeminent form of diversity among the loyalist refugees. Loyalists had never been uniformly "loyal." Their political beliefs did and would continue to range widely, in ways that defied the suggestion of placid obedience implied in this image. To the extent that loyalists had left the colonies believing in the king and the preservation of empire, Britain's postwar ascent and triumph in 1815 was something they both welcomed and benefited from. But many loyalist refugees also sought reform and expanded rights within the empire, only to find themselves time and again clashing with imperial authority. Importing political sensibilities from colonial America into the postrevolutionary British Empire, loyalist refugees turned out to be vectors of imperial *dissent* as conspicuously as they embodied loyal consent.

While loyalists' personal laments may have faded, their languages of protest lived on. In the Bahamas, for instance, conflicts over the regulation of slaves continued to divide American refugee planters and imperial officials. In 1817 Lord Dunmore's onetime antagonist William Wylly, now attorney general, precipitated a three-year standoff between planters and authorities when he blocked a loyalist planter from exporting a slave to the United States—precisely the sort of issue that, back in 1772, had led to the demise of slaveowning in Britain.[5] (Wylly himself moved to St. Vincent some time later; but the ruins of his New Providence plantation, strewn along a modern highway, are a rare surviving vestige of the loyalist planter period in the Bahamas.) In Jamaica, another loyalist legacy reverberated through the massive slave rebellion that rocked the western part of the island in 1831. One of the revolt's leaders was a self-taught black Baptist preacher who had done just what white authorities had always feared George Liele would do, and used his prayer meetings to help organize the rising. Liele himself probably would not have approved of the Baptist War, as the episode became known, had he lived to see it. (He died in the 1820s.) But as the first black Baptist preaching to Jamaican slaves, he had played a pivotal role in inspiring it.[6] There was poetic justice in the fact that this rebellion, drawing on rhetoric introduced by a freed American slave, accelerated the abolition of slavery in the British Empire as a whole.

But it was British North America, which had absorbed the majority of refugees, that became the most vigorous arena for loyalist-influenced debate. In 1837–38, ongoing struggles about rights and liberties erupted in linked antigovernment rebellions in Upper and Lower Canada. Though they were triggered by local circumstances, at base these protests turned on complaints that sounded strikingly similar to those of American patriots—and disgruntled loyalist refugees. Both the rebellions and the British response—the Durham Report of 1839, which promoted the concept of "responsible government"—are seen as foundational to the Canadian liberal tradition. But they had still wider repercussions, by framing ideas of provincial governance that would eventually culminate in calls for home rule. For neither the first nor the last time, British North America thus served as a laboratory for imperial reforms.[7]

So how does one square the loyalists' participation in the "spirit of 1783" with these more contentious legacies? The answer is that while refugees were often successfully assimilated into a refurbished British Empire, making up for their losses by finding—and founding—imperial alternatives, they also widened (if not introduced) cracks in the postrevolutionary empire's foundations. Provincial understandings of rights had prevailed over metropolitan ones in the American Revolution. Analogous discourses of rights, inflected in part and in places by loyalist refugees, would eventually prevail once more. And there was one further way that loyalist refugees anticipated future imperial upheavals. Dispersed by the British Empire's first great war of independence, they anticipated the still larger and more violent displacements caused by twentieth-century decolonization.

Unsurprisingly, the endings of many of the lives in these pages present a similarly mixed picture of things lost and found. By 1815 many refugees had died, while others settled into place, like Elizabeth Johnston and Phil Robinson, both of whom died in comfortable retirement in their eighties, in Nova Scotia and Britain respectively. Of all the imperial officials who influenced the loyalists' fate, Lord Cornwallis—the man who lost America—died in the best position, professionally speaking, as governor-general of India in 1805. He rests in a beautifully proportioned neoclassical mausoleum that looks more like something one would expect to find on the grounds of an English stately home than on the edge of the provincial Indian town of Ghazipur, where it stands. The lengthy epitaph praises Cornwallis's feats in India, and says nothing at all of his time in America. There, in the new center of British imperial power, it simply didn't need to. Yet as with so many such British monuments in India, the structure's grandiose heft seems also a rather sad attempt to compensate for its locale, so far from home.

Guy Carleton, first Baron Dorchester, died on one of his three English estates in 1808, old (eighty-four), rich, if somewhat embittered by his clashes with political rivals. His hard-won barony became extinct by the end of the century, though his political legacies in Canada arguably endured longer. Lord Dunmore died the following year—of "decay," aged seventy-eight—significantly less rich, and likely more bitter. He spent his last years in the seaside resort of Ramsgate, Kent, supported in part by his daughter Augusta, who had married one of King George III's sons without permission and been cut off by the royal family in disgrace. In what turned out to be Dunmore's final meeting with King George III, in 1803, the earl grew so enraged when the king denounced their joint grandchildren as "Bastards! Bastards!" that it took all the self-control he could muster to refrain from assaulting his own sovereign.[8]

Dunmore's loyalist protégés John Cruden and William Augustus Bowles both died prematurely (in 1787 and 1805 respectively), their visionary ambitions for new states in the American southwest unfulfilled. Their own "loyal" projects had seen them branded at times as traitors, at others as hopeless dreamers. What their stories captured best, however, was the dynamism and possibility created by a world of warring empires. Had they lived into later middle age, they would have seen American and British filibusters undertake initiatives similar to theirs—to say nothing of a wave of revolutions that brought down most of the Spanish American empire by the end of the 1820s.

Joseph Brant, meanwhile, experienced a different sort of afterlife. He died in 1807, at his house at Burlington Bay on Lake Ontario, thoroughly disillusioned with the British Empire. In 1850 his body was exhumed and carried by relay to Grand River, where he was formally reburied in "a proper tomb" next to the white clapboard church in Brantford (as Brant's Town had been renamed). It was the beginning of a sort of apotheosis. At the centennial of the loyalist exodus, some twenty thousand people assembled in Brantford's Victoria Park to see a statue of Brant unveiled, cast from the bronze of donated British cannon.[9] While his name continued to signify savagery in the United States, Brant was taken up in Canada as a national hero and celebrated for his loyalty to empire, his "civilizing" influence among the Indians, and his contribution to the Canadian ethnic mosaic.

David George died in Freetown in 1810. There is no trace today of his church, though a living reminder of the black loyalists' influence can still be heard in the American-inflected creole they developed, Krio, the lingua franca of Sierra Leone today. Of all the sites of loyalist emigration, Freetown has had by far the most violent and tragic subsequent history. But at the time of George's death, it was positively flourishing compared to the place he had left: Shelburne, Nova Scotia. When government subsidies ended in the 1790s and cheap labor fell away (notably with the black migration), this onetime rival to Halifax collapsed almost as quickly as it had risen. Within a decade of its founding, the boomtown had become a ghost town, and some of its residents returned to New York.[10]

The very range of these endings makes an important concluding statement about the diversity of these American refugees, and the varied traces they left in the British Empire. That said, looked at together they also reveal a strikingly consistent pattern. If there is something bittersweet about many of these people's stories, that surely owes something to the tensions embedded in the "spirit of 1783" that shaped their world, an empire in which what they wanted was not always what they got. It also stems from contradictions inherent in the loyalist refugee condition. They were provincial settlers who became international migrants. They were British subjects who proved their loyalty in one setting and resisted imperial authority in others. They were Americans who failed or refused to find a place in the republic.

They were refugees who never became stateless persons in the modern sense. And they were exiles who *could* go home again, thanks to post-war reconciliation, by later returning to the United States.

So it was that in 1816, with peace restored between the British Empire and the United States, Beverley Robinson Jr. at last fulfilled his sons' oft-repeated invitations to visit them in New York City. His brother Phil had recently gone to the Hudson Highlands to see their childhood home, and Beverley Jr. eagerly anticipated his own excursion to those familiar spots where he and his siblings had "gambolled and gallopped a thousand times." He enjoyed his reunion with his sons, spending time with a bevy of American-born grandchildren he barely knew, and receiving visits from old friends he had not seen in thirty years or more. But Robinson's homecoming was abruptly cut short when he fell ill in New York and within days was dead. In his sixty-two years, Robinson had traveled from privilege through privation to fortune restored. He had seen two of his sons killed in the service of the British Empire, and two others flourish in the United States. He was buried in his "native city"—under a tablet that described him as "late of Fredericton in the Province of New Brunswick."[11] Robinson died as he was born, at once an American and a British subject. As his life's full circle suggests, for all that loyalists lost, they found some consolations too.

STANDARD ESTIMATES cited by historians for the size of the loyalist migration range from 60,000 to 100,000—but nobody has ever provided justification for these numbers.[1] How can one come up with a plausible figure of the number of loyalists and slaves who left? There are no documents that systematically record how many civilians evacuated from the British-held cities at the end of the war. Nor are there comprehensive registers of arrivals in different sites. It is especially hard to count the refugees who fled individually or in clusters throughout the war; while the fact that so many loyalists moved more than once further complicates reckonings.

Triangulating among a variety of extant documents, however, one can nevertheless construct a reasonable estimate of the proportions of the exodus as it stood in about 1785. The most informative records by far are the various musters compiled by government inspectors of refugees in British North America. These musters listed loyalists by place of settlement, gender, and age group (adult or child); they also denoted "servants," a term often (but not always) used to describe black slaves. Nothing so thorough exists for refugees settled in other regions. Another vital source lies in the surviving evacuation records from New York, Savannah, Charleston, and East Florida. These provide tallies of emigrants broken down by race (black and white), and list their stated destinations. There are also some lists that denote the ships used during these evacuations; but correlating these against ship muster books yields at best haphazard information about loyalist passengers traveling as supernumeraries.[2]

The migration of black loyalists can be documented at least as well as the flight of whites.[3] (The vast majority of blacks listed on the evacuation returns were of course enslaved, making these the best sources for calculating the loyalist export of slaves.) Both the evacuation of blacks from New York in 1783 and the movement of black loyalists from the Maritimes to Sierra Leone can be quantified not only in aggregate but also parsed by categories such as place of origin and reasons for leaving. Historians have previously estimated the number of runaway slaves to be as high as 80–100,000. Through careful analysis of the Book of Negroes and British military records, though, Cassandra Pybus has authoritatively replaced these reckonings with a far more modest but supportable figure of 20,000 black runaways, 8,000 to 10,000 of whom survived to evacuate in freedom with the British.[4]

Given the difficulty of establishing the sum total of loyalist migrants to each destination, it is hardly surprising that coming up with more detailed demographic breakdowns (by amount of property owned, occupation, religion, or more) proves considerably more difficult. The files of the Loyalist Claims Commission, though the best single archive relating to the loyalist experience during the war, are also—as discussed in chapter 4—a very unreliable guide to refugee demographics because the procedures involved in lodging claims privileged certain kinds of people. Wherever possible in this book, I have drawn on the few extant records that *do* give insight into the social profile of migrants, such as the certificates filed for tax exemption by loyalists in Jamaica. But analyzing the refugee population in concrete quantitative categories—to say nothing of measuring the statistical incidence of multiple migration—remains an elusive goal, especially for Jamaica and Britain, where loyalists did not compose a majority of the population.

The Maritimes

The majority of refugees settled in Nova Scotia and New Brunswick, and almost all of them arrived there from New York City at the end of the war. An evacuation return from New York produced in October 1783 counted 27,009 people going to Nova Scotia (14,162 of whom were bound for what became New Brunswick). A return dated November 24, 1783, the day before Evacuation Day, raised the total to 29,244.[5]

Not everybody listed on the registers necessarily sailed (although the higher figure was made just a day before the last ships headed out), but the numbers correlate well with records produced on the ground in the Maritimes. Musters of loyalists performed across Nova Scotia and New Brunswick between May and July 1784 counted a total of 26,757 men, women, and children entitled to receive provisions from government stores—a bounty granted only to loyalist refugees.[6] At the end of the summer of 1784, the surveyor Colonel Robert Morse used these musters to report that 28,347 loyalists had settled in the region.[7] This also conforms to the estimate delivered by Governor John Parr to

Lord Shelburne, in December 1783, that "the great emigration of Loyalists from New York" did "not fall short of 30,000 souls." In August 1784, Parr repeated this figure to Lord Sydney, saying that "the number of souls located amount to near thirty thousand."[8] The figure of 26,757 also corresponds closely to a 1785 muster of loyalists in Nova Scotia, New Brunswick, Cape Breton Island, and Saint John's Island (now called Prince Edward Island), which listed 26,317 individuals still receiving government rations.[9]

These musters noted only those loyalists entitled to receive provisions. There were also refugees who had settled in the Maritimes and did not get rations. A comment on the 1785 muster explains that 942 "Loyalists and Disbanded Soldiers have been struck off the Provision List . . . being considered as unworthy of a Continuance of the Bounty." The lists do not account, either, for all the refugees who would already have migrated to Nova Scotia during the war. At least 1,100 traveled to Halifax following the British evacuation of Boston in 1776, while others such as Jacob Bailey made their way there later. The evacuation of East Florida brought a further 725 white refugees to the Maritimes after these musters were completed.[10]

It is not entirely clear whether these musters included all 3,000 of the free blacks who traveled north. The October 1783 New York evacuation register lists 822 members of "black companies." The Nova Scotia musters include 791 and 785 "servants" respectively—a term typically used in connection with blacks—while Colonel Morse's 1784 report confidently estimates the total number of "servants" in the province to be 1,232. What portion of these servants were free and what portion enslaved remains ambiguous: a note by the 1784 muster-master for Chedebucto, for instance, explains that 228 of the town's 991 settlers were "Negro settlers exclusive of the Blacks employed as servants," of whom there were sixty-two. These registers also do not separately account for the black population at Birchtown, recorded in a 1784 muster as 1,485.[11]

Combining these data, one can safely estimate the minimum number of refugees in the Maritimes after the war to be 30,000. But given all the lacunae in the records—those 725 refugees from Florida, for instance, and however many of the Boston refugees still remained—combined with the documentable presence of just under 30,000 refugees on the New York returns alone, it seems fair to suggest that the total number of refugees in the Maritimes around 1785 could have ranged on the order of 10 percent higher.

Quebec

Refugees trickled into Quebec throughout the war. The number of loyalists receiving provisions in the province steadily inched up from 853 in July 1779, to 1,023 in October 1779, to 1,394 in November 1781, to 1,699 in January 1782, to 3,204 in November 1783.[12] A muster of loyalists in Quebec toward the end of 1784 listed a total of 5,628 individuals (including 130 "servants") to be settled on government land grants.[13] This squares with an undated document, probably from the summer of 1784, that describes the quantity of land required to locate the men of five disbanded loyalist regiments and their families, amounting to 5,251 people in total.[14]

The latter tally did not include the Mohawks, whose land claims on Grand River are described in the same document. A 1785 census revealed nearly 2,000 Indians living at Grand River, of whom about four hundred were Mohawks. Another group of at least a hundred Mohawks lived at the Bay of Quinte.[15] These musters may also leave out some of the refugees who had arrived in the province during the war but *not* received land grants, such as the refugees who had settled at Machiche (present-day Yamachiche, near Trois-Rivières).[16]

Between the 5,628 individuals listed on the 1784 muster, the further contingent of Mohawks, and those who emigrated without getting land grants, one can easily justify a minimum population figure of 6,000 refugees in Quebec—and again plausibly imagine the total number to have been up to 10 percent higher.

East Florida

As in the Maritimes and Quebec, loyalists and slaves arrived in East Florida throughout the war, though precise numbers can only be pinned down following the evacuations of Savannah and Charleston. By the end of 1782, an inspector of refugees in East Florida counted 2,917 white loyalists and 4,448 blacks who had arrived from Georgia and South Carolina.[17] Another report dating from mid-1783 set the number of new arrivals at 5,000 whites and 6,500 blacks.[18] It seems fair, then, to accept Governor Patrick Tonyn's description, in May 1783, of "a late accession of near twelve thousand loyalists"—assuming that his calculation represents the combined number of loyalists and slaves.[19]

(Tonyn also later estimated the population of the province "at about sixteen thousand," a figure that included East Florida's several thousand prewar inhabitants as well.)[20]

Records of the evacuation of East Florida support those figures. The embarkation commissioner appointed in East Florida documented 3,398 whites and 6,540 blacks who left the province. In addition to these, he noted that "there was supposed to be about 5000 more souls in the Province mostly back country people, who are imagined to have gone over the Mountains to the States &c."[21] Similar figures were also cited by Tonyn, who reported "that the entries on the Commissioners Books" indicated "about ten thousand souls" would emigrate, while "it is concluded more than four thousand, have passed into the interior parts of America among the Mountains; and that at least three thousand, have gone into the American States."[22]

One can safely assert, then, that 5,000 white loyalists arrived in East Florida before 1784, and at least 6,500 blacks, of whom the vast majority were enslaved. The outmigration of East Florida refugees to Britain, the Bahamas, and Jamaica will be reckoned in the tallies for those locations below. In addition to those outflows, the East Florida evacuation return showed 196 whites and 714 blacks bound for "Jamaica and the Spanish Main"—many of whom settled in British possessions in Central America—and 225 whites and 444 blacks bound for Dominica.[23]

Britain

The best calculation of the loyalist migration to Britain has been performed by Mary Beth Norton, who traced the arrivals of 1,440 loyalist heads of household from the colonies between 1775 and 1784. From these she projected an estimate of 7,000 to 8,000 (almost all white) loyalists who immigrated to Britain during and after the war. This figure rightly does not double-count refugees who crossed the Atlantic more than once, nor does it include those who traveled to Britain for a short time only to file a loyalist claim. Nevertheless, it is likely to be an underestimate. Based largely on one of the two collections of loyalist claims documents (Audit Office Series 12), it excludes a number of refugees settled in Britain, especially women, whose claims did not advance to a further stage of the review process. It also leaves out a number of the white loyalists who, like the Johnston family, went to

Britain from East Florida in or after 1784. Thus, the higher figure of 8,000 can safely be taken as a minimum for what was quite probably a larger white refugee population.[24]

Norton's estimates also exclude one major category of migrants to Britain: the very large number of black loyalists who ended up there toward the end of the war. Cassandra Pybus calculates these to have been approximately 5,000.[25]

Bahamas

The October 1783 evacuation return from New York indicated that 941 people had already embarked for Abaco.[26] A New York evacuation return from November 1783 put the total number of Abaco settlers at 1,458.[27] Loyalists from East Florida began to sail for the Bahamas in the spring of 1784, amounting to 1,033 whites and 2,214 blacks according to the Florida embarkation commissioner.[28]

A report presented in the Bahamas house of assembly in April 1789 stated that 1,200 white refugees and 3,600 blacks had arrived from the former colonies in 1784 and 1785, and that a further four hundred whites and 2,100 blacks came to the islands from different parts of the region between 1786 and 1789. The Bahamas population rose from about 1,700 whites and 2,300 blacks at the beginning of 1784, to 3,300 whites and 8,000 blacks in 1789.[29] At much the same time, Solicitor-General William Wylly noted that the "new" inhabitants who had arrived since the revolution included 330 white heads of household, and 3,761 slaves.[30]

Adding together the New York and East Florida refugees, it seems fair to conclude that as many as 2,500 white loyalists immigrated to the Bahamas. They brought with them on the order of 4,000 slaves. This figure is slightly lower than Michael Craton's "best guess" of about 8,000 loyalist and slave immigrants to the islands; but as he rightly observes, "no-one will ever know exactly how many went."[31]

Jamaica

No musters exist to document the number of loyalists who relocated to Jamaica, but evacuation records once again give some indication of the quantity involved. W. H. Siebert scrutinized the returns from Savannah to suggest that some 5,000 blacks and "four hundred white families" traveled to Jamaica from there; another return lists 1,278 whites and 2,613 blacks who embarked for Jamaica from Charleston.[32] A handful of refugees also traveled to Jamaica from East Florida.[33]

If a "family" consisted of an average of four individuals, then more than 3,000 whites and up to 8,000 black slaves seem to have relocated to Jamaica directly. This estimate, like so many others, does not include the migration of loyalists who may have gone to Jamaica from New York or during the course of the war (like Alexander Aikman). It might be noted that population estimates for the island show a marked rise in both the black and white populations between 1774 and 1788: an increase of 44,567 blacks (or 17.5 percent) and 5,610 whites (or 30 percent).[34]

Total Emigration

To add up the minimum totals by region ca. 1785: 30,000 white and black loyalists had traveled to the Maritimes; 6,000 refugees to Quebec, including five hundred Mohawks; 13,000 refugees to Britain (of whom some 5,000 were free blacks); 2,500 white loyalists to the Bahamas; and 3,000 white loyalists to Jamaica. This comes to 54,500 individuals. In addition, one must add the documented clusters of refugees heading from East Florida to Central America and Dominica, as well as the few who ventured still farther afield to locations such as India. Including such people would raise the sum to between 55,000 and 55,500.

These figures fail to account in any way for the manifest occurrence of unregistered migration. As suggested above, in every case the quantifiable numbers are likely to fall short of the actual total, in some instances by as much as 10 percent. This tally also places the number of black loyalists evacuated from the colonies at the bottom end of Pybus's estimated range of 8,000–10,000 migrants. Factoring in a plausible underestimate on the British North American refugee population alone brings a fair figure for the total loyalist migration to 59,000. Adding in some or all of the further 2,000 free blacks easily tips the balance toward 60,000. The fact is that no numbers can ever perfectly enumerate this swirling population on the move. But they can indicate its proportions. It thus seems safe to estimate the total loyalist emigration from revolutionary America at 60,000 individuals—and just as safe to eliminate outright the substantially higher figures of 80,000 or 100,000.

Slave Exports

The records of loyalist migration also give good insight into the number of slaves exported by loyalists. At the top of the list come the convoys leaving Savannah and Charleston, which carried nearly 8,000 blacks straight to Jamaica. Only a tiny minority of these Jamaica-bound blacks (unlike those heading for Nova Scotia or Britain) would have been free, like George Liele. The evacuation from East Florida indicated another 3,527 blacks leaving for different British colonies. The estimate of 3,600 slaves brought by loyalists to the Bahamas surpasses the 2,200 recorded as having been exported from East Florida, which suggests that a further 1,400 loyalist-owned slaves arrived in the islands by different routes. Loyalists brought a minimum of 1,232 "servants" into the Maritimes, according to Morse's estimates; the total number was doubtless higher.[35] Another several hundred slaves were imported by loyalists into Quebec.[36] A conservative estimate of the number of loyalist-owned slaves in British North America would stand at around 2,000. In addition to these larger clusters, loyalists also carried a small number of slaves into Britain (where slaveowning was by then unenforceable) as "servants," such as Elizabeth Johnston's maid Hagar. Finally, there were the many loyalist-exported slaves who ended up in the slave markets of Tortola and other West Indian islands.

Though not properly part of a reckoning of loyalist-owned slaves exported into the British Empire, a further important testament to the volume of loyalist slave trafficking can be found in the number of blacks taken back into the United States following the evacuation of East Florida. The embarkation commissioner counted 2,516 such persons; there would also have been a high percentage of blacks among those 5,000 East Floridians who made their own way back into the American states.

Adding together these various quantities of slaves yields a total of 14,927. This number, again a conservative estimate, doubtless falls short of the actual volume of slaves exported by loyalists—not least those taken temporarily into East Florida. It seems entirely legitimate to conclude that loyalists carried some 15,000 slaves out of the United States.

ACKNOWLEDGMENTS

WHILE WRITING THIS BOOK I have been repeatedly struck by how interconnected its subjects remained, despite the great distances they traveled. Letters linked friends and family members across oceans; neighbors in one setting became neighbors again in others. My own research has been consistently helped along by analogous small-world connections, whether through the wonders of technology or the still more wondrous generosity of colleagues, students, friends, and sometimes strangers. In the process I have racked up deeper and more numerous debts than these few pages can adequately express.

Many of those acknowledged below read portions of this manuscript, and my first thanks goes to them for their suggestions, as well as to the numerous audiences who responded to this project as a work in progress. For especially extensive readings of earlier drafts, I am grateful to David Armitage, Joyce Chaplin, Nicholas Dawidoff, Sam Haselby, Sheila Jasanoff, Jill Lepore, Peter Marshall, Marco Roth, Laurel Ulrich, and Megan Williams. Linda Colley not only read the entire manuscript but has continued to provide me with exceptional encouragement, advice, and inspiration. Jerry Bannister, Michel Ducharme, and Amani Whitfield offered invaluable assistance with Canadian history. I have also been the lucky beneficiary of the wisdom and support of other scholars who have so expertly traced these routes before me, particularly Mary Beth Norton, Cassandra Pybus, and Simon Schama.

I wrote this book in two centers of revolutionary America, each of which has left its mark on the final product. I began it as a member of the history department at the University of Virginia. I cannot imagine a more sympathetic environment in which to have had the privilege of beginning my teaching career. Among the many colleagues with whom I enjoyed memorable conversations on matters historical and otherwise, I want to thank Rich Barnett, Lenard Berlanstein, Claudrena Harold, Krishan Kumar, Chuck McCurdy, Christian McMillen, Elizabeth Meyer, Joe Miller, Duane Osheim, Sophie Rosenfeld, and Mark Thomas. Andrew O'Shaughnessy has been an unfailingly gracious interlocutor, and kindly lent me the Roosevelt Cottage as I began my revisions. One of the special pleasures of my time at Virginia was to work alongside my very first teacher of eighteenth-century British history, Paul Halliday, a model scholar and friend. Another was to gain firsthand appreciation of Peter Onuf's extraordinary capacity for mentorship. Peter, together with Charlottesville's lively group of early Americanists, has profoundly influenced my understanding of this subject.

At Harvard, I have had the equally great privilege of finishing this book in an academic setting that has exposed me to exciting new ways of seeing international and global history. My gratitude extends to all my departmental colleagues, notably Ann Blair, Sugata Bose, Vincent Brown, Joyce Chaplin, Caroline Elkins, Alison Frank, Peter Gordon, Andy Jewett, Mary Lewis, Erez Manela, Ian Miller, Emma Rothschild, Rachel St. John, and Judith Surkis; and my chairs Lizabeth Cohen, Andrew Gordon, and James Kloppenberg. To David Armitage, Niall Ferguson, and Mark Kishlansky my debts are especially copious. They have greatly enriched my approach to British history and how to write it, and given me much good counsel and conversation along the way. I also want to acknowledge those who have facilitated my life at Harvard in more practical respects, including Paul Dzus, Janet Hatch, Cory Paulsen, Anna Popiel, and Sandy Selesky; and several students who have contributed to this endeavor in various technical ways: Sarah Burack, Christa Dierksheide, Erik Linstrum, Noah McCormack, and Tim Rogan.

This book could not have been completed as fully or efficiently without ample support from Harvard and the University of Virginia; the National Endowment for the Humanities; the John W. Kluge Center at the Library of Congress; the Robert H. Smith International Center for Jefferson Studies; the MacDowell Colony; and a Charles A. Ryskamp Fellowship from the American Council of Learned Societies. A fellowship at the New York Public Library's Dorothy and Lewis B. Cullman Center for Scholars and Writers did more than fund my work. It allowed me to join a vibrant creative and intellectual community under the expert leadership of Jean Strouse. My warmest thanks to Jean, Betsy Bradley, Pamela Leo, Adriana Nova, and my fellow fellows—especially David Blight, Jim Miller, Jim Shapiro, Jeff Talarigo, and Sean Wilentz—for an unforgettable year.

From Toronto and London to Kingston and Nassau, I was fortunate to enjoy the hospitality of, among others, Stephen Aranha, Richard Bourke, Simon Dickie, and my dear friends and too-frequent hosts in London, Michael Dresser and Martin Reading. Julian Gardner and his family gave me a memorable welcome in Kasganj. My research in Sierra Leone could not have taken place without the incredible help extended to me by Freddy "Shabaka" Cole, Aminatta Forna, Peter Hanson-Alp, Alpha Kanu, Abu Koroma, Philip Misevich, Joe Opala, Ambassador June Carter Perry, Danna Van Brandt, and everybody at Country Lodge.

At Knopf, Carol Janeway has once again brought her sage editorial touch to this book. Further thanks go to the fantastically capable Liz Lee for stewarding it through publication, and to Knopf's superb production team for all their dedication and patience. At HarperPress, I have enjoyed the special pleasure of being published by my old friend Arabella Pike; and am grateful for the contributions of Sophie Goulden and others involved in this project at Harper, as well as to Mitzi Angel for her early participation. Without the magnificent Andrew Wylie, and his tremendous staff on both sides of the Atlantic, this book might never have appeared in the first place.

Throughout this project I have been engaged, enlightened, and entertained by conversations with my friends and fellow historians Jeffrey Auerbach, Michael Dodson, Richard Drayton, François Furstenberg, Durba Ghosh, Evan Haefeli, David Hancock, Lorenz Lüthi, Philip Stern, Robert Travers—and the late Stephen Vella, who is missed. William Dalrymple has been a strong believer in this project from the outset and I have gained much from his continuing friendship and his writerly example. Among my many debts for congenial company in Charlottesville, New York, and Cambridge, some fall due to Nuri Akgul, Sabri Ates, Douglas Fordham, Healan Gaston, Sam Haselby, Glenn Horowitz, Andy Jewett, Adam Kirsch, Remy Holzer Kirsch, John Nemec, Basharat Peer, Bahare Rashidi, Ananya Vajpeyi, and Heidi Voskuhl.

It would take another book to express my gratitude for the sustaining friendship—in the ether, the airwaves, and locations too numerous to itemize—of Duncan Chesney, Anna Dale, Josiah Osgood, Marco Roth, Neil Safier, Jesse Scott, Kirk Swinehart, Megan Williams, Nasser Zakariya, and Julie Zikherman. Indeed, I might never have formulated this topic without Kirk, who introduced me to Molly and Joseph Brant in my first week of graduate school. I can only hope that the years ahead will hold ample chances for me to return at least some of these accumulated favors.

This book is about families dispersed and displaced—a theme that must have attracted me in part because of my own mixed and immigrant heritage. So it has been a marvelous accident of history to find myself completing it with my immediate family all living within the same square mile. Alan, Luba, and Nina have given me fresh perspectives and many happy hours of domestic distraction. My parents Jay and Sheila have again been unfailing sources of everything from home-cooked meals to editorial input—and the title—as well as bedrocks of understanding and support. Sadly the journeys of my grandmothers Edith Jasanoff and Kamala Sen ended before this book was done. Their tales of earlier lives in other worlds kindled my own first instincts as a storyteller, and I dedicate this result to their memory.

NOTES

Introduction: The Spirit of 1783

1. The order of procession was printed in a broadside, November 24, 1783, Early American Imprints, Series 1, no. 44426. See, among other newspaper accounts, *Pennsylvania Evening Post*, November 28, 1783, pp. 261–62.

2. There was one small glitch in the proceedings, when the American soldiers found the British royal ensign billowing at the top of Fort George's flagpole. The British troops had not only refused to strike their flag: they had actually nailed it to the post, cut its halyards, and greased the flagpole. After several comic efforts by soldiers to shimmy up the pole, a nimble captain used cleats to scramble up and tear off the offending ensign. James Riker, *"Evacuation Day," 1783, Its Many Stirring Events: with Recollections of Capt. John Van Arsdale of the Veteran Corps of Artillery* (New York: Printed for the Author, 1883).

3. Judith L. Van Buskirk, *Generous Enemies: Patriots and Loyalists in Revolutionary New York* (Philadelphia: University of Pennsylvania Press, 2002), p. 183.

4. Toasts listed in *Rivington's New-York Gazette*, November 26, 1783, p. 3.

5. *New-York Packet*, January 15, 1784, p. 3.

6. Clifton Hood, "An Unusable Past: Urban Elites, New York City's Evacuation Day, and the Transformations of Memory Culture," *Journal of Social History* 37, no. 4 (Summer 2004): 883–913.

7. A contemporary newspaper account commented on the unsettling "compound of joy and pity" felt by patriots on seeing "so many hundreds made immediately happy" by the evacuation contrasted with "others made wretched by having new habitations to seek, in a comfortless region, and at a stormy season." *New-York Packet*, January 15, 1784, p. 3.

8. Historians widely cite the figure of 2.5 million as an estimated colonial population in 1775. The U.S. Census Bureau estimates that the population of the future United States in 1780 stood at about 2,780,000, while the first U.S. census, performed in 1790, recorded a population of 3,929,625. See Robert V. Wells, "Population and Family in Early America," in Jack P. Greene and J. R. Pole, eds., *A Companion to the American Revolution* (Malden, Mass.: Blackwell Publishing, 2000), p. 41.

9. "Rev. J. Bailey's explanation of his Conduct in sending political notice," March 1, 1775, LOC: Jacob Bailey Papers. See also James S. Leamon, "The Parson, the Parson's Wife, and the Coming of the Revolution to Pownalborough, Maine," *New England Quarterly* 82, no. 3 (September 2009): 514–28.

10. William S. Bartlet, *The Frontier Missionary: A Memoir of the Life of the Rev. Jacob Bailey, A.M.* (Boston: Ide and Dutton, 1853), p. 111.

11. Jacob Bailey to John Pickering, August 26, 1778, and Jacob Bailey to Mrs. [?], November 24, 1778, "Letters to various persons March 21st 1777 to Decr 30 1778," PANS: Jacob Bailey Fonds, MG 1 (reel 14895), item 21, pp. 59–74, 112–14.

12. Bartlet, pp. 129–31. Jacob Bailey, "A journal containing a variety of incidents," June 21, 1779, PANS: Jacob Bailey Fonds, MG 1 (reel 14900), vol. IV, p. 13.

13. Jacob Bailey, "A journal containing a variety of incidents," June 21, 1779, PANS: Jacob Bailey Fonds, MG 1 (reel 14900), vol. IV, pp. 6, 21–22.

14. Two classic studies remain indispensable to understanding revolutionary loyalism: Bernard Bailyn, *The Ordeal of Thomas Hutchinson* (Cambridge, Mass.: Harvard University Press, 1974), and Robert M. Calhoon, *The Loyalists in Revolutionary America, 1760–1781* (New York: Harcourt, Brace, Jovanovich, 1973). For non-elite loyalists, see, e.g., Robert M. Calhoon, Timothy M. Barnes, and George A. Rawlyk, eds., *Loyalists and Community in North America* (Westport, Conn.: Greenwood Press, 1994); Joseph S. Tiedemann, Eugene R. Fingerhut, and Robert W. Venables, eds., *The Other Loyalists: Ordinary People, Royalism, and the Revolution in the Middle Colonies, 1763–1787* (Albany: State University of New York Press, 2009).

15. Massachusetts governor Thomas Hutchinson noted how "tory" was "always the term of reproach." Quoted in Wallace Brown, *The Good Americans: The Loyalists in the American Revolution* (New York: Morrow, 1969), p. 30. A good analogy would be the use of the term "aristo" to label French émigrés, despite the fact that they were overwhelmingly non-aristocratic. While loyalist refugees and their slaves accounted for about one in forty members of the American population, the number of émigrés leaving revolutionary France was closer to one in two hundred.

16. The estimate of one in five is supplied by Paul H. Smith, based on enrollment in loyalist regiments: Paul H. Smith, "The American Loyalists: Notes on Their Organization and Numerical Strength," *William & Mary Quarterly* 25, no. 2 (April 1968): 259–77. The figure of one in three, frequently used as a benchmark by historians, is sometimes traced to an 1815 letter by John Adams in which he famously suggested that at the start of the revolution a third of the population was loyal, a third patriots, and another third "rather lukewarm." John Adams to James Lloyd, January 1815, in John Adams, *The Works of John Adams*, ed. Charles Francis Adams, 10 vols. (Boston: Little, Brown and Company, 1856), X, p. 110. There is some debate over whether Adams was referring to the American or to the French revolution in that par-

ticular letter. In other writings, however, Adams repeated the estimate, saying that "about a third of the people of the colonies were against the revolution" (quoted in Thomas McKean to Adams, January 1814, in Adams, X, p. 87), and that British ministers had "seduced and deluded nearly one third of the people of the colonies" into supporting them (Adams to Dr. J. Morse, December 22, 1815, in Adams, X, p. 193). Describing the membership of the First Continental Congress in 1774, Adams said, "To draw the characters of them all . . . would now be considered as a caricature-print; one-third tories, another whigs, and the rest mongrels." (John Adams to Thomas Jefferson, November 12, 1813, in Adams, X, p. 79.)

17. A valuable recent exception is Jim Piecuch, *Three Peoples, One King: Loyalists, Indians, and Slaves in the Revolutionary South, 1775–1782* (Columbia: University of South Carolina Press, 2008).

18. Attempts to generalize a social and psychological profile of loyalists include: William Nelson, *The American Tory* (Oxford: Oxford University Press, 1961); Kenneth S. Lynn, *A Divided People* (Westport, Conn.: Greenwood Press, 1977); N. E. H. Hull, Peter C. Hoffer, and Steven L. Allen, "Choosing Sides: A Quantitative Study of the Personality Determinants of Loyalist and Revolutionary Political Affiliation in New York," *Journal of American History* 65, no. 2 (September 1978): 344–66.

19. Although the portrayal of the revolution as a civil war has not deeply penetrated American popular consciousness, it has been widely described as such in historical works ranging from John Shy, *A People Numerous and Armed: Reflections on the Military Struggle for American Independence*, rev. ed. (Ann Arbor: University of Michigan Press, 1990), to Kevin Phillips, *The Cousins' Wars: Religion, Politics, and the Triumph of Anglo-America* (New York: Basic Books, 1999). See also Robert M. Calhoon, "Civil, Revolutionary, or Partisan: The Loyalists and the Nature of the War for Independence," in Robert M. Calhoon et al., *The Loyalist Perception and Other Essays* (Columbia: University of South Carolina Press, 1989), pp. 147–62; Allan Kulikoff, "Revolutionary Violence and the Origins of American Democracy," *Journal of the Historical Society* 2, no. 2 (March 2002): 229–60.

20. Thus, where Barry Cahill has sharply contested the idea that runaway slaves can be termed "loyalists," on the grounds that they did not necessarily share loyalist ideology, I nevertheless include such figures within the category of loyalist refugees. See Barry Cahill, "The Black Loyalist Myth in Atlantic Canada," *Acadiensis* 29, no. 1 (Autumn 1999): 76–87; James W. St. G. Walker, "Myth, History and Revisionism: The Black Loyalists Revised," *Acadiensis* 29, no. 1 (Autumn 1999): 88–105.

21. Notes throughout this book cite the relevant regional literature. One valuable essay, however, sets the loyalist emigration in a wider Atlantic context: Keith Mason, "The American Loyalist Diaspora and the Reconfiguration of the British Atlantic World," in Peter Onuf and Eliga Gould, eds., *Empire and Nation: The American Revolution in the Atlantic World* (Baltimore: Johns Hopkins University Press, 2005), pp. 239–59.

22. Lorenzo Sabine, *The American Loyalists, or, Biographical Sketches of Adherents to the British Crown in the War of Revolution*, 1st ed. (Boston: Charles C. Little and James Brown, 1847), p. iii.

23. The classic statement of this kind is R. R. Palmer, *The Age of the Democratic Revolution: A Political History of Europe and America*, 2 vols. (Princeton, N.J.: Princeton University Press, 1959–64). Leading recent efforts to internationalize U.S. history include David Armitage, *The Declaration of Independence: A Global History* (Cambridge, Mass.: Harvard University Press, 2007), and Thomas Bender, *A Nation Among Nations: America's Place in World History* (New York: Hill and Wang, 2006).

24. Judge Peter Oliver carried a treasured family sugar box with him to England, now in the Winterthur collection. (On loyalist material culture, see the 2009 Harvard Ph.D. dissertation by Katherine Rieder.) Frances Wentworth, wife of Nova Scotia governor John Wentworth, used American recipes in Halifax. ("Memorandum of Cash Expended for the use of Mrs. Wentworth's House," September 1786, PANS: RG1, vol. 411 [reel 15457], item 10.) John and William Charles Wells used the printing press in Florida and the Bahamas. (Wilbur Henry Siebert, *Loyalists in East Florida, 1774 to 1785: The Most Important Documents Pertaining Thereto, Edited with an Accompanying Narrative*, 2 vols. [Deland: Florida State Historical Society, 1929], I, p. 189.)

25. I do not mean to suggest that these principles sprang fully formed from the American Revolution; the Seven Years' War had already made the British Empire indisputably multiethnic, while many of these features were clarified in the French Revolutionary–Napoleonic wars ahead. See especially P. J. Marshall, *The Making and Unmaking of Empires: Britain, India, and America, c. 1750–1783* (Oxford: Oxford University Press, 2005), and C. A. Bayly, *Imperial Meridian: The British Empire and the World, 1780–1830* (London: Longman, 1989).

26. I draw my understanding of the revolution's consequences for the British Empire in part from: Marshall, *Making and Unmaking*; Eliga Gould, *The Persistence of Empire: British Political Culture in the Age of the American Revolution* (Chapel Hill: University of North Carolina Press, 2000); Stephen Conway, *The British Isles and the War of American Independence* (Oxford: Oxford University Press, 2000); H. T. Dickinson, ed., *Britain and the American Revolution* (Harlow: Addison Wesley Longman, 1998); Kathleen Wilson, *The Sense of the People: Politics, Culture, and Imperialism in England, 1715–1785* (Cambridge, U.K.: Cambridge University Press, 1995); Linda Colley, *Britons: Forging the Nation, 1707–1837* (New Haven, Conn.: Yale University Press, 1992); Christopher Leslie Brown, *Moral Capital: Foundations of British Abolitionism* (Chapel Hill: University of North Carolina Press, 2006).

27. Alan Frost, *The Precarious Life of James Mario Matra: Voyager with Cook, American Loyalist, Servant of Empire* (Carlton, Victoria: Miegunyah Press, 1995).

28. Jeremy Adelman, "An Age of Imperial Revolutions," *American Historical Review* 113, no. 2 (April 2008): 319–40. For a fascinating early comparison of the American and French revolutions, which characterizes the former as "defensive" and legitimate and the latter as "offensive" and violent, see Friedrich Gentz, *The Origin and Principles of the American Revolution, Compared with the Origin and Principles of the French Revolution* (Philadelphia: Asbury Dickins, 1800).

29. Cf. Peter S. Onuf, "Federalism, Democracy, and Liberty in the New American Nation," in Jack P. Greene, ed., *Exclusionary Empire: English Liberty Overseas, 1600–1900* (Cambridge, U.K.: Cambridge University Press, 2010), pp. 132–59; David C. Hendrickson, *Peace Pact: The Lost World of the American Founding* (Lawrence: University Press of Kansas, 2003); Alison LaCroix, *The Ideological Origins of American Federalism* (Cambridge, Mass.: Harvard University Press, 2010).

30. On constitutionalism in India, see Robert Travers, *Ideology and Empire in Eighteenth-Century India: The British in Bengal* (Cambridge, U.K.: Cambridge University Press, 2007). Of course American constitution-making itself had thoroughly British antecedents: see Daniel J. Hulsebosch, *Constituting Empire: New York and the Transformation of Constitutionalism in the Atlantic World, 1664–1830* (Chapel Hill: University of North Carolina Press, 2005).

31. The 1707 Act of Union with Scotland created the "United Kingdom of Great Britain," while the 1800 Act of Union with Ireland enlarged this to the "United Kingdom of Great Britain and Ireland." A precedent for these "United" entities may have

been found in the name of the Dutch United Provinces, constituted in 1581, though Americans did not invoke the Dutch example in formulating the Declaration of Independence: Armitage, pp. 42–44.

32. On migration, slavery, and revolution in the eighteenth-century Atlantic world, see especially Bernard Bailyn, *The Peopling of British North America: An Introduction* (New York: Knopf, 1986); Bernard Bailyn, *Voyagers to the West: A Passage in the Peopling of British North America on the Eve of the Revolution* (New York: Knopf, 1986); Marcus Rediker and Peter Linebaugh, *The Many-Headed Hydra: Sailors, Slaves, Commoners, and the Hidden History of the Revolutionary Atlantic* (Boston: Beacon Press, 2000); Stephanie E. Smallwood, *Saltwater Slavery: A Middle Passage from Africa to American Diaspora* (Cambridge, Mass.: Harvard University Press, 2007); Alexander X. Byrd, *Captives and Voyagers: Black Migrants across the Eighteenth-Century British Atlantic World* (Baton Rouge: Louisiana State University Press, 2008); Sarah M. S. Pearsall, *Atlantic Families: Lives and Letters in the Later Eighteenth Century* (Oxford: Oxford University Press, 2008).

Chapter One: Civil War

1. The celebrated naturalist William Bartram described this as "the most magnificent forest I had ever seen." William Batram, *Travels through North and South Carolina, Georgia, East and West Florida* (Philadelphia: James and Johnson, 1791), pp. 53–56, 259–62.

2. "The Supplemental Memorial of Lieutenant Colonel Thomas Brown," Nassau, April 21, 1788, NA: AO 13/34 (Part 1), f. 100.

3. "The Supplemental Memorial of Lieutenant Colonel Thomas Brown," Nassau, April 21, 1788, NA: AO 13/34 (Part 1), f. 100.

4. Thomas Brown to Lord Cornwallis, July 16, 1780, NA: PRO 30/11/2, f. 308.

5. Edward J. Cashin, *The King's Ranger: Thomas Brown and the American Revolution on the Southern Frontier* (Athens: University of Georgia Press, 1989), pp. 28–29.

6. The black legend of Brown entered history books as early as 1784, with Hugh McCall's *The History of Georgia* (Atlanta: A. B. Caldwell, 1909 [1784]), and was sustained by the eminent nineteenth-century historian Charles Colcock Jones. "Of all the inhuman characters developed during this abnormal period so replete with murder, arson, theft, brutality and crimes too foul for utterance," said Jones, "none can be named more notorious than Thomas Brown." Charles Colcock Jones Jr., *The History of Georgia*, 2 vols. (Boston: Houghton Mifflin, 1883), II, p. 475. For reappraisals, see Cashin, passim; Bernard Bailyn, *Voyagers to the West: A Passage in the Peopling of America on the Eve of the Revolution* (New York: Vintage, 1988), pp. 555–58; Jim Piecuch, *Three Peoples, One King: Loyalists, Indians, and Slaves in the Revolutionary South, 1775–1782* (Columbia: University of South Carolina Press, 2008), pp. 4–5.

7. These include Bernard Bailyn's classic *The Ideological Origins of the American Revolution* (Cambridge, Mass.: Harvard University Press, 1967) and Gordon S. Wood, *The Radicalism of the American Revolution* (New York: Knopf, 1991). For a rowdier, bottom-up perspective, see, e.g., Ray Raphael, *A People's History of the American Revolution: How Common People Shaped the Fight for Independence* (New York: New Press, 2001); Gary B. Nash, *The Unknown American Revolution: The Unruly Birth of Democracy and the Struggle to Create America* (New York: Viking, 2005); T. H. Breen, *American Insurgents, American Patriots: The Revolution of the People* (New York: Hill and Wang, 2010).

8. For an excellent overview of the meanings of loyalism in this period, see Jerry Bannister and Liam Riordan, "Loyalism and the British Atlantic, 1660–1840," in Jerry Bannister and Liam Riordan, eds., *The Loyal Atlantic: Remaking the British Atlantic in the Revolutionary Era* (Toronto: University of Toronto Press, forthcoming 2011). I am grateful to Jerry Bannister for an advance copy of this essay. On loyalist ideology, see, among others, Robert M. Calhoon et al., *The Loyalist Perception and Other Essays* (Columbia: University of South Carolina Press, 1989), Part I; Bernard Bailyn, *The Ordeal of Thomas Hutchinson* (Cambridge, Mass.: Harvard University Press, 1974); Carol Berkin, *Jonathan Sewall: Odyssey of an American Loyalist* (New York: Columbia University Press, 1974); John E. Ferling, *The Loyalist Mind: Joseph Galloway and the American Revolution* (University Park, Pa.: Pennsylvania State University Press, 1977); Janice Potter-MacKinnon, *The Liberty We Seek: Loyalist Ideology in Colonial New York and Massachusetts* (Cambridge, Mass.: Harvard University Press, 1983).

9. Bailyn, *Voyagers*, pp. 26, 552–53.

10. Benjamin H. Irvin, "Tar, Feathers, and the Enemies of American Liberties, 1768–1776," *New England Quarterly* 76, no. 2 (June 2003): 197–238. "Sons of Liberty" was first used in a speech by the Irish-born MP and "friend of America" Isaac Barré in a parliamentary speech opposing the Stamp Act. "Isaac Barré," q.v., *DNB*.

11. John Adams, *The Works of John Adams*, ed. Charles Francis Adams, 10 vols. (Boston: Little, Brown, and Company, 1865), II, pp. 363–64.

12. The definitive treatment of Galloway is Ferling, *The Loyalist Mind*.

13. Galloway's speech is reproduced in Joseph Galloway, *Historical and Political Reflections on the Rise and Progress of the American Rebellion* (London, 1780), pp. 70–81. For the text of the plan, see Worthington Chauncey Ford, ed., *Journals of the Continental Congress, 1774–89*, 4 vols. (Washington: Government Printing Office, 1904), pp. 49–51.

14. Benjamin Franklin to Joseph Galloway, February 25, 1775, in Jared Sparks, ed., *The Works of Benjamin Franklin* (Chicago: Townsend McCoun, 1882), VIII, pp. 144–48.

15. Franklin conveyed a similar sentiment still more vividly in a cartoon he circulated following the Stamp Act controversy, showing the British Empire as a dismembered female body, with its amputated limbs representing the colonies.

16. Galloway, p. 81. For the debate, see John Adams's notes: Adams, II, pp. 387–91.

17. Adams, II, p. 390.

18. Ferling, p. 26. Nothing appears to survive to indicate which colonies voted for and against. Galloway claimed that the debate over his plan had been intentionally "expunged" from the congressional record, consigning it to the ignorance of posterity. But the neglect may have been procedural: see Robert M. Calhoon, " 'I Have Deduced Your Rights': Joseph Galloway's Concept of His Role, 1774–1775," in Calhoon et al., p. 89.

19. "Declaration and Resolves of the First Continental Congress," The Avalon Project at Yale Law School, http://avalon.law.yale.edu/18th_century/resolves.asp, accessed October 7, 2009.

20. The phrase comes from Emerson's 1837 "Concord Hymn," though the first shots were exchanged in Lexington.

21. On the ramifications of the war for British identities, see especially Dror Wahrman, "The English Problem of Identity in the American Revolution," *American Historical Review* 106, no. 4 (October 2001): 1236–62; Stephen Conway, "From Fellow Nationals to Foreigners: British Perceptions of the Americans, circa 1739–1783,"

William & Mary Quarterly 59, no. 1 (January 2002): 65–100; Linda Colley, *Britons: Forging the Nation* (New Haven, Conn.: Yale University Press, 1992), pp. 137–45.

22. Rick J. Ashton, "The Loyalist Congressmen of New York," *New-York Historical Society Quarterly* 60, no. 1 (January–April 1976): 95–106. See also Joseph S. Tiedemann, *Reluctant Revolutionaries: New York City and the Road to Independence, 1763–1776* (Ithaca, N.Y.: Cornell University Press, 1997).

23. For a list of documented cases see Irvin, pp. 233–37.

24. Catherine Skinner Robinson, *Lady Robinson's Recollections* (London: Barrett, Sons and Co., Printers, 1842), pp. 19–20. (I accessed a copy of this privately printed book in LAC: Lady Catherine Robinson Fonds, Microfilm A-1985.) "Cortlandt Skinner," q.v., *DNB*.

25. For the evacuation of Boston, see David McCullough, *1776* (New York: Simon and Schuster, 2005), pp. 97–105; Piers Mackesy, *The War for America, 1775–83* (Cambridge, Mass.: Harvard University Press, 1964), p. 80. A list of 926 Boston evacuees appears in Samuel Curwen, *The Journal and Letters of Samuel Curwen, 1775–1783*, ed. George Atkinson Ward (Boston: Little, Brown and Company, 1864), pp. 485–88.

26. Quoted in Lorenzo Sabine, *The American Loyalists: Or, Biographical Sketches of Adherents to the British Crown in the War of the Revolution* (Boston: Charles C. Little and James Brown, 1847), p. 14.

27. [Charles Inglis], *The True Interest of America, Impartially Stated, in Certain Strictures on a Pamphlet Called Common Sense* (Philadelphia: James Humphreys, 1776), pp. vi, 34, 51.

28. [Inglis], p. vi.

29. Isaac Kramnick, "Editor's Introduction," in Thomas Paine, *Common Sense*, ed. Isaac Kramnick (New York: Penguin, 1986), pp. 8–9. But for more conservative publication estimates see Trish Loughran, *The Republic in Print: Print Culture in the Age of U.S. Nation-Building* (New York: Columbia University Press, 2007), pp. 33–58.

30. Charles Inglis, "Breif [*sic*] Notes or Memoirs of Public & various Other Transactions: Taken to assist my Memory, & begun Jan. 1775," February 20, April 4, May 8, June 14, June 22, 1776, LAC: Charles Inglis and Family Fonds, Microfilm A-710. The Inglis pamphlet burned in New York was an earlier version of *The True Interest* called *The Deceiver Unmasked; or, Loyalty and Interest United: in Answer to a Pamphlet called Common Sense* (New York: Samuel Loudon, 1776).

31. Brendan McConville, *The King's Three Faces: The Rise and Fall of Royal America, 1688–1776* (Chapel Hill: University of North Carolina Press, 2006), pp. 306–11. On Bowling Green, see Inglis, "Breif Notes," July 9, 1776, LAC: Charles Inglis and Family Fonds, Microfilm A-710; and Holger Hoock, *Empires of the Imagination: Politics, War, and the Arts in the British World, 1750–1850* (London: Profile Books, 2010), pp. 49–54.

32. Quoted in Judith L. Van Buskirk, *Generous Enemies: Patriots and Loyalists in Revolutionary New York* (Philadelphia: University of Pennsylvania Press, 2002), p. 18.

33. Even before the battle they had been rowing out to the fleet to seek protection: Thomas Moffat Diary, July 3, July 8, August 6, November 23–24, December 1, 1776, LOC.

34. Mary Beth Norton, *The British-Americans: The Loyalist Exiles in England, 1774–1789* (London: Constable, 1974), p. 32. For the larger context of loyalism in New York, with assessments of the strength of loyalism in the colony, see Philip Ranlet, *The New York Loyalists* (Knoxville: University of Tennessee Press, 1986).

35. Benjamin L. Carp, "The Night the Yankees Burned Broadway: The New York City Fire of 1776," *Early American Studies* 4, no. 2 (Fall 2006): 471–511.

36. On loyalist-British relations see Van Buskirk, esp. chapter 1, and Ruma Chopra, "New Yorkers' Vision of Reunion with the British Empire: 'Quicken Others by our Example,' " Working Paper 08–02, International Seminar on the History of the Atlantic World, Harvard University, 2008.

37. "Loyalist Declaration of Dependence," November 25, 1776, NYHS.

38. R. W. G. Vail, "The Loyalist Declaration of Dependence of November 28, 1776," *New-York Historical Society Quarterly* 31, no. 2 (April 1947): 68–71. I have also relied on the annotated "Transcription and Partial List of the Signatories of the New York Loyalist Declaration of Dependence of November 28, 1776," prepared by the staff of the New-York Historical Society.

39. Diary of Sir Frederick Philipse Robinson, RMC, p. 5.

40. "Minutes of the Committee for Detecting Conspiracies," February 22, 1777, Richard B. Morris, ed., *John Jay: The Making of a Revolutionary; Unpublished Papers, 1745–1780* (New York: Harper and Row, 1975), p. 348.

41. Beverley Robinson to John Jay, March 4, 1777, in Morris, ed., pp. 349–50.

42. Aaron Nathan Coleman, "Loyalists in War, Americans in Peace: The Reintegration of the Loyalists, 1775–1800" (Ph.D. dissertation, University of Kentucky, 2008), pp. 41–52, 246–48.

43. Jay to Susanna Philipse Robinson, March 21, 1777, in Morris, ed., pp. 352–54.

44. Diary of Sir Frederick Philipse Robinson, RMC, p. 6.

45. Charles A. Campbell, "Robinson's House in the Hudson Highlands: The Headquarters of Washington," *Magazine of American History* 4 (February 1880): 109–17.

46. Colin G. Calloway, *The American Revolution in Indian Country: Crisis and Diversity in Native American Communities* (Cambridge, Mass.: Cambridge University Press, 1995). For the longer context of Indian participation in the revolution, see Richard White, *The Middle Ground: Indians, Empires, and Republics in the Great Lakes Region, 1650–1815* (Cambridge, U.K.: Cambridge University Press, 1991).

47. For a treatment of the American Revolution as frontier war, see Patrick Griffin, *American Leviathan: Empire, Nation, and Revolutionary Frontier* (New York: Hill and Wang, 2007).

48. On the formative impact of Indian war in forging early American identity, see Peter Silver, *Our Savage Neighbors: How Indian War Transformed Early America* (New York: Norton, 2008); Jill Lepore, *The Name of War: King Philip's War and the Origins of American Identity* (New York: Knopf, 1998).

49. Brown to Cornwallis, July 16, 1780, NA: PRO 30/11/2, f. 308.

50. Karim M. Tiro, "The Dilemmas of Alliance: The Oneida Indian Nation in the American Revolution," in John Resch and Walter Sargent, eds., *War and Society in the American Revolution: Mobilization and Home Fronts* (DeKalb: Northern Illinois University Press, 2007), pp. 215–34.

51. Daniel Claus to Frederick Haldimand, August 30, 1779, BL: Add. Mss. 21774, f. 58.

52. "The first letter written by Hannah Lawrence Schieffelin to her parents after her marriage. Written from Navy Hall opposite Fort Niagara to her father John Lawrence, New York, December 4, 1780," NYPL: Schieffelin Family Papers, Box 1.

53. "List of Loyalists Against Whom Judgments Were Made Under the Confiscation Act," NYPL.

54. "Sir William Johnson," q.v., *DNB*; Alan Taylor, *The Divided Ground*, pp. 3–45. I owe much of my understanding of the Johnsons and Brants to Kirk Davis Swinehart: see "This Wild Place: Sir William Johnson Among the Mohawks, 1715–1783" (Ph.D.

dissertation, Yale University, 2002) and Kirk Davis Swinehart, "Object Lessons: Indians, Objects, and Revolution," *Common-Place* 2, no. 3 (April 2002), http://www.history cooperative.org/journals/cp/vol-02/no-03/lessons/, accessed December 30, 2009.

55. William Leete Stone, *Life of Joseph Brant (Thayendanegea)*, 2 vols. (Albany, N.Y.: J. Munsell, 1865), II, p. 247.

56. Taylor, p. 75; Charles Inglis, "Journal of Occurrences, beginning, Wednesday, October 13, 1785," October 13, 1785, LAC: Charles Inglis and Family Fonds, Microfilm A-709.

57. *The London Magazine* 46 (July 1776).

58. Barbara Graymont, *The Iroquois in the American Revolution* (Syracuse, N.Y.: Syracuse University Press, 1972), pp. 146–49.

59. Linda Colley, *Captives: Britain, Empire and the World, 1600–1850* (London: Jonathan Cape, 2002), pp. 228–31.

60. Mackesy, pp. 130–41.

61. These measures are summarized in Claude Halstead Van Tyne, *The Loyalists in the American Revolution* (New York: Macmillan, 1902), appendices B and C, pp. 318–41.

62. Claus to Haldimand, August 30, 1779, BL: Add. Mss. 21774, ff. 57–58.

63. Charles H. Lesser, ed., *The Sinews of Independence: Monthly Strength Reports of the Continental Army* (Chicago: University of Chicago Press, 1976).

64. Andrew Jackson O'Shaughnessy, *An Empire Divided: The American Revolution and the British Caribbean* (Philadelphia: University of Pennsylvania Press, 2000); Jack P. Greene, *Pursuits of Happiness: The Social Development of the Early Modern British Colonies and the Formation of American Culture* (Chapel Hill: University of North Carolina Press, 1988).

65. Elizabeth Lichtenstein Johnston, *Recollections of a Georgia Loyalist* (New York: M. F. Mansfield and Company, 1901), pp. 41, 45–46. Memorial of John Lightenstone, NA: AO 13/36B, Georgia H-M, f. 441.

66. Johnston, pp. 48–49, 52.

67. John Graham to William Knox, March 8, 1779, NA: AO 13/36A, Georgia H-M, ff. 69–70.

68. Johnston, pp. 52–57. William's student antics earned him numerous chastising letters from his father: see Lewis Johnston to William Martin Johnston, July 17, 1773, September 6, 1773, November 17, 1773, February 5, 1774, July 15, 1774, PANS: Almon Family Papers, reel 10362.

69. Johnston gave a somewhat disorganized account of the siege: Johnston, pp. 57–63. See also Mackesy, pp. 277–78.

70. Alexander Chesney, *The Journal of Alexander Chesney, a South Carolina Loyalist in the Revolution and After*, ed. E. Alfred Jones (Columbus: Ohio State University Press, 1921), p. 10; Mackesy, pp. 340–43.

71. "A Memoir of the Life of William Charles Wells, M.D., Written by Himself," in William Charles Wells, *Two Essays: One upon Single Vision with Two Eyes; the Other on Dew* (London: Printed for Archibald Constable and Co., 1818), p. xviii. One John Wells signed a loyalty certificate on June 24, 1780, and a John Wells Jr. on June 23, 1780. NA: CO 5/527.

72. NA: CO 5/527. This is one of several volumes of loyalty oaths from Charleston.

73. See for instance Cruden's announcement of the seizure of patriot estates in the *Pennsylvania Packet*, January 20, 1781, p. 3.

74. Johnston, pp. 64–66.

75. Cashin, pp. 114–19; Jones, II, pp. 455–59; McCall, pp. 483–87. Andrew Johnston's obituary is available online: http://www.royalprovincial.com/military/rhist/kcarrng/kcrngobit.htm, accessed October 7, 2009.

76. Cashin observes that King's Mountain, recognized as a turning point in the southern war, grew out of the siege of Augusta. Cashin, pp. 120–21.

77. For a landmark interpretation of the American Revolution as a war over slavery and black liberation, see Sylvia R. Frey, *Water from the Rock: Black Resistance in a Revolutionary Age* (Princeton, N.J.: Princeton University Press, 1991).

78. "An Account of the Life of Mr. David George. . . . ," reprinted in Vincent Carretta, ed., *Unchained Voices: An Anthology of Black Authors in the English-Speaking World of the Eighteenth Century* (Lexington: University of Kentucky Press, 1996), pp. 333–34.

79. The municipal officials of Williamsburg immediately presented Dunmore with a written protest, reprinted in various colonial newspapers, e.g., *Newport Mercury*, May 15, 1775, p. 2.

80. James Corbett David, "A Refugee's Revolution: Lord Dunmore and the Floating Town, 1775–1776," Working Paper 08–04, International Seminar on the History of the Atlantic World, Harvard University, 2008.

81. *Pennsylvania Evening Post*, November 4, 1775, Supplement, p. 507. The same paper had earlier ridiculed Dunmore for his maritime exploits: "Lord Dunmore, we hear, keeps cruising about (wandering like Cain) and at the time of the late storm was up in James river." (*Pennsylvania Evening Post*, September 19, 1775, p. 426.)

82. Philip Morgan and Andrew Jackson O'Shaughnessy, "Arming Slaves in the American Revolution," in Christopher Leslie Brown and Philip Morgan, eds., *Arming Slaves: From Classical Times to the Modern Age* (New Haven, Conn.: Yale University Press, 2006), pp. 188–89; Frey, pp. 49–80. Slaves themselves had on several occasions justified rebellion by citing the rumor that the king intended to free them: McConville, pp. 175–82.

83. Proclamation, November 7, 1775, Early American Imprints, Series 1, no. 14592.

84. Cassandra Pybus, *Epic Journeys of Freedom: Runaway Slaves of the American Revolution and Their Global Quest for Liberty* (Boston: Beacon Press, 2006), pp. 13–20; Cassandra Pybus, "Jefferson's Faulty Math: The Question of Slave Defections in the American Revolution," *William & Mary Quarterly* 62, no. 2 (April 2005): paras. 11–15.

85. Archibald Campbell, *Journal of an Expedition against the Rebels of Georgia*, ed. and intr. Colin Campbell (Darien, Ga.: Ashantilly Press, 1981), pp. 52–53. On receiving favorable overtures from Galphin, Campbell sent the slaves to Savannah "to be preserved for Mr. Golphin, in Case he continued to act the same friendly part toward us" (Campbell, p. 56). Galphin died the following year.

86. "Account of the Life of David George," in Carretta, ed., pp. 334–36; Pybus, *Epic Journeys*, pp. 38–40; Walter H. Brooks, *The Silver Bluff Church: A History of Negro Baptist Churches in America* (Washington, D.C.: R. L. Pendleton, 1910).

87. Morgan and O'Shaughnessy, p. 191. Stiele's deposition is reproduced online: http://www.royalprovincial.com/Military/rhist/blkpion/blklet4.htm, accessed September 11, 2010.

88. Mackesy, pp. 409–12.

89. Elizabeth A. Fenn, *Pox Americana: The Great Smallpox Epidemic of 1775–82* (New York: Hill and Wang, 2001), pp. 126–33; Pybus, *Epic Journeys*, pp. 49–51.

90. Cornwallis to Sir Henry Clinton, September 16, 1781, NA: PRO 30/11/74, f. 91.

91. Patriots interpreted Cornwallis's expulsion of the sick as an act of biological warfare: Fenn, pp. 131–32.

92. Cornwallis to Clinton, October 20, 1781, NA: PRO 30/11/74, ff. 106–10; Henry Dearborn Diary, October 16 and 17, 1781, NYPL; Pybus, *Epic Journeys*, pp. 51–53; Johann Ewald, *Diary of the American War: A Hessian Journal*, trans. and ed. Joseph P. Tustin (New Haven, Conn.: Yale University Press, 1979), pp. 334–37.

93. Articles of surrender published in *Pennsylvania Packet*, October 25, 1781, p. 3.

94. On the ballad and its afterlives, see Christopher Hill, *The World Turned Upside Down: Radical Ideas during the English Revolution* (London: Penguin, 1991), pp. 379–81.

95. Articles of Capitulation "Done in the Trenches before York," October 19, 1781, NA: PRO 30/11/74, ff. 128–32.

Chapter Two: An Unsettling Peace

1. Nathaniel William Wraxall, *Historical Memoirs of My Own Time* (London: Kegan, Paul, Trench, Trübner and Co., 1904), p. 398.

2. William Smith, *Historical Memoirs of William Smith, 1778–1783*, ed. W. H. W. Sabine (New York: New York Times and Arno Press, 1971), p. 461.

3. Smith, pp. 461–63.

4. Simon Schama, *Rough Crossings: Britain, the Slaves, and the American Revolution* (London: BBC Books, 2005), pp. 124–25. John Cruden to Lord Dunmore, January 5, 1782, NA: CO 5/175. (I am grateful to Jim David for a copy of this document.) In April 1782, William Smith heard Dunmore still talking about raising "several Corps of Blacks upon the Promise of Freedom." Smith, p. 497.

5. Robert M. Calhoon, " 'The Constitution Ought to Bend': William Smith Jr.'s Alternative to the American Revolution," in Robert M. Calhoon et al., *The Loyalist Perception and Other Essays* (Columbia: University of South Carolina Press, 1989), pp. 14–27.

6. For an important reappraisal of these peace initiatives, see Andrew Jackson O'Shaughnessy, "Lord North and Conciliation with America," unpublished manuscript.

7. King George III to Lord North, January 21, 1782, *The Correspondence of King George the Third with Lord North from 1768 to 1783*, ed. W. Bodham Donne, 2 vols. (London: John Murray, 1867), II, pp. 403–4.

8. On these events see Ian R. Christie, *The End of Lord North's Ministry, 1780–82* (London: Macmillan, 1958); John Cannon, *The Fox-North Coalition: Crisis of the Constitution, 1782–84* (London: Cambridge University Press, 1969).

9. Debate of February 22, 1782, *Cobbett's Parliamentary History of England*, 36 vols. (London: R. Bagshaw, 1806–20), XXII, columns 1028–29.

10. Debate of February 27, 1782, *Parliamentary History*, XXII, columns 1071, 1085.

11. Debate of March 15, 1782, *Parliamentary History*, XXII, column 1199.

12. Horace Walpole, *Journal of the Reign of King George the Third from the Year 1771 to 1783*, 2 vols. (London: Richard Bentley, 1859), II, p. 521.

13. Walpole, p. 500.

14. For Carleton's early career, see Paul David Nelson, *General Sir Guy Carleton, Lord Dorchester: Soldier-Statesman of Early British Canada* (Madison, N.J.: Fairleigh Dickinson University Press, 2000), pp. 17–27.

15. Quoted in Nelson, pp. 45–46.

16. Quoted in Nelson, p. 55.

17. Philip Lawson, *The Imperial Challenge: Quebec and Britain in the Age of the American Revolution* (Montreal: McGill–Queen's University Press, 1989). See also Hilda Neatby, *Quebec: The Revolutionary Age, 1760–1791* (Toronto: McClelland and Stewart, 1966), chapter 9.

18. Nelson, pp. 58–60.

19. Neatby, chapter 10.

20. Nelson, p. 136; Neatby, pp. 151–52.

21. Quoted in Nelson, p. 102.

22. Christie, pp. 291–94.

23. Nelson, pp. 142–43.

24. I have drawn biographical information on William and Benjamin Franklin from Sheila L. Skemp, *William Franklin: Son of a Patriot, Servant of a King* (New York: Oxford University Press, 1990); Sheila L. Skemp, *Benjamin and William Franklin: Father and Son, Patriot and Loyalist* (Boston: Bedford Books of St. Martin's Press, 1994); Walter Isaacson, *Benjamin Franklin: An American Life* (New York: Simon and Schuster, 2003).

25. For minutes and other documents relating to the Board of Associated Loyalists see NA: CO 5/82, ff. 23–88, 178–203.

26. Skemp, *William Franklin*, pp. 256–63; Smith, pp. 499–521 passim; Schama, pp. 141–44; Nelson, pp. 152–55.

27. Smith, p. 545; Skemp, *William Franklin*, pp. 263–66.

28. Daniel Claus to Frederick Haldimand, August 30, 1779, BL: Add. Mss. 21774, f. 58.

29. For these later campaigns, see Barbara Graymont, *The Iroquois in the American Revolution* (Syracuse, N.Y.: Syracuse University Press, 1972), pp. 192–258.

30. "Return of Prisoners & Killed, by the Different Partys under the Direction of Captain Brant, In Augt. 1780—of Col. Johnsons Departmt," BL: Add. Mss. 21769, f. 70.

31. Peter Silver, *Our Savage Neighbors: How Indian War Transformed Early America* (New York: W. W. Norton, 2008), pp. 268–74. Few whites who learned about the Indian reprisal, in turn, would easily forget it. Delawares seized an American colonel and painstakingly tortured him to death: gouging him with burning sticks, forcing him to walk over hot coals, firing "squibs of powder" at him until "he begged of . . . a white renegade who was standing by, to shoot him, when the fellow said, 'Don't you see I have no gun.' " Soon enough he would be scalped, his body tossed into the embers and coals shoveled over him till he was finally dead. Maj. William Croghan to Col. William Davies, Fort Pitt, July 6, 1782, LAC: William A. Smy Collection, MG31 G36.

32. Edward J. Cashin, *The King's Ranger: Thomas Brown and the American Revolution on the Southern Frontier* (New York: Fordham University Press, 1999), pp. 143–44; Hugh McCall, *The History of Georgia* (Atlanta: A. B. Caldwell, 1909 [1784]), pp. 532–33; Elizabeth Lichtenstein Johnston, *Recollections of a Georgia Loyalist* (New York: M. F. Mansfield and Company, 1901), pp. 69–73.

33. William Moultrie, *Memoirs of the American Revolution: So Far as It Related to the States of North and South Carolina and Georgia*, 2 vols. (New York: David Longworth, 1802), II, p. 336.

34. David Fanning, *The Adventures of David Fanning in the American Revolutionary War*, ed. A. W. Savary (Ottawa: Golden Dog Press, 1983).

35. Moultrie, II, p. 355. For a detailed description of these post-Yorktown engagements, see Jim Piecuch, *Three Peoples, One King: Loyalists, Indians, and Slaves in the Revolutionary South* (Columbia: University of South Carolina Press, 2008), pp.272–327.

36. Cashin, pp. 150–53.

37. Sir Guy Carleton to Alexander Leslie, July 15, 1782, quoted in *Report on American Manuscripts in the Royal Institution of Great Britain*, 4 vols. (London: HMSO, 1904), III, p. 19.

38. Carleton to Leslie, May 23, 1782, NYPL: Alexander Leslie Letterbook.

39. Leslie to Alured Clarke, June 4, 1782, and Leslie to Sir James Wright, June 4, 1782, NYPL: Alexander Leslie Letterbook.

40. Wright to Lord Shelburne, September 1782, quoted in Charles Colcock Jones, *The History of Georgia*, 2 vols. (Boston: Houghton Mifflin Company, 1883), II, p. 526.

41. Wright to Carleton, July 6, 1782, quoted in *Report on American Manuscripts*, III, p. 11.

42. "To the Citizens of Charles-Town, South-Carolina," August 9, 1782, LOC: "American Papers Respecting the Evacuation of Charlestown 1782," George Chalmers Collection.

43. Piecuch, pp. 292–98.

44. For South Carolina's act: Thomas Cooper, ed., *The Statutes at Large of South Carolina* (Columbia, S.C.: A. S. Johnston, 1838), IV, pp. 516–23. The names were published in the *Royal Gazette* (Charleston), March 20, 1782. For Georgia (text quoted here): Allen D. Candler, ed., *The Revolutionary Records of the State of Georgia* (Augusta, Ga.: Franklin-Turner Company, 1908), I, pp. 373–97; Robert S. Lambert, "The Confiscation of Loyalist Property in Georgia, 1782–1786," *William & Mary Quarterly* 20, no. 1 (January 1963): 80–94.

45. Jones, II, pp. 516–17.

46. "Proceedings of the Merchants & Citizens of Charlestown upon a Report that the Garrison was shortly to be evacuated; with the Letters and other Papers which passed between them Genls. Leslie, Govr Mathews &c," LOC: "American Papers Respecting the Evacuation of Charlestown 1782," George Chalmers Collection.

47. Moultrie, II, p. 279; Lambert, p. 230. For lists of refugees receiving handouts, see Murtie June Clark, *Loyalists in the Southern Campaign of the Revolutionary War*, 3 vols. (Baltimore: Genealogical Publishing Company, 1981), I, pp. 512–29.

48. Thomas Paine, *Common Sense* (New York: Penguin, 1986), p. 120. Fanning, p. 60.

49. Patrick Tonyn to Lord George Germain, May 1, 1782, NA: CO 5/560, p. 421.

50. "Address of the Upper and Commons Houses of Assembly to Lieut. Gen. Alexander Leslie," June 16, 1782, quoted in *Report on American Manuscripts*, II, p. 527; Tonyn to Carleton, June 20 and 21, 1782 (*Report on American Manuscripts*, II, p. 529, p. 531). See also address from General Assembly to Tonyn, June 19, 1782, NA: CO 5/560, p. 752.

51. Leslie to Carleton, June 28, 1782, NYPL: Alexander Leslie Letterbook.

52. Henry Nase Diary, July 11, 1782, NBM, p. 13.

53. "An Account of Several Baptist Churches, consisting chiefly of Negro Slaves: particularly of one at Kingston, in Jamaica; and another at Savannah, in Georgia," reprinted in Vincent Carretta, ed., *Unchained Voices: An Anthology of Black Authors in the English-Speaking World of the Eighteenth Century* (Lexington: University of Kentucky Press, 1996), pp. 326–27.

54. I have drawn sailing dates from the diary of Henry Nase, July 20–27, 1782, NBM, pp. 13–14.

55. Michael John Prokopow, " 'To the Torrid Zones': The Fortunes and Misfortunes of American Loyalists in the Anglo-Caribbean Basin, 1774–1801," (Ph.D. dis-

sertation, Harvard University, 1996), pp. 17–20. Leslie had asked Carleton for enough shipping to carry fifty whites and nineteen hundred blacks to Jamaica. Leslie to Carleton, July 6, 1782, NYPL: Alexander Leslie Letterbook.

56. "Nathaniel Hall," q.v., "A List of Loyalists in Jamaica," NLJ: MS 1841, p. 14. Claim of Sir James Wright in *Report of Bureau of Archives*, II, p. 1306.

57. "A Return of Refugees, with their Negroes, who came to the Province of East Florida in consequence of the evacuation of the Province of Georgia," n.d., NA: CO 5/560, pp. 806–8.

58. John Graham to Carleton, July 20, 1782, quoted in *Report on American Manuscripts*, III, p. 30. A contemporary newspaper report claimed that Brown, his twelve hundred men, and three hundred Indians traveled with three thousand blacks. *New England Chronicle*, September 19, 1782, p. 3.

59. Elizabeth Johnston to William Johnston, May 25, 1781, PANS: Almon Family Papers, reel 10362.

60. William Johnston to John Lichtenstein, May 20, 1781, PANS: Almon Family Papers, reel 10362.

61. Elizabeth Johnston to William Johnston, September 3 and September 2, 1781, PANS: Almon Family Papers, reel 10362.

62. Leslie to Sir Henry Clinton, March 27, 1782, quoted in *Report on American Manuscripts*, II, p. 434. See also Leslie to Clinton, April 17, 1782, quoted in *Report on American Manuscripts*, II, p. 457.

63. Leslie to Carleton, September 8, 1782, NYPL: Alexander Leslie Letterbook.

64. Autobiography of Stephen Jarvis, NYHS, p. 78.

65. Henry Nase Diary, November 20, 1782, NBM, p. 15.

66. Clark, ed., I, pp. 545–50.

67. Lambert, p. 254. "Return of the Loyal Inhabitants within the British Lines at Charles Town South Carolina who have given in their names as intending to leave that Province. . . . ," August 29, 1782, *Report on American Manuscripts*, III, p. 97. Schama, p. 134.

68. Leslie to Carleton, June 27, 1782, quoted in *Report on American Manuscripts*, II, p. 544; Leslie to Carleton, August 16, 1782, NYPL: Leslie Letterbook.

69. Carleton to Leslie, July 15, 1782, quoted in *Report on American Manuscripts*, III, p. 20.

70. Leslie to Carleton, August 10, 1782, NYPL: Alexander Leslie Letterbook.

71. Samuel Rogers to Joseph Taylor, May 1, 1782, LOC: Lovering-Taylor Family Papers. Cruden's father, William, was minister of the Scottish Presbyterian Church in Crown Court, Covent Garden. "William Cruden," q.v., *DNB*; Alexander Chesney, *The Journal of Alexander Chesney*, ed. E. Alfred Jones (Columbus: Ohio State University Press, 1921), p. 91.

72. John Cruden, *Report on the Management of the Estates Sequestered in South Carolina, by Order of Lord Cornwallis, in 1780–82*," ed. Paul Leicester Ford (Brooklyn, N.Y.: Historical Printing Club, 1890), pp. 13–14. Jeffrey J. Crow, "What Price Loyalism? The Case of John Cruden, Commissioner of Sequestered Estates," *North Carolina Historical Review* 58, no. 3 (July 1981): 215–33.

73. John Cruden to Robert Morris, August 15, 1782, LOC: Lovering-Taylor Family Papers.

74. "Articles of a Treaty, Respecting Slaves within the *British* Lines, *British* Debts, Property secured by Family Settlements, &c.," LOC: "American Papers Respecting the Evacuation of Charlestown 1782," George Chalmers Collection.

75. Leslie to Carleton, October 18 and November 18, 1782, NYPL: Alexander

Leslie Letterbook. Leslie to Carleton, "Secret," October 18, 1782, quoted in *Report on American Manuscripts*, III, pp. 175–76. Moultrie, II, pp. 343–52.

76. "Commission for the examination of Negroes," n.d., NYPL: Alexander Leslie Letterbook.

77. Cassandra Pybus, *Epic Journeys of Freedom: Runaway Slaves of the American Revolution and Their Global Quest for Liberty* (Boston: Beacon Press, 2006), p. 60. Moultrie and others insisted that twenty-five thousand blacks had been taken away from Charleston, many of them illegally.

78. Pybus, p. 59; "An Account of the Life of Mr. David George . . . ," in Carretta, ed., p. 336. Carretta's note that George left for Nova Scotia with Major General James Patterson cannot be supported: Patterson was in Halifax throughout this period, and could not have been the "Major P." George names as a patron in Charleston. Both Pybus and Carretta state that George left on November 19, but the only recorded Halifax convoy appears to have sailed in October—with almost exactly the number of loyalists George estimated.

79. Report of numbers of loyalists leaving Charleston for Halifax, October 20, 1782, in *Report on American Manuscripts*, III, p. 179.

80. Henry Nase Diary, November 27 and 30, 1782, p. 15, NBM.

81. William Johnston is named in the "Commission for the examination of Negroes," n.d., NYPL: Alexander Leslie Letterbook. Johnston, p. 74.

82. Major P. Traille to Brigadier General Martin, January 29, 1783, NYPL: Carleton Papers, Box 29, no. 6835. Carleton ordered that the bells be returned, as unlawfully confiscated American property.

83. A return of evacuated civilians is reprinted in Joseph W. Barnwell, "The Evacuation of Charleston by the British," *South Carolina Historical and Genealogical Magazine* 11, no. 1 (January 1910): 26. For the order of evacuation, see *Magazine of American History with Notes and Queries*, vol. 8 (New York: A. S. Barnes and Company, 1882), pp. 826–30.

84. Cruden to Morris, August 15, 1782, LOC: Lovering-Taylor Family Papers.

85. Richard B. Morris, *The Peacemakers: The Great Powers and American Independence* (New York: Harper and Row, 1965). Oswald's career is explored in detail by David Hancock, *Citizens of the World: London Merchants and the Integration of the British Atlantic Community, 1735–85* (Cambridge, U.K.: Cambridge University Press, 1995).

86. John Jay, "The Peace Negotiations of 1782–1783," in Justin Winsor, ed., *Narrative and Critical History of America* (Boston: Houghton Mifflin, 1888), p. 137.

87. See Shelburne to Henry Strachey, October 20, 1782, LOC: Papers of Henry Strachey, ff. 93–94.

88. Adams, quoted in Isaacson, p. 414.

89. Benjamin Franklin to Richard Oswald, November 6 and 26, 1782, in Benjamin Franklin et al., *Memoirs of Benjamin Franklin* (Philadelphia: McCarty & Davis, 1834), I, pp. 460–64.

90. "The Last Will and Testament of Benjamin Franklin," http://sln.fi.edu /franklin/family/lastwill.html, accessed December 27, 2009.

91. Isaacson, p. 415.

92. Henry Laurens, "Journal of Voyage, Capture, and Confinement," NYPL. Laurens's treatment was not improved by the friendly overtures made by his fellow inmate Lord George Gordon—an anti-Catholic demagogue who had incited the greatest riots in London history—who invited Laurens to take a walk with him around the Tower. The prison governor "swore like a Trooper" on the news and forbade Laurens

from walking anywhere beyond his cell door. Laurens got into further trouble when Gordon sent him a piece of cake.

93. Morris, pp. 381–82.

Chapter Three: A New World Disorder

1. Thomas Townshend to Sir Guy Carleton, February 16, 1783, NYPL: Carleton Papers, Box 30, no. 6917.

2. William Smith, *Historical Memoirs of William Smith, 1778–1783*, ed. W. H. W. Sabine (New York: New York Times and Arno Press, 1971), p. 574.

3. Townshend to Carleton, February 16, 1783, NYPL: Carleton Papers, Box 30, no. 6917.

4. Carleton to Lord Sydney, March 15, 1783, NYPL: Carleton Papers, Box 30, no. 7139.

5. John Parr to Sydney, Halifax, June 6, 1783, NA: CO 217/56, f. 89.

6. "Return of Ordinance proposed for Roseway," March 2, 1783, NYPL: Carleton Papers, Box 30, no. 7049.

7. "List of items sent out to Nova Scotia," NYPL: Carleton Papers, Box 32, no. 7631.

8. Carleton to Parr, April 26, 1783, NYPL: Carleton Papers, Box 32, no. 7557.

9. "Memoirs of the Life of Boston King, a Black Preacher," reproduced in Vincent Carretta, ed., *Unchained Voices: An Anthology of Black Authors in the English-Speaking World of the Eighteenth Century* (Lexington: University of Kentucky Press, 1996), pp. 352–56.

10. Early American Imprints, Series 1, no. 44375.

11. For a published edition of the Book of Negroes, see Graham Russell Hodges, ed., *The Black Loyalist Directory: African Americans in Exile after the American Revolution* (New York: Garland Publications, 1995). The April fleet carried 660 black men, women, and children to Nova Scotia. Cassandra Pybus, *Epic Journeys of Freedom: Runaway Slaves of the American Revolution and their Global Quest for Liberty* (Boston: Beacon Press, 2006), p. 66.

12. Smith, pp. 585–87.

13. George Washington to Carleton, May 6, 1783, and Carleton to George Washington, May 12, 1783, NYPL: Carleton Papers, Box 32, nos. 7637 and 7666.

14. Christopher Leslie Brown, "Empire without Slaves: British Concepts of Emancipation in the Age of the American Revolution," *William and Mary Quarterly* 56, no. 2 (April 1999): 276–81. Carleton had personally recruited Morgann from the Earl of Shelburne's office, recognizing Morgann's remarkable talents. The Welsh polymath had also ventured into Shakespeare criticism, penning an influential treatise on the character of Sir John Falstaff.

15. Quoted in Catherine S. Crary, ed., *The Price of Loyalty: Tory Writings from the Revolutionary Era* (New York: McGraw-Hill, 1973), pp. 391–92.

16. Carleton to Townshend, May 27, 1783, NYPL: Carleton Papers, Box 32, no. 7783.

17. Deposition of Oliver De Lancey, May 20, 1783, NYPL: Carleton Papers, Box 32, no. 7727. See also depositions of John Fowler (no. 7728) and Robert Hunt (no. 7738).

18. Newspaper report, May 23, 1783, NYPL: Carleton Papers, Box 32, no. 7796.

19. "TO All Adherents to the British Government and Followers of the British

Army Commonly called TORIES Who are present Within the City and County of New-York," August 15, 1783, Early American Imprints, Series 1, no. 44464.

20. "Extract of a Letter from Port Roseway, dated May 25," *Royal Gazette* (New York), June 7, 1783.

21. "Extract of a Letter from Port Roseway . . . dated the 29th June 1783," *Royal Gazette* (New York), July 19, 1783.

22. "Extract of a letter from a gentleman in St. John's, Bay of Fundy. . . . ," *Royal Gazette* (New York), August 9, 1783.

23. "To those LOYAL REFUGEES who either have already left, or who hereafter may leave their respective Countries, in search of other Habitations," *Royal Gazette* (New York), April 20, 1783.

24. *Royal Gazette* (New York), June 28, 1783, p. 3.

25. "Extract of a late Letter from New-York," *Providence Gazette*, September 6, 1783.

26. "Account of sundry Stores sold at public auction, by order of the Commissary General, and pr. Particular account in his Office," July 24, 1783, NYPL: Carleton Papers, Box 35, no. 8515.

27. See advertisement in *Royal Gazette* (New York), August 16, 1783.

28. "List of Sundry distressed Loyalists who have take[n] Refuge within the British Lines at New York to whom the following allowances are recommended for their support from 4th January to 31 March 1783 inclusive," NYPL: Carleton Papers, Box 31, no. 7258. In the second quarter of 1783, the commissioners paid £7,400 to 454 refugees: "List of Persons recommended by the Board appointed by His Excellency the Commander in Chief to consider the circumstances and claims of distressed Loyalists, for their support from 1st April to 30th June 1783 inclusive," NYPL: Carleton Papers, Box 34, no. 8252. Over the second half of 1782, British officers had paid £12,000 sterling in relief for New York refugees. See précis in NYPL: Carleton Papers, Box 29, no. 6843.

29. Diary of Sir Frederick Philipse Robinson, n.d., RMC, pp. 10–11.

30. Beverley Robinson to Sir Henry Clinton, quoted in Judith L. Van Buskirk, *Generous Enemies: Patriots and Loyalists in Revolutionary New York* (Philadelphia: University of Pennsylvania Press, 2002), p. 157.

31. Cortlandt Skinner to Lord Sydney, March 7, 1783, NA: FO 4/1, f. 18; Skinner to Lord North, October 5, 1783, BL: North Papers, Add. Mss. 61864, f. 34.

32. Beverley Robinson to Carleton, June 6, 1783, NYPL: Carleton Papers, Box 33, no. 7911.

33. For these figures see the appendix; cf. Philip Ranlet, *The New York Loyalists* (Knoxville: University of Tennessee Press, 1986), pp. 193–94.

34. Diary of Sir Frederick Philipse Robinson, n.d., RMC, p. 13.

35. Smith, pp. 615–16.

36. Elizabeth Johnston to William Johnston, January 3, 1783, PANS: Almon Family Papers, reel 10362.

37. Elizabeth Lichtenstein Johnston, *Recollections of a Georgia Loyalist* (New York: M. F. Mansfield and Company, 1901), pp. 74–75.

38. A total of 2,917 whites and 4,448 blacks arrived on the convoys from Georgia and South Carolina: "A Return of Refugees and their Slaves arrived in the Province of East Florida from the Provinces of Georgia and South Carolina taken upon Oath to the 23rd December 1782," NA: CO 5/560, p. 507. "A Return of Refugees & their Slaves arrived in this Province from Charlestown, at the time of the Evacuation thereof & not included in the last return, the 31st Decembr 1783 [*sic*]," April 20, 1783,

NYPL: Carleton Papers, Box 31, no. 7468. The estimate of twelve thousand was widely offered by contemporaries: see, for instance, Lord Hawke's "Observations on East Florida," in John Walton Caughey, ed., *East Florida, 1783–85: A File of Documents Assembled, and Many of Them Translated by Joseph Byrne Lockey* (Berkeley and Los Angeles: University of California Press, 1949), pp. 120–21.

39. Patrick Tonyn to Lord Shelburne, November 14, 1782, NA: CO 5/560, pp. 469–70.

40. Bernard Bailyn, *Voyagers to the West: A Passage in the Peopling of British North America on the Eve of the Revolution* (New York: Vintage, 1988), p. 440. Charles Loch Mowat, *East Florida as a British Province, 1763–1784* (Berkeley and Los Angeles: University of California Press, 1943), pp. 60–61.

41. Carole Watterson Troxler, "Refuge, Resistance, and Reward: The Southern Loyalists' Claim on East Florida," *Journal of Southern History* 55, no. 4 (November 1989): 586–87. William Johnston's brothers Andrew and Lewis Johnston Jr. had as early as November 1776 signed a petition to Tonyn requesting tracts of land to settle on: Wilbur Henry Siebert, *Loyalists in East Florida, 1774 to 1785: The Most Important Documents Pertaining Thereto, Edited with an Accompanying Narrative*, 2 vols. (Deland: Florida State Historical Society, 1929), I, p. 48.

42. Bailyn, pp. 451–61; Linda Colley, *The Ordeal of Elizabeth Marsh: A Woman in World History* (London: HarperPress, 2007), pp. 124–32.

43. Edward J. Cashin, *The King's Ranger: Thomas Brown and the American Revolution on the Southern Frontier* (New York: Fordham University Press, 1999), p. 159.

44. Troxler, pp. 587–90.

45. "A Memoir of the Life of William Charles Wells, Written by Himself," in William Charles Wells, *Two Essays: One on Single Vision with Two Eyes; the Other on Dew* (London: Constable, 1818), pp. xx–xxii. The *East Florida Gazette* was published under John Wells's name, but William Charles Wells's memoir clarifies his own involvement. Three issues survive: see *Facsimiles of the extant issues of the first Florida newspaper. . . .*, intr. Douglas C. McMurtrie (Evanston, Ill.: privately printed, 1942).

46. John Cruden to C. Nisbet, March 25, 1783, NYPL: Carleton Papers, Box 30, no. 7213.

47. James Clitherall to John Cruden, May 25, 1783, NYPL: Carleton Papers, Box 32, no. 7766.

48. Clitherall to Cruden, May 31, 1783, NYPL: Carleton Papers, Box 32, no. 7834; Cruden to J. K. Rutledge, David Ramsay, Ralph Izard, and John Lewis Gervais, May 31, 1783, NYPL: Carleton Papers, Box 32, no. 7832; and Cruden to Major MacKenzie, June 5, 1783, NYPL: Carleton Papers, Box 33, no. 7891. Cruden also placed an advertisement in the *East Florida Gazette* of May 3, 1783, "ordering all persons holding negroes that were sequestrated, in Carolina to give in a list of their names and also the names of their owners."

49. See Cruden to Lord North, August 22, 1783, NA: FO 4/1, ff. 63–66.

50. This was the spirit in which Cruden approached patriot Robert Morris, who had essentially bankrolled the American war effort, with a scheme to corner the Atlantic tobacco market. "I could lay before you a Variety of matters that would give you sattisfaction, & that might prove highly beneficial to you as an individual & to your family for Ever," he hinted mysteriously. John Cruden to Robert Morris, August 15, 1782, LOC: Lovering-Taylor Family Papers. Morris responded favorably to Cruden's scheme: Morris to Cruden, August 5 and 13, 1782, in John Catanzariti and E. James Ferguson, eds., *The Papers of Robert Morris, 1781–84*, vol. 6 (Pittsburgh: University of Pittsburgh Press, 1984), pp. 137, 157.

51. Elizabeth Johnston to William Johnston, April 20, 1783, PANS: Almon Family Papers, reel 10362. Johnston misremembered the year as 1784 in her memoir (Johnston, p. 75).

52. John Cruden, "An Address to the Monarchical and Thinking Part of the British Empire," BL: North Papers, Add. Mss. 61864, f. 141.

53. J. Mullryne Tattnall to John Street, May 30–August 28, 1783, NA: CO 5/560, ff. 483–86. This formula echoes, however unconsciously, George III's valedictory words to Lord North.

54. David Fanning, *The Adventures of David Fanning in the American Revolutionary War*, ed. A. W. Savary (Ottawa: Golden Dog Press, 1983), p. 64.

55. "Substance of Talks delivered at a conference by the Indians to His Excellency Governor Tonyn, Colonel McArthur, and the Superintendent," May 15, 1783, NA: CO 5/560, pp. 617–19.

56. On the McGillivray family, see, among others, Edward J. Cashin, *Lachlan McGillivray, Indian Trader: The Shaping of the Southern Colonial Frontier* (Athens: University of Georgia Press, 1992); John Walton Caughey, *McGillivray of the Creeks* (Norman: University of Oklahoma Press, 1938); and Claudio Saunt, *A New Order of Things: Property, Power and the Transformation of the Creek Indians, 1733–1816* (Cambridge, U.K.: Cambridge University Press, 1999), pp. 67–89.

57. Alexander McGillivray to Thomas Brown, August 30, 1783, NA: CO 5/82, f. 405.

58. Brown to Carleton, April 26, 1783, NYPL: Carleton Papers, Box 32, no. 7556.

59. Brown to Carleton, May 15, 1783, NYPL: Carleton Papers, Box 32, no. 7688. Colin G. Calloway, *The American Revolution in Indian Country: Crisis and Diversity in Native American Communities* (Cambridge, U.K.: Cambridge University Press, 1995), p. 248.

60. Quoted in Calloway, pp. 26.

61. Cashin, *The King's Ranger*, pp. 163–67; William S. Coker and Thomas D. Watson, *Indian Traders of the Southeastern Spanish Borderlands: Panton, Leslie & Company and John Forbes & Company, 1783–1847* (Pensacola: University of West Florida Press, 1986), pp. 49–55.

62. Tonyn to Sydney, December 6, 1784, quoted in Caughey, ed., *East Florida*, pp. 324–25.

63. Quoted in Thomas Nixon to Evan Nepean, October 22, 1783, NA: CO 5/560, p. 848.

64. Tonyn to North, September 11, 1783, NA: CO 5/560, p. 685.

65. Tonyn to Sydney, May 15, 1783, NA: CO 5/560, pp. 585–86.

66. Lewis Johnston to unknown recipient, July 14, 1783, NA: CO 5/560, pp. 927–33. On Johnston in St. Kitts, see Alexander A. Lawrence, *James Johnston: Georgia's First Printer* (Savannah: Pigeonhole Press, 1956), p. 3.

67. Elizabeth Johnston to William Johnston, October 11, 1783, November 10, 1783, January 2, 1784, January 15, 1784, PANS: Almon Family Papers, reel 10362.

68. Elizabeth Johnston to William Johnston, February 12, 1784, PANS: Almon Family Papers, reel 10362.

69. Elizabeth Johnston to William Johnston, April 6, 1784, PANS: Almon Family Papers, reel 10362.

70. Elizabeth Johnston to William Johnston, November 10, 1783, and February 3, 1784, PANS: Almon Family Papers, reel 10362.

71. "Return of Persons who Emigrated from East Florida to different parts of the British Dominions," William Brown, May 2, 1786, NA: CO 5/561, f. 407.

72. Tattnall to Street, May 30–August 28, 1783, NA: CO 5/560, ff. 483–86.

73. Cruden was referring here to the legend of Madoc, the Welsh prince believed to have discovered America in the twelfth century. For a contemporary discussion of Welsh Indians, see John Williams, L.L.D., *An Enquiry into the Truth of the Tradition, Concerning the Discovery of America, by Prince Madog ab Owen Gwynedd, about the Year, 1170* (London: J. Brown, 1791).

74. Fragment dated June 30, 1784, LOC: East Florida Papers, Reel 82, Bundle 195M15.

75. Tonyn to Cruden, St. Augustine, May 26, 1784, quoted in Caughey, ed., *East Florida*, pp. 195–96.

76. Vicente Manuel de Zéspedes to Bernardo de Gálvez, July 16, 1784, quoted in Caughey, ed., *East Florida*, p. 231.

77. James Cruden to Sir Robert Keith, November 24, 1784, BL: Add. Mss. 35533, f. 141.

78. Quoted in Siebert, I, p. 169.

79. "Petition of the Loyalists to the Spanish King," October 28, 1784, LOC: East Florida Papers, Reel 82, Bundle 195M15. A copy of this text appears in Caughey, ed., *East Florida*, pp. 301–2.

80. Cruden to Carlos Howard, December 8, 1784, LOC: East Florida Papers, Reel 82, Bundle 195M15. A copy of this text appears in Caughey, ed., *East Florida*, pp. 431–32.

81. Cruden to Howard, March 10, 1785, and Cruden to Zéspedes, March 10, 1785, quoted in Caughey, ed., *East Florida*, pp. 485–87.

82. Zéspedes to Gálvez, March 23, 1785, quoted in Caughey, ed., *East Florida*, p. 484.

83. Cruden to North, May 16, 1785, BL: North Papers, Add. Mss. 61864, ff. 133–34.

84. Zéspedes imputed as much when he wrote to Tonyn that "I cannot but think it strange that Senr Cruden in a Manifesto dated in the month of November last appears to be informed of part of the contents of my letter to your Excellency" (Zéspedes to Tonyn, April 11, 1785, quoted in Caughey, ed., *East Florida*, pp. 587–88). He found the ex-governor "hypercritical and suspicious," and discovered "a number of intrigues" plotted by Tonyn's friends and presumably "entered into with his approval." (Zéspedes to Gálvez, June 6, 1785, quoted in Caughey, ed., *East Florida*, pp. 552–53).

85. "Return of Persons who Emigrated from East Florida to different parts of the British Dominions," William Brown, May 2, 1786, NA: CO 5/561, f. 407.

86. Tonyn to Sydney, April 4, 1785, quoted in Caughey, ed., *East Florida*, p. 500; Tonyn to Sydney, August 29, 1785, NA: CO 5/561, f. 353; Tonyn to Sydney, August 10, 1785, NA: CO 5/561, f. 235; Tonyn to Sydney, September 15, 1785, quoted in Caughey, ed., *East Florida*, p. 721; Tonyn to Sydney, November 10, 1785, quoted in Caughey, ed., *East Florida*, pp. 738–39.

87. Tonyn to Lord Hawke, April 4, 1785, quoted in Caughey, *East Florida*, ed., p. 536.

88. Siebert, I, p. 177.

Chapter Four: The Heart of Empire

1. Louisa Susannah Wells, *The Journal of a Voyage from Charlestown to London* (New York: Arno Press, 1968; repr. New-York Historical Society, 1906), pp. 61–62, 78.

2. Mary Beth Norton and Eliga Gould, among others, cite this quote as typical of

loyalist attitudes about Britain; but my own research suggests that it is quite exceptional. Eliga Gould, *The Persistence of Empire: British Political Culture in the Age of the American Revolution* (Chapel Hill: University of North Carolina Press, 2000), p. 205; Mary Beth Norton, *The British-Americans: The Loyalist Exiles in England, 1774–1789* (London: Constable, 1974), p. 42. My analysis in this chapter owes much to Norton's definitive study.

3. Americans visiting Britain before the revolution often expressed a similar feeling that "home" reinforced their provincial identities: Susan Lindsey Liveley, "Going Home: Americans in Britain, 1740–1776" (Ph.D. dissertation, Harvard University, 1996). For the loyalist response, see Norton, esp. pp. 41–61.

4. Quoted in Lively, pp. 277–78.

5. Diary of Edward Oxnard, October 5, 1775, March 21, 1776, UNB: MIC-Loyalist FC LFR.09E3J6.

6. Oxnard, November 29, 1775, UNB: MIC-Loyalist FC LFR.09E3J6.

7. Oxnard, March 27, 1776, UNB: MIC-Loyalist FC LFR.09E3J6.

8. Samuel Curwen, *The Journal of Samuel Curwen, Loyalist*, ed. Andrew Oliver, 2 vols. (Cambridge, Mass.: Harvard University Press, 1972), I, p. 37.

9. Oxnard, November 13, 1775, UNB: MIC-Loyalist FC LFR.09E3J6.

10. Oxnard, October 18, 1776, UNB: MIC-Loyalist FC LFR.09E3J6.

11. Curwen, I, p. 162.

12. Oxnard, February 8, 1776, UNB: MIC-Loyalist FC LFR.09E3J6; Norton, pp. 73–76. He also attended a meeting of the Robin Hood Society, a debating society, at which the question was posed "whether it is equitable & Right that the Congress should confiscate the Estates of the Refugees in England." The measure was "determined to be unjust by a great majority" (September 14, 1775).

13. See, among others, Oxnard's lament on his thirtieth birthday: "May Heaven grant me a happy sight of my native land before the return of another Birth day. Driven by the unhappy situation of my once happy Country, to see that peace in a foreign Clime, which was denied me in my own, my anxiety since I left it is not to be expressed by words." Oxnard, July 30, 1777, UNB: MIC-Loyalist FC LFR.09E3J6; John Watts to Robert Watts, April 19, 1779, NYHS: Robert Watts Papers, Box 2; Curwen, II, p. 607.

14. John Watts to Robert Watts, March 31, 1784, NYHS: Robert Watts Papers, Box 2.

15. Stephen Conway, *The British Isles and the War of American Independence* (Oxford: Oxford University Press, 2000), p. 54. For an excellent summary of the effects of the war on Britain, see John Cannon, "The Loss of America," in H. T. Dickinson, ed., *Britain and the American Revolution* (Harlow, U.K.: Addison Wesley Longman, 1998), pp. 233–57.

16. Diary of Sir Frederick Philipse Robinson, n.d., RMC, p. 14. Oxnard, September 13, October 26, 1775, UNB: MIC-Loyalist FC LFR.09E3J6.

17. Diary of Samuel Shoemaker, October 10, 1784, NYHS, pp. 248–50.

18. Linda Colley, *Britons: Forging the Nation, 1707–1837* (New Haven, Conn.: Yale University Press, 1992), chapter 5.

19. There were of course pre-revolutionary precedents: see Brendan McConville, *The King's Three Faces: The Rise and Fall of Royal America, 1688–1776* (Chapel Hill: University of North Carolina Press, 2006). On the cultivation of imperial royalism after 1783, see C. A. Bayly, *Imperial Meridian: The British Empire and the World, 1780–1830* (London: Longman, 1989); David Cannadine, *Ornamentalism: How the British Saw Their Empire* (New York: Oxford University Press, 2001); Bernard Cohn, "Representing Authority in Victorian India," in Eric Hobsbawm and Terence Ranger, eds., *The*

Invention of Tradition (Cambridge, U.K.: Cambridge University Press, 1992), pp. 165–209; Miles Taylor, "Queen Victoria and India, 1837–61," *Victorian Studies* 46, no. 2 (Winter 2004): 264–74.

20. Debate of February 17, 1783, *Cobbett's Parliamentary History of England*, vol. 23 (London: T. C. Hansard, 1814), columns 452–53 (North), 460 (Mulgrave), 468 (Burke), 524 (Bootle), 481 (Sheridan), 492 (Lee).

21. Debate of February 17, 1783, *Parliamentary History*, vol. 23, columns 503, 571. The original motion of censure came in two parts, the first challenging the territorial concessions, and the second stating that "this House do feel the regard due from this nation to every description of men, who, with the risk of their lives, and the sacrifice of their property, have distinguished their loyalty." Once the first motion passed, the second was withdrawn.

22. Debate of February 17, 1783, *Parliamentary History*, vol. 23, column 438.

23. Debate of February 17, 1783, *Parliamentary History*, vol. 23, columns 564–70. Wilmot is sometimes confused with his father, Sir John Eardley Wilmot, chief justice of the Court of Common Pleas—see, e.g., Simon Schama, *Rough Crossings: Britain, the Slaves, and the American Revolution* (London: BBC Books, 2005), p. 177. In 1812 Wilmot added "Eardley" to his surname by royal license to become John Eardley Eardley-Wilmot, under which name he published his memoir of service on the Loyalist Claims Commission. His son, Sir John Eardley Eardley-Wilmot, pursued the family career trajectory as a lawyer, member of Parliament, and colonial governor. See "Sir John Eardley Wilmot," "John Eardley Eardley-Wilmot," "Sir John Eardley Eardley-Wilmot," q.v., *DNB*.

24. Norton, pp. 54–55, 111–15, 119; John Eardley-Wilmot, *Historical View of the Commission for Enquiring into the Losses, Services, and Claims of the American Loyalists*, intr. George Athan Billias (Boston: Gregg Press, 1972), pp. 15–22. Samuel Curwen described the procedure in his diary entries for late October 1782: Curwen, II, pp. 864–66.

25. Francis Green to Ward Chipman, February 7, 1783, LAC: Ward Chipman Fonds, Reel C-1179, p. 608.

26. *The Case and Claim of the American Loyalists, Impartially Stated and Considered, Printed by Order of their Agents* (London, 1783). Galloway raised very similar points in his *Observations on the Fifth Article of the Treaty with America, and on the Necessity of appointing a Judicial Enquiry into the Merits and Losses of the American Loyalists, Printed by Order of their Agents.* (London: G. Wilkie, 1783)—hence my suggestion that he may have had a hand in writing *The Case and Claim*.

27. On the Marsh family, see Linda Colley, *The Ordeal of Elizabeth Marsh: A Woman in World History* (London: HarperPress, 2007).

28. *The Parliamentary Register,* 112 vols. (London: J. Debrett, 1775–1813), vol. 10, pp. 204–5, pp. 308–9; Norton, p. 192; Eardley-Wilmot, p. 45.

29. H. T. Dickinson, "The Poor Palatines and the Parties," *English Historical Review* 82, no. 324 (July 1967): pp. 464–85; Daniel Statt, *Foreigners and Englishmen: The Controversy over Immigration and Population, 1660–1760* (Newark: University of Delaware Press, 1995), chapters 5–6.

30. George Chalmers, *Opinions on Interesting Subjects of Public Law and Commercial Policy, Arising from American Independence* (London, 1784), p. 8.

31. On Robinson's land: Peter Wilson Coldham, *American Migrations: The Lives, Times, and Families of Colonial Americans Who Remained Loyal to the British Crown* (Baltimore: Genealogical Publishing Company, 2000), p. 327. This volume serves as an invaluable index to the loyalist claims.

32. Beverley Robinson to Ann Barclay Robinson, February 24, 1784, NBM: Robinson Family Papers, Folder 2.

33. Joanna Robinson to Beverley Robinson Jr., February 6, 1784, NBM: Robinson Family Papers, Folder 7; Joanna Robinson to Ann Barclay Robinson, March 9, 1784, and October 29 [1784], NBM: Robinson Family Papers, Folder 10.

34. Frederick Philipse Robinson to Beverley Robinson Jr., n.d. NBM: Robinson Family Papers, Folder 14.

35. Joanna Robinson to Ann Barclay Robinson, October 29 [1784], NBM: Robinson Family Papers, Folder 10.

36. Joanna Robinson to Beverley Robinson Jr., February 6, 1784, NBM: Robinson Family Papers, Folder 7.

37. Beverley Robinson to Ann Barclay Robinson, November 29, 1784, NBM: Robinson Family Papers, Folder 2.

38. Joanna Robinson to Beverley Robinson Jr., February 6, 1784, NBM: Robinson Family Papers, Folder 7.

39. Joanna Robinson to Ann Barclay Robinson, October 29 [1784], NBM: Robinson Family Papers, Folder 10.

40. See, e.g., Bourdieu, Chollet, and Bourdieu to Alexander Wallace, September 27, 1783, LOC: Papers of Nicholas Low, Container 3.

41. Shoemaker Diary, January 30 and February 17, 1784, NYHS, pp. 42, 55.

42. Shoemaker Diary, January 17, 1784, NYHS, p. 28. Another loyalist remarked that "by contrary winds & calms we were tossed on the Ocean for Six Weeks before we reach'd Dover, & must now add that ever since my arrival I have been equally disagreeably toss'd about from one public office to another, & Heaven only knows when I shall get safe into Harbour." (Jonathan Mallet to Robert Watts, July 12, 1784, NYHS: Robert Watts Papers, Box 2.)

43. Isaac Low to Nicholas Low, March 3, 1784, LOC: Papers of Nicholas Low, Container 1.

44. Isaac Low to Nicholas Low, February 6, 1784, LOC: Papers of Nicholas Low, Container 1.

45. Isaac Low to Nicholas Low, March 3, 1784, LOC: Papers of Nicholas Low, Container 1.

46. Isaac Low to Nicholas Low, April 7, 1784, LOC: Papers of Nicholas Low, Container 1.

47. Isaac Low to Nicholas Low, August 4, 1784, LOC: Papers of Nicholas Low, Container 1.

48. Isaac Low to Nicholas Low, September 1, 1784, LOC: Papers of Nicholas Low, Container 1.

49. Isaac Low to Nicholas Low, November 30, 1784, LOC: Papers of Nicholas Low, Container 1.

50. Isaac Low to Nicholas Low, January 31, 1784. Isaac Jr. showed off his fancy education in a letter to his uncle Nicholas—written in French. There were only eight boys in the select academy, he said, "deux desquels sont Américains & avec qui j'étois dans la même Classe à la nouvelle Yorke." Isaac Low Jr. to Nicholas Low, May 4, 1785, LOC: Papers of Nicholas Low, Container 1.

51. Petition of Alicia Young, December 23, 1785, NA: AO 13/67, f. 633. Claim of Alicia Young, in Coldham, p. 375.

52. Claim of Sarah Baker, in Coldham, p. 46.

53. Claim of Donald McDougal, in Coldham, p. 629.

54. Claim of Archibald McDonald, in Coldham, p. 770.

55. Memorial of Shadrack Furman, NA: AO 13/59, ff. 658–59.

56. Claim of Benjamin Whitecuffe, in Coldham, p. 368; Cassandra Pybus, *Epic Journeys of Freedom: Runaway Slaves of the American Revolution and Their Global Quest for Liberty* (Boston: Beacon Press, 2006), pp. 79–81; Schama, pp. 174–77.

57. Quoted in Schama, pp. 179–80.

58. Gilbert Francklyn, *Observations, Occasioned by the Attempts Made in England to Effect the Abolition of the Slave Trade, Shewing the Manner in which Negroes are Treated in the British Colonies, in the West Indies* (Kingston and Liverpool: A. Smith, 1788), p. vi.

59. Stephen J. Braidwood, *Black Poor and White Philanthropists: London's Blacks and the Foundation of the Sierra Leone Settlement, 1786–91* (Liverpool: University of Liverpool Press, 1994), pp. 64–66.

60. Braidwood, pp. 63–69.

61. Braidwood, pp. 70–93.

62. Braidwood, pp. 97–102.

63. Eardley-Wilmot, p. 50. For pound sterling value conversions, I have used the purchasing power calculator at http://www.measuringworth.com/ppoweruk/, which estimates that £1 in 1784 had the purchasing power of £97.44 in 2007.

64. It must be noted that different figures available for the total number of loyalist claims do not always square with one another. The figure of 3,225 comes from the commission's "Statement of the Claims and Losses of the American Loyalists up to the 25th of March 1790" presented to Parliament in that year (Eardley-Wilmot, p. 90). This number seems in keeping with the figure of 3,157 claims presented in the commission's last formal report, of June 1789 (Eardley-Wilmot, appendix VIII, pp. 196–97). But a "general statement" of the number of claims submitted to the commission lists 5,072 "Claims including those in Nova Scotia and Canada," of which 954 were "withdrawn, or not prosecuted" (Eardley-Wilmot, appendix IX, p. 199). And Coldham's summary of claims by province yields 5,656 claims for the thirteen colonies (Coldham, appendix IV, p. 834).

65. For a thorough analysis see Wallace Brown, *The King's Friends: The Composition and Motives of the American Loyalist Claimants* (Providence, R.I.: Brown University Press, 1965).

66. Eugene R. Fingerhut, "Uses and Abuses of the American Loyalists' Claims: A Critique of Quantitative Analysis," *William & Mary Quarterly* 25, no. 2 (April 1968): 245–58.

67. Traveling to London to file a claim served as the opening gambit for a picaresque novel about the American Revolution, *Adventures of Jonathan Corncob, loyal American refugee* (London, 1787).

68. Mary Beth Norton, "Eighteenth-Century American Women in Peace and War: The Case of the Loyalists," *William & Mary Quarterly*, 3rd ser., 33, no. 3 (1976): 388; Mary Beth Norton, "The Fate of Some Black Loyalists of the American Revolution," *Journal of Negro History* 58, no. 4 (October 1973): 417. Pybus puts the number of black claimants at forty-five (Pybus, *Epic Journeys*, p. 81).

69. I counted 281 based on the précis of claims provided in Coldham.

70. One pair in County Down who filed late pleaded illiteracy and the fact that they lived "in remote parts where newspapers were seldom received." Claims of Thomas Burns and William Henry, in Coldham, pp. 452–53, 464.

71. Claim of Lewis Johnston Jr., NA: AO 13/36A, ff. 82–89.

72. "A Loyalist," *Directions to the American Loyalists, in Order to Enable Them to State Their Cases, by Way of Memorial, to the Honourable the Commissioners Appointed (by Statute the 23. Geo. III. C. 80.) to Inquire into the Losses and Services of Those Persons Who Have*

Suffered, in Consequences of Their Loyalty to This Majesty, and Their Attachment to the British Government, by a Loyalist (London: W. Flexney, 1783), pp. 22–24.

73. Eardley-Wilmot, pp. 45–49, 58. Their notes have been published in Alexander Fraser, *Second Report of the Bureau of Archives for the Province of Ontario*, 2 parts (Toronto: L. K. Cameron, 1904–5).

74. William Smith, *The Diary and Selected Papers, 1784–1793*, ed. L. F. S. Upton, 2 vols. (Toronto: Champlain Society, 1963–65), I, pp. 34–35.

75. Thomas Coke, *A History of the West Indies*, 3 vols. (Liverpool: Nutter, Fishall, and Dixon, 1808), pp. 132, 246–47, 353–54.

76. Smith, I, p. 207.

77. Shoemaker Diary, July 16, 1784, NYHS, p. 177.

78. Shoemaker Diary, December 9, 1784, NYHS, 292; Coke, pp. 283–84.

79. William Jarvis to Munson Jarvis, May 23, 1787, NBM: Jarvis Family Collection, Folder 27.

80. Nine, according to the 1789 report (Eardley-Wilmot, appendix VIII, p. 188). A conspicuous fraud was the claim of John Ferdinand Dalziel Smyth, author of the 1784 *A Tour in the United States of America*, known for his predilection for exaggeration. Smyth later adopted the surname Stuart and purported to be a descendant of Charles II. ("John Ferdinand Smyth Stuart," q.v., *DNB*; Coke, pp. 127–32.) Shoemaker Diary, July 31, 1784, p. 191.

81. Isaac Low to Nicholas Low, September 3, 1785, LOC: Papers of Nicholas Low, Container 1.

82. Shoemaker Diary, December 9, 1784, NYHS, p. 292.

83. Smith, II, pp. 36, 63–64.

84. Claim of William Cooper, in Coldham, p. 672.

85. Pybus, *Epic Journeys*, pp. 76–79.

86. Norton, "Eighteenth-Century American Women," pp. 396–97.

87. Coke, pp. 53–55; Claim of Jane Gibbes, NYPL: Loyalist Transcripts, vol. 52, pp. 365–85.

88. Claim of Jane Stanhouse, in Coldham, p. 649.

89. John Watts to Robert and John Watts, February 2, 1785, NYHS: Robert Watts Papers, Box 2.

90. Isaac Low to Nicholas Low, September 3, 1785, LOC: Papers of Nicholas Low, Container 1.

91. Alexander Wallace to Nicholas Low, September 15, 1785, LOC: Papers of Nicholas Low, Container 2.

92. Quoted in Eardley-Wilmot, pp. 142–44.

93. John Watts to Robert Watts, March 26, 1787, NYHS: Robert Watts Papers, Box 2.

94. William Jarvis to Munson Jarvis, July 9, 1787, NBM: Jarvis Family Collection, Folder 27.

95. Alexander Wallace to Nicholas Low, August 18, 1786, LOC: Papers of Nicholas Low, Container 2.

96. Alexander Wallace to Nicholas Low, June 14, 1785, LOC: Papers of Nicholas Low, Container 2.

97. Alexander Wallace to Nicholas Low, September 15, 1785, LOC: Papers of Nicholas Low, Container 2.

98. Alexander Wallace to Nicholas Low, August 17, 1786, and February 16, 1787, LOC: Papers of Nicholas Low, Container 2.

99. Alexander Wallace to Nicholas Low, October 2, 1787, and February 4, 1788, LOC: Papers of Nicholas Low, Container 2.

100. Isaac Low to Nicholas Low, August 15 and October 3, 1786, LOC: Papers of Nicholas Low, Container 1.

101. Coldham, p. 277.

102. Isaac Low to Nicholas Low, September 7, 1786, LOC: Papers of Nicholas Low, Container 1.

103. Isaac Low to Nicholas Low, September 7, 1786, LOC: Papers of Nicholas Low, Container 1.

104. Isaac Low to Nicholas Low, June 28, 1790, LOC: Papers of Nicholas Low, Container 1.

105. Isaac Low to Nicholas Low, October 16, 1787, LOC: Papers of Nicholas Low, Container 1.

106. Isaac Low Jr. to Nicholas Low, September 5, 1791, LOC: Papers of Nicholas Low, Container 1.

107. Eardley-Wilmot, pp. 90–91; Norton, *The British Americans*, pp. 227–29.

108. *The Trial of Warren Hastings, Late Governor-General of Bengal* (London, 1788), pp. 7–8.

109. *Parliamentary Register*, vol. 23, pp. 597–609.

110. On continuities with the pre-revolutionary empire, see P. J. Marshall, *The Making and Unmaking of Empires: Britain, India, and America, c. 1750–1783* (Oxford: Oxford University Press, 2005), esp. chapter 11. I am expanding on the concept of "moral capital" advanced by Christopher Leslie Brown, *Moral Capital: Foundations of British Abolitionism* (Chapel Hill: University of North Carolina Press, 2006).

111. James Mario Matra, "A Proposal for establishing a Settlement in New South Wales," BL: Add. Mss. 47,568, f. 244.

112. Matra, ff. 242–43. On Matra's life see Alan Frost, *The Precarious Life of James Mario Matra: Voyager with Cook, American Loyalist, Servant of Empire* (Carlton, Victoria: Miegunyah Press, 1995).

113. Pybus provides the only in-depth treatment of loyalists in Australia in *Epic Journeys*.

114. *Parliamentary Register*, vol. 24, pp. 51, 55.

115. Eardley-Wilmot, pp. 98–99.

116. Kirsty Carpenter, *Refugees of the French Revolution: Emigrés in London, 1789–1802* (Basingstoke, U.K.: MacMillan, 1999), pp. 45–47. The committee assisted Catholic priests in particular, a group whom an earlier generation of Britons would have regarded with great suspicion, but who looked positively good to Britons anxious about the threat of godless Jacobins. The Loyalist Claims Commission was explicitly cited as the model for a "Commission for the Relief of Suffering Loyalists" established by the Irish parliament after the rebellion of 1798. See Thomas Bartlett, "Clemency and Compensation: The Treatment of Defeated Rebels and Suffering Loyalists after the 1798 Rebellion," in Jim Smyth, ed., *Revolution, Counter-Revolution, and Union: Ireland in the 1790s* (Cambridge, U.K.: Cambridge University Press, 2000), pp. 119–27.

117. Twelfth Report and Liquidation of Claims, NA: AO 12/109, ff. 112–13.

118. William Henry Robinson to Beverley Robinson Jr., July 22, 1789, NBM: Robinson Family Fonds, Box 1, Folder 6.

119. Diary of Sir Frederick Philipse Robinson, n.d., RMC, pp. 17–22.

120. Sheila L. Skemp, *William Franklin: Son of a Patriot, Servant of a King* (New York: Oxford University Press, 1990), pp. 274–76.

121. Claire Brandt, *The Man in the Mirror: A Life of Benedict Arnold* (New York: Random House, 1994), pp. 259–64.

122. Twelfth Report and Liquidation of Claims, NA: AO 12/109, ff. 73–74, 79–80.

123. Elizabeth Lichtenstein Johnston, *Recollections of a Georgia Loyalist* (New York: M. F. Mansfield and Company, 1901), pp. 78–80.

124. Johnston, p. 79.

125. Elizabeth Johnston to William Johnston, September 11, 1785, PANS: Almon Family Papers, reel 10362.

126. Johnston, p. 80.

Chapter Five: *A World in the Wilderness*

1. Charles Inglis, "Journal of Occurrences, beginning, Wednesday, October 12, 1785," October 16, 1787, LAC: Charles Inglis and Family Fonds, Microfilm A-709.

2. Petition to Sir Guy Carleton, July 22, 1783, NYPL: Carleton Papers, Box 35, no. 8500. Neil MacKinnon, *This Unfriendly Soil: The Loyalist Experience in Nova Scotia, 1783–91* (Kingston, Ont.: McGill–Queen's University Press, 1986), pp. 87–88.

3. Brian Cuthbertson, *The First Bishop: A Biography of Charles Inglis* (Halifax, N.S.: Waegwoltic Press, 1987), pp. 15, 60–61.

4. Cuthbertson, p. 62.

5. Inglis, "Journal," May 30, 1786, LAC: Charles Inglis and Family Fonds, Microfilm A-709.

6. Cuthbertson, pp. 79–89. Judith Fingard, *The Anglican Design in Loyalist Nova Scotia, 1783–1816* (London: SPCK, 1972), chapter 2.

7. Inglis, "Journal," October 16, 1787, LAC: Charles Inglis and Family Fonds, Microfilm A-709.

8. Inglis, "Journal," October 27 and November 5, 1787, LAC: Charles Inglis and Family Fonds, Microfilm A-709.

9. Inglis, "Journal," July 16, 26, 27, 1788, LAC: Charles Inglis and Family Fonds, Microfilm A-709.

10. Cornelia's brother wrote movingly about how "My dear Sister DeLancey is tossed about at the will and pleasure of an unfeeling man, first to the Bahamas and then to cross that wide Atlantic ocean, never I suppose more to behold that man to whom she has place her affection, and Good God who is he a savage who dispises her, who treats her with Disdain." Anthony Barclay to Ann Barclay Robinson, September 15, 1792, NBM: Robinson Papers, Folder 21.

11. Inglis, "Journal," July 28–29, 1788, LAC: Charles Inglis and Family Fonds, Microfilm A-709.

12. Inglis, "Journal," August 1–2, 1788, LAC: Charles Inglis and Family Fonds, Microfilm A-709.

13. The classic treatment of this process remains William J. Cronon, *Changes in the Land: Indians, Colonists and the Ecology of New England* (New York: Hill and Wang, 1983).

14. John Mack Faragher, *A Great and Noble Scheme: The Tragic Story of the Expulsion of the French Acadians from Their American Homeland* (New York: W. W. Norton, 2005), p. 6.

15. The name was bestowed by King James I in 1621, in a grant to its first (Scottish) proprietor, Sir William Alexander. For fresh perspectives on Anglo-French rivalry in Acadia, see John G. Reid, Maurice Basque, Elizabeth Mancke, Barry Moody, Geoffrey Plank, and William Wicken, *The "Conquest" of Acadia, 1710: Imperial, Colonial, and Aboriginal Constructions* (Toronto: University of Toronto Press, 2004).

16. John G. Reid has made the case, however, that indigenous power remained a serious force to be reckoned with in Nova Scotia well into the eighteenth century

(later than has conventionally been recognized), and was only swept away decisively by the loyalist influx. See John G. Reid, "*Pax Britannica* or *Pax Indigena?* Planter Nova Scotia (1760–1782) and Competing Strategies of Pacification," *Canadian Historical Review* 85, no. 4 (December 2004): 669–92; and Emerson W. Baker and John G. Reid, "Amerindian Power in the Early Modern Northeast: A Reappraisal," *William & Mary Quarterly* 61, no. 1 (January 2004): 77–106.

17. Thomas B. Akins, *History of Halifax City* (Halifax, N.S.: n.p., 1895), pp. 5–11. Faragher, pp. 249–51.

18. Faragher, p. 252.

19. Faragher, p. 344.

20. Faragher, pp. 354, 359.

21. Faragher, p. 357.

22. John Bartlet Brebner, *The Neutral Yankees of Nova Scotia: A Marginal Colony during the Revolutionary Years* (New York: Columbia University Press, 1937), p. 94.

23. Planter Nova Scotia has been the subject of several edited volumes: see, e.g., Margaret Conrad, ed., *Making Adjustments: Change and Continuity in Planter Nova Scotia, 1759–1800* (Fredericton, N.B.: Acadiensis Press, 1991).

24. John Robinson and Thomas Rispin, *Journey through Nova-Scotia* (Sackville, N.B.: Ralph Pickard Bell Library, Mount Allison University, 1981; repr. York, 1774).

25. The Micmac population in 1780 has been estimated at three thousand. Philip K. Bock, "Micmac," in Bruce G. Trigger, ed., *Handbook of North American Indians* vol. 15, *The Northeast* (Washington, D.C.: Smithsonian Institution, 1978), p. 117.

26. Jacob Bailey, "A journal containing a variety of incidents," June 21, 1779, PANS: Jacob Bailey Fonds, MG 1 (reel 14900), vol. IV, pp. 4–6, 19–30. Parts of this journal are reproduced in William S. Bartlet, *The Frontier Missionary: A Memoir of the Life of the Rev. Jacob Bailey, A.M.* (Boston: Ide and Dutton, 1853).

27. Bailey, "A journal containing a variety of incidents," June 21, 1779, PANS: Jacob Bailey Fonds, MG 1 (reel 14900), vol. V, p. 10.

28. Bartlet, pp. 168–69.

29. Jacob Bailey to Benjamin Palmer, June 24, 1779, PANS: Jacob Bailey Fonds, MG 1 (reel 14900), item 26, pp. 9–10.

30. Bailey to Major Godwin, June 25, 1779, PANS: Jacob Bailey Fonds, MG 1 (reel 14900), item 26, p. 21.

31. Akins, pp. 75–76.

32. Proceedings of Nova Scotia Council, October 9 to December 23, 1776, NA: CO 217/53, f. 94.

33. Samuel Rogers to Joseph Taylor, June 27, 1776, LOC: Lovering Taylor Papers, Box 1.

34. Elizabeth Mancke, *The Fault Lines of Empire: Political Differentiation in Massachusetts and Nova Scotia, 1760–1830* (New York, Routledge, 2005), pp. 87–94.

35. Mancke, p. 78.

36. "Fragment of a journal of journey to Cornwallis, 1779," August 16, 1779, PANS: Jacob Bailey Fonds, MG 1 (reel 14900), item 27.

37. There are three major studies of revolutionary Nova Scotia. Brebner's classic *The Neutral Yankees of Nova Scotia* stresses the province's isolation and commercial ties to Britain as reasons for neutrality (see esp. chapter 10). Gordon Stewart and George Rawlyk point to the significance of the Great Awakening in turning "Yankees" into "Nova Scotians": Gordon Stewart and George Rawlyk, *A People Highly Favored of God: The Nova Scotia Yankees and the American Revolution* (Toronto: Macmillan of Canada, 1972). Elizabeth Mancke's *Fault Lines of Empire* argues that Nova Scotian loyalism

emanated from the divergent political cultures of Nova Scotia and New England (see esp. chapter 4).

38. MacKinnon, p. 11.

39. John Parr to Charles Grey, quoted in Brebner, p. 352, and MacKinnon, p. 12.

40. Parr to Townshend, October 26, 1782, NA: CO 217/56, f. 2.

41. Parr to Townshend, February 20, 1783, NA: CO 217/56, f. 61.

42. Parr to Townshend, January 15, 1783, NA: CO 217/56, f. 60. The Minute Book of the Port Roseway Association lists 1,507 subscribers to the scheme for 1783. LAC: Shelburne, Nova Scotia Collection, Microfilm H-984, pp. 3–23.

43. Parr to Lord Sydney, June 6 and August 23, 1783, September 30, 1783, NA: CO 217/56, ff. 89, 93, 98.

44. Parr to Sydney, November 20, 1783, NA: CO 217/56, f. 115.

45. "A General Description of the Province of Nova Scotia ... done by Lieutenant Colonel Morse Chief Engineer in America, upon a Tour of the Province in the Autumn of the year 1783, and the summer 1784. Under the Orders and Instructions of His Excellency Sir Guy Carleton ... Given at Head Quarters at New York the 28th Day of July 1783," LAC: Robert Morse Fonds, f. 44.

46. For estimates of black migrants, see James W. St. G. Walker, *The Black Loyalists: The Search for a Promised Land in Nova Scotia and Sierra Leone, 1783–1870* (London: Longman, 1976), pp. 32, 40. Walker's portrayal of free blacks as "black loyalists" has attracted a sharp critique from Barry Cahill, "The Black Loyalist Myth in Atlantic Canada," *Acadiensis* 29, no. 1 (Autumn 1999): 76–87. On loyalist-owned slaves, see Harvey Amani Whitfield, "The American Background of Loyalist Slaves," *Left History* 14, no. 1 (Spring-Summer 2009): 58–87.

47. S. S. Blowers to Ward Chipman, September 23, 1783, LAC: Chipman Fonds, Microfilm C-1179, p. 95.

48. Blowers to Chipman, November 8, 1783, LAC: Chipman Fonds, Microfilm C-1179, p. 102.

49. Edward Winslow to Chipman, November 19, 1783, LAC: Chipman Fonds, Microfilm C-1180, p. 1314.

50. Edward Winslow to Chipman, January 1, 1784, LAC: Chipman Fonds, Microfilm C-1180, p. 1327.

51. "A General Description," LAC: Robert Morse Fonds, pp. 11–15, 26–32, 34–36.

52. Quoted in Bartlet, p. 193. Bailey estimated the population to be 120 at the time of his arrival (Bartlet, p. 192).

53. Parr to Lord North, November 20, 1783, NA: CO 217/56, f. 115.

54. Parr to Sydney, July 26, 1784, NA: CO 217/59, f. 193.

55. Proceedings of Nova Scotia Council, July 2, 1779, to March 11, 1780, NA: CO 216/55, f. 20.

56. Samuel Seabury to Colonel North, London, July 21, 1783, NA: CO 217/35, f. 333.

57. Major General John Campbell to Lord North, January 1, 1784, NA: CO 217/41, f. 35.

58. "General Return of all the Disbanded Troops and other Loyalists who have lately become Settlers in the Provinces of Nova Scotia and New Brunswick, made up from the Rolls taken by the several Muster Masters," Halifax, November 4, 1784, NA: CO 217/41, ff. 163–64.

59. Campbell to Lord North, April 1, 1784, NA: CO 217/41, ff. 63 and 65.

60. Sydney to Campbell, June 7, 1784, NA: CO 217/41, ff. 89–90.

61. Parr to Lord North, September 30, 1783, NA: CO 217/56, f. 98. For a list of escheats see Parr to Sydney, June 3, 1786, NA: CO 217/58, f. 159.

62. Wentworth to Lt. Jonathan Davidson, November 27, 1783, PANS: Letterbook of Sir John Wentworth, 1783–1808, RG 1, vol. 49 (reel 15237), p. 17.

63. Wentworth to Grey Elliott, April 10, 1784, and Wentworth to Commissioners of the Navy, April 16, 1786, PANS: Letterbook of Sir John Wentworth, 1783–1808, RG 1, vol. 49 (reel 15237), p. 32 and no page.

64. Faragher, pp. 288–90; Akins, p. 10.

65. MacKinnon, pp. 13–14, 21–23, 96.

66. Bailey to Dr. William Morice, November 6, 1783, quoted in Bartlet, p. 196.

67. Diary of Henry Nase, December 25, 1783, NBM, p. 19.

68. "Hannah Ingraham Recalls the Snowy Reception at Fredericton," in Catherine S. Crary, ed., *The Price of Loyalty: Tory Writings from the Revolutionary Era* (New York: McGraw-Hill, 1973), p. 402.

69. D. G. Bell, *Early Loyalist Saint John: The Origin of New Brunswick Politics, 1783–1786* (Fredericton: New Ireland Press, 1983), p. 63.

70. Overseers of the Poor of Halifax to Governor Parr, n.d., 1784, PANS: Phyllis R. Blakeley Fonds, MG 1, vol. 3030.

71. "A General Description," LAC: Robert Morse Fonds, pp. 41–44.

72. Winslow to Chipman, April 26, 1784, LAC: Ward Chipman Fonds, pp. 1335–36.

73. Brook Watson to Evan Nepean, March 3, 1784, NA: CO 217/56, f. 380.

74. The definitive history of this settlement is Marion Robertson, *King's Bounty: A History of Early Shelburne Nova Scotia* (Halifax: Nova Scotia Museum, 1983). A popular account is provided by Stephen Kimber, *Loyalists and Layabouts: The Rapid Rise and Faster Fall of Shelburne, Nova Scotia, 1783–1792* (Toronto: Doubleday Canada, 2008).

75. Diary of Benjamin Marston, November 24, 1776, http://www.lib.unb.ca/ Texts/marston/marston3.html, accessed November 28, 2009. The entirety of Marston's diary is available online: up to 1778 in the electronic transcript cited above, and from 1778 onward in page images through the Winslow Papers, vols. 20–22: http:// www.lib.unb.ca/winslow/browse.html, accessed November 28, 2009. (Henceforth cited as Marston Diary.)

76. Marston Diary, December 13–30, 1781, UNB: Winslow Papers, vol. 21, pp. 138–42.

77. Marston Diary, September 8, 1782, UNB: Winslow Papers, vol. 22, p. 57.

78. Marston Diary, April 21–May 3, 1783, UNB: Winslow Papers, vol. 22, pp. 70–72.

79. Joseph Durfee, report on meeting with Sir Guy Carleton, March 24, 1783, LAC: Shelburne, Nova Scotia Collection, Microfilm H-984, pp. 94–95.

80. Marston Diary, May 24, 1783, UNB: Winslow Papers, vol. 22, pp. 81–82.

81. Marston Diary, May 16, 1783, UNB: Winslow Papers, vol. 22, pp. 76–77.

82. Marston Diary, May 16 and June 9, 1783, UNB: Winslow Papers, vol. 22, pp. 77, 89–90.

83. Marston Diary, May 26 and June 4, 1783, UNB: Winslow Papers, vol. 22, pp. 83, 87.

84. Marston Diary, May 8, 1783, and May 18, 1784, UNB: Winslow Papers, vol. 22, pp. 74, 153.

85. Marston Diary, May 21 and May 29, 1783, UNB: Winslow Papers, vol. 22, pp. 80, 84.

86. Marston Diary, August 2, 1783, UNB: Winslow Papers, vol. 22, p. 103.

87. Benjamin Marston to Edward Winslow, February 6, 1784, in William Odber Raymond, ed., *Winslow Papers, A.D. 1776–1826* (Boston: Gregg Press, 1972), p. 164.

88. Marston Diary, July 22 and July 20, 1783, UNB: Winslow Papers, vol. 22, pp. 100–101.

89. A 1791 census put the Halifax population at just 4,897, though this represented a decline from the population of 1784 (Akins, p. 103). Several musters place the Shelburne population in 1784 at around eight thousand, including the fifteen hundred free blacks.

90. Parr to Lord Shelburne, December 16, 1783, NA: CO 217/56, f. 126.

91. Marston Diary, January 19, 1784, UNB: Winslow Papers, vol. 22, p. 141.

92. "An Account of the Life of Mr. David George . . . ," in Vincent Carretta, ed., *Unchained Voices: An Anthology of Black Authors in the English-Speaking World of the Eighteenth Century* (Lexington: University Press of Kentucky, 1996), p. 337.

93. Marston Diary, August 28, 1783, UNB: Winslow Papers, vol. 22, p. 111.

94. "Persons Victualled at Shelburne the 8th January 1784," PANS: Negro and Maroon Settlements, RG 1, vol. 419 (reel 15460), p. 108. The August 1784 muster shows 1,521 "negroes" at Shelburne: "Those Mustered at Shelburne, NS in the Summer of 1784. . . . ," LAC: Shelburne, Nova Scotia Collection, Microfilm H-984, vol. 3, p. 4.

95. "Memoirs of the Life of Boston King," in Carretta, ed., p. 356.

96. Marston Diary, June 19, 1783, UNB: Winslow Papers, vol. 22, p. 92.

97. Luke 8:5–8.

98. "Memoirs of the Life of Boston King," in Carretta, ed., pp. 356–58.

99. Parr to Nepean, January 22, 1783, NA: CO 217/59, f. 14.

100. "An Account of the Life of Mr. David George," in Carretta, ed., pp. 336–37.

101. "An Account of the Life of Mr. David George," in Carretta, ed., p. 337.

102. Walker, p. 40.

103. "A General Description," LAC: Robert Morse Fonds LAC: Robert Morse Fonds, p. 69.

104. "An Account of the Life of Mr. David George," in Carretta, ed., p. 338.

105. Parr to Evan Nepean, April 11, 1784, NA: CO 217/59, f. 105.

106. Marston Diary, September 19, 1783, UNB: Winslow Papers, vol. 22, pp. 118–19.

107. Marston Diary, July 26–27 and August 4, 1784, UNB: Winslow Papers, vol. 22, pp. 157–59.

Chapter Six: Loyal Americas

1. Lord Sydney to John Parr, March 8, 1785, NA: CO 217/57, ff. 28–29.

2. Edward Winslow to Ward Chipman, April 26, 1784, AO: Ward Chipman Papers, Microfilm C-1180, ff. 1343–44. Winslow must have been referring to an earlier letter of Sydney's that used much the same formulation as the March 1785 text quoted above. The Winslow Papers, the richest collection of personal papers on loyalist settlement in the Maritimes, are available online through the University of New Brunswick Library: http://www.lib.unb.ca/winslow, accessed December 24, 2009.

3. The best account of the partition movement is provided by Ann Gorman Condon, *The Envy of the American States: The Loyalist Dream for New Brunswick* (Fredericton, N.B.: New Ireland Press, 1984), pp. 97–120. Winslow laid out the scheme in full in his letter to Chipman of April 26, 1784, cited above.

4. Condon, pp. 112–19.

5. Cf. Seymour Martin Lipset, *Continental Divide: The Values and Institutions of the United States and Canada* (New York: Routledge, 1990), p. 1. As will become clear below, however, I disagree with Lipset's reductionist understanding of the United States as "the country of revolution, Canada of the counterrevolution."

6. For this influential narrative of Canadian history, see Ian McKay, "The Liberal Order Framework: A Prospectus for a Reconnaissance of Canadian History," *Canadian Historical Review* 81, no. 3 (December 2000): 617–45; and the valuable volume of critical essays edited by Jean-François Constant and Michel Ducharme, *Liberalism and Hegemony: Debating the Canadian Liberal Revolution* (Toronto: University of Toronto Press, 2009). On the loyalists' foundational role in the liberal order, see the insightful contribution of Jerry Bannister, "Canada as Counter-Revolution: The Loyalist Order Framework in Canadian History, 1750–1840," in Constant and Ducharme, eds., pp. 98–146.

7. Winslow to Sir John Wentworth, December 26, 1784, *Winslow Papers*, p. 260. On the progress of building in the city, see D. G. Bell, *Early Loyalist Saint John: The Origin of New Brunswick Politics, 1783–1786* (Fredericton, N.B.: New Ireland Press, 1983), pp. 48–49.

8. Quoted in "Thomas Carleton," q.v., *Dictionary of Canadian Biography Online*, http://www.biographi.ca, accessed December 24, 2009.

9. In contrast to his prolific and well-archived brother, Thomas Carleton produced little documentation—that survives at least—to help flesh out his personality and career. But a short précis Carleton wrote of his military service is reproduced in the *New Brunswick Magazine*, vol. 2 (Saint John, N.B.: William Kilby Reynolds, 1899), pp. 75–76. See also "Thomas Carleton," q.v., *Dictionary of Canadian Biography Online*, http://www.biographi.ca, accessed December 24, 2009.

10. The original candidate for the position was General Henry Fox, brother of Charles James Fox and leading advocate for the partition of Nova Scotia; but Fox declined the post for personal and political reasons. Esther Clark Wright, *The Loyalists of New Brunswick* (Fredericton, N.B.: n.p., 1955), p. 139.

11. William Odber Raymond, ed., *Winslow Papers, A.D. 1776–1826* (Boston: Gregg Press, 1972), p. 251; Beamish Murdoch, *A History of Nova Scotia, or Acadie*, 3 vols. (Halifax, N.S.: James Barnes, 1867), III, pp. 38–39; Bell, pp. 94–95.

12. Winslow to Chipman, July 7, 1783, in Raymond, ed., p. 100.

13. Thomas Carleton to Sydney, February 12, 1785, PANB: Thomas Carleton Letterbook.

14. Instructions to Thomas Carleton, n.d., NA: CO 188/1, f. 90.

15. Marston Diary, January 18, 1785, UNB: Winslow Papers, vol. 22, p. 177.

16. "Hannah Ingraham Recalls the Snowy Reception at Fredericton," in Catherine S. Crary, ed., *Tory Writings from the Revolutionary Era* (New York: McGraw-Hill, 1973), p. 402.

17. Thomas Carleton to Sydney, April 25, 1785, PANB: Thomas Carleton Letterbook.

18. Beverley Robinson Jr., "Receipt and Memorandum Book begun 24th Decr 1783," p. 75, NBM: Robinson Family Papers, Box 1, Folder 3.

19. See chapter 5, n. 2. For the New Brunswick response, see Condon, pp. 89–90.

20. Quoted in Bell, p. 65.

21. Quoted in Bell, p. 74.

22. Winslow to Wentworth, December 26, 1784, in Raymond, ed., p. 260. Thomas Carleton to Sydney, June 25, 1785, PANB: Thomas Carleton Letterbook.

23. Thomas Carleton to Sydney, June 25, 1785, PANB: Thomas Carleton Letterbook.

24. Thomas Carleton to Sydney, October 25, 1785, PANB: Thomas Carleton Letterbook; Bell, p. 57.

25. Thomas Carleton to Sydney, November 20, 1785, PANB: Thomas Carleton Letterbook.

26. Marston Diary, July 24 and November 17, 1785, UNB: Winslow Papers, vol. 22, pp. 189–90, 204–5.

27. Bell, pp. 104–5.

28. Thomas Carleton to Sydney, November 20, 1785, PANB: Thomas Carleton Letterbook.

29. Bell, p. 112.

30. Bell, pp. 113, 148–49.

31. Bell, p. 151.

32. Bell, p. 117.

33. Sydney to Thomas Carleton, April 19, 1786, NA: CO 188/3, ff. 189–90.

34. Thomas Carleton to Sydney, November 20, 1785, PANB: Thomas Carleton Letterbook.

35. On this theme see Jack P. Greene, ed., *Exclusionary Empire: English Liberty Overseas, 1600–1900* (Cambridge, U.K.: Cambridge University Press, 2010), esp. Philip Girard, "Liberty, Order, and Pluralism: The Canadian Experience," pp. 160–90.

36. *Cobbett's Weekly Political Pamphlet* 32, no. 36 (December 13, 1817): cols. 1148–50. See also Bell, pp. 130–31, 142–44.

37. Cobbett was a notoriously unreliable autobiographer. See David A. Wilson, *Paine and Cobbett: The Transatlantic Connection* (Kingston, Ont.: McGill–Queen's University Press, 1988), esp. (for New Brunswick) pp. 99–105.

38. Alan Taylor, *The Divided Ground: Indians, Settlers, and the Northern Borderland of the American Revolution* (New York: Knopf, 2006), pp. 112–13.

39. Quoted in Barbara Graymont, *The Iroquois in the American Revolution* (Syracuse, N.Y.: Syracuse University Press, 1972), p. 260.

40. Quoted in Taylor, p. 113.

41. The site had originally been dubbed "Loyal Confederate Valley" in June 1782. Graymont, p. 254.

42. Quoted in Taylor, p. 113.

43. "Abstract of poor Refugee Loyalists that stand in need of Clothing," [1783] BL: Add. Mss. 21822, f. 62. Another document reckoned that the government needed to supply 3,204 pairs of stockings and "Canadian shoes" (a set for each loyalist), and sixteen thousand yards of linen and wool to clothe the refugees. "Estimate of clothing required to Clothe the above number of Refugees, agreeable to the Proportions heretofore granted," BL: Add. Mss. 21826, f. 103. On the travails of Quebec refugees, see Janice Potter-MacKinnon, *While the Women Only Wept: Loyalist Refugee Women* (Montreal: McGill–Queen's University Press, 1993).

44. Memorandum, Montreal, March 6, 1782, BL: Add. Mss. 21825, f. 5.

45. Robert Mathews to Abraham Cuyler, November 18, 1782, BL: Add. Mss. 21825, f. 25.

46. Petition by "His Majesty's Faithful Subjects Emigrated Under the Conduct of Captain Michael Grass from New York to this place," Sorel, September 29, 1783, BL: Add. Mss. 21825, ff. 147–48.

47. Stephen Delancey to Mathews, April 26 and May 4, 1784, BL: Add. Mss. 21825, ff. 233–35.

48. Daniel Claus to General Haldimand, December 15, 1783, BL: Add. Mss. 21774, ff. 344–45.

49. Haldimand to Claus, December 17, 1783, BL: Add. Mss. 21774, f. 346.

50. "Return of disbanded Troops & Loyalists settled upon the King's Lands in the Province of Quebec in the Year 1784," BL: Add. Mss. 21828, f. 141.

51. Haldimand to Sir John Johnson, May 26, 1783, BL: Add. Mss. 21775, f. 122. Isabel Thompson Kelsay, *Joseph Brant, 1743–1807: Man of Two Worlds* (Syracuse, N.Y.: Syracuse University Press, 1984), p. 350.

52. Alan Taylor observes that the Mohawks were "the exception that proved the rule" about British neglect of Indian allies (p. 120). I would suggest that British perceptions of Mohawks as loyalists was what accounted for that difference.

53. Kelsay, pp. 366–67; Stone, pp. 243–45.

54. Kelsay, pp. 345–46.

55. Copy of grant by Haldimand, AO: Simcoe Family Papers, F-47-1-1 (MS 1797).

56. Quoted in William L. Stone, *Life of Joseph Brant (Thayendanegea)*, 2 vols. (Albany, N.Y.: J. Munsell, 1865), II, p. 253.

57. Joseph Brant to Sydney, January 4, 1786, quoted in Stone, II, pp. 252–53.

58. Stone, II, pp. 259–60.

59. Sydney to Brant, April 6, 1786, quoted in Stone, II, pp. 255–56.

60. Kelsay, pp. 385–91.

61. John Stuart to William White, September 4, 1788, LAC: John Stuart Papers, pp. 46–47.

62. Stuart to White, September 4, 1788, LAC: John Stuart Papers, pp. 46–47.

63. Isaac Weld, *Travels through the States of North America and the Provinces of Upper and Lower Canada, during the Years 1795, 1796, and 1797* (London: John Stockdale, 1800), pp. 485–89.

64. Taylor, p. 123; Kelsay, pp. 370–71.

65. Brant to Samuel Kirkland, March 8, 1791, AO: Simcoe Family Papers, Series F-47-1-1.

66. Paul David Nelson, *General Sir Guy Carleton, Lord Dorchester: Soldier-Statesman of Early British Canada* (Madison, N.J.: Fairleigh Dickinson University Press, 2000), pp. 174–76.

67. Quoted in Nelson, p. 184.

68. Nelson, pp. 176–87; Condon, pp. 118–19. He did not get the title of governor-general, reflecting the wariness British ministers retained about creating such a powerful position.

69. William Smith, *The Diaries and Selected Papers of Chief Justice William Smith*, ed. L. F. S. Upton, 2 vols. (Toronto: Champlain Society, 1963), II, p. 105.

70. William Smith estimated the population of Quebec at 130,000 in 1788 (Nelson, p. 209). According to the 1790 U.S. census, New York State had 340,241 residents.

71. Nelson, pp. 208–9.

72. *Diaries of William Smith*, II, p. 163.

73. "Report of the Council Committee on Education," in *Diaries of William Smith*, II, p. 266; Nelson, p. 205.

74. For a nuanced picture of Anglo–French Canadian relations in this period, see Donald Fyson, *Magistrates, Police, and People: Everyday Criminal Justice in Quebec and Lower Canada, 1764–1837* (Toronto: University of Toronto Press, 2006).

75. Gerald M. Craig, *Upper Canada: The Formative Years, 1784–1841* (Toronto: McClelland and Stewart, 1963), pp. 13–19. For the text of the act, see Adam Shortt

and Arthur C. Doughty, eds., *Documents Relating to the Constitutional History of Canada,
1759–1791* (Ottawa: S. E. Dawson, 1907), pp. 694–708. On the authoritarian turn, see
C. A. Bayly, *Imperial Meridian: The British Empire and the World, 1780–1830* (London:
Longman, 1989).

76. Fox criticized the bill's creation of an aristocracy and mocked Burke's sympathy
for an institution that had been eliminated in France. Burke passionately insisted that
he would uphold his defense of British constitutionalism to the end of his life, and
"with his last words exclaim, 'Fly from the French constitution!' " Fox was heard to
mutter that "there was no loss of friends," to which Burke responded "Yes, there was a
loss of friends . . .—their friendship was at an end." Fox rose to speak, "but his mind
was so much agitated, and his heart so much affected by what had fallen from Mr.
Burke, that it was some minutes before he could proceed. Tears trickled down his
cheeks." Debate of May 6, 1791, *The Parliamentary History of England* (London: T. C.
Hansard, 1817), vol. 29, columns 359–430, esp. 387–88.

77. At the risk of falling into semantic debate, I should note that my understanding
of this act conforms to the use of "counter-revolution" put forward by Eliga Gould,
"American Independence and Britain's Counter-Revolution," *Past & Present* 154 (February 1997): 107–41; Eliga Gould, "Revolution and Counter-Revolution," in David
Armitage and Michael J. Braddick, eds., *The British Atlantic World, 1500–1800* (Basingstoke, U.K.: Palgrave Macmillan, 2002), pp. 196–213; and Bannister, "Canada as
Counter-Revolution."

78. Quoted in Elizabeth Jane Errington, *The Lion, the Eagle, and Upper Canada: A
Developing Colonial Ideology* (Kingston, Ont.: McGill–Queen's University Press, 1987),
p. 30.

79. *Diaries of William Smith*, II, p. 163.

80. William Smith to Lord Dorchester, February 5, 1790, in *Diaries of William
Smith*, II, pp. 270–76.

81. McKay, pp. 632–33. See also Phillip A. Buckner, *The Transition to Responsible
Government: British Policy in British North America, 1815–1850* (Westport, Conn.:
Greenwood Press, 1985). A response to the 1837–38 Canadian rebellions, the union of
the Canadas also resembled the union of Great Britain and Ireland in 1801, as another
attempt to contain a recently rebellious Catholic population within a Protestant polity.

82. Nelson, pp. 211–15.

83. For this characterization of Simcoe's policies, see, among others, Errington,
chapter 2; Craig, pp. 20–22.

84. Quoted in Jeffrey L. McNairn, *The Capacity to Judge: Public Opinion and Deliberative Democracy in Upper Canada, 1791–1854* (Toronto: University of Toronto Press,
2000), p. 23.

85. Craig, pp. 20–22.

86. Quoted in Mary Beacock Fryer and Christopher Dracott, *John Graves Simcoe,
1752–1806: A Biography* (Toronto: Dundurn Press, 1998), p. 121. J. Ross Robertson,
ed., *The Diary of Mrs. John Graves Simcoe* (Toronto: William Briggs, 1911), p. 180.

87. *Diary of Mrs. Simcoe*, pp. 121–63.

88. *Diary of Mrs. Simcoe*, pp. 180–84.

89. Quoted in Errington, p. 31.

90. Craig, p. 35; *Diary of Mrs. Simcoe*, pp. 184–200; Fryer and Dracott, pp. 162–63.

91. On shifts in the meaning of loyalism see David Mills, *The Idea of Loyalty in
Upper Canada, 1784–1850* (Kingston, Ont.: McGill–Queen's University Press, 1988);
Norman Knowles, *Inventing the Loyalists: The Ontario Loyalist Tradition and the Creation
of Usable Pasts* (Toronto: University of Toronto Press, 1997).

92. Alan Taylor, "The Late Loyalists: Northern Reflections of the Early American Republic," *Journal of the Early Republic* 27, no. 1 (Spring 2007): 5.

93. Taylor, "Late Loyalists," pp. 5–6.

94. *Diary of Mrs. Simcoe*, pp. 136–39.

95. Elizabeth Jane Errington, "British Migration and British America," in Phillip Buckner, ed., *Canada and the British Empire* (Oxford: Oxford University Press, 2008), pp. 140–46. Up to the U.S. Civil War, the primary destination for British immigrants to North America continued to be the United States.

96. The British traveler Isaac Weld (an enthusiastic proponent of immigration to Canada) noted that "it is a fact worthy of notice, which banishes every suspicion relative to the diminution of the inhabitants by emigrations into the States, that great numbers of people actually emigrate into Canada annually, whilst none of the Canadians, who have it in their power to dispose of their property, emigrate into the United States, except, indeed, a few of those who have resided in the towns." (Weld, p. 287.) The white population of Upper Canada doubled from about seven thousand (largely refugees) in 1784 to fourteen thousand in 1791, and then multiplied fivefold to seventy thousand between 1791 and 1811. To the extent that loyalist refugees moved back to the United States (and I have found no evidence to suggest that they did so in large numbers), returnees in no way compromised provincial growth. Taylor, "Late Loyalists," pp. 4, 19.

97. I draw my interpretation of Upper Canada as an "American" province from the illuminating work of Elizabeth Jane Errington: see esp. *The Lion, the Eagle, and Upper Canada*, chapter 3. For a case study in how imperial rule could appeal to a quintessential early U.S. individualist, see J. I. Little, "American Sinner/Canadian Saint?" in *Journal of the Early Republic* 27, no. 2 (Summer 2007): 203–31.

98. Stuart to White, September 8, 1788, AO: John Stuart Papers, p. 46.

99. Taylor, "Late Loyalists," p. 7.

100. Egerton Ryerson, *The Loyalists of America and Their Times: From 1620 to 1816*, 2 vols. (Toronto: William Briggs, 1880), II, p. 474.

101. Stuart to White, October 14, 1783, AO: John Stuart Papers, p. 18.

102. Craig, pp. 28–31.

103. For a suggestive investigation of loyalism and religious culture, see Christopher Adamson, "God's Divided Continent: Politics and Religion in Upper Canada and the Northern and Western United States, 1775 to 1841," *Comparative Studies in Society and History* 36, no. 2 (July 1994): 417–46.

104. Louis Hartz, *The Founding of New Societies: Studies in the History of the United States, Latin America, South Africa, Canada, and Australia* (New York: Harcourt, Brace, and World, 1964), p. 91; Gad Horowitz, "Conservatism, Liberalism, and Socialism in Canada: An Interpretation," *Canadian Journal of Economics and Political Science/Revue canadienne d'economique et de science politique* 32, no. 2 (May 1966): 143–71.

105. Bannister, pp. 102, 126–27. For critiques see also S. F. Wise, "Liberal Consensus or Ideological Battleground: Some Reflections on the Hartz Thesis," in S. F. Wise, *God's Peculiar Peoples: Essays on Political Culture in Nineteenth-Century Canada* (Ottawa: Carleton University Press, 1993), pp. 199–211; Janet Ajzenstat and Peter J. Smith, eds., *Canada's Origins: Liberal, Tory, or Republican?* (Ottawa: Carleton University Press, 1995).

Chapter Seven: Islands in a Storm

1. John Cruden to Joseph Taylor, November 25, 1786, LOC: Lovering Taylor Papers, Box 3.

2. [John Cruden], "An Address to the Monarchial and Thinking Part of the British Empire," [1785], BL: North Papers, Add. Mss., 61864, f. 138; Cruden to Taylor, November 25, 1786, LOC: Lovering Taylor Papers, Box 3.

3. [John Cruden], "An Address to the Monarchial and Thinking Part of the British Empire," [1785], BL: North Papers, Add. Mss., 61864, f. 139–47. Cf. John Cruden, *An Address to the Loyal Part of the British Empire, and the Friends of Monarchy Throughout the Globe* (London, 1785).

4. Cruden to Rev. William Cruden, May 16, 1785, NA: PRO 30/11/7, Cornwallis Papers, Box 7, f. 52.

5. Cruden to Taylor, November 25, 1786, LOC: Lovering Taylor Papers, Box 3.

6. S. S. Blowers to Taylor, November 7, 1786, LOC: Lovering Taylor Papers, Box 3.

7. Cruden to Taylor, November 11 and 25, 1786, LOC: Lovering Taylor Papers, Box 3.

8. John Cruden to Rev. William Cruden, May 16, 1785, NA: PRO 30/11/7, Cornwallis Papers, Box 7, f. 52.

9. [John Cruden], "An Address to the Sons of Abraham, Containing thoughts on the Prophecys respecting the restoration of the Jews . . . by a British American Royalist," May 16, 1785, NA: PRO 30/11/7, Cornwallis Papers, Box 7, ff. 59–71.

10. Michael Craton, *A History of the Bahamas* (London: Collins, 1968), pp. 31–34. There is considerable dispute over which island Columbus actually touched first, but conventional wisdom holds that his San Salvador is present-day Watlings Island.

11. Craton, pp. 56–64.

12. Sandra Riley, *Homeward Bound: A History of the Bahama Islands to 1850 with a Definitive Study of Abaco in the American Loyalist Plantation Period* (Miami: Island Research, 1983), pp. 42–43.

13. Craton, p. 166.

14. For a good contemporary description of the Bahamas, see Johann David Schoepf, *Travels in the Confederation [1783–1784]*, trans. and ed. Alfred J. Morrison, 2 vols. (New York: Bergman Publishers, 1968), II, pp. 259–316.

15. Quoted in Riley, p. 101.

16. Craton, pp. 149–57; Riley, pp. 98–103.

17. Quoted in Riley, p. 131. Firebrand loyalist colonel David Fanning recruited thirty men for the expedition, only to miss the boat when Deveaux sailed without him. David Fanning, *The Adventures of David Fanning in the American Revolutionary War*, ed. A. W. Savary (Ottawa: Golden Dog Press, 1983), pp. 60–61.

18. Quoted in Riley, p. 132.

19. See Craton, pp. 160–61; Riley, pp. 131–34; Andrew Deveaux to Sir Guy Carleton, June 6, 1783, NYPL: Carleton Papers, Box 33, no. 7906.

20. Riley, p. 133.

21. The expedition and terms of peace were reported simultaneously in the pages of the *East Florida Gazette*, May 3, 1783, and in Patrick Tonyn to Lord Sydney, May 15, 1783, NA: CO 5/560, pp. 583–88.

22. Deveaux set an example himself by claiming 250 prime acres of land on New Providence (Craton, p. 161).

23. Returns indicate a total of 1,458 prospective Abaco settlers: *Report on American Manuscripts in the Royal Institution of Great Britain*, 4 vols. (London: HMSO, 1904), IV, p. x.

24. Tonyn to Carleton, May 15, 1783, NYPL: Carleton Papers, Box 32, no. 7691.

25. Lewis Johnston to unknown recipient, July 14, 1783, NA: CO 5/560, pp. 928–33. Sir Guy Carleton commissioned a survey of the islands at the same time,

which offered somewhat more favorable prospects for the cultivation of cotton in particular (Craton, p. 163).

26. Lord North to Tonyn, December 4, 1783, NA: CO 5/560, p. 724.

27. North to Tonyn, December 4, 1783, NA: CO 5/560, pp. 724–25; Craton, p. 163. The purchase was formally completed in 1787.

28. Like Parr and the Carletons, Maxwell was an Irish Protestant military officer. In 1779 his wealthy wife of three years sought to divorce him, on the grounds that he had never consummated the marriage. A. P. W. Malcolmson, *In Pursuit of the Heiress: Aristocratic Marriage in Ireland, 1740–1840* (Belfast: Ulster Historical Foundation, 2006), pp. 74–75.

29. John Maxwell to Sydney, June 19, 1784, NA: CO 23/25, f. 139.

30. In addition to the 1,458 New Yorkers bound for Abaco, 1,033 whites and 2,214 blacks left from East Florida for the Bahamas, according to the "Return of Persons who Emigrated from East Florida to different parts of the British Dominions," May 2, 1786, NA CO: 5/561, f. 407. See population table in Craton, p. 166.

31. James Powell to Tonyn, June 9, 1785, and Tonyn to Powell, August 25, 1785, in John Walton Caughey, ed., *East Florida, 1783–85: A File of Documents Assembled, and Many of Them Translated by Joseph Byrne Lockey* (Berkeley and Los Angeles: University of California Press, 1949), pp. 695–97.

32. Cruden to Maxwell, October 28, 1784, NA: CO 23/25, ff. 247–48. Maxwell to Cruden, November 25, 1784, NA: CO 23/25, ff. 247–49.

33. Tonyn to Maxwell, May 10, 1784, NA: CO 23/25, f. 133. Maxwell to Tonyn, June 5, 1784, NA: CO 23/25, f. 135.

34. Schoepf, II, pp. 262–64.

35. Riley, p. 143.

36. Arthur McArthur to Sydney, March 1, 1784, NA: CO 23/25, ff. 75–76.

37. Maxwell to Sydney, March 29, 1784, NA: CO 23/25, f. 83.

38. "To His Excellency John Maxwell Esq. Captain General Governor and Commander in Chief of the Bahama Islands," enclosed in Maxwell to Sydney, May 17, 1784, NA: CO 23/25, ff. 113–14.

39. Maxwell to Sydney, May 17, 1784, NA: CO 23/25, f. 111.

40. Enclosed in Maxwell to Sydney, June 4, 1784, NA: CO 23/25, f. 117.

41. Maxwell to Sydney, June 20, 1784, NA: CO 23/25, f. 143.

42. Wilbur Henry Siebert, *Loyalists in East Florida, 1774 to 1785: The Most Important Documents Pertaining Thereto, Edited with an Accompanying Narrative*, 2 vols. (Deland: Florida State Historical Society, 1929), I, p. 189.

43. Enclosed in Maxwell to Sydney, June 4, 1784, NA: CO 23/25, f. 119.

44. Maxwell to Sydney, September 4, 1784, NA: CO 23/25, f. 172.

45. Maxwell to Sydney, November 20, 1784, NA: CO 23/25, f. 238.

46. Maxwell to Sydney, May 17, 1784, NA: CO 23/25, f. 111.

47. Maxwell to McArthur, June 9, 1784, NA: CO 23/25, f. 141; Maxwell to Sydney, June 4, 1784, NA: CO 23/25, f. 115.

48. Gail Saunders, *Bahamian Loyalists and Their Slaves* (London: Macmillan Caribbean, 1983), p. 58.

49. The handbill, along with identifications of its signers, is enclosed in Maxwell to Sydney, July 29, 1784, NA: CO 23/25, ff. 155, 210.

50. Maxwell to Sydney, September 4, 1784, NA: CO 23/25, f. 171. On the lawyers' grievance, see, among others, Stephen Haven to Tonyn, December 6, 1784, in Caughey, ed., pp. 433–34; Maxwell to Sydney, September 4, 1784, NA: CO 23/25, f. 171; Maxwell to Sydney, November 20, 1784, NA: CO 23/25, f. 238.

51. Maxwell to Sydney, September 7, 1784, NA: CO 23/25, f. 178.

52. Maxwell to Sydney, October 9, 1784, NA: CO 23/25, f. 224.

53. Maxwell to Sydney, August 26, 1784, NA: CO 23/25, f. 165.

54. Maxwell to Sydney, September 29, 1784, NA: CO 23/25, f. 188.

55. Sworn testaments to George Bunch, Justice of the Peace, September 29, 1784, NA: CO 23/25, ff. 211–12.

56. Maxwell to Sydney, October 15, 1784, NA: CO 23/25, ff. 226–27.

57. [William Wylly], *A Short Account of the Bahamas Islands, Their Climate, Productions, &c. . . .* (London, 1789), p. 13. Charles Colcock Jones, *The History of Georgia*, 2 vols. (Boston: Houghton Mifflin, 1883), II, p. 420.

58. Powell to Sydney, May 11, 1785, NA: CO 23/25, f. 318.

59. Proceedings of April 4, 1785, *Journal of the House of Assembly of the Bahamas, 12 May 1784 to 29 September 1794*, NAB, pp. 28–30.

60. Proceedings of April 26, 1785, *Journal of the House of Assembly of the Bahamas, 12 May 1784 to 29 September 1794*, NAB, pp. 42, 45.

61. Loyalist memorial to Powell, May 18, 1785, NA: CO 23/25, ff. 321–24.

62. Sydney to Powell, July 18, 1785, NA: CO 23/25, f. 331.

63. Powell to Loyalists, n.d., NA: CO 23/25, f. 325. Proceedings of May 13, 1785, *Journal of the House of Assembly of the Bahamas, 12 May 1784 to 29 September 1794*, NAB, pp. 50–60.

64. Sydney to Maxwell, August 6, 1784, NA: CO 23/25, ff. 162–63.

65. For a fuller exposition of the effects of personal trauma on Bahamian loyalists, see Michael J. Prokopow, " 'To the Torrid Zones': The Fortunes and Misfortunes of American Loyalists in the Anglo-Caribbean Basin, 1774–1801" (Ph.D. dissertation, Harvard University, 1996), pp. 221–29. On Brown: Edward J. Cashin, *The King's Ranger: Thomas Brown and the American Revolution on the Southern Frontier* (New York: Fordham University Press, 1999), p. 179.

66. Schoepf, II, p. 271.

67. J. Leitch Wright, "Dunmore's Loyalist Asylum in the Floridas," *Florida Historical Quarterly* 49, no. 4 (April 1971): 370–79.

68. Sydney to Maxwell, June 1786, NA: CO 23/25, ff. 418–19.

69. "Plan of the Town of Nassau and Environs on the Island of New Providence Surveyed by Order of the General Assembly of the Bahamas, by Captain Andrew Skinner, 1788," NAB. The city was resurveyed in 1785 to incorporate all the new dwellings. *Journal of the House of Assembly of the Bahamas, 12 May 1784 to 29 September 1794*, p. 93.

70. Schoepf, II, p. 263.

71. The Book of Negroes names eighty blacks bound for Abaco on the ships *William* and *Nautilus*: http://www.blackloyalist.com/canadiandigitalcollection /documents/official/book_of_negroes.htm, accessed December 30, 2009. Riley, appendix D, pp. 266–69; Michael Craton and Gail Saunders, *Islanders in the Stream: A History of the Bahamian People*, 2 vols. (Athens: University of Georgia Press, 1999), I, pp. 183–84. On Brother Amos, see Whittington B. Johnson, *Race Relations in the Bahamas, 1784–1834: The Nonviolent Transformation from a Slave to a Free Society* (Fayetteville: University of Arkansas Press, 2000), pp. 56–58.

72. Saunders, p. 20; Cashin, *The King's Ranger*, pp. 174–79; Thelma Peters, "The American Loyalists and the Plantation Period in the Bahama Islands" (Ph.D. dissertation, University of Florida, 1960), pp. 69–70.

73. See list of land grants, NAB: Registrar General, Land Grants, Book C1 (1789–90).

74. Riley, pp. 180–85; [Wylly], p. 7.

75. [Wylly], p. 3.

76. G. Barry to Anthony Stokes, June 30, 1786, NA: CO 23/26, f. 225.

77. Memorial of John Cruden, January 14, 1786, *Journal of the House of Assembly of the Bahamas, 12 May 1784 to 29 September 1794*, NAB, pp. 110–11.

78. Siebert, p. 191. I derive this ratio from Wylly's 1788 population estimate, counting four whites for each male head of family.

79. "An Account of the present Situation of affairs in the Bahama Islands," n.d., NA: CO 23/28, f. 150.

80. Lord Dunmore to Sydney, November 28, 1787, NA: CO 23/27, f. 75.

81. Quoted in Riley, p. 170.

82. "An Account of the present Situation of affairs in the Bahama Islands," n.d., NA: CO 23/28, f. 151.

83. [Wylly], pp. 21–23, 40–41; Riley, pp. 169–70; Craton and Saunders, p. 187.

84. Petitions reproduced in [Wylly], pp. 33–39; for originals see NA: CO 23/26, ff. 102–21, 153–54.

85. For the documents and depositions in this affair, see NA: CO 23/28, ff. 105–6, 149–74.

86. Dunmore to Sydney, February 29, 1788, NA: CO 23/26, ff. 103–4.

87. Quoted in Riley, p. 172.

88. [Wylly], p. 16.

89. Craton, pp. 176–77; Craton and Saunders, p. 203.

90. [Wylly], pp. 30–31.

91. [Wylly], p. 24.

92. On this—and a fresh interpretation of Lord Dunmore's career in general—see James Corbett David, "Dunmore's New World: Political Culture in the British Empire, 1745–1796" (Ph.D. dissertation, College of William and Mary, 2010). I am grateful to Jim David for sharing with me portions of this work while in progress.

93. On Creek marriage customs and houses, see William Bartram, *Travels* (Philadelphia: James and Johnson, 1791), pp. 396–97, 514–15; Kathryn E. Holland Braund, *Deerskins and Duffels: The Creek Indian Trade with Anglo-America, 1685–1815*, 2nd ed. (Lincoln: University of Nebraska Press, 2008), pp. 12–13, 15–17.

94. The definitive biography of Bowles is by J. Leitch Wright, *William Augustus Bowles: Director General of the Creek Nation* (Athens: University of Georgia Press, 1967). See also Elisha P. Douglass, "The Adventurer Bowles," *William & Mary Quarterly* 6, no. 1 (January 1949): 3–23; and the hagiographic contemporary biography by Benjamin Baynton, *Authentic Memoirs of William Augustus Bowles* (London, 1791).

95. Wright, p. 13; Cashin, p. 184; William S. Coker and Thomas D. Watson, *Indian Traders of the Southeastern Spanish Borderlands: Panton, Leslie & Company and John Forbes & Company, 1783–1847* (Pensacola: University of West Florida Press, 1986), p. 114.

96. Philip Waldeck Diary, transcribed and translated by Bruce E. Burgoyne, LOC, f. 217A.

97. Journal of Zachary Macaulay, May 28, 1798, Zachary Macaulay Papers, Henry E. Huntington Library [Harvard College Library: Microfilm A 471, Reel 3]; Baynton, pp. 12–13.

98. Among the most prominent were George Galphin, David George's onetime master and a patriot; and Alexander McGillivray's loyalist father, Lachlan. On the place of white and mixed-ethnicity individuals in Creek culture, see Andrew Frank, *Creeks and Southerners: Biculturalism on the Early American Frontier* (Lincoln: University

of Nebraska Press, 2005), esp. pp. 26–45, 77–95; and Claudio Saunt, *A New Order of Things: Property, Power, and the Transformation of the Creek Indians, 1733–1816* (Cambridge, U.K.: Cambridge University Press, 1999), esp. pp. 2–3, 46–89.

99. Baynton, p. 29.

100. Deposition of William Augustus Bowles, April 9, 1788, NA: CO 23/27, ff. 158–59. However suspect Bowles's testimony may be, the paraphrase he provided of Cruden's letters does bear notable echoes with Cruden's surviving letters. That said, no documents appear to suggest that Cruden proposed an outright overthrow of the Bahamas government. He seems, rather, to have spent late 1786 and early 1787 trying to persude the Duke of York to make some of the islands crown colonies and settle them with "the most industrious inhabitants of the Northern States." See James Cruden to General R. Grenville, August 8, 1786, BL: Add. Mss. 70959, f. 89.

101. Henceforth Cruden's younger brother James, once charged with promoting John's ambitious plans across the courts of Europe, pursued the family's claim for a lost fortune of £40,000 from the Loyalist Claims Commission. Claim of James Cruden, NYPL: Loyalist Transcripts, vol. 48, pp. 528–55.

102. Saunt, pp. 38–63.

103. Saunt, pp. 70–75, 83–88; Coker and Watson, pp. 115–16. McGillivray's brother-in-law Louis LeClerc de Milfort remarked on how, in London, "Bowles dressed like the Indians to give a semblance of reality to his story." Louis LeClerc de Milfort, *Memoir, or a Cursory Glance at My Different Travels & My Sojourn in the Creek Nation* (Chicago: Lakeside Press, 1956). The portrait was painted by Thomas Hardy on Bowles's 1791 visit to London; another member of his party sat for William Hodges, the painter who had first made his name as artist on Captain Cook's second voyage, and subsequently traveled to India.

104. When not enough men volunteered for the expedition Dunmore released a handful of criminals from the Nassau jail to join it. Petition from "Subscribers late of the Party under the Command of Col. Bowles from Nassau," November 24, 1788, LOC: East Florida Papers, reel 82, bundle 195M15.

105. Wright, pp. 30–35; Coker and Watson, pp. 117–20. Vicente Manuel de Zéspedes to Alexander McGillivray, St. Augustine, October 8, 1788, quoted in Caughey, *McGillivray*, pp. 202–3.

106. McGillivray to John Leslie, November 20, 1788, quoted in Caughey, *McGillivray*, p. 207; McGillivray to William Panton, February 1, 1789, quoted in Caughey, *McGillivray*, p. 217; Milfort, pp. xxxi–xxxiv, 82–83.

107. Baynton, p. 67; Wright, pp. 37–38.

108. Parr subvented Bowles's travel and lodging. See Parr to Lords Commissioners of the Treasury, Halifax, May 10, 1791, PANS: RG1, vol. 221 (reel 15328), no. 164.

109. Douglas Brymner, ed., *Report on Canadian Archives* (Ottawa: Brown Chamberlin, 1891), pp. 255–56.

110. Petition of William Bowles, January 3, 1791, reprinted in Frederick Jackson Turner, "English Policy toward America," *American Historical Review* 7, no. 4 (July 1902): 726–28.

111. Cruden to North, May 16, 1785, BL: North Papers, Add. Mss. 61864, ff. 133–34.

112. Bowles to Lord Grenville, January 19, 1791, reprinted in Turner, pp. 728–33.

113. Grenville to Dunmore, April 1, 1791, NA: CO 23/31, f. 7.

114. Bowles to Dunmore, February 6, 1792, NA: CO 23/31, f. 153.

115. Panton to Indian chiefs, February 19, 1792, in Caughey, p. 309.

116. Wright, pp. 56–70; Coker and Watson, pp. 148–56.

117. Wright, pp. 71–92.

118. *Votes of the Honourable House of Assembly* (Nassau: John Wells, 1796); Craton and Saunders, pp. 203–11; David, chapter 5.

119. The travails of a middle-class loyalist planter are well described in Charles Farquharson, "A Relic of Slavery: Farquharson's Journal for 1831–32," typescript, NAB. See also Peters, pp. 148–54.

120. Cashin, *The King's Ranger*, p. 197.

121. Craton, pp. 176–78.

Chapter Eight: False Refuge

1. Maria Nugent, *Lady Nugent's Journal of Her Residence in Jamaica from 1801 to 1805*, ed. Philip Wright (Kingston: Institute of Jamaica, 1966), p. 10.

2. William Beckford, *A Descriptive Account of the Island of Jamaica*, 2 vols. (London, 1790), I, pp. 21–22, 80; II, p. 401. This William Beckford (1744–1799) is not to be confused with William Thomas Beckford (1760–1844), son of Alderman William Beckford (1709–1770), one of Jamaica's largest absentee landowners, builder of Fonthill Abbey, and the author of the Gothic novel *Vathek*. Beckford the historian was Alderman Beckford's nephew. He wrote his *Descriptive Account* while imprisoned for debt in the Fleet prison.

3. Bryan Edwards explained, "The whole of the scenery is . . . superlatively fine, nor can words alone (at least any that I can select) convey a just idea of it." Bryan Edwards, *The History Civil and Commercial of the British Colonies in the West Indies*, 2 vols. (London, 1793), I, pp. 180–83.

4. Louisa Susannah Wells, *The Journal of a Voyage from Charlestown to London* (New York: Arno Press, 1968 [1906]), pp. 48, 111–12.

5. See especially Alexander X. Byrd, *Captives and Voyagers: Black Migrants Across the Eighteenth-Century British Atlantic World* (Baton Rouge: Louisiana State University Press, 2009).

6. On Aikman's career, see Frank Cundall, "The Early Press and Printers in Jamaica," *Proceedings of the American Antiquarian Society* 26 (April–October 1916): 290–354.

7. Richard S. Dunn, *Sugar and Slaves: The Rise of the Planter Class in the English West Indies, 1624–1713* (Chapel Hill: University of North Carolina Press, 1972), pp. 149–87. Edward Ward, *A Trip to Jamaica with a True Character of the People of the Island* (London, 1700), pp. 13, 16.

8. Sidney W. Mintz, *Sweetness and Power: The Place of Sugar in Modern History* (New York: Penguin, 1985), pp. 39, 67.

9. Beckford, I, pp. 50–51.

10. Trevor Burnard, *Mastery, Tyranny, and Desire: Thomas Thistlewood and his Slaves in the Anglo-Jamaican World* (Chapel Hill: University of North Carolina Press, 2004), pp. 13–16.

11. Mintz, pp. 46–52.

12. J. R. Ward, "The British West Indies, 1748–1815," in P. J. Marshall, ed., *The Oxford History of the British Empire*, vol. 2, *The Eighteenth Century* (Oxford: Oxford University Press, 1998), p. 433. Barbados, however, had a larger and more settled white population, with a slave to white ratio of about four to one.

13. Burnard, p. 156; Douglas Hall, *In Miserable Slavery: Thomas Thistlewood in Jamaica, 1750–1786* (London: MacMillan, 1989), p. 72.

14. Burnard, pp. 150–51; Vincent Brown, *The Reaper's Garden: Death and Power in the World of Atlantic Slavery* (Cambridge, Mass.: Harvard University Press, 2008), pp. 140–41.

15. Edwards, I, p. 230.

16. Burnard, pp. 16–18.

17. Quoted in Brown, p. 13. Burnard, p. 16.

18. Edwards, I, p. 227.

19. Kamau Brathwaite, *The Development of Creole Society in Jamaica, 1770–1820* (Oxford: Clarendon Press, 1971), p. 86; Lowell Ragatz, *The Fall of the Planter Class in the British Caribbean, 1763–1833: A Study in Social and Economic History* (New York: Octagon Books, 1963 [1928]), pp. 180–82, 189–90. Brown notes that the high estimate of slave deaths offered a convenient way for planters to explain falling numbers in the slave population (p. 184).

20. Beckford, I, pp. 103–4.

21. R. R. Palmer, *The Age of the Democratic Revolution: A Political History of Europe and America, 1760–1800*, 2 vols. (Princeton, N.J.: Princeton University Press, 1959–64).

22. I am grateful to Josiah Osgood for his analysis of this inscription.

23. For a comprehensive discussion of this topic see Andrew Jackson O'Shaughnessy, *An Empire Divided: The American Revolution and the British Caribbean* (Philadelphia: University of Pennsylvania Press, 2000).

24. O'Shaughnessy, pp. 151–54.

25. "Memoir Relative to the Island of Jamaica by Major General Archibald Campbell," 1782, NLJ: MS 16.

26. O'Shaughnessy, pp. 232–37.

27. Frank Cundall, "Sculpture in Jamaica," *Art Journal* (March 1907): 65–70. On commemorative efforts in Britain, see Holger Hoock, *Empires of the Imagination: Politics, War, and the Arts in the British World, 1750–1850* (London: Profile Books, 2010), pp. 67–71.

28. O'Shaughnessy, pp. 217–32; Ragatz, pp. 160–63.

29. Beckford estimated the population in 1790 at eight thousand whites, fifteen hundred free people of color, and fourteen thousand slaves (Beckford, I, p. xxii). A report commissioned by the Kingston parish vestry gave the population of Kingston as 6,539 whites, 2,690 free people of color (listed as "brown"), 590 free blacks; and 16,659 slaves. Kingston Vestry Minutes, February 28, 1788, NAJ: 2/6/6. (These numbers are also quoted by Edwards, I, p. 213.) Both sets of figures of course date from after the loyalist influx. Edward Long estimated Kingston's population at five thousand whites, twelve hundred free blacks and people of color, and five thousand slaves (see Edward Long, *The History of Jamaica. Or, General Survey of the Antient and Modern State of That Island . . .*, 3 vols. [London: T. Lowndes, 1774], II, p. 103).

30. Long, II, pp. 102–18.

31. Kingston Vestry Minutes, November 5, 1784, NAJ: 2/6/6, f. 118.

32. Quoted in Michael John Prokopow, " 'To the Torrid Zones': The Fortunes and Misfortunes of American Loyalists in the Anglo-Caribbean Basin, 1774–1801" (Ph.D. dissertation, Harvard University, 1996), p. 29.

33. House of Assembly Journals, February 11–14, 1783, NAJ: 1B/5/1/31.

34. House of Assembly Journals, December 2, 1783, NAJ: 1B/5/1/32.

35. See "A List of Loyalists in Jamaica," NLJ: MS 1841. Prokopow gives a breakdown by place of origin, pp. 32–33.

36. "A List of Loyalists in Jamaica," NLJ: MS 1841, pp. 9, 16, 24–25, 27, 31–32, 34.

37. "A List of Loyalists in Jamaica," NLJ: MS 1841, pp. 9–10, 14, 17, 25, 35, 40–41.

38. Kingston Vestry Minutes, March 11, 1783, NAJ: 2/6/6, f. 65; Kingston Vestry Minutes, October 11, 1784, NAJ: 2/6/6, f. 116.

39. Kingston Vestry Minutes, November 5, 1784, NAJ: 2/6/6, f. 118.

40. Kingston Vestry Minutes, November 28, 1785, NAJ: 2/6/6, ff. 156–57.

41. Ragatz, pp. 190–91.

42. This thesis was most famously advanced by Lowell Ragatz and by Eric Williams, *Capitalism and Slavery* (Chapel Hill: University of North Carolina Press, 1944). A recent modification of Williams places equal emphasis on the Haitian Revolution as a cause of planter decline: David Beck Ryden, *West Indian Slavery and British Abolition, 1783–1807* (Cambridge, U.K.: Cambridge University Press, 2009), esp. chapter 9. For a demonstration of how the war affected one major planter family, see Michael Craton and James Walvin, *A Jamaican Plantation: The History of Worthy Park, 1670–1970* (London: W. H. Allen, 1970), pp. 154–79.

43. The 1783 petition is quoted in Prokopow, p. 36. See also *To the King's Most Excellent Majesty in Council, the Humble Memorial and Petition of the Council and Assembly of Jamaica* (Kingston, 1784).

44. Quoted in Prokopow, p. 61.

45. Prokopow, p. 69.

46. Petition of loyalists in Jamaica to Carleton, April 8, 1783, NYPL: Carleton Papers, Box 31, no. 7357.

47. Brown, pp. 21–22. Simon Taylor's house Prospect Park was later purchased by Alexander Aikman, and is now the residence of the Jamaican prime minister (Cundall, "Early Press," p. 310).

48. Simon Taylor to Chaloner Arcedeckne, September 9, 1782, Cambridge University Library: Vanneck Papers, 3A/1782/36. I am indebted to Vince Brown for references from the Taylor letters.

49. Taylor to Arcedeckne, September 3, 1787, Cambridge University Library: Vanneck Papers, 3A/1787/14. "Dirt-eating" was a poorly understood if widespread practice among West Indian slaves. Eighteenth-century observers like Taylor often saw it as a degenerate, voluntary practice; recent medical opinion (though still not unanimous) suggests it may be symptomatic of mineral deficiencies. Sheridan, pp. 216–19.

50. A searchable database of Atlantic slave trade data is available at http://www.slavevoyages.org/tast/index.faces, accessed December 26, 2009.

51. Prokopow, pp. 62–63. Of the 102 transported out of Savannah, thirty children had been born, but only seventy-six survived in 1786 to be sold, of which only twenty-five, in turn, were deemed sellable in Charleston. Leland J. Bellot, *William Knox: The Life and Thought of an Eighteenth-Century Imperialist* (Austin: University of Texas Press, 1977), pp. 198–99.

52. Long, II, p. 189.

53. Proceedings for November 13, 1784, *Journals of the Assembly of Jamaica* (Kingston: Alexander Aikman, 1804), VIII, p. 22.

54. Proceedings for December 21, 1784, *Journals of the Assembly of Jamaica*, VIII, pp. 82–83. The fullest treatment of this scheme is in Prokopow, pp. 65–100. "Frog" had long been used as a slang term for the Dutch, as well as for Jesuits and the French.

55. Prokopow, pp. 87–88. On Frogg, see "A List of Loyalists in Jamaica," NLJ: MS 1841, p. 12. He managed to receive at least some official succor, with a 1787 commis-

sion to make the uniforms for the Kingston town guard (Kingston Vestry Minutes, June 28, 1787, NAJ: 2/6/6).

56. "Return of Persons who Emigrated from East Florida to different parts of the British Dominions," signed by William Brown, May 2, 1786, NA: CO 5/561, f. 407. At least fifty whites and two hundred blacks from Florida transited through Jamaica to the Mosquito Coast in the summer of 1784: Alured Clarke to Sydney, August 15, 1784, NA: CO 137/84, f. 157.

57. "Extract of a Letter from Governor Orde, to the Right Honble Lord Sydney, dated Dominica Novr. 25th 1784," NA: T1/610, f. 192.

58. Boyd Alexander, *England's Wealthiest Son: A Study of William Beckford* (London: Centaur Press, 1962), pp. 210–15. Beckford later sued the Wildmans to recover the plantation, Quebec, near Port Maria. Alexander notes that James Wildman's "letters and handwriting indicate an almost illiterate man unable to express himself on paper." On returning to England in 1794, Wildman used his fortune to buy Chilham Castle in Kent.

59. Allan Karras, *Sojourners in the Sun: Scottish Migrants in Jamaica and the Chesapeake, 1740–1800* (Ithaca, N.Y.: Cornell University Press, 1992), pp. 55–56.

60. Brown, pp. 181–90; Sheridan, chapters 7–8, passim. For ameliorative efforts in Jamaica see Christa Breault Dierksheide, "The Amelioration of Slavery in the Anglo-American Imagination, 1770–1840" (Ph.D. dissertation, University of Virginia, 2009), chapters 5–6.

61. Sheridan, p. 46–47, 83–95, 192, 295–312. See also Craton and Walvin, pp. 125–34.

62. Sheridan, pp. 9–11; Elizabeth Lichtenstein Johnston, *Recollections of a Georgia Loyalist* (New York: M. F. Mansfield and Company, 1901), pp. 82–83. Dr. Johnston's former teacher Benjamin Rush famously applied both treatment methods to yellow fever victims in Philadelphia that same year, though to little avail.

63. Sheridan, pp. 250–63. When Maria Nugent's daughter was vaccinated from the arm of "a nice little mulatto child" in Spanish Town a decade later, it was using the safer Jenner method of vaccination with cowpox virus (p. 177).

64. Johnston, pp. 84–85.

65. Johnston, pp. 85, 89, 105. The details of Catherine's departure are not explained in Johnston's narrative. Catherine accompanied her mother to Jamaica in 1786 (p. 80), but Elizabeth later lamented that Lewis Johnston had "taken her from me, thinking to benefit her by the advantages she would gain in Edinburgh," when Catherine was ten, i.e. in 1792–93 (p. 105).

66. Johnston, p. 90.

67. Johnston, pp. 85–86.

68. On the postwar revival in Jamaica, see Sylvia R. Frey and Betty Wood, *Come Shouting to Zion: African American Protestantism in the American South and British Caribbean to 1830* (Chapel Hill: University of North Carolina Press, 1998), chapter 5; Brown, chapter 6; Mary Turner, *Slaves and Missionaries: The Disintegration of Jamaican Slave Society, 1787–1834* (Chicago: University of Illinois Press, 1998), chapter 1.

69. "An Account of several Baptist Churches, consisting chiefly of Negro Slaves: particularly of one at Kingston, in Jamaica; and another at Savannah in Georgia," in "Letters Showing the Rise and Progress of the Early Negro Churches of Georgia and the West Indies," *Journal of Negro History* 1, no. 1 (1916): 71. This and Liele's other letters first appeared in the *Baptist Annual Register* of 1790–93.

70. Quotations from "An Account of several Baptist Churches," and George Liele to John Rippon, May 18, 1792, in "Letters Showing the Rise," pp. 71–73, 81. See also

Cox, II, p. 13. John W. Pulis, "Bridging Troubled Waters: Moses Baker, George Liele, and the African American Diaspora to Jamaica," in John W. Pulis, ed., *Moving On: Black Loyalists in the Afro-Atlantic World* (New York: Garland Publishing, 2002), pp. 183–222.

71. "An Account of several Baptist Churches," in "Letters Showing the Rise," pp. 73–74. On Liele as a leader and institution-builder, see Frey and Wood, pp. 115–17.

72. "An Account of several Baptist Churches," in "Letters Showing the Rise," p. 71.

73. Stephen Cooke to Rippon, November 26, 1791, in "Letters Showing the Rise," pp. 75–76.

74. Julius Sherrard Scott III, "The Common Wind: Currents of Afro-American Communication in the Era of the Haitian Revolution" (Ph.D. dissertation, Duke University, 1986), pp. 209–12.

75. Scott, pp. 213–14.

76. Scott, pp. 51–58.

77. Scott, pp. 182–83.

78. R. C. Dallas, *The History of the Maroons*, 2 vols. (London, 1803); John N. Grant, *The Maroons in Nova Scotia* (Halifax, N.S.: Formac, 2002); Brathwaite, pp. 248–51.

79. Scott, p. 231. Anna Maria Falconbridge, whose abolitionist husband was involved in the Sierra Leone settlement scheme, arrived in Kingston not long afterwards and remarked on how much "it would have hurt me" to see Wilberforce "coupled with such an incendiary." A. M. Falconbridge, *Narrative of Two Voyages to the River Sierra Leone during the Years 1791–1792–1793*, 2nd ed. (London: L. I. Higham, 1802), pp. 234–35.

80. Francis Augustus Cox, *History of the Baptist Missionary Society, from 1792 to 1842*, 2 vols. (London: T. Ward and Co., and G. J. Dyer, 1842), II, pp. 13–15; Brathwaite, p. 253.

81. Brathwaite, p. 255.

82. Clement Gayle, *George Liele: Pioneer Missionary to Jamaica* (Kingston: Jamaica Baptist Union, 1982), p. 19.

83. On paternalism as exercised on Jamaican plantations, see Byrd, pp. 78–85.

84. Thomas Coke, *A History of the West Indies*, 3 vols. (Liverpool: Nutter, Fishall, and Dixon, 1808), I, p. 445; Frey and Wood, p. 136.

85. Thomas Nicholas Swigle to [John Rippon], May 1, 1802, "Letters Showing the Rise," pp. 88–89.

86. On the nineteenth-century history of Baptism in Jamaica, see especially Catherine Hall, *Civilising Subjects: Colony and Metropole in the English Imagination, 1830–1867* (Chicago: University of Chicago Press, 2002).

87. Nugent, *Lady Nugent's Journal*, pp. 1, 10–11, 253.

88. Nugent, p. 184.

89. In October, 1803, Nugent noted that "Mrs. and the Misses Johnstone were the ladies at dinner to-day," but gave no first names. (Nugent, p. 179.)

90. Nugent, p. 23.

91. Johnston, pp. 91–95, 105–7.

92. Johnston, p. 107.

93. Johnston, pp. 96–97.

94. Johnston, p. 108.

95. On U.S. commerce with the Caribbean in this period, see Michelle Craig Mac-Donald, "From Cultivation to Cup: Caribbean Coffee and the North American Economy, 1765–1805" (Ph.D. dissertation, University of Michigan, 2005), chapter 5.

96. Johnston, pp. 110–11.

97. On loyalists in Belize, see especially the work of St. John Robinson, "Southern Loyalists in the Caribbean and Central America," *South Carolina Historical Magazine* 93, no. 3–4 (July–October 1992): 205–20; and Prokopow, section III.

Chapter Nine: Promised Land

1. "An Account of the Life of Mr. David George . . . ," in Vincent Carretta, ed., *Unchained Voices: An Anthology of Black Authors in the English-Speaking World of the Eighteenth Century* (Lexington: University of Kentucky Press, 1996), pp. 338–40.

2. "An Account of the Life of David George," in Carretta, ed., pp. 340, 348 n. 48.

3. James W. St. G. Walker, *The Black Loyalists: The Search for a Promised Land in Nova Scotia and Sierra Leone, 1783–1870* (London: Longman, 1976), pp. 23–32; Ellen Gibson Wilson, *The Loyal Blacks* (New York: Capricorn, 1976), pp. 100–102, 108–11 (Peters quote p. 109); Robin W. Winks, *The Blacks in Canada: A History*, 2nd ed. (Montreal: McGill-Queen's University Press, 1997), p. 36.

4. "Memoirs of the Life of Boston King," in Carretta, ed., p. 360.

5. Walker, pp. 40–41; Winks, pp. 37–38. The terminological slippage makes it hard to know how many of the 396 "servants" listed in 1784 musters of Shelburne and Birchtown were actually enslaved.

6. John Clarkson's Memorandum Book, BL: Add. Mss. 41626B, ff. 15–16. This volume contains notes on a number of abuses cited by black loyalists in Nova Scotia.

7. Walker, pp. 50–51. On slavery in loyalist Nova Scotia, see Barry Cahill, "Habeas Corpus and Slavery in Nova Scotia: *R. v. Hecht, ex parte Rachel, 1798*," *University of New Brunswick Law Journal* 44 (1995): pp. 179–209.

8. Wilson, pp. 95–96.

9. The dinner party anecdote was reported by Thomas Clarkson, and is quoted in Wilson, pp. 177–78.

10. "Memorial of Thos. Peters and Others to the Rt. Honl. W. W. Grenville one of His Majesty's principal Secretaries of State," NA: FO 4/1, ff. 421–23.

11. He must have left Nova Scotia at more or less the same time that William Augustus Bowles also sailed from Nova Scotia, in search of British support for Muskogee. This leads Wilson to suggest fancifully that they may have traveled on the same ship. Wilson, pp. 179–80.

12. Wilson, pp. 149–50.

13. The fullest account of the Black Poor project is provided in Stephen J. Braidwood, *Black Poor and White Philanthropists: London's Blacks and the Foundation of the Sierra Leone Settlement, 1786–91* (Liverpool: University of Liverpool Press, 1994), pp. 129–60. But see also Wilson, pp. 144–53; Simon Schama, *Rough Crossings: Britain, the Slaves, and the American Revolution* (London: BBC Books, 2005), pp. 190–97; Cassandra Pybus, *Epic Journeys of Freedom: Runaway Slaves of the American Revolution and Their Global Quest for Liberty* (Boston: Beacon Press, 2006), pp. 111–19; Alexander X. Byrd, *Captives and Voyagers: Black Migrants across the Eighteenth-Century British Atlantic World* (Baton Rouge: Louisiana State University Press, 2008), pp. 139–53. Equiano discussed the scheme in his autobiography: Olaudah Equiano, *Interesting Narrative of the Life of Olaudah Equiano* (New York: Penguin Books, 2003), pp. 226–31.

14. "Treaty for 1788," NASL.

15. Granville Sharp, *A Short Sketch of Temporary Regulations (Until Better Shall be Proposed) for the Intended Settlement on the Grain Coast of Africa, Near Sierra Leona*, 2nd ed. (London: H. Baldwin, 1786), p. 34.

16. David Hancock, *Citizens of the World: London Merchants and the Integration of the British Atlantic Community, 1735–1785* (Cambridge, U.K.: Cambridge University Press, 1995), pp. 1–2.

17. A. M. Falconbridge, *Narrative of Two Voyages to the River Sierra Leone during the Years 1791–1792–1793*, 2nd ed. (London: L. I. Higham, 1802), pp. 32–33.

18. Falconbridge, p. 64.

19. "Manuscript Orders from the Directors of the Sierra Leone Company," ca. 1791, NASL, p. 5.

20. Sir Henry Clinton to Evan Nepean, December 26, 1790, NA: FO 4/1, f. 416.

21. Memorial of Thomas Peters to Lord Grenville, ca. December 24, 1790, NA: FO 4/1, ff. 419–20.

22. Henry Dundas to Thomas Carleton, August 6, 1791, NA: CO 188/4, f. 215.

23. Quoted in Wilson, p. 186.

24. William Wilberforce to John Clarkson, August 8, 1791, BL: Add. Mss. 41262A, f. 5; Thomas Clarkson to John Clarkson, August 28, 1791, f. 11; Henry Thornton to John Clarkson, December 30, 1791, f. 44; Thomas Clarkson to John Clarkson [January 1792], ff. 64–74.

25. Carleton to Dundas, December 13, 1791, NA: CO 188/4, ff. 239–40.

26. Clarkson Diary, October 8, 1791, NASL, p. 16. The originals of Clarkson's diary have been dispersed and some portions lost. I have drawn citations from Clarkson's diary for March–December 1791 from the manuscript original in the National Archives of Sierra Leone. Citations from December 1791–March 1792 are drawn from a microfilm in the New-York Historical Society of Charles Bruce Fergusson, ed., *Clarkson's Mission to America, 1791–1792* (Halifax: Public Archives of Nova Scotia, 1971); and citations for March–August 1792 are from a microfilm, also in the New-York Historical Society, of the original. Clarkson's diary for August–November 1792 has been published in *Sierra Leone Studies* 8 (1927): 1–114.

27. A copy of this handbill can be found in PANS: RG 1, vol. 419 (reel 15460), item 1.

28. "Memoirs of the Life of Boston King," in Carretta, ed., pp. 363–64.

29. Lorenzo Sabine, *Biographical Sketches of Loyalists of the American Revolution*, 2 vols., 2nd ed. (Boston: Little, Brown and Company, 1864), II, pp. 307–8.

30. Stephen Skinner to Colonel William Shirriff, November 2, 1791, NYHS: Stephen Skinner Letterbook.

31. John Clarkson Memorandum Book, BL: Add. Mss. 41262B, f. 15.

32. "An Account of the Life of David George," in Carretta, ed., p. 340.

33. Clarkson Diary, October 25, 1791, NASL, p. 32.

34. Clarkson Diary, October 26, 1791, NASL, pp. 33–34.

35. Clarkson Diary, October 26, 1791, NASL, p. 37.

36. Clarkson Diary, November 2, 1791, NASL, p. 41.

37. Clarkson Diary, October 28, 1791, NASL, p. 38.

38. Byrd, pp. 177–99.

39. "Bill of fare—for Victualling the free Blacks to Sierra leone," PANS: RG 1, vol. 419 (reel 15460), item 18.

40. Thomas Peters and David Edmons to Clarkson, December 23, 1791, BL: Add. Mss. 41262A, f. 24.

41. Clarkson Diary, December 23 and 26, 1791, NYHS, pp. 115, 118.

42. Wilson, p. 225.

43. Clarkson Diary, December 13, 1791, NYHS, p. 104.

44. "An Account of the Life of David George," in Carretta, ed., p. 340; "Memoirs of the Life of Boston King," in Carretta, ed., p. 364; Clarkson Diary, January 15 to March 6, 1792, NYHS, pp. 161–68.

45. "An Account of the Life of David George," in Carretta, ed., p. 340.

46. Clarkson Diary, March 11, 1792, NYHS, p. 171; "An Account of the Life of David George," in Carretta, ed., p. 340.

47. Clarkson Diary, March 6, 1792, NYHS, p. 168.

48. Clarkson Diary, March 7, 1792, NYHS, p. 169.

49. Clarkson Diary, March 18, 1792, NYHS, pp. 180–81.

50. Lots are itemized in a list of "Names of Settlers Located on the 1st Nova Scotian Allotment," NASL.

51. Clarkson Diary, March 20 and 27, 1792, NYHS, pp. 8, 37. Anonymous Journal, March 15, 1792, BL: Add. Mss. 41264, f. 13. Falconbridge, p. 162.

52. Falconbridge, p. 148.

53. "Memoirs of the Life of Boston King," in Carretta, ed., p. 364.

54. Clarkson Diary, April 5, 1792, NYHS, p. 74.

55. Clarkson Diary, May 4, 1792, NYHS, p. 169.

56. Clarkson Diary, March 27, 1792, NYHS, p. 43.

57. Wilson, pp. 240–44. The alcoholics were Dr. Bell, the surgeon, and Alexander Falconbridge, commercial agent.

58. Clarkson Diary, June 23, 1783, NYHS, p. 312.

59. Clarkson Diary, March 22, 1792, NYHS, pp. 20–21.

60. Clarkson Diary, June 15, 1792, NYHS, p. 293.

61. Clarkson Diary, April 8, 1792, NYHS, p. 86.

62. Clarkson Diary, June 26, 1792, NYHS, p. 324.

63. Clarkson Diary, May 19, 1792, NYHS, pp. 221–22.

64. Clarkson Diary, May 29, 1792, NYHS, p. 248.

65. Clarkson Diary, April 8, 1792, NYHS, pp. 81–84.

66. Anonymous Journal, April 11, 1792, BL: Add. Mss. 41264, f. 27.

67. Clarkson Diary, July 25, 1792, NYHS, pp. 388–89.

68. Clarkson Diary, July 30, 1792, NYHS, p. 400.

69. Walker, p. 181; Wilson, p. 293.

70. Falconbridge, p. 169.

71. Prayer and List of Gifts, BL: Add. Mss. 41262A, ff. 210–20; Journal of Isaac DuBois, BL: Add. Mss. 41263, f. 1.

72. "Farewell Petition," November 28, 1792, in Christopher Fyfe, ed., *"Our Children Free and Happy": Letters from Black Settlers in Africa in the 1790s* (Edinburgh: Edinburgh University Press, 1991), pp. 30–31.

73. "An Account of the Life of David George," in Carretta, ed., p. 341.

74. Journal of Zachary Macaulay, September 28, 1794, Zachary Macaulay Papers, Henry E. Huntington Library [Harvard College Library: Microfilm A 471, reel 3]; Schama, pp. 368–71; Wilson, pp. 317–20; David George to John Rippon, November 12, 1794, in Carretta, ed., pp. 343–44.

75. Wilson, pp. 318, 21.

76. Luke Jordan, Moses Wilkinson et al., November 19, 1794, in Fyfe, ed., pp. 43–44.

77. Luke Jordan and Isaac Anderson to Clarkson, June 28, 1794, in Fyfe, ed., p. 42.

78. James Liaster to Clarkson, March 30, 1796, in Fyfe, ed., pp. 49–50.

79. Christopher Fyfe, *A History of Sierra Leone* (Oxford: Oxford University Press, 1962), pp. 49–50; Walker, p. 176; Wilson, p. 288.

80. Falconbridge, p. 205.

81. Falconbridge, p. 210.

82. Journal of Isaac DuBois, January 7, 1793, BL: Add. Mss. 41263, f. 3. The couple had a son, Francis Blake DuBois, one of whose sons in turn was named John Clark-

son DuBois. The African-American intellectual W. E. B. DuBois, who was partly descended from white Bahamians, surmised that his forebears were loyalists, and wondered if he was perhaps related to Isaac DuBois, whom he knew held a land grant in the Bahamas. The connection is all the more intriguing given that DuBois spent his last years in West Africa, attracted there by his black ancestry—little knowing that, in Isaac DuBois, he may have had a white ancestor who lived on the continent too. W. E. B. DuBois, *Dusk of Dawn: An Essay Toward an Autobiography of a Race Concept* (New Brunswick, N.J.: Transaction Books, 1984), p. 105.

83. "Settlers' Petition," in Fyfe, ed., p. 38.

84. Falconbridge, p. 255.

85. Wilson, pp. 295–97.

86. Walker, pp. 178–80; Pybus, pp. 178–80.

87. Nathaniel Snowball and James Hutcherson to Clarkson, May 24, 1796, in Fyfe, ed., p. 52.

88. Walker, p. 205.

89. Sir Guy Carleton to Sydney, March 15, 1783, NYPL: Carleton Papers, Box 30, no. 7139. Walker, p. 219.

90. Boston King to Clarkson, June 1, 1797, BL: Add. Mss. 41263, f. 147.

91. Pybus, pp. 189–90.

92. This document is reproduced in Fyfe, ed., pp. 63–64.

93. Walker, pp. 208–9.

94. Pybus, pp. 198–202; Walker, pp. 228–35; Wilson, pp. 393–95.

95. Quoted in Fyfe, p. 87.

96. By 1811 there were already 807 Maroons to 982 Nova Scotians. "Houses and Population within the Walls of Sierra Leone taken by Order of Governor Columbine, April 1811," in Liverpool to Maxwell, November 20, 1811, NASL: Secretary of State Despatches, 1809-[1811], pp. 155–56; Fyfe, pp. 114–15.

97. Philip Beaver, *African Memoranda: Relative to an Attempt to Establish a British Settlement on the Island of Bulama* (London: C. and R. Baldwin, 1805), pp. 115–16. Deirdre Coleman, *Romantic Colonization and British Anti-Slavery* (Cambridge, U.K.: Cambridge University Press, 2005), pp. 80–89.

98. On black loyalism as a process, see Byrd, pp. 245–46.

99. "Memoir of the Life of Boston King," in Carretta, ed., pp. 365–66.

100. "Memoir of the Life of Boston King," in Carretta, ed., p. 360.

101. Journal of Zachary Macaulay, May 28, 1798, Zachary Macaulay Papers, Henry E. Huntington Library [Harvard College Library: Microfilm A 471, reel 3]. This was the version of events Bowles presented to Macaulay, though another story suggested that his ship was attacked by the Royal Navy. J. Leitch Wright, *William Augustus Bowles: Director General of the Creek Nation* (Athens: University of Georgia Press, 1967), pp. 93–94.

102. This image is reproduced as the frontispiece in Thomas Winterbottom, *Account of the Native Africans in the Neighbourhood of Sierra Leone*, 2 vols. (London: C. Whittingham, 1803).

Chapter Ten: Empires of Liberty

1. For the later careers of Morris, John, and Phil Robinson, see Julia Jarvis, *Three Centuries of Robinsons: The Story of a Family* (Toronto: T. H. Best, 1967), pp. 85–111. William Henry Robinson's career is described in Catherine Skinner Robinson, *Lady Robinson's Recollections* (London: Barrett, Sons and Co., Printers, 1842).

2. F. P. Robinson to Beverley Robinson Jr., December 3, 1799, NBM: Robinson Family Papers, Folder 14.

3. Henry Robinson to Beverley Robinson Jr., October 10, 1801, NBM: Robinson Family Papers, Folder 7.

4. F. P. Robinson to Beverley Robinson Jr., May 1, 1801, NBM: Robinson Family Papers, Folder 14.

5. Henry Robinson to Beverley Robinson Jr., April 21, 1802, NBM: Robinson Family Papers, Folder 7.

6. Henry Robinson to Beverley Robinson Jr., April 21, 1802, NBM: Robinson Family Papers, Folder 7.

7. Henry Robinson to Ann Barclay Robinson, May 27, 1802, NBM: Robinson Family Papers, Folder 8.

8. F. P. Robinson to Beverley Robinson Jr., n.d. [Autumn 1804], NBM: Robinson Family Papers, Folder 14.

9. Henry Robinson to Beverley Robinson Jr., June 1, 1803, NBM: Robinson Family Papers, Folder 7.

10. Henry Robinson to Ann Barclay Robinson, June 11 and August 22, 1804, NBM: Robinson Family Papers, Folder 8.

11. R. Burnham Moffat, *The Barclays of New York: Who They Are, and Who They Are Not* (New York: Robert Grier Cooke, 1904), p. 106.

12. Ann Barclay Robinson to Susan Robinson, August 20, 1805, NBM: Robinson Family Papers, Folder 10.

13. F. P. Robinson to Beverley Robinson Jr., May 1, 1805, NBM: Robinson Family Papers, Folder 14.

14. F. P. Robinson to Beverley Robinson Jr., July 3, 1805, NBM: Robinson Family Papers, Folder 14.

15. Beverley Robinson III to Ann Barclay Robinson, October 29 [1796], NBM: Robinson Family Papers, Folder 5.

16. Henry Robinson to Ann Barclay Robinson, March 12, 1802, NBM: Robinson Family Papers, Folder 8.

17. Jonathan J. Bean, "Duer, William"; http://www.anb.org.ezp-prod1.hul.harvard.edu/articles/10/10–00470.html; *American National Biography Online*, February 2000, accessed March 14, 2010. Craig Hanyan, "Duer, William Alexander"; http://www.anb.org.ezp-prod1.hul.harvard.edu/articles/11/11–00259.html; *American National Biography Online*, February 2000, accessed March 14, 2010. Devonshire-born William Duer Sr. had served as Robert Clive's secretary in India before immigrating to New York. Their maternal grandfather was William Alexander, Lord Stirling.

18. Beverley Robinson III to Beverley Robinson Jr., July 21 and August 6, 1806, NBM: Robinson Family Papers, Folder 4.

19. The absence of violence against loyalists in particular might also be partly explained by the presence of violence in the early republic more generally. See Allan Kulikoff, "Revolutionary Violence and the Origins of American Democracy," *Journal of the Historical Society* 2, no. 2 (March 2002): 229–60.

20. James H. Kettner, *The Development of American Citizenship, 1608–1870* (Chapel Hill: University of North Carolina Press, 1978), pp. 173–209, 245–46.

21. Aaron Nathan Coleman, "Loyalists in War, Americans in Peace: The Reintegration of the Loyalists, 1775–1800" (Ph.D. dissertation, University of Kentucky, 2008), p. 90. On loyalist reintegration see also David Edward Maas, "The Return of the Massachusetts Loyalists" (Ph.D. dissertation, University of Wisconsin, 1972), chapters 8–11; Robert M. Calhoon, "The Reintegration of the Loyalists and Disaffected," in Robert M. Calhoon, et al., *The Loyalist Perception and Other Essays* (Colum-

bia: University of South Carolina Press, 1989), pp. 195–215; Rebecca Nathan Brannon, "Reconciling the Revolution: Resolving Conflict and Rebuilding Community in the Wake of Civil War in South Carolina, 1775–1860" (Ph.D. dissertation, University of Michigan, 2007).

22. Coleman, pp. 89–116.

23. Daniel J. Hulsebosch, *Constituting Empire: New York and the Transformation of Constitutionalism in the Atlantic World, 1664–1830* (Chapel Hill: University of North Carolina Press, 2005), p. 192.

24. Hulsebosch, pp. 192–202.

25. "Letters from Phocion," Letter II, in Alexander Hamilton, *The Works of Alexander Hamilton*, ed. Henry Cabot Lodge, 12 vols. (New York: G. P. Putnam's Sons, 1904), IV, p. 289.

26. George Washington to Charles Cotesworth Pinckney, August 24, 1795, in George Washington, *The Writings of George Washington*, ed. Worthington Chauncey Ford, 14 vols. (New York: G. P. Putnam's Sons, 1892), XIII, p. 95.

27. On debts, see Kettner, pp. 186–87.

28. Robert W. Tucker and David C. Hendrickson, *Empire of Liberty: The Statecraft of Thomas Jefferson* (New York: Oxford University Press, 1990), p. 67.

29. Peter Silver, *Our Savage Neighbors: How Indian War Transformed Early America* (New York: W. W. Norton, 2009), chapter 9.

30. Isabel Thompson Kelsay, *Joseph Brant, 1743–1807: Man of Two Worlds* (Syracuse, N.Y.: Syracuse University Press, 1984), pp. 564, 601.

31. Alan Taylor, *The Divided Ground: Indians, Settlers, and the Northern Borderland of the American Revolution* (New York: Knopf, 2006), pp. 326–41.

32. The Venezuelan creole Francisco de Miranda was also in London again, wooing American and British support for his plan to foment a revolution across Spanish America. Alexander Hamilton suggested that "a fleet of Great Britain, an army of the U. States" could collaborate in assisting Miranda. (Alexander Hamilton to Francisco de Miranda, August 22, 1798, in Charles R. King, *The Life and Correspondence of Rufus King*, 6 vols. [New York: G. P. Putnam's Sons, 1894–1900], II, p. 659.) When Miranda finally did launch his expedition to liberate Venezuela, he did it not from London but New York, and recruited volunteers among former patriots and loyalists alike. James Biggs, *The History of Don Francisco de Miranda's Attempt to Effect a Revolution in South America, in a Series of Letters* (Boston: Edward Oliver, 1812), identifies a number of the participants, who included John Adams's grandson William Steuben Smith, acting as Miranda's aide-de-camp, as well as several loyalists. See also James Leitch Wright, *William Augustus Bowles, Director General of the Creek Nation* (Athens: University of Georgia Press, 1967), pp. 98–99.

33. Wright, pp. 96–106.

34. Claudio Saunt, *A New Order of Things: Property, Power, and the Transformation of the Creek Indians, 1733–1816* (Cambridge, U.K.: Cambridge University Press, 1999), p. 139.

35. For a comparison of these diasporas, see my "Revolutionary Exiles: The American Loyalist and French Émigré Diasporas," in David Armitage and Sanjay Subrahmanyam, eds., *The Age of Revolutions in Global Context, c. 1760–1840* (Basingstoke, U.K.: Palgrave Macmillan, 2010), chapter 3.

36. Wright, pp. 124–41, 146–49.

37. Saunt, pp. 233–72.

38. Quotations from Jon Latimer, *1812: War with America* (Cambridge, Mass: Harvard University Press, 2007), p. 29; Jon Meacham, *American Lion: Andrew Jackson in the*

White House (New York: Random House, 2008), p. 31. See also Anthony Wallace, *The Long, Bitter Trail: Andrew Jackson and the Indians* (New York: Hill and Wang, 1993).

39. Taylor, pp. 357–65; Kelsay, pp. 564, 601, 615–52.

40. For the centrality of imperial models in early U.S. political thought, see Hulsebosch, esp. pp. 213–19; David Hendrickson, *Peace Pact: The Lost World of the American Founding* (Lawrence: University Press of Kansas, 2003). On Jefferson and empire, see Peter Onuf, *Jefferson's Empire: The Language of American Nationhood* (Charlottesville: University of Virginia Press, 2001), esp. chapter 2; Tucker and Hendrickson, esp. part III.

41. Beverley Robinson III to Beverley Robinson Jr., November 5, 1809, NBM: Robinson Family Papers, Folder 4.

42. Morris Robinson to Beverley Robinson Jr., February 14, 1806, NBM: Robinson Family Papers, Folder 13.

43. Morris Robinson to Beverley Robinson Jr., April 5, 1806, NBM: Robinson Family Papers, Folder 13.

44. Latimer, pp. 17, 32.

45. Latimer, p. 42.

46. Latimer, pp. 45–46.

47. J. I. Little, *Loyalties in Conflict: A Canadian Borderland in War and Rebellion, 1812–1840* (Toronto: University of Toronto Press, 2008).

48. Norman Knowles, *Inventing the Loyalists: The Ontario Loyalist Tradition and the Creation of Usable Pasts* (Toronto: University of Toronto Press, 1997), p. 21. The idea was that loyalists would place the initials "U.E." after their names as an honorific. The provincial Land Boards started keeping lists of United Empire Loyalists, but these were not systematically maintained.

49. Gerald M. Craig, *Upper Canada: The Formative Years, 1784–1841* (Toronto: McClelland and Stewart, 1963), pp. 57–70; Elizabeth Jane Errington, *The Lion, the Eagle, and Upper Canada: A Developing Colonial Ideology* (Kingston, Ont.: McGill–Queen's University Press, 1987), pp. 64–67; George Sheppard, *Plunder, Profits, and Paroles: A Social History of the War of 1812 in Upper Canada* (Montreal: McGill-Queen's University Press, 1994), pp. 27–29, 41–42.

50. Sheppard, pp. 56–65; Latimer, p. 107.

51. Errington, pp. 70–80.

52. Craig, p. 72.

53. A. J. Langguth, *Union 1812: The Americans Who Fought the Second War of Independence* (New York: Simon and Schuster, 2006), p. 174.

54. Donald R. Hickey, *The War of 1812: A Forgotten Conflict* (Urbana: University of Illinois Press, 1989), pp. 80–90; Errington, p. 80; Latimer, pp. 51, 64–83.

55. Hickey, pp. 129–30; Latimer, pp. 131–33. Quote from Sheppard, *Plunder, Profit, and Paroles*, p. 102.

56. Duncan Andrew Campbell, *Unlikely Allies: Britain, America and the Victorian Origins of the Special Relationship* (London: Hambledon Continuum, 2007), p. 29.

57. Latimer, pp. 304–22.

58. Latimer, pp. 349–60. For excerpts from Robinson's account of the battle, see C. W. Robinson, "The Expedition to Plattsburg, Upon Lake Champlain, Canada, 1814," *Journal of the Royal United Service Institution* 61 (August 1916): 499–521. Published in the middle of World War I, when large numbers of Canadian volunteers joined the British on the Western Front, this article offers a good statement of how later generations of Canadians responded to the War of 1812, seeing it as a moment when "those links of loyalty and devotion which bind Canada to the Mother Country were cemented with blood" (p. 499).

59. Latimer, pp. 386–87.

60. Quoted in Harvey Amani Whitfield, *Blacks on the Border: The Black Refugees in British North America, 1815–1860* (Burlington: University of Vermont Press, 2006), p. 33.

61. Whitfield, pp. 31–40; Robin W. Winks, *The Blacks in Canada: A History*, 2nd ed. (Montreal: McGill–Queen's University Press, 1997), pp. 114–16. The *Times* of London described Cochrane's proclamation as "addressed to Negro Slaves in Southern States," even though the actual text did not mention slaves at all. Malcolm Bell Jr., *Major Butler's Legacy: Five Generations of a Slaveholding Family* (Athens: University of Georgia Press, 1987), p. 171.

62. Winks, p. 115.

63. Richard White, *The Middle Ground: Indians, Empires, and Republics in the Great Lakes Region, 1650–1815* (Cambridge, U.K.: Cambridge University Press, 1991), esp. chapters 10–12; Taylor, passim. Jeremy Adelman and Stephen Aron also interpret the War of 1812 as "the last gasp of the Great Lakes borderland" (p. 823): Jeremy Adelman and Stephen Aron, "From Borderlands to Borders: Empires, Nation-States, and the Peoples in between in North American History," *American Historical Review* 104, no. 3 (June 1999): pp. 814–41.

64. William S. Coker and Thomas D. Watson, *Indian Traders of the Southeastern Borderlands: Panton, Leslie & Company and John Forbes & Company, 1784–1847* (Pensacola: University of West Florida Press, 1986), pp. 302–9; Saunt, pp. 273–90.

65. Key's uncle, Philip Barton Key, had been a loyalist who had served as one of Ensign Bowles's commanding officers in the Maryland Loyalists. Philip Key noted in his loyalist claim that his brother (Francis Key's father) "was a firm Rebel. It was not recommended to the two Brothers to take different sides." He returned to the United States in 1785 and was later a Federalist congressman. Daniel Parker Coke, *The Royal Commission on the Losses and Services of American Loyalists, 1783–1785*, ed. Hugh Edward Egerton (New York: B. Franklin, 1971), pp. 387–88; "Philip Barton Key," q.v., Biographical Directory of the United States Congress, http://bioguide.congress .gov/scripts/biodisplay.pl?index=K000159, accessed July 22, 2009.

66. This is not to say that the border remained undisturbed—witness the Canadian rebellions of 1837–38, which included raids launched from the United States, and the Fenian raids of 1866 and later. The United States maintained well-developed plans for the invasion of Canada until the 1930s: Latimer, pp. 407–8.

67. In the words of Egerton Ryerson, for instance, the War of 1812 "illustrate[d] the Loyalist spirit and courage of the Canadians, French as well as English, and even true Americans; for the American settlers in Canada were, with a few exceptions, as loyal subjects and as bold defenders of their adopted country as the U.E. Loyalists themselves." Egerton Ryerson, *The Loyalists of America and Their Times: From 1620 to 1816*, 2 vols. (Toronto: William Briggs, 1880), II, p. 317.

68. Though there is broad consensus about the war's foundational role in popular memory, there is a rich literature on how precisely its effects played out during the nineteenth century. See among others, David Mills, *The Idea of Loyalty in Upper Canada, 1784–1850* (Kingston, Ont.: McGill–Queen's University Press, 1988), esp. pp. 12–33; S. F. Wise, "The War of 1812 in Popular History," in S. F. Wise, *God's Peculiar Peoples: Essays on Political Culture in Nineteenth-Century Canada* (Ottawa: Carleton University Press, 1993), pp. 149–67; Errington, pp. 55–86; Little, pp. 11–56; Knowles, pp. 14–25.

69. Mills, pp. 34–51.

70. Frederick Philipse Robinson to John Beverley Robinson, January 4, 1816, AO: Sir John Beverley Robinson Papers, MS 4, Reel One.

71. John Beverley Robinson Diaries, October 31, 1815, AO: Sir John Beverley Robinson Papers, MS 4, Reel Two, pp. 62–63.

72. Knowles, p. 14; S. F. Wise, "Upper Canada and the Conservative Tradition," in Wise, pp. 169–84. On the loyalist tradition see also J. M. Bumsted, *Understanding the Loyalists* (Sackville, N.B.: Centre for Canadian Studies, Mount Allison University, 1986).

73. Diary of Sir Frederick Philipse Robinson, RMC, pp. 278–79.

74. Catherine Skinner Robinson, *Lady Robinson's Recollections* (London: Barrett, Sons and Co., Printers, 1842), pp. 24–25.

75. Benson John Lossing, *The Pictorial Field Book of the Revolution*, 2 vols. (New York: Harper & Brothers, 1852), II, pp. 140–41. Charles A. Campbell, "Robinson's House in the Hudson Highlands: The Headquarters of Washington," *Magazine of American History* 4 (February 1880): 109–17. The house, later owned by New York senator Hamilton Fish, burned down in 1892.

76. Diary of Sir Frederick Philipse Robinson, RMC, pp. 279–80.

77. William Henry Robinson to Susan Robinson, February 6, 1810, NBM: Robinson Family Papers, Folder 9.

78. About twenty officers serving in this period born in various parts of America are listed in V. C. P. Hodson, *List of the Officers of the Bengal Army, 1758–1834*, 4 vols. (London: Constable, 1927–47).

79. Maria Nugent, *A Journal from the Year 1811 till the Year 1815, Including a Voyage to and Residence in India*, 2 vols. (London: T. and W. Boone, 1839), I, p. 126. The nephews were Cortlandt Skinner Barberie, a son of her sister Euphemia, and Philip Kearny Skinner, a son of her eldest brother. For their cadet papers, see APAC: L/MIL/10/25/255 and L/MIL/12/70/1.

80. Nugent, I, pp. 386–87.

81. Benedict Arnold to Jonathan Bliss, September 19, 1800, NBM: Arnold Papers, Folder One.

82. He then imagined packing the poor woman off to New Brunswick, where with "the first snow storm she will kick the Bucket or the devil is in her." William Henry Robinson to Susan Robinson, June 20, 1811, NBM: Robinson Family Papers, Folder 9.

83. Sophia's husband Pownall Phipps had an unusual background of his own, raised largely in France and spending several years under virtual house arrest in Caen during the French Revolution; his first wife was French, he spoke English with a French accent, and he was sent to India because his family wanted to put him "beyond the reach of French fascination" (that is, of defecting to the French side). He was already engaged to Sophia Arnold by the time Nugent met her in 1812. Pownall William Phipps, *The Life of Colonel Pownall Phipps* (London: Richard Bentley and Son, 1894), pp. 43–44, 90.

84. On these relationships see Durba Ghosh, *Sex and the Family in Colonial India: The Making of Empire* (Cambridge, U.K.: Cambridge University Press, 2006); William Dalrymple, *White Mughals: Love and Betrayal in Eighteenth-Century India* (New York: Viking, 2003); Maya Jasanoff, *Edge of Empire: Lives, Culture, and Conquest in the East, 1750–1850* (New York: Knopf, 2005), chapters 2–3.

85. Will of Lt. Edward Shippen Arnold, APAC: L/AG/34/29/26, Bengal Wills 1814, p. 193.

86. Will of Lt. Col. George Arnold (1829), APAC: L/AG/34/29/44, Bengal Wills 1829, vol. 1, pp. 22–23. The will provoked a suit in Chancery (Arnold v. Arnold, 1836–37) and a challenge to Louisa's bequest.

87. Phipps, pp. 152, 167. Phipps made no reference to Louisa's Indian mother.

Parents often worried about how best to raise bicultural children in this period. David Ochterlony, for instance, worried that "My children . . . are uncommonly fair but if educated in the european manner they will in spite of Complexion labour under all the Disadvantages of being known as the 'Natural Daughters of Ochterlony by a Native Woman.'" (David Ochterlony to Major Hugh Sutherland, ca. 1804, APAC: Letterbook of Robert Sutherland, MS Eur D 547, f. 133.)

88. Dalrymple, pp. 23–24. "Sir David Ochterlony," q.v., *DNB*.

89. In 1828 a public subscription was taken up to raise a memorial to Ochterlony on the Calcutta Maidan. Because of Ochterlony's attraction to Muslim culture, it was said, the monument was built in a Muslim architectural style: a fluted pillar 165 feet high, with a small onion dome at the top. The Ochterlony Monument has now been renamed the Shahid Minar (martyrs' tower), in honor of fighters for Indian independence.

90. Among the connections were Gardner's second cousins Frances and Henrietta Duer, who married Phil's nephews Bev and Morris Robinson respectively.

91. For Gardner's actions at Charleston, see *Independent Ledger* (Boston), June 19, 1779, p. 2. "Major Gardner of the 16th, his Lady and family" were among the prisoners taken to Boston in September 1779: *New Jersey Gazette* (Burlington, N.J.), September 29, 1779, p. 2. (The paper explained that Gardner "commanded the light corps of Col. Campbell's army in Georgia, and is *well known there* by the name of the *short regiment, humane* Commandant.") William Smith (whose wife was a Livingston) met Valentine and Alida Gardner in New York in late December 1779, after Valentine was released on parole. Smith later deployed Alida Gardner in an effort to persuade the loyalist-leaning Livingstons "to a Reconciliation with Great Britain." William Smith, *Historical Memoirs of William Smith, 1770–1783*, ed. William H. W. Sabine (New York: Arno Press, 1971), pp. 202, 258. There are scattered references to Valentine Gardner in the NYPL Carleton Papers.

92. As the above details help demonstrate, the suggestion that Gardner went to France with his mother as early as 1774 (Lionel J. Gardner, *The Sabre and the Spur: An Account of Colonel Gardner of Gardner's Horse [1770–1835]* [Chandigarh: Siddharth Publications, 1985], pp. 6–7) and the *DNB*'s statement that he "was brought up in France" are both wrong. Gardner himself said, "After the Peace we all came to England," confirming the view that they left with the evacuation of New York. Narinder Saroop, *Gardner of Gardner's Horse* (New Delhi: Palit and Palit, 1983), p. 11. On his Continental education: Saroop, pp. 14–15.

93. Fanny Parkes, *Wanderings of a Pilgrim in Search of the Picturesque*, 2 vols. (Karachi: Oxford University Press, 1975), I, pp. 417–18.

94. Another American who had been in Maratha service, John Parker Boyd of Massachusetts, returned to the United States—leaving his half-Indian daughter behind—where he fought Tecumseh at Tippecanoe and the British in the War of 1812. Ronald Rosner, "John Parker Boyd: The Yankee Mughal," *Asian Affairs* 34, no. 3 (November 2003): 297–309.

95. Quoted in Saroop, p. 97.

96. Emma Roberts, *Scenes and Characters of Hindostan*, 3 vols. (London: William H. Allen and Co., 1835) III, p. 142. Parkes, I, p. 348. An earlier version of Roberts's sketch appeared in the press, and Gardner wrote a letter to the *Asiatic Journal and Monthly Register* to correct errors in the portrait—particularly the suggestion that his female descendants would have trouble finding European husbands because of their complexions. *Asiatic Journal* 38 (1835): pp. 60–61.

97. Nugent, II, p. 9.

98. Parkes, I, pp. 185, 230.

99. Parkes, I, p. 185.

100. William Linnaeus Gardner to Edward Gardner, August 21, 1821, National Army Museum, London: Gardner Papers, p. 241. I am grateful to William Dalrymple for his transcripts from the Gardner letters.

Conclusion: Losers and Founders

1. I share the interpretation of this period suggested by Jeremy Adelman, "An Age of Imperial Revolutions," *American Historical Review* 113, no. 2 (April 2008): 319–40, which reinterprets the "age of democratic revolutions" proposed by R. R. Palmer as an age of imperial revolutions, fortifying empires at least as much as it furthered the fortunes of nation-states. See also C. A. Bayly, *The Birth of the Modern World, 1780–1914: Global Connections and Comparisons* (Malden, Mass.: Blackwell, 2004), chapter 3.

2. On the two images see Helmut von Erffa and Alan Staley, eds., *The Paintings of Benjamin West* (New Haven, Conn.: Yale University Press, 1986), pp. 219–22, 565–67.

3. Elizabeth Lichtenstein Johnston, *Recollections of a Georgia Loyalist* (New York: M. F. Mansfield and Company, 1901), p. 164. Although the preface states that Johnston wrote her recollections in 1836, she refers in her text to an event that took place in 1837. Johnston's daughter Eliza married Thomas Ritchie, a barrister elected to the Nova Scotia assembly. Her son John was also a member of the assembly. Her youngest son, James William Johnston, served as longtime leader of the Nova Scotia Conservative Party, premier of Nova Scotia, and was named Nova Scotia's lieutenant governor in 1873, but died before he could assume office.

4. See, e.g., discussions produced around the bicentennial of the emigration: J. M. Bumsted, *Understanding the Loyalists* (Sackville, N.B.: Centre for Canadian Studies, Mount Allison University, 1986); Wallace Brown and Hereward Senior, *Victorious in Defeat: The American Loyalists in Exile* (New York: Facts on File, 1984); Christopher Moore, *The Loyalists: Revolution, Exile, Settlement* (Toronto: Macmillan of Canada, 1984).

5. Michael Craton, *A History of the Bahamas* (London: Collins, 1968), pp. 194–96.

6. Mary Turner, *Slaves and Missionaries: The Disintegration of Jamaican Slave Society, 1787–1834* (Urbana: University of Illinois Press, 1982), chapter 6.

7. Ian McKay, "The Liberal Order Framework: A Prospectus for a Reconnaissance of Canadian History," *Canadian Historical Review* 81, no. 3 (December 2000): 632; Philip Girard, "Liberty, Order, and Pluralism: The Canadian Experience," in Jack P. Greene, ed., *Exclusionary Empire: English Liberty Overseas, 1600–1900* (Cambridge, U.K.: Cambridge University Press, 2010), pp. 177–81; Robin W. Winks, *The Relevance of Canadian History: U.S. and Imperial Perspectives* (Toronto: Macmillan of Canada, 1979).

8. James Corbett David, "Dunmore's New World: Political Culture in the British Empire, 1745–1796" (Ph.D. dissertation, College of William and Mary, 2010).

9. Isabel Kelsay, *Joseph Brant* (Syracuse, N.Y.: University of Syracuse Press, 1984), p. 658; Norman Knowles, *Inventing the Loyalists: The Ontario Loyalist Tradition and the Creation of Usable Pasts* (Toronto: University of Toronto Press, 1997), p. 119.

10. Marion Robertson, *King's Bounty: A History of Early Shelburne, Nova Scotia* (Halifax: Nova Scotia Museum, 1983), chapter 15. For a negative appraisal of the loyalists' fate in Nova Scotia, see Neil MacKinnon, *This Unfriendly Soil: The Loyalist Experience in Nova Scotia, 1783–1791* (Montreal: McGill–Queen's University Press, 1986), chapter 10.

11. Beverley Robinson Jr. to Frederick Robinson (son), June 17, 1816, NBM: Robinson Family Papers, Folder 6. Charles A. Campbell, "Robinson's House in the Hudson Highlands: The Headquarters of Washington," *Magazine of American History* 4 (February 1880): 115.

Appendix: Measuring the Exodus

1. Mary Beth Norton, *The British-Americans: The Loyalist Exiles in England, 1774–1789* (London: Constable, 1974), p. 9 (60–80,000); Esmond Wright, ed., *Red, White, and True Blue: The Loyalists in the Revolution* (New York: AMS Press, 1976), p. 2 (80,000); Wallace Brown, *The Good Americans: The Loyalists in the American Revolution* (New York: Morrow, 1969), p. 2 (100,000); John Ferling, *A Leap in the Dark: The Struggle to Create the American Republic* (Oxford: Oxford University Press, 2003), p. 257 (100,000).

2. The shipping lists can be found in NA: ADM 49/9.

3. I use the phrase "black loyalist" here, as throughout this book, to denote those slaves who ran away to the British in response to promises of freedom, not to suggest a uniform ideological position.

4. Cassandra Pybus, "Jefferson's Faulty Math," *William & Mary Quarterly* 62, no. 2 (April 2005): 243–64.

5. "Returns of Loyalists &c. gone from New York to Nova Scotia &c. p returns in the Commissary General's Office," New York, October 12, 1783, NA: CO 5/111, f. 118. "Return of Loyalists &c. gone from New York to Nova Scotia, Quebec & abbacoe as per Returns in the Commissary General's Office at New York," New York, November 24, 1783, NA: CO 5/111, f. 236.

6. "General Return of all the Disbanded Troops and other Loyalists who have lately become Settlers in the Provinces of Nova Scotia and New Brunswick, made up from the Rolls taken by the several Muster Masters," Halifax, November 4, 1784, NA: CO 217/41, ff. 163–64. The New York muster of October 1783 shows 1,328 refugees bound for Quebec (NA: CO 5/111, f. 118). These musters suggest that Philip Ranlet's skepticism of the New York evacuation figures may be overstated: Philip Ranlet, *The New York Loyalists* (Knoxville: University of Tennessee Press, 1986), pp. 193–94.

7. "A General Description of the Province of Nova Scotia . . . done by Lieutenant Colonel Morse Chief Engineer in America, upon a Tour of the Province in the Autumn of the year 1783, and the summer 1784. Under the Orders and Instructions of His Excellency Sir Guy Carleton . . . Given at Head Quarters at New York the 28th Day of July 1783," LAC: Robert Morse Fonds, MG 21, p. 43.

8. John Parr to Lord Shelburne, December 16, 1783, and Parr to Lord Sydney, August 13, 1784. NA: CO 217/56, f. 126 and f. 216.

9. "General Return of all the Disbanded Troops and other Loyalists settling in Nova Scotia and New Brunswick who are now receiving the Royal Bounty of Provisions," Halifax, November 25, 1785, NA: CO 217/41, f. 238.

10. "Return of Persons who Emigrated from East Florida to different parts of the British Dominions," signed by William Brown, Commissioner, London, May 2, 1786, NA: CO 5/561, f. 407.

11. "Muster-Book of Free Black Settlement of Birchtown 1784," LAC: Shelburne, Nova Scotia Collection, MG 9, B 9–14, Microfilm Reel H-984, ff. 172–207.

12. "An Effective List of all the Loyalists in Canada receiving provisions from the King's Store, that are not Charged for the same; with an exact accompt of the Number

of their Families, their age, & Sex, & the quantity of provisions pr day, with remarks opposite their Respective Names," July 1, 1779; "Return of Royalists & their families who receive provisions, not paying for the same at following places, Commencing the 25th day of September 1779 & Ending the 24th of October followg. Inclusive"; "Return of Families of Loyalists Receiving Provisions out of the Different magazines or Depots in the District of Montreal from the 25th of Octbr to the 24th of Novembr 1780"; "Return of Unincorporated Loyalists and Families who Received their Provisions gratis from Government from the 25th of Decembr 1781 to the 24th Janr 1782 Inclusive"; "Return of Unincorporated Refugee Loyalists in the Province of Quebec, exclusive of those at the upper Ports," November 3, 1783, BL: Haldimand Papers, Add. Mss. 21826, ff. 10–13, 24–30, 33–44, 62–69, 103.

13. "Return of disbanded Troops & Loyalists settled upon the King's Lands in the Province of Quebec in the Year 1784." BL: Haldimand Papers, Add. Mss. 21828, f. 141.

14. "Estimate of the Quantity of Lands that may be required to settle the K. R. R. New York, the Corps of Loyal, and King's Rangers, and Refugee Loyalists in the Province of Quebec, including those who have lately Arrived from New York," BL: Haldimand Papers, Add. Mss. 21829, f. 62.

15. Alan Taylor, *The Divided Ground: Indians, Settlers, and the Northern Borderland of the American Revolution* (New York: Knopf, 2006), pp. 122–23. J. M. Bumsted, *A History of the Canadian Peoples* (Toronto: Oxford University Press, 1998), p. 91.

16. Already receiving provisions there in 1778 were 191 refugees: "List of the Loyalists and their Families lodged at Machiche, 2d December 1778," BL: Add. Mss. 21826, f. 3.

17. "A Return of Refugees and their Slaves arrived in the Province of East Florida from the Provinces of Georgia and South Carolina taken upon Oath to the 23rd December 1782," NA: CO 5/560, f. 507. (Cf. an earlier account of 2,165 white and 3,340 black refugees, in "A Return of Refugees and their Slaves arrived in East Florida from Georgia and South Carolina taken upon Oath to the 14th November 1782," NA: CO 5/560, f. 477.) "A Return of Refugees & their Slaves arrived in this Province from Charlestown, at the time of the Evacuation thereof & not included in the last return, the 31st December 1783 [*sic*]," April 20, 1783, NYPL: Carleton Papers, Box 31, no. 7468. My figure differs from that provided by W. H. Siebert, who adds together the numbers provided in the musters of November 14 and December 23, 1782. I see no reason to assume, as Siebert does, that these represented separate populations, rather than a cumulative figure. W. H. Siebert, *Loyalists in East Florida 1774 to 1785: The Most Important Documents Pertaining Thereto, Edited with an Accompanying Narrative*, 2 vols. (Deland: Florida State Historical Society, 1929), I, pp. 130–31.

18. Lord Hawke, "Observations on East Florida," enclosed in Bernardo del Campo to Conde del Floridablanca, June 8, 1783. John Walton Caughey, ed., *East Florida, 1783–85: A File of Documents Assembled, and Many of Them Translated by Joseph Byrne Lockey* (Berkeley and Los Angeles: University of California Press, 1949), pp. 120–21. For a more detailed analysis of slave ownership among these refugees, see Carole Watterson Troxler, "Refuge, Resistance, and Reward: The Southern Loyalists' Claim on East Florida," *Journal of Southern History* 55, no. 4 (November 1989): 580–85.

19. Patrick Tonyn to Sydney, May 15, 1783, NA: CO 5/560, f. 584.

20. Tonyn to Admiral Digby, September 10, 1783, NA: CO 5/560, f. 698.

21. "Return of Persons who Emigrated from East Florida to different parts of the British Dominions," May 2, 1786, NA: CO 5/561, f. 407.

22. Tonyn to Sydney, April 4, 1785, quoted in Caughey, ed., pp. 498–99.

23. "Return of Persons who Emigrated from East Florida to different parts of the British Dominions," May 2, 1786, NA: CO 5/561, f. 407.

24. Norton, *The British-Americans*, pp. 36–37; Mary Beth Norton, "Eighteenth-Century American Women in Peace and War: The Case of the Loyalists," *William & Mary Quarterly* 33, no. 3 (July 1976): 386–409. Mary Beth Norton, personal communication, January 5, 2010.

25. Pybus, "Jefferson's Faulty Math."

26. "Returns of Loyalists &c. gone from New York to Nova Scotia &c. p returns in the Commissary General's Office," New York, October 12, 1783, NA: CO 5/111, f. 118.

27. W. H. Siebert, "The Legacy of the American Revolution to the British West Indies and Bahamas," *Ohio State University Bulletin* 17, no. 27 (April 1913): 21. This figure comes from a copy in the Carleton Papers. The "Return of Loyalists &c. gone from New York to Nova Scotia, Quebec & abbacoe as per Returns in the Commissary General's Office at New York," New York, November 24, 1783, NA: CO 5/111, f. 236—is damaged and the data for Abaco no longer legible.

28. "Return of Persons who Emigrated from East Florida to different parts of the British Dominions," May 2, 1786, NA: CO 5/561, f. 407.

29. *Journal of the House of Assembly of the Bahamas*, April 28, 1789. Department of Archives, Nassau: *Journal of the House of Assembly of the Bahamas, 12 May 1784 to 20 September 1794*, p. 248. Cf. Michael Craton, *A History of the Bahamas* (London: Collins, 1968), pp. 165–66.

30. [William Wylly], *A Short Account of the Bahamas Islands, Their Climate, Productions, &c.* (London, 1789), p. 7.

31. Craton, p. 164.

32. Siebert, "Legacy," p. 15.

33. "Return of Persons who Emigrated from East Florida to different parts of the British Dominions," May 2, 1786, NA: CO 5/561, f. 407.

34. Trevor Burnard, "European Migration to Jamaica, 1655–1780," *William & Mary Quarterly* 53, no. 4 (October 1996): 772.

35. Harvey Amani Whitfield, "Black Loyalists and Black Slaves in Maritime Canada," *History Compass* 5, no. 6 (October 2007): 1980–97.

36. As stated by Robert Morse, "A General Description of the Province of Nova Scotia," LAC: Robert Morse Fonds, MG 21, p. 43. On numbers for the Maritimes, see James W. St. G. Walker, *The Black Loyalists: The Search for a Promised Land in Nova Scotia and Sierra Leone, 1783–1870* (London: Longman, 1976), pp. 11–12. For Quebec, see Robin W. Winks, *The Blacks in Canada* (Montreal: McGill–Queen's University Press, 1997), pp. 33–34.

BIBLIOGRAPHY

Printed Primary Sources

Adams, John. *The Works of John Adams.* 10 vols. Edited by Charles Francis Adams. Boston: Little, Brown and Company, 1856.

Adventures of Jonathan Corncob, loyal American refugee. London, 1787.

Bartlet, William S. *The Frontier Missionary: A Memoir of the Life of the Rev. Jacob Bailey, A.M.* Boston: Ide and Dutton, 1853.

Bartram, William. *Travels through North and South Carolina, Georgia, East and West Florida.* Philadelphia: James and Johnson, 1791.

Baynton, Benjamin. *Authentic Memoirs of William Augustus Bowles.* London, 1791.

Beaver, Philip. *African Memoranda: Relative to an Attempt to Establish a British Settlement on the Island of Bulama.* London: C. and R. Baldwin, 1805.

Beckford, William. *A Descriptive Account of the Island of Jamaica.* 2 vols. London, 1790.

Brymner, Douglas, ed. *Report on Canadian Archives.* Ottawa: Brown Chamberlin, 1891.

Campbell, Archibald. *Journal of an Expedition against the Rebels of Georgia.* Edited by Colin Campbell. Darien, Ga.: Ashantilly Press, 1981.

Candler, Allen D., ed. *The Revolutionary Records of the State of Georgia.* Augusta, Ga.: Franklin-Turner Company, 1908.

Carretta, Vincent, ed. *Unchained Voices: An Anthology of Black Authors in the English-Speaking World of the Eighteenth Century.* Lexington: University of Kentucky Press, 1996.

The Case and Claim of the American Loyalists, Impartially Stated and Considered, Printed by Order of Their Agents. London, 1783.

Caughey, John Walton, ed. *East Florida, 1783–85: A File of Documents Assembled, and Many of Them Translated by Joseph Byrne Lockey.* Berkeley and Los Angeles: University of California Press, 1949.

Chalmers, George. *Opinions on Interesting Subjects of Public Law and Commercial Policy, Arising from American Independence.* London, 1784.

Chesney, Alexander. *The Journal of Alexander Chesney, a South Carolina Loyalist in the Revolution and After.* Edited by E. Alfred Jones. Columbus: Ohio State University Press, 1921.

Clark, Murtie June, ed. *Loyalists in the Southern Campaign of the Revolutionary War.* 3 vols. Baltimore: Genealogical Publishing Company, 1981.

Clarkson, John. "Diary of Lieutenant J. Clarkson, R.N. (Governor, 1792)." *Sierra Leone Studies* 8 (1927): 1–114.

Cobbett, William. *Parliamentary History of England.* 36 vols. London, 1806–20.

Coke, Daniel Parker. *The Royal Commission on the Losses and Services of American Loyalists, 1783–1785.* Edited by Hugh Edward Egerton. New York: B. Franklin, 1971.

Coke, Thomas. *A History of the West Indies.* 3 vols. Liverpool: Nutter, Fishall, and Dixon, 1808.

Coldham, Peter Wilson, ed. *American Migrations: The Lives, Times, and Families of Colonial Americans Who Remained Loyal to the British Crown.* Baltimore: Genealogical Publishing Company, 2000.

Cooper, Thomas, ed. *The Statutes at Large of South Carolina.* Columbia, S.C., 1838.

Cox, Francis Augustus. *History of the Baptist Missionary Society, From 1792 to 1842.* 2 vols. London: T. Ward and Co., and G. J. Dyer, 1842.

Crary, Catherine S., ed. *The Price of Loyalty: Tory Writings from the Revolutionary Era.* New York: McGraw-Hill, 1973.

Cruden, John. *An Address to the Loyal Part of the British Empire, and the Friends of Monarchy Throughout the Globe.* London, 1785.

———. *Report on the Management of the Estates Sequestered in South Carolina, by Order of Lord Cornwallis, in 1780–82.* Edited by Paul Leicester Ford. Brooklyn, N.Y.: Historical Printing Club, 1890.

Curwen, Samuel. *The Journal and Letters of Samuel Curwen, 1775–1783.* Edited by George Atkinson Ward. Boston: Little, Brown and Co., 1864.

Dallas, R. C. *The History of the Maroons.* 2 vols. London, 1803.

Directions to the American Loyalists, in Order to Enable Them to State Their Cases . . . to the Honourable the Commissioners Appointed . . . to Inquire into the Losses and Services of Those Persons Who Have Suffered, in Consequences of Their Loyalty to This Majesty. London: W. Flexney, 1783.

Donne, W. Bodham, ed. *The Correspondence of King George the Third with Lord North from 1768 to 1783.* 2 vols. London: John Murray, 1867.

Eardley-Wilmot, John. *Historical View of the Commission for Enquiring into the Losses, Services, and Claims of the American Loyalists.* Introduction by George Athan Billias. Boston: Gregg Press, 1972 [1815].

Edwards, Bryan. *The History Civil and Commercial of the British Colonies in the West Indies.* 2 vols. London, 1793.

Equiano, Olaudah. *Interesting Narrative of the Life of Olaudah Equiano.* New York: Penguin, 2003.

Ewald, Johann. *Diary of the American War: A Hessian Journal.* Edited and translated by Joseph P. Tustin. New Haven: Yale University Press, 1979.

Falconbridge, A. M. *Narrative of Two Voyages to the River Sierra Leone during the Years 1791–1792–1793.* London: L. I. Higham, 1802.

Fanning, David. *The Adventures of David Fanning in the American Revolutionary War.* Edited by A. W. Savary. Ottawa: Golden Dog Press, 1983.

Fergusson, Charles Bruce, ed. *Clarkson's Mission to America, 1791–1792.* Halifax: Public Archives of Nova Scotia, 1971.

Ford, Worthington Chauncey, ed. *Journals of the Continental Congress, 1774–89.* 4 vols. Washington, D.C.: Government Printing Office, 1904.

Francklyn, Gilbert. *Observations, Occasioned by the Attempts Made in England to Effect the Abolition of the Slave Trade, Shewing the Manner in which Negroes are Treated in the British Colonies, in the West Indies.* Kingston and Liverpool: A Smith, 1788.

Franklin, Benjamin. *Memoirs of Benjamin Franklin, Written by Himself and Continued by his Grandson.* 2 vols. Philadelphia: McCarty and Davis, 1834.

———. *The Works of Benjamin Franklin.* 10 vols. Edited by Jared Sparks. Chicago: Townsend McCoun, 1882.

Fraser, Alexander. *Second Report of the Bureau of Archives for the Province of Ontario.* Toronto: L. K. Cameron, 1904–5.

Fyfe, Christopher, ed. *"Our Children Free and Happy": Letters from Black Settlers in Africa in the 1790s.* Edinburgh: Edinburgh University Press, 1991.

Galloway, Joseph. *Historical and Political Reflections on the Rise and Progress of the American Rebellion.* London, 1780.

———. *Observations on the Fifth Article of the Treaty with America, and on the Necessity of Appointing a Judicial Enquiry into the Merits and Losses of the American Loyalists, Printed by Order of Their Agents.* London: G. Wilkie, 1783.

Gentz, Friedrich. *The Origin and Principles of the American Revolution, Compared with the Origin and Principles of the French Revolution*. Philadelphia: Asbury Dickins, 1800.

Hodges, Graham Russell, ed. *The Black Loyalist Directory: African Americans in Exile after the American Revolution*. New York: Garland Publications, 1995.

House of Assembly. *Journals of the Assembly of Jamaica*. Kingston: Alexander Aikman, 1804.

House of Assembly. *Votes of the Honourable House of Assembly*. Nassau, Bahamas, 1796.

[Inglis, Charles]. *The Deceiver Unmasked; or, Loyalty and Interest United: in Answer to a Pamphlet Called Common Sense*. New York: Samuel Loudon, 1776.

[————]. *The True Interest of America, Impartially Stated, in Certain Strictures on a Pamphlet Called Common Sense*. Philadelphia: James Humphreys, 1776.

Jay, John. *John Jay: The Making of a Revolutionary; Unpublished Papers, 1745–1780*. Edited by Richard B. Morris. New York: Harper and Row, 1975.

————. "The Peace Negotiations of 1782–1783." In *Narrative and Critical History of America*, edited by Justin Winsor. Boston: Houghton Mifflin, 1888.

Johnston, Elizabeth Lichtenstein. *Recollections of a Georgia Loyalist*. New York: M. F. Mansfield and Company, 1901.

Lesser, Charles H., ed. *The Sinews of Independence: Monthly Strength Reports of the Continental Army*. Chicago: University of Chicago Press, 1976.

"Letters Showing the Rise and Progress of the Early Negro Churches of Georgia and the West Indies." *Journal of Negro History* 1, no. 1 (1916): 69–92.

Long, Edward. *The History of Jamaica. Or, General Survey of the Antient and Modern State of That Island. . . .* 3 vols. London: T. Lowndes, 1774.

Lossing, Benson John. *The Pictorial Field Book of the Revolution*. 2 vols. New York: Harper & Brothers, 1852.

McCall, Hugh. *The History of Georgia*. Atlanta: A. B. Caldwell, 1909 [1784].

de Milfort, Louis LeClerc. *Memoir, or a Cursory Glance at My Different Travels & My Sojourn in the Creek Nation*. Chicago: Lakeside Press, 1956.

Moultrie, William. *Memoirs of the American Revolution: So Far as It Related to the States of North and South Carolina and Georgia*. 2 vols. New York: David Longworth, 1802.

Nugent, Maria. *A Journal from the Year 1811 till the Year 1815, Including a Voyage to and Residence in India*. 2 vols. London: T. and W. Boone, 1839.

————. *Lady Nugent's Journal of Her Residence in Jamaica from 1801 to 1805*. Edited by Philip Wright. Kingston: Institute of Jamaica, 1966.

Paine, Thomas. *Common Sense*. Edited by Isaac Kramnick. New York: Penguin, 1986.

Parkes, Fanny. *Wanderings of a Pilgrim in Search of the Picturesque*. 2 vols. Karachi: Oxford University Press, 1975.

Raymond, William Odber, ed. *Winslow Papers, A.D. 1776–1826*. Boston: Gregg Press, 1972.

Roberts, Emma. *Scenes and Characters of Hindostan*. 3 vols. London: William Allen and Co., 1835.

Robertson, J. Ross, ed. *The Diary of Mrs. John Graves Simcoe*. Toronto: William Briggs, 1911.

Robinson, Catherine Skinner. *Lady Robinson's Recollections*. London: Barrett, Sons and Co., Printers, 1842.

Robinson, C. W. "The Expedition to Plattsburg, Upon Lake Champlain, Canada, 1814." *Journal of the Royal United Service Institution* 61 (August 1916): 499–521.

Robinson, John, and Thomas Rispin. *Journey through Nova-Scotia*. Sackville, N.B.: Ralph Pickard Bell Library, Mount Allison University, 1981 [1774].

Royal Commission on Historical Manuscripts. *Report on American Manuscripts in the Royal Institution of Great Britain*. 4 vols. London: HMSO, 1904.

Schoepf, Johann David. *Travels in the Confederation [1783–1784]*. Edited and translated by Alfred J. Morrison. 2 vols. New York: Bergman Publishers, 1968.

Sharp, Granville. *A Short Sketch of Temporary Regulations . . . for the Intended Settlement on the Grain Coast of Africa*. London: H. Baldwin, 1786.

Shortt, Adam, and Arthur C. Doughty, eds. *Documents Relating to the Constitutional History of Canada, 1759–1791*. Ottawa: S. E. Dawson, 1907.

Siebert, Wilbur Henry. *Loyalists in East Florida, 1774 to 1785: The Most Important Documents Pertaining Thereto, Edited with an Accompanying Narrative*. 2 vols. Deland: Florida State Historical Society, 1929.

Smith, William. *Diaries and Selected Papers of Chief Justice William Smith, 1784–1793*. Edited by L. F. S. Upton. 2 vols. Toronto: Champlain Society, 1963–65.

———. *Historical Memoirs of William Smith, 1776–1778*. Edited by William H. W. Sabine. New York: Colburn & Tegg, 1958.

———. *Historical Memoirs of William Smith, 1778–1783*. Edited by William H. W. Sabine. New York: New York Times and Arno Press, 1971.

Stone, William L. *Life of Joseph Brant (Thayendanegea)*. 2 vols. Albany, N.Y.: J. Munsell, 1865.

Talman, James J., ed. *Loyalist Narratives from Upper Canada*. Toronto: Champlain Society, 1946.

The Trial of Warren Hastings, Late Governor-General of Bengal. London, 1788.

To the King's Most Excellent Majesty in Council, the Humble Memorial and Petition of the Council and Assembly of Jamaica. Kingston, 1784.

Walpole, Horace. *Journal of the Reign of King George the Third from the Year 1771 to 1783*. 2 vols. London: Richard Bentley, 1859.

Ward, Edward. *A Trip to Jamaica with a True Character of the People of the Island*. London, 1700.

Washington, George. *The Writings of George Washington*. Edited by Worthington Chauncey Ford. 14 vols. New York: G. P. Putnam's Sons, 1892.

Weld, Isaac. *Travels through the States of North America and the Provinces of Upper and Lower Canada, during the Years 1795, 1796, and 1797*. London: John Stockdale, 1800.

Wells, Louisa Susannah. *The Journal of a Voyage from Charlestown to London*. New York: Arno Press, 1968 [1906].

Wells, William Charles. *Two Essays: One upon Single Vision with Two Eyes; the Other on Dew*. London: Printed for Archibald Constable and Co., 1818.

Williams, John. *An Enquiry into the Truth of the Tradition, Concerning the Discovery of America, by Prince Madog ab Owen Gwynedd, about the Year, 1170*. London: J. Brown, 1791.

Winterbottom, Thomas. *Account of the Native Africans in the Neighbourhood of Sierra Leone*. 2 vols. London: C. Whittingham, 1803.

Wraxall, Nathaniel William. *Historical Memoirs of My Own Time*. London: Kegan, Paul, 1904.

[Wylly, William]. *A Short Account of the Bahamas Islands, Their Climate, Productions, &c. . . .* London, 1789.

Secondary Works

Adamson, Christopher. "God's Divided Continent: Politics and Religion in Upper Canada and the Northern and Western United States, 1775 to 1841." *Comparative Studies in Society and History* 36, no. 2 (1994): 417–46.

Adelman, Jeremy. "An Age of Imperial Revolutions." *American Historical Review* 113, no. 2 (2008): 319–40.

Adelman, Jeremy, and Stephen Aron. "From Borderlands to Borders: Empires, Nation-States, and the Peoples in between in North American History." *American Historical Review* 104, no. 3 (1999): 814–41.

Ajzenstat, Janet, and Peter J. Smith, eds. *Canada's Origins: Liberal, Tory, or Republican?* Ottawa: Carleton University Press, 1995.

Akins, Thomas B. *History of Halifax City*. Halifax, N.S., 1895.

Armitage, David. *The Declaration of Independence: A Global History*. Cambridge, Mass.: Harvard University Press, 2007.

Ashton, Rick J. "The Loyalist Congressmen of New York." *New-York Historical Society Quarterly* 60, no. 1 (January–April 1976): 95–106.

Bailyn, Bernard. *The Ideological Origins of the American Revolution*. Cambridge, Mass.: Harvard University Press, 1967.

———. *The Ordeal of Thomas Hutchinson*. Cambridge, Mass.: Harvard University Press, 1974.

———. *The Peopling of British North America: An Introduction*. New York: Knopf, 1986.

———. *Voyagers to the West: A Passage in the Peopling of America on the Eve of the Revolution*. New York: Vintage, 1988.

Baker, Emerson W., and John G. Reid. "Amerindian Power in the Early Modern Northeast: A Reappraisal." *William & Mary Quarterly*, 3rd ser., 61, no. 1 (2004): 77–106.

Bannister, Jerry, and Liam Riordan. "Loyalism and the British Atlantic, 1660–1840." In *The Loyal Atlantic: Remaking the British Atlantic in the Revolutionary Era*, edited by Jerry Bannister and Liam Riordan. Toronto: University of Toronto Press, forthcoming 2011.

Barnwell, Joseph W. "The Evacuation of Charleston by the British." *South Carolina Historical and Genealogical Magazine* 11, no. 1 (1910): 1–26.

Bayly, C. A. *The Birth of the Modern World, 1780–1914: Global Connections and Comparisons*. Malden, Mass.: Blackwell, 2004.

———. *Imperial Meridian: The British Empire and the World, 1780–1830*. London: Longman, 1989.

Bell, D. G. *Early Loyalist Saint John: The Origin of New Brunswick Politics, 1783–1786*. Fredericton, N.B.: New Ireland Press, 1983.

Bender, Thomas. *A Nation among Nations: America's Place in World History*. New York: Hill and Wang, 2006.

Berkin, Carol. *Jonathan Sewall: Odyssey of an American Loyalist*. New York: Columbia University Press, 1974.

Bethell, A. Talbot. *Early Settlers of the Bahamas and Colonists of North America*. Westminster, Md.: Heritage Books, 2008 [1937].

Braidwood, Stephen J. *Black Poor and White Philanthropists: London's Blacks and the Foundation of the Sierra Leone Settlement, 1786–91*. Liverpool: University of Liverpool Press, 1994.

Brandt, Claire. *The Man in the Mirror: A Life of Benedict Arnold*. New York: Random House, 1994.

Brathwaite, Kamau. *The Development of Creole Society in Jamaica, 1770–1820*. Oxford: Clarendon Press, 1971.

Braund, Kathryn E. Holland. *Deerskins and Duffels: The Creek Indian Trade with Anglo-America, 1685–1815*. Lincoln: University of Nebraska Press, 2008.

Brebner, John Bartlet. *The Neutral Yankees of Nova Scotia: A Marginal Colony during the Revolutionary Years*. New York: Columbia University Press, 1937.

Breen, T. H. *American Insurgents, American Patriots: The Revolution of the People*. New York: Hill and Wang, 2010.

Brooks, Walter H. *The Silver Bluff Church: A History of Negro Baptist Churches in America*. Washington, D.C.: R. L. Pendleton, 1910.

Brown, Christopher Leslie. "Empire without Slaves: British Concepts of Emancipation in the Age of the American Revolution." *William & Mary Quarterly*, 3rd ser., 56, no. 2 (1999): 273–306.

———. *Moral Capital: Foundations of British Abolitionism*. Chapel Hill: University of North Carolina Press, 2006.

Brown, Vincent. *The Reaper's Garden: Death and Power in the World of Atlantic Slavery*. Cambridge, Mass.: Harvard University Press, 2008.

Brown, Wallace. *The Good Americans: The Loyalists in the American Revolution*. New York: Morrow, 1969.

———. *The King's Friends: The Composition and Motives of the American Loyalist Claimants*. Providence, R.I.: Brown University Press, 1965.

Brown, Wallace, and Hereward Senior. *Victorious in Defeat: The American Loyalists in Exile*. New York: Facts on File, 1984.

Buckner, Phillip A. *The Transition to Responsible Government: British Policy in British North America, 1815–1850*. Westport, Conn.: Greenwood Press, 1985.

———, ed. *Canada and the British Empire*. Oxford: Oxford University Press, 2008.

Bumsted, J. M. *A History of the Canadian Peoples*. Toronto: Oxford University Press, 1998.

———. *Understanding the Loyalists*. Sackville, N.B.: Centre for Canadian Studies, Mount Allison University, 1986.

Burnard, Trevor. *Mastery, Tyranny, and Desire: Thomas Thistlewood and His Slaves in the Anglo-Jamaican World*. Chapel Hill: University of North Carolina Press, 2004.

Byrd, Alexander X. *Captives and Voyagers: Black Migrants across the Eighteenth-Century British Atlantic World*. Baton Rouge: Louisiana State University Press, 2009.

Cahill, Barry. "The Black Loyalist Myth in Atlantic Canada." *Acadiensis* 29 (Autumn 1999): 76–87.

———. "Habeas Corpus and Slavery in Nova Scotia: *R. v. Hecht, ex parte Rachel, 1798*." *University of New Brunswick Law Journal* 44 (1995): 179–209.

Calhoon, Robert M. *The Loyalists in Revolutionary America, 1760–1781*. New York: Harcourt, Brace, Jovanovich, 1973.

Calhoon, Robert M., in collaboration with Timothy M. Barnes, Donald C. Lord, Janice Potter, and Robert M. Weir. *The Loyalist Perception and Other Essays*. Columbia: University of South Carolina Press, 1989.

Calhoon, Robert M., Timothy M. Barnes, and George A. Rawlyk, eds. *Loyalists and Community in North America*. Westport, Conn.: Greenwood Press, 1994.

Calloway, Colin G. *The American Revolution in Indian Country*. Cambridge, U.K.: Cambridge University Press, 1995.

Campbell, Charles A. "Robinson's House in the Hudson Highlands: The Headquarters of Washington." *Magazine of American History* 4 (February 1880): 109–17.

Campbell, Duncan Andrew. *Unlikely Allies: Britain, America and the Victorian Origins of the Special Relationship*. London: Hambledon Continuum, 2007.

Cannon, John. *The Fox-North Coalition: Crisis of the Constitution, 1782–84*. London: Cambridge University Press, 1969.

Carp, Benjamin L. "The Night the Yankees Burned Broadway: The New York City Fire of 1776." *Early American Studies* 4, no. 2 (Fall 2006): 471–511.

Cashin, Edward J. *The King's Ranger: Thomas Brown and the American Revolution on the Southern Frontier*. New York: Fordham University Press, 1999.

———. *Lachlan McGillivray, Indian Trader: The Shaping of the Southern Colonial Frontier*. Athens: University of Georgia Press, 1992.

Caughey, John Walton. *McGillivray of the Creeks*. Norman: University of Oklahoma Press, 1938.

Christie, Ian R. *The End of Lord North's Ministry, 1780–82*. London: Macmillan, 1958.

Clark, J. C. D. "British America: What If There Had Been No American Revolution?" In *Virtual History: Alternatives and Counterfactuals*, edited by Niall Ferguson. New York: Basic Books, 1997.

Coker, William S., and Thomas D. Watson. *Indian Traders of the Southeastern Spanish Borderlands: Panton, Leslie & Company and John Forbes & Company, 1783–1847*. Pensacola: University of West Florida Press, 1986.

Coleman, Deirdre. *Romantic Colonization and British Anti-Slavery*. Cambridge, U.K.: Cambridge University Press, 2005.

Colley, Linda. *Britons: Forging the Nation, 1707–1837*. New Haven, Conn.: Yale University Press, 1992.

———. *Captives: Britain, Empire and the World, 1600–1850*. London: Jonathan Cape, 2002.

———. *The Ordeal of Elizabeth Marsh: A Woman in World History*. London: Harper-Press, 2007.

Condon, Ann Gorman. *The Envy of the American States: The Loyalist Dream for New Brunswick*. Fredericton, N.B.: New Ireland Press, 1984.

Conrad, Margaret, ed. *Making Adjustments: Change and Continuity in Planter Nova Scotia, 1759–1800*. Fredericton, N.B.: Acadiensis Press, 1991.

Constant, Jean-François, and Michel Ducharme, eds. *Liberalism and Hegemony: Debating the Canadian Liberal Revolution*. Toronto: University of Toronto Press, 2009.

Conway, Stephen. *The British Isles and the War of American Independence*. Oxford: Oxford University Press, 2000.

———. "From Fellow Nationals to Foreigners: British Perceptions of the Americans, circa 1739–1783." *William & Mary Quarterly*, 3rd ser., 59, no. 1 (2002): 65–100.

Craig, Gerald M. *Upper Canada: The Formative Years, 1784–1841*. Toronto: McClelland and Stewart, 1963.

Craton, Michael. *A History of the Bahamas*. London: Collins, 1968.

Craton, Michael, and Gail Saunders. *Islanders in the Stream: A History of the Bahamian People*. 2 vols. Athens: University of Georgia Press, 1999.

Craton, Michael, and James Walvin. *A Jamaican Plantation: The History of Worthy Park, 1670–1970*. London: W. H. Allen, 1970.

Cronon, William J. *Changes in the Land: Indians, Colonists and the Ecology of New England*. New York: Hill and Wang, 1983.

Crow, Jeffrey J. "What Price Loyalism? The Case of John Cruden, Commissioner of Sequestered Estates." *North Carolina Historical Review* 58, no. 3 (1981): 215–33.

Cundall, Frank. "The Early Press and Printers in Jamaica." *Proceedings of the American Antiquarian Society* (April-October 1916): 290–354.

———. "Sculpture in Jamaica." *Art Journal* (March 1907): 65–70.

Cuthbertson, Brian. *The First Bishop: A Biography of Charles Inglis*. Halifax, N.S.: Waegwoltic Press, 1987.

Dalrymple, William. *White Mughals: Love and Betrayal in Eighteenth-Century India*. New York: Viking, 2003.

Davis, David Brion. "American Slavery and the American Revolution." In *Slavery and Freedom in the Age of the American Revolution*, edited by Ira Berlin and Ronald Hoffman. Charlottesville: University of Virginia Press, 1983.

DeMond, Robert O. *The Loyalists in North Carolina During the Revolution*. Durham, N.C.: Duke University Press, 1940.

Dickinson, H. T. ed. *Britain and the American Revolution*. Harlow, U.K.: Addison Wesley Longman, 1998.

———. "The Poor Palatines and the Parties." *English Historical Review* 82, no. 324 (1967): 464–85.

Douglass, Elisha P. "The Adventurer Bowles." *William & Mary Quarterly*, 3rd ser., 6, no. 1 (1949): 3–23.

Dunn, Richard S. *Sugar and Slaves: The Rise of the Planter Class in the English West Indies, 1624–1713*. Chapel Hill: University of North Carolina Press, 1972.

Errington, Elizabeth Jane. *The Lion, the Eagle, and Upper Canada: A Developing Colonial Ideology*. Kingston, Ont.: McGill–Queen's University Press, 1987.

Faragher, John Mack. *A Great and Noble Scheme: The Tragic Story of the Expulsion of the French Acadians from their American Homeland*. New York: Norton, 2005.

Fenn, Elizabeth A. *Pox Americana: The Great Smallpox Epidemic of 1775–82*. New York: Hill and Wang, 2001.

Ferling, John E. *A Leap in the Dark: The Struggle to Create the American Republic*. New York: Oxford University Press, 2003.

———. *The Loyalist Mind: Joseph Galloway and the American Revolution*. University Park: Pennsylvania State University Press, 1977.

Fingard, Judith. *The Anglican Design in Loyalist Nova Scotia, 1783–1816*. London: SPCK, 1972.

Fingerhut, Eugene R. "Uses and Abuses of the American Loyalists' Claims: A Critique of Quantitative Analysis." *William & Mary Quarterly*, 3rd ser., 25, no. 2 (1968): 245–58.

Fischer, David Hackett. *Washington's Crossing*. New York: Oxford University Press, 2004.

Flick, Alexander C. *Loyalism in New York During the American Revolution*. New York: Columbia University Press, 1901.

Frank, Andrew. *Creeks and Southerners: Biculturalism on the Early American Frontier*. Lincoln: University of Nebraska Press, 2005.

Frey, Sylvia. *Water from the Rock: Black Resistance in a Revolutionary Age*. Princeton, N.J.: Princeton University Press, 1991.

Frey, Sylvia R., and Betty Wood. *Come Shouting to Zion: African American Protestantism in the American South and British Caribbean to 1830*. Chapel Hill: University of North Carolina Press, 1998.

Frost, Alan. *The Precarious Life of James Mario Matra: Voyager with Cook, American Loyalist, Servant of Empire*. Carlton, Victoria: Miegunyah Press, 1995.

Fryer, Mary Beacock, and Christopher Dracott. *John Graves Simcoe, 1752–1806: A Biography*. Toronto: Dundurn Press, 1998.

Fyfe, Christopher. *A History of Sierra Leone*. Oxford: Oxford University Press, 1962.

Gayle, Clement. *George Liele: Pioneer Missionary to Jamaica*. Kingston: Jamaica Baptist Union, 1982.

Ghosh, Durba. *Sex and the Family in Colonial India: The Making of Empire*. Cambridge, U.K.: Cambridge University Press, 2006.

Gould, Eliga H. "American Independence and Britain's Counter-Revolution." *Past & Present* 154 (February 1997): 107–41.

———. *The Persistence of Empire: British Political Culture in the Age of the American Revolution*. Chapel Hill: University of North Carolina Press, 2000.

———. "Revolution and Counter-Revolution." In *The British Atlantic World, 1500–1800*, edited by David Armitage and Michael J. Braddick. Basingstoke, U.K.: Palgrave Macmillan, 2002.

Grant, John N. *The Maroons in Nova Scotia*. Halifax, N.S.: Formac, 2002.

Graymont, Barbara. *The Iroquois in the American Revolution*. Syracuse, N.Y.: Syracuse University Press, 1972.

Greene, Jack P. ed. *Exclusionary Empire: English Liberty Overseas, 1600–1900*. Cambridge, U.K.: Cambridge University Press, 2010.

———. *Pursuits of Happiness: The Social Development of the Early Modern British Colonies and the Formation of American Culture*. Chapel Hill: University of North Carolina Press, 1988.

Griffin, Patrick. *American Leviathan: Empire, Nation, and Revolutionary Frontier*. New York: Hill and Wang, 2007.

Hall, Catherine. *Civilising Subjects: Colony and Metropole in the English Imagination, 1830–1867*. Chicago: University of Chicago Press, 2002.

Hall, Douglas. *In Miserable Slavery: Thomas Thistlewood in Jamaica, 1750–1786*. London: Macmillan, 1989.

Hancock, David. *Citizens of the World: London Merchants and the Integration of the British Atlantic Community, 1735–85*. Cambridge, U.K.: Cambridge University Press, 1995.

Hartz, Louis. *The Founding of New Societies: Studies in the History of the United States, Latin America, South Africa, Canada, and Australia*. New York: Harcourt, Brace, 1964.

Hendrickson, David C. *Peace Pact: The Lost World of the American Founding*. Lawrence: University Press of Kansas, 2003.

Hickey, Donald R. *The War of 1812: A Forgotten Conflict*. Urbana: University of Illinois Press, 1989.

Hoock, Holger. *Empires of the Imagination: Politics, War, and the Arts in the British World, 1750–1850*. London: Profile Books, 2010.

Hood, Clifton. "An Unusable Past: Urban Elites, New York City's Evacuation Day, and the Transformations of Memory Culture." *Journal of Social History* 37, no. 4 (2004): 883–913.

Horowitz, Gad. "Conservatism, Liberalism, and Socialism in Canada: An Interpretation." *Canadian Journal of Economics and Political Science* 32, no. 2 (1966): 143–71.

Hull, N. E. H., Peter C. Hoffer, and Steven L. Allen. "Choosing Sides: A Quantitative Study of the Personality Determinants of Loyalist and Revolutionary Political Affiliation in New York." *Journal of American History* 65, no. 2 (1978): 344–66.

Hulsebosch, Daniel J. *Constituting Empire: New York and the Transformation of Constitutionalism in the Atlantic World, 1664–1830*. Chapel Hill: University of North Carolina Press, 2005.

Irvin, Benjamin H. "Tar, Feathers, and the Enemies of American Liberties, 1768–1776." *New England Quarterly* 76, no. 2 (2003): 197–238.

Isaacson, Walter. *Benjamin Franklin: An American Life*. New York: Simon and Schuster, 2003.

Jarvis, Julia. *Three Centuries of Robinsons: The Story of a Family.* Toronto: T. H. Best, 1967.

Jasanoff, Maya. *Edge of Empire: Lives, Culture, and Conquest in the East, 1750–1850.* New York: Knopf, 2005.

———. "Revolutionary Exiles: The American Loyalist and French Émigré Diasporas." In *The Age of Revolutions in Global Context, c. 1760–1840,* edited by David Armitage and Sanjay Subrahmanyam. Basingstoke, U.K.: Palgrave Macmillan, 2010.

Johnson, Whittington B. *Race Relations in the Bahamas, 1784–1834: The Nonviolent Transformation from a Slave to a Free Society.* Fayetteville: University of Arkansas Press, 2000.

Jones, Charles Colcock. *The History of Georgia.* 2 vols. Boston: Houghton Mifflin, 1883.

Kammen, Michael. *A Season of Youth: The American Revolution in the Historical Imagination.* New York: Knopf, 1978.

Karras, Allan. *Sojourners in the Sun: Scottish Migrants in Jamaica and the Chesapeake, 1740–1800.* Ithaca, N.Y.: Cornell University Press, 1992.

Kelsay, Isabel Thompson. *Joseph Brant, 1743–1807: Man of Two Worlds.* Syracuse, N.Y.: Syracuse University Press, 1984.

Kettner, James H. *The Development of American Citizenship, 1608–1870.* Chapel Hill: University of North Carolina Press, 1978.

Kimber, Stephen. *Loyalists and Layabouts: The Rapid Rise and Faster Fall of Shelburne, Nova Scotia, 1783–1792.* Toronto: Doubleday Canada, 2008.

Kirk-Greene, Anthony. "David George: The Nova Scotian Experience." *Sierra Leone Studies* 14 (1960): 93–120.

Knowles, Norman. *Inventing the Loyalists: The Ontario Loyalist Tradition and the Creation of Usable Pasts.* Toronto: University of Toronto Press, 1997.

Kulikoff, Allan. "Revolutionary Violence and the Origins of American Democracy." *Journal of the Historical Society* 2, no. 2 (March 2002): 229–60.

LaCroix, Alison. *The Ideological Origins of American Federalism.* Cambridge, Mass.: Harvard University Press, 2010.

Lambert, Robert S. "The Confiscation of Loyalist Property in Georgia, 1782–1786." *William & Mary Quarterly,* 3rd ser., 20, no. 1 (1963): 80–94.

Langguth, A. J. *Union 1812: The Americans Who Fought the Second War of Independence.* New York: Simon and Schuster, 2006.

Larkin, Edward. "What Is a Loyalist?" *Common-Place* 8, no. 1 (2007), http://www.common-place.org/vol-08/no-01/larkin/.

Latimer, Jon. *1812: War with America.* Cambridge, Mass.: Harvard University Press, 2007.

Lawrence, Alexander A. *James Johnston: Georgia's First Printer.* Savannah: Pigeonhole Press, 1956.

Lawson, Philip. *The Imperial Challenge: Quebec and Britain in the Age of the American Revolution.* Montreal: McGill–Queen's University Press, 1989.

Leamon, James S. "The Parson, the Parson's Wife, and the Coming of the Revolution to Pownalborough, Maine." *New England Quarterly* 82, no. 3 (2009): 514–28.

Lepore, Jill. *The Name of War: King Philip's War and the Origins of American Identity.* New York: Knopf, 1998.

Lipset, Seymour Martin. *Continental Divide: The Values and Institutions of the United States and Canada.* New York: Routledge, 1990.

Little, J. I. "American Sinner/Canadian Saint?" *Journal of the Early Republic* 27, no. 2 (2007): 203–31.

————. *Loyalties in Conflict: A Canadian Borderland in War and Rebellion, 1812–1840*. Toronto: University of Toronto Press, 2008.

Loughran, Trish. *The Republic in Print: Print Culture in the Age of U.S. Nation-Building*. New York: Columbia University Press, 2007.

Lynn, Kenneth S. *A Divided People*. Westport, Conn.: Greenwood Press, 1977.

Mackesy, Piers. *The War for America, 1775–83*. Cambridge, Mass.: Harvard University Press, 1964.

MacKinnon, Neil. *This Unfriendly Soil: The Loyalist Experience in Nova Scotia, 1783–91*. Kingston, Ont.: McGill–Queen's University Press, 1986.

Magee, Joan. *Loyalist Mosaic: A Multi-Ethnic Heritage*. Toronto: Dundurn Press, 1984.

Mancke, Elizabeth. *The Fault Lines of Empire: Political Differentiation in Massachusetts and Nova Scotia, 1760–1830*. New York: Routledge, 2005.

Marshall, P. J. *The Making and Unmaking of Empires: Britain, India, and America, c. 1750–1783*. Oxford: Oxford University Press, 2005.

————, ed. *The Oxford History of the British Empire*, vol. 2, *The Eighteenth Century*. Oxford: Oxford University Press, 1998.

Mason, Keith. "The American Loyalist Diaspora and the Reconfiguration of the British Atlantic World." In *Empire and Nation: The American Revolution in the Atlantic World*, edited by Peter Onuf and Eliga Gould. Baltimore: Johns Hopkins University Press, 2005.

McConville, Brendan. *The King's Three Faces: The Rise and Fall of Royal America, 1688–1776*. Chapel Hill: University of North Carolina Press, 2006.

McCullough, David. *1776*. New York: Simon and Schuster, 2005.

McKay, Ian. "The Liberal Order Framework: A Prospectus for a Reconnaissance of Canadian History." *Canadian Historical Review* 81, no. 3 (2000): 617–45.

McNairn, Jeffrey L. *The Capacity to Judge: Public Opinion and Deliberative Democracy in Upper Canada, 1791–1854*. Toronto: University of Toronto Press, 2000.

Meacham, Jon. *American Lion: Andrew Jackson in the White House*. New York: Random House, 2008.

Mills, David. *The Idea of Loyalty in Upper Canada, 1784–1850*. Kingston, Ont.: McGill–Queen's University Press, 1988.

Mintz, Sidney W. *Sweetness and Power: The Place of Sugar in Modern History*. New York: Penguin, 1985.

Moore, Christopher. *The Loyalists: Revolution, Exile, Settlement*. Toronto: Macmillan of Canada, 1984.

Morgan, Philip, and Andrew Jackson O'Shaughnessy. "Arming Slaves in the American Revolution." In *Arming Slaves: From Classical Times to the Modern Age*, edited by Christopher Leslie Brown and Philip Morgan. New Haven, Conn.: Yale University Press, 2006.

Morris, Richard B. *The Peacemakers: The Great Powers and American Independence*. New York: Harper and Row, 1965.

Mowat, Charles Loch. *East Florida as a British Province, 1763–1784*. Berkeley: University of California Press, 1943.

Nash, Gary B. *The Unknown American Revolution: The Unruly Birth of Democracy and the Struggle to Create America*. New York: Viking, 2005.

Neatby, Hilda. *Quebec: The Revolutionary Age, 1760–1791*. Toronto: McClelland and Stewart, 1966.

Nelson, Paul David. *General Sir Guy Carleton, Lord Dorchester: Soldier-Statesman of Early British Canada*. Madison, N.J.: Fairleigh Dickinson University Press, 2000.

Nelson, William. *The American Tory*. Oxford: Oxford University Press, 1961.

Norton, Mary Beth. *The British-Americans: The Loyalist Exiles in England, 1774–1789*. London: Constable, 1974.

———. "Eighteenth-Century American Women in Peace and War: The Case of the Loyalists." *William & Mary Quarterly*, 3rd ser., 33, no. 3 (1976): 386–409.

———. "The Fate of Some Black Loyalists of the American Revolution." *Journal of Negro History* 58, no. 4 (1973): 402–26.

Onuf, Peter S. *Jefferson's Empire: The Language of American Nationhood*. Charlottesville: University of Virginia Press, 2001.

O'Shaughnessy, Andrew Jackson. *An Empire Divided: The American Revolution and the British Caribbean*. Philadelphia: University of Pennsylvania Press, 2000.

Palmer, R. R. *The Age of the Democratic Revolution: A Political History of Europe and America*. 2 vols. Princeton, N.J.: Princeton University Press, 1959–64.

Pearsall, Sarah M. S. *Atlantic Families: Lives and Letters in the Later Eighteenth Century*. Oxford: Oxford University Press, 2008.

Phillips, Kevin. *The Cousins' Wars: Religion, Politics, and the Triumph of Anglo-America*. New York: Basic Books, 1999.

Piecuch, Jim. *Three Peoples, One King: Loyalists, Indians, and Slaves in the Revolutionary South, 1775–1782*. Columbia: University of South Carolina Press, 2008.

Potter-MacKinnon, Janice. *The Liberty We Seek: Loyalist Ideology in Colonial New York and Massachusetts*. Cambridge, Mass.: Harvard University Press, 1983.

———. *While the Women Only Wept: Loyalist Refugee Women*. Montreal: McGill–Queen's University Press, 1993.

Pulis, John W., ed. *Moving On: Black Loyalists in the Afro-Atlantic World*. New York: Garland Publishing, 2002.

Pybus, Cassandra. *Epic Journeys of Freedom: Runaway Slaves of the American Revolution and their Global Quest for Liberty*. Boston: Beacon Press, 2006.

———. "Jefferson's Faulty Math: The Question of Slave Defections in the American Revolution." *William & Mary Quarterly*, 3rd ser., 62, no. 2 (April 2005): 243–64.

Ragatz, Lowell. *The Fall of the Planter Class in the British Caribbean, 1763–1833: A Study in Social and Economic History*. New York: Octagon Books, 1963.

Ranlet, Philip. *The New York Loyalists*. Knoxville: University of Tennessee Press, 1986.

Raphael, Ray. *A People's History of the American Revolution: How Common People Shaped the Fight for Independence*. New York: New Press, 2001.

Rediker, Marcus, and Peter Linebaugh. *The Many-Headed Hydra: Sailors, Slaves, Commoners, and the Hidden History of the Revolutionary Atlantic*. Boston: Beacon Press, 2000.

Reid, John G. "*Pax Britannica* or *Pax Indigena*? Planter Nova Scotia (1760–1782) and Competing Strategies of Pacification." *Canadian Historical Review* 85, no. 4 (2004): 669–92.

Reid, John G., Maurice Basque, Elizabeth Mancke, Barry Moody, Geoffrey Plank, and William Wicken. *The "Conquest" of Acadia, 1710: Imperial, Colonial, and Aboriginal Constructions*. Toronto: University of Toronto Press, 2004.

Riker, James. *"Evacuation Day," 1783, Its Many Stirring Events: with Recollections of Capt. John Van Arsdale of the Veteran Corps of Artillery*. New York: Printed for the Author, 1883.

Riley, Sandra. *Homeward Bound: A History of the Bahama Islands to 1850 with a Definitive Study of Abaco in the American Loyalist Plantation Period*. Miami: Island Research, 1983.

Robertson, Marion. *King's Bounty: A History of Early Shelburne, Nova Scotia*. Halifax: Nova Scotia Museum, 1983.

Robinson, St. John. "Southern Loyalists in the Caribbean and Central America." *South Carolina Historical Magazine* 93, no. 3–4 (1992): 205–220.

Ryden, David Beck. *West Indian Slavery and British Abolition, 1783–1807*. Cambridge, U.K.: Cambridge University Press, 2009.

Ryerson, Egerton. *The Loyalists of America and Their Times: From 1620 to 1816*. 2 vols. Toronto: William Briggs, 1880.

Sabine, Lorenzo. *The American Loyalists, or, Biographical Sketches of Adherents to the British Crown in the War of Revolution*. Boston: Charles C. Little and James Brown, 1847.

Saroop, Narinder. *Gardner of Gardner's Horse*. New Delhi: Palit and Palit, 1983.

Saunders, Gail. *Bahamian Loyalists and Their Slaves*. London: Macmillan Caribbean, 1983.

Saunt, Claudio. *A New Order of Things: Property, Power and the Transformation of the Creek Indians, 1733–1816*. Cambridge, U.K.: Cambridge University Press, 1999.

Schama, Simon. *Rough Crossings: Britain, the Slaves, and the American Revolution*. London: BBC Books, 2005.

Sheppard, George. *Plunder, Profits, and Paroles: A Social History of the War of 1812 in Upper Canada*. Montreal: McGill–Queen's University Press, 1994.

Shy, John. *A People Numerous and Armed: Reflections on the Military Struggle for American Independence*. Ann Arbor: University of Michigan Press, 1990.

Siebert, Wilbur. *The Legacy of the American Revolution to the British West Indies and Bahamas: A Chapter Out of the History of the American Loyalists*. Columbus: Ohio State University Press, 1913.

Silver, Peter. *Our Savage Neighbors: How Indian War Transformed Early America*. New York: Norton, 2008.

Skemp, Sheila L. *Benjamin and William Franklin: Father and Son, Patriot and Loyalist*. Boston: Bedford Books, 1994.

———. *William Franklin: Son of a Patriot, Servant of a King*. New York: Oxford University Press, 1990.

Smith, Paul H. "The American Loyalists: Notes on Their Organization and Numerical Strength." *William & Mary Quarterly*, 3rd ser., 25, no. 2 (1968): 259–77.

Statt, Daniel. *Foreigners and Englishmen: The Controversy over Immigration and Population, 1660–1760*. Newark: University of Delaware Press, 1995.

Stewart, Gordon and George Rawlyk. *A People Highly Favored of God: The Nova Scotia Yankees and the American Revolution*. Toronto: Macmillan of Canada, 1972.

Stone, William L. *Life of Joseph Brant (Thayendanegea)*. 2 vols. Albany, N.Y.: J. Munsell, 1865.

Swinehart, Kirk Davis. "Object Lessons: Indians, Objects, and Revolution." *Common-Place* 2, no. 3 (2002), http://www.historycooperative.org/journals/cp/vol-02/no-03/lessons/.

Taylor, Alan. *The Divided Ground: Indians, Settlers, and the Northern Borderland of the American Revolution*. New York: Knopf, 2006.

———. "The Late Loyalists: Northern Reflections of the Early American Republic." *Journal of the Early Republic* 27, no. 1 (Spring 2007): 1–34.

Tiedemann, Joseph. *Reluctant Revolutionaries: New York City and the Road to Independence, 1763–1776*. Ithaca, N.Y.: Cornell University Press, 1997.

Tiedemann, Joseph S., Eugene R. Fingerhut, and Robert W. Venables, eds. *The Other Loyalists: Ordinary People, Royalism, and the Revolution in the Middle Colonies, 1763–1787*. Albany: State University of New York Press, 2009.

Tiro, Karim M. "The Dilemmas of Alliance: The Oneida Indian Nation in the American Revolution." In *War and Society in the American Revolution: Mobilization and Home Fronts*, edited by John Resch and Walter Sargent. DeKalb: Northern Illinois University Press, 2007.

Travers, Robert. *Ideology and Empire in Eighteenth-Century India: The British in Bengal*. Cambridge, U.K.: Cambridge University Press, 2007.

Troxler, Carole Watterson. "Refuge, Resistance, and Reward: The Southern Loyalists' Claim on East Florida." *Journal of Southern History* 55, no. 4 (1989): 563–95.

Tucker, Robert W., and David C. Hendrickson. *Empire of Liberty: The Statecraft of Thomas Jefferson*. New York: Oxford University Press, 1990.

Turner, Frederick Jackson. "English Policy toward America." *American Historical Review* 7, no. 4 (1902): 706–35.

Turner, Mary. *Slaves and Missionaries: The Disintegration of Jamaican Slave Society, 1787–1834*. Chicago: University of Illinois Press, 1998.

Vail, R. W. G. "The Loyalist Declaration of Dependence of November 28, 1776." *New-York Historical Society Quarterly* 31, no. 2 (1947): 68–71.

Van Buskirk, Judith L. *Generous Enemies: Patriots and Loyalists in Revolutionary New York*. Philadelphia: University of Pennsylvania Press, 2002.

Van Tyne, Claude Halstead. *The Loyalists in the American Revolution*. New York: Macmillan, 1902.

Von Erffa, Helmut, and Alan Staley, eds. *The Paintings of Benjamin West*. New Haven, Conn.: Yale University Press, 1986.

Wahrman, Dror. "The English Problem of Identity in the American Revolution." *American Historical Review* 106, no. 4 (October 2001): 1236–62.

Walker, James W. St. G. *The Black Loyalists: The Search for a Promised Land in Nova Scotia and Sierra Leone, 1783–1870*. London: Longman, 1976.

———. "Myth, History and Revisionism: The Black Loyalists Revised." *Acadiensis* 29, no. 1 (Autumn 1999): 88–105.

Wells, Robert V. "Population and Family in Early America." In *A Companion to the American Revolution*, edited by Jack P. Greene and J. R. Pole. Malden, Mass.: Blackwell Publishing, 2000.

White, Richard. *The Middle Ground: Indians, Empires, and Republics in the Great Lakes Region, 1650–1815*. Cambridge, U.K.: Cambridge University Press, 1991.

Whitfield, Harvey Amani. "The American Background of Loyalist Slaves." *Left History* 14, no. 1 (2009): 58–87.

———. "Black Loyalists and Black Slaves in Maritime Canada." *History Compass* 5, no. 6 (October 2007): 1980–97.

———. *Blacks on the Border: The Black Refugees in British North America, 1815–1860*. Burlington: University of Vermont Press, 2006.

Williams, Eric. *Capitalism and Slavery*. Chapel Hill: University of North Carolina Press, 1944.

Wilson, David A. *Paine and Cobbett: The Transatlantic Connection*. Kingston, Ont.: McGill–Queen's University Press, 1988.

Wilson, Ellen Gibson. *The Loyal Blacks*. New York: Capricorn, 1976.

Wilson, Kathleen. *The Sense of the People: Politics, Culture, and Imperialism in England, 1715–1785*. Cambridge, U.K.: Cambridge University Press, 1995.

Winks, Robin W. *The Blacks in Canada: A History*. Montreal: McGill–Queen's University Press, 1997.

———. *The Relevance of Canadian History: U.S. and Imperial Perspectives*. Toronto: Macmillan of Canada, 1979.

Wise, S. F. *God's Peculiar Peoples: Essays on Political Culture in Nineteenth-Century Canada*. Ottawa: Carleton University Press, 1993.

Wood, Gordon S. *The Radicalism of the American Revolution*. New York: Knopf, 1991.

Wright, Esmond, ed. *Red, White, and True Blue: The Loyalists in the Revolution*. New York: AMS Press, 1976.

Wright, Esther Clark. *The Loyalists of New Brunswick*. Fredericton, N.B., 1955.

Wright, J. Leitch. "Dunmore's Loyalist Asylum in the Floridas." *Florida Historical Quarterly* 49, no. 4 (April 1971): 370–79.

———. *William Augustus Bowles: Director General of the Creek Nation*. Athens: University of Georgia Press, 1967.

Unpublished Secondary Works

Brannon, Rebecca Nathan. "Reconciling the Revolution: Resolving Conflict and Rebuilding Community in the Wake of Civil War in South Carolina, 1775–1860." Ph.D. dissertation, University of Michigan, 2007.

Chopra, Ruma. "New Yorkers' Vision of Reunion with the British Empire: 'Quicken Others by Our Example.' " Working Paper 08–02, International Seminar on the History of the Atlantic World: Harvard University, 2008.

Coleman, Aaron Nathan. "Loyalists in War, Americans in Peace: The Reintegration of the Loyalists, 1775–1800." Ph.D. dissertation, University of Kentucky, 2008.

David, James Corbett. "Dunmore's New World: Political Culture in the British Empire, 1745–1796." Ph.D. dissertation, College of William and Mary, 2010.

———. "A Refugee's Revolution: Lord Dunmore and the Floating Town, 1775–1776." Working Paper 08–04, International Seminar on the History of the Atlantic World: Harvard University, 2008.

Dierksheide, Christa Breault. "The Amelioration of Slavery in the Anglo-American Imagination, 1770–1840." Ph.D. dissertation, University of Virginia, 2009.

Liveley, Susan Lindsey. "Going Home: Americans in Britain, 1740–1776." Ph.D. dissertation, Harvard University, 1996.

Maas, David Edward. "The Return of the Massachusetts Loyalists." Ph.D. dissertation, University of Wisconsin, 1972.

MacDonald, Michelle Craig. "From Cultivation to Cup: Caribbean Coffee and the North American Economy, 1765–1805." Ph.D. dissertation, University of Michigan, 2005.

O'Shaughnessy, Andrew Jackson. "Lord North and Conciliation with America." Unpublished manuscript.

Prokopow, Michael John. " 'To the Torrid Zones': The Fortunes and Misfortunes of American Loyalists in the Anglo-Caribbean Basin, 1774–1801." Ph.D. dissertation, Harvard University, 1996.

Scott, Julius Sherrard. "The Common Wind: Currents of Afro-American Communication in the Era of the Haitian Revolution." Ph.D. dissertation, Duke University, 1986.

Swinehart, Kirk Davis. "This Wild Place: Sir William Johnson Among the Mohawks, 1715–1783." Ph.D. dissertation, Yale University, 2002.

INDEX

Page numbers in *italics* refer to illustrations.

Page 1   Beverley Robinson House. Widener Library, Harvard College Library, US 13.5 (V.4, 1880).

Page 1   Portrait of Joseph Brant by George Romney. National Gallery of Canada, Ottawa, Ontario, Canada/The Bridgeman Art Library.

Page 2   Portrait of Elizabeth Lichtenstein Johnston. Widener Library, Harvard College Library, US 4503.72.

Page 2   Dunmore Proclamation. Library of Congress, Rare Book and Special Collections Division.

Page 3   Portrait of Sir Guy Carleton. Library and Archives Canada/Credit: Mabel B. Messer/Mabel Messer collection/C-002833.

Page 3   Black Loyalist Certificate/NSARM. Nova Scotia Archives and Records Management.

Page 4   William Booth, *A Black Wood Cutter at Shelburne*, 1788. Library and Archives Canada/Credit: W. Booth/W. H. Coverdale collection of Canadiana, Manoir Richelieu collection/C-040162.

Page 4   William Booth, *Part of the Town of Shelburne in Nova Scotia*, 1789. Library and Archives Canada/Credit: William Booth/William Booth collection/C-010548.

Page 5   James Peachey, *Encampment of the Loyalists at Johnstown*, 1784. Library and Archives Canada/Credit: James Peachey/James Peachey collection/C-002001.

Page 5   Elizabeth Simcoe, *Mohawk Village on the Grand River*, ca. 1793. Mohawk Village on the Grand River [ca. 1793], Archives of Ontario, F 47-11-1-0-109.

Page 6   Mohawk Chapel, Brantford. Author photograph.

Page 6   Portrait of William Augustus Bowles by Thomas Hardy. © NTPL/Angelo Hornak.

Page 6   Rodney Memorial, Spanish Town. Author photograph.

Page 7   Sierra Leone Company Handbill. Nova Scotia Archives and Records Management.

Page 7   Sketch of Freetown. Widener Library, Harvard College Library, Afr 6143.16.2A.

Page 8   Gardner Family Tomb. Author photograph.

Page 8   Benjamin West, "The Reception of the American Loyalists by Great Britain." Widener Library, Harvard College Library, US 4503.22.1.

MAPS

Page 20   After Thomas Pownall, *A General Map of the Middle British Colonies, in America*, 1776, and Bernard Romans, *A General Map of the Southern*

British Colonies in America, 1776. Library of Congress, Geography and Map Division.

Page 51 *Plan of York Town and Gloucester in Virginia, Shewing the Works Constructed for the Defence of Those Posts by the Rt. Honble: Lieut. General Earl Cornwallis, with the Attacks of the Combined Army of French and Rebels,* 1781. Library of Congress, Geography and Map Division.

Page 54 William Faden, *A Map of South Carolina and a Part of Georgia,* 1780. Library of Congress, Geography and Map Division.

Page 82 William Faden, *The United States of North America with the British and Spanish Territories According to the Treaty,* 1783. Library of Congress, Geography and Map Division.

Page 112 Thomas Kitchin, *A Compleat Map of the British Isles,* 1788. David Rumsey Map Collection, www.davidrumsey.com.

Page 146 Jedidiah Morse, *A New Map of Nova Scotia, New Brunswick and Cape Breton,* 1794. David Rumsey Map Collection, www.davidrumsey.com.

Page 167 *Captain Holland, Plan of Port Roseway Harbor,* 1798. Nova Scotia Archives and Records Management.

Page 176 Robert Campbell, *A Map of the Great River St. John & Waters,* 1788. Library and Archives Canada/Credit: Robert Campbell, Surveyor/n0000254.

Page 212 G. H. Van Keulen, *A New and Correct Chart of the Coast of East Florida,* 1784. Courtesy of the John Carter Brown Library at Brown University.

Page 244 Thomas Jefferys, *Jamaica, from the Latest Surveys,* 1775. David Rumsey Map Collection, www.davidrumsey.com.

Page 278 William Dawes, *Plan of the River Sierra Leone,* 1803. Widener Library, Harvard College Library, Afr 6143.16.

Page 310 Samuel Lewis, *A Correct Map of the Seat of War,* 1815. Library of Congress, Geography and Map Division.

Page 336 James Rennell, *A Map of Bengal, Bahar, Oude, & Allahabad,* 1786. David Rumsey Map Collection, www.davidrumsey.com.

A NOTE ON THE TYPE

This book was set in Janson, a typeface long thought to have been made by the Dutchman Anton Janson, who was a practicing type-founder in Leipzig during the years 1668–1687. However, it has been conclusively demonstrated that these types are actually the work of Nicholas Kis (1650–1702), a Hungarian, who most probably learned his trade from the master Dutch typefounder Dirk Voskens. The type is an excellent example of the influential and sturdy Dutch types that prevailed in England up to the time William Caslon (1692–1766) developed his own incomparable designs from them.

Composed by North Market Street Graphics,
Lancaster, Pennsylvania
Printed and bound by Berryville Graphics
Berryville, Virginia
Designed by Virginia Tan